SATURDAY AFTERNOONS
AT THE OLD MET

Ezio Pinza as Don Giovanni.

SATURDAY AFTERNOONS
AT THE OLD MET

The Metropolitan
Opera Broadcasts
1931–1950

by

Paul Jackson

AMADEUS PRESS
Reinhard G. Pauly, General Editor
Portland, Oregon

Copyright © 1992 by Amadeus Press
(an imprint of Timber Press, Inc.)
All rights reserved.

ISBN 0-931340-48-9
Printed in Hong Kong
Designed by Sandra Mattielli

Amadeus Press
9999 S.W. Wilshire, Suite 124
Portland, Oregon 97225

Library of Congress Cataloging-in-Publication Data

Jackson, Paul, 1927-
    Saturday afternoons at the old Met : the Metropolitan Opera
broadcasts, 1931-1950 / by Paul Jackson.
        p. cm.
    Includes bibliographical references and index.
    ISBN 0-931340-48-9
    1. Metropolitan Opera (New York, N.Y.) 2. Opera--New York
(N.Y.)--20th century.   3. Radio and music. I. Title.
ML1711.8.N3M434   1992
782.1'09747'1--dc20   91-33533
                                                          CIP
                                                          MN

For Lee, my wife

Contents

Illustrations

Lucrezia Bori as the Duchess of Towers in *Peter Ibbetson*. Photography by Mishkin.

Preface

To most American opera lovers the story is a familiar one. On a snowy after-noon in a small town on Michigan's upper peninsula, a thirteen-year-old randomly twists the Philco dial. His ear, already tuned by a half-dozen years of piano lessons, is caught and held by a lively exchange between a high-flying soprano and a meaty bass: 'Rataplan' growls Salvatore Baccaloni, 'Rataplan' echoes Lily Pons in the drum duet from *La Fille du Régiment*. The year is 1940, the Texas Company's first season of broadcasts "direct from the stage of the Metropolitan Opera in New York City" on NBC's Blue Network. From that day to the present, except when traveling in Europe, Saturday afternoons were spent at the opera. I was a bit confounded on the next Saturday when Donizetti's sparkling comedy was succeeded by *Tannhäuser*, but Flagstad and Melchior, Thorborg and Janssen were convincing proponents. I stayed with it. Other afternoons of that first season brought Martinelli, Tibbett, Albanese, Warren, Moore, Pinza, Swarthout, Maison, Thomas, Bampton, Castagna—they seemed as familiar as friends. I remember keeping a record in a special notebook of all their names and their roles and a brief outline of each plot.

The opera broadcasts have significance not only for individuals. In their variously preserved states they offer a unique aural history of the Metropolitan Opera from the early 1930s to the present day. So-called private pressings (the pejorative is "pirate," a term that Met Librarian Mapleson might not like), discs released in Europe, the Rodgers and Hammerstein Archives of Recorded Sound at Lincoln Center, and lately the Metropolitan Opera's own series of Historic Broad-cast recordings—together these provide an overview of the company's character and quality. True, the visual aspects of operatic production are lacking: not only the sets and costumes but, even more important, the actor's stage action, his carriage, and his mien—all of which should add immeasurably to (but have been known to detract moderately from) both the singer's conception of the role and his actual per-formance. But was not the radio audience, vast in numbers, of greater importance in the formulation of operatic taste, and in the evaluation of opera and artists, than the three or four thousand people who heard and saw the performance in the house? What has been preserved on the often primitive tapes and records of those broad-casts is fairly typical of what that large public heard; it represents the substance of our national opera, at least before the advent of regularly televised Met performances in

1977. Over the years an occasional evaluation, or more often a brief mention, of a particular broadcast has appeared in print, yet the sizable aural documentation of the company warrants a detailed critical survey.

In my survey I have sought to maintain an overall chronology of seasons, though where dictated by fruitful comparisons, a grouping of the body of an artist's work, or the narrative itself, I have deemed these more valuable than rigorous preservation of chronology. The survey should serve as a counterbalance to the necessarily brief evaluations (often a single sentence) of performances and artists in Kolodin's history of the Metropolitan. Brevity, too, is often the curse of the entries on singers in the several biographical dictionaries where the evaluation, if any is attempted, is confined to a few generalities; usually artists' capabilities in contrasting roles or at various stages of their careers are not elaborated upon. As will be seen in the following chapters, a given artist can wear quite different faces, even in separate performances of the same role. From these accumulated individual performances rather than from a career flattened into an average, collective statement come not only a more illuminating but also a fairer appraisal of an artist's abilities and overall career. In describing each broadcast I have tried to relate only what was heard on that particular afternoon, and though homage should be paid at the conclusion of a singer's long career, and often is, readers will also be able to formulate their own assessment of the artist from these detailed critiques. A fuller and, I hope, more appreciative picture of each artist (and of the Met's standard of performance) should emerge.

I was fortunate to have access to the correspondence of Gatti-Casazza, Edward Ziegler, Edward Johnson, and Rudolf Bing, and where appropriate, I have used their words and the words of their correspondents to enhance the narrative.

Some readers may find my assessments excessively detailed or too technical; I have felt, in line with the previous remarks, that a few specifics better reveal the nature of a performance than an overbrush of abstractions without reference to particular moments in the interpretation. At the other extreme, I have tried to avoid what I call the "thesis" review in which the critic formulates a central proposition and then interprets all events accordingly, selecting those elements which conform and ignoring the contraries. Dumping everything into a collective bin may make for unity in an article, but too often it results in a violent distortion of particular elements of a performance.

The survey divides into two sections. The first section covers four years of broadcasts during the Gatti regime (1931–1935); the second details the full fifteen-season Johnson era (through 1950). For this nineteen-year period I have surveyed by far the majority of the surviving records of the broadcasts, but undoubtedly some others will turn up, since a few have surfaced while this study was in progress. Many of these early records or tapes are decidedly primitive in sound quality, marred by static, wow and flutter, and even major pitch deviations. Cuts are sometimes extensive, and portions of one aria can intrude on another without warning. A variable pitch control was an essential tool throughout the study, and it was necessary to constantly check for the pitch accuracy of each act, often of each aria, and sometimes even within an aria. While all these blemishes make many broadcasts unlikely candidates for commercial marketing, other performances (both early and late) are of quite acceptable sound quality.

The examination of the first nineteen broadcast seasons holds the most interest as a historical study. Over two hundred performances are preserved, in whole or in part. Before the advent of the long-playing (LP) record (about 1950), few Metropolitan artists recorded many or any of their roles in toto. Frequently not even a single aria of a seldom-performed role made it to commercial discs, so the broadcasts often represent the only documentation of the singers' conceptions. As time goes on these documents of forty, fifty, even sixty years ago gain in historical importance, not only as mirrors of the artists' capabilities but also as records of style.

The coming of LP records, and later of tape recordings, made complete roles of major artists more often available on commercial pressings. The preservation of broadcasts, too, became comprehensive; the Metropolitan itself retains a complete record of broadcast performances from 1950 on. Except for the first season or so, for which no aural documentation survives, I have confined my comments to those performances which are preserved in sound; it would be idle to merely replicate casts in prose.

Readers may find a few anomalies in the written forms of operas and artists' names. In a book about the Metropolitan Opera, I have deemed it appropriate to follow Metropolitan usage (and that of its organ, *Opera News*). Thus, *La forza del destino* is converted to *La Forza del Destino*, just as *La fille du régiment* is elevated to *La Fille du Régiment*. When cited without his given name, Giuseppe de Luca becomes De Luca. While Lakmé wears her crowning mark, no accent graces Gerald or Mimi, and even Kurwenal turns into a phonetic Kurvenal at the old Met.

The primary source materials for this work have been the broadcasts themselves and material from the Metropolitan Opera Archives. Some of the many secondary sources are cited in the Select Bibliography, where several useful periodicals, including *Opera News*, are also mentioned. For decades many radio listeners have relied on *Opera News* to supplement broadcast enjoyment. Though published by the Metropolitan Opera Guild, the magazine served as the unofficial organ of the Metropolitan Opera, and at least until the 1970s its coverage was admittedly pro-Met. Now and then I have quoted from a contemporary issue of *Opera News* when it suggests the flavor of the period, as it often did when it was edited by Mrs. Peltz, a favorite of longtime listeners to the Opera Quiz. On the other hand, I have seldom quoted from contemporary newspaper reviews since they almost invariably refer to a first performance rather than to the broadcast performance; the latter's value is sustained when treated as a distinct alternative to the newspaper review. Even when reviews of an actual broadcast performance exist, I have refrained from using them because what is heard in an in-house performance is often colored by what is seen. My concern is solely with what went out over the airwaves into the ears and hearts of the radio public, though fortunately this by no means negates the acting component for many artists.

One of the rewards of authorship is the right to acknowledge those individuals and institutions that have provided assistance. Of the many, several are noted with particular gratitude. The Drake University Research Council, when I was Dean of the College of Fine Arts, awarded a grant that made possible the early stages of this study more than a decade ago. Robert Tuggle, Director of the Metropolitan Opera Archives, was most generous in opening the extensive resources of the Archives to me. I am greatly indebted to him for permission to quote from the unpublished correspondence of the managers of the Metropolitan and the documents that trace the negotiations with NBC. Grateful acknowledgement is made to the Rodgers and Hammerstein Archives of Recorded Sound of the New York Public Library at Lincoln Center, where archives director David Hall first introduced me to the

Preliminary List of Audio Documentation Metropolitan Opera Broadcasts, 1931/32–1949/50. I especially wish to thank Texaco, Inc. for permission to use quotations from the live intermission features of the Metropolitan Opera broadcasts. Ellen Godfrey, Associate Radio Producer of the Metropolitan Opera, was instrumental in gaining that permission. My thanks to G. Palmer LeRoy, Managing Director of the Metropolitan Opera Guild, who readily granted permission to reprint a number of quotations from *Opera News.* It is a pleasure to express my appreciation to Madame Jarmila Novotna for sharing her memories of Mozart performances at the Metropolitan.

The Metropolitan Opera Archives, through the good offices of Assistant Archivist John Pennino, provided photographs of Bjoerling, Castagna, Steber, and Traubel (Elsa). I am grateful to Andrew Farkas, Director of Libraries and Professor of Library Science at the University of North Florida, for the loan of the Tibbett (Rigoletto) and autographed Kipnis (Boris) photographs and to Adrienne Auerswald, Professor Emeritus of Music, Smith College, for the loan of the Mario (Gretel) photograph. All other photographs and memorabilia are from the author's collection. Many persons provided assistance in assembling the collection. In particular I wish to thank Bob Salmon of Benedikt & Salmon Record Rarities of San Diego, and Bill Safka of Safka & Bareis in Forest Hills, N.Y. Additional items were obtained from the Librairie de l'Abbaye in Paris, V. A. Heck in Vienna, Walter R. Benjamin Autographs, La Scala Autographs, Paul C. Richards Autographs, the Opera Box, and JB Muns, Fine Arts. During my visits to the Metropolitan Opera Archives, Gail Pam Frohlinger aided access to research materials. The Dartmouth College music library, Baker Library (also at Dartmouth College), and the Vermont Technical College library allowed me the use of their facilities, and their staffs were ever helpful. The Randolph, Vermont Public Library provided interlibrary loan assistance.

I must again cite Texaco to express my gratitude for its largesse in sponsoring the Metropolitan Opera broadcasts over the past half century. And for their preservation of early broadcasts we all must acknowledge those recordists (be they pirateers, network engineers, or studio technicians preserving a role at the request of a particular artist) who, whether for personal pleasure or gain, saved all or a portion of a performance for posterity.

Since 1954 my wife has been the only person with whom I could or would have wished to share Saturday afternoons at the opera. To her I give my thanks and my love.

PART I
The Gatti Years

Rosa Ponselle as Norma. Photography by Mishkin.

CHAPTER ONE

Convincing Gatti

"Everyone was terrible nervous; the whole world could hear us!"[1] Madame Manski was recalling Christmas Day 1931 when she played the Witch in *Hänsel und Gretel* on the first Metropolitan Opera broadcast. The holiday matinee fell on Friday so the radio public and Saturday afternoons at the Metropolitan were not mated until the following day, 26 December, when the final two acts of *Norma* were aired. Rosa Ponselle, Gladys Swarthout, Giacomo Lauri-Volpi, Ezio Pinza, Tullio Serafin—the names of the 1931 *Norma* broadcast conjure up a fabled age of opera. For the first time Americans throughout the land could be a part of it.

Outside the opera house in that year, the shadow of the depression continued to darken the lives of Americans, robbing them of material security and suppressing their inherent optimism, while within the tarnished walls of the old Metropolitan Opera House on the corner of Broadway and Thirty-ninth Street a worthy experiment was beginning that would provide a new national pastime for millions of Americans. Less than a decade later Mrs. August Belmont, the *grande dame* of the Metropolitan and the radio broadcasts, could write with characteristic fervor, "Opera has grown from a private luxury to a national necessity."[2] For many of the unseen radio audience the hyperbole of the erstwhile actress turned social leader was close to the truth. An independent survey in 1939 estimated that 10,500,000 listeners in America tuned in the opera each Saturday.[3] Some of them seemed to echo Mrs. Belmont's zeal. That same year the National Broadcasting Company, in cooperation with the Opera Association and the Metropolitan Opera Guild, sponsored a letter-writing contest—an effective if slightly shopworn symbol of American marketing technique—which as much as anything confirmed the progress of the effort to democratize opera. The call had gone forth: "What the Metropolitan Opera Broadcasts Mean to Me." There were more than 17,000 responses. Giving the ring of truth to Mrs. Belmont's claim, a telephone company worker from Cleveland wrote, "On Saturday afternoons, a third-floor walk-up becomes a Seventh Heaven where one listens and lives and grows."[4] She won an all-expense-paid three-day visit to New York for the 1940 opening night of *Un Ballo in Maschera*. Opera did indeed seem to have become part of the American Dream.

No comparable zeal for the broadcasts was evident on the part of the Metropolitan itself in 1931. Giulio Gatti-Casazza, the gray eminence of the Metropolitan and its general manager since the days of Caruso and Toscanini, first had to be challenged and then vanquished by the American businessman Merlin H. Aylesworth, president of the National Broadcasting Company. Aylesworth was the prime mover in the plan to put the Met on the air.

As told by Milton Cross, announcer of the Met broadcasts from the beginning until his death in 1975, the first time Aylesworth spoke to Gatti about the project he received a "flat and ringing 'No.' "[5] Aylesworth persisted while Gatti held firm with that taciturn intractability for which he was famous. "Gatti wouldn't even give reasons for his refusal," Cross continued. "He wasn't used to being asked for reasons. When he said 'No,' it was final." Aylesworth, however, proved a Merlin in more than name only by magically converting the skeptical general manager. A backward glance at the history of opera broadcasting indicates how much he had to overcome.

A few years earlier on 21 January 1927, the Chicago Opera Company had aired the garden scene from *Faust* with Edith Mason, Charles Hackett, Richard Bonelli, and Vanni Marcoux, conducted by Giorgio Polacco. This was the first live broadcast on a national network in America. (The National Broadcasting Company had been organized less than five months earlier.) The Metropolitan turned a deaf ear, declaring that the transmission was "not opera."[6] Previous to this pioneering effort there had been a number of regional and local broadcasts. According to NBC's research department, the scene of the first "official" opera broadcast was the Manhattan Opera House in New York City—at one time the home of the Oscar Hammerstein Manhattan Opera Company, which from 1906–10 gave the Metropolitan the only serious competition in its long history. Wagner's *Der Fliegende Holländer*, performed by a visiting German troupe, was broadcast from there over station WJZ on 17 February 1923.[7] Local, nonprofessional performances had been aired even earlier. Cedric Hart claims priority in this area with the broadcast of *La Bohème* on 5 September 1922 from station KDYL in Salt Lake City, Utah. The size of the orchestra (seven or eight pieces including piano) and a mother-son team as Mimi and Rodolfo (the latter just out of high school) proclaim amateur night at the opera, and the employment of "an elocutionist, who explains, in English, as the action goes on what the characters are doing and the progress of the action"[8] affirms how little new there is under the sun.

During the 1920s, broadcasts of opera moved from the curiosity stage of local, condensed versions, to one-hour look-ins on the Chicago Civic Opera, to the production of operas for the radio audience by NBC's National Grand Opera Company (thirty programs) and presentations of the major Puccini operas.[9] NBC's early efforts were capped by rebroadcasts of opera from Dresden in 1930 and from Covent Garden and Salzburg in 1931. Decidedly, the Metropolitan was the reluctant bridegroom in the wedding of radio and opera. When the marriage finally occurred, however, it lasted.

In fact, two efforts from the stage of the Metropolitan preceded the December 1931 inaugural broadcast. On 21 April of that same year, while the Metropolitan company was on tour, the League of Composers' performance of Stravinsky's *Oedipus Rex* with the Philadelphia Orchestra conducted by Leopold Stokowski was broadcast. One cannot know if the Metropolitan management considered it "not opera" (at least the oratoriolike nature of *Oedipus* would have given greater credibility to the denial), but they jealously guarded the hallowed stage from airwaves pollution, causing H. B. Schaad of NBC Artists Services to pen a hasty apology to the Met's Assistant Manager, Edward Ziegler:

> In accepting the invitation from Mr. Stokowski to broadcast this concert from the Metropolitan we assumed he had covered with you the matter of your permission to allow this broadcast to emanate from your House, and that had we any thought of this not being the case you would have been consulted in the matter prior to my publicity release in regard to the event.[10]

Stokowski's sleight of hand paid off and the broadcast went on. It was not an auspicious beginning for the future union of the Metropolitan and NBC.

Had Mr. Gatti prowled backstage, as was his wont, on 12 and 13 January 1910, in the second year of his reign, he surely must have been aware of the very first attempts to broadcast live from the Metropolitan. A young engineer, Lee de Forest, self-proclaimed in his autobiography as the "Father of Radio," had nursed his appetite for grand opera in Chicago. During the winter of 1909–10 De Forest (now in New York) met with Gatti's co-director, Andreas Dippel.[11] Dippel had been a leading tenor at the Met for two decades (the Wagner heroes were his specialty). Unlike the reluctant Gatti of the 1930s, the "kindly, bright-eyed, energetic"[12] Dippel was fascinated by De Forest's project and eagerly aided his test efforts. Gatti, too had an (unwilling) role to play: he desired to hear the performances on stage via telephone wire in his office. By chance, at the time of De Forest's visit, an Acousticon microphone was being installed on stage by the National Dictograph Company. De Forest installed a small carbon-arc transmitter in the attic of the Metropolitan, "rigged up a temporary bamboo mast on the roof, lashed it to one of the short flagpoles there, rigged up the largest antenna that was practical for such a situation and ran the lead-in wire down through a ventilator to the transmitter."[13] Wire went down through the backstage area and hooked up with the microphone, to which De Forest taped an ordinary telephone receiver.

This was the primitive vehicle which carried the voices of the golden age as far as Newark, New Jersey. Though opera broadcast by wireless telephone would prove short-lived, hundreds of people within a fifty-mile radius became the first unseen audience of the Metropolitan as, on 12 January they heard Olive Fremstad struggle with the vile Scarpia of Pasquale Amato in the second act of Puccini's *Tosca*. Seeking greater réclame, for his second attempt on 13 January, De Forest had special listening stations set up throughout the Manhattan area, including receivers in the city room of the *World* and on the Royal Mail Steamer Avon anchored off Thirteenth Street. According to the *Sun*, 260 special guests aboard the steamer "took turns fitting the receivers over their ears, and one or two of them thought they heard a tenor. They were not positive."[14] When the tenor was Enrico Caruso in *Pagliacci* it may have been worth the effort. Amato and Bella Alten joined Caruso, while Emmy Destinn and Riccardo Martin taunted one another in *Cavalleria Rusticana*. Preliminary notices of these events in the *World* on 9 January promised that "you may now listen to the Grand Opera's greatest singers in your distant home."[15] The marvel of "messages picked out of the air without towers" promised that "grand opera . . . by connection with a wireless-telephone is shown to be no longer a dream."[16] The assessment was overly optimistic.

Editha Fleischer as Hänsel in *Hänsel und Gretel*. Photography by Mishkin.

Queena Mario as Gretel in *Hänsel und Gretel*.

We do not know what Gatti thought of these efforts, but twenty years later he was still a nonbeliever. Fortunately Merlin Aylesworth's tenacity matched Gatti's intractability. Aylesworth was "not a man to give up easily,"[17] as Deems Taylor, the commentator of the first season of Met broadcasts, recounts.

> People thought the idea of putting opera on the air was "madness." They saw no sense to it at all. There was one major exception, however—Mr. Merlin H. Aylesworth. . . . He firmly believed that the opera belonged on the radio and he meant to get it there whatever the opposition. . . . Time after time he spoke to Gatti and finally Gatti broke down to the point of explaining the reasons why the Met shouldn't be broadcast. . . . He was skeptical of the fidelity of a broadcast from the stage. He didn't think that radio would do justice to his singers or his orchestra.

Once aware of the problem, Aylesworth, with his business acumen, "hit on a plan." According to Cross, "he decided to rig up a demonstration broadcast for Gatti alone. He would get the impresario to his office one evening and make him listen to the opera being performed that night."[18]

Charles Gray, NBC engineer in charge of the technical aspects of the first season of broadcasts, was the man on the spot for the demonstration for Gatti. He brought his equipment to the opera house on the evening of 23 December for the performance of *Madama Butterfly* featuring Maria Müller, Giovanni Martinelli, Ina Bourskaya, and Antonio Scotti, with Vincenzo Bellezza at the helm.[19] The equipment was the same as he used when broadcasting a dance band—nothing special about it. But Gray was well aware of the importance of the occasion.

> I knew that if Gatti weren't sold this first time he never would be. . . . The opera started . . . and I was in constant touch with Mr. Aylesworth in his office. Soon he told me that Gatti had asked to hear more orchestra—so I increased the volume. Gatti still wasn't satisfied, so I increased it some more. This time it was too much and I had to cut the orchestra down. But Gatti was convinced.[20]

With insight into a technique which would enable the sound engineer of the future to rival the conductor in the pit, Gray proudly notes that Gatti "had heard the proof that the engineer could control the sound from the stage and make appropriate adjustments when necessary." It did not occur to Gray to voice Hamlet's regret: "O cursed spite that ever I was born to set it right," though we might think so today.

Perhaps it was a triumph not without alloy, but Gray rejoiced that "Mr. Aylesworth had won his fight and the Met was going on the air." In the photograph taken on the afternoon of the historic first broadcast on Christmas Day, the *Hänsel und Gretel* cast (Editha Fleischer and Queena Mario in the title roles, Dorothee Manski as the Witch, Henrietta Wakefield and Gustav Schützendorf, the parents, with Pearl Besuner and Dorothea Flexer as Dewman and Sandman—all under Karl Riedel's direction) was joined by Taylor and the mild-appearing Aylesworth, who looked like anything but the hero he was. As for Mr. Gatti, he too consented to be photographed with them, his dour countenance successfully masking any pleasure he felt in the occasion.

Dorothee Manski as the Witch in *Hänsel und Gretel*. Photography by Mishkin.

Giulio Gatti-Casazza. Photography by Mishkin.

CHAPTER TWO

The Money Factor

Gatti's initial opposition to the broadcasts was certainly real, but one can doubt that the future of Metropolitan Opera broadcasts hung in the balance on the evening of the trial performance of 23 December. The *Butterfly* test was more in the nature of a rehearsal for the airing of *Hänsel und Gretel* on 25 December; the Metropolitan and NBC had completed contractual agreements for the broadcasts six months earlier.

Ziegler handled all matters relative to the broadcasts since Gatti confined himself to Italian in speech and on paper throughout his twenty-seven year tenure. Negotiations with Aylesworth were well under way by mid-May 1931. At that time NBC prepared an agreement whose conditions had been approved in earlier conferences:

> Metropolitan Opera Company, or its successors, agree that for a period of two (2) seasons, beginning November 1, 1931, each of the seasons to consist of approximately twenty-four (24) weeks, National Broadcasting Company, Inc., shall have the exclusive right to broadcast, by means of wired or wireless radio, and from such station or stations as it may desire, the operas, operettas, and performances of whatsoever kind and nature presented under the management of the Metropolitan Opera Company, upon the terms and conditions embodied herein.[1]

Only one broadcast per week would be permitted unless the Met should consent in writing to a greater number. Nor would the network be obliged to broadcast every week but would "at the option of the Metropolitan Opera Company be entitled to an equal number of additional broadcasts during a subsequent week or weeks." The Met was to choose the opera of each week and to notify NBC of its decision "no later than one week in advance of each broadcast." NBC agreed to pay the Metropolitan "the sum of $120,000.00 per season for each of the two seasons, which is at the rate of $5,000.00 per broadcast for twenty-four broadcasts during each season" in amounts of $10,000 or $20,000 each month throughout the season.

Although the first broadcast seasons would be sustaining programs without commercial sponsorship, NBC covered the possibility of sponsorship while granting the opera company approval of the sponsor:

> The rights hereby granted to National Broadcasting Company, Inc., shall
> include the right to sell such broadcasts to its clients, subject to the
> approval of the Metropolitan Opera Company, upon the condition, how-
> ever, that the price to the client for each broadcast shall be not less than
> Ten Thousand ($10,000.00) Dollars unless the Metropolitan Opera
> Company consent in writing to a sale or sales for a lesser amount.

If and when the broadcasting rights were sold, the Met would receive "the sum of
such contract price in excess of $5,000.00 for each broadcast."

Though commercial television was at least a decade away, all audio-visual
reproduction rights were denied NBC.

> It is expressly understood that no sound record or disc shall be made of
> such broadcast for phonograph reproduction, or reproduction by any
> other device or process. It is also expressly understood that National
> Broadcasting Company, Inc., shall not have the right to televise any per-
> formance or part of a performance under this agreement.

During the negotiations, Gatti had returned to Italy (the 1930–31 season
having ended in Rochester on 4 May). On 18 May Ziegler cabled his boss in Milan:

> Have new broadcasting proposition guaranteeing minimum one hundred
> twenty thousand per year for one evening hour each week during season
> STOP We have right to select opera to be broadcast each week also we have
> right to choose and change evening on which to broadcast upon two
> weeks notice STOP This avoids conflict with Puccini and other restricted
> operas and artists STOP Kahn advises accepting for two years Cable
> Regards[2]

The imprimatur of Otto Kahn, which Ziegler's crafty foresight had provided,
should have provoked an immediate response from Gatti. Kahn was the Metropolitan's beneficent Maecenas, member of the opera board since 1903, its chairman
from Gatti's inaugural year of 1908, and—as owner of eighty-four percent of the
opera company stock—the power behind the throne. Receiving no reply, Ziegler
again cabled Gatti on 21 May, this time to Naples. "Am awaiting your reply to my
cable about broadcasting,"[3] the impatient Ziegler began. The next day Gatti, still
reluctant, replied from Milan:

> I agree regarding broadcasting proposition STOP However would like well
> defined case in which we might be compelled to change at last hour a per-
> formance already settled to a Ricordi or other restricted opera or with an
> artist not obliged to broadcast STOP[4]

It was business as usual for Gatti, who concluded his cable with "Will hold audition
with Bodanzky May twentyeighth Milan. Dor [*sic*, Doe], Ljungberg, Lippe possible;
also Cebotari, Kullman. Regards." (The Met Archives teem with "might-have-
beens"; Maria Cebotari, only twenty-one and fresh from her Dresden debut, never
made it to the Met.)

On 25 May Ziegler wrote to Aylesworth, "If you find it possible to incorporate
these [several enclosed paragraphs] and if in the third line of Paragraph 2 of your
agreement we can change the wording to read, 'It is understood that the Metropolitan Opera Company shall choose *the day* [italics added] and opera each week of
such broadcast,' then I think the matter will be closed this morning." In response to
Gatti's reservations concerning operas whose broadcast was restricted by the pub-

lisher Ricordi, Ziegler requested and gained approval for an addition to the agreement:

> The failure of the Metropolitan Opera Co. to furnish in any one or more weeks an act of opera or portion of an opera for broadcast shall submit the Metropolitan Opera Company to no damages except that the Metropolitan Opera Co. shall reimburse the National Broadcasting Company, Inc., $5,000.00 for every such failure, unless it furnishes a substitute broadcast.[5]

With Ziegler continuing to safeguard the Met's hegemony, the final contract also included the stipulation that NBC "agrees not to advertise that it has an exclusive license to broadcast Metropolitan Opera Company artists or performances," though this was patently the case. Under date of 27 May the final contract was achieved. Kahn immediately cabled Aylesworth from Paris:

> Ziegler just cabled me the conclusion of negotiations between you and him. I am delighted at this first step in what I trust will be a close and mutually propitious relationship between your great organization and the Metropolitan. It is a particular satisfaction to me to think that this relationship will increase my opportunities for personal contact with one whom I hold in such cordial regard and high esteem as I do yourself. Kindest regards[6]

The whole affair now took on the aspect of bonhomie, Ziegler writing to Aylesworth re Kahn's cable: "It is so like him in thoughtfulness and appreciation, and I hope that this agreement may be the means of bringing you in closer contact with him." He looked forward to seeing Aylesworth "tomorrow for luncheon at the Ritz at one o'clock."[7]

The camaraderie would be short-lived, however, for in the face of the deepening shadow of the depression Kahn unexpectedly relinquished the chairmanship of the board in October of the same year. His role at the Met diminished yearly until his death in March 1934. Mistaken is Martin Mayer's supposition (in the official Metropolitan Opera Guild Centennial book)[8] that it was Paul D. Cravath, Kahn's successor as chairman of the board and lawyer for both RCA and Kahn, who engineered the agreement with NBC after his accession in October. The project had been all wrapped up the previous summer. In fact, on 1 June 1931 Aylesworth sent Ziegler the initial payment of $10,000 called for "upon the signing of this agreement."[9] Additional payments of $10,000 (1 October) and $20,000 (15 November and 15 December) followed.

On 11 December NBC informed Ziegler that they hoped to start broadcasts of the Met on or about Saturday, 19 December.[10] (Under this timetable *Tosca* with Maria Jeritza, Giovanni Martinelli, and Antonio Scotti would have usurped the fairy tale *Hänsel und Gretel* in pride of place.) The Met responded that they would try, but "our chief difficulty is the fact that our repertoire is only definitely made up about two weeks in advance."[11]

Planning a season in Gatti's time was considerably different from modern practice. Now productions and artists' contracts are arranged three and four years in advance. Before the advent of air travel (particularly the jet plane) artists came to America to stay for the season, or a major part of it, and were bound to the Metropolitan for lengthy periods of time. They contracted for a minimum number of performances, but actual dates of their appearances were not known more than a week or two ahead of time. Moreover, the Metropolitan had a good deal of control over most singers' concert and symphonic appearances. The Met received a commission on these engagements, an arrangement going back to the earliest days of the company. Here, too, was bait for NBC—bait perhaps more enticing than the broadcasts themselves. In a second agreement of the contract of 27 May 1931, NBC showed its hand by agreeing to pay the Met $30,000 per annum for the "franchise" on Met artists' services:

> Inasmuch as your contracts with your artists contain a clause forbidding them from rendering artistic services to anyone without your consent, you hereby grant us the exclusive right to negotiate with and employ any artist (under contract with the Metropolitan Opera Company) for concerts or recitals to be broadcast by radio, whether said broadcasts be sponsored or unsponsored.[12]

The dates of the concert broadcasts were subject to artists' prior engagements at the Met, and each of the artists (singers and conductors) could broadcast "on not more than four occasions during any one year" without written consent from the Met. The Met contractee was required to sign a declaration, or waiver, that the Met's approval of the radio appearance "shall not be construed as a waiver or relinquishment by [the Met] to enforce any or all covenants or rights which [the Met] may have under any contract with any such artist, especially any clause prohibiting any artist from singing at radio performances at any other occasion or occasions."[13]

Such was the notorious franchise which caused so many struggles between artists and corporate entities during the next decade. The interlocking institutional relationship and uncertain economic conditions of the depression years are laid bare in July, months before the launching of the opera broadcasts themselves, in a letter to Ziegler from H. B. Schaad, associate managing director of NBC Artists Service. Prophetically, it concerns tenor Beniamino Gigli, whose financial dispute with the Met at the end of the season would cause a public scandal. Schaad inquired about the availability of Gigli for a radio concert.

> As you know there still remains considerable doubt as to whether Atwater Kent will return to the air at all and if so, no definite guarantee that he will resume with as expensive a program as formerly. Nor can we foresee at this time, in view of the continued gravity of the business situation, what probable sponsors there will be for the Metropolitan franchise.
>
> In undertaking Gigli's management, we as you know, had to give very substantial assurances in regard to engagements, two of which are radio dates at a most liberal figure. We need badly to assure ourselves of the sale of these two dates and even if Atwater Kent resumes, there is a question of their using Gigli's services for last season. When we notified them of the new price, they expressed themselves as being unwilling to engage him at this fee.
>
> Now, in the meantime, we had an inquiry from the Household Finance Corporation in Chicago regarding the possible use of Gigli's services on one of their programs. They have been using the best concert artists obtainable, outside of the Metropolitan Opera artists, and in every way it is a high-grade program. It was in connection with this inquiry that we cabled you as George [Engles, NBC Artists managing director] and I felt that if there was any way possible for you to make this exception in view of the very uncertain conditions, it would be most helpful to us and at least, afford us an outlet for one of the Gigli radio dates; waiting for the other until the allocation of your franchise for next year was further along.

Lucrezia Bori as Magda and Beniamino Gigli as Ruggero in *La Rondine*. Photography by Mishkin.

> We would very much appreciate your giving this your best consideration and in our opinion, the appearance of Gigli for this one time would not in any way complicate our situation in meeting general conditions in connection with your franchise. Please give this your liberal interpretation.[14]

Radio's place in the operatic scheme, even in the early stages of the relationship, was potent. We see it again a few months later when Ziegler relayed basso Ezio Pinza's plaint to Engles after the Telephone Company had approached Pinza concerning a radio appearance. Ziegler had told Pinza he could not have permission "but he [Pinza] asks why he has never been given a chance to appear on the air under your [NBC] direction. . . . Could you see your way to including him in one of your radio broadcasts?"[15] The next day Engles assured Ziegler that "Unfortunately only a very limited demand comes for a bass in connection with broadcast programs."[16] This must have been a surprise to the future matinee idol of the Broadway stage; but Engles knew his trade and added the requisite balm: "I shall certainly be pleased to endeavor to sell the services of Mr. Pinza, who is a very fine artist."[17]

If the bass voice was taboo for radio, the baritone was well within range. On 12 December Firestone Tire and Rubber Co. eagerly sought the services of Lawrence Tibbett for a series of thirteen broadcasts (4 January to 22 March 1932). NBC received $7500 for securing "authorization for us to negotiate for services of Tibbett" and having the "program and sponsorship" approved by the Metropolitan.[18] Not only were the radio engagements financially rewarding to artist and commerce alike, but radio exposure would play a major role in creating the box-office opera stars of the future. For the Metropolitan the marriage of opera and radio had both positives and negatives: radio stars stimulated ticket sales for their performances at the opera, but the demand for them in more lucrative concert and radio engagements increasingly limited their availability for opera.

Maria Jeritza as Helena in *Die Ägyptische Helena*.

CHAPTER THREE

1931–32
On the Air

At last the Metropolitan is on the air and Madame Manski's Witch crisps away in her gingerbread oven at the close of the Christmas broadcast of *Hänsel und Gretel.* While the designation "Saturday afternoon broadcast" eventually became proverbial, only sixteen broadcasts of the 1931–32 season occurred on Saturday afternoon; three Thursday and six Friday afternoon broadcasts completed the radio schedule. (In the original negotiations Ziegler had favored an evening hour!) The week following the Christmas Day opening brought the Friday matinee airing of acts one and two of the New Year's Day *La Bohème.* Ziegler was pleased, for he wrote to Aylesworth, "I thought yesterday's Bohème was probably the best that has come over so far."[1]

Aylesworth had had two radios installed at the Met, one for Gatti, the other for Ziegler. Ziegler thought them "excellent in quality of tone, but we suffer very much from being near an electric generating station on 39th street."[2] He hoped Aylesworth could eliminate the problem. The ever resourceful NBC president did, adding, "I have heard many favorable comments on Bohème."[3] After thanking both Ziegler and Gatti for their kindness, Aylesworth's optimism surfaced: "It is not hard to make great progress with the kind of cooperation you have given." Ziegler confirmed the general air of benevolence: "We are very happy with the broadcasts; as happy as you are, and we hope they will stimulate interest in us. Publicity has already followed the broadcasts.'[4]

The Saturday afternoon series began most auspiciously on 26 December with that all-star cast in the final acts of Bellini's *Norma.* The following Saturday, 2 January, the opera airwaves were silent, though in the house Suppé's *Donna Juanita* had its first Metropolitan performance. Gatti cancelled the previously announced airing, evidently not considering the opera "suitable broadcast material"[5] in spite of the presence of the incandescent Maria Jeritza in the cast. Thereafter, each Saturday matinee was broadcast through the final week of the season when *Tannhäuser* was given a second airing on 16 April. The era showed no deficiency of vocal wealth—the 12 February *Tannhäuser* offered Jeritza, Gertrude Kappel as Venus, Lauritz Melchior, Friedrich Schorr, Michael Bohnen as the Landgrave, and Fleischer as the Shepherd, while the April broadcast retained Melchior and featured Elisabeth Rethberg as Elisabeth and Lawrence Tibbett as Wolfram. Artur Bodanzky was at the helm for both.

METROPOLITAN OPERA·HOUSE

METROPOLITAN OPERA COMPANY

GIULIO GATTI~CASAZZA
General Manager

PROGRAM
GRAND OPERA
SEASON 1931~1932

TRIUNE PRINTING COMPANY · PUBLISHER · NEW YORK

Fifteenth Week—Feb. 8 to Feb. 14, 1932

METROPOLITAN OPERA HOUSE

GRAND OPERA SEASON 1931-1932

GIULIO GATTI-CASAZZA -- GENERAL MANAGER

FRIDAY AFTERNOON, FEBRUARY 12, 1932, AT 1.45 O'CLOCK

First Performance in the Wagner Cycle

TANNHÄUSER

UND DER SÄNGERKRIEG AUF WARTBURG

OPERA IN THREE ACTS (FOUR SCENES)

(IN GERMAN)

BOOK AND MUSIC BY RICHARD WAGNER

LANDGRAF HERMANN..MICHAEL BOHNEN
TANNHAEUSER..LAURITZ MELCHIOR
WOLFRAM..FRIEDRICH SCHORR
WALTHER..HANS CLEMENS
BITEROLF..ARNOLD GABOR
HEINRICH..GIORDANO PALTRINIERI
REINMAR..JAMES WOLFE
ELISABETH..MARIA JERITZA
VENUS..GERTRUDE KAPPEL
A YOUNG SHEPHERD..EDITHA FLEISCHER

Act I, "Bacchanale," by CORPS DE BALLET
Arranged by AUGUST BERGER
Three Graces: LILYAN OGDEN, JESSIE ROGGE, MARTHA HENKEL

CONDUCTOR..ARTUR BODANZKY

CHORUS MASTER..GIULIO SETTI
STAGE DIRECTOR..HANNS NIEDECKEN-GEBHARD
STAGE MANAGER..ARMANDO AGNINI

POSITIVELY NO ENCORES ALLOWED

PROGRAM CONTINUED ON NEXT PAGE

CORRECT LIBRETTOS FOR SALE IN THE LOBBY
KNABE PIANO USED EXCLUSIVELY

Program for the broadcast of *Tannhäuser* on 12 February 1932.

The large number of non-Saturday offerings was occasioned by the Thursday matinee Wagner cycle (the four operas of the *Ring, Tannhäuser*, and *Tristan und Isolde*) and a Good Friday performance of *Parsifal.* The emphasis on Wagner was inevitable since the decade of the thirties was the heyday of modern Wagner performances at the Metropolitan. Except for its earliest days, the Metropolitan has generally been regarded as an Italian house. And yet, in the first season of the great democratic experiment, only seven of the twenty-five offerings were Italian operas. The current roster certainly contained first-rank artists for the Italian repertory: Lucrezia Bori, Lily Pons, Rosa Ponselle, Elisabeth Rethberg, Carmela Ponselle, Beniamino Gigli, Giacomo Lauri-Volpi, Giovanni Martinelli, Francesco Merli, Giuseppe Danise, Giuseppe de Luca, Lawrence Tibbett, Ezio Pinza, and Tancredi Pasero—all were company members. Many of them appeared in the four Verdi works (*Trovatore, Traviata, Aida*, and the revival of *Simon Boccanegra*) plus one opera each for Bellini, Rossini (*Barbiere*), and Puccini (*Bohème*). The matinee Wagner cycle guaranteed primacy to the German wing for a total of eleven broadcasts. Even more surprising are the five broadcasts in French (*Lakmé, Manon, Roméo, Faust*, and *Sadko*,—the latter, though Russian in origin, was sung in French). Perversely, *L'Africaine,* monumental relic of French grand opera, was offered in Italian.

How unlike was this repertory to that of future decades: the predominance of Wagner, the abundance of French opera, the presence of an American opera (Deems Taylor's *Peter Ibbetson*), the absence of Mozart and Strauss, the paucity of Puccini. Obeisance to familiar Verdi was paid, however, and the broadcast of *Boccanegra* was a harbinger of the future direction of the repertory.

The *Boccanegra* airing reveals the potentiality of the broadcast experiment. On 28 January 1932 the audience in the house heard the first Metropolitan performance of Verdi's little-known opera (performed in the revised version of 1881). The second performance on 6 February was broadcast, and immediately Verdi's work gained a greater réclame than decades of earlier performances in the house could have provided. Radio was destined to play a major role in increasing both the number and knowledgeableness of opera lovers; of equal merit was the exposure of a more experienced public to little-known works.

There were other American premieres in the Metropolitan season which, regrettably, were not broadcast—Weinberger's *Schwanda*, Montemezzi's *La Notte di Zoraima*, as well as the Suppé opus recalled by Gatti. The radio broadcasts were still considered rather a harmless parasite to the main business of opera in New York. Nevertheless, listeners found plenty of novelty in the broadcast repertory. *Peter Ibbetson* (world premiere in February 1931) continued to charm in the portrayals of Bori and Edward Johnson; Rimsky-Korsakov's *Sadko* was offered on 12 March with French tenor Georges Thill; Meyerbeer's *L'Africaine* on 19 March enlisted the formidable trio of Rethberg, Gigli, and Pinza. Over the next half century of broadcasts *Sadko* would not reappear; in fact, Russian opera was all but ignored for decades. The Pons phenomenon eventually necessitated a revival of Rimsky's fairy-tale opera, *Le Coq d'Or* (Munsel sang the only broadcast in 1945), and his molding, meddling hand was clearly audible in his oft-broadcast revision of Mussorgsky's *Boris Godunov*, but that was it. Even less fortunate was Meyerbeer, whose epic operas (after a repeat of *L'Africaine* in 1934) remained off the boards for four decades until the Met mounted *Le Prophète* for Marilyn Horne in 1977.

All three of the season's novelties were under the baton of Tullio Serafin, who also conducted four other broadcasts. Artur Bodanzky was naturally at the helm for

all ten of the Wagner operas, with Louis Hasselmans in charge of the French repertory and Vincenzo Bellezza presiding over *Bohème, Trovatore*, and *Barbiere*. To Karl
Riedel went the honor of conducting the first broadcast on Christmas day.

When Madame Manski's Witch met her gruesome fate, the radio audience
shared with the holiday crowd in the opera house the rescue of the truant Hänsel and
Gretel. The fate of many other heroes, heroines, and villains in that season's twenty-
five broadcasts, however, remained in doubt for radio listeners. The Humperdinck
work was the only opera to be broadcast complete that year (though *Das Rheingold*
may also have been heard in its entirety).

Most other broadcasts were only an hour long. Usually only a single act of the
Wagner operas was aired, but normally two acts of the Italian and French operas
could be included. The effort to broadcast as much of an opera as possible resulted in
"some riotous scenes,"[6] recalled Deems Taylor. "If two acts of an opera lasted no
more than an hour we presented them both without an intermission." While the
singers extended their bows, the stagehands frantically changed the scenery. In their
correspondence Ziegler and Gerald Chatfield of NBC let us in on the give-and-take
of early opera broadcasting. For the broadcast of act two of *Tristan* on 18 February,
Chatfield wrote that NBC would "go on the air at 3:00 and will be obliged to fade out
and sign off at about 3:59. Your timing runs 3:11 to 4:10. If you can shorten up the
intermission ahead of this act, it will help make a better broadcast."[7] For the broadcast of acts three and four of *Traviata* on 20 February (3:30 to 4:45) Chatfield asked
Ziegler "to hold up the start of the third act for about three minutes to give Mr.
Taylor a chance to start." Intermissions were a problem. Chatfield, writing about the
17 March *Götterdämmerung* offered the Met an option: after noting that the times of act
one were 1:00 to 2:55 and act two 3:17 to 4:21, Chatfield adds, "We shall fade in at
2:00 and fade out at 4:00. . . . If Mr. Taylor does not wish to fill this entire intermission, we can switch back to the studio for a fill in by the string quartet."[8]

Is it any wonder that the broadcasters initially were regarded as interlopers by
the paying customers? Engineer Charles Gray remembered twenty-five years later
that "in those days, very few people around here liked us" and that a member of the
NBC program department was needed to act as a buffer against the Met forces.[9] After
the broadcast of *Trovatore* on 16 January, a vice-president of Chase National Bank and
holder of Box 46 in the Grand Tier raised his not inconsiderable voice against the
interlopers. Ziegler frantically sent the boxholder's comments to Aylesworth:

> As you know, box #44 is used for broadcasting purposes and this has not
> annoyed us in our box in any way until Saturday when, after they had
> finished broadcasting, three or four men gathered in the anteroom of the
> box and left the temporary door open and conversed in tones that ruined
> the first scene of the last act for Mrs. Sackett and me and for our guests.
> This was undoubtedly due to thoughtlessness, but you will do me a very
> great favor if you will ask these people hereafter to hold their business
> meeting outside of the box. It so happened that Ponselle's singing in the
> first scene of the last act was the best of the whole opera, and it was unfor-
> tunate that we were disturbed.[10]

Banker Charles A. Sackett showed his astuteness as an opera critic, but Ziegler
thought he might have merely called an usher to quiet the disturbance. He did ask
Aylesworth to take care of the matter with his personnel, while he himself would
"write to Mr. Sackett, assuring him that no repetition of this will occur."[11]

At least the broadcasting trio was as uncomfortable as the audience, for they had no radio booth. Taylor recalls: "We were all huddled together in Box 44 in the Grand Tier. There wasn't even a glass enclosure. We were out in the open, . . . Mr. Gray in the front of the box, Mr. Cross and myself cramped inside of the cloak room in the back."[12] Taylor commented while the opera was actually in progress. For those within range in the auditorium, hearing him give the first line of an aria or herald Mme Manski's entrance with "now the Witch rides in on a broomstick" must have been as disquieting as it eventually proved to the radio audience. Gray would cut down the music in order that Taylor's comments might be heard. These interruptions to the music were eliminated in later seasons, though one high-minded listener considered "Mr. Taylor's remarks of interest and his running comment of real benefit. He is too fine a musician to be a party to any proceeding that would mar the artistic appeal of such an undertaking."[13] As to the quality of broadcast reproduction, the Staten Islander admitted that it was "not perfect perhaps (there have been times when I have wished for a little more judicious use of the mixing controls)." Nor was that the only evidence of the listener's clairvoyance; he hoped complete broadcasts would soon become a reality: "Chopping off at the end of a quarter or half hour period absolutely ruins the effect."

Though the truncated performances were frustrating, the radio public was given a full measure of the great vocalists of the Metropolitan. In addition to her Norma, Ponselle was heard as Leonora in *Trovatore*; Rethberg appeared as Marguerite, Aida, and Selika, as well as Elisabeth; and Bori portrayed Mimi, Violetta, and the Duchess of Towers. Pons (in her second Met season) offered her Rosina and Lakmé, the latter opera not heard since 1917 and revived especially for her. The American soprano Grace Moore (in only her third season with the company) was deemed suited to the French heroines of Manon and Juliette, while the Bohemian Maria Müller offered not only the expected Elsa but the Italian Amelia in *Boccanegra*. Gertrude Kappel dominated the heroic roles of the Wagner repertory, with Göta Ljungberg as an occasional alternate and Karin Branzell as Ortrud and Fricka. The seventy-year-old Ernestine Schumann-Heink's final appearance on the Met stage occurred in the *Siegfried* of 11 March.

In the male wing, the indispensable Melchior sang seven of the Wagner leads, spelled only by Rudolf Laubenthal's Siegmund and Loge and Max Lorenz's Lohengrin. Martinelli, oddly enough, though appearing frequently in New York, had only Gabriele in the *Boccanegra* broadcast, while his rival Gigli (who would soon leave the company) was prominent in both the French and Italian broadcasts. Famed French tenor Georges Thill filled the remaining French slots as Faust, the *Lakmé* Gerald, and Sadko. Single broadcasts were allotted to Johnson (Ibbetson), Armand Tokatyan (Count Almaviva), and Frederick Jagel (Alfredo). Lauri-Volpi, displaying his heroic voice and style as Pollione and Manrico, and debutant Francesco Merli as Radames completed the tenor list.

Pinza and Léon Rothier dominated the Italian and French bass roles; Siegfried Tappolet and Gustav Schützendorf, the German. Schorr and Bohnen displayed their widely contrasted styles in the German repertory, Bohnen appearing in baritone as well as bass roles. The American Clarence Whitehill, in his last Met season, bade farewell as Amfortas and Kurvenal. New baritone Armando Borgioli (Amonasro) and the departing Mario Basiola (Valentin, Nelusko) were outdistanced by the triumvirate of De Luca (Lescaut, Figaro, Mercutio, Marcello, Germont), Danise (in a single broadcast as Di Luna), and the American Tibbett (heard as the Italian

Boccanegra, the German Wolfram, and Colonel Ibbetson in Taylor's American opera.)

What Gigli's flight meant to the company may be imagined from the good fortune of the radio audience who heard the tenor as Rodolfo, Vasco da Gama, Roméo, and Massenet's Des Grieux in the first broadcast season. Gigli had joined the company in 1920, and the mantle of Caruso, cut down to size, had settled on his shoulders in the decade since the great tenor's death in 1921 (though Martinelli and Lauri-Volpi both staked their claims). The sweet-voiced Gigli, however, had not inherited the good nature of his noble predecessor. When the economic woes of the depression threatened the Metropolitan's existence (the 1931–32 season ended with a deficit of $497,213),[14] and all personnel were requested to take a salary cut for the 1932–33 season, Gigli refused. His contract would have run until 1935, and though he bravely defended his decision, his colleagues (including nearly all the illustrious members of the company—Bori, Pons, Ponselle, De Luca, Martinelli, Pinza) found his conduct "inexcusable."[15] He was accused of disturbing "the harmony of the Metropolitan" and showing lack of esprit de corps. Gigli offered, among other concessions, to sing his radio broadcast without an additional fee, though his contract called for this remuneratic n. (Even in the first season the monetary returns from the radio experiment meant something to the individual artists as well as to the institution.) But the door was effectively closed to Gigli when Gatti wrote to Ziegler from Milan during the summer of 1932:

> Frankly, I cannot understand what the desire of Gigli to make peace means. It is not a matter of peace or war, but it is simply a matter of letting Mr. Gigli stay where he voluntarily put himself, i.e., away from the Metropolitan. It will be a historic and exemplary precedent for the effect that it will have in these extremely difficult times. . . . In any case, if he will come to see me, I shall tell him that for the coming season nothing can be done because we already have contracted for too many performances for tenors and that as to the future it rests on the knees of Jove and nothing can be said now.[16]

A brief coda was added to Gigli's Metropolitan career in the 1939–40 season when the radio audience heard him as Radames; only the final two acts of that performance remain as a souvenir of his lengthy Met career. We are even less fortunate in regard to Jeritza, who was heard only as Elisabeth in *Tannhäuser* during the first broadcast season, her last at the Metropolitan.[17]

The vocal riches of the first season of broadcasts underline the largesse of the NBC experiment. By the end of the season the Metropolitan's attitude had completely altered. With the sound of the final broadcast of *Tannhäuser* in his ears, on 16 April Ziegler wrote again to Aylesworth:

> With today's broadcast, our official connection ceases for the season, and I wish to tell you that it was a joy and privilege to contract with you, and in working with your organization we found nothing but sympathetic cooperation.
>   I personally am very happy and proud of this connection, and look forward to continuing it in another year.[18]

Aylesworth responded in kind—"very glad to have lunch with you when you return to New York from tour."[19] But the more vivid sign of approval had occurred months earlier when the faithful Ziegler wrote to Aylesworth:

A few days ago Mr. Gatti-Casazza expressed the desire to have a radio set installed in his apartment at the Savoy-Plaza, which I communicated to Mr. Chatfield.

I wish to report that this request was most promptly and effectively granted, for which Mr. Gatti and I thank you.[20]

Even Gatti had at last gone over.

When viewed from the distance of more than a half century, the repute of these early performances is formidable. Writing in 1936, Kolodin, the sometimes dour chronicler of the Met's history, was not always enthralled. He cited the *Faust* of 13 February (a Saturday broadcast) where the now venerated Thill and the all-but canonized Rethberg were "in obviously bad voice, and the tenor could not manage his C in 'Salut! demeure,' nor approach within plausible distance of it."[21] How we might view that performance today we cannot judge, for no recordings of the first broadcast season have come to light. This is particularly regrettable since 1931–32 offered the only opportunity to hear "live" portions of Ponselle's Norma, for instance, and it was the final Met season for such legendary performers as Bohnen and Jeritza. We have some consolation in that a few of the first season's performances are closely replicated in later seasons where they may be heard in their entirety rather than in the single hour of radio time originally allotted. One can hear Kappel and Melchior in *Tristan* (in 1933–34); Kappel and Branzell in *Walküre* (1933–34); Bori, Johnson, and Tibbett in *Peter Ibbetson* (1933–34); and Tibbett, Martinelli, and Pinza in *Boccanegra* (1934–35). Although there remains no audible record of the first broadcast season, the prospect thereafter invites us, offering the opportunity for aural appraisal. The 1932–33 season provides only two examples, but the amazing sound record grows significantly thereafter, both in quantity and in sound quality.

Lauritz Melchior as Tristan in *Tristan und Isolde*. Photography by Carlo Edwards.

CHAPTER FOUR

1932–33
Money Troubles

When the 1932–33 season opened, the Metropolitan found itself in a deep financial crisis. The economic depression forced the board to shrink the season by one-third (from twenty-four weeks to sixteen) and to reorganize the Opera Company into the Metropolitan Opera Association, thereby qualifying it eventually for tax-exemption as a nonprofit institution which merely subleased the theater. In so doing the board took the first step along the path toward democratization of the opera which became the dominant theme of the next two decades.

That the new board chairman was interested more in the financial savings than the movement toward a people's opera is evident in Cravath's response to Bodanzky's undiplomatic outburst to the press on his return from Europe. The conductor railed against "those who use opera for their own social ends. It was the artists who saved this distinctly great American institution from going to the wall. The bankers and the backers—why, they quit!"[1] In spite of having profited from seventeen seasons of association with bankers and backers, Bodanzky planned to confer with Ziegler and Gatti to take "the Metropolitan out of the hands of the wealthy few and put it in the hands of the appreciative public."[2] Cravath, whose Met associations went back even further, immediately countered with a confidential note to Ziegler asking him or Gatti "to caution Bodanzky not to talk to the newspapers any more. . . . He can talk to the newspapers every day if he will give them the kind of foolish talk that he gave out on his arrival. I am wondering whether I belong to the 'wealthy few' or to the 'bourgeoisie'."[3]

It soon became clear that an appreciative public already existed in the unseen audience. The curtailment of the season, the salary cuts proposed by Gatti, and Cravath's reorganization would prove insufficient to sustain the company. Ziegler, clearly seeing the hard path ahead, had written to Gatti in July 1932:

> The financial conditions and general business conditions are considerably worse than they were when you left, nor has the choice of the Democratic Presidential Nominee met with approval, so I am inclined to think that the presidential election will have very little effect on improving conditions, and I fear that this recovery is going to be a very slow one and will probably stretch out over a period of years.[4]

Ziegler proved more accurate in forecasting the duration of the economic plight than in his evaluation of incoming president Franklin Delano Roosevelt. In fact, Ziegler would have opted for a more radical change in government, adding to Gatti (who was in Milan) that he was convinced "our present form of government has proven a failure at this time and I believe what we need here is what you have in Italy, namely a dictator."[5] In Ziegler's defense, others of far greater political experience at the time were similarly beguiled by Mussolini's air of efficiency.

When the 1932–33 season opened, the effect of its curtailment on the radio broadcasts was uncertain. On 1 December 1932 Aylesworth wrote Ziegler that the actual number and duration of the broadcasts "are somewhat dependent on circumstances. Our broadcasts may increase in number each week. . . . We may need more time than we had last year; we may need less. We must proceed experimentally and I count on your cooperation to this end."[6] The precarious nature of the experiment was again evident as Aylesworth noted the amount to be paid to the Met would have "to await the outcome of events and be subject to mutual agreement thereafter." By this time the establishment of a Guaranty Fund to preserve the Metropolitan became a necessity, and NBC was prepared to be a part of the effort. Though on 12 January 1933[7] the original contract of 27 May 1931 was altered to eliminate payments of $20,000 each on 15 January and 15 February, what the right hand took away the left hand restored. Aylesworth had ended his 1 December letter to Ziegler:

> It is definitely understood, however, that in spite of the reduction of the season to 16 weeks, the total amount the NBC pays for the broadcasting privilege and the control of your artists for broadcasting purposes, and on account of our subscription to the Metropolitan Opera Association Guaranty Fund, will not, without our written consent, exceed the total amount paid last year under our two contracts but will, on the other hand, at least equal the amount paid last year.[8]

In effect, NBC contributed the balance to the drive to save the Metropolitan. The actual broadcast season, however, did consist of twenty-four broadcasts since (in the contractual revision of 12 January) Aylesworth had provided that "we shall have the right to broadcast the operas more than once each week providing that we do not make more than twenty-four broadcasts during the 1932–33 season." Ziegler responded that "we are in accord with your understanding of the case, and will do our utmost to help you work things out."[9] Thus the season included fourteen Saturday matinees (the 2 January *Mignon* and 4 March *Trovatore* were not broadcast) and eight midweek matinees (Wednesday, Thursday, or Friday) of the Wagner operas, plus Thursday matinees of *Lakmé* and *La Bohème* on Thanksgiving and Christmas Eve.

Unlike later practice, the broadcast season coincided with the opening and closing of the New York season. Pons' ascendancy is apparent in her four broadcasts. On 24 November she opened the broadcast season on a Thursday matinee (act two of *Lakmé* with Swarthout, Martinelli, Rothier; Hasselmans), followed on Saturday, 26 November, by the first of Pons' fourteen broadcasts of *Lucia* (acts two and three). One doubts she was ever again so well partnered, for Tito Schipa sang Edgardo and De Luca appeared as Enrico Ashton. Later in the season she played Amina in *La Sonnambula*, last heard at the Met with Maria Barrientos in 1916 and revived in March 1932 for Pons. Lauri-Volpi and Pinza joined her in the Bellini work. Gilda in *Rigoletto* completed her broadcast efforts; also in the cast were De Luca, Lauri-Volpi, and Pasero.

Lakmé and *Lucia* were not broadcast in their entirety. The practice of incomplete offerings of the first season continued for eleven of the twenty-four broadcasts of the 1932–33 season. Wagner's *Götterdämmerung* (played twice), *Lohengrin, Parsifal, Siegfried, Walküre*, and the *Tristan* of 3 March plus *Pelléas* and *Boccanegra* were the other incomplete operas. (*Tristan* on 11 March was broadcast complete—at least in performance time, if not in terms of Wagner's score.) For the first time the radio public heard complete Metropolitan performances of *The Bartered Bride* (Rethberg, Laubenthal, Hofmann; Bodanzky), *Bohème, Don Giovanni, Elektra* (Kappel, Ljungberg, Branzell, Schorr; Bodanzky), *Rigoletto, Sonnambula, Tannhäuser* (Rethberg, Olszewska, Melchior, Schorr), *Traviata, Tristan*, and the one-act *Emperor Jones*. (*Hänsel* was again heard in its entirety).

The second season's repertory mix was not much changed. There were ten Wagner broadcasts with *Elektra, Hänsel*, and *Die Verkaufte Braut* (The Bartered Bride) bringing the German total to thirteen—more than half the season. Bodanzky was on the podium for all of them except Riedel's Humperdinck preserve. In the French repertory, only *Lakmé, Pelléas*, and *Manon* were heard, and the Italian offerings remained a meager seven operas (Verdi's *Rigoletto, Traviata*, and *Boccanegra*, the perennial *Bohème*, and *Lucia* and *Sonnambula* for the popular Pons). The Italian language list included the first broadcast of a Mozart opera, *Don Giovanni*, with Serafin guiding a fabled cast: Pinza, Ponselle, Müller, Fleischer, Schipa, Pasero, and Rothier. This was Ponselle's only broadcast of the season, though the gifted Müller was favored with Mimi and Amelia as well. Rethberg added Elsa and Elisabeth to her Marie, and Miss Bori could be heard in her familiar Violetta, plus Mélisande (with Johnson as Pelléas) and Manon. Making his Met debut as an elegant Chevalier des Grieux on the 25 February broadcast was the young American tenor Richard Crooks, already familiar to the radio audience as a popular singer of songs.

The reference to radio is apt, for the *Manon* broadcast was the occasion of the initial solicitation by the Metropolitan for funds from the radio audience. The honor of the first of many solicitations to the radio public over the years fell prophetically to Edward Johnson (along with Bori and Tibbett, artist members of the Committee for Saving the Metropolitan Opera). The 1933–34 season was in jeopardy. Aylesworth wanted Bori to momentarily leave off the courtesan Manon's finery and step before the curtain during intermission to speak to the audience in the house, stating that "while the National Broadcasting Company is contributing to the Opera fund so that the radio listeners may hear the Opera, it has become necessary for those who attend Opera, and desire to support the Opera, to come to the rescue of the Metropolitan Opera."[10] Aylesworth further requested, "If those who are listening today, as well as those in the house, will write Lucretia [*sic*] Bori, Metropolitan Opera Company, New York, she will be very glad to send you detailed information of what is required to sustain the Opera for the coming season."[11] The appeal to the radio audience was continued by other artists during the intermissions of the remaining three broadcasts (former diva Geraldine Farrar joined current members on one occasion). NBC reaffirmed its commitment to the opera (though its two years of bearing all costs of the broadcasts without commercial sponsorship was perhaps evidence enough) by providing the Committee for Saving the Metropolitan with the opportunity to rouse the radio audience on a special Sunday afternoon program on 4 March.

It was Cravath himself who now was content to embrace the bourgeoisie. On 2 March Ziegler forwarded to NBC a copy of a "suggested talk which Mr. Cravath is to use in his remarks introducing Miss Bori:"[12]

The National Broadcasting Company, who through their contract with the Opera Company under which they have received the right to broadcast opera, have contributed largely to the support of the Opera Company. This kind of support the National Broadcasting Company are prepared to continue so that you who have listened to the opera broadcasts this year may again have the opportunity to do so next winter. Realizing however that the opera cannot be broadcast unless it is produced, and believing that their clients are anxious and eager to hear opera over the air, the National Broadcasting Company have placed this hour at the disposal of the "Save the Opera Committee" so that Miss Bori may have an opportunity to tell you what she wants you to do.[13]

What Miss Bori wanted was the financial assistance of the radio audience; the public responded with contributions totaling $100,000 (one-third of the $300,000 Guaranty Fund).[14]

Though the precarious financial situation affected the artists' remuneration, it had little effect on the make-up of the company during the 1932–33 season. The financial crunch had obliged Gigli to quit, but Lauri-Volpi remained to sing Rodolfo in addition to partnering Pons as Elvino and the Duke of Mantua. There was good fortune in Schipa's coming to the Met in the wake of Gigli's departure, but the Met would again lose one of its stellar tenors at the end of the 1932–33 season. Lauri-Volpi continued to sing in Europe until the early 1950s and partnered Callas in some of her early performances, but he sang no more at the Met.

Of the lower voices, amazingly the repertory provided no need for an Italianate mezzo (Swarthout appeared only as Mallika), but the male wing was in good hands again with Tibbett (Germont and Boccanegra) and De Luca (Rigoletto and Lescaut), plus the American Richard Bonelli, in his first Metropolitan season, as Marcello. Pinza continued to do yeoman's service as Fiesco, Colline, the *Sonnambula* Count, Don Giovanni, and his first assumption of Golaud, the latter taken over from the departed Clarence Whitehill. Melchior and Schorr of course dominated the Wagner performances with six and nine hearings respectively. Melchior's brief absence fortunately allowed Gustaav de Loor only Lohengrin and Siegfried, which were evidently more than enough, for he did not return. Schützendorf, Hofmann, and Tappolet filled the remaining roles much as in the previous season. Spelling Bodanzky in his conducting marathon were Serafin (*Boccanegra, Giovanni, Emperor Jones, Traviata, Sonnambula*) and Bellezza, with Hasselmans in charge of the three French works.

A few stellar artists again escaped before recorded sound captured their Metropolitan broadcasts. But the arrival of Europe's premier Wagnerian soprano, Frida Leider, for the 1932–33 season is some compensation, not only for contemporary radio listeners but for our grateful ears. Of the three known recordings of that season's broadcasts, two capture portions of Leider's Isolde. New also to the Metropolitan was the celebrated singing-actress Maria Olszewska, long a favorite of audiences in Vienna, Berlin and London; we hear her as the broadcast Brangäne.

The weekday matinees of the Metropolitan's 1933 Wagner cycle brought a broadcast (incomplete) of *Tristan* on 3 March with Leider and Olszewska in company with Melchior, Schorr, and Ludwig Hofmann (also new to the company) as King Marke. When the opera was again given (complete) on the Saturday matinee of 11 March, Schützendorf was the Kurvenal. Bodanzky guided both performances. While Melchior's Tristan and Schorr's Kurvenal under the leadership of Bodanzky would continue to be prized possessions of the radio audience for years to come, capturing

Tristan und Isolde
3 March 1933

Isolde
Frida Leider

Brangäne
Maria Olszewska

Tristan
Lauritz Melchior

Kurvenal
Friedrich Schorr

Marke
Ludwig Hofmann

Conductor
Artur Bodanzky

Frida Leider as Isolde in *Tristan und Isolde.*

Maria Olszewska. Photography by Setzer.

Leider's Isolde and Olszewska's Brangäne on records is fortuitous since their Metropolitan careers were so short-lived. Leider returned only for the next season, and Olszewska departed the year after. Moreover, these were Olszewska's and Leider's sole broadcasts of these roles.

Tristan und Isolde
11 March 1933
Isolde
Frida Leider
Brangäne
Maria Olszewska
Tristan
Lauritz Melchior
Kurvenal
Gustav Schützendorf
Marke
Ludwig Hofmann
Conductor
Artur Bodanzky

Since the Metropolitan in the 1930s was, more than anything, a stronghold of Wagnerian performance, justice is served by the preservation of portions of *Tristan* as the earliest "live" recordings of the company (always excepting Metropolitan Opera librarian Lionel Mapleson's minuscule but invaluable efforts at the turn of the century). While Melchior and Schorr were the indispensable pillars of the male wing, and Bodanzky was invariably the presiding priest, the Metropolitan luxuriated in a profusion of majestic voices and varied interpretations for the Wagner heroines. Florence Easton, Margarete Matzenauer, and Elisabeth Ohms had departed by 1932, but the female roster was still resplendent with Kappel, Rethberg, Jeritza, Müller, Grete Stückgold, and Branzell. On the horizon were Lotte Lehmann (1933–34), Anny Konetzni and Kirsten Flagstad (1934–35), Marjorie Lawrence (1935–36), and Kerstin Thorborg (1936–37).

The engagement of Leider and Olszewska caused considerable displacement in the Wagner radio casts—Gertrude Kappel, for the last half-dozen years the favored Wagner soprano, was granted only the broadcast of Elektra. Göta Ljungberg sang the *Götterdämmerung* Brünnhilde and the *Rheingold* Freia, while Dorothee Manski shed her Witch's garb for the *Siegfried* Brünnhilde and Gutrune. But it was Leider who garnered the lioness' share of the heroic Wagner roles, first appearing as the *Walküre* Brünnhilde on 2 February and following it with *Götterdämmerung* on 17 February before her two March broadcasts of Isolde. Olszewska's lot was even larger in quantity, for she appeared as the broadcast Erda in *Rheingold* and *Siegfried*, Fricka (*Walküre*), Waltraute, Venus, and the two Brangänes, while the stalwart Branzell held on only to Ortrud and another Waltraute (though she gained Strauss' Klytemnestra).

In heralding the debuts of Leider and Olszewska, Lawrence Gilman, longtime (and by now somewhat jaded) critic of the *Herald Tribune*, belittled "the trustful belief of many operagoers whose credulity outran their knowledge"[15] as they accepted the Metropolitan's boast that it housed the foremost opera singers in the world. Not without Leider and Olszewska it didn't, Gilman opined. Leider, after a brief sojourn in provincial theaters following her 1915 debut as Venus ("I was a dramatic soprano right from the beginning"[16]—no soubrette dalliance à la Flagstad for her), had reigned for two decades in Berlin (her home house), Milan, Paris, Vienna, London, Bayreuth, and Buenos Aires in the Wagner operas. Some, Gilman among them, thought her the greatest contemporary Isolde. One can hear the evidence in the live broadcast, evidence more substantial than that of the recording studio or the printed review.

Of the earlier performance (3 March) about thirty-five minutes of the opera are preserved—half an hour from act one and only four minutes from act two. The act-one excerpts begin with Isolde's 'Mir erkoren' just before 'Todgeweihtes Haupt' and continue through Tristan's first appearance, 'Was wohl erwidertest du?' (about ten minutes of music). The major excerpt is Isolde's Narrative and Curse beginning at 'Tod! uns beiden' on through Tristan's reappearance and 'Ehrfurcht hielt mich in Acht.' The brief act-two excerpt again highlights Isolde, this time feverishly awaiting Tristan ('Dem Freund zulieb'' through 'die sie webt aus Lust'). The 11 March performance was broadcast complete, and recorded excerpts total an hour and fifteen minutes. They essentially duplicate the act-one material but precede it with a few measures of the prelude and Isolde's imperious 'Nimmermehr! Nicht heut', noch morgen!' ending at 'Zerschlag' es.' The act-two material is again similar to 3 March, but added is an important minute at the climax of the love duet ('Soll der Tag noch Tristan wecken?') plus several brief moments for Tristan and King Marke at the very end of the act. The major additions are in act three, including the lengthy scene of Tristan's delirium 'Ich war, wo ich von je gewesen' (with brief performance cuts) through Kurvenal's 'was je Minne sich gewinnt!' and a second lengthy scene 'Kurwenal, wie du säh'st sie nicht?' through the actual sighting of the ship, the entrance of Isolde, and on (again with minor performance cuts) through the Liebestod—all in all about thirty-five minutes of the act. The body of the evidence is thus substantial, though the quality of the sound recording almost rivals Mapleson's 1901–03 cylinders in noise.

While the contributions of Melchior and Schorr can be more fully examined in several later complete performances, the lengthy third-act scenes of Melchior do provide the earliest glimpse of his live performances. By Melchior's own words we owe to Mme Charles Cahier his conversion from journeyman baritone; in the Di Luna–Azucena duet he struck a high C, and Madame named him "tenor"—"I can honestly say it was her influence that decided me."[17] After Canio and Radames at the Copenhagen Opera, a second conversion occurred when Cosima and Siegfried Wagner persuaded him that Bayreuth was his spiritual home (Parsifal in 1924); he came to the Met as Tannhäuser two years later where, after a lukewarm reception, press and public recognized him as sui generis. His baritone beginnings were an asset, he claimed: "It is easier to build from the bottom than from the top."[18] And evidently it was, for the voice is incredibly beautiful in the *Tristan* broadcast excerpts, the baritonal lower tones carrying immediate emotional impact and his vocal staying powers throughout Tristan's delirium never in doubt. His final voicing of 'Isolde' seems to be more falsetto than head tone. Surprisingly, it is the excellence of his musicianship and the deep commitment of his characterization which register most strongly; dynamic markings are carefully observed and he is always alive to textual implications. Schützendorf's 11 March Kurvenal has a rough bluffness that may be appropriate in terms of the vassal's character, but his barking is the strongest contrast to Schorr's beautiful voicing of the first-act 'Frisch und froh!' in the earlier broadcast.

The ladies warrant closer examination. Even in Brangäne's limited recorded passages Olszewska projects her characterization through many masterful touches: the almost coy toying with Tristan in the first-act exchange, the sudden *piano* on 'entsandt' when she questions Isolde, the contrasting angry outbursts of tone ('Entsetzen! Schone mich Arme!'). This is no mere handmaiden but a very knowing, authoritative Brangäne. Upon hiring Olszewska, Gatti had informed Ziegler that she was "an extraordinarily sensitive artist and in a way sensational in her interpretations."[19] She does not disappoint. Vocally, too, Olszewska shows her years of experience; the voice is not always rock firm, and an occasional threadbareness thins the tone.

It is Leider who makes the most vivid impression in these excerpts. One is taken by the singular beauty of the voice itself, the melding of noble tone with affective coloration; the two are almost inseparably bound together, the coloration not merely appliquéd for certain effects or at emotive words. In these live performances Leider's voice, especially in the 3 March performance where her voice is in slightly better condition, radiates greater emotional conviction than in many of her admirable records.

While reveling in the Leider sound, one notes that she is decidedly fond of *portamento*—almost alarmingly so for modern ears. Of course, as far as the venerable vocal devices are concerned, we live in an aural desert. But strangeness need not dilute the pleasure we derive from the warm curve of a well-executed *portamento*, and their abundance in the song of Olszewska, and Ludwig Hofmann as well, obviously confirms their stylistic acceptability (though it is late enough in time if one recalls that Emma Eames, recoiling from the abuse of *portamento* by De Reszke and Caruso, decisively eliminated all but the essential ones from her scores). Melchior seems relatively immune from the disease in his readings, however, and one wishes Leider would be just a bit less generous. Actually, her *portamenti* unduly intrude only in the final section of the Liebestod where repetitions of the phrase-shape 'soll ich atmen, soll ich lauschen?' cause them to multiply too quickly.

Nevertheless, the dominant face of Leider's characterization of the Irish princess is one of moderation; her rage is not demonic nor her passion unbridled. Everywhere her long experience dictates a sure control, but it serves not to inhibit but rather to give her Isolde a larger dimension, a heightened stature. Her conception admits many expressive details: the imperious firmness of her decision not to reach Cornwall's shore ('Nimmermehr!'); the Lotte Lehmann–like immediacy of emotive sound and textual pathos in 'Der Mutter Rat gemahnt mich recht' as she asks Brangäne to fetch her mother's potion; the lovely, enchanted quality which suddenly penetrates her tone as she tells Brangäne 'Diesen Trank! In die gold'ne Schale giess' ihn aus,' rendered even more poignant as it gives way to the drained, hollow declamation of 'Der Tod nun sag' ihr Dank.' When Leider's Isolde asks Kurvenal to bring Tristan to her, the vocal color and attitude change from woe to calm authority, the contrasts always within the zones of her patrician conception. She employs coloristic effects sparingly, and they are all the more affecting when they suddenly appear, like the shaft of light on the words 'Lichtes letzten Schein!' as Isolde awaits Tristan's arrival in act two. As Isolde falls under Frau Minne's spell, knowing that life and death are subject to her power, the earlier containment of Leider's conception magnifies the poignancy of her submission. The Liebestod emanates a quiet tenderness. Leider begins with maximum mildness, shaping the early phrases meaningfully (with a strong glottal stroke on 'Auge'). She doesn't shy from deploying her full, dark sound at the climaxes, but over all she wafts a more fragile, feminine tone, as though taking her cue from 'die so wundervoll und leise.' The *portamenti* quicken; she breathes before the final 'Lust,' and the apotheosis is momentarily weakened. While the Leider Isolde has a full measure of nobility and more than a hint of something beyond the human, she means her 'Irische Maid' not only to be admired but to be loved.

To Stew —
— now he's a wrestler
"Wrestling Bradford" in "Merry Mount"
erstwhile
Lawrence Tibbett
Jan / 34

Lawrence Tibbett as Wrestling Bradford in *Merry Mount*.

1933-34
Deities, Premieres, and Farewells

The initial two-year agreement between the Metropolitan and NBC had run its course. In spite of the dire financial condition of the opera company and the country, the experiment was a success and a boon to both, and in May 1933, NBC and Ziegler entered into negotiations for a new broadcast contract.

Arrangements covering both the broadcasting of opera performances and the franchise of radio appearances by Met artists were now incorporated into a single agreement for the 1933-34 season, with a renewal option for 1934-35. Other changes were necessitated by the shortening of the New York season from sixteen to fourteen weeks. NBC initially suggested two broadcasts per week, but Ziegler cautioned "this would prove an impossibility in the number of weeks. Outside of the regular Saturday matinee performances and the six Wagner Cycle performances the other matinee performances given are invariably benefits for charities and as such pass from our control, so that we would have no right to broadcast them."[1] Twenty broadcasts were eventually agreed upon (though "as many additional broadcasts as prove possible" could be included). Ultimately only seventeen broadcasts were aired.

The original $150,000 figure of 1931 was now reduced to $100,000, though the Metropolitan's profit-and-loss statement for the season shows receipts from NBC of $113,000[2] (including $3,000 for the broadcast of *Pelléas* from Boston[3]). The Met's financial crisis was far from over. Ziegler expressed his fears for the future of the company (in regard to the proposed option for 1934-35) when he wrote to Engels that "no season is assured for 1934-35, and it is conceivable that if our financial condition is not bettered during the next year, and if the opera attendance does not increase enormously, the season of 1934-35 might in that event be a very brief one." But Ziegler went on to reaffirm "the close cooperation of the two organizations, with the presence on these two boards of Mr. [Cornelius] Bliss, with Mr. Aylesworth's confidence in Mr. Cravath and in us . . . a divorce in this widespread family is rather difficult to contemplate."[4] (Difficult, yes, but not impossible—the divorce was half a dozen years in the future.) As a result of Ziegler's concern, the contract draft of 19 June gave NBC the option of a second season, conditioned upon the season being the same length, with the right of first refusal to contract for the altered season on the same terms as offered by other bidders.

Under the new agreement the Metropolitan itself would receive from NBC "the entire amount it receives from its [NBC's] clients from the sale of any opera broadcasts other than the amounts received for its announcing, technical and broadcasting facilities."[5] This would reduce NBC's payment by an equal amount, less any increased fees the Met might pay to artists, should commercial sponsorship materialize. The Met also was to secure licenses and pay copyright fees for operas restricted by copyright.

But problems with the franchise portion of the agreement were more troublesome. Ziegler wanted the exclusive NBC broadcast of artists to be confined to "regular" artists since "we have this year engaged a number of artists who can only be given a very limited number of performances, and therefore they cannot be held to comply with the restriction clause in our regular artist contract."[6] NBC wanted to protect its lucrative right to the exclusive broadcast of concert services of Metropolitan artists. NBC understood that the Metropolitan "may not be able to grant this right with respect to artists [John Charles] Thomas, Crooks, Lehman [*sic*], Muzio, [Cyrena] Van Gorden, [Paul] Althouse, [Charles] Hackett, [Nino] Martini and Bodanzky," but the Met was to "use its best endeavors to secure such rights" for NBC. Failing that, the Met was not to permit its name or the phrase "Metropolitan Star" to be used on any broadcasts of these artists unless NBC and the Met agreed. The formal agreement went further by turning tenor Martini into "Exhibit A"; any engagement of Martini by the Met must be in accordance with its provisions. Commercial radio rivalry now enters into the personnel policies of the Metropolitan. Martini was under contract to the Columbia Broadcasting Company until 21 November 1933. But the tenor was "desirous of being engaged with the Metropolitan Opera Company," so discussions of 19 April 1933 were incorporated as "Exhibit A" of the agreement for the broadcast season of 1933–34. Madame Maria Gay, erstwhile Met contralto and current personal agent for Martini, was to secure Martini's release from any further option with CBS, thereupon enabling NBC to step into the breach. If this should prove impossible, "Exhibit A" stipulated that "the Metropolitan has the right to engage said Martini . . . but upon the condition that during the period of his engagement . . . said Martini is not to broadcast over any system other than National Broadcasting Company."[7] Martini came to the Met as the *Rigoletto* Duke on 28 December 1933 and later that season sang the broadcast *Lucia* with Pons (who had been brought to the attention of the Met by the omnipresent Mme Gay). Though an operatic artist of no special abilities, Martini had been a film star in Italy since 1929, and his American films and extensive radio engagements made him "recognized by millions,"[8] to use his own words. The likeable tenor was no flash in the pan, however, for he remained with the Met until 1946.

The commercial value of radio and film personalities (apparent in the complicated maneuvers of NBC) dictated NBC's interference in the internal management of the opera company and the Metropolitan acceded to the demands. The interlocking realms of radio and talking (hence "singing") pictures would continue to weaken the hegemony of the opera company throughout the next decade.

Meanwhile, a national public continued to enjoy opera over the airwaves. In a repeat of the scenario of two years earlier, a Christmas Day *Hänsel und Gretel* inaugurated the 1933–34 broadcast season. Neither it nor the 30 December *Mignon* (superlatively cast with Bori, Pons, Swarthout, Schipa, and Rothier) is preserved; once again it is the Wagner wing which is immortalized in sound.

Gertrude Kappel had preceded Leider as the first broadcast Isolde in the premiere season of broadcasts. Now she followed Leider in the role on the broadcast

Gertrude Kappel as Isolde in *Tristan und Isolde*.
Photography by A. Sahm.

of 6 January 1934 (with Doris Doe, Melchior, Schorr, Hofmann; Bodanzky). The
recorded excerpts are similar to those of 11 March 1933, with the second-act excerpt
now extending through Tristan's entrance (but ending too soon at Kappel's rather
infantile 'Endlich! Endlich!'); the Liebestod is abruptly appended to the lengthy act-
three scenes of Tristan. The recorded sound marks a slight improvement over the
1933 performances.

Kappel is one of those artists whose name is repeatedly heard, but of whom
recorded evidence is limited and commentary conflicting. (Kolodin denied her any
historic importance[9] while Robert Lawrence, survivor of many a broadcast quiz,
repeatedly championed her as "the most diversely hued, sensitively projected
Wagner-Strauss voice in recall."[10] Before beginning her Met career as Isolde in 1928,
Kappel used Hanover as home base for twenty-one seasons; Covent Garden, Vienna,
Berlin, and Munich were all favored by her well-judged Wagner and Strauss
portrayals. The heroic was always her lot from her debut as Fidelio (1903, age
nineteen!) to her controversial Elektra in the 1932 Met premiere. At the time of her
1934 broadcast Isolde, she was fifty years old and near the end of her distinguished
international career. With the memory of Leider's compact tone, firm legato, and
sense of dramatic and musical proportion still fresh in one's ears, Kappel's Isolde
immediately registers as more overtly dramatic—individual words are vividly treated,
her manner is more insistently "girlish" (she sends her greetings to Tristan in act one

Tristan und Isolde
6 January 1934

Isolde
Gertrude Kappel
Brangäne
Doris Doe
Tristan
Lauritz Melchior
Kurvenal
Friedrich Schorr
Marke
Ludwig Hofmann
Conductor
Artur Bodanzky

with no apparent concern for the fateful meeting), and the emotional framework is more impetuous (as at 'Lösche den scheuchenden Schein' in act two). On the other hand, Kappel's *portamenti* are far less intrusive. All these elements find cause in the voice itself, which is essentially a lyric instrument; therefore, she does not draw as resolute a line in this heroic music as do other Isoldes. But her phrasing in itself is often captivating; a certain delicious fluidity infects it. She scrupulously observes the *subito piano* on 'nicht' after a lovely embracing *forte* at the beginning of 'Frau Minne will: es werde Nacht.' In the Liebestod, 'seht ihr's, Freunde?' and 'Säht ihr's nicht?' are really heard as questions, and Kappel sends off 'wie er leuchtet' with a soaring curve; she shapes and shades the ensuing phrases with warmth and intimacy. Although she, too, occasionally converts a *portamento* into a scoop, her Liebestod reaches a splendid climax on 'in des Welt-Atems.' In spite of her subtle artistry, the vocal resources at her command seem somewhat slight for Isolde's music, and more tonal security and firmness of line would be welcome.

The act-three scenes featuring Melchior and Schorr are the most memorable portions of these 1934 excerpts. The hopelessness of 'Wie schwand mir seine Ahnung?' is mirrored in Melchior's dark, wooly tone. And this time he sings 'göttlich ew'ges Ur-Vergessen!' in correct rhythm (unlike the broadcast of 11 March 1933) suggesting that he did not make the same mistakes all the time; he was not so reliable as the old saw would have it. 'Wonnen und Wunden hab' ich des Trankes Gifte gefunden!' is magnificently declaimed—at least for the radio audience Melchior qualifies as a great actor. Schorr is equally impressive. When he sings 'wer einst dir Merolds Wunde schloss' (act three) with peerless legato, perfectly focused tone, bright top, and solid bottom, we suddenly find ourselves in bel canto land. His most affecting moments come after Tristan's final outburst, where he drains all color from his tone at 'holdester Wahn!' and then immediately suggests Kurvenal's compassion and grief as he sweetly intones 'der wonnige Mann.'

Two other Wagner performances from the 1933–34 season amplify regard for these several artists. A month after Kappel's Isolde, she appeared as Sieglinde to Leider's Brünnhilde in the *Walküre* broadcast of 3 February 1934. Often enough one hears two celebrated sopranos in these widely contrasted roles (Flagstad and Lehmann, Nilsson and Rysanek are justly famous pairings) but seldom does one have the chance to hear the era's foremost portrayers of Isolde and the Brünnhildes in such provocative juxtaposition. The recording is far from complete: act one terminates before Sieglinde's return; in act two the entire Fricka scene is missing, as is the Sieglinde-Siegmund exchange; a larger portion of act three is preserved.

Die Walküre
3 February 1934
Sieglinde
Gertrude Kappel
Brünnhilde
Frida Leider
Fricka
Karin Branzell
Siegmund
Paul Althouse
Wotan
Ludwig Hofmann
Hunding
Emanuel List
Conductor
Artur Bodanzky

From her first entrance Kappel impresses as being in finer vocal fettle; she is authoritative and secure, yet always one is conscious of a soft womanliness in the substance of the voice. Her call to prevent Siegmund from leaving ('O bleibe hier') begins with splendid conviction of voice and manner, though the end is marred by some unsteadiness. The women's ranks are further strengthened by the Fricka of Karin Branzell, a stalwart of the mezzo roster, now at the midpoint of her twenty-two Met seasons. But the male first-team is absent on this occasion: Ludwig Hofmann moves up to Wotan, newcomer Emanuel List makes a rich-voiced but not quaver-free Hunding, and Paul Althouse is Siegmund. A native of Reading, Pennsylvania, Althouse had sung Italian and French roles with the company since his 1913 debut (age twenty-three) as Dimitri. After a ten-year European sojourn he returned as a Wagnerian. His dry, somewhat throaty voice (dark at the bottom—but not holding the desirable baritonal richness—and rather insecure and colorless at the top) makes for only a serviceable Siegmund, though his sound improves as he progresses through the opera and thus better communicates his honest characterization. Althouse's best repute was to come as teacher of many Met luminaries of the next decades; Tucker, Steber, Huehn, Varnay, and Harshaw, among others, frequented his studio.

Courageous bassos who weary of the lugubrious depths of Wagner's rulers and giants are occasionally prompted to attempt the *Walküre* Wotan. The result is usually mixed, as is the case with Hofmann. The heft and bright color of the estimable Hofmann's normal range provide a welcome thrust to Wotan's frequent rages in the lower voice but all the high Es and Fs are a trial, for us as well as for him. In the lengthy scenes which conclude the opera, Wotan's role is critical; when Wotan laments the inability of father and daughter to share their counsel, the open roughness of some of his tones does not complement his affecting phrasing. His Farewell makes an impact with manly, full-throated sound, but he can only counterfeit the requisite tenderness and ease in the upper range. At the end, he summons Loge magisterially.

Again it is the two heroines who command our interest. At her entrance Leider is just short of the desired amplitude of tone; the top tones are taken as quickly as possible and the octave leaps are maximum upward *portamenti*. But one cannot ignore the lovely warmth of the voice (even in the execrable sonics of the tape). Best of all are the astonishing trills, each note distinctly separate and evenly articulated, with color intact. One would have to reach back to Lilli Lehmann (perhaps Nordica) at the turn of the century to duplicate them. And how lovingly she articulates the text as she asks Wotan to confide in her—the words remain a part of the legato, yet the meaning is perfectly sounded. Leider's vocal style and the voice itself represent a centrality which enables one to respond without reservation to her portrayals; everything is within the zones, nothing is exaggerated, nothing underplayed. Her responses to Siegmund allow Wagner's music and her own womanly, full-toned vocalism to speak for themselves. Yet in the scene with her Walküre sisters and Sieglinde, we find a marvelously agitated Brünnhilde who blazes out with sure shafts of resplendent tone. 'Fort denn, eile' is superbly energized, the Siegfried theme powerfully proclaimed; but still the tones remain liquid, and she names Siegfried with a cherishable *piano* attack.

Now comes the opportunity to hear Kapell's Sieglinde in a focal moment. As she asks Brünnhilde to allow her to die, her plea is full of pathos, the emotive lower tones slightly veiled, giving way to a strong, piercing but lovely top (the instrument and abandon in its use may best be compared to that of Leonie Rysanek). Kapell hurls out the climactic phrases of 'O hehrstes Wunder' with tones of silvery splendor in response to the equally passionate Leider. The encounter is fascinating in its flaming intensity (though sonically the documentation at this point approaches the nadir of the Mapleson cylinders).

The final half hour of the opera, beginning with Leider's musicianly 'War es so schmählich,' is virtually complete. Though Leider feels compelled to break some of the phrases, the care with which she attacks each one combines with the constancy of warm color throughout the entire range to convey the urgency of Brünnhilde's plea without indulgence in treacly self-pity. Brünnhilde's final plea to surround her exposed rock is passionately and nobly limned. Though one or two ultimate top tones skitter slightly, she never overextends herself vocally. Fortunately, as compensation for Hofmann, Bodanzky's way with the final pages of the opera is satisfying in its easy pace and flow of feeling.

Unlike some later periods where great conductors of moderate to immense repute were guests for brief or lengthy sojourns, in the 1930s the Metropolitan staff consisted of a half-dozen regulars, two of whom were in charge of the major portion of the repertory: Serafin in the Italian sphere and Bodanzky in the German. Louis Hasselmans held the reins in the French realm, and two or three lesser lights spelled the regulars and were assigned certain productions where the challenges were considered surmountable. While the system courted the abuses of routine, it could provide the virtues of continuity, perfection of ensemble, and musically disciplined performances. The system was, moreover, an absolute necessity in a repertory house like the Metropolitan where a different opera was played each night of the week. A more practical compensation was the possibility of fewer rehearsal hours, a critical consideration for management during the depression years.

When the principal conductors were of the first caliber, the results could be quite satisfying. Serafin and Bodanzky both had major reputations sustained by merit—still, there were drawbacks to their hegemony. In particular, Bodanzky's tenure was of such long duration (he came to the Met in 1915 after a decade's seasoning on the main European circuit and remained until 1939) that by the thirties the suspicion of boredom was an ever-present spectre. When the cocky young Erich Leinsdorf became Bodanzky's lieutenant in 1937, he divined that the old man was "fed up with his work, and only excited by his card games, skat and bridge."[11] Another inhibiting factor was the minimal rehearsal time alloted before placing an opera before the public (one three-hour rehearsal per Wagner act was the norm, according to Leinsdorf). Leinsdorf's captivating behind-the-scenes particulars, however, give way to the evidence of the preserved Bodanzky performances and the curious paradox that, whatever defects of precision and internal detail occasionally surface, in actual performance Bodanzky's overbold temperament generates both musical and dramatic vitality. Most often he offers a gratifying plasticity of musical expression which effectively complements the stage drama. Critical darts were also aimed at Bodanzky for his rather extensive system of cuts, anathema to the true Wagnerite. Bodanzky in turn maintained that his cuts were largely those devised by Gustav Mahler, the composer and deified conductor of German opera at the Metropolitan from 1907 to 1910. (Bodanzky had been Mahler's assistant in Vienna in the early years of the century.) If Bodanzky was himself bored, his prime aim was to avoid inflicting it on others, and if he succeeds, the extensive cuts and heady pace are contributing factors. In a Bodanzky performance "the sap ran free, the watercourses flowed with new refreshment,"[12] to quote from the Bodanzky obituary written by Mary Ellis Peltz, the irrepressible editor of *Opera News*. The sap would run free through fifty-two performances in the first eight broadcast seasons until Bodanzky's death just before the opening of the 1939 season.

Of course Bodanzky was at the helm for the other two Wagner offerings of the 1933–34 season. (Unlike earlier seasons, NBC did not broadcast the *Ring* cycle; thus the Wagner performances were reduced from ten to four). One of these was significant as the first opportunity for the larger American public to meet one of the legendary artists of the first half of the century, soprano Lotte Lehmann, heard as Elisabeth in the *Tannhäuser* broadcast of 24 February 1934 with Olszewska, Melchior, Schorr, and Hofmann. Her only previous Met performance was her debut as Sieglinde on 11 January. Amazingly, Lehmann had been contracted for only two performances at $600 each.[13] (A third performance as Eva was added later.) This was to be the pattern of Lehmann's Met career—wild acclaim but few performances. She was already approaching her forty-sixth birthday when she came to the Metropolitan, an artist of vast experience. Early on, the lyric heroines of the Italian and French repertory were hers, but her unique qualities shone best in more magisterial fare such as Fidelio, Ariadne and Sieglinde. Though Lehmann's radiant artistry would be heard in *Lohengrin* and *Walküre* broadcasts in the next few years, until the 1938 airing of her most notable characterization, the Marschallin, there is little record of her performances.

One final Wagner recording from the first three broadcast seasons (*Lohengrin* on 24 March 1934) provides a better glimpse of Olszewska's vocal magnetism than the brief *Tristan* excerpts. Schützendorf and Hofmann join Melchior, heard here in the first of his ten broadcast farewells to the swan. Here, too, is our first encounter with one of the glories of the Metropolitan of the twenties and thirties, the silvery-voiced Elisabeth Rethberg. As the Herald, young George Cehanovsky's firm tones summon Elsa to her defense. Having made his Met debut in 1926, Cehanovsky remained for forty seasons, appearing in character roles on innumerable broadcasts until his final radio appearance as Handsome (apt epitaph for his career) in *Fanciulla* during the last season at the old Met. And after a lifetime of devotion, he gained Rethberg as his wife.

As was the case with the earlier *Walküre* one can now move beyond the struggle with deficiencies of sound and abrupt shifting from snippet to snippet of the opera to a genuine feel of the performance. More than an hour and a half (quite evenly divided among the acts) is preserved. Act two offers the most vivid memento of Olszewska's Ortrud. Here the true beauty of her voice impresses as she pleads with Elsa to aid her; supplication is evident in every tone. The registers are well blended, color is still opulent, and she matches Rethberg in legato spin. No black-toned Ortrud she, but one whose evil resides in the bewitching line of her phrasing and vocal color. Left alone on stage, her 'Entweihte Götter!' flashes out into the house, not shouted or squeezed out but actually sung with brilliant tone. In no way is the voice recalcitrant. Olszewska provides another thrilling episode in the following scene where Ortrud drops her mask and reveals her true intent; the wear of a long career momentarily appears in a slight tonal blowziness as Olszewska begins to rage, but soon her charges against Elsa are delivered with pointed tone and to maximum effect.

The overall virtue of this treasured performance resides in the sheer beauty of the singing of the principals (excepting Schützendorf)—they actually *sing* the Wagnerian lines with plenty of vocal heft but full tonal beauty. Hofmann (King Henry) is very impressive in the dream sequence of act one with no hint of vocal wobble, the color most sympathetic. His Wotan would have profited from comparable sensitivity. But for Wagner singing of utmost musicality and vocal blandishment one turns again and again to Melchior and Rethberg. In 1915 Fritz Reiner had thrust the serious young soprano onto the stage of the Dresden Opera; soon she triumphed as Agathe, and all the European capitals claimed her. A favorite at the Salzburg Festivals, she created Strauss' *Ägyptische Helena* at Dresden in 1928. Her coming to the Met in 1922 (Aida) resulted from a chance audition with Bodanzky in Berlin—she was merely idling between trains. Rethberg leaves nothing to chance, however, in her vocalism.

The beauty of Rethberg's honeyed tones in the broadcast *Lohengrin* replicates her best recordings, but the rather detached manner of the recordings gives way on this afternoon to a performance that is not merely live but alive. Rethberg's response to Ortrud's plea in act two has rhythmic vitality and forward thrust without being unduly aggressive, and when Olszewska turns on her, Rethberg is strong and ani-

Lohengrin
24 March 1934

Elsa
Elisabeth Rethberg
Ortrud
Maria Olszewska
Lohengrin
Lauritz Melchior
Telramund
Gustav Schützendorf
King Henry
Ludwig Hofmann
Conductor
Artur Bodanzky

mated in her answer. With Lohengrin, too, in the final moments of the bridal chamber duet, there is nothing stolid about her; the attack is pointed, her phrasing bold and questioning. One is startled by her unsparing spending of voice in the cutting frenzy of these moments. She abandons her bravura manner briefly but effectively at 'Ach nein'; the color suddenly turns warm and softly full as she pulls back from asking the fateful questions of her husband.

Overall, it is the familiar Rethberg sound which continues to entrance; by her tone and phrasing she holds us in suspended time during the lengthy dream sequence. When she spins out the phrase 'mein Aug' ist zugefallen, ich sank in süssen Schlaf' with the most wonderful, dreamlike *piano*, we almost share the sweet sleep of her dream. And her vocal manner changes to "awake" as she is pressed for her champion's appearance. Bodanzky aids in giving thrust to these moments, his penchant for accelerandi (Wagner's *immer schneller* this time) finally becoming excessive at the end of the first act where he whips up the choral passages to a fast gallop. Rethberg's singing in the balcony scene is of matchless beauty. In 'Euch Lüften' she wafts a perfect legato (the older style of *portato,* the tone carried from note to note); the pace is leisurely—one feels she must be thinking "line, line" not "word, word." Her *portamenti* are judiciously measured and apportioned. One might occasionally wish for a wider range of dynamics—she has a strong preference for *mezzo piano*—yet she often surprises with subtle modulations, as at the first voicing of 'der Wang', in Lieb erglüht.' When she reaches the magical phrases of 'Es gibt ein Glück' Olszewska joins her, firmly but discreetly conducting the line, and the two similar voices intertwine to lovely effect. Rethberg's voice and temperament seem perfectly matched with the role of Elsa.

When Lohengrin tells Elsa of his love in act one ('Elsa' sung with a proud *forte*, 'Ich liebe dich' softly voiced) Melchior floods the text with belief. The initial Farewell to the Swan is rather remote (perhaps due to the placement of the tenor on stage); then Melchior presents himself to the court with a plenitude of voice, rich and full, unblemished by the excessive vocal squeeze which often invades his technique. In the excerpts from the next two acts Melchior offers an impressive range of dynamics and vocal coloration. His performance is free from stolidity, and his attitude toward Elsa is implicit in his choice of vocal color and volume. When in act two he begs her not to torment herself and him, his dark-toned, emotion-laden delivery of the climactic phrases seems wrenched from his inner being. The tenor's vocal equipment is so monumental that his musical sensitivity has been too often slighted; on this occasion his reading of 'In fernem Land' reveals his thorough grasp of its architectural layout. Later he employs those affective head tones of his to gently chastise Elsa, and at 'Kommt er dann heim" successively applies a different weight and color for 'dies Horn,' 'dies Schwert,' and 'den Ring.' On our part, too, remembering Farrar's characterization of Elsa as "a silly goose," we can only repeat the unspoken question "With such a Lohengrin, Elsa, how could you?"

A different set of artists from the German wing peoples another 1933-34 broadcast of which record remains. Richard Strauss' *Salome* was aired on 10 March with Schorr as Jokanaan, Manski as Herodias, and tenor Max Lorenz, an infrequent Met visitor, as Herod. Swedish soprano Göta Ljungberg is Salome, the role which sustains her fame. And for the first time we have an all but complete performance, lacking only a few measures and the orchestral Dance of the Seven Veils. The performance has particular interest since the revival of 13 January 1934 (with the identical cast of the broadcast two months later) was the first Metropolitan Salome since the ill-fated Metropolitan premiere on 22 January 1907 with the remarkable Olive Fremstad as the Judean princess. At that time the Board of Directors, their moral wrath fanned by J. P. Morgan's sense of righteousness, found the stage action too decadent; the opera was withdrawn after a single performance, leaving a bitter taste on more than Salome's lips. Unlike Fremstad, Mme Ljungberg's performance of 13 January was not well regarded by the press. Kolodin opines that she "labored diligently with the role, but she could not give it the intensity it demanded. Moreover, her performance was not well-sung."[14] Olin Downes, writing closer in time, found her singing variable, occasionally eloquent. Only Bodanzky and Schorr were praised, the major blame being fixed on the tame dramatic action on stage.

The radio audience does not have to contend with visual inadequacies, and the broadcast records preserve a musical reading of high calibre. Bodanzky's work is indeed monumental—the pieces of the musical puzzle are masterfully put together, the layering of motifs is achieved with utmost clarity, and the forward thrust of the drama is purposefully maintained at all times in the orchestra. The lower brass playing is wonderfully plangent, yet not overblown. And the radio audience could hear with startling clarity the celebrated four notes in the high register of the solo double bass as Salome hovers over the cistern waiting for the Executioner's blow to fall. Schorr sings as well as ever—the passages from the cistern are nobly intoned. Occasionally we sense that the Strauss orchestral sonorities cause an uncharacteristic touch of vocal strain, as in the phrases just before the Baptist returns to the cistern. In spite of (or perhaps because of) his intelligence and vocal security, a certain squareness to Schorr's reading obtrudes—perhaps he is ill at ease in this decadent court, too far from home, too nobly Godlike for the Baptist's feverish denunciations, and yet he is more human than Salome deserves. Lorenz is always in the dramatic picture, and his voice owns a bright color and powerful ring—a superior Herod (*pace* Kolodin). Herod can be *sung* and still be effectively frenetic, as Lorenz proves.

Ljungberg comes over the airwaves as an impressive Salome. Whatever her stage appearance, she has a Salome voice—the white, silvery, girlish sound in the upper octave suggestive of the silvery moon of Wilde's text, a voice capable of moving up and down the Strauss vocal stairs with ease. Interpretively, she responds deftly to Salome's shifting moods and suggests her volatility as early as the opening scene with Narraboth. In the great scene with Jokanaan her voice cuts through the orchestral fabric like 'the ivory knife which cuts the pomegranate.' In this scene one first notes an occasional skittering top note, like a nail scraping on glass, and this defect unfortunately mars the final minute of the opera, robbing us of that hypnotic involvement which *Salome* can induce. But such failings are few. For the most part Ljungberg meets the demands of the concluding monologue head-on, with a vivid feel for pace and color and a sensitive response to the text. When Salome dwells on the mystery of love and death, the soprano applies a pregnant play of color; conversely, as she begins the final series of phrases ('Ich habe deinen Mund geküsst') she momentarily drains all color from the voice, as though madness inhabits the tone itself. Metropolitan audiences had waited over a quarter of a century for this able Salome; the radio audience would wait another fifteen years before hearing the opera again when the 1949 broadcast would introduce a Salome worthy of the Fremstad mantle.

While questions of morality no longer kept *Salome* from public view, lack of filthy lucre might have kept it off the airwaves. Operas restricted by copyright were

Salome
10 March 1934
Salome
Göta Ljungberg
Herodias
Dorothee Manski
Herod
Max Lorenz
Narraboth
Hans Clemens
Jokanaan
Friedrich Schorr
First Nazarene
Emanuel List
Conductor
Artur Bodanzky

girded by inhibiting financial considerations. Publishers Fuerstner and Fuerstner requested a broadcast fee of $7500, payable in advance, for the *Salome* airing. Their American agent wrote Ziegler: "I can realize the reason for this fee. They know the broadcast will be over a chain of seventy-five or one hundred stations and this would make it about $100 per station, which is not a large sum considering they must exchange our dollars for marks. . . . If you are able to ascertain the amount the broadcasters will pay, I will endeavor to bring about a mutual agreement."[15] Two months later the publishers agreed upon a $4000 fee for the broadcast.[16] Yet another new cost born by NBC was a payment to the Metropolitan orchestra; the broadcasts were now sponsored, and each union member received $12 per broadcast. The tab for the initial *Mignon* was $828 (69 players), but *Aida* (102 players) tallied $1224, and *Tristan* topped the schedule at $1284 for 107 players.[17] *Salome*, with its enormous orchestral force and costly copyright restriction, bore a double burden, which NBC gamely assumed.

Salome was Mme Ljungberg's final Metropolitan broadcast, but earlier in the season she had been heard in the unlikely role of Lady Marigold Sandys in the world premiere of the American opera *Merry Mount*, broadcast on 10 February 1934. The important occasion has been preserved virtually complete.

Mr. Gatti, who had been considered antipathetic to the German repertory when he arrived on American shores in the company of Toscanini in 1908, demonstrated a catholicity of national tastes during his long tenure. In his penchant for novelties he had not neglected the cultivation of native American opera. *Merry Mount* was, in fact, the fifteenth American work he had produced at the Met, the list including Walter Damrosch's *Cyrano de Bergerac* (1913), Victor Herbert's *Madeleine* (1914), and our radio friend Deems Taylor's *The King's Henchman* (1927). None of these works was fated to enjoy a long public life, but in addition to the premiere of *Merry Mount,* two American operas from earlier seasons remained in the repertory in the 1933–34 season; both of them had a radio hearing. The premiere of Louis Gruenberg's *The Emperor Jones*, a one-act opera based on the Eugene O'Neill play, was broadcast on Saturday afternoon, 7 January 1933. The other American work, Deems Taylor's *Peter Ibbetson*, enjoyed a slightly longer existence than any of Gatti's other American operas. Following its premiere in February 1931, *Ibbetson* was heard by the radio public during the first broadcast season and again on the broadcast of 17 March 1934.

Two oddly paired musicians were central to the Metropolitan's mounting of these American works: the conductor of the Italian repertory, Tullio Serafin, and the American singing actor, Lawrence Tibbett. For all three works, Serafin was at the helm and Tibbett had the baritone lead—indeed, *Jones* and *Merry Mount* were virtually one-man operas.

Lacking Toscanini, Serafin was no mean substitute. (As a youth in Ferrara, he had served as Toscanini's stand-in on the podium.) From a viola post in the La Scala orchestra at the turn of the century, Serafin rose to become principal conductor at that august house before joining the Met in 1924. He believed that singers of an earlier age relied on "less shouting and more shading,"[18] but the clue to his success as a revered mentor to vocal artists may have been his view that "a true conductor can impose what the composer wants on the singer and let him think the idea is his own."[19] Tibbett, of course, did have ideas of his own. He must have, for he had parlayed a walk-on as Lovitzky in *Boris* in his 1923 Met debut into unchallenged status as the premier baritone, not only of the Metropolitan stage, but (through radio and films) of a much broader public.

The Emperor Jones was fashioned by Russian-American Gruenberg in a jazz idiom. The setting is the Caribbean, and Negro spirituals are also incorporated into the score. In fact, the principal souvenir of the opera is an excellent commercial record by Tibbett of the final scene, which culminates in 'Standin' in the Need of Prayer.' A curious, privately processed memento of the opera purports to be a portion of the actual radio premiere (and is so listed by the Rodgers and Hammerstein Library of Recorded Sound at Lincoln Center).[20] The opera is about an hour and a quarter in length and enjoyed considerable box-office success due to Tibbett's magnetic presence. The twenty-five minute record is an encapsulation of the score and consists mostly of spoken monologues by Tibbett over a pulsating drum background. The baritone moves convincingly back and forth between the spoken text and accompanied recitative (frequently on a single pitch). O'Neill's language sounds decidedly odd now, with its profusion of "dats" and "dereabouts" and unfortunately even so masterful an interpreter as Tibbett cannot help calling up the ghost of Mantan Moreland and other hapless Hollywood caricatures of blacks in the thirties. But more often Tibbett is powerful in expressing the growing terror of the black who went 'from stowaway to emperor in two years—dat's goin' some.' Jones, a petty thief, is now set up as a god on his island kingdom of blacks, but through the connivance of Henry Smithers, a cheap Cockney who fears and hates him, he is soon to be challenged by the people. Jones eventually goes on the run and, in 'Da moon's risin',' turns to song (to this point Tibbett has whistled more than he has sung). But Gruenberg provides no buildup of musical form or feeling for Tibbett to latch onto. The opera turns again to *melodrama* (spoken dialogue with instrumental accompaniment), and here Tibbett is intensely dramatic and quite moving. As Jones moves into a hallucinatory state, imagining that he sees the prison guard he killed, the music finally gathers force ('Don't whip me—I'se workin' as hard as I can. I'll kill you— prison guard.'). Now the climax of the opera begins ('Lord Jesus, hear my prayer'), but after all the frantic speaking and shouting, the baritone is in poor vocal condition for 'It'sa me, O Lord, standin' in the need of prayer.' His tone is wide open and worn, and Tibbett sharps on the final top note. The mighty will fall and the Emperor does too, against a drum ostinato ('You was real A-one paten' leather, too. Look at you now, Emperor. You gettin' mighty low.'). Gruenberg provides a hugely dissonant orchestral climax as the mob is heard in the background while the Emperor uses his 'silver bullet' to end his life, crying 'I'se Emperor—Lord Jesus.' Grotesque and ultimately unsatisfying (a one-time experience only), the opera nevertheless provided Tibbett with a showy vehicle for his theatrical skills, and he triumphed.

With its lengthy choral scenes, elaborate ballets, and full-scale orchestration, Howard Hanson's *Merry Mount*, in four acts and five scenes, was a far more ambitious work than *Jones*. Grandiose in conception, the possibility of failure was correspondingly greater. Dr. Hanson was the director of the Eastman School of Music in Rochester, New York, a post which he held for forty years. His influence extended far beyond the eastern school, for he provided strong, imaginative leadership for American music education and served as a champion of young American composers, often conducting their works in his orchestral appearances. A prolific composer, several of his compositions have earned a place in the hierarchy of American music. *Merry Mount* is not one of them.

Uneasiness mixed with optimism is reflected in Ziegler's advance words, written to Gatti (in Milan) in May concerning the first concert performance at Ann

The Emperor Jones
7 January 1933

Native Woman
Pearl Besuner
Jones
Lawrence Tibbett
Smithers
Marek Windheim
Witch Doctor
Hemsley Winfield
Conductor
Tullio Serafin

Merry Mount
10 February 1934

Marigold
Göta Ljungberg
Plentiful
Gladys Swarthout
Gower
Edward Johnson
Bradford
Lawrence Tibbett
Conductor
Tullio Serafin

Arbor, Michigan. Ziegler called the reports "rather reassuring" but with characteristic pragmatism admitted, "of course, the composer and librettist are enthusiastic, but from other sources, not prejudiced, I hear that the music is really very beautiful and the orchestration is effective."[21] A stage performance proved to be another matter. Edward Johnson, the tenor lead of the Met premiere, after two weeks of rehearsal confessed that he was "pretty well fed up with it. . . . *Merry Mount* is a very pretentious, ineffective work."[22] After hearing the broadcast tape there is no reason to question his behind-the-scenes judgment.

Set in the Massachusetts Bay Colony in the early seventeenth century, Richard Stokes' libretto brought together Hawthorne's assortment of Puritans, Cavaliers, and Indians in a series of genre scenes which give the opera the air of a pageant. 'A company of merry gentlemen,' as the libretto has it, descends upon the God-fearing Puritans and scandalizes them by performing May dances. The ascetic clergyman, Wrestling Bradford, who provides the only dramatic focus in the opera, does indeed wrestle with his own soul as he develops an unholy passion for the beautiful Lady Marigold Sandys. At the opera's end, Bradford seeks redemption by leaping into the flames with Lady Marigold clasped in his arms. With this scenario (the word apt for its Hollywood connotations), Hanson concentrated upon the clash of cultures at the expense of individuals. The chorus is prominent throughout, and several extensive dance scenes give Hanson the opportunity to write purely instrumental occasional pieces. His incessant drumbeat ostinati and repetitive fanfares ultimately relegate a large portion of the score to the realm of background music. Hanson establishes no distinctive sound signature either in the predictably Polovetzian choral and ballet sections or in his monochromatic vocal writing for the principals. Bradford has an effective act-one monologue ('Tis an Earth Defiled'), but for the most part the composer has not found a telling declamatory style which enhances the text; we hear spoken pitches rather than communicative, heightened speech. If the aria format is to be eschewed successfully, as Mussorgsky, Debussy, and Poulenc have done, the reciting style itself must be evocative; Hanson's is not. Moreover, not until the beginning of the third act does the composer bring the human equation adequately into the picture and engage our interest. There Lady Marigold has a brief aria and Bradford responds with a quiet, moving prayer. But the mood all too soon gives way to a series of frenzied dances. Announcer Cross describes it as "a fascinating and weird, wild and wicked scene of the Devil's Den with its . . . devils and beautiful courtesans." With charming schoolboy horror and a treasurable naiveté mirrored in his voice, Cross exclaims, "What a scene that was! My goodness, we could say plenty about that and I daresay it will be discussed a great deal." (Johnson had written to his daughter that the third-act ballet had less impact even though it "inclined to nudity."[23]) Though the choral writing was generally praised by contemporary critics (little else was), Hanson is overfond of lengthy choral vocalizations on 'Ah'; too often the music calls to mind the trappings of a Hollywood soundtrack. After Bradford's penitential immolation, a final choral apotheosis, accompanied by the inevitable drums, brings the opera to a close. One must echo Johnson's lament that all their labors and money had "gone for nothing."[24] (Hanson later salvaged an orchestral suite from the opera.)

The Metropolitan had gone all out for the production. In addition to Tibbett, Johnson, and Ljungberg, the cast includes Gladys Swarthout, Irra Petina, George Cehanovsky, and Louis d'Angelo. After the second act with its elaborate maypole dances, Cross comments that "the Metropolitan certainly does things in a great. way and with a lavish hand in this premiere." Obviously, you had to be there.

Undoubtedly the visual effect of the scenery and ballet was an asset; in fact, the largest applause of the afternoon comes after the second-act ballet. With his establishment loyalty securely in place even in these early days, Cross, at the end of the first act, ventures to play the role of critic: "Listen to that applause. The audience liked it. Well, we knew they would."

We know the radio audience liked the ebullient Cross, whose voice was "probably more familiar to the ten million men and women who hear him every Saturday afternoon than that of any other American citizen with the possible exceptions of President Roosevelt and Charlie McCarthy."[25] For more than forty-three seasons Cross would be the constant feature of the opera broadcasts, completely at home in Box 44 of the old Metropolitan Opera House before the move to Lincoln Center in 1966. A native New Yorker, Cross was, not surprisingly, himself a frustrated singer who began his radio career in 1921 as a tenor at the Westinghouse studio of WJZ. He quickly became announcer and Jack-of-all-trades (including substitute reader of Uncle Wiggly stories for children).[26] When WJZ became the nucleus of the newly formed National Broadcasting Company in 1926, Cross continued to expand his broadcast activities. The 1930 RCA Radiotron Station Directory assures us that "Down New York way they rate Milton ace high." They ought to, for in 1929 he had won the gold medal of the American Academy of Arts and Letters "for speaking the English language more nearly as it should be spoken than any other announcer." Milton himself, however, had his folksy side; "I've been on the air so long . . . my family tells me that I can't even say 'please pass the butter' without sounding like a radio announcer." Maybe it was more than his voice; he had a "large and benign presence," and according to the RCA Directory, "The ladies swear by him and no one ever swears at him."[27] His Metropolitan assignment was the logical outcome of Cross' broadcasts of the Chicago Opera from the old Chicago Auditorium; there the announcer's habitat was the cellar where he had no eye contact with the stage.

At the Metropolitan, Cross moved from the cellar up to the Grand Horseshoe and into the hearts of millions of listeners who unabashedly dubbed him "Mr. Opera." He was very much a gentleman of the old school, and for many his speech served as "the final refutation of the fallacy that good enunciation is necessarily highbrow, and sloppy diction is the only language of good fellowship."[28] In the early years of the Met broadcasts, intermission features were somewhat spasmodic; Cross would occasionally be required to provide as much as twenty minutes of commentary and would sometimes, as a last resort, reenact scenes from the opera of the day.[29] Cross' compatibility with the task was already apparent in his *Merry Mount* comments. His characteristic optimism continued to be an endearing part of his radio personality over the next four decades. But even he, on that day in 1934, could not make *Merry Mount* live up to its title.

As Wrestling Bradford, Tibbett makes a mighty effort. Commitment and belief are the touchstones of all the work done by this most admirable of American artists. Tibbett's violent declamation exposes the maniacal tyranny of the preacher—he plays at a dangerously high pitch throughout the afternoon. But give him even the briefest of moments for affective pathos or lyrical expansion ('Save me from evil spirit . . . whilst my soul is damned forevermore' at the conclusion of the act-one monologue), and he seizes it and touches our hearts. Particularly effective is his change of vocal color on the words 'Sanctify me' at the end of act three. He stays with, and vanquishes, the high tessitura and seems vocally fresh at the opera's end. Johnson, too, in a role he called "simply lousy," is effective in declamation and occasionally manages to inject a modicum of dramatic tension into the piece. And he sends out a sterling high B-flat in the second-act scene of the cavaliers. The diction of both Canadian Johnson and American Tibbett is admirable, but hardly a word of the Swedish Ljungberg comes through. Still, she manages to convey the changing moods of her act-three aria, and while a few of her top tones are unattractive, the middle voice carries emotional weight. Overall, though, her contribution to the opera is disappointing.

The track record of *Merry Mount* for its single season is impressive. The opera was given five more times plus three performances out of town, with its final exposure in the hometown of the composer on the company's spring tour. Like so many attempts at contemporary American opera, the aftermath is bittersweet, as reflected in Hanson's brave words to Ziegler six months after the premiere. The composer expresses his disappointment that *Merry Mount* will not figure in the next season's repertory:

> In fairness to myself and to American opera and, as well, to the Metropolitan I should now like to have the opportunity of taking the work and making those changes which would show the profit that has been derived from the excellent performance of last season, after which I should then appreciate a revival of the work in its new form. This seems the only way in which American opera will ever be written.[30]

Ziegler was more alive to the practicalities of the opera house when two days later he informed Gatti (via Villa, his secretary) that he had written Hanson and Stokes "that it does not of necessity mean that it [*Merry Mount*] would disappear entirely from the repertoire of the Metropolitan." Villa was to "please ask Mr. Gatti if he does not think it advisable to let the opera remain in the prospectus as one of the operas in our repertoire. He has carried other operas this way, although he had not [*sic*] idea of presenting them."[31] Hanson's forlorn hope for a revival was not realized. Though the composer proved not to be a prophet, fortunately the revered Dr. Hanson continued to enjoy honor for decades on his own turf.

The Rochester *Merry Mount* also proved to be the final Metropolitan appearance of Serafin, for years the principal conductor of the Italian wing. The Metropolitan tenure of the regnant Italian maestro was considerably shorter than that of his German colleague, and when he quit the house after ten years of superior music-making, it was not death but dollars that spurred his exit. (He did later complain bitterly to Johnson about Bodanzky's "porcheria" in the Met orchestra.)[32] Successive salary reductions in the early thirties caused the high-priced Serafin to leave the Met to become director of the Royal Opera in Rome and, in later years, once again principal conductor at La Scala. The time span of his career paralleled that of Toscanini. Not only did Serafin guide the Metropolitan's home-grown premieres during his New York decade, but also, in a similar vein, he nurtured the careers of American singers, most notably Rosa Ponselle and (much later) Maria Callas. And Serafin's interests extended beyond the Italian and American territory, ranging from Rimsky-Korsakov's *Sadko* and Mussorgsky's *Fair at Sorochintzy* to Meyerbeer's *L'Africaine* and Mozart's *Don Giovanni*. Seventeen of his performances were aired during the first three broadcast seasons.

Johnson had one final jibe for *Merry Mount*, confiding to friends "Give me *Peter Ibbetson* any day, or *Pelléas*."[33] In fact the Met had given him *Peter Ibbetson* as his exclusive property during the four seasons it remained in the repertory. Taylor's opera had enjoyed a marked popular success, bringing almost $150,000 into the Metropolitan's needy coffers during its first season. Though the critics had been more chary of their approval, Gatti had chosen *Ibbetson* to open the 1933–34 season, perhaps in tribute to the trio of stars who had contributed so much to its success: the beloved Spanish soprano Lucrezia Bori, the personable Canadian tenor Edward Johnson, and the ubiquitous American baritone Tibbett. Though Johnson and Bori would abandon their stage careers in the next year or so, all three would remain among the most familiar figures to the radio public in the ensuing decade and a half.

The Metropolitan production of *Ibbetson* was a very elegant affair. Based on the novel by George du Maurier, the opera is set in the crinoline period of the Victorian era with English country houses and Parisian suburban gardens to please the eye. An aura of romance hovers over the whole, for the opera was calculated to capture the Bori-Johnson brand of elegance and sophistication already nurtured in numerous appearances together as Juliette and Roméo, Mélisande and Pelléas. The libretto had been skillfully wrought from her play by the redoubtable Constance Collier, veteran of many Shakespearean encounters with John Barrymore. (Even today one may revel in the tart acuity of Collier's character portrayals through television reruns of her films from the 1930s.) With Taylor, who also had a hand in the libretto, Miss Collier transformed the novel into a stageworthy piece and its appeal is modestly potent even without colorful visual assets. The action of the opera alternates between scenes of rediscovery by the adult Ibbetson and Mary (now the Duchess of Towers) in England and flashbacks to their childhood near Paris. Though finally separated in life by Peter's unintentional murder of his cruel uncle, Colonel Ibbetson, the couple 'dream true' to eventual union in death. The dream device is well suited to the operatic milieu, and since in the imagination of the radio listener dreams are unencumbered by stagecraft, the dream sequences are quite evocative.

Precisely because Taylor has written a period piece, the opera is somewhat palatable today (perhaps more so than at the time of its premiere when the need for originality and newness made it more than suspect). Like Peter, we 'may see and listen' but must never touch these dreams 'for they are dead and gone and touch or speech will veil the dream, like breaths upon a windowpane.' But, keeping our distance, we can experience the calculated sentiment so surely concocted by Miss Collier and the conventional musical palette skillfully blended by Taylor until, in the best scenes, some of the enchantment of du Maurier envelops us too. The music may be ordinary, but it allows the story to speak—no mean compliment. Perhaps the most notable element of Taylor's achievement is his setting of the text so that it may be fully understood. Johnson and Tibbett were masters of clear diction, but a 1960 performance of the opera at the Empire State Music Festival (Albanese, Wainner, Van Ginkel; Pelletier) also proves the deftness of Taylor's textual setting. Every word is comprehensible. (In that more recent performance the thread of aural history is tidily drawn: Wilfred Pelletier had prepared the Met production and conducted the final Met performance of *Ibbetson* on 27 February 1935; Bori had coached her friend Licia Albanese in the role of Mary; composer Taylor is heard as announcer for the performance; and 1960 is the year when Bori and Tibbett died.) But Taylor's achievement goes beyond textual setting. He understands the conventions of opera and is not afraid to make good use of them: he delays the prima donna's entrance in act one; he utilizes dance music to provide musical continuity (in the manner of Verdi in *Traviata* and *Rigoletto*); he causes Colonel Ibbetson to 'recite' a poem, which is not only a key element in the plot but also provides a prime vocal opportunity for Tibbett (à la

Peter Ibbetson
17 March 1934
Mary
Lucrezia Bori
Mrs. Deane
Gladys Swarthout
Peter
Edward Johnson
Colonel Ibbetson
Lawrence Tibbett
Duquesnois
Léon Rothier
Conductor
Tullio Serafin

Andrea Chénier): he writes (sometimes overlong) interludes to connect the scenes (after *Pelléas*—in harmony and orchestration, as well); he carefully positions the dramatic and musical climaxes—the love duets at the end of acts two and three, the murder of the Colonel at the beginning of act three; and finally, he closes with chorus a capella (as Gounod used it following Valentin's death in *Faust*). Of course the idiom is largely dissonance-free and often enough the musical substance misses the mark, as in the jaunty orchestral epilogue which comes hard on the heels of Colonel Ibbetson's murder.

The opera contains vivid opportunities for singing actors in the lesser parts as well as in the principal roles. Mezzo Gladys Swarthout is an appealing Mrs. Deane, her fresh voice uniquely dusky in timbre and without the glottal stops which mar her singing in later years. Character tenor Angelo Bada, a longtime mainstay of the Met, does a virtuoso turn as the French waiter at the inn at Passy, and old Léon Rothier, member of the company since 1910, is impressive in his act-two scene as Major Duquesnois. His cumbersome bass voice is appropriately weary as he dejectedly begins, but as the Major recalls other days, the voice quickens in rhythm and gathers firmness of tone and line. The portrait has the authority of the *grand seigneur*. And well it might, for Rothier, who had begun his career at the Opéra Comique in 1899, studied his roles with Saint-Saëns, Massenet, Thomas, Charpentier, and Debussy and was so highly regarded for his mastery of the French manner that Met colleagues Farrar, Homer, Ponselle, Amato, and Johnson all coached with him.

Tibbett's role does not often hold center stage, but the dramatic moments are effective and he does his set pieces beautifully. He employs the darker colors of his voice to suggest the Colonel's pomposity at the beginning of the French verse 'La bien-aimée' before succumbing to the need to display his vocal wares (his awesome and usually flawless mezza voce is momentarily ruffled at the climactic 'jamais').

The Duchess of Towers was one of Bori's most highly regarded creations, its poetry and refinement ideally mated to her abilities in the declining years of her career. Born a Borja (the Spanish branch of the Italian Borgias) and convent reared, Miss Bori possessed a legendary self-discipline that was severely tried by her enforced withdrawal from the opera stage in 1915 due to nodules on her vocal cords. Her career had had a storybook beginning: following a 1908 Rome debut as Micaela and early honor in the Italian houses (the first Octavian at La Scala), Gatti had called her to Paris as a last-minute replacement for Lina Cavalieri as Manon Lescaut in the Met's 1910 visit. The home house first heard her in 1912. After a five-year exile, she returned in 1921 to enslave the Metropolitan public which remained unshakably fond of her for the next decade and a half. In her forty-seventh year at the time of the 1934 broadcast, she is occasionally stretched by the tessitura—particularly as she tires. In the final-act apostrophe for Mary alone, several top tones are decidedly unpleasant. (Composer Taylor, awake to the problem, eliminates this episode in the 1960 performance and ends the opera far more appropriately with the moment when Peter joins Mary in death.) But then, top tones were never Miss Bori's strong suit; her aural appeal rested on the piquant quality of her voice, musky in flavor but flashed with acerbity like a fine old wine. Almost excessively collected, the acid tone can bite the ear and does so in the climactic phrases which give us the moral of the opera: 'Life is a dream, death the awakening.' Too often her diction leaves us in doubt precisely when the dialogue is of greatest importance; she frequently makes a choice in favor of legato over word clarity. But what a beautiful legato it is as she etches the line into the delicate and meaningful contours, filled with bewitching and subtle *portamenti*. The

Léon Rothier as Dr. Miracle in *Les Contes d'Hoffmann*. Photography by Mishkin.

cameo-like outline of her vocalism reflects a bygone age of elegance of manner, both personal and musical. Other prima donnas might be familiarly hailed as Rosa or Gerry, but the Spanish patrician was always Miss Bori.

Much of the time her vocal means are equal to the role. 'How fleet is time,' an old-fashioned entrance aria for the prima donna, is entirely lovely and climaxed by a superb high B-flat. When she bids Peter 'au revoir' at the end of the dream sequence in act two, the combination of resignation and longing for the past penetrates her tone. She is most communicative in the renunciation scene at the end of the act, summoning the genuine pathos native to her Violetta and Manon as she owns to Peter 'We shall never meet again—I am not free. I shall think of you always.' It is a telling moment, and Taylor grasps the emotion of it and expands on it in the orchestral phrases which conclude the act. Serafin's fine hand is apparent in moments like this. Time after time he galvanizes the drama by pointing up a critical moment (the killing of Colonel Ibbetson), and he gives the interludes a significant profile.

If Johnson rightly bewailed his role in *Merry Mount*, Taylor has given him ample recompense in the title role of *Ibbetson*. The Welsh-Irish tenor, born in Guelph, Ontario, youthful Broadway star of *The Waltz Dream* in 1908, reincarnated as Edoardo di Giovanni for his 1912 Padua debut (Chénier), Wagnerian at La Scala, and converted back to Edward Johnson for his 1922 Met debut as Avito (opposite Miss Bori, of course), contributed during the next decade some remarkably stylish portraits in French, Italian, and American opera. "Something more than a voice"[34] one critic had called him at his debut, and so he is as the broadcast Peter. In between Tibbett's French air and Bori's entrance aria, the composer fashioned a lengthy narrative for the tenor, skillfully molded to Johnson's strengths. Johnson tells the story of Peter's youth in forthright and remarkably clear declamation, offering an occasional colorful head tone, as when we first learn of 'dreaming true.' He eschews a shaping legato, and the voice may be monochromatic in color but it retains a sound metal, considering the late stage of his career. Johnson's intelligence is everywhere apparent: regret can invade his tone when he recalls that Mimsey is 'Gone—lost, like all the rest'; at moments of excitement, such as his recognition of Major Duquesnois in act two, he adopts an animated, strongly rhythmic delivery yet maintains vocal quality; 'I did not mean to kill him,' he tells Mary at fever pitch, and we believe him. If Johnson fails to suggest by sheer beauty of tone or smoothness of phrasing the romantic young dreamer that is Peter Ibbetson, his clarity of enunciation and intelligent portrayal redress the loss.

How fortunate we are to have this vivid memento of Bori's and Johnson's stage manner. Often pure chance dictates the existence of these records—a letter in the Met Archives tells how some came to be. Five days before her *Ibbetson* broadcast, Bori received a letter (hastily relayed by her to the Metropolitan management). Speak-O-Phone Recording Studios tells all to "My dear Mme. Bori":

> Again we take pleasure in writing you to say that on Saturday we made a beautiful set of records of "Pagliacci" for Queena Mario.
> Also we have just received a lovely letter from Maria Gay Zenatello who says that "Nino Martini is very satisfied with the Speak-O-Phone records" which we made directly from the air of the broadcast of "Lucia di Lammermoor" a week or two ago. Mme. Eida [*sic*] Norena also was so pleased with her records of "Faust" that she took them with her to Europe. Likewise the other artists for whom we recorded the various operas were extremely happy with the results.

> This is the fifth week that we have made these recordings directly from the air and delivered them immediately after the performance to the artist's home, complete and ready to be played on any phonograph.[35]

Then comes the pitch. "Perhaps this week you too would enjoy having us record your selections from 'Peter Ibbetson' and if you will call us on the telephone, we will be pleased to quote you a very special rate, either for the whole opera or for your particular part." The phrase "your particular part" explains the fragmentary nature of so many surviving records of this vintage. Whether Bori (ever the good soldier) was horrified at this poaching of Met property or, like so many artists then and now, delighted at being preserved "live on disc," most operaphiles will think kindly of all the Speak-O-Phone entrepeneurs of the thirties.

Cross later recalled that, unlike Taylor in his radio commentaries of the 1931–32 season, he confined his comments to before and after each act; but as late as the *Ibbetson* broadcast of 1934, Cross can be heard relating the plot during the orchestral interludes of Taylor's own opera. During the first scene of act three, he interjects a needless explanation of a stage action between passages of sung dialogue; and at the climax of the opera, where the composer draws the emotion of the love duet into a moving orchestral peroration, the moment is marred by Cross informing us of the epilogue which will close "our Lucky Strike broadcast today." Commercial sponsorship of the broadcasts had begun on 30 December 1933 when Bori's Mignon was supported not only by Pons and Schipa on stage but by the American Tobacco Company, which had paid nearly $100,000 to the Metropolitan management for the 1933–34 season's broadcasts.[36] John B. Kennedy joined Cross as intermission commentator.

Gone now were the broadcasts of the midweek Wagner matinee cycle; the tradition of the Christmas Day *Hänsel und Gretel* was the only exception to the Saturday afternoon sequence which became the norm for future seasons. In compensation, the 1933–34 season was extended beyond the normal New York season by the first out-of-town broadcast, Debussy's *Pelléas et Mélisande*, from the stage of the Boston Opera House on 7 April. Although NBC withheld permission for Boston-area listeners to hear the opera over Boston station WAAB (NBC Boston outlet WBZ had "a complete coverage of New England"), the network paid the Metropolitan an additional $3,000 for the nationwide airing.[37]

The occasion marked the Metropolitan's first appearance in Boston in sixteen years. Johnson and Bori continued their romantic partnership as Pelléas and Mélisande, with Pinza as Golaud, Rothier as Arkel, and Bourskaya as Geneviève. The only cast change from the broadcast of the previous season was Ellen Dalossy as Yniold. This time, however, we have a remote and quite noisy (but nevertheless informative) recording of the entire performance.

"The first voice we hear," to use the words of Milton Cross familiar to millions of radio listeners, is Ezio Pinza in the unlikely role of Golaud—a part normally assigned to a baritone. One might not expect to find the stalwart Italian bass among the half-mists inhabited by Maeterlinck's nebulous creatures nor musically at ease in Debussy's world of demitints and subtle imagery. But Golaud is the one character in the play who struggles against the fatalism of Maeterlinck's philosophy. He is the man of action, futile though his actions must be, and thus Pinza, who became opera's quintessential symbol of virility during the thirties and forties, is able to make a powerful impression in the role.

Pinza's Golaud considerably expands our concept of this magnetic artist's

Pelléas et Mélisande
7 April 1934
Mélisande
Lucrezia Bori
Geneviève
Ina Bourskaya
Pelléas
Edward Johnson
Golaud
Ezio Pinza
Arkel
Léon Rothier
Conductor
Louis Hasselmans

capabilities. He handles the upper range of the role with complete security and no sacrifice of tone quality. How effectively he uses the warm tones of his basso cantante as he tries to discover the reasons for Mélisande's unhappiness! A sweet sadness dwells in his silken, somber tones—but the voice quickly becomes menacing as he compels her to search for the lost ring in the gloomy cave. In the more overtly dramatic scenes, of course, he is superb, whether spying with young Yniold (a fine conception by Dalossy) or flying into a frenzy as he brutalizes Mélisande. When he movingly cries 'Je suis trop vieux; et puis je ne suis pas un espion,' an agonized 'Ah' escapes from him (one of the few ugly sounds Pinza ever condescended to utter). Old Rothier is still in the picture as Arkel, though the all-important 'Si j'étais Dieu, j'aurais pitié du coeur des hommes' is unaccountably missing from the tapes. Bourskaya's voice is perhaps not sufficiently dark-hued for Geneviève, but her tones have a lovely color and fluidity.

The performance takes on added historical resonance since Johnson and Bori were the first interpreters of the roles at the Metropolitan (in 1924), and they were the only Pelléas and Mélisande in the intervening years. Too, Johnson had prepared his role with Jean Périer, the original Pelléas. It was generally regarded as his finest portrayal, though the later Ibbetson was also universally acclaimed. The tenor was just a few months shy of his fifty-sixth birthday at the time of the broadcast, and age has invaded his tones if not his girth. (Critics and admirers of Johnson always wrote of "seeing" his performances; the visual aspect was undoubtedly a prime factor in his success.) From his first appearance in act one to the death scene in the park, Johnson's voice sounds worn and less vibrant than as Ibbetson a few months before. Lack of support sometimes gives a curious flatness and tremulousness to his tone. One can still admire his beautiful articulation of the text and, above all, his stylistic restraint. Because he adheres to the subtle framework of his conception, his few climaxes are the more effective: 'Ah! voici la clarté' flashes out from the dark subterranean grotto, and as he demands to touch Mélisande's hair in the tower scene, he imperiously cries 'Donnez, donnez,' his voice rising to a strong *forte* climax at 'Ils m'aiment plus que toi.'

This was the Canadian tenor's final broadcast. A year later to the day, Johnson's Met career ended in Boston as Peter Ibbetson, his final New York appearance having occurred as Pelléas on 20 March 1935. From Boston he was summoned to become the general manager of the Metropolitan, and a new and more important chapter in his life began.

Though her career, too, was fast coming to a close, in the mid thirties Miss Bori was still a very active artist whose presence was of critical importance to the Metropolitan. She had opened the current season, and Johnson would grant her the opening night *Traviata* in 1935, her final season with the company. She could still offer great satisfaction in a number of roles; the week before the *Pelléas* broadcast she was heard in the broadcast *Manon* with the American tenor Richard Crooks again offering his distinguished Des Grieux. The worn record grooves of the *Pelléas* performance are less kind to her than to the male singers; it is not easy to know her Mélisande. J. B. Steane, in his invaluable critique of commercial vocal records, *The Grand Tradition*, voices the opinion that her preserved stage performances "tell us little";[38] on the contrary, several moments of her Mélisande are well worth remembering. The castle scene in act two, the concluding act, and especially the opening of the tower scene all tell us a good deal about the "live" Bori. The voice is perfectly poised in the act-two scenes; the dusky color of her low register is effectively employed after the ring has been lost at the well, and in the castle scene with Golaud, 'Je suis malade ici' is uttered with utmost delicacy. Bori's charm is palpable in these moments. The final act is delivered entirely in a voice of childish wonder ('Non, non; nous n'avons pas été coupables,' she tells Golaud), and at the end she achieves a lovely pathos by introducing a more liquid tone into her final words to Arkel. The most valuable memento in the opera, however, is Bori's voicing of the little song which opens the tower scene. For a brief moment one feels that this is how Bori must have actually sounded in the theatre. So often on records a pinched, metallic quality dilutes her celebrated charm, but here the voice, full and warm, seems to sail out into the auditorium with utmost freedom. The strangely seductive quality of her middle low range is fully captured. This is the kind of moment for which one searches during hours of listening to scratchy records in the hope of finding a clue to a long-gone artist's greatness.

Two years later, a scene from Bori's farewell performance will reveal even more of her special qualities. Her only broadcast of the 1934–35 season was *Don Pasquale* with the memorable cast of Schipa, De Luca, and Pinza under Panizza's baton. Bori had been slated for the Metropolitan premiere of Cimarosa's *Il Matrimonio Segreto*, but the toll of a long career prevented her assumption of a final new role (new at least for the Met; she had sung it elsewhere early in her career). Her deteriorating vocal estate and steadfast character are equally apparent in Ziegler's frantic cable to Gatti in mid-summer 1934:

> Today Bori telephoned saying impossible sing Matrimonio unless entire opera is transposed full tone in ensembles and solos STOP Says she works daily with result that she is losing her voice STOP None of my arguments carry any weight as she is convinced she cannot sing it without transposition tessitura too high STOP Cable what to do.[39]

Ziegler went further in defense of Bori when he wrote to Villa that same day:

> You can imagine what a shock this is to me, but you also know that Bori is a serious woman and would not place us in an awkward position if she could possibly help herself. She told me that she was terribly distressed over the whole matter; says that she cannot sleep nights worrying about it, but at the same time she was utterly convinced that she could not sing this music.[40]

The new production was dropped and Cimarosa's opera did not reach the Metropolitan until 1937 when young American singers performed it in English.

In her final season Bori turned again to the favored roles of her late career: Mignon (4 January 1936 with Antoine, Crooks, and Pinza) and Magda in Puccini's sentimental and slight but flavorful *La Rondine*, broadcast on 21 March 1936 in the final week of the New York season. (The Rodgers and Hammerstein Archives listing of Metropolitan recorded broadcasts provided by David Hall includes this performance of *La Rondine* (followed by a question mark), but the preserved performance is not from the Met but that of 10 August 1934 by the San Francisco Opera with Bori and Mario Chamlee. It consists of act two only.) Puccini's "swallow" is denied us, but there does exist a souvenir of Bori and Pinza in the swallow duet ('Légères hirondelles') from the *Mignon* broadcast. (The fragment is not specifically identified as such; elimination of other possibilities plays a large part in tracking down and identifying fragments from the early broadcasts.) Pinza begins in rather wooly fashion, but Bori is deftly birdlike and she executes the little ornaments

Mignon
4 January 1936

Mignon
Lucrezia Bori
Lothario
Ezio Pinza
Conductor
Louis Hasselmans

beautifully. In the middle section of the duet her phrases are full of animation, though capped by a rather skittish high A. The finest feature of the excerpt is her exquisite diminuendo on the penultimate note of the main section and its reprise.

But the jewel of all mementos of Bori's stage performances is the Saint-Sulpice scene from *Manon*, her final effort on the Met stage, broadcast on the evening of 29 March 1936. In honor of Bori, the company's leading artists (including Flagstad and Melchior, Rethberg and Pinza, Ponselle, Martinelli, and Tibbett) had earlier performed scenes from several operas, and Bori herself had begun the evening with the second act of *Traviata*. None of these excerpts was broadcast. The apogee of the gala was Bori's appearance as Manon. As she enters the 'silent walls and cold atmosphere' of Saint-Sulpice, her declamation thrills. Then come the perfectly sculpted, cameo-like tone and phrasing of 'Pardonnez-moi, Dieu de toute puissance,' ending with a fine high B, characteristically narrow and contained as she always handled her top voice. Her seduction scene conveys not only the exquisite refinement normally associated with Bori; as she demands response from Des Grieux (Crooks), Bori is also a very experienced and insistent charmer, and her vocal attack is securely posited as well. Though Bori depicts the hapless Manon in appropriate phrases ('Hélas! l'oiseau qui fuit'), passion and vibrancy dominate her conception to a surprising degree. 'Regardez-moi' becomes a command rather than a supplication. Unlike her recordings, it is the brio of Bori's stage work which remains in the memory.

Also preserved are the ceremonies which followed the *Manon* scene. Now the announcer (surprisingly not Milton Cross) conjures up "soft amber lights, the old gold of the finish, and the huge majestic gold curtains" of the old opera house while Miss Bori walks "along the length of the stage gathering her bouquets that have rained out of the tiers." This is the house where the twenty-four-year-old soprano had made her debut as Manon Lescaut opposite Caruso on the opening night of the 1912 season, where she had appeared on 473 occasions (an additional 155 performances on tour). It is the house which she had worked tirelessly to save in the depression years by her leadership of the campaign to solicit funds. It is the house she is destined to continue to serve as the first artist ever to be named to the Board of Directors.

General Manager Johnson spoke for the entire company (assembled on stage) who "wish to pay you homage and to express admiration for you as an artist, affection as a colleague, and deep regret at your retirement from this circle in which you have been so deeply beloved." Her arms laden with gifts and flowers, Bori addressed her public: "My friends, my heart is in such a turmoil that I do not know how to express the great emotion I am feeling." She specifically thanked Mr. Ziegler "who for so many years has been so patient, listening to all my troubles." After thanking the artists and the entire staff, she turned to the general manager. It was a moment those intimate with the house must have awaited. "And to you, Mr. Johnson, my thanks and my affection and my good wishes to you as the general manager of the great Metropolitan Opera," and here, for the only time, audible emotion penetrates the legendary control of the Spanish lady as, her voice breaking, she continued, "which will always be so close to my heart." Although she would not sing again in opera, she avowed "I shall be here again to sing for the Metropolitan Opera Guild. I am supremely happy, supremely grateful to you all and still supremely sad" (each repetition resonantly drawn out to 'supreeemly'). In perhaps a knowing paraphrase of Violetta's act-two renunciation, she embraced her public, assuring them that "I shall be there, sitting with you, yes, one of you. Let me say 'au revoir.'"

Manon
29 March 1936

Manon
Lucrezia Bori
Des Grieux
Richard Crooks
Count
Léon Rothier
Conductor
Louis Hasselmans

Lucrezia Bori as Manon. Photography by Mishkin.

As the gala evening ends, the ladies are "crying into their handkerchiefs," the announcer tells us. Years later in a radio interview, Bori recalled that evening. "I never will forget that when I have to thank everybody (and I was afraid not to forget them) my voice break in the middle of my little speech. And you know I am not a speaker and to improvise and try not to forget anybody—it was a great, great effort that I make." And then with that gusto which always startles one coming from this patrician artist: "But I *did* it!"

The popular triumvirate of Bori, Johnson, and Tibbett was now dismembered as the soprano and tenor moved behind the scenes. Tibbett remained center stage. No matter how prominent Tibbett was in the American operas, his lasting réclame was in the great roles of nineteenth-century Italian opera. He had initially staked his claim to this territory in his celebrated assumption of Ford in Verdi's *Falstaff* a decade earlier, to the chagrin of the veteran Falstaff, Antonio Scotti. Not quite yet a case of 'Le roi est mort, vive le roi,' Tibbett would fully assume the royal crown with the doge's robes in the 1932 revival of *Boccanegra*. Both Germont (1925) and Tonio (1926) were early steps in this progression, and the repellent player in Leoncavallo's *Pagliacci* provides our first opportunity to hear him in this repertory. *Pagliacci* served as curtain raiser to the *Salome* previously cited on the broadcast of 10 March 1934, with Martinelli as Canio, Queena Mario as Nedda, and Cehanovsky (stepping out of the comprimario ranks) as Silvio, a role which he often sang in his early Met career.

What a splendid introduction to Tibbett's Italian manner his singing of the Prologue provides. From the modulated differentiation between 'Signore, Signori,' through the beautiful, poised head tones on 'Un nido di memorie,' to the ringing high A-flat on 'voi' (both vowels articulated) that closes the monologue, the prologue shows the baritone in the fullest command of his powers. If there is a hint of too-open tone and a slight sense of no-reserve-in-the-vocal-tank as he expansively lays out the D-flat section, any concern for his vocal health lies far in the future. One can only savor the generosity of this vocal spendthrift. He is entirely in character as he play-acts throughout the opera (he removes all vibrato from his voice, for instance, in the second-act exchanges with Colombina). Perhaps his finest moment is the haunting mezza voce he employs at 'Or via. Bisogna a fingeri' as Tonio urges Canio to pretend, and wait to entrap Nedda. Evil so subtly and musically expressed is the coin of Iago, the role with which Tibbett will complete his conquest of the Italian repertory in the late 1930s.

Tibbett's companion player, Giovanni Martinelli, is a worthy partner. The irrepressible tenor, eldest of a Paduan cabinetmaker's fourteen children and a budding clarinetist, had appeared at twenty-five as Ernani (Milan) before singing at all the major Italian houses and Covent Garden (where he was much admired). He joined the Metropolitan in 1913 (Cavaradossi in Philadelphia, Rodolfo in New York) and, in the years after Caruso's death, had homesteaded a portion of the Caruso territory for himself. Canio is certainly part of that domain; Martinelli's incredible vocal stamina and brilliance of declamation are prime assets for the role. The voice is all there, bottom to top, as he demonstrates with the ringing high B of 'Ventitré ore' at his entrance. Whatever one's reaction to the voice as an instrument of beauty (and there were widely divergent opinions about that), his dramatic intensity and, more important, his musical integrity are most impressive. The recitative before 'Vesti la giubba' is nobly set forth; this is no grubby sobster—one can give a strong affirmative to his 'sei tu forse un uom?' The aria itself is taken at the slowest possible pace, but Martinelli is more than equal to sustaining the tension of the line throughout.

Pagliacci
10 March 1934
Nedda
Queena Mario
Canio
Giovanni Martinelli
Tonio
Lawrence Tibbett
Silvio
George Cehanovsky
Conductor
Vincenzo Bellezza

Each note seems dragged out from his anguished heart, yet the line never sags. His breath control is remarkable: he achieves an incredible crescendo on the climactic 'Ah! Ridi, Pagliaccio,' and, like a man possessed, he keeps returning to the high As—all without any vocal strain. To hear this often tawdry moment become genuinely tragic in Martinelli's reading is a searing experience. We can forgive him two cries of 'Infamia' which he interpolates at the end of the postlude.

Martinelli's greatest merit is his absolute control over the tensile strength of the musical line; one notes it again in the concluding section of 'No, Pagliaccio non son' (again the high B-flats are entirely secure). His abrupt, quietly spoken 'La commedia è finita!' reflects the broken spirit of the man—no need for grandstanding now.

Soprano Queena Mario was often heard in leading roles in these early broadcasts, and her Nedda certainly is well routined. The quintessential American product, Mario (born Tillotson) had come to the Met in 1922 and remained the ingénue soprano throughout her seventeen seasons. (When her old teacher, Sembrich, became ill in 1931, Mario had assumed her duties at Curtis, in turn producing Bampton and Jepson for the Metropolitan—she had plenty of mettle off stage). On stage her conception of Nedda is more doll-like than impassioned, her silvery top compensating for insufficient vocal mass and a rather unpleasant whine in the middle voice. The trills in the *Ballatella* are neat (plenty of *portamenti* here) and she knows how to mix coyness with scorn in her treatment of Tonio. Mario contributes to a pedestrian love duet with Cehanovsky, who lacks the necessary vocal goods for the climaxes while his rather congested nasal coloring proves monotonous. Bellezza misses some of the excitement of the act-one chase but is at his best in the quickly changing moods of the play-within-a-play.

Martinelli's qualifications for the verismo Canio made unlikely his broadcast appearance a few weeks earlier as Faust (Norena, Swarthout, Tibbett, Pinza; Hasselmans). Yet Faust and Don José were among the five most frequently performed of Martinelli's thirty-eight Metropolitan roles (the others were the expected Radames, Canio, and Manrico); unfortunately no live souvenirs of these French roles have come to light. Pons' popular Lucia was heard again this season with radio tenor Nino Martini and veterans De Luca and Rothier, and Rethberg repeated her Aida, joined by Branzell, Borgioli, and Carlo del Corso as Radames. Rosa Ponselle sang Selika in the broadcast *L'Africaine* with Borgioli, Rothier, and young American tenor Frederick Jagel, whose two-decade-plus Metropolitan career would be of far longer duration than Del Corso's single season.

While these aural jewels are denied us, a precious memento of Ponselle as Mozartian (for there are no commercial records) remains in the *Don Giovanni* of 20 January 1934. The quality of the recording, unfortunately, is perhaps the poorest of all surviving broadcasts; it wows, sputters, fades in and out at the most exasperating moments, and clips off arias and ensembles in mid-phrase—a supreme test of an audiophile's ability to 'listen through.' Not only Ponselle makes it worthwhile, for the gnawed grooves contain the earliest documentation of one of opera's legendary portrayals—Pinza as Giovanni—and the only preserved Met broadcast by tenor Tito Schipa, a survivor from the earliest decade of twentieth-century operatic performance. *Don Giovanni* had been broadcast in 1932 (with virtually the same cast) and would be heard again in 1935, 1938, and 1939, but only the 1934 performance survives as guide to the Metropolitan's Mozart style in the thirties.

Serafin's Mediterranean manner molds the performance. The portentous rising and descending scales of the overture signal the overt nature of the performance: the

Don Giovanni
20 January 1934

Donna Anna
Rosa Ponselle

Donna Elvira
Maria Müller

Zerlina
Editha Fleischer

Don Ottavio
Tito Schipa

Don Giovanni
Ezio Pinza

Leporello
Virgilio Lazzari

Masetto
Louis D'Angelo

Commandant
Emanuel List

Conductor
Tullio Serafin

Rosa Ponselle as Selika in *L'Africaine.*

musical gestures will be broad, the closing ritards baroque in extent and pace, the fluctuations of tempo within arias and ensembles at the service of textual impera- tives. Thus the careful geometry of the Mozartean landscape is disturbed, and the dynamic spirit of nineteenth-century Italian opera hovers over Seville. Yet, if the manner is sometimes oppressive, the characters come vividly to life. (At least one is spared the vocal mincing which came into favor in later generations.) And while it is true that the classic profile of eighteenth-century opera seria (and a good deal of opera buffa) is preserved by an orderly progression in its closed forms, the musical gestures of the seria must be grandly assertive if the composer's rhetoric is to speak. One may carp at a number of Ponselle and Schipa's bits of vocal business, but one cannot mistake their intent.

Pinza's Giovanni was initially (1929) deemed deficient in the vocal elegance and personal magnetism of the confident seducer; after five years of Met performances, the basso has more than made up the difference. The sheer brio and energy of his per- formance are sometimes overpowering. One occasionally wishes for a little less center-stage posturing and more vocal reticence (the champagne aria is wonderfully articulated but the accents on the downbeats thunder). How unlikely this Don Giovanni's lack of success seems as Pinza manipulates all about him with superb self- confidence. One would not want to forgo his vibrancy of tone, clarity of diction, and suavity of line; the Serenade, in particular, is hypnotically attractive. The first-act duet with Editha Fleischer (a competent, if not distinctive, Zerlina) tells the story of contemporary Mozart style: characterization takes precedence over mere correctness as Pinza pushes his phrases urgently on and Fleischer holds back the movement of hers. Serafin signals the reprise of 'Là ci darem' by a broad ritard and takes the 6/8 coda at a much quicker tempo than the body of the duet.

Virgilio Lazzari's musicianly recitation of the catalog of conquests alleviates the initial stolid impression of his Leporello. He employs an effective *piano* at 'è ognor vezzosa' but also some questionable pitches at the repeated 'quel che fa' insinuations which conclude the aria. Although Maria Müller is shortchanged by the absence of two of her arias, her Elvira could be the most satisfying portrayal of the afternoon. This distinguished soprano had pursued a career in central Europe following her 1919 debut (Elsa) at Linz, and her Wagnerian bent led to the Met (1925, Sieglinde) and Bayreuth in the thirties. She is a fine Mozartean as well. In Elvira's entrance aria she is forceful but never strident and manages the parodic coloratura with complete aplomb. Her Lemnitz-like voice sounds perfectly equalized throughout its scale, and she has an easy top. Perhaps some remnant of the 1787 Prague premiere of *Don Giovanni* has lingered long enough to inform the Bohemian soprano's musicianship, leaving its mark on her deft handling of the recitatives and stylish ensemble singing.

Oddly enough one cannot be quite so enthusiastic about Schipa. For a quarter century—at La Scala, Monte Carlo (where he created Ruggero in *La Rondine* in 1917), Chicago, and San Francisco—Schipa's nuanceful song and probity of characterization had rightfully commanded near-idolatry. Fortunately, virtually all of his Ottavio is captured here, and most of it is elegantly declaimed and well sung. When upon discovering the murdered commandant he swears to assist Anna in her vengeance ('Lo giuro al nostro amor'), he is the epitome of the noble cavalier, the polished vocal patrician. 'Dalla sua pace' is beautifully turned and solidly round in tone, not crooned; he even manages to suggest unsuspected strength of character in the firm 'morte mi dà' (though the upward leap on 'morte' has a curious and ugly burr on the *r*). All is well in the ensembles, and Schipa would seem to have earned his niche among the memorable Ottavios until he confronts 'Il mio tesoro.' Surely the forty-five-year-old tenor can perform this test piece with greater accuracy! Schipa's reading captures the grace of Mozart's *andante grazioso*, but his very slow tempo turns the aria into a long walk indeed. Again the conductor and singer seem to have agreed upon fluctuating tempos to suit the varied moods of the text; the emphatic rhythms of 'Ditele che i suoi torti' are in strong contrast to the body of the piece. The famous test phrase is badly mangled: Schipa several times omits a pair of the sixteenth notes in the figuration and breathes twice. All sense of shape is lost. Troubled no doubt by the weakness of his low range, he omits the low D in the concluding 'nunzio' after altering Mozart's carefully plotted musical arch at 'tornar.' (Schipa merely repeats the descending scale E-flat to F rather than taking the sequence down a third.) Ponselle, too, is guilty of musical sleight of hand at critical points in her act-one aria, but hers is a mere misdemeanor and not the felony perpetrated by Schipa. Still, Schipa's lack of graceful fioriture cannot permanently blemish the memory of his refined art; if Ottavio fits him ill on this occasion he is better remembered for his cherishable Nemorino, Fritz, Ernesto, Elvino, Des Grieux, and Wilhelm Meister, all carefully tailored to his vocal size. Schipa had come late to the Metropolitan (1932), like Leider and Olszewska a refugee from the defunct Chicago Opera where the bulk of his American career was spent. He remained for only three seasons, but would return for a lonely pair of Ottavios in 1941 and then be heard no more at the Metropolitan.

Tito Schipa as Don Ottavio in *Don Giovanni*.

And what of "our Rosa," as Mr. Cross called her on a later broadcast? In her decade and a half before the Metropolitan public no alloy had debased Ponselle's golden instrument. Elvira (*Ernani*), the Leonoras (*Trovatore* and *Forza*), Santuzza, Gioconda, and above all, Bellini's Druid priestess, Norma—the grand roles were her vocal playground. Only thirty-seven at the time of the *Giovanni* broadcast, Ponselle would quit the opera stage three seasons later, her voice, except for a receding top, still in prime condition. By the time of the *Giovanni* broadcast, Anna had been in her repertory for five years, and she is in full command of this notoriously demanding role. The voice is not fully focused in the opening scene; occasional sharp pitches, whitish tone, and disjunct top notes in fast passage work are telltale signs of lack of complete vocal poise. These minor imperfections soon disappear, and artist and role seem perfectly mated. She understands the architecture of Mozart's constructions, effectively contrasting dual-phrase components in the act-one duet ('Fuggi, crudele, fuggi! lascia che mora anch'io). Nor does she fail to single out Anna's salient moment of pathos in the accompanied recitative where she colors her isolated cry of 'Padre mio' with deep longing. Similarly, the varied rhythmic landscape of the great recitative preceding the honor aria is astutely plotted. Her vengeance aria is not bound by a single affect as it so often is (and probably correctly so, since the aria is a throwback to the older seria manner); Ponselle repeatedly drops to a *piano* dynamic and noticeably lays on her legato at each remembrance of her father ('che il padre mi tolse'). The top As are all secure and refulgent, though she drops the consonants in her approach to them; in the final ascending arpeggios of 'Vendetta ti chiedo, la chiede il tuo cor' she consistently leaves out the first eighth note (high A) on 'la.' A giant ritardando buttresses the final four phrases; is it dictated by Serafin's predilection, or by an attempt to ease the pressure of the tessitura for Ponselle? The mask trio marks the high point of Ponselle's portrayal; her seamless legato and burnished tone are bewitching, ascending and descending scale passages are beautifully and effortlessly negotiated, and the soft top B-flats are executed with perfect ease. Dare one use the cliché "golden-age singing"? Unfortunately, the lengthy second-act act aria 'Non mi dir' is not preserved, but we have the preceding accompanied recitative, apparently transposed down a half step. The top A of 'abbastanza' is taken in a strong, secure *forte*—not the preferred *piano*—and the whole scene is realistically declaimed. In the concluding vaudeville Ponselle's notorious fear of top tones proves needless as she blithely takes a fleeting high B in stride.

But Ponselle's fear of the high C was real, and in the *Traviata* broadcast of the following season (5 January 1935) 'Sempre libera' is transposed down a whole tone and even 'Ah fors'è lui' is down a half step. "They [high notes] had become an obsession with me," she confided to the radio audience during an intermission interview two decades later. "The whole idea of this opera [*Norma*] on stage made me tremble. . . . It wasn't only *Norma* that gave me that feeling of responsibility. Almost everything that I did or had to sing had that same sense of urgency—that's why I envied the mezzo sopranos. I used to stand in the wings and how I wanted to sing Amneris and Laura and Dalila—my voice was dark enough, you know, in color, low enough in range, too, and I could have let myself go dramatically without worrying about the next high C coming up. . . . Every time I studied a new score I'd look through it first to see how many high Cs there were."[41] She owned that they did not *sound* difficult because "I worked hard and I had a technique that always stood by me, thank God." Actually, the shadow of Ponselle's nervous distress was present from the beginning of her career (despite her years on the vaudeville circuit with sister

Carmela), for she had fainted dead away midway through 'Casta Diva' at her 1918 Metropolitan audition before Gatti, De Luca, and Mardones. In spite of her collapse she won the season's opening night in the Met's first *Forza*—the twenty-one-year-old soprano's first appearance on any opera stage.

Transpositions were not the only demerit with which the critics had saddled Ponselle's Violetta when first heard in New York in 1931. The press deemed her too declamatory, insufficiently lyrical, inelegant; she was accused of making "violent onslaughts on Verdi's melodic line."[42] Bori's elegance and the delicate creation of pansy-voiced Galli-Curci had fixed the current Metropolitan norm for *Traviata*. But Ponselle's demimondaine had found great favor in London; British critics equated it with her Norma. What does the 1935 broadcast reveal?

The broadcast was the first *Traviata* of the season, with the mature Tibbett as papa Germont and Brooklyn-born, Milan-trained Jagel as a rather raw Alfredo. (Better in the *forte* passages of the later acts than in the lyric moments, Jagel was still an unfinished talent, though he had been with the company since his debut as Radames in 1927.) Serafin having departed following his salary dispute, the new conductor of the Italian wing, Ettore Panizza, is in charge. Buenos Aires–born Panizza had been Toscanini's right-hand man at La Scala during the 1920s, and one anticipates the imprint of the old master (textual fidelity, tension of line, dynamic propulsion) on Panizza's music-making. Such a concept certainly was not Ponselle's, however, and a comparison with Panizza's later *Traviata* broadcasts featuring various prima donnas indicates that there was more than a little meeting of minds in the interpretation of Ponselle and Panizza. The conductor betrays a fondness for some very slow tempi (in most of the second-act duet and 'Parigi, o cara,' for example). Ponselle moves even farther afield in frequent extensions of phrase and brief fermati, which Panizza's later interpreters (Sayão, Bovy, Jepson, Novotna) eschew. In the livelier and more dramatic portions of the opera some of the welcome virtues of the old man from Parma are discernible: the precision and bite of the violin trills which decorate the main love theme of the prelude give us the first hint; then come the rhythmic brio and momentum of the dance music. Wherever Panizza is free to exercise dynamic thrust, he makes good use of the opportunity: the taut excitement of the stretta as the chorus leaves the stage, the accompaniment to 'Non sapete,' the orchestral fury supporting both Violetta's 'Amami, Alfredo' and the confrontation scene that culminates Flora's party. In the long line of the act-four (at the Met) prelude, Panizza achieves a noble grandeur—perhaps a mite too grand for the intimate character of this chamber opera but a fitting framework for Ponselle's Violetta.

Gioconda, Donna Anna, and Santuzza were the intensely dramatic roles which occupied Ponselle when she was not singing Violetta in the 1934–35 season, yet how she modulates her tones for the frail courtesan! Seldom does any heaviness overweight her singing (she uses little chest tone, for example), and she achieves the finely floated line which is Violetta's province. Her legato is a constant wonder, the vocal color is often ravishing, and the act-one fioriture are well articulated (better than by most light-voiced Violettas). She knows her way around the often slighted turns in the Brindisi, too. On the negative side are the frequent tempo distortions: the andantino of both 'Ah fors'è lui' and 'Dite alla giovine' becomes an adagio, and in 'Parigi, o cara' (marked *andante mosso*) all sense of movement gradually is lost. In addition to her predilection for slow tempi, Ponselle (and Jagel, too—perhaps of necessity in his case) often pushes key phrases beyond their logical shapes. Where a mere nod at a cadence will do, she opts for a giant ritardando ('croce e delizia'); where

La Traviata
5 January 1935

Violetta
Rosa Ponselle

Alfredo
Frederick Jagel

Germont
Lawrence Tibbett

Conductor
Ettore Panizza

the climactic curve of a line needs only a fond caress, she may choose to grapple it to her bosom. In a current reassessment of Ponselle, Michael Scott (in his estimable, often provocative *Record of Singing*) draws attention to "a peculiarity of her voice production . . . compromising the purity of the vowels and obscuring them with that characteristic diphthonged 'ow' which is present in all her singing."[43] Throughout act one this slightly metallic sound is sometimes evident, though to my ears it is more an "ahrr" than an "ow." One first hears it in the low descending run in the duet ('amor'). The "ahrr" surfaces again in the double aria, especially on the open *e* vowels which sound like they come from a person singing in a cistern. But this metallic burr is entirely absent from Ponselle's work in the remainder of the opera—there the utmost beauty and warmth of tone prevail.

One notes, for instance, the opening of 'Ah fors'è lui,' lightly sung and full of exquisite diminuendi and *portamenti*, and the succession of three melting recitative phrases at the beginning of the scene with the elder Germont ('Or amo Alfredo,' 'O come dolce,' 'era felice troppo'). Indeed, the entire duet is vocalized with lyrical restraint by both Ponselle and Tibbett. The American baritone is superb throughout this scene, singing all of 'Pura siccome un angelo' in a vibrant mezza voce. A sympathetic warmth invades his tones when the text warrants ('bella voi siete e giovane,' 'consolatore'. Tibbett does not bellow 'Di Provenza' nor play it as the big vocal moment; again his mezza voce suggests the 'vecchio genitor' who suffers with his son. He ends the aria with the gentlest of head tones, the F taken *mezzo piano* with a crescendo not only of volume but of feeling.

In the gambling scene the slender *fil di voce* of Ponselle's 'Alfredo, di questo core' contrasts strongly with her dominance in the big ensemble. Best of all is her final act, a constant stream of vocal glories. She speaks the letter without affectation—the famous booming tones which were Ponselle's normal speaking voice are forsworn, and her tempo (for once) is apt for the farewell aria. Ponselle's characterization is well conceived throughout the opera, and everywhere she matches vocal color and dramatic intent, no more so than in 'Addio del passato.' 'Se una pudica vergine' is softly and simply delivered. Seldom in the opera does she call upon her commanding chest voice, but she deploys it most effectively at 'per lei sarà' just before 'Dite alla giovine' and again at 'salvarmi è dato' in the final act. In fact, the only overplayed moment in her performance is a nonvocal one in the denunciation scene with Alfredo. Here Ponselle writes her own scenario, engaging in a wild emotionalism, crying, squealing, and speaking where Verdi was content to let Alfredo do the ranting. Aside from this outburst, Ponselle nowhere overpowers the role and, because of her lyrical approach, makes a convincing and moving Violetta. Had she modified her conception since it was first revealed in 1931? Or were the critics, subject to preconceptions, not listening?

Just two seasons after the *Traviata* broadcast, the forty-year-old diva bade farewell to the Metropolitan and the lyric stage. But before leaving, Ponselle took on yet another controversial role, Carmen. Four performances of her gypsy were broadcast during this period, and two of them are preserved: one (28 March 1936) on private records, the other (17 April 1937) issued by the Metropolitan Opera. (The 1936 records contain some foreign portions which have been interpolated to make a complete performance—Morales suddenly changes from Cehanovsky to Wilfred Engelman, for example.) Both are tour performances, the first in Boston, the latter in Cleveland and of some historical moment as the soprano's final performance in opera (though this was not known at the time).

Carmen
28 March 1936
Carmen
Rosa Ponselle
Micaela
Susanne Fisher
Don José
René Maison
Escamillo
Ezio Pinza
Conductor
Louis Hasselmans

Few portrayals have gained so notorious a repute as Ponselle's Carmen, as though it were a personal affront that the Druid priestess should stoop to portray an earthy gypsy. She certainly did not conquer, at least in the press, which considered it a disaster. "We have never heard Miss Ponselle sing so badly and have seldom seen the part enacted in such an artificial and generally unconvincing manner" was Olin Downes' infamous verdict in the *Times* of 28 December 1935.[44]

How had it ended? Ponselle's final broadcast reveals the vocal and musical integrity of her Carmen in its later performances. And in the earlier broadcast (just three months after her first Carmen on 27 December 1935) much is of interest. In the 1937 farewell, Gennaro Papi's straightforward conducting often plods; thus the overall performance is less vivid than the 1936 *Carmen* under Louis Hasselmans. The French conductor offers greater fluidity of tempo and occasionally whips up the orchestra to considerable excitement, sometimes to Ponselle's discomfort (as in the second verse of the Gypsy Song where the diva falls almost a measure behind). But in the Flower Song and similar passages, Hasselmans' players achieve a welcome plasticity of line.

Ponselle's colleagues are less than memorable in the 1936 broadcast. In his debut season, the admirable Belgian tenor René Maison is hard-pressed in the upper range. (His pitch in the Flower Song is on the low side, and the high B-flat is painful.) Nevertheless, Maison is a convincing antihero and unexpectedly lyrical in the act-one duet. He cannot be faulted for finding the Micaela of Hilda Burke dull, for she sings with firm tone but virtually no characterization. Pinza's assumption of the Toreador (another flirtation with baritone roles in his early career) seems dictated more by his physical attributes than vocal suitability. Of course, he gives it his all and provides the expected panache in the Toreador Song; the scene with José in the mountains is highly charged as well. While the little act-four duet with Ponselle is sumptuous in tone, elsewhere the top tones are often strained. Yet one must prize this single opportunity to hear Pinza in a role he sang quite frequently during his early career (thirty-four appearances with the Metropolitan).

And now for Ponselle—first the 1936 portrayal. Her occasional preference for soprano pitch alternatives is no surprise; a greater detraction is her compulsion to add spoken dialogue of her own creation at moments of tension. These mistaken attempts to heighten the realism of her portrayal (at the conclusion of act three and in the final struggle with José) are mere self-indulgence on Ponselle's part. Had she in mind a reversion to the original spoken dialogue of the 1875 premiere?—rather unlikely, though she had wanted to do the opera without the accompanied recitatives. In act two the fleet pace of Bizet's setting engenders some white, squawky tones. But there are fine moments. The Habanera is well sung, the Seguidilla even better, deftly and lightly done on through the held high B at the close. Her little-girl speaking voice in the recitatives before the Seguidilla is effective. "And Rosa waves her peach-colored handkerchief to the audience," Cross tells us during the first-act curtain calls, bringing the visual aspect to the radio audience as he describes in detail Ponselle "in her yellow blouse . . . black skirt dotted with colored flowers, four ruffles each trimmed with a red-ribboned border."

The card scene is marvelously vocalized in rich, firm low tones with full attention to the text. Ponselle makes good use of her impressive chest voice in the final confrontation with José—clearly a Carmen unwilling to accept her fate without a struggle. Though both Ponselle and Maison indulge in a good deal of snarling, Carmen's anger and disdain are tellingly presented. All in all, the 1936 reading provokes a mixed response, and one regrets, along with Walter Legge, that Ponselle chose to play it "tough."[45] One turns to the 1937 performance with more than usual interest. Will the broad interpretation be further coarsened, or will the musical and dramatic instincts which informed her best achievements gain the upper hand?

In 1937 Maison is in better vocal form and manages a more cogent Don José. The young American baritone, Julius Huehn, offers a sturdy but rather raw Toreador, while Thelma Votipka and Cehanovsky contribute some telling touches as Frasquita and Dancairo. As to the vocal condition of the soon-to-retire soprano, she is in splendid voice, her tone all smoldering bronze, never displaced (as occasionally occurred in 1936) and as full-bodied as that remembered from her earliest recordings. And the conception has been modified for the better. Occasionally the effects are still painted with too broad a brush (the vocal equivalent of a hip swing in the 'tra la la' just before the Seguidilla). But the emotional ad libbing against the orchestral background is generally abandoned in favor of grand vocal effects.

The first-act arias are well contrasted. Ponselle declaims the Habanera in a very public manner (chest tone much in evidence) while the Seguidilla is a private thing, intimately directed at José, especially in the playful recitatives. At the end of the aria she merely mouths the ascending scale of *tra la*s but caps it with a ringing high B. Examples of her superb vocal estate abound: the soft caress of the final 'prends garde à toi!' swells to a menacing *forte*; the voluptuous curve of 'Je suis amoureuse' smolders in the midst of what must be the dullest, slackest quintet on record (Papi's enervating baton is the culprit—later, as she taunts José for his devotion to duty, Ponselle tries to urge on her conductor). Her conception is exceptionally well planned here; quietly but portentously she repeats 'Non, tu ne m'aimes pas!' and delivers 'Là-bas, là-bas' with insinuating calm. Her ringing 'La liberté' (alternate high notes) brings the act to a close in a burst of theatrical excitement. In a few of the old grooves of these Met broadcasts the impression of actually being in a large house is suddenly captured; this is one of them. One can well understand why Ponselle took comfort in the great popular success of her Carmen in the face of the critical barrage which undermined her confidence and contributed to her early retirement.

The card scene represents the climax of Ponselle's farewell performance. Like an indomitable earth goddess she pours out her dark, lustrous tone in an undistorted, measured cadence. The registers are skillfully mixed—no shifting of vocal gears here. The final act is equally well conceived, for the coarseness of the 1936 performance has given way to a nobler stance. In her beautifully modulated legato line (as the scene opens) one can sense the dignity of the ancient race which allows Carmen to remain calm in the face of impending death. 'Non. Je ne t'aime plus,' she tells José, the 'Non' uttered matter of factly with the utmost simplicity. Only at 'frappe-moi donc, ou laisse-moi passer' does Carmen's control break; her disdain and impatience seem to demand the final death blow.

Like Carmen, Ponselle managed her exit with her pride intact. But when Johnson refused her request for *Adriana Lecouvreur*, pride combined with hurt, and the greatest of all American prima donnas chose a premature and permanent retirement.

Carmen
17 April 1937
Carmen
Rosa Ponselle
Micaela
Hilda Burke
Don José
René Maison
Escamillo
Julius Huehn
Conductor
Gennaro Papi

Kirsten Flagstad as Isolde in *Tristan und Isolde*.

CHAPTER SIX

1934-35
A Mighty Quartet
and a Norse Goddess

The 1934-35 season of broadcasts required further negotiations between NBC and the opera company. The only matter for dispute regarding the broadcasting of the operas themselves was NBC's insistence that "in the event the broadcasting again becomes a commercial one" the Met would pay the additional fees to the orchestra musicians (a sustaining program did not require salary beyond the regular performance rate paid by the Met). Ziegler found this demand "not just" since NBC would receive additional revenue whereas "the Met does not profit in any way by the sale of the hour."[1] NBC capitulated. The Met in turn granted NBC the option to extend the agreement to include the 1935-36 season "provided the Metropolitan Opera Association, Inc. functions for the season 1935-36."[2]

But the troublesome franchise area remained a major point of contention. Of the total payment of $100,000, NBC designated $28,000 as the cost of the franchise rights. If the artists' contract rights could not be extended beyond the close of the 1934-35 season (April 1935) a six-month period would remain before the termination (31 October) of the agreement with NBC. If the Met "ceased to function" after the close of the 1934-35 season, NBC wanted a rebate of a prorated portion of the $28,000. Ziegler hoped NBC would forgo the possibility of a rebate if the Met placed at its disposal an additional number of broadcast opera performances. But Ziegler was no longer dealing with his lunching companion, opera devotee Merlin Aylesworth. The stern words of NBC's executive vice-president, Richard Patterson, convey the new tone in the "family" relationship: NBC could not consider adding to its schedule "as we do not have the time available for such additional opera broadcasts, and we shall do well if in the course of the fourteen weeks of the opera season we are able to take the number of opera broadcasts mentioned in the agreement."[3] Gone were the days when a cycle of six or eight lengthy Wagner operas could be fitted into the midweek radio schedule. If the Met should cease to function at the close of the season, Patterson saw a rebate by the Met of seven-twelfths of $28,000 as the only "practical way" to settle the matter. That such a relatively small sum (a little over $16,000) was critical to the Met is evident in Ziegler's continuing efforts with Patterson. When Lambert Pharmaceutical was firmly on board as sponsor, he tried again to have the rebate waived "in view of the economic plight this institution finds itself in."[4] The problem eventually proved moot (the 1935–36 season took place), but the plight of the Met remained dire. In mid-March 1935 Ziegler informed Patterson that "inasmuch as over 90% of our disbursements are for labor—artistic and otherwise" he felt compelled to request advance payment of the final $20,000 due 31 March since "this would help us very much in solving our financial problems."[5]

No doubt the franchise was a prime asset for NBC, especially when it involved major artists. One example will show how the process worked. NBC granted the firm of Young and Rubicam the right to negotiate with Tibbett, conductor Wilfred Pelletier, and other Metropolitan artists for a series of broadcasts sponsored by Packard Motor Cars between 18 September and 18 December 1934; in return NBC would receive $250 for each broadcast, the total sum not to exceed $6,000 should the series run twenty-six weeks. (The fee was $150 if only one Met artist appeared per program.)[6] But by 1934 the pivotal clause of the franchise which gave NBC the exclusive right to broadcast Met artists was showing signs of further disintegration. Ponselle, Crooks, Bodanzky, and Doe had contracts which permitted them to broadcast; Louise Homer and John Charles Thomas had no restriction clauses in their contracts. Oddly, Tibbett had the "right to televise, but no mention of broadcast" while the number of artists who were excluded from the franchise due to their very limited number of Met appearances was growing (in addition to those mentioned above, Jepson, Bampton, Dino Borgioli, Johnson, Hackett, and others were now listed as having only a few performances).[7]

The franchise issue would continue to cloud relations between NBC and the Metropolitan throughout the thirties. But NBC reaffirmed its support for the 1934–35 season, and the annual series of opera broadcasts went on without interruption. The network was able to air the fourteen Saturday matinees of the shortened New York season; in fact, a fifteenth broadcast was added, though it is not noted in any of the Metropolitan surveys. On 24 April 1935 Ziegler acknowledged NBC's check for $1250 "representing payment for the broadcast of *Faust* on Saturday afternoon, April 6"[8] from Boston. The performance featured Rethberg, Swarthout, Martinelli, Tibbett, and Pinza, with Hasselmans conducting. Perhaps it was aired locally only, since the Met had wished to allow the local committee of sponsors to permit broadcast by the Columbia network outlet in Boston. The performance had been a cause of friction between NBC's executive vice-president and the Metropolitan. On 20 February Patterson's velvet words to Ziegler hardly concealed his displeasure:

> In view of the very cordial and productive association between the Metropolitan Opera Company and the National Broadcasting Company, we sincerely hope that you will see a way out of what appears to be an embarrassing situation.
>
> For several years, as sustaining and under sponsorship, the National Broadcasting Company has carried your opera from coast to coast on all its stations. I am certain you will agree with us that it would be most annoying, to say the least, to have a competitor carry a performance of your company when it is generally recognized that the National Broadcasting Company has the exclusive franchise for the Metropolitan.

Patterson drove his point home by coldly juxtaposing NBC's continued support with his request:

> We have always been anxious to cooperate for the furtherance of your company's welfare and will continue to do so. In fact, we seem rather

"blood relations." I do hope that there will be no broadcast of "Faust" in Boston.[9]

NBC's payment to Ziegler indicates that they, rather than CBS, took over the *Faust* broadcast and no blood was spilled.

Following the ritual Christmas Day Humperdinck offering, Pons opened the 1934–35 Saturday broadcast season as Lucia and returned later in *La Sonnambula.* But Elisabeth Rethberg garnered the largest number of broadcast assignments. This was an Italian season for the Dresden soprano. On 19 January she briefly acquired squatter's rights to what had been Ponselle's exclusive property—Leonora di Vargas in *La Forza del Destino.* She was heard again as Aida (Ponselle had long ago fled from the naked exposure of the 'O patria mia' high C after having sung only two Aidas in the New York house) and took over from Müller another role in the Verdi canon, Maria Boccanegra. She closed the broadcast season with one of only five house appearances as Puccini's Mimi.

Simon Boccanegra had been one of the most successful revivals of Gatti's tenure and already had been heard twice by the radio audience under Serafin's baton. Panizza was in charge of the 16 February broadcast with the familiar male contingent of Tibbett, Martinelli, and Pinza. (The same formidable lineup would be heard in the next *Boccanegra* broadcast in 1939.) The performance is one of the most significant documents of the early broadcasts. Four of the world's greatest vocal artists—the Italian equivalent of the peerless Wagnerian casts of the 1930s—are heard in a performance which had solidified under Serafin's knowing hand and was now revived by the Toscanini surrogate, Panizza. How eagerly the radio listener anticipates those performances when all the principal roles are cast from maximum strength. With fear we await Cross' introductory remarks, dreading the possible change of cast which will mar the perfect occasion, aware that never will the performance be bettered (or even equaled) by the substitution. (Well, almost never—there was that rare afternoon in 1974 when the announced Amara-Pavarotti *Bohème* by air time became Caballé-Corelli, the Spanish soprano's only Metropolitan Mimi.) How blemished would *Boccanegra* be if Rethberg had given way to Leonora Corona, the aging Martinelli to Jagel, or Tibbett to Armando Borgioli. Pinza, of course, would never give way. All fears proved needless in this case, and we have intact the matchless quartet.

Indeed they were both matchless and well matched. One is struck by the homogeneous musical manner of these artists, most evident in their treatment of the Verdi line. Everywhere the arch of Verdi's vocal melody is probed and shaped and extended to produce a mournful nobility of feeling. In 1857, after the fiasco of the premiere, Verdi had written the Countess Maffei, "The music of Boccanegra is of the kind that does not make its effect immediately. . . . It is very elaborate, written with the utmost exquisite craftsmanship and needs to be studied in all its details."[10] In the radio performance one feels the study had been made and the details conquered and absorbed into a meaningful whole. Of course, it is the 1881 revision which the Metropolitan performs, with its foreshadowing of *Otello* in the masterful scene in the council chamber—one of the peaks of Italian opera. Panizza's control of the alternate tension and release in this scene is worthy of the composer's conception and conveys the requisite excitement. Here, too, Tibbett is magisterial with his authoritative tones

Simon Boccanegra
16 February 1935
Maria/Amelia
Elisabeth Rethberg
Gabriele
Giovanni Martinelli
Simon
Lawrence Tibbett
Fiesco
Ezio Pinza
Conductor
Ettore Panizza

and breadth of phrasing, very much the beleaguered Doge but seizing every possible moment for human expression. When he cries out for peace and love, our hearts, in company with the plebeians and patricians of Genoa, must succumb. Tibbett's 'E vo gridando: pace! E vo gridando: amor!' rises so naturally and movingly out of the ensemble mass and is so sweepingly declaimed that we, like Hamlet, "stand like wonder-wounded hearers." The sheer emotive power of Tibbett's conception throughout, achieved by the most thorough probing of the "details" of the music and text, makes this the American baritone's crowning achievement. He is mighty in the recitative of the Doge which concludes the council chamber scene. Though coming in the train of one of Verdi's greatest ensembles (regrettably heard in alternately muffled or boxy sound), the baritone allows no sense of anticlimax. He toys with the guilty Paolo in tonal colors of awesome variety: his voice pales as he describes how the villain suffers ('e impallidisce in volto'); 'Io so il suo nome' is nastily grisly in tone. With the aid of Panizza's forceful management of the brass, Tibbett fully realizes the *tremenda maestà e violenza sempre più formidabile* of Verdi's stage direction. Yet it is his constant revelation of the human in Boccanegra's makeup which ultimately captures us: the ravishing mezza voce as he recounts Petrarch's desire for peace ('ei per Venezia supplica pace'), the sweetness of his request to Amelia to tell of the kidnapping ('Amelia, di' come tu fosti rapita'). In his commercial recording of the ensemble one can hear the love creep into his tones at 'Tutta l'alma mia parla d'amore'; unfortunately, this striking effect is curiously lacking in the complete performance.

Rethberg is uninhibitedly dramatic as she recounts Amelia/Maria's childhood. Earlier I noted a contrast between some of Rethberg's commercial records and her live performances; perhaps she felt it improper to completely mesh the dramatic with the musical in the recording studio. The broadcast performances broaden and alter our concept of her artistry. Her recordings, while ethereally beautiful in tone, at times convey an overall placidity and generality of conception, both in musical phrasing and dramatic motivation. By the time Rethberg voices Amelia's childhood narrative, her tone has become fully rounded, the honeyed viola-like middle range capped by sudden silvery shafts. Her prominent ensemble line is firmly drawn and the final trill well executed—no lack of vocal focus or pitch problems here, both of which detract from her opening aria in the first scene. One would like to think the veiled quality of the middle voice in 'Come in quest'ora bruna' is the singer's imaginative response to the 'tears of sorrow' in Piave's text, but the effect (except for the glinting top tones) is as though she were heard through a scrim; the flatness and weariness of tone are particularly prominent from F up to C in the lower octave. But as soon as Martinelli arrives, she comes alive, almost aggressively so. In the concluding phrases of their duet the two singers are in fine form.

The noble mood of *Simon Boccanegra* comes to the fore in the *duettino religioso* for Gabriele and Fiesco, and here Martinelli and Pinza grasp the intent of Verdi's conception, singing in an almost instrumental fashion, Martinelli's muted trumpet topping Pinza's sonorous cello. The great recognition scene, when Amelia discovers she is the daughter of the Doge, is lovingly done. Rethberg effectively covers her low voice to suggest the sorrow of her youth ('Orfanella il tetto umile') while Tibbett's vocal palette changes from hope at 'Se la speme' (though here some sense of vocal effort intrudes) to animated joy at 'Figlia! A tal nome palpito.' Rethberg has the *forte* high B-flat well in hand, an apt foil for the softly glowing 'Figlia' with which Tibbett closes the scene.

Veteran Martinelli comes into his own in Gabriele's scene in act two. As

Gabriele falls victim to Paolo's false accusations against the innocent Amelia, Martinelli's depiction of the torment of jealousy provides a prophetic glimpse of his Otello, now two years in the future. Alone with his anguish, Martinelli lets loose 'O inferno' like the cry of a wounded animal. From the low-lying tessitura in the opening phrases of the aria, he resolutely climbs in pitch and agony to a delirium worthy of the Moor. (Recall that Tamagno had sung Gabriele in the premiere of the revised version at La Scala, just four years before he created Otello.) In 'Pietà, gran Dio' Martinelli squeezes out his tones in veristic fashion, but the tenor's scrupulous sense of line mitigates the tonal flintiness. His upward *portamenti* in the cantabile ('Cielo, pietoso') are marvelously sculpted. When he reaches 'Priva di sue virtù, ch'io non la vegga più,' the self-torture is almost uncomfortably vivid. He trumpets the final phrase brazenly out into the house, provoking a wild demonstration of shouts and applause. Martinelli had a unique capacity for embracing the grand dimension in his portrayals, seizing on the crucial moment of passion and exposing the soul in its naked agony. The astringent vocal manner of his later years contributes to, rather than detracts from, the powerful impression he creates. His vocal cords were undoubtedly of steel as Marguerite d'Alvarez thought, but when she noted that "he swung on them like a fox terrier on a bone,"[11] she was graphic but cruelly incomplete in her description. Tenacity he had, and intensity of commitment, but there was nothing small about him—if he gnawed at all, he was a noble Doberman Pinscher.

The grand decrescendo which marks the entire opera after the tenor's violent scene gives a curiously pathetic tone to the work, a pathos perfectly mirrored in Tibbett's vocalism. At his entrance in act two he manages with a single word ('Figlia') to suggest the weariness of an old man full of sorrows. Tibbett's lengthy unaccompanied recitative is colored by a tender sadness—his weary limbs ('Stanche le membre') are reflected in his murmuring mezza voce. His transition to the sleeping Boccanegra is a splendid example of vocal acting. Nor does Martinelli blatantly disturb the mood, managing to modulate his stentorian tones to a discreet *piano* at his entrance. Although Pinza's warmth of tone is seemingly at odds with Fiesco's character, he is able to suggest the granitic severity of old Fiesco by rhythmic emphasis in the terrible act-three confrontation between the two men. When the reconciliation occurs, it is doubly effective; Boccanegra's 'Balsamo all'alma mia' is vocal balm in Tibbett's dulcet voicing. The elegiac mood is sustained in the final trio; Rethberg may be a little insensitive in her initial entries, but thereafter both soprano and tenor skillfully execute the difficult half-tone descents. Tibbett's musico-dramatic sensitivity never falters. When, with incredible sweetness, he extends his final benediction, he seems to waste away.

This remarkable portrait is captured again four years later, with far better audio, in the broadcast tapes of 21 January 1939. In the prologue Pinza splendidly intones Fiesco's 'Il lacerato spirito.' Verdi had noted that the near-fanatic Fiesco must have a "voice of steel,"[12] certainly no description of Pinza's mellifluous instrument. But Pinza understands the character; he even refuses to modify Fiesco's angry denunciation of the Virgin in his opening recitative as so many basses misguidedly do. Superbly resonant singing by Tibbett and Pinza in the act-two duet confirms the continued healthy state of these voices throughout the decade of the thirties. Tibbett is in even better voice than in 1935, everywhere at the height of his powers. At 'O de' Fieschi implacata' he introduces successive changes of weight and color of tone in response to the text. 'Plebe! Patrizi!' wears an even greater spaciousness. He does everything on a grander scale, especially the baiting of Paolo, which rolls out

Simon Boccanegra
21 January 1939

Maria/Amelia
Elisabeth Rethberg
Gabriele
Giovanni Martinelli
Simon
Lawrence Tibbett
Fiesco
Ezio Pinza
Paolo
Leonard Warren
Conductor
Ettore Panizza

splendidly as Tibbett spends his vocal capital in the most generous fashion; as he tells Paolo of his need for him, Tibbett adds a malicious, quiet snarl ('Bramo l'ausilio tuo'). Though Tibbett was in perfect vocal form on this occasion, he appears to be less completely immersed in the character of the Doge than in the 1935 performance, and he employs much less of the unique mezza voce which gave such a haunting twilight tint to his earlier portrayal.

Martinelli, too, retains sufficient vocal life to color his lines. One appreciates all the more his expressive molding of 'Angiol che dell'empireo' after Rethberg's rather pedestrian voicing of the opening of their act-one duet. No denying that he finds it a shade harder going this time around in the great outburst of act two—some of the metal has worn away, and the tensile strength of line, always his most notable possession, grows slack now and then. Rethberg is basically in fine voice, yet the tone is perhaps a little breathier, and middle-voice gurgle a little more prominent in her opening scene (with attendant pitch problems); but thereafter the lower octave is firmly grounded. As she ascends in pitch she often grows overly assertive, punching at the top curve of phrases and (occasionally) squeezing out the very top tones. Yet her soft singing invariably remains lovely. And Panizza's pliant hand unites all elements in a performance still remarkable for musical and dramatic impact.

The inevitable vocal decline which the implacable years visit upon all but a few vocal artists had not appreciably settled upon Rethberg, however, in her Italian season of 1934–35. Her rare appearance as Mimi in the *Bohème* broadcast of 23 March 1935 is a case in point. Opera historians[13] would have us believe that the German soprano, at one time hailed as the world's greatest singer, was but a pale shadow of her former self by the mid thirties. But the records of this live performance show that she is by no means a negligible vocal artist. Surprisingly, the unfamiliar terrain of carefree Bohemian life in the Latin Quarter is not uncongenial to her; she even makes some concessions to realistic vocal acting. Her entrance lines have a weary pathos induced by her ascent of the stairs, and 'Vivo sola, soletta' is very much *a piacere*. Rethberg has assimilated the traditional *accenti* of the role, and the first-act narrative is full of lovely little *portamenti* which give definition to the line. She has a habit of altering final *e* vowels to 'ah' and the B-flat–C area in her middle voice still lacks focus (as at the first 'senza rancor' in the farewell aria). For the most part she evades the "Hausfrau" identity and is certainly romantic enough for the sturdy but prosaic Rodolfo of Frederick Jagel. No matter how earnest his efforts, lack of spin in the voice and deficient charm of vocal manner rob him of the poetry essential to Rodolfo's claimed profession. He has the high B, however (the aria is taken a half tone down), and manages a commendable diminuendo on the A-flat of 'alla stagion dei fior' in the quartet.

The high point of the performance is the act-three duet of Mimi and Marcello, with Rethberg fully committed to Mimi's distress and De Luca authoritative in response. De Luca's easy vocalism and jaunty delivery of the text, in fact, exemplify an authentic manner which neither Rethberg nor Jagel can match. De Luca never overplays. His opening 'Questo Mar Rosso' is almost offhand, and his designation of Musetta as 'Vipera! Strega!' must be the most gentlemanly ever heard. But when grace and charm are needed, he supplies them with consummate ease, making us notice the simplest phrases through a sudden sweetness of tone ('Povera Mimì') or by giving a capricious lilt to a single word ('canto' in 'Musetta insegna il canto ai passeggieri') or finding the exact mixture of friendly ire as he berates friend Rodolfo ('noioso, cocciuto').

La Bohème
23 March 1935
Mimi
Elisabeth Rethberg
Musetta
Nina Morgana
Rodolfo
Frederick Jagel
Marcello
Giuseppe de Luca
Colline
Ezio Pinza
Conductor
Vincenzo Bellezza

Giuseppe de Luca as Figaro in *Il Barbiere di Siviglia*. Photography by Mishkin.

Bellezza has it all in hand, the livelier sections generally taken somewhat slower than expected (the chilly Bohemians can thank him for the slow chordal passages which accompany the burning of Rodolfo's play). Nina Morgana and Pinza round out the cast in this performance, of which only the first (absent the duet) and third acts are preserved.

If Puccini could feel confident about portraying Bohemian life in nineteenth-century Paris, warring families of Renaissance Verona would seem fair game for Charles Gounod. Though the results were unequal, *Roméo et Juliette* continued to find favor with management and public throughout the thirties and forties. The broadcast of 26 January 1935 shows "the reason why." De Luca is again on hand as friend to another American tenor, Charles Hackett, who sings Roméo. To the Norwegian soprano Eidé Norena (Juliette), add Swarthout and D'Angelo, and the polyglot character of the casts of French opera, even this early, is apparent.

Happily, the odd mix is belied in this instance by the apposite style of the performance itself, proving that stylistic know-how, not nationality, is the essential. With old Rothier lending the genuine article to Friar Laurence's pronouncements, the performance has an aura of stylistic rightness and dramatic credibility seldom heard in presentations of French opera in recent times.

Norena, of course, had been a fixture of the Paris Opéra since 1928, and America's own French company, housed in Chicago but with its heart in Paris, claimed both her and Hackett as members. Hackett, now in his late forties, is one of those artists about whom one knows relatively little but would like to hear much more. He had joined the Metropolitan as early as 1918 after a successful Italian career. Upon leaving the Met in 1921, he appeared at Paris, Covent Garden, and La Scala before rejoining the company in 1934 for another five-year stint. Hackett had taken part in some historic performances; he appeared as Roméo in act two of Melba's farewell at Covent Garden in 1926, and the following year he sang Faust with the Chicago Opera in the first nationwide opera broadcast in America. His experience and authority are never in doubt in this performance; he gives the impression of being completely at home on stage and fully comfortable in Roméo's togs. An occasional vocal frog and a few reluctant top tones notwithstanding, he casts an aura of genuine vocal glamour, parading his array of demitints in elegant French to excellent effect. Both he and Norena begin in labored fashion, but soon the voices are sufficiently lubricated to do justice to Gounod's sensuous lyricism. (Kolodin cites this performance as "ill-sounding"[14] with all principals except Swarthout beset by vocal problems. Perhaps his penchant for neat packaging interfered with perception on this occasion.)

At the end of the first act, announcer Cross reminds us that radio opera is again enjoying commercial support. He refers to "our Listerine Antiseptic broadcast"—the reference is surely to the product and not a critical comment on the performance. The Lambert Pharmaceutical Company paid NBC $375,000 to sponsor the season; thus the previous year's cigarette-making sponsor gave way to the throat-soothing mouthwash, demonstrating once again the know-how of American business. But we left "the good-looking Charles Hackett" (as Cross calls him) bemoaning that he should love a Capulet.

The second act reveals his best qualities. He begins (and ends) the act with exquisite mezza voce effects; in the aria, after scooping the opening 'Ah,' he sings the piece with ardent feeling and compelling style, ending with a resonant high B-flat. The apostrophe which concludes the act is the high point of his performance; with

Roméo et Juliette
26 January 1935

Juliette
Eidé Norena
Stephano
Gladys Swarthout
Roméo
Charles Hackett
Mercutio
Giuseppe de Luca
Friar Laurence
Léon Rothier
Conductor
Louis Hasselmans

Gigli-like sweetness of tone, he sustains the dreamy atmosphere of night by subtly weighting the reiterated C's. (One remembers that *Sun* critic W. J. Henderson had compared Hackett in his debut season to Alessandro Bonci.) Hackett is equally effective in the dramatic declamation of the street scene in act three; he defends himself to the Duke in manly fashion before becoming overtly heartsick as he contemplates exile. Not having the vocal metal to sustain the taut lines of the ensemble, he substitutes a not-ineffective broken declamation (and fortunately eschews a final top C). In reserve, however, is plenty of firm-voiced tone for the bedroom scene, and the tomb scene provides another high point. Now the declamation is nobly elegiac, his sorrow touched by an elegant dignity; once again the chains of reiterated notes are magically inflected. If he totters occasionally on the edge of lachrymosity or falters on a top tone, one can forgive anything for the haunting loveliness of his high B (a genuine *piano*) before he expires.

Though the broadcast is most notable for Hackett's idiomatic (if imperfect) Roméo, Norena, at fifty no longer young, exerts a strange fascination. Already familiar to the radio audience for her Marguerite, Norena came to the Met at Cravath's instigation, though at the time Ziegler opined that "she is not a singer of distinction and while the voice is a nice lyric quality, I don't think it would make much impression in the vast spaces of the Metropolitan."[15] In her Juliette, the listener may well decry the infantile quality of the low voice (in her entrance music) or the acidulous point of certain top tones or a momentary smudge of legato. But then one falls victim to her unique vocal coloring, the exotic middle voice often flowing like citrus-tainted honey (as in the 'Ange adorable' duet of act one). We are compelled to nod appreciatively at her accurate graces as she begins the waltz song and to admire the clean rush of scales which ends the aria. She and Hasselmans take the middle section at a much slower tempo (*pace* Emma Eames, who maintained that Gounod taught her to sing the aria absolutely in time), and the final trills and high C are a trial. The music of the balcony scene fairly droops with the languid longing of her tones; her initial 'Hélas' is a wail and the *portamenti* are heavy indeed. Yet her coloring of these phrases gives a pungency to Gounod's supposedly cloying melodies that seems exactly right. A pity that only this broadcast Juliette survives of her Met career, for she is an interesting artist of a type no longer in vogue. Ziegler confirmed the approaching end to her Met career of six seasons when he contracted for only two performances for the 1936-37 season. (The Met was to be reimbursed for her fees by a friend of Norena's who would make a contribution to the Metropolitan Opera Fund.) Ziegler wrote Johnson "I told [Norena's friend] frankly that our public was not enthusiastic about her."[16] But as late as 1984, one auditor of her 1930 Met performances recalled Norena as a "soprano who at her best possessed a magisterial vocal technique."[17]

The American mezzo, Gladys Swarthout, in her fourth season and embarking on a film career which would upgrade her status in the opera house, makes a fine Stephano. 'Que fais-tu, blanche tourterelle' is accurate and done with care—the piece would profit from more animation. Swarthout's tone is that of an ingénue, not the more flavorful dusky quality much admired in later seasons. Rothier, "the grand old bass" in Cross' fond words, gives perhaps his best preserved performance as Friar Laurence, bringing not just his customary authority but also solid steady tone, obviously of sizable sonority. No sign here of the quavers and struggles of vocal age which one hears in a number of his broadcasts (after all, he made his Met debut as Méphistophélès in 1910 with Farrar). And there is something really grand about his priest. The same cannot be said for D'Angelo's Capulet or Bada's Tybalt.

De Luca, too, is in the final stages of a long career; his debut at the Met had occurred in 1915, but he had sung with Caruso in Italy as far back as 1897. This was to have been his final Met season, but he returned five years later at age 64 for a full complement of performances including a broadcast *Bohème.* One would not want to bid him a last farewell on this afternoon, for his Mercutio moves on 'the wings of grasshoppers' when the fifty-nine-year-old sprite trippingly tosses off the ballad of Queen Mab. And he makes something of this thankless role throughout the afternoon.

The Met's chief historian considered the *Roméo* broadcast one of the performances which clouded "the sunset glow" of Gatti's last season.[18] Certainly other performances have more consistent vocalism, but few are as flavorful or as fascinating as this imperfect memento of what seems a remote time indeed. It was a time when Gatti's twenty-seven-year tenure was hastening to a close. Yet the well-remembered event of the season was not his leave-taking but the cometlike arrival of an artist with the vocal endowment of a Caruso. This time it was no Mediterranean songbird but a Nordic goddess fit to inhabit the lofty peaks of Wagnerian music drama—the Norwegian soprano, Kirsten Flagstad.

We know that the Met's Wagner wing did not lack for first-rank interpreters; the radio audience heard them frequently during the first three broadcast seasons. But now the matinee Wagner cycle was no longer aired, so the season of Flagstad's arrival saw only three Wagner broadcasts. She was not yet on board for the *Tannhäuser* of 12 January 1935, the fifth airing of the opera but the first of which any documentary material remains, slight though it is. (The material is not listed in the *Rodgers and Hammerstein Preliminary List of Audio Documentation.*) About thirty-five minutes from the second and third acts are preserved in generally poor sound; groove wear is the principal irritant. Included are Wolfram's Address and Tannhäuser's outburst from act two, the third-act meeting of Wolfram and Elisabeth, and much of the lengthy scene for Tannhäuser which ends the opera. Melchior had sung all the previous *Tannhäuser* broadcasts and is again the reluctant penitent, always undaunted by the high tessitura. He is splendidly outgoing in his final evocation of Venus, but saves the purest of headtones for a magical naming of 'Elisabeth.' Maria Müller joins the list of notable broadcast Elisabeths (Jeritza, Rethberg, Lehmann) portraying a more girlish saint than we are accustomed to, and one more indulgent in self-pity ('mein Herz sich abgewandt von dir') than internally devout in her prayer. Yet her *pianissimo* 'Nimm dich gnädig meiner an!' is very lovely, and her singing gains quietude as she nears heavenly grace. The radio audience would hear this engaging artist again in *Don Giovanni* before her Metropolitan career of eleven seasons ended.

The most notable feature of these acoustically variable excerpts is the portrayal of Wolfram by the American baritone, Richard Bonelli. After twenty years of appearances in Europe and America, Bonelli found refuge at the Met when the Chicago Opera collapsed. Now in his third Metropolitan season, Bonelli normally inhabited the Italian repertory (he had been heard earlier in the season on the broadcast *Lucia*), but his noble voice and scrupulous artistry—a student of Jean de Reszke, no less—make him a perfect Wartburg contestant. Judging from the superbly lyrical cast of his singing on this occasion, Elisabeth should have been his prize. Wolfram's 'heart begins to glow' in the hall of song, and Bonelli's vocal line, too, expands in the simplest, most noble fashion. He alters the dark richness of his tone to a ravishing mezza voce at 'und hold und tugendsam' and sweetens 'lieblicher Blüthen' in the manner of Heinrich Schlusnus. The voice may flutter unduly in the last half of the

Tannhäuser
12 January 1935
Elisabeth
Maria Müller
Venus
Dorothee Manski
Tannhäuser
Lauritz Melchior
Wolfram
Richard Bonelli
Landgrave
Ludwig Hofmann
Conductor
Artur Bodanzky

Address (or is this merely poor audio quality?), but his response to Tannhäuser's outburst is firm-toned and passionate. The excerpts from act three are equally fine. The voice itself comes over best at the beginning of the act where it is completely unforced, its darkly vibrant and manly color constantly shaded by perfectly formed vowels. Wagner's music is treated with utmost sensitivity. And yet not even a mention of this American singer is found in Steane's admirable anthology, *The Grand Tradition*. Was it simply that the age was crowded with great baritones? Tibbett was at the peak of his powers, dominating the likely Bonelli roles; De Luca had moved on, but yet another stalwart American, John Charles Thomas, had long been standing in the wings waiting to step onto the Metropolitan stage. At that, Bonelli would appear far more often than Thomas during the next decade; we can look forward to his several broadcasts of the big Italian roles.

When *Tannhäuser* would next be heard, the name of Flagstad would be added to that line of memorable Elisabeths. Frida Leider's occupancy of the Wagnerian throne proved to be brief at the Metropolitan, though her displacement was of her own choosing and as much of a surprise to the Metropolitan as was Flagstad's subsequent triumph. Negotiations for Leider's hoped-for return were still in progress at the end of summer, 1934. The correspondence between Ziegler and Villa (for Gatti) recounts the progressive deterioration of these efforts as well as the manner of Flagstad's engagement.

On 14 August Luigi Villa (Gatti's amanuensis) informed Ziegler that Leider had not yet signed her contract and that "she is trying everything to find any excuse not to come to America this winter. Mr. Gatti and Mr. Bodanzky are now in touch with her, but Mr. Gatti writes me that he feels that he will be compelled to replace her for the coming season."[19] Three days later the prospects were even more pessimistic. From St. Moritz Gatti had written to Villa in Cossato, Italy, reaffirming the need for Leider's release. Villa informed Ziegler,

> It seems that her substitution is made practically necessary because they Mr. Gatti, Maestro Bodanzky and Mr. Simon [the Met's European agent] are all convinced that Leider has decided not to go to America in the coming season whatever we may do. Mr. Gatti adds that they are considering the Swedish [*sic*] soprano Kirsten Flagstad, who is now singing with success in Bayreuth and of whom they have had good reports, to replace Leider.[20]

But the attempt for a rapprochement with Leider went on. On 6 September Gatti himself wrote (via Villa's English translation),

> I have to inform you that it has not been possible to come to an arrangement with Frida Leider, although Bodanzky and Simon used their best efforts too and I had made several concessions going even beyond the limits of our interests, but all to no avail.
>
> Therefore when I realized that it was impossible to come to an understanding with Leider, I invited Mme. Kirsten Flagstad to come to St. Moritz and sing an audition for Bodanzky and me. She made an excellent impression and I have engaged her for the period left vacant by Leider, viz., nine weeks, from January 28 to March 31, at a weekly salary of $550, for an average of two appearances per week. Ten days preliminary rehearsal and our right to prolong for one or more weeks, upon the same terms.[21]

Though the "excellent impression" of Flagstad's audition contradicts popular belief, Gatti's final words to Ziegler place it in perspective from the manager's viewpoint: "This will mean a substantial economy over the Leider contract."[22] But on 10 September Villa included Flagstad's name among those whose contracts had not yet been signed.[23]

On 7 September Ziegler tried further to illuminate Leider's reluctance. From the soprano's friend Mr. Neuer, who had spoken with her on the telephone in Bayreuth, he learned of Leider's belief that "behind her back the Metropolitan had engaged [Anny] Konetzni." Neuer supposed "it is this more than anything else which is dictating her present attitude."[24] Villa, however, informed Ziegler of Gatti's desire to minimize the conflict:

> Mr. Gatti adds that in case some newspaper critic should ask questions regarding the "Leider case," you should answer that the reason Leider is not returning is because of the forced long delay with which the final contracts were sent to the artists for the coming season.[25]

Die Walküre
2 February 1935
Sieglinde
Kirsten Flagstad
Siegmund
Paul Althouse
Hunding
Emanuel List
Conductor
Artur Bodanzky

Ziegler was directed merely to say that he had "found a substitute." The radio audience thus shared with New Yorkers the discovery of the substitute on the broadcast of *Die Walküre* on 2 February 1935.

Melchior, reigning Heldentenor (and last of his line), was not on stage to welcome the new soprano who would share so many Metropolitan performances with him. That honor fell to Althouse, fortunately in much stronger form than in his last broadcast. The tenor makes a sturdy, respectable Siegmund. Particularly admirable is his baritonal delivery of the 'Wehwalt' narrative of the Wälsungs; he is less effective in the higher range and seldom realizes the poetry of the love passages because his voice loses its coloration at the softer dynamics. List's appropriately black and solid tone is again impressive in Hunding's stern music. Kappel, Olszewska, and Schorr complete this notable cast, but regrettably, since only act one has been preserved, our concern remains the brother-sister-husband triangle.

Flagstad enters not as the heroic Brünnhilde, which would seem her more natural province (as it would soon become), but as the womanly Sieglinde. From the first it is apparent that her attributes are more godlike than human. Even so, her Sieglinde is a revelation. As she utters her first words upon discovering Siegmund on her husband's hearth, Sieglinde's surprise is modest compared to that of her unprepared auditors upon first hearing this completely unheralded singer. She was there only by default after all, and in spite of her "excellent impression," the Met management was not fully prepared for this vocal phenomenon, at least not until she sang a *Götterdämmerung* rehearsal in mid-January. The small carpeted room in St. Moritz had concealed the extent of her vocal amplitude. Beyond that, Flagstad herself offered a clue to the riddle when she wrote of her work during the interim between her audition and her debut months later: "In between [performances of *Fidelio* in Sweden] I worked either on the Brünnhildes or Isolde. Every moment was jammed with work and study.... You can imagine how I used my voice. I felt it growing stronger and larger under constant pressure."[26] Oscar Thompson, having heard and greatly admired her Isolde in Oslo in 1932, voiced concern for the size of her voice. The Flagstad voice we know today was not fully developed until the period shortly before her debut; the impact could not have been anticipated. Just short of her fortieth birthday, Flagstad was the somewhat weary veteran of a twenty-year career in the Scandinavian provincial opera houses where she had sung everything from Micaela to Minnie, Agathe to Aida. Only recently had she ventured onto the Wagnerian terrain in her native Oslo. Far from being an international star, her only major appearances had been at Bayreuth in 1933 as Ortlinde (*Walküre*) and the Third Norn, these small parts earning her advancement to Sieglinde and Gutrune in the 1934 festival.

After her St. Moritz audition, the Metropolitan sent Flagstad to George Szell in Prague for coaching in the Wagner roles which would be her Metropolitan lot. Whether the Szell inculcation was calculated merely to bring her to an acceptable Metropolitan standard or whether he actually burnished the gem-in-the-rough to the luster she revealed at her Met debut remains conjecture. But no doubt clouds the effect Flagstad had upon the public and professional critics at her debut on that February afternoon in 1935.

Years of hearing the Flagstad voice at its most mature make it difficult to recapture the sensations which that first audience experienced. In the early moments of the opera the density of the middle and lower voice captures attention. Later in the act, one notes how she lessens the pressure in her middle upper voice, producing a brighter, less dense sound (more oboe than her customary clarinet or English horn), which suits the soft womanliness of Sieglinde. (This rare vocal coloration, particularly striking in the passage beginning 'So bleibe hier!' will be heard less and less as Flagstad's career continues; one regrets its absence in so many of her recordings.) The purely vocal impact is complemented by the naturalness of her utterance, the text clearly articulated with no vowel manipulation for tonal amplitude—there simply is no need.

Flagstad's reading of 'Der Männer Sippe' is the finest episode in the act. She treats the phrase 'O merke wohl, was ich dir melde' as though it were the conclusion of a seria recitative, laying it out rather squarely; it is exactly right. Her diction throughout the narrative is exemplary, and the vocal colorations are varied in response to the text. As she recalls Wotan's entry at her wedding, an unusual sweetness invades her tone; it happens again at 'mir allein weckte das Auge' and again when she shows Siegmund the sword left by Wotan. Then comes the inevitable moment of the Flagstad vocal takeoff, skillfully planned in the approach to the high-lying 'O fänd ich ihn heut'.' Here was the moment when the live audience of 1935 must have realized the full grandeur of the singer's resources, resources not even fully expended, resources which enable her to master the outsized architecture of Wagner's music dramas. If she doesn't quite capture the rapture of spring, the beautiful color and amplitude of voice were undoubtedly more than enough for a first hearing. In the final exchanges with Siegmund she is again most communicative. A few lovely lighter effects suggest youthful delight; but now she first unveils a curious legato, the briefest smearing of the adjacent tones as though the voice must be marshalled from note to note. Though today we remember Flagstad as the matronly figure of her later years, critics of this period repeatedly comment on the girlishness of this forty-year-old soprano's stage figure. A similar welcome slenderness of voice occasionally comes to the fore in this performance; in turn it allows a wider range of color, a vocal manner more in tune with Sieglinde's nature. In limning that nature Flagstad does not employ artificial effects for dramatic emphasis—no breathy excess of surprise for her upon discovering the stranger. True, there remains a remnant of 'winter's ice-bound days' as this Sieglinde proclaims her newfound lover to be the spring ('Du bist der Lenz'); intoxication was not the Norwegian soprano's forte and probably not her intent—she left that to her auditors who were consumed by the

Tristan und Isolde
9 March 1935
Isolde
Kirsten Flagstad
Brangäne
Karin Branzell
Tristan
Lauritz Melchior
Kurvenal
Friedrich Schorr
Marke
Ludwig Hofmann
Conductor
Artur Bodanzky

splendor of her voice. Perhaps it is better that way.

Flagstad's gifts were more fully apparent in her second broadcast of 1935. On 9 March Melchior and Flagstad joined forces for the first of their nine consecutive broadcast portrayals of Tristan and Isolde, this time in company with Branzell, Schorr, and Hofmann. A new era of Wagnerian grandeur begins.

Though Schorr seems slightly below his very best on this occasion (a pair of high F's are decidedly speculative in act three), his low range is surprisingly impressive. As he begins his vigil over the wounded Tristan, Schorr reminds us that, if the singer has them at his disposal, Wagner allows for legato, varied tonal weights, and mezza voce. Ludwig Hofmann, too, is impressive with his firm dark tones and no hint of the aging bass wobble which so often makes Marke's monologue a marathon. He even wakens our sympathy when, in climactic tones, he describes his gracious Isolde; better yet, he substitutes genuine anguish for self-pity as he asks 'Warum mir diese Schmach?'

Branzell's Brangäne benefits from her splendid vocal amplitude—she pours out rich tone effortlessly, the phrases as seamless as a stream of brown molasses. The homely simile is apt, for subtlety is not her main concern. But her musicianly performance has many fine moments from the lovely soft 'Ungeminnt?' (incredulous that anyone should not love her Isolde) to the brave manner of her responses as she carries forward the excitement engendered by Flagstad in Isolde's first-act narrative. Curiously, she begins the pivotal second-act warning a little blowzily and sounds slightly sharp throughout—Brangäne's perch aloft in this scene can often play tricks on the singer, as well as on us. The two utterances of 'Habet acht' which later interrupt the love duet, however, are perfectly poised. While Bodanzky's first act seems less angular and hurried than before (especially Kurvenal's song and the long orchestral treatment of the heroic Tristan motive before Tristan comes to Isolde), in the climactic moments of the later acts he is intent on whipping up orchestral excitement (in both velocity and mass); his *fortissimi* press even these Wagnerian stalwarts.

When first heard on 6 February (just four days after her debut) Flagstad's Isolde had caused a sensation. We can closely approximate that experience since the broadcast of 9 March is Flagstad's very next appearance in the role. Melchior's knight is already familiar to the radio audience, but the 1935 broadcast provides our first opportunity to hear him in a complete Wagnerian role. The sense of discovery may therefore be nearly as great in regard to the Danish tenor as for the new Norwegian soprano; in fact, this proves to be the case.

Flagstad's Isolde was not only new to the Metropolitan stage but, like most of her Wagnerian assumptions, relatively new to her repertory. She first sang the part (in Norwegian) in Oslo in 1932 with infrequent repetition thereafter and never in an international house. Recall again the emphasis critics placed on Flagstad's youthfulness, her slender womanliness, during her debut season. The primary impression one gains from hearing the 1935 Isolde complements that visual image: a surprisingly virginal sound (always within the tonal colors of the English horn and the chalumeau register of the clarinet, of course), the resonances kept high. She rarely, almost never, calls upon the dark fullness of her middle low voice—she avoids it, for instance, at 'Ungeminnt den hehrsten Mann.' Nor is the brilliant opacity of the highest notes, which became her trademark in later years, often heard. The very first scene epitomizes her manner: 'Brangäne, du? Sag', wo sind wir?' is voiced in a questioning, dreamlike softness; 'Welches Land?' is uttered with girlish simplicity. Her lengthy

Karin Branzell as Brangäne in *Tristan und Isolde*. Photography by Mishkin.

narrative is no seething torment but is notable for the wonderful float and suspension of tone ('er sah mir in die Augen'), her recall of events consistently and appropriately full of revery, which in turn makes doubly effective the sure, swordlike thrust of the final high B ('gab er es preis') as her thoughts turn to Tristan's betrayal. Within this gentler conception, Flagstad is matchless when the phrases require a grander, more extended line ('Für tiefstes Weh'). Her manner with Tristan is suitably enigmatic when he appears. Two contrasting phrases tell the tale: 'das schwur ich nicht!' blazes forth, followed by the quiet, pregnant 'Zu schweigen hatt' ich gelernt.' And she manages to imbue the primarily instrumental cast of her voice with sensuous color and line as she invites Tristan to drink to friendship.

More startling is the intimacy in the opening scene of the second act. Here the rustling leaves whisper no more than Flagstad herself, and as she quietly revels in the welcome sound of the departing hunting horns which will give the lovers their freedom, a wondrous womanly aura surrounds her. This is precisely the aura which was absent in large part from her broadcast Sieglinde and it is all the more surprising here. An immense sense of repose envelops this Isolde; Flagstad nurtures a very "inner" conception. Sometimes a greater sense of movement in the plotting of her music would in fact be welcome, for not even the Irish princess' eagerness to brandish the torch calls forth passionate agitation.

Bodanzky plays his part well in this act, with skillfully charted surges of tempo which prepare Tristan's arrival. In the convulsive music of the lovers' greeting Flagstad touches the high Cs lightly (the first is surer than the second). When at last the lovers join in the lengthy duet, it is Melchior who gains our attention. He has been impressive in the opening scenes of the opera, his first tones a perfect balance of baritone splendor and pointed head resonance, the tone free and open with no squeezing of the vowels. As he offers Isolde his life on his sword, his tones become clouded and murky. Just before the fateful potion is drunk, Melchior again shows his command of tonal variety as he colors each of Tristan's pronouncements ('Ehre höchste Treu'!'). And Flagstad, having snatched the potion from Tristan for her rightful share, emits a marvelously soft 'Treuloser Holder!' (no hint of her normal woodwind color), as if she has been transformed by the magical drink.

As the lovers meet in the second act, however, the spell of the potion continues to work most potently upon Melchior. When, in the love duet, one hears Flagstad and Melchior side by side, it is Melchior who consistently sounds the note of nocturnal rapture which encompasses the lovers. Both provide ravishing vocal effects, but he is the one completely immersed in the dream world of 'O sink' hernieder.' In contrast to her reposeful, straightforward phrases, Melchior knows the value of subtle crescendi and diminuendi, of phrase expansion, of minutely altering pace and color by inflecting the text—in short, he knows how to enhance and deepen the mood. Both make memorable the closing phrase in sixths ('Nie wieder erwachens wahnlos holdbewusster Wunsch'), their tones perfectly mated. Flagstad's 'Lausch', Geliebter!' is as soft as the flutter of a hovering hummingbird in this most intimate of dialogues; yet her very next phrase ('Neid'sche Wache!') is commonplace next to Melchior's emotionally full 'Nie erwachen!' Could this be subtle dramatic perception on Flagstad's part—Isolde as the interrogator while Tristan remains lost in ecstasy in his languorous, lagging 'Lass den Tag dem Tode weichen!'? Again Melchior observes every dynamic marking in the lengthy passage beginning 'So starben wir, um ungetrennt'—the pain of ecstasy is in his voice as they contemplate eternal love even in death. In their alternating phrases, again it is Melchior who sustains the mood against Flagstad's matter-of-fact responses. One cannot gainsay the beauty of tone she spins at 'Lass den Tag dem Tode weichen!' but even that is surpassed by the *subito piano* of Melchior's 'Soll ich lauschen?' In the concluding passages both supply plenty of brilliant tone, volume, and intensity, and for once the singers have the requisite staying power to carry them through the rising chromatic passages (Flagstad is particularly impressive in this high tessitura).

After a half-dozen years' experience in the role, Melchior's Tristan is fully formed. He is superb in his response to his king in act two, the voice tightly collected, the resonances perfectly mixed. How perceptively he grasps the significant moment in a phrase, revealing it by a sudden increase in line, in legato, in dark color ('das dunkel nächt'ge Land')! His final act is most full, its alternating moods of despair and agitated hope easily compassed by Melchior, who caps his performance with a ravishing, incredibly gentle voicing of 'Isolde,' the notes imperceptibly creeping out of the orchestral fabric as he expires. The concluding episode of the opera is admirably suited to Flagstad's restrained conception. She repeatedly floats mezza voce phrases of ethereal beauty in her middle upper range; the ascending and descending *portamenti* in the passage beginning 'So bange Tage' are subtle indeed. Her Liebestod is excessively gentle, the vocal weights judiciously chosen, particularly in the shaping of the first climax ('wie er leuchtet') and in her dolce naming of Tristan ('Freunde'). Only once does she employ her remarkable chalumeau color (near the end, at 'unbewusst'); otherwise she is content to take her cue from Isolde's words: 'süsser Atem sanft entweht,' her 'sweet breath softly stirring.'

The impression remains that Flagstad's Isolde, vocally fluent, is not yet fully developed interpretively. In act one, when Flagstad repeats 'Wie lenkt' er sicher den Kiel zu König Markes Land?' no bitterness, no inflection of any kind intrudes, though Wagner marks it *schmerzlich bitter.* Her broadly gauged, sustained blocks of solid tone in the curse are stylized symbols rather than towering human rage. One recalls Leider's vocal caress on 'die gold'ne Schale' with nostalgia. Yet even in her initial Metropolitan season it is apparent that Flagstad's dramatic and musical restraint, her emphasis on the architectural layout of Wagner's music from the smallest phrases to the overall arch of an act or an entire opera are essential counterparts to the amplitude of her vocal equipment. We may respond to the characterful, fervid declamation of a Lehmann and revel in the warmth of tone of a Traubel, for they and their like are worthy alternatives to the cool monumentality of Flagstad's conceptions. But undoubtedly one can safely amend Farrar's dictum about classifying singers: "There are two you must put aside: one is Caruso, the other is Rosa Ponselle. Then you may begin."[27] That duo must be enlarged to include Kirsten Flagstad.

There will be other Flagstad Isoldes in the years ahead. One of the greatest rewards to be gained from the extensive series of Metropolitan broadcasts, as opposed to a single commercial recording, is the opportunity to observe an artist's changing conception through repeated assumptions of a role over the years. Often the conception deepens as the singer lives with the role; sometimes a fully realized portrayal's finest aspects become caricatured upon excessive repetition; and occasionally the artist keeps intact the purity of the original conception. Seventeen of Melchior's twenty broadcast Tristans are preserved, and we have Albanese's ten Violettas, Traubel's ten Isoldes, Steber's six Contessas, and nine of Warren's Rigolettos. All provide apt opportunity for role-watching, but none is more fascinating than the progress of Flagstad's nine broadcast Isoldes from 1935 to 1941.

Geraldine Farrar as Carmen. Photography by Mishkin, probably a copy of a still from her silent film.

CHAPTER SEVEN

Coda: Exit Gatti

The *Tristan* performance of 9 March 1935 is the climax of the broadcast season, perhaps the summit of all the radio performances of these early years. In a few weeks Gatti-Casazza, now at the end of his long tenure of twenty-seven seasons, would leave the Metropolitan. Flagstad would remain. One might think that Gatti's foresight had obligingly provided the new management with its most valuable asset; but just as Flagstad's coming was an accident, her retention was a stroke of luck, for amazingly, the departing manager took no initiative regarding her contract for the 1935–36 season.

Gatti did consent to appear, however, on the season's final broadcast (*Bohème* on 23 March) to deliver a brief farewell message, in "barely understandable English."[1] As to the quality of that English, Miss Farrar would have it otherwise. The redoubtable Geraldine, for sixteen years (1906–1922) the darling of the Metropolitan public and (with Caruso) the company's prime box-office attraction, served as the season's commentator while Cross continued to handle the technical chores. She recounts that Gatti paid several visits to her broadcast booth—"an especially equipped loge in the upper tier of the opera house" arranged for her use, "a little salon such as would please any woman in her own home."[2] Farrar's ensconcement was quite a change from the cramped male trio huddled together during the first broadcast season. But then, as Farrar noted, "my personal relations had been pleasantly social with the President of the Lambert Company [makers of Listerine], Mr. J. L. Johnston." After all, the soprano had been the favorite of the German crown prince at the turn of the century, and undoubtedly enough charm remained at middle age for the mere president of an American business company.

The willful charm of the ageless diva was further apparent in the contretemps over her piano. Knabe was the official piano of the Metropolitan (paying the Met $15,000 per annum for the exclusive privilege), and Ziegler informed NBC that Knabe had prepared a small piano, one which enabled "its user to lock it when through," that would fit "in the Foyer of the box in which Miss Farrar will broadcast."[3] Knabe forbade the introduction of any other piano "whether built especially or by an accredited maker." Ziegler pitifully asked Gerald Chatfield, NBC's liaison for the broadcasts, "what is to be done in this situation, as I have heard it said that Miss Farrar would like to use the piano which she used in her private car? [Farrar always

Gatti's official card with signature.

traveled in style on the railways during her concert tours]. . . . It seems to me that this is a matter to be straightened out entirely between Miss Farrar's business representative and Wm. Knabe & Company."[4] In the end, it was Knabe that was put straight. A week later their representative advised Ziegler of their capitulation, noting "the most essential part of the entire subject is that nothing be said, nor any piano name be printed or broadcast or pictures be issued which would indicate that any other piano but the Knabe is the official piano of the Metropolitan Opera House."[5] With Miss Farrar, where there was a will there was a way, and the way had always been hers.

When Gatti visited Farrar in her radio booth during her brief tenure, it was to observe how she conducted her share of the broadcast. She gives us an intimate portrait of the fearsome director in her radio lair.

> Gatti was a big man and trod heavily; curious about the coils and wires scattered all over, he stumbled against the microphones, dislocating practically all the fuses, breathing loudly over my shoulder all the while. On these occasions, I wondered if the listeners might not fancy that I was wheezing with laryngitis or struggling in a fog with the hoot of a boat whistle in the offing, so muddy was the reception in the sensitive microphone, under the circumstances. His remarks were priceless anent the mechanics involved.[6]

Up to now, no one had been able to persuade Gatti to speak on the air. Concerning the final broadcast of the season, John Royal, NBC vice-president in charge of programs, informed Gatti that NBC was "planning to make this occasion a gala one for the radio audience and have invited officials of the Metropolitan Opera and of the Radio Corporation; Mr. Johnston, President of the Listerine Company, and, of course, Miss Geraldine Farrar to speak briefly during the intermissions." Royal gingerly approached the possibility of Gatti joining in the celebration. "We would consider it a real privilege if you could join us in Box 42 Saturday afternoon,

3/23/35 with A.H.Reid

METROPOLITAN OPERA HOUSE

METROPOLITAN OPERA ASSOCIATION
INCORPORATED

GIULIO GATTI-CASAZZA
GENERAL MANAGER

O

THE PROGRAM - METROPOLITAN OPERA HOUSE - PUBLISHED BY TRIUNE PRINTING CO - NEW YORK

Thirteenth Week—Mar. 18 to Mar. 24, 1935

Program cover for Gatti's final season showing Triumphal Scene from *Aida*.

and, if you cared to, say a few words to our audience." Acknowledging Gatti's monumental reserve, Royal assured him that "if you would prefer not to speak, we do hope that you will honor us with your presence so that you may hear the complimentary remarks of our important guests."[7]

Farrar claims that she gained Gatti's consent for the brief interview at the farewell matinee. "I promised his part of the interview would be brief, and I would write it according to what he desired to say. . . . He begged me to compose what I thought would be fitting for the occasion." She gave Gatti the script a week ahead of time, and he carefully rehearsed his phonetics with backstage officials. When the moment came, Gatti "covered himself with glory in carefully enunciated phrases of appreciation and farewell good wishes. Suddenly he broke into mellifluous ex tempore Italian, and concluded with a hearty smack on my cheek, after a tremendous clearing of the throat. . . . He was as excited as a boy."[8] One may choose between Kolodin's "barely understandable English" and Farrar's critique of the occasion; I personally prefer the prima donna's more flavorful account. After all, she was on the scene.

Gatti's consent to his farewell speech, inveigled by the crafty Farrar, confirms how far toward legitimacy the radio broadcasts had travelled since his grudging approval of the initial season. Whereas the coming of Flagstad was the notable artistic event of the 1930s, the most far-reaching aspect of Gatti's final years was the move toward democratization of the Metropolitan. No event was more crucial in that trend than the commencement of the radio broadcasts. Like Flagstad, they had been forced on Mr. Gatti, and again like Flagstad, they would prove to be a great boon for the survival of the house. A larger opera public was beginning to develop throughout the country, and more immediate results were apparent as well. Foremost among these was the financial gain to the Metropolitan through active solicitation of the radio audience during the hard-pressed years of the depression.

In addition to the direct compensation which the Metropolitan received either from NBC or commercial sponsors of the radio season, the Metropolitan over the years has made repeated use of the airwaves to solicit dollars from the listening audience. The custom began early when, it its second season of broadcasts, the Met had incurred so large a deficit that the next season was endangered. A most acute observer who would soon be known to all the radio audience, the ubiquitous Mrs. Belmont, later recalled that "the general public appeared apathetic to the dire emergency that confronted grand opera. Doubtless the fact that the Opera House was privately owned and operated by rich families contributed to the unconcern."[9] In significant words, which in their mild expression contain a weight of condemnation quite unusual for the public Mrs. Belmont, she averred that "these families felt that under existing conditions they could, or would, no longer carry such a heavy burden." The time was ripe for new public initiatives which would establish a broader base of support for the opera.

PART II
The Johnson Era

Edward Johnson. Photography by Mishkin.

CHAPTER EIGHT

Prologue

In the spring of 1935 the Metropolitan began to prepare for new leadership; bass Herbert Witherspoon was selected to succeed Gatti as general manager. Ziegler would continue at his old post and our friend, tenor Edward Johnson, would abandon his career before the footlights in favor of a new administrative position as assistant manager. Johnson's principal task would be to oversee a new supplementary season to provide opportunities for American singers, a condition of the Juilliard Foundation's continued financial support. It was the same old story—the 1935–36 season had been in doubt, and the Juilliard Foundation had stepped into the breach with a $150,000 guarantee and several provisos, the most important for radio auditors being the development of the supplementary season from which three operas were to be broadcast.

An unspecified condition of the Juilliard sponsorship may have been the naming of Witherspoon, a former member of the Juilliard faculty, as Gatti's successor. (John Erskine, Juilliard's president, specified Witherspoon as general manager in the plan he presented to the Met and Juilliard trustees).[1] In his planning for the 1935–36 season, Witherspoon appears to have adhered to the Juilliard's demand for a nondeficit budget. He resolved to eliminate a number of the company's most expensive (and greatest) stars. Although recognizing that "our German wing is probably the strongest in the world," he specified the need for "another German baritone, at a small price, to eventually take the place of Schorr, who is beginning to fail and who can no longer do parts like Talramund [*sic*] and Kurvenal. His high voice is practically gone and even Bodanzky acknowledges this, but he is still a very fine artist."[2] (In spite of Witherspoon's judgment, Schorr would continue to perform with memorable artistry until 1942; the opera world is still waiting for his equal.)

But for Witherspoon "the most serious question regarding the personnel of the company is concerned with the Italian wing, which is lamentably weak . . . really a disasterous [*sic*] condition." And here Witherspoon took on two of the Met favorites. "There is an absolute rebellion over the entire city against the retaining of De Luca and Martinelli. . . . There is very little for De Luca to do and his price is high . . . and we can get an inexpensive baritone to take the place of Bergioli [*sic*], who is very bad." And De Luca, after twenty consecutive seasons in New York, would leave. Martinelli was more tenacious, for even Witherspoon acknowledged the scarcity of dramatic tenors. "The question of Martinelli is serious . . . because strong Italian tenors are hard to find. However, I have several in mind and I think no contract should be made with Mr. Martinelli except for a few performances which he will probably not accept, until I have been in Europe and have heard what we can obtain." (Two years later Martinelli would have his greatest Metropolitan triumph in the long awaited revival of *Otello*, an impersonation fortunately well documented in several recorded radio broadcasts.)

The dual demands of Juilliard's guarantee easily coalesced in Witherspoon's mind. He concluded that "by eliminating De Luca and Martinelli we can save a lot of money, and also have the opportunity to bring young fresh voices who will interest the public and I am certain there is no use in trying to sell these two men to the public again." Among his projected needs was "the best possible coloratura we can find"— one could save money on Pons, too. In view of the housecleaning of old favorites no wonder Witherspoon felt that "whoever takes the management should have a guarantee of two or three years."

Witherspoon certainly had no problem with making hard decisions, and some of his projected plans were decidedly attractive.[3] Concerning the radio broadcasts he wrote, "I have many ideas about this. Radio should aid the company much more than it has." But his statement that "the plain truth is that the opera has been dead for years" is in vivid contrast to Johnson's opinion a month or so later that "the Metropolitan has a d——fine organization."[4] For it was Johnson who was to be at the helm for the 1935–36 season and the next fourteen years. Ziegler was witness to Witherspoon's sudden death on 10 May 1935 due to a heart attack "just at the threshold of my office—the door leading into Villa's office—and it seemed a little bit too much for me,"[5] he informed Gatti, now comfortably retired in Italy. By this time Johnson was in command and Ziegler confided his sense of relief to his old boss:

> I hope that you will agree that Johnson's appointment is a very wise one. He has completely won the Board of Directors which, of course, will make his task much easier. He is calm, but enthusiastic, and he and I have been working together much in the same manner that it was my pleasure to work with you.[6]

There could be no higher commendation to Ziegler's mind, quite in contrast to his fearsome comment on Witherspoon's plans:

> So I am completely happy, except for the fact that the Witherspoon commitments are still exerting a serious influence. If he had continued, I am perfectly certain that we would have found ourselves in the most tragic state imaginable.[7]

More reassuring, at least to Ziegler's ears, was Johnson's promise to "proceed along lines of evolution rather than revolution."[8] Gatti had mounted a tremendous repertory, as large as forty to fifty operas a season, including many works new to the Metropolitan stage. Normally these operas received only a few performances in a single season. The radio audience had heard some of these novelties (*Sadko*, the three American premieres, *L'Africaine*) but others were not broadcast (*Schwanda, Signor Bruschino, Linda di Chamounix*). In words which would prove true with a vengeance, Johnson proclaimed "There will be no costly experiments with doubtful outcome— better to produce standard works with great casts than to experiment at great cost."[9] More cryptic was his intention "to concentrate on performances and not on star performers, and give more emphasis to the composer than to the interpreter."[10] Unlike Gatti he was not at all reluctant about the role of radio in the Metropolitan scheme. Fortunately, NBC was willing to continue the arrangements of the previous year. In the period of indecision over the continuance of the Metropolitan, NBC board chairman David Sarnoff had informed Cornelius Bliss he would "be prepared to say at Friday's meeting [of the Met board] that despite the fact that NBC has been unable to secure a client for next year's opera broadcasts nevertheless NBC will agree to take up its option and pay $100,000."[11] The network requested options for three additional years "in view of the initiative taken by NBC in developing and promoting the broadcasting of the operas of the Metropolitan."[12] Undoubtedly foreseeing the eventual demise of the franchise, Ziegler protected the long-range interests of the Met by having the allocation for the broadcast of operas ($70,000) and the individual artists' franchise ($30,000) altered to $80,000 and $20,000.[13]

But the franchise continued to be a bone of contention in regard to artists not subject to the agreement. Ziegler did not think it reasonable that Crooks who "sings very few performances with us" should be expected "to pay a franchise on all of the broadcasts he does when he is not in our employ."[14] He felt the same about John Charles Thomas, Pons, and Ponselle "who has only eight performances with us." But NBC's Daniel S. Tuthill drove home his point:

> The reason for our desiring "the exclusive right to negotiate with and employ artists for concerts or recitals to be broadcast by radio" is the same as it has always been, namely to aid us in the sale of our facilities through our possession of exclusive rights in connection with Metropolitan artists and Metropolitan opera performances.[15]

As late as 21 January 1936 the agreement still was not signed.

Though the franchise would eventually die from natural causes, NBC had shown greater foresight in its early stipulation regarding the inclusion of television rights:

> Our feeling is that television as part of the Metropolitan performances when this becomes possible, will create an added interest in the Opera on the part of the public for the reason that they will be able to sense to a greater degree the dramatic value of operatic performances, and as a result of this, be more anxious to patronize the boxoffice.[16]

Interim attempts would be made, but television patronage was four decades in the future. In the meantime, radio would do. Though there would be no commercial sponsor for his first season of broadcasts, in mid-December Johnson had boasted that the Metropolitan itself would pay for them "because radio broadcasting makes the Metropolitan no longer a local affair; radio nationalizes whatever it touches and that makes the Met the central operatic theatre of the United States. The operatic situation is nationalized, with the Met as the hub."[17]

The new manager's admonition about star performers proved to be mere managerial discretion. There was a period shortly after Johnson's appointment when the status of the more celebrated artists, including Pons, Tibbett, and Ponselle, remained in doubt. Upon Witherspoon's death Ziegler picked up the pieces, informing Johnson that Tibbett's contract "had not yet been definitely agreed because of special conditions regarding broadcasting. I understand however that he was to be engaged for 15 performances @ $800."[18] As late as 6 June, Johnson had told Pons' agent that "it would be beneficial if Miss Pons returned to the Metropolitan next season" though the Met could only offer her "a very small cachet" of $500 per performance with a minimum of five and maximum of eight performances (Pons had requested eight performances at $1000 each).[19] The broadcasts of the thirties would be difficult to imagine without the attractions of Tibbett and Pons. Happily, negotiations with most of the major artists were completed in time, though often their appearances turned out to be less numerous than their artistry (or fame) warranted. Still, in the fifteen broadcasts by the main company, the radio audience heard its full share of leading artists during Johnson's inaugural season.

Elisabeth Rethberg as Eva in *Die Meistersinger von Nürnberg*.

CHAPTER NINE

1935–36
Wagner and a Coloratura Soprano

Lohengrin opened the broadcast season on 21 December, 1935 with a cast which confirmed the continued supremacy of the German wing.

The occasion marked the first Metropolitan Ortrud of the Australian soprano Marjorie Lawrence, who had made her debut three days earlier as the *Walküre* Brünnhilde. Melchior, Schorr, and Bodanzky were the old hands, while Lotte Lehmann sang Elsa, one of only three Met appearances in the role. A tantalizing glimpse of her portrayal has surfaced—a short portion of the bridal chamber duet. Her partner, Melchior, sounds young and involved, and this time he is careful not to unduly cover his tones with gummy resonance. Lehmann's rather imperious delivery is such that one feels Lohengrin surely must answer her fatal questions on the spot. The voice is very secure, the tone rather metallic but always carrying its potent emotive dose. Her really excessive *portamenti* (and I do like *portamento*) are rescued by a sudden caress of a word ('süss') while the quickly snatched breaths are washed from memory by the consuming love for her knight which her singing conveys. Yet, with all those sudden *piano*s and little *Luftpausen* the suspicion of overinterpretation arises, making Elsa seem almost guileful.

Flagstad was very much in evidence throughout the season. She repeated her Isolde on 8 February (Branzell, Melchior, Huehn) and sang her first Met *Fidelio* on the broadcast of 7 March 1936 (Maison, Huehn, List; Bodanzky). Once again we are lacking aural documentation of these performances. But we can hear her in a new role in the broadcast of *Tannhäuser* on 18 January. Also new to the airwaves is the Wolfram of Tibbett, though he had first sung the role at the Met a full decade earlier. The American baritone was an infrequent visitor to the Wagner terrain, however, Wolfram being the only Wagner role he essayed in New York (a few Telramunds with the touring company tease the imagination). Margaret Halstead as Venus, List as the Landgrave, and Melchior as the errant knight complete the cast.

The overture offers a first opportunity to follow Bodanzky through a lengthy orchestral work. Predictably, he is at his best in his incisive treatment of the Venusberg themes, increasing the tempo at sequential passages and moving precipitously into the Hymn to Venus. A delicious amalgamation of control and *Schwung* is served

Lohengrin
21 December 1935
Elsa
Lotte Lehmann
Lohengrin
Lauritz Melchior
Conductor
Artur Bodanzky

Tannhäuser
18 January 1936
Elisabeth
Kirsten Flagstad
Venus
Margaret Halstead
Tannhäuser
Lauritz Melchior
Wolfram
Lawrence Tibbett
Landgrave
Emanuel List
Conductor
Artur Bodanzky

up by Bodanzky, and the orchestra plays well for him, the strings' articulation clear and precise, the winds neatly poised throughout. Melchior is always adept at suggesting a narcotic state, and his veiled tones capture Tannhäuser's mix of ecstasy and pain before his longing for earthly joys bursts forth at 'Die Nachtigall hör' ich nicht mehr.' His Hymn to Venus may be a shade bumpy in its rhythmic current but it is surely vibrant, which cannot be said of Halstead's Venus. Her pallid attempt to float the seduction music explains her uneventful Met career of five seasons. Delectable, however, is the vocal piping of the young Shepherd, Editha Fleischer, whose unexpectedly piquant middle range and insouciant manner suggest why she was the favorite broadcast Hänsel. The chorus experiences a few intonational vagaries as the pilgrims wend their way on and off stage.

Bass Emanuel List made a modest impression in the 1934 *Walküre* broadcast, but he warrants more attention on this afternoon. After this erstwhile Viennese tailor's son had forsaken cutting cloth to join a touring vaudeville company during the First World War, he had accumulated a quota of engagements on prime stages (Berlin, Salzburg, Bayreuth, Covent Garden) before joining the Met. The leap to the Vienna Volksoper (1922) was natural enough, and praise from Furtwängler (for Wagner) and Strauss (for Ochs) was not long delayed. List's right to inhabit the Met's Wagner Valhalla is apparent throughout the *Tannhäuser* broadcast. Firm-toned and properly authoritative among his knights, he turns intimate and solicitous with Elisabeth. Moreover, he is wobble-free; he doesn't growl or merely lay out the usual heavy sonority that afflicts so many dull Wagnerian bass portrayals—he sings. The fruity admixture of his resonance lends a natural richness and impressive weight to his pronouncements (particularly as he prescribes Rome for the impious hero), and his declamation is more noble than knotty. In his hands the Landgrave becomes a major role.

To hear Tibbett sing Wagner is to discover another facet of his art, a simplicity of utterance, a directness of manner entirely right for Wolfram. His is a more manly characterization of the gentle knight than is often heard. Whenever the situation warrants, he summons a strong, straightforward tone—in fact, at his initial appearance one has the feeling he may be attempting to certify his credentials of Wagnerian tonal heft. It is Wolfram's virility which Tibbett's vocal manner emphasizes by the healthy sonority of his middle low voice as he urges Tannhäuser to remain with his friends and by his austere praise of spiritual love in the song contest. Then, in the second strophe, comes the typical Tibbett moment where he begins to work his heartfelt magic, sweetening the tone and binding the phrases in seamless legato. The Hymn to the Evening Star sustains his characterization; in control of mezza voce and subtle gradations of tone it is a model of vocal mastery, yet the overall effect is one of simplicity and directness. Compare this moment with his 1934 commercial recording, and one hears the difference between mere fine vocalism combined with rather matter-of-fact interpretation (on the record) and melding of tone and word into musico-dramatic expression of the highest order. This Wolfram is no shadowy, hopeless languisher after Elisabeth but a man of strength and intensity of feeling.

Flagstad's Elisabeth would require such a man, for her portrayal has its magisterial moments. The rock-bottom security of the triadic intervals in her greeting to the Hall of Song conveys an impressive assurance; seldom does one hear such purity of pitch in the leaps with which the aria abounds. The audience, in uncharacteristic fashion for a Wagner opera, honors her with applause, both at her entry and at the end of the aria (but then 'Dich, teure Halle' seems to cry out for applause in the best tradition of a prima donna's entrance aria). Bodanzky takes the lengthy orchestral introduction at a flying clip, but the unconstrained weight of Flagstad's voice soon anchors the piece. Never was the glow of the Flagstad instrument more evident than in this moment, its refulgent mix of French horn and middle woodwind colors blended into the most compact, yet glossy, sonority. After the initial thrust of joy, she skillfully lowers the intensity and projects a momentary sorrow as she recalls Tannhäuser's desertion. No breathless agitation invades the final repetitions of 'Sei mir gegrüsst,' but her effortless vault to the high B is sufficient evidence of her joy. In the scene with Tannhäuser, Flagstad is at her most communicative, tenderly modifying her mass of sound in a variety of inflections—she successfully registers girlhood confusion, subtly varies the weight of the top tones, and as she tries to fathom her lover's behavior, floats a pair of deliciously seductive *Heinrich*s. The romantic manner of Wagner's early operas clearly allows her greater play in the management of line and voice.

In the quick movement of the duet with its troublesome turns, both Flagstad and Melchior avoid the usual scramble and project with clarity—by no means an easy feat in this passage. Brünnhilde's strength is unleashed momentarily as she wards off Tannhäuser's accusers, but Elisabeth's woe returns when Flagstad pleads for him; she brings the atmosphere down to a listener's hush. This is some of the loveliest singing in the entire Flagstad canon—the voice is so gentle and filled with sorrow. In contrast to Müller's emotionalism in the third-act prayer, Flagstad concentrates on absolute fidelity to Wagner's dynamic markings; the gradation from the opening *fortissimo* of 'Allmächt'ge Jungfrau' down to the *piano* at the end of the phrase is masterful. Most interestingly, the static quality which governs her commercial voicing of this moment is successfully avoided through control of dynamics and fluid manipulation of quietly vibrating tone. In sum, the entry of Elisabeth into the Flagstad broadcast gallery provides one of her most sensitive portrayals, notable for her frequent rejection of heroic dimensions in favor of fresh buoyancy of song.

Throughout the opera Melchior successfully negotiates the high tessitura of this most trying of Wagner tenor roles (always excepting Siegfried), though even he betrays some slight effort in his appeal for forgiveness at the end of the second act. The Rome Narrative provides any singing-actor with the challenge of projecting a wide range of emotions as Tannhäuser recounts the failure of his pilgrimage: anger, confusion, hopelessness, near-madness succeed one another until only the craving for Venus remains. Here Melchior reveals the enormous range of expression of his splendid instrument: now his tones fill with scorn as he responds to Wolfram 'Wer ich bin?'; now their bright metal rings like a well-struck anvil as he recounts his journey; now his dulcet head voice fairly weeps as he recalls his 'Engel' Elisabeth; now the plangent baritonal timbre piles up the stern repeated notes of the Pope's rejection—all of it a telling progression to the wild propulsion of his call to Venus. The image of the lazy clown which distorts the repute of Melchior in later years is completely at variance with the reality of these early performances. Melchior's Tannhäuser deserves his redemption.

The tenor was also on hand for the first *Götterdämmerung* of the season, the broadcast matinee of 11 January 1936 with the usual Wagnerian stalwarts—Schorr (Gunther), Hofmann (Hagen), and Manski (Gutrune). In Bodanzky's hands celerity governs the performance to an alarming degree, robbing certain key segments of stature (the oaths on the spear and the immolation scene). On the other hand, the pace and manner of the Rhine Journey complement the blithe assuredness of Siegfried on

Götterdämmerung
11 January 1936
Brünnhilde
Marjorie Lawrence
Gutrune
Dorothee Manski
Waltraute
Kathryn Meisle
Siegfried
Lauritz Melchior
Gunther
Friedrich Schorr
Alberich
Eduard Habich
Hagen
Ludwig Hofmann
Conductor
Artur Bodanzky

the march. The surviving tapes are of very poor quality due to groove wear and occasional pitch fluctuation (with even a few gaps bridged by the insertion of fragments of a later Flagstad-Melchior performance). Even so, some telling moments pierce the aural rubble. Melchior again must be singled out for his characterful play of tone color; particularly notable is the dreamy, erotic, covered tone as, recalling Brünnhilde, he pledges his undying love just before Siegfried and Gunther launch the blood-brother duet. And in this duet the still puissant Schorr proves a mighty match; when the two join voices, Melchior blends and phrases in Italianate style (what a *Forza* Don Alvaro he might have been). His oath on the spear is solid and baritonal (some Bayreuth bark intrudes) and he captures the joy of his approaching wedding to Gutrune in long, splendidly flowing phrases. The variety of Melchior's characterization is apparent again in the free-and-easy charm of his exchange with the Rhinemaidens, all in his best young Siegfried manner (and Bodanzky for once adopts an appropriately leisurely tempo). The 'Hei-o' calls to Gunther and Hagen are unbelievably plangent, and Melchior stuns us with a high C of incredible size and brilliance—a breathtaking effect. Surely no Wagnerian tenor (and almost no Italianate tenor) has ever duplicated it.

Melchior's narration of Siegfried's life provides the climax of the performance. No baritonal fogs here as he summons the bright sound of youth, effortlessly negotiates the jagged lines, and ascends to the myriad high As with consummate ease. As Hagen's potion restores Brünnhilde's image, his transition from marcato to legato singing is striking, and he achieves a perfect blending of tenor and baritone resonance (especially on a sustained E) in the final phrases of the narrative before Hagen's spear finds Siegfried's back. From the veiled pain of 'Heilige Braut!' to the noble, dark tones of farewell, Melchior's final greeting to the absent Brünnhilde catches the heart.

While Hofmann has the necessary black sonority for Hagen's villainies, Eduard Habich is merely another in that endless line of expendable Alberichs, and Kathryn Meisle has neither the vocal timbre (she is more soprano than alto) nor plenitude for the grandeur of Waltraute's Narrative. There remains, however, one other sterling element in this *Götterdämmerung*: the Brünnhilde of the Australian soprano Marjorie Lawrence.

Though only in her mid twenties Lawrence came well prepared to her Metropolitan debut. Unlike Flagstad, whose approach to acclaim was tortoiselike through twenty years of mostly provincial appearances, Lawrence's ascent was as precipitous as was its near-termination by polio within the decade. Her career was Paris-based, both in study and performance; after a few forays into provincial houses at Monte Carlo and Lille, she had made her debut as Ortrud at the Paris Opéra in February 1933. During two years of multiple appearances in the most demanding roles at the Opéra (the Brünnhildes, Salome—both Strauss and Massenet—Aida, Rachel in *La Juive*, and Donna Anna) the young singer's career had acquired the glitter of stardom. Early on Gatti had approached her about the Metropolitan. Later Witherspoon, in preparing for his aborted takeover, wrote that he had in mind "Marjorie Lawrence . . . considered by Gatti, Ziegler, and Bodanzky and others to be very fine, and from all reports she may be as good as Flagstad, only with a more brilliant voice." Of moment to him was his belief that "we can get her for a very small price . . . thereby eliminating Kappel, who is now old and who will be worse next season. Bodanzky and I are thoroughly in accord on this."[1] Witherspoon, like most impresarios, certifies Lear's lament: "The younger rises and the old doth fall."

Fortunately Johnson was equally intrigued with Lawrence, though he insisted on an audition which the Paris prima donna felt was beneath her, for she advised the Met's talent scout to tell Johnson that "I am at the Paris Opéra. He may come and hear me there."[2] But on 15 June Johnson was able to verify her qualities as prescribed: "Marjorie Lawrence gave an excellent audition and Mr. Bodanzky is very pleased with her. However she does not know as yet her Wagner in German." While all Lawrence's European appearances had been in French, Johnson nevertheless prophesied "the voice will probably 'get' our public" even though the language "may make her at times uncertain."[3]

At the Opéra, Lawrence had successfully challenged the predominance of the longtime favorite, Germaine Lubin, whose repertory she shared. In spite of Witherspoon's optimism, Lawrence's encounter with Flagstad's newly won supremacy would prove more problematic. After her debut as the *Walküre* Brünn-hilde and her broadcast Ortrud, Lawrence was assigned the first performance of both the *Siegfried* and *Götterdämmerung* Brünnhildes (although Flagstad was currently in residence). Quite in keeping with the almost reckless pace of her career, Lawrence's biggest splash with the press resulted from her leaping onto the horse Grane and riding him into the flames of Siegfried's pyre at the close of the *Götterdämmerung* broadcast. Wagner had so prescribed, but evidently no prima donna had been able to comply until the young warrior from "down under" delivered.

Of more lasting merit is the quality of her vocal performance. In the opening scene with Siegfried the sensuous sheen of the Lawrence voice markedly differs from the remembered Flagstad and other soprano Wagnerians; hers is a voice of sufficient size and thrust to cut through, rather than surmount, the Wagnerian orchestral horde. Pliant in the extreme, it soars to silvery top tones with laserlike efficiency. Such fluid vocal movement amplifies the youthful impetuosity of her interpretation. Tonal density is not hers, certainly not in the lowest tones where a slightly breathy dullness lodges—at least until the instrument becomes all of a piece as it does later in the afternoon. (Comparison with Flagstad is unavoidable since the tape fills in a gap in the first-act duet with a portion of a later Flagstad-Melchior performance. The body and splendor of the Flagstad tones are unmistakable, but the comparison is not invidious; if Flagstad sculpts with a massive blade, Lawrence paints with a fluent brush, its tip touched with crimson.) In the exchange with Waltraute some harshness intrudes upon Lawrence's tones, but she manages a ravishing expansion of line as she ecstatically proclaims that while love lasts, she will love. This Brünnhilde is obviously a woman who has known love, and her emotional response to situations of betrayal, anger, and grief have a human spontaneity. Genuine sorrow gathers in her well-collected middle voice as she joins Gunther and Hagen in the plot to kill Siegfried.

Her Immolation has immense pathos. She begins with sweet, pure sound and a lovely point to the tone, then betrays more anger than is usually registered at the apocalyptic moment (some glancing blows at top tones are less than fully poised). The match of 'Ruhe' with the French horns is exquisite—a lovely soft velvet encircles the tone, and the voice shimmers with a fine, light vibrato. Grane is summoned with purposeful intent, and Bodanzky (opposed to and unaware of Lawrence's equestrian purpose) spurs her on at a hectic pace before pulling back for a sufficiently serene apotheosis by the strings. Lawrence's warrior maid has all the virtues of youth and remarkably few of the blemishes. (The closest approximation to Lawrence's portrayal for modern audiences is Hildegard Behrens' quite admirable assumption of

Die Meistersinger von
Nürnberg
22 February 1936

Eva
Elisabeth Rethberg
Magdalene
Karin Branzell
Walther
René Maison
David
Hans Clemens
Hans Sachs
Friedrich Schorr
Beckmesser
Eduard Habich
Pogner
Emanuel List
Conductor
Artur Bodanzky

these roles—there is a similar seductive quality to the voice, though unlike Behrens, Lawrence's instrument is palpably that of a genuine dramatic soprano and betrays no signs of wear.)

Though Schorr had little to contribute but his dependability in the role of the hapless Gunther, he is the hero of the final Wagner broadcast in the 1935–36 season, *Die Meistersinger*, which was heard by the radio audience for the first time on 22 February. In company with Chaliapin's Boris, Richard Mayr's Baron Ochs, and Pinza's Don Giovanni, Schorr's Hans Sachs is one of the unmatched portrayals of the century. He was now only 47 years old, far from the end of the line for a Wagner baritone. But he had begun early with the heaviest roles of the repertory, making his debut at Graz as the *Walküre* Wotan at age 22—"Baby Wotan," the critics called him.[4] Oddly enough, Chicago heard him in small roles the following year. In his mid twenties he sang the major Wagner roles at Prague and Berlin until, in 1923, he ventured to New York with the ill-fated German Grand Opera. Luckily, the Met called him for a *Tannhäuser* debut in 1924, the *Tribune* noting his Wolfram as "marked by a delicacy of coloring, refinement, and warmth of tone too seldom met in Wagnerian performances."[5] A dozen years later, his performance offers no reason to revise that estimate; half a century later, the lament gains increasing force.

In the broadcast *Meistersinger* the preserved sound is again below par—but sublime is the word for Schorr's Sachs. In the lengthy act-one scene with the mastersingers, Schorr is the only one who proves a worthy member of the guild (though the young American Julius Huehn is a Kothner of sufficient Wagnerian bulk). Even List (Pogner) does not impress in the Johannistag Address, sung mostly marcato with the voice not rolling forth in his customary manner. Thus each phrase of Sachs is like a shaft of light in the vocal umbra. Schorr rings all the changes of Sachs' character in the second act. He begins with a forthright 'Was duftet doch der Flieder,' the 'Lenzes Gebot' section voiced with intimacy and sentiment and crowned by a lovely dolcissimo tone at 'Dem Vogel.' Real surprise invades his voice as Eva enters, and as though vivified by Eva's encouragement of the widower in the marriage market, no sign of age weights his ringing 'Jerum.' Schorr's greatest asset in the Wagner repertory is the natural size of his instrument—he doesn't need to puff up his tone with a rough burr in order to give it sufficient mass. No tonal roughness disturbs the warm humanity of his cobbler poet.

Schorr completely dominates the final act, introducing a rich sonority into his low voice in the 'Wahn' monologue (a vivid contrast to the perfect mezza voce employed at 'Ein Kobold'). His conversational manner as he teaches Walther is natural, and in the Beckmesser scene he seems genuinely amused—a delightful shine illumines his voice. Throughout the act Schorr's instrument takes on added color and vibrancy—the pregnant *Tristan und Isolde* reference is deftly underlined. He even permits himself a little sob of emotion as he thanks the *Meister* for their greeting ('mich von euch geliebt'), and thanks to two major cuts in Sachs' music ('Hat man mit dem Schuhwerk' and 'Schon grosse Ehr' ward mir erkannt'), he never falters in his full-voiced paean to German art which brings the opera to a close ('Habt Acht!' is sung with dark, powerful tone). How willingly one joins the guilds and populace in congratulating Sachs-Schorr.

Bodanzky justly paces the entire last act, from the lovingly shaped quiet solo lines that begin the act through the contrasted tempi and styles of the several guilds: he summons precision and spirit for the forthright cobblers, a *bürgerlich* bump for the tailors, and a delightful gemütlichkeit for the dance of the prentices. Unfortunately,

Friedrich Schorr as Hans Sachs in *Die Meistersinger von Nürnberg*.

the overture (marked *sehr mässig bewegt*) careens along in a similarly bumptious fashion, all movement and no moderation.

Though Hans Clemens' mature David is more gone-to-seed than in-the-bud, Habich's Beckmesser is sung, not caricatured, and Branzell is unexpectedly light-toned and sprightly as Magdalene. The Belgian tenor, René Maison, had made his house debut three weeks earlier as Walther von Stolzing. Though we know him from partnering Ponselle in *Carmen*, this is his broadcast debut. Product of the Paris Conservatoire and, after his 1922 debut in Geneva, protégé of Mary Garden at the Opéra Comique (Alfano's *Resurrection*) and her own Chicago company, Maison will serve the Metropolitan well over the next eight seasons.

If he is hard-pressed on an occasional top tone (the long held As at the conclusion of the Prize Song verses are more a triumph of tenacity than vocal prowess), he makes a convincing suitor, impetuous in manner and bright of tone, with a foundation of baritonal color at the bottom of his range and a Tauber-like point to the upper voice at *forte* levels—the latter a boon in the climaxes of the Prize Song. (The third verse is cut in this performance). Maison is a master of the long phrase and conducts Walther's line with surety. Two brief moments in the third act demonstrate his ability to delineate character: he leaves off his earlier rash manner and quietly recounts his dream to Sachs, but when the *Meister* at last offer approval, his cry of refusal cuts through like a sword.

Rethberg is a very determined Eva when first met—one feels quite certain she will have the knight of her choice. In the second act she overtly reveals her frustation and anger as things don't go right for Eva. (List returns to form in this scene with his daughter and produces some gentle, soft effects.) Rethberg is in lovely voice throughout; the role lies for the most part in her middle range, which on this afternoon is mellow and natural in color with no hint of veiled tone or insecurity of pitch. Eva's finest moments occur in the final act, and here Rethberg is splendid, her outburst to Sachs flooding forth full of passion and love ('Ja, lieber Meister'). (Curiously, Johnson, upon hearing the soprano in *Schwanda* at Covent Garden a few months earlier, could summon up no more flattering words than "our good, reliable" Rethberg.)[6] She leads the quintet with firm, quiet tones devoid of sentimentality. The scenes between Rethberg and Schorr are notable for vocal poise and dramatic conviviality, the seemingly spontaneous interplay born of long acquaintance and self-confident artistry.

Though many of the lengthy Wagner operas of this season are preserved almost complete, the Italian and French repertory is less well served. Nothing remains of *Aida* (Rethberg, Wettergren, Jagel, John Charles Thomas), *La Bohème* (Moore, Kullman, Morelli, Pinza), *Gianni Schicchi* nor Bori's final *Rondine*. We do have a fragment from the *Trovatore* of 15 February 1936—the final scene of the opera, where the demented Azucena is calmed to sleep by the filial love of Manrico. Kathryn Meisle is again a hard-pressed mezzo with a short, pinched top voice and insufficient color and weight in the lower range. Though the gypsy's hallucinatory outbursts are beyond her, she is capable of some appealing *piano* singing in the mid range, and 'Ai nostri monti' is quite affecting in its childlike simplicity. Martinelli is briefly heard in one of his greatest roles (performed sixty-nine times with the Metropolitan alone). How pleasant to discover (in the opening recitative) that his middle voice still retains a lively sheen. 'Riposa o madre' is spun out with perfect breath control and lovely color, though some might find it a shade steely in tone for a lullaby. Of course, he is unequaled in the torrential rage with which he confronts Leonora's supposed

Il Trovatore
15 February 1936

Leonora
Elisabeth Rethberg
Azucena
Kathryn Meisle
Manrico
Giovanni Martinelli
Di Luna
Richard Bonelli
Conductor
Gennaro Papi

betrayal; the entire episode beginning 'Parlar non vuoi' is laid out on the broadest scale, the imprecation thundered out as he successfully surmounts the orchestral mass. Under such an attack any Leonora might be unnerved, and Rethberg's agitation is only too palpable in her harsh tone. Her rapid declamation is scratchy and often she punches at the line, rather than guiding it. At lower dynamic levels ('Prima che d'altri vivere') she regains tonal beauty. Fortunately, all three singers prove adept in the quiet coda to the trio before the rapid denouement at Bonelli's entrance.

Another extant broadcast of the Italian repertory (*Pagliacci* on 29 February) offers opportunity to enjoy Bonelli in a complete portrayal. (The decade's only broadcast of *Gianni Schicchi* followed, the Juilliard influence apparent in the American cast and English translation.) The recorded sound of *Pagliacci* is the best thus far. Bonelli's masterful voicing of the Prologue makes one wonder who is the premier Italian baritone of the era—he combines all the fat, rolling tone of Thomas and the point and dramatic flavor of Tibbett. Bonelli owns a voice of ravishing, darkly sensuous color, full and even throughout the entire range, with menacing bite at the bottom and absolute freedom at the top (the interpolated A-flat is perfectly poised, no tenor tone but harboring the same rich claret hue as the rest of the voice). His cantabile ('E voi, piuttosto') is woven with a girdling legato and subtle use of *portamento*. Memories of the golden age of Italian baritones surface—Amato, even a touch of Ruffo potency—though Bonelli never pushes beyond the zones of musical taste. In the opera proper he completely leaves off his primo baritono stance and plays the character; how he enjoys watching Nedda with her lover. He moves quickly from the menace of 'si tradisca' to the sudden *piano* of 'fingere' as he advises Canio to wait, to pretend; and he is all fool in the play-within-a-play.

Apart from Martinelli's anguished clown, the other players are negligible. Mario is in much poorer voice than in her earlier Nedda, all nose and chest in her lower octave with little thrust in the upper range. She knows how to play the coquette, though. She and Cehanovsky are overmatched by the love duet, and Paltrinieri is barely adequate as Beppe. The orchestra plays well under Papi in spite of his tarnished reputation; spirit and precision quicken the scherzolike episodes. As for Martinelli, his middle voice is a little less collected, but the upper octave is in exemplary shape. All the topmost tones have a decided ring, and once again one marvels at his inexhaustible flow of breath in the climactic unbroken phrases of 'Vesti la giubba'—Leoncavallo demands *piena voce, straziante* and the tortured Martinelli complies. He is less involved in 'No! Pagliaccio non son' but supplies the expressive cantabile of 'Sperai, tanto il delirio.' Time is not yet Martinelli's foe.

Within the time spectrum of an artist's career, Lily Pons was clearly in her nonage, though already in the sixth season of a Metropolitan affiliation which would span twenty-eight years. She had been heard by the radio audience as Rosina in the first broadcast season and regularly thereafter as Lakmé, Lucia, Amina, Gilda, and Philine, but our first souvenir is a much truncated *Rigoletto* of 28 December 1935. The preserved excerpts were probably made for tenor Frederick Jagel since almost all of his role is recorded. And worth preserving it is, for the American tenor unexpectedly does some of his best work as the light-hearted Duke of Mantua. The very top tones still give one the feeling that Radames has mistakenly wandered into this Renaissance court, but he makes every effort to sing artistically, and by the time the quartet is reached, he is singing with a good deal of suavity. On this afternoon he owns a ringing, well-poised high B-flat which he applies to 'Parmi veder le lagrime' (all the *accenti* in place); in 'La donna è mobile' he negotiates a lovely diminuendo on 'd'accento' and

Pagliacci
29 February 1936

Nedda
Queena Mario
Canio
Giovanni Martinelli
Tonio
Richard Bonelli
Silvio
George Cehanovsky
Conductor
Gennaro Papi

Rigoletto
28 December 1935

Gilda
Lily Pons
Maddalena
Helen Olheim
Duke
Frederick Jagel
Rigoletto
Lawrence Tibbett
Sparafucile
Virgilio Lazzari
Conductor
Ettore Panizza

Richard Bonelli as Tonio in *Pagliacci*.

observes the *pianissimo leggiero* marking of 'e di pensier' before ruining it all with a graceless cadenza. Try as he will, the voice itself is just not innately ingratiating. Helen Olheim is a very well-behaved slut in the quartet, but Lazzari has enough menace in his tone for Sparafucile. Earlier, as he first offers his services to Rigoletto, Lazzari lacks a resonant low F and sacrifices the legato which would complement the low strings' jaunty tune and confirm the black humor of their interchange.

Tibbett is the one who captures the fantastical character of the assassin's interview by the soft hush of his questions. Indeed, the performance is most notable for Tibbett's first Metropolitan Rigoletto, one of those precious gifts of broadcast history wherein we hear an artist's debut in one of his most famous roles. Tibbett had waited a dozen years before taking on this most demanding of baritone parts, years filled with many Met appearances as Ford, Germont, Tonio, Amonasro, Jack Rance, Scarpia, and Boccanegra. The portrayal is not quite as fine as one might hope. (True, the recorded portrayal is incomplete—we, and he, are shortchanged by the absence of the two lengthy scenes with Gilda.)

The accompanied recitative in which Verdi sets forth the dark side of the hunchback's character is played most freely by Tibbett; he takes plenty of time to caricature (excessively) Monterone and fills in the spaces with much laughter. 'Pari siamo' is also slowly paced; the huge *portamenti* on 'oh rabbia' and 'è solo' are rather stagey, but they do not dilute the deep sorrow which permeates much of the reading. After Gilda's abduction he enters the hostile courtiers' domain with the lightest 'La rà, La rà,' thereby suggesting the indifference prescribed by Verdi—each repetition of the 'La rà' refrain takes on increased agitation and fear. Some of the forward movement of the scene is lost (Panizza not keeping a firm enough rein), for Tibbett is always one to stretch *a piacere* to maximum individuality. The 'Cortigiani' double aria is somewhat disappointing, appropriately declamatory in the opening section, rather plodding in 'Miei signori perdono' (no problem for the cello figurations at this slow tempo), and tonally not quite blandishing. Tibbett momentarily loses the text at 'ridonarla a voi,' mouthing some non-Italian; in fact, the performance has more than its share of high jinks, for Pons omits 'vi fece a me' in the love duet and Jagel gets the opera off to a perilous start by muffing his initial lines, he and his Borsa (Paltrinieri) scrambling over a dozen measures to find their way back on track. All this points up the oft-heard accusation of opera thrown on stage with insufficient preparation during the thirties and forties at the Met, though it is hard to believe that Tibbett's first Rigoletto would have been so cavalierly treated by management.

Tibbett is fiercely commanding as he sends off the courtiers when Gilda appears. At the reappearance of Monterone, Tibbett takes on a lordly manner, weights his tone with resolution, and caps the episode with a long interpolated E-flat superbly diminished from *fortissimo* down to the softest *piano* ('un vindice avrai'). Panizza really takes off at the final repetition of the theme, with Tibbett and Pons at odds in the concluding cadence as she vaults to the E-flat. Tibbett interpolates, too, and not just the high note which ends the tragedy, but plenty of *cielo*s and *Dio*s en route. The baritone is always in earnest in this initial Metropolitan effort and has fine moments. But the portrait is one-sided. The recorded scenes largely depict the violent emotions of sadistic torture, hatred, and vengeance—we lack those affecting scenes between father and daughter which must have summoned a more sensitive response from Tibbett. Certainly, the jester is as yet no equal to the doge.

Pons' Gilda is even more abbreviated in these excerpts—almost none of Gilda's great moments in act one are available. Tonally she vacillates between a delicate, chiming attack and tremulous tones in the lower octave. When we finally hear her at some length in the 'Vendetta' duet, the fragile Pons voice is pitted against the raging orchestra and a full-voiced Tibbett, so she distorts every phrase by beginning with an anticipatory gulp to provide dramatic emphasis; 'huh-balenarvi, huh-di perdono' are ugly effects, indeed. Nor does the interpolated (and slightly breathy) high E-flat compensate. The last half of the quartet is more satisfying as she attacks each of the two sixteenth-note interjections with the dexterity and accuracy of a toe dancer, but without a shred of Gilda's anguish ('Infelice cor tradito, per angoscia non scoppiare'). Though 'Lassù in cielo' is again marred by a careless error (she enters one beat too soon at 'benedite'), she is properly angelic in tone as Gilda's strength wanes.

Is this the Pons who generated so great a public and critical response only a few years earlier? Child of a French father and Italian mother, Pons had been a teenage piano student (first prize at fifteen) at the Paris Conservatoire, then turned soprano for a debut as Lakmé at Mulhouse in 1928 (age thirty!). After three years' labor in the French provinces she was so little known that her first records bore labels marked "chanteuse légère des casinos de Cannes et Deauville." Her 1931 Met debut changed all that. Pons' prominence in these early broadcasts (and a sense of fairness) prompts immediate examination of her next *Rigoletto* broadcast on 11 March 1939 where she is again partnered by Tibbett, Lazzari, and Olheim, this time under Papi's baton. The performance is complete, but the sound is remote and tubby in the extreme, making judgment of tonal quality suspect. Even so, enough is audible to allow reevaluation of the now complete portrayals of Pons and Tibbett.

Tibbett's jester is fleshed out to a more affecting characterization, and a Boccanegra-like humanity permeates his scenes with Gilda. The earlier license of the *a piacere* moments in the accompanied recitatives is kept within bounds. 'Ah! Deh non parlare al misero' is spun out in a superb mezza voce—the sound of love in the voice itself; unfortunately, a performance cut is made of the initial 'Ah! veglia, o donna.' The great scene of the second act is much more impressive than four years earlier. Now 'Cortigiani' moves at a faster pace, and Tibbett molds the broken phrases into a convincing whole; 'Miei signori' is replete with plaintive supplication (the diminuendo on 'tu taci' is particularly fine). As he comforts the distraught Gilda ('Ah! Piangi!'), Tibbett suggests a nobility which raises the scene above the level of sentimentality, and even Pons seems to feel it as her phrases, too, take on expansive shape. The episode marks the performance peak. Overall, Tibbett indulges in less grandstanding, even in the moments of anger and rage. As he discovers Gilda's body, no tatters are evident; the moment holds the utmost intimacy for the wretched father and dying daughter—'Dio tremendo' is sculpted, not shouted. Mezza voce and bel canto line are the prominent features of the baritone's Rigoletto on this afternoon, for truth to tell, Tibbett now approaches full-voice top tones rather gingerly; sometimes they own little baritone ring, though he does sound a high A-flat at the end of 'Sì, vendetta.'

Olheim still hasn't learned any wicked ways since 1935 (she doesn't attempt the accents in the storm trio which should give impetus to her line). Under Papi the chorus delivers a most accurate 'Zitti, zitti' but neither conductor nor courtiers capture the sardonic bite of the act-two chorus as they inform the Duke of Gilda's abduction—it rolls along in jolly fashion with little dynamic contrast.

Polish tenor Jan Kiepura, though the rage of the Vienna Staatsoper in the 1930s, is an enigma as the Duke. He certainly knows his way around not only Mantua but also the role. He has as much of the impertinent swagger as any libertine could

Rigoletto
11 March 1939

Gilda
Lily Pons
Maddalena
Helen Olheim
Duke
Jan Kiepura
Rigoletto
Lawrence Tibbett
Sparafucile
Virgilio Lazzari
Conductor
Gennaro Papi

Lawrence Tibbett as Rigoletto.

handle; in fact, the vocal narcissism of his portrayal proves vexing as he repeatedly bends the music out of shape. The voice thins decidedly as it approaches the top, he is excessively fond of a diminuendo to a reedy falsetto, and he holds the final B at the reprise of 'La donna è mobile' forever, an affront to the dramatic impact of Rigoletto's horrible discovery. Kiepura deftly manages the cabaletta of the love duet and allows a modicum of sincerity to invade 'Parmi veder le lagrime,' though the bleat on sustained tones annoys. At the Met for six seasons, he appeared earlier in *Manon* and another *Rigoletto* broadcast, but this is our only available portrayal.

Happily, Pons is in much better form than in the 1935 matinee. Everything she tries is on the mark, her attack always quick and sure, the staccati and fioriture precise (one must acknowledge even the precision of her aspirates while regretting their necessity). The little trills in 'Caro nome' are neatly outlined, and the final interpolated high E maintains color. In the charming coda to the aria she substitutes for the lengthy trill a slowly rising arpeggio to another (slightly glassy) high E. All is in place in this very stylized account of Gilda's role—even the anticipatory gulps in 'Sì, vendetta' are mercifully reduced to a paltry few. Of course, she cannot provide tragic accents, and when she tries (only once at 'color che m'han rapita' in 'Tutte le feste') the voice simply refuses to withstand the pressure—for the first time a quaver invades her tone. But in the latter regard we hail good tidings—with the single noted exception, her singing is entirely free of the tremulousness which was so prevalent in 1935. She achieves a delicious bell-like attack on each note and lovingly etches all the lines of Gilda's music (by far the majority is of a cantabile cast) with complete security, even in the lowest portion of the staff.

Jan Kiepura as the Duke of Mantua in *Rigoletto*.

Now we can approach some of Pons' interim performances with keener anticipation and some confidence. Pons was most acclaimed for her Lucia, the role of her sensational 1931 debut and, over a period of twenty-four years, her most frequent broadcast portrayal. Her repute in the role is well sustained by her first preserved Lucia (27 February 1937); she is in excellent form from beginning to end.

Pons is again partnered by the reliable Jagel, with Pinza as Raimondo and the Australian baritone John Brownlee making his debut as Lucy's brother. Brownlee, a worthy enough artist in the right roles, had first appeared ten days earlier as Rigoletto, the Metropolitan management having seriously misjudged the nature of his vocal equipment. He is little better suited to the run-of-the-mill bluster of Enrico Ashton (this is in fact his only house performance of the role in his twenty-one Met seasons). He offers a solid, stout portrayal, but all beer and no vino. Brownlee rarely attempts legato, the timbre is inherently wooden, and the top notes turn hollow in Ashton's big opening scene. The audience is decidedly unresponsive. He is a shade more effective in the scene with Lucia where Ashton is allowed to be more sympathetic. Jagel is in good form (for him), occasionally strangled as he approaches the upper range and also short on suavity, but ever the fine musician. Not until the final scene does his portrayal obtain any distinction—there he delivers an excellent 'Fra poco a me ricovero' with a neat cadenza, and though Papi allows the orchestra to plod through 'Tu che a Dio,' Jagel manages the relentless ascent of the final phrases with honor. Papi's tempi are rather unpredictable throughout. In the opening, the chorus is almost routed by the wild brio of Papi's beat, but the slow-moving sextet nearly grinds to a halt in an attempt at grandeur. Pinza is the only one of the afternoon's performers who seems capable of any dynamic modification, though he chooses an uncommonly stentorian heraldic manner for his announcement of Lucia's crime, thundering out 'In ciel'' in response to Edgardo's inquiry as to her whereabouts. But his vocal richness is balm in this desert of tonal vacuity.

With Pons one must accept the monochromatic color of her singing and recognize that she knows exactly what she can do with her voice and attempts nothing else. It is folly to look for subtle gradations of tone, vocal coloring in keeping with the text, or any large-scale emotional response either in volume or dramatic emphasis. She is the eternal *jeune fille*, with "pretty" as the only appropriate adjective—but at least "pretty" is not "ugly." One must admire how she utilizes what she has in a secure, professional manner and relish the pleasure which she thereby provides—a pleasure comparable to viewing the most expensive and delicate Meissen figurine, not great art but a wonder of its kind, perfect in its way, as Pons is in this Lucia. She never falters, her tones are tremolo-free, few aspirants intrude in fioriture (oddly we hear them in slow cantabile—'Alfin son tu-hoo-a'), she is ever on pitch, her *attacca* is quick and accurate. Her technical arsenal does not include a real trill—the minute ornaments in 'Regnava nel silenzio' are indistinct and the longer trills barely acceptable shakes. She etches (as opposed to spins) Donizetti's graceful melodies with utmost care. Even the low-lying cantabile of 'Soffriva nel pianto,' in which Lucia longs for death, is firmly drawn though far removed from the tragic lament we know it to be. No Gothic mystery shades her tale of the ghostly maiden, but the line of 'Regnava nel silenzio' is nicely sculpted and the stratospheric recall of 'Verranno a te' in the cadenza of the mad scene has surprising fullness of tone. Moreover, she often gains a brilliance in the upper octave and a half that is quite extraordinary, and an occasional upward flight of staccati (in the mad scene) strikes with rapierlike precision. "Our Provençal nightingale," as Cross calls her, concludes the first section of the mad scene

Lucia di Lammermoor
27 February 1937

Lucia
Lily Pons
Edgardo
Frederick Jagel
Enrico Ashton
John Brownlee
Raimondo
Ezio Pinza
Conductor
Gennaro Papi

Frederick Jagel as Edgardo in *Lucia di Lammermoor*.

with a stunning F in alt, brilliant in color, round in tone and held until the "thunderous applause" drowns her out. But Cross assures us that "her melodious raving" will continue, and it surely does. In fact, every D, E-flat and F scattered throughout the opera is rung with precision by Pons. A Pons artifice is her habit of pausing a fraction of a beat or more (while the orchestra waits) before launching some of the more spectacular roulades or high notes, thus compelling the audience to join her in a conspiracy of suspense. The audience clearly doted on her and would continue to do so until Maria Callas taught us that we really could care about mad Lucy and her tragic fate.

Radio audiences had already come to dote on Mr. Cross as well, and at this point in his radio tenure, he has adopted a folksy manner. Following the final curtain of *Lucia*, he urges "all of you good radio neighbors" who are enjoying the broadcast to "draw up an easy chair and listen in" again next week. Fortunately, urbanity was more his style and we hear little of his down-home ways hereafter.

To continue our perusal of Pons, we turn to the *Barber of Seville* broadcast of 22 January 1938. It is a rather ragged performance, for Papi mistakenly substitutes accelerandi for brio with a consequent ill effect on ensemble. The recording is incomplete but most of the major numbers are included.

Though very slight in weight, Bruno Landi's tenorino is welcome for its dulcet sound, adequate fioriture, and refined style in music that has been badly mangled by many another singer of greater repute. Pompilio Malatesta's Bartolo is just an ordinary buffo off the ready-to-perform rack. Pinza brings off "La calunnia' in customary blustery fashion, though only coming within range of the climactic E-flat. American baritone John Charles Thomas, favorite son of the radio concert audience, is a remarkably self-indulgent Figaro, flagrantly strewing interpolated phrases and laughter about the stage in his entrance aria. Kolodin called his performance a "burlesque."[7] Thomas is always willing to substitute four or five *piano, piano*s when Rossini's one will do, but he does evoke Figaro's spontaneous nature. His rendition is certainly preferable to the labored efforts at vivacity and the lack of vocal ease of most baritones in this test piece—Thomas tosses it off as casually as though he were licking a lollipop. Less praiseworthy are his badly smudged fioriture in the 'Dunque io son' duet—eventually he just gives up on most of them and, since he got away with it, repeats the offense in the opera's concluding 'Di si felice innesto.'

Pons would seem ideally suited to Rosina's high spirits, if one is willing to accept a light-voiced soprano for Rossini's intended *mezzo con estensione*. Only recently have we been weaned into correctness on this point—Pons had plenty of precedence for her altitudinous decorative effects in a role earlier traced by Patti, Sembrich, Melba, Tetrazzini, and Galli-Curci. Oddly enough she appeared in only three broadcasts of the opera, of which the 1938 offering is the second. Once again she dispatches Rosina's music expeditiously but without quite the tonal blandishment of her Lucia broadcast. The voice seems more fragile, slightly breathy in the lower octave; the aspirates are particularly profuse, and she occasionally teeters on the flat side of sustained notes. In short, her singing sounds a shade worn—as though the voice, not the will, is not in its healthiest state. She does execute a neat *messa di voce* on the high C preceding her F in alt at the end of 'Una voce poco fa' (unlike most opera singers, Pons always transposed up). In the duet with Figaro, Pons begins to ornament in the opening measures and succumbs to the ubiquitous need to improve on Rossini by adding a spoken 'Figaro' before handing over her letter ('Eccolo qua'). With Papi pushing ever onward and Thomas ignoring the filigree, little of the charm of this episode survives. The practice of offering the audience a little concert of one's own choosing in the lesson scene is still in effect, and Pons elects Constanze's first-act aria from Mozart's *Die Entführung aus dem Serail* (sung in Italian with some rather pinched tone). She is more successful in her encore, Dell'Acqua's 'Villanelle,' sung in French; the concert warhorse provokes one of Pons' infrequent attacks of abandon—she sings with great fluency, more compact tone, and indulges in a cadenza with flute that, in length and complexity, rivals that of Lucia's mad scene. And there we leave her, where she seems happiest—perched on a neat E-flat in alt.

Il Barbiere di Siviglia
22 January 1938

Rosina
Lily Pons
Almaviva
Bruno Landi
Figaro
John Charles Thomas
Basilio
Ezio Pinza
Dr. Bartolo
Pompilio Malatesta
Conductor
Gennaro Papi

Bidú Sayão as Violetta in *La Traviata*.

CHAPTER TEN

1936–37
Italian and French Favorites;
A Spring Bouquet

For the 1936–37 season, commercial sponsorship of the broadcasts was again obtained, albeit with a little nepotistic sleight of hand. The Radio Corporation of America, close relative of NBC, enriched the Met coffers by $100,000 for "the honor" of hosting the Met broadcasts; the company was honored in return by Cross' endorsement of the RCA Victor Magic Voice radio, "an instrument altogether worthy of the program." In the belief that a natural affinity existed between the recording-radio industry and the opera artists whose record sales had helped make the company, the *Lucia* broadcast (27 February 1937) was closed with a five-minute panegyric in praise of assorted RCA products, including the "modern high-quality receiving set" (the radio audience was encouraged to go to the RCA outlet and listen to the forthcoming *Traviata* broadcast for audio quality), and the *Stars of the Metropolitan* RCA record album ("only $10"). The listener was also asked to tune in on Sunday to the RCA-sponsored "Magic Key Hour"—an hour of music, entertainment, and news featuring Maurice Evans, a Broadway comedienne, a film star, and a new Metropolitan artist to be featured in the next week's broadcast of *La Traviata*, Bidú Sayão. To give RCA its due, the company also offered a thirty-two page illustrated booklet calculated to bring home to the radio audience "the tradition and romance behind the Metropolitan."

Now the courting of the radio audience begins in earnest. The new general manager had eagerly embraced the concept of the recently formed Opera Guild, finding in Mrs. Belmont a worthy ally to brave "the atmosphere of emergency and depression confronting the big House on Broadway and Thirty-ninth Street."[1] By the end of the 1935–36 season, Ziegler was able to inform NBC that 850 of the Guild's 2600 members lived outside the Metropolitan area, that out-of-towners purchased twenty-five percent of the tickets and had contributed "about one-fourth" of the "Save the Opera" fund receipts.[2] The time was ripe for Mrs. Belmont to enlarge the field and take her campaign to the unseen audience.

The seed was sown with the creation of the Guild organ, a four-page flyer titled *Opera News*, which was first offered to Guild members in the 1936–37 season. Over the next few years the flyer grew in size and devoted ever-increasing space to the broadcast of the week. The plan worked, and by 1939 the Guild membership had increased sixfold to fifteen thousand members, the majority of them far removed from the New York area. Yet another tie with the radio audience was the commercially sponsored "Metropolitan Opera Auditions of the Air," inaugurated during the 1935–36 season, with Johnson himself as master of ceremonies. Sponsored by the Sherwin-Williams Paint Company, the program would bring to the attention of the Metropolitan management many talented Americans, while audience interest was piqued by the suspense of singers contesting for a Metropolitan contract.

The Metropolitan's soprano debutante, Bidú Sayão, was as diminutive as Pons and similarly slight of vocal mass—but not of means. The Brazilian soprano's stage persona was far from the stylized automaton so profitably cultivated by Pons. Sayão was adept at coloratura (she sang both Lucia and Sonnambula in Europe and became a favorite Rosina and Gilda at the Met), but her coming to the Metropolitan was dictated by the vacuum in the lyric repertory occasioned by the retirement of Lucrezia Bori. And Sayão would shine in a number of Bori roles (Manon, Violetta, Mimi, Juliette, Norina, Mélisande). No artist replicates another, however, and Sayão had to be taken on her own terms. Bori had eschewed the coloratura turf (Violetta's rapid flights in 'Sempre libera' were a trial for her) but she extended her conquest of the full lyric repertory as the Puccini Manon, Nedda, Louise, and Antonia and occasionally ventured beyond into the weightier territory of Fiora, Iris, Giulietta, and Alice Ford. The realm of Sayão's unquestioned supremacy proved to be the slighter traceries of the soubrette (call her a *dugazon*, as the French do, and avoid any pejoratives). She was an unmatched Norina, Zerlina, and Adina. But the salient point remains that with natural resources as minimal as Pons', Sayão chose the path of a Bori—the path of truthful dramatic and musical communication. And she wanted even more. Many years later, in an opera broadcast intermission, she cried, "My life was renunciation—total renunciation."[3] She longed to play Butterfly, Manon Lescaut, Desdemona. In that longing lies the fascinating dichotomy of her portrayals where passion and often an almost veristic intensity govern; but the soubrette always lurks in the shadows and sometimes, forced by vocal imperatives, reveals herself at unexpected moments. At least in her early Metropolitan appearances, Sayão is most remembered for the charm and elegance of her manner and vocalism, but her powerful commitment to the dramatic situation is equally striking.

She shows her mettle in her very first Met appearance as the French Manon, broadcast on 13 February 1937. The management had intended to provide her with a well-matched partner in Richard Crooks, but to her surprise, she was greeted on stage by the throaty bellow of American tenor Sydney Rayner, a graduate of the Juilliard-sponsored supplementary seasons. His portrayal of Des Grieux offers sincerity but no variation of color or dynamics ('Le rêve' is no dream), and his vocal squeeze often pushes him off pitch. Bonelli is stalwart in tone and manner as cousin Lescaut, though the role offers little opportunity for his best qualities. Cehanovsky's excellence in the second act shows why he is the Brétigny of all twelve *Manon* broadcasts from the old Met, and American bass Chase Baromeo delivers the Count's advice to his wayward (both into and out of sin) son with splendid dark tone and a stern paternity which makes one believe he could later allow the police to cart his son off to prison.

New conductor Maurice de Abravanel had come well recommended. Johnson had written Ziegler that "Furtwängler and Walter each gave him great praise"; cryptically, and prophetically, he added, "in Lisbonne [*sic*] they had not even heard of

Manon
13 February 1937

Manon
Bidú Sayão
Des Grieux
Sydney Rayner
Lescaut
Richard Bonelli
Count
Chase Baromeo
Conductor
Maurice Abravanel

him. Perhaps he is Portuguese like I am Irish!"[4] Abravanel was expected to do double duty, relieving Bodanzky of some Wagner chores and taking over a portion of the French repertory—and there was a good deal of the latter this season, eight broadcasts of six operas. Abravanel proves more responsive to Massenet's surging orchestral line than to the score's more delicate moments; Manon's coquetry seldom finds an echo in the orchestral figurations. The orchestral introduction and women's chorus in the seminary scene betray ensemble problems and (though Natalie Bodanya, Charlotte Symons, and Irra Petina are a neat trio of skittish actresses) the frenetic undercurrent of the gambling scene is wanting until the denouement, when Guillot accuses Des Grieux of cheating; there the conductor achieves a strong dramatic climax. But Abravanel's emphasis on the expansiveness of the score works against Sayão's limited vocal resources in the later acts of the opera.

Any conjecture as to how Sayão's small but perfectly produced voice would fare in the great spaces of the Metropolitan is speedily allayed. Her affinity for the French style (she had spent several years studying with Jean de Reszke in southern France) and a decade's experience in European houses enabled her to set foot on the Met stage with a portrayal fully formed—not entirely the "flighty French girl, too young to know the ways of the world" of Mr. Cross' description, but much closer to Prévost's sphinxlike charmer. Her delivery of the first-act arias is surprisingly full-toned, with little of the spinning flutter on sustained tones which later became a Sayão trademark. The abandon of her laughter and the tripping charm of Manon's entrance aria contrast vividly with the pathos of 'Voyons, Manon,' but in the latter the rather nasal quality of the low voice surfaces. Her spoken voice as she reads Des Grieux's letter in act two startles with its low, serious tone. In contrast to the finely controlled delicacy of her commercial recording of 'Adieu, notre petite table,' she fills the aria to the full with 'mes larmes'—a very emotional rendition. (Sayão did in fact regard the microphone as "something cold—that you can't give yourself, but when you have an audience in front of you, you transmit what you feel to them and if they accept what you offer them, that is a big, big thing."[5]) In the *forte* high B of the preceding recitative and a few other climaxes her resources are fully extended (the C-sharp in alt of act three is close to a scream as she struggles to surmount the ensemble).

The delicious fragility of Sayão's Manon returns in her declamation of 'Ces murs silencieux' at Saint-Sulpice—horror and despair are remote as she momentarily becomes a helpless, lost waif; nor could she expect her prayer for pardon to be answered since there is little sense of urgency on her part. She seems vocally somewhat overwhelmed by the passionate demands of 'Oui! Je fus cruelle et coupable.' But Sayão has a full battery to direct at Des Grieux and convincingly converts into a full-blooded seductress as she delivers 'N'est-ce plus ma main' with hypnotic charm and skill. The reprise with Des Grieux again finds her somewhat hard pressed; the voice stiffens, the pitch moves sharp, and one becomes aware that she must depend excessively on the vocal sob for dramatic accent. (The situation was difficult—Sayão confirmed that her first private meeting with Rayner was before the Saint-Sulpice scene when Abravanel "got us together to rehearse a little.")[6]

Met Manons of this period cannot promenade on the Cours la Reine, but the Gavotte is interpolated into the gambling scene. The piece is tailor-made for Sayão's gifts, and her second verse is beautifully controlled with an easy cadenza to the high D. At the close of the Hotel Transylvania ensemble, she murmurs 'Ah! c'en est fait! je meurs!' with infinite pathos. Her final act is completely satisfying; by now her lower tones blend well with the rest of the voice and she sings her part of the duet with firm tone. One notes particularly her noble declamation of 'Ah! je sens une pure flamme' and the ecstatic wonder of 'Ah! le beau diamant!' Dramatically, Sayão's overt representation of Manon's fears and hopes as death approaches tips her interpretation precariously close to the veristic.

Fullness of character portrayal and the dramatic thrust of her singing remain the dominant features of Sayão's debut in what was perhaps her finest role. As Manon she could give full reign to her passionate nature, exploit to the full the charming femininity of her person, and yet, for the most part, remain within the boundaries which, of necessity, governed her exquisite soprano.

Just three weeks later the broadcast audience heard the Brazilian soprano as yet another courtesan, one less exacting than Manon in her grasping after worldly goods but even more stringent in vocal demands. On 6 March 1937 Sayão stepped onto the Met stage (for only the second time) in the role of Violetta, with Brownlee singing his first Met Germont and Kullman as Alfredo.

Unlike many young Americans who came to the Metropolitan during the Johnson era, Charles Kullman did not have to be tutored in matters of operatic practice, for he had a backlog of European experience in Berlin, Vienna, Salzburg, Florence, and Covent Garden. Coupled with a fine intelligence nurtured at Yale (where he had been soloist with the Glee Club while preparing for a medical career), Juilliard, and a faculty appointment at Smith College, his capabilities would prove extremely useful to the Metropolitan, particularly during the war years, for he was able in all operatic styles. Faust, Cavaradossi, Dimitri in *Boris Godunov*, Tamino, Walther von Stolzing, and Parsifal were just a few of his thirty-four roles during twenty-five consecutive Met seasons. Though often cited for his versatility and reliability, he was more than a journeyman tenor—after all, in his pre-Met career Toscanini had chosen him for the Verdi Requiem and *Meistersinger*, Bruno Walter for Mahler's *Das Lied von der Erde*. As early as 1931 Gatti had shown interest in the young tenor.[7] Johnson, who heard Kullman in Weinberger's *Schwanda* at Covent Garden in 1935 and signed him for the Met, provided Ziegler with an astute assessment of the young Yankee "in a role too heavy for him" but showing a "lyric tenor voice of good quality, at times uneven in production, but facile and pleasant—a good figure, easy manner with a tendency to move too much, but in general quite sympathetic."[8]

Kullman's Alfredo reveals a musicality which lends distinction to a role too often ineffectual. Kullman understands the architectonics of 'De' miei bollenti spiriti' (which frequently merely bumps along in a profusion of huffs and puffs) and reveals it to us through varied articulation of the phrases and rhythmic play; when he enthusiastically repeats the climactic 'Io vivo quasi in ciel' we can believe in his ardor. Though both Sayão and Kullman perform the Brindisi like two well-bred acquaintances at a tea party, 'Un dì felice' has a fine sincerity on Kullman's part. When Violetta agrees to see him on the morrow his 'Io son felice' has the ring of happiness in it. One soon notes his predilection for a slight sob where no dramatic motivation warrants, but the vocal quality is distinctive, an odd combination of sweetness and nose which is immediately identifiable and pleasant to my ears. In the demanding denunciation of Violetta in the gambling scene Kullman is overmatched at the climax, but Panizza's plodding tempo and constant expansion of phrase are no help—the tension and momentum inevitably lapse.

Judging by the orchestral figures which accompany Brownlee's entrance as a very angry father, Panizza pictures an excessively pompous Germont. The cantabile

La Traviata
6 March 1937

Violetta
Bidú Sayão

Alfredo
Charles Kullman

Germont
John Brownlee

Conductor
Ettore Panizza

of 'Pura siccome un angelo' suits Brownlee better than does Ashton's bluster, and his top voice is adequate throughout, but the monochromatic timbre and lack of suavity do little to mitigate the squareness which Verdi laid on 'Di Provenza.'

Sayão's Violetta is a vivid creation and exceedingly well sung throughout. Oddly enough, she is considerably more reticent in deploying her vocal resources as a Verdi heroine, so there is little of that sense of overextension which occasionally marred her Manon. Does that mean she is deficient in passion or dramatic thrust? On the contrary, although all her moves are kept within her own well-defined scale. She turns the coloratura of the first act into a dramatic device just as Verdi intended— even the descending three-note flourishes with which she responds to Alfredo's confession of love are laced with an unusual cutting edge. The 'gioir's in the recit preceding 'Ah fors'è lui' become angry flourishes, but she clothes her repetition of Alfredo's love theme with a genuine wonder and sense of longing. Throughout the performance she employs her lovely tonal spin (flutter) with far greater frequency than as Manon. Panizza adopts a moderate tempo for the cabaletta, but he can't prevent Sayão from turning 'Sempre libera' into a fervid delirium; the attack and rapidity of the descending scales, the splendid reiterated high Cs, the precision and ease of coloratura—all convey an abandon in strong contrast to her very lovely but rather chaste commercial recording of this scene (though the interpolated high E-flat is rather hard-toned in the live performance). Sometimes in the recording studio Sayão seems to be merely play-acting (and she is sovereign at it), but little sense of pretense intrudes on her stage portrayals.

Her second act doesn't quite measure up. Too often Sayão must be content with pathos where dramatic directness is required ('Era felice troppo'), and she returns to the upper-octave B-flat at the end of 'L'uom implacabile per lei sarà' (the one-note alteration is critical, for we are robbed of Violetta's graphic plunge into despair). For 'Dite alla giovine' Panizza adopts a Ponselle tempo that necessitates a Ponselle weight, and Sayão is forced to indulge in multiple little gulped attacks which violate the line. At this most truthful of moments the soubrette intrudes; it is the weakest part of Sayão's performance. Many a tear must stain her farewell note to Alfredo, but she knows how to manage the frenzied phrases leading to 'Amami, Alfredo' without becoming vocally unstrung. The final outburst is, of necessity, a little tame. Nor is the thrice-repeated 'Ah, perchè venni, incauta!' phrase drawn out of her throat as an arch of pain (but then Panizza ignores the *agitato* marked by Verdi). Panizza's constant plucking at the tempo is most intrusive in the prelude to the final act where expressive freedom degenerates into a succession of slowdowns and speedups. Sayão is superb throughout the final act. She reads Germont's letter forcefully, throws off a tragic 'È tardi,' and delivers an exquisite 'Addio del passato' (barring some undesirable aspirants at 'della'); the finely controlled phases of 'Or tutto, tutto' mark the emotional climax, all capped by a shimmering top A. The tragic moments are convincingly played: she utters 'Prendi, quest'è l'immagine' almost as a *pronunciamento*, and predictably, an abundance of lovely tone affirms the line of 'Se una pudica vergine.' Violetta's momentary renascence of strength at the opera's close is almost defiantly conveyed.

In spite of the obvious merits of Sayão's demimondaine, its miniature proportions prompted the Metropolitan to continue its search for a definitive Violetta. The following season Belgian soprano Vina Bovy was the broadcast *Traviata*, and in 1939 American Helen Jepson sang the first of her two consecutive *Traviata* broadcasts.

Panizza and the comprimarios are constant in all three performances, but we

La Traviata
23 December 1939

Violetta
Helen Jepson
Alfredo
Richard Crooks
Germont
Lawrence Tibbett
Conductor
Ettore Panizza

are treated to a parade of Germonts, *père et fils*. The gloss of radio and film stardom of the thirties shines on the sequence: Nino Martini, Richard Crooks, John Charles Thomas, and Lawrence Tibbett all earned a large public following outside the opera house in the popular media.

Helen Jepson, too, had made the trip to Hollywood where the California Barnum, Sam Goldwyn, had featured her singing of 'Sempre libera' in the *Goldwyn Follies*, qualification enough in the Met's mind for her assumption of the role that had challenged the greatest actresses of opera and stage. Garbed in gowns by Hollywood's Omar Kiam, Jepson's physical beauty undoubtedly made for an attractive stage picture, but the radio audience heard only a schoolgirl courtesan, devoid of passion or interpretive insight. "Hearty as her own garden in the Catskills, reliable and businesslike as a career girl in industry"[9] (the description is from the "Personality of the Week" in *Opera News*) were admirable attributes of the American girl who made good—but not quite in the line of Verdi's lady of the camellias (though there may be something apt about "career girl"). The lady from New Jersey is healthy of voice as well as of person with an evenly produced lyric soprano of lovely, if not individual, timbre. She certainly possesses adequate technique for the fioriture of act one. But no more anguish pierces Jepson's cry of 'Preferirò morir' to father Germont than if she had been forbidden attendance at the high school prom. Nor does any of Verdi's *debolissima* or *passione* invade her fresh tone as death approaches. One is always grateful for clean vocalism (her farewell to the past is delivered with firm tone and fine breath control), but the absence of musical subtleties and dramatic temperament make the purchase of this virginal Violetta too costly.

The male members of this American trio are another matter entirely. Media fame had not tinseled their artistry, though the financial lure of radio concerts and the resultant increase in recital engagements did diminish the number of their opera appearances. Crooks' weekly radio concerts ("The Voice of Firestone") had made him a household name, and even his few Met appearances were made, as Ziegler pointed out to NBC, "at a most reasonable rate and a sacrifice."[10] The Metropolitan name was not without commercial value to even the most sought-after radio singer, but nevertheless, the financial sacrifice on Crooks' part implies a dedication to the operatic muse which is confirmed in all of his opera broadcasts.

Backed by European study and opera appearances in Hamburg (debut as Cavaradossi in 1927), Berlin, Holland, and Belgium, Crooks—through his lyric voice (with its unique command of *voix mixte*) and his musical sensitivity—lent much-needed style to performances of French opera during his Metropolitan decade. In the Italian repertory, too, Crooks shone as Charles in *Linda di Chamounix*, Don Ottavio, and Alfredo. No more elegant Germont *fils* is to be heard in the entire broadcast history. In Crooks' throat the shopworn Brindisi has the subtlety of an art song—delicious *piano* phrases contrast with manly outbursts, for he is no lily-livered tenorino. 'Un dì felice' has a sincerity just right for the young provincial, the phrases articulated and shaped with care, the tone full of gradations of weight and color. Panizza's moderate tempo in the aria enables Crooks to voice the text with intensity (one does notice the occasional American *r*, and the vowels are unduly open at *forte* levels at the top of the range). In contrast to his full-voiced denunciation in the gambling scene, one relishes the pure head tones in place of the usual bellow at 'De' corsi affanni' in the final duet, but not the way Jepson trivializes the melody by straightening out the dotted rhythms. (Is Crooks' lovely *portamento* to the high A-flat a demeaning falsetto?)

Tibbett's sterling Germont buttresses the performance. An unintentional sound of age touches his angry remarks to Violetta, but by the time he reaches 'Pura siccome un angelo' all is vocal beauty, notwithstanding an occasional throaty *forte* tone. His mezza voce is particularly fine in the reprise of 'Dite alla giovine' (Panizza is still anchored to a dismally slow tempo here, but elsewhere the languors of Ponselle's tempi have mercifully been abandoned—much of the final act, especially at Germont's entrance, positively races.) More than most baritones Tibbett observes at least some of Verdi's markings in 'Di Provenza,' pouring the gentlest breath into the timeworn melody. The *acciaccaturas* are perfectly articulated, and he ends the first verse with a beautifully controlled diminuendo ('guidò') in contrast to the brilliant, full-voice conclusion to the second verse where the top rings out with splendor. He even adds a strong high A-flat as Alfredo rushes off.

Turning back to the *Traviata* broadcast of 11 December 1937, we again find popular media stars on stage. The handsome film star and radio favorite Nino Martini (he whom NBC was so anxious to corral in the 1933–34 contract) makes an excellent impression in the Brindisi with the natural flow of his Italian timbre and diction, but satisfaction is soon dissipated by his tendency to sing under the pitch (throughout the entire 'Un dì felice'). The aria is no improvement, but the last act finds him in better form. Bovy's timbre is curiously like that of Pons with its glassy sheen (a less welcome similarity is the tremulousness of her lower voice), but her singing has more emotional content. On the other hand, she does not command Pons' line in cantilena; thus some of the score's most affecting moments are victimized by choppy emotionalism (both 'Alfredo, di questo core' and 'Parigi, o cara' are picked to pieces). And she opens all the vowel sounds to excess, which makes for some odd Italian. Bovy whirls with aplomb through 'Sempre libera' (preceded by a delightful tinkling laugh), but to little dramatic purpose. On the other hand, the incisive, knifeedged top voice is wedded to a surprisingly full lower octave, and in the scene with Germont her voice is less skittish and she achieves some lovely affects. 'Non sapete' is quietly limned for mood, and she employs an affecting *portamento* at 'Gran Dio' and manages 'Così alla misera' in one breath; often enough Bovy works an odd combination of fragility and strength which somehow strikes home. Fortunately, by this season Panizza allows 'Dite alla giovine' to flow at a reasonable pace for a lyric voice. Where Sayão's 'va all'istante!' was an emphatic command to Annina, Bovy chooses a forlorn hopelessness and leaves all the tears to the clarinet. 'Addio del passato' is in the pathetic, rather than tragic, mood; again the overlay of emotionalism seems excessive. A more satisfying solidity of tone and line pervades the remainder of the act, but her stylized cries of 'rinasce' do not quite ring true.

Traviata may be one of the ultimate star vehicles for sopranos, but the star of this performance is undoubtedly John Charles Thomas' sonorous Germont. His lasciviously fat tone and rolling cantilena envelop the entire confrontation scene; Thomas doesn't trifle with Verdi and offers a generalized, dignified presence whose conversational manner gives the scene a welcome spontaneity. 'Bella voi siete,' he cries with surprise, as though he has only just recognized Violetta's beauty. By the time he reaches the duet proper he has grown impatient with Panizza's lethargy, and their *Piangi*s are in decided disagreement. One notices how his legato is overmagnified by his tendency to sing on the consonants ('vinnncero'), a carryover mannerism from the colloquial diction he employs as a justly admired singer of American songs. By the end of the scene Thomas is conducting with the voice, and Panizza and Bovy are forced to tag along with his ground swell of tone as he sprints through to the end.

La Traviata
11 December 1937
Violetta
Vina Bovy
Alfredo
Nino Martini
Germont
John Charles Thomas
Conductor
Ettore Panizza

'Di Provenza' is the vocal highlight of the afternoon. Though Verdi's frequent *dolce* and *pianissimo* markings are all but ignored, the breadth of line and resplendent top voice are nigh irresistible; as if to prove he can be subtle if he chooses, he trots out a delicious diminuendo on the final tonic of the aria. Verdi's high tessitura holds no terrors for Thomas—for him, singing is as easy as falling off a log.

Les Contes d'Hoffmann
23 January 1937
Olympia, Giulietta,
Antonia, Stella
Vina Bovy
Hoffmann
René Maison
Lindorf, Coppelius,
Dappertutto, Dr. Miracle
Lawrence Tibbett
Conductor
Maurice Abravanel

If Bovy's Violetta was upstaged by John Charles' portly Germont, she had had an earlier opportunity to more than hold center stage. In the only other broadcast of her brief Met career, Bovy took on all four roles in *Les Contes d'Hoffmann* on 23 January 1937. This is a far more satisfying effort by Bovy (and luckily heard by the radio audience who were spared the incredibly feeble lineup of Andreva, Halstead, and Burke in the multiple roles at the season's premiere). Though planned as a vehicle for Tibbett (who played all four baritone roles in all the season's performances) Bovy's one-time-only appearance is the feature of the preserved portions of the opera (the doll aria and most of the Venice and Munich acts, but no prologue or epilogue).

Tibbett is betrayed by the low tessitura of the villains, and his few excerpts hold little distinction—the menace throughout is too generalized. Two moments have a face of their own: the finely spun mezza voce as Dr. Miracle entices Antonia to sing again, and Dappertutto's aria, sung in the original key and ending with a brilliant (though not effortless) G-sharp. The lacklustre heaviness of the aria is occasioned by its schizophrenic tessitura; once quit of the lower octave of the first section Tibbett is much happier in the high range of the piece's final moments, but even so, the lack of bright French vowel sounds robs the piece of éclat. Tibbett's deficiency in idiomatic diction is abundantly clear when Bovy and René Maison are before us.

Both tenor and soprano are natives of Belgium (where the French language dominates the artistic scene) and denizens of many a French operatic stage. The seduction scene of act two (where Maison contributes one of his best purely vocal achievements in 'O Dieu, de quelle ivresse'—the heroic tone takes on a real glint) has plenty of panache and contrasts effectively with the easy, intimate exchanges between Antonia and Hoffmann in act three. The coloratura mechanics of Bovy's doll aria may not run on precision bearings (though the echo effects are neatly achieved) but she projects a vivid aural image of a red-cheeked marionette. Abravanel's waltz music has the appropriate lilt; his conducting throughout is decidedly propulsive (too much so in the trio which ends the opera proper). Antonia's duet with Hoffmann marks the high point of the afternoon, both artists pouring out quantities of ringing tone. D'Angelo (Crespel) and Anna Kaskas (Mother's Voice) both contribute to the security of the final scene where Bovy's febrile delivery makes clear Antonia's agitated state. Tonally, Bovy is at her best here, but unfortunately she has no trill in reserve when Antonia, like Bovy's Met career of only two seasons, comes to an untimely end.

Samson et Dalila
26 December 1936
Dalila
Gertrud Wettergren
Samson
René Maison
High Priest
Ezio Pinza
Old Hebrew
Emanuel List
Conductor
Maurice Abravanel

Another artist of similarly brief tenure is the Swedish mezzo, Gertrud Wettergren, who launched the Saturday series of the 1936–37 season as Dalila in the first broadcast of Saint-Saëns' problematic opera-oratorio. Over the next several decades the radio audience might be able to ignore the pitfalls of staging this dramatically static work, but the felicitous casting of both title roles in the same performance would prove elusive. A visually satisfying temptress too often is deficient in vocal allure, particularly in the warm deeps of Dalila's three arias. Over the airwaves, Wettergren's voice has the necessary velvet for the seduction scenes, and she manages an easy, musical flow in the arias. The warmth of color and seamless blend of register, however, are not matched by sufficient weight to permit the *espansione* which

Saint-Saëns called for at the climactic moments (the too-familiar 'Réponds' phrases in 'Mon coeur' become episodic), and in her scenes with the High Priest her efforts are often dwarfed by the rolling grandeur of Pinza's tones. Another opportunity to hear Pinza in a role little associated with him (he sang only the five performances of this single Met season) is as rewarding as it is welcome. He is in splendid voice, rhythmically invigorating (the melismas in the temple scene are incisive barbs), and he throws out line after line of ravishing tone in this ungrateful part. He does not seem to have found the secret of elisions in French, so there is an emphasis on marcato singing and a too vigorous (and indiscriminate) attack on syllables without regard to dramatic or musical motivation. But Dalila's acquiescence to her mentor is perfectly plausible in the face of Pinza's potent vitality. No matter how minor the role, Pinza can't help but take command.

The Bacchanal and earlier choral episodes are not preserved, but Abravanel's energetic approach to the score is clear in the storm episode and the frenzy of the temple scene.

Appropriately, the hero of the performance is Maison; Samson is the best of all his broadcast performances. Anchored in the middle voice, the tessitura of the role is readily conquered, and his command of French declamation is a powerful asset in the troubled utterances of the Israelite leader—'Vois ma misère' is a masterful combination of wretchedness and dignity. The burnished copper shine of his heroic tenor is most attractive throughout the afternoon. The exchanges of Wettergren and Maison in the second act have a spontaneity and surging impetus which negates the static nature of the work, and Maison raises the temperature of the scene with a ringing high B-flat in the duet coda of Dalila's aria. To those in the opera house, the Belgian tenor's giant physical proportions made him visually an ideal Samson, while for the radio audience the integrity of his conception and his imposing tone and style prove equally satisfying.

Wettergren's broadcast debut had been as Amneris the previous season, but the Italian repertory will be far better and longer served by the decade of Bruna Castagna's dominance of the mezzo realm. Castagna, too, first appeared as Amneris in the 1935–36 season; she essayed the Egyptian princess in the supplementary-season broadcast of *Aida* in May, an indication of management's ambivalent appraisal of her abilities. Her first New York opera appearances had been at the popular-priced Hippodrome, not the most prestigious port of entry for a future Met star. But when the next *Aida* broadcast rolled around, Castagna was on the throne which she would occupy for all seven of the *Aida* airings through 1943. Not so fortunate in Metropolitan longevity is her equally gifted rival in love, the celebrated dramatic soprano, Gina Cigna, who made her Metropolitan debut as Aida on the broadcast of 6 February 1937. Born in Paris in 1900 (and named Geneviève), longtime pupil of the legendary Emma Calvé, debutante at La Scala in 1927, for twenty years a leading figure on the Italian stages in all the great dramatic parts, Cigna was an artist of formidable intelligence and temperament. She included in her repertory Strauss, Gluck, Monteverdi, Mozart, and Rossini, but was especially renowned for Gioconda, Turandot, and Norma.

With Cigna and Castagna, Martinelli and Morelli, Pinza and Panizza, *Aida* promises to be an afternoon of idiomatic Italian opera. Carlo Morelli is the under-sized member of the quintet, pleasant of timbre but deficient in the dramatic accents necessary to quell a wayward daughter. In another of his service roles, Pinza again makes much of little. Pinza's resonant tones, rhythmic bite, and dramatic conviction

Aida
6 February 1937
Aida
Gina Cigna
Amneris
Bruna Castagna
Radames
Giovanni Martinelli
Amonasro
Carlo Morelli
Ramfis
Ezio Pinza
Conductor
Ettore Panizza

rivet our attention and elevate our level of belief—he turns every priest into a God. Martinelli is a wonder in his opening aria, the bane of tenors for its early placement, difficult ascending lines, and quiet close. He can't manage the latter but does suggest the dolcissimo of 'Il tuo bel cielo.' He knows the exact flow and shape of those ascending lines (as well he might, for he had been singing Radames at the Met since his debut season of 1913), and he ends each of them with a deft *portamento*. On this afternoon the years have robbed his tone of a good deal of its lustre, but Radames' music on the Nile is still favored by his robust manner.

Though Castagna was accused of a lack of refinement in her early Met career, her Amneris is a model of musical and dramatic rectitude. Nothing seems calculated for the gallery; one might even wish for a bit less reticence in her judgment scene. In the first act her lightly floated tones fully satisfy Verdi's *grazioso* marking—this Amneris could deceive even the most experienced of tenors. For once, Amneris' trio of high-flying phrases (as act two opens) holds no terrors—Castagna's tone is as seductively warm as the text demands, and her subtle *morendo* close of the phrases suggests a trancelike state. As well as she conveys Amneris' honest emotion, Castagna is equally practiced in deceit; her cantabile in 'Io son l'amica tua' reeks of sincerity. Provincial huffs or chest tones never intrude, but she is properly explosive as she names herself 'tua rivale figlia de' Faraoni.' Castagna's judgment scene fills out her conception of the Egyptian princess: even when scorned, she is no whirling dervish of fury, but a woman who desires and is worthy of love (Panizza's stately tempi enhance her rather sedate interpretation). Castagna's approach to her top voice is ever easy and assured; her velvety Mediterranean timbre is constant throughout the entire range as she makes the judgment scene a musical experience, not merely a star turn.

Against the poised assurance of Castagna, the volatility of newcomer Cigna is particularly riveting. Her mercurial manner ensures that the dramatic monologue of the first act will be more satisfying than Aida's recall of her homeland, where vocal purity is paramount. "I always preferred temperament and interpretation to voice alone,"[11] she opined late in life. Such prima donna pronouncements, whether dictated by technical deficiencies or a matter of choice, may be taken in good faith in Cigna's case. 'Ritorna vincitor' is indeed a searing experience. The opening declamation is meaningfully shaped, she maintains a fine line in 'L'insana parola,' and the *fortissimo* high B-flat has a nice edge to it. Panizza allows her complete freedom in the 'l'amor mio' section (is this what is meant by idiomatic performance?) where Cigna spins and plays with the tone at will, expressively evoking the memory of Radames' love. The final prayer to the gods for pity is much drawn out, but very lovely. Aida's monologue, with its widely swinging moods, is an ideal vehicle for Cigna's temperament, and with it she makes an impressive entrance into the Metropolitan galaxy.

By the second act Cigna is in full command of her top voice (an excellent full-voiced high C), and she surmounts the ensemble with a knifelike brilliance—hers is not a plushy instrument. Panizza substitutes accelerandi for momentum in portions of the triumphal scene and the maestoso mood gives way to a feverish pace (not unlike that of a horse on the way home to the barn after an outing). 'O patria mia,' with its exposed cantabile, requires complete control; the aria is a fearsome test for any soprano on any occasion, let alone a Metropolitan debut, broadcast to an audience of millions. Cigna meets it head-on. The result is a draw, with the high C (*mezzo forte*) reasonably vanquished. As she admirably seeks the *piano* dynamics required by Verdi, Cigna's tone takes on a glassy whiteness, whereas at the other end of the spectrum, excessive pressure at *forte* levels exaggerates her quick vibrato into a disturbing flutter. But by now the audience is obviously much taken with the soprano, and once past the aria, Cigna is decidedly effective in a variety of ways: her fury as her father suggests betrayal is wonderfully telling, yet she maintains control over the forceful utterances; unlike most Aidas, her seduction of Radames in 'Là tra foreste' is not only vocally lovely but suggestive of a real temptress as she languorously tampers with the vocal line. Best of all is the tomb scene; here both Cigna and Martinelli evoke an ethereal beauty. Verdi's quietly vaulting lines are usually hard going for tenors and sopranos who can meet the robust demands of other portions of the opera (especially when the final scene is taken at Panizza's inert pace). But age has not robbed Martinelli of the ability to conduct a line with precision and care, and his B-flats are nicely colored and finely drawn throughout. Cigna is even better as she lightly traces 'Vedi? di morte l'angelo' (though oddly Panizza hurries her at this point), and 'O terra addio' is exquisitely controlled with a beguiling spin (but no *piano*) on 'raggio.' Perhaps it is the refinement of this elegiac close, after all, that spells Italian opera. The moment is one of the high points of the broadcasts.

Patently sharing this opinion is Marcia Davenport, novelist daughter of old-time Met soprano Alma Gluck and co-host with Cross of the 1936–37 broadcasts. She hastily interrupts Cross after the third act with a paean of praise for Cigna (who has received a lengthy ovation extending over several solo calls). Davenport excitedly hails the "extraordinary piece of news going on here today . . . the biggest news that's hit the Italian wing of the Metropolitan in some time, and the house is really having a very exciting afternoon. Madame Cigna is a *beautiful* artist. . . . They're yelling, they're calling 'Cigna' and 'brava'—and she deserves *every* bit of it." Turning critic in a fashion never heard in later broadcasts, where opinions about the artists performing are resolutely taboo, Davenport notes that Cigna has a "beautiful, clear, pure voice, that she is a *marvelous* musician . . . she has a beautiful vocal control, she phrases magnificently well, her singing is accurate and musical, and of course we've all been thrilled by the perfect purity of her high notes." Perhaps unnerved by this show of partiality, the decidedly torpid Cross contents himself with the observation that the debutante "has only been singing professionally for eight years—just think of that!" But Davenport is closer to the mark, for she knows that "the discovery and the debut of a *real* top-notch Italian prima donna is always a thrilling occasion and *this is it.*"

Cigna's debut was aptly timed; ten days later Rosa Ponselle, for two decades imperatrix of dramatic sopranos, sang her final performance at the Metropolitan—would Cigna achieve a similar dominance in the ensuing decades? The comparison was apropos, for only two weeks after her broadcast debut, Cigna essayed her first Met Norma, Ponselle's greatest role. Once again the radio audience was in on the premiere.

For several seasons the Metropolitan had been seeking a new Druid priestess now that the terrors of Norma's demands had vanquished Ponselle to a less altitudinous terrain. At first the palm seemed certain to go to the Met's new prima donna Kirsten Flagstad who, while ruling supreme in the German wing, seemed willing to extend her domain. At the close of her first season, Ziegler wrote to Flagstad at her home in Norway: "Mr. [Earl] Lewis told me that you heard the one act of *Norma* at the special performance given here [act two with Ponselle and Swarthout in the gala performance at Gatti's farewell] and said that you were keen to sing it here." Hardly concealing his joy, Ziegler assured her "that we will be very keen to have you sing it. . . . I frankly see a great triumph in this for you."[12] But this was only the beginning

Norma
20 February 1937

Norma
Gina Cigna
Adalgisa
Bruna Castagna
Pollione
Giovanni Martinelli
Oroveso
Ezio Pinza
Conductor
Ettore Panizza

of the Met's diligent but futile campaign to achieve a Flagstad Norma. In the same letter Ziegler quotes from a telegram in which Flagstad's husband stated that his wife is "overworked mostly in bed cannot therefore presently decide *Norma* STOP Please send all necessary material to Norway STOP She will then decide."[13] Six weeks later Ziegler cabled Johnson that Flagstad could not sing Norma "if she must study Senta, Fidelio."[14] Ziegler felt neither *Holländer* nor *Fidelio* was "good box office STOP Flagstad thinks she can do Norma if relieved of other roles STOP If she sings Norma it will also relieve the congestion in dramatic soprano department."[15] Johnson eliminated *Holländer*, but the congestion was not to be relieved, for Flagstad never undertook the role whose varied requirements included skill in florid song.

The following season Johnson, still intent on bringing *Norma* back into the repertory, evidently remembered a performance of the opera he had heard in Florence in 1935 under Vittorio Gui. At the time he had written Ziegler:

> Cigna . . . was a fine figure in the robes of the daughter of the Druids. The voice is full and has great range, but the emission is uneven and the agility is heavy. After the "Casta Diva" her nerves quieted down, but even so— well, it seems to me a very fine success for Rosa Ponselle.[16]

In fairness to Cigna, Johnson found the whole performance (Merli, Pasero) "most interesting." Once again we have aural evidence enabling us to monitor Johnson's evaluation, which, though mixed, did not deter him from subsequently engaging the Italian prima donna. At the Met, Cigna's skills were certainly well tested; in the two weeks between her debut as Aida and the Norma of 20 February she had sung Leonora (*Trovatore*) and Gioconda, not winning the whole-hearted approval of the critics but evidently building a rabid public following. This broadcast once again joins Castagna, Martinelli, Pinza, and Cigna for 'idiomatic Italian opera' under Panizza's pliant and perceptive leadership.

In the first half century of Metropolitan history the challenge of Norma had been undertaken (and happily met) by only two sopranos: Ponselle and Lilli Lehmann, legendary interpreter of the late nineteenth century. Why the paucity of interpreters? Bellini built into the role contrasting imperatives: he fused the liquid cantilena and florid flights of the bel canto tradition with the impassioned accents of a Medea-like heroine who successively seeks vengeance for betrayal in love, contemplates and rejects infanticide, and finally achieves serenity through a Wagner-like immolation. Thus its dramatic and interpretive demands dictated a voice of ample size and a command of tragic utterance, yet one capable of considerable agility. In modern times nearly all vocal types from the soprano leggiero to the pushed-up mezzo soprano have seen fit to undertake Norma, often with disastrous results. (Sayão, who knew well how to coax a riposte from the then dowager 'regina della casa,' once said to Milanov, a justly famed Norma of the forties, that a certain singer had told her it was "easy" to sing Norma; the inimitable Zinka replied "It is easy if you sing it badly."[17]) As if to affirm the simple wisdom of Milanov's pronouncement, Cigna's Norma succeeds; evidently the role is not that easy for her (obvious effort sits on some of her fioriture), but she has all the requirements for the role, and she grows in vocal ease throughout the performance.

Though the great accompanied recitative at Norma's entrance is unduly squally (Italianate sopranos of this period never shrink from incisive tone when authoritative accents are required), both tone and phrase amplify as the aria nears; the address to the moon is quite splendid with no excessive flutter, and the top voice is indeed

Gina Cigna.

refulgent. (Critic W. J. Henderson should not have accorded Cigna the honor of singing 'Casta Diva' in the original key,[18] for like most sopranos, her key is F—a full tone lower.) Clearly, the soprano prefers (and achieves) a slower tempo than Panizza's, one which allows her to expressively manipulate Bellini's cantilena. The turns in the opening phrase are smudged, but her concluding cadenza is on the mark. The cabaletta is far less satisfying, for she hurls her voice at the craggy coloratura with more determination than skill. The glottal disease again infects her anguished recitative at the opening of the scene with Adalgisa. But their duet has the genuine aura of bel canto—not quite the well-tuned machine of more recent singers, but rather two woebegone human beings breathing and sighing and feeling together with here and there a *messa di voce* and radiant top tones gracing the aural landscape. Later, Cigna's

Bruna Castagna as Adalgisa in *Norma*.

steely tone serves her well as she voices her anger with Pollione. She is not afraid to propel the big tune of the trio with rhythmic waltz inflections, and she even adds a stentorian, stony high D as the curtain falls.

By the time Norma contemplates the murder of her children, Cigna is in full command of her resources; her performance grows both in authority and vocal beauty on through the denouement. Now Cigna achieves a greater repose for Bellini's melodies. Her control of color and volume throughout the entire 'Mira, o Norma' scene is remarkable, and Panizza well knows how to waft the accompanying arpeggios to allow the singers a supple rubato. In the final scene Cigna achieves some authentic bursts of virtuosity, even though her liberal use of chest register disturbs the melodic continuity of 'In mia man alfin tu sei.' The menace and tension which Cigna generates here are noteworthy. An artist of such extrovert tendencies often skirts the line between crudity and majesty, but there is no trespass in this instance. The intricate coloratura patterns of 'Già mi pasco' momentarily elude her, but the grand manner of the concluding pages is native terrain to her. Her confusion is first voiced in pitiful *pianissimo* tones with a moving *messa di voce* as she admits her guilt ('Son io'). In her controlled *piano* voicing of 'Deh non volerli vittime' we hear the best of Cigna's art; her entire range is suffused with a shimmering color which prepares us for Norma's immolation.

Ultimately a Cigna performance is more than the sum of its parts. One feels the satisfaction of an encounter with an authentic Druid priestess and a woman who has loved.

Castagna's Adalgisa is a more restrained portrayal, appropriate to the gentler maiden's distress. It is also more perfectly vocalized. She adopts a delightfully girlish tone in her entrance aria, reserving an effective chest voice and Italianate sob for the closing 'Perduta io son.' In her first encounter with Norma the chest voice does become excessive at the expense of appropriate float for 'Sola furtiva.' Castagna's well-oiled vocal mechanism and Cigna's occasionally recalcitrant instrument seem not inappropriate to their contrasted dramatic stance in the great duet scenes. Castagna's top tones (either *piano* or *forte*) are especially lovely in 'Mira, o Norma.'

In his third consecutive venture as a servant of the gods, Pinza is again in top form. He manages to aurally provide a different priestly manner for each of them, turning Ramfis into a straightforward political negotiator, playing *Samson*'s High Priest as the intriguer who is both threatening and enticing, and through noble tone and grand line, imbuing Norma's father with serenity. For once Oroveso's opening scene is no mere treading of water until the prima donna appears. In 'Ah! del Tebro' the volcanic outpouring of tone suggests that Pinza may be carrying his own built-in amplifier (Albanese said he sounded "as if he had a microphone in his throat.")[19]

Oddly enough, the 1937 broadcast is Martinelli's first Metropolitan Pollione. Though a mite huffy in his opening recitative and at later emphatic points in the opera, 'Meco all'altar di Venere' is exactly right in fervor and bright, burnished tone; the rhythmic vigor of Martinelli's style is well suited to the angular outlines of Bellini's warrior. He makes a passionate plea out of 'Vieni in Roma' and, as may often be observed in his performances, employs a long crescendo on a single note (in the second-act trio) to musical and dramatic effect.

If Flagstad had remained keen on the *Norma* assignment, it is difficult to imagine her at home in the alternating graces and fervor of this Italianate performance. Nor would one anticipate Dresden's Elisabeth Rethberg at the center of a Sicilian vendetta in *Cavalleria Rusticana*. Rethberg performed only three Santuzzas with the

Cavalleria Rusticana
10 April 1937

Santuzza
Elisabeth Rethberg
Lola
Irra Petina
Turiddu
Sydney Rayner
Alfio
Carlo Morelli
Conductor
Gennaro Papi

Metropolitan, the first in 1927 and the last a decade later, on 10 April 1937, while on tour in Boston. Ponselle had been singing all the Santuzzas of the tour but was indisposed, so Rethberg was unexpectedly called into service. The loss of one more Ponselle interpretation is hardly mitigated by Rethberg's capable performance.

For many years Rethberg had successfully spanned an international repertory which included, in the Italian sphere, Maddalena, the *Trovatore* Leonora, and Amelia Grimaldi; she was the prime Aida of the house. But her forays into verismo territory had been of the gentler kind (Nedda, Mimi, Butterfly, Iris). She never undertook Tosca, and the Santuzza assignment remains an anomaly. (An even less likely combination is the broadcast pairing of *Cavalleria Rusticana* with *Hänsel und Gretel*—but then, a measure of violence taints *Hänsel* as well, if one remembers that oven). Papi conducts a taut, fast-paced performance. The 'Regina Coeli' is given a particularly rousing choral climax to which Rethberg contributes, but her 'Voi lo sapete' is merely serviceable. She is surprisingly adept at exchanging parlando epithets with Turiddu and manages a goodly amount of full, round tone in voicing her anguish. But her quiet pleas are more convincing than the anticlimactic curse—no wonder Turiddu was undeterred. So it goes, moments of finely spun tone (in the confrontation with Alfio) alternating with rather scratchy bursts of anger. Though one is again impressed by her overt commitment to the drama, Rethberg is not a gratifying shouter. Tenor Sydney Rayner is, however. The brutal behavior of Turiddu fits his vocal manner, and he pours out a steady volume of solid tone quite effectively in his farewell to Mamma, but without a dram of the sensuous charm which should pervade the offstage Siciliano. Irra Petina's piquant vocalism as Lola, Morelli's more than adequate Alfio, and Anna Kaskas' exceptionally sturdy Mamma Lucia are worthy enough contributions.

The broadcast season of the main company concluded a week later with Ponselle's farewell in *Carmen*. In all, there were eight airings of French opera—more than a third of the total and the high water mark of all broadcast seasons for Gallic tastes. On 20 March Jepson, Crooks, Bonelli, and Pinza had been heard in *Faust*; the week before had brought the first of the season's two airings of Ambroise Thomas' fragant period piece, *Mignon*. The departed Bori having relinquished her exclusive hold on the gentle gypsy, the role descended upon a trio of mezzos: Gladys Swarthout, Jennie Tourel, and in 1938, Risë Stevens.

Swarthout had played the minor pants part of Frederic to Bori's Mignon in the 1933 broadcast, but by now her sleek beauty had taken her to Hollywood (*Rose of the Rancho, Give Us This Night*, and *Ambush*), so her elevation to prime star status at the Metropolitan was preordained. An intelligent artist, with a voice of singularly distinctive and appealing timbre, the lovely singer was unfortunately deficient in temperament. She seemed unable to give her characterizations a strong dramatic profile (thus belying her birthplace—Deep Water, Missouri).

Mignon
13 March 1937

Mignon
Gladys Swarthout
Philine
Josephine Antoine
Wilhelm
Charles Hackett
Lothario
Ezio Pinza
Conductor
Wilfred Pelletier

Swarthout's Mignon is vocally fluent. 'Connais-tu le pays' benefits from an abundance of dusky tone, but 'C'est là que je voudrais vivre' is no cry of passionate longing. Glottal strokes mar the Styrienne, and the voice proves slightly unwieldly in rapid song. She startles with the size and security of the high B-flats as Mignon contemplates suicide. Still, her best moments come at the opera's end where her affinity for quiet, gentle song brings Lothario to himself again. Pinza's minstrel is a full-scale portrait. In the duets with Swarthout he lightens his tone ('Légères hirondelles' is a marvel of buoyant grace, while 'As-tu souffert?' is simply and movingly voiced). When Lothario echoes Mignon's desire to see the castle in flames, it takes Pinza only two words to convey all the crazed determination of his intent. The high point of his performance is the Berceuse, his tone perhaps excessively covered, but as dulcet as bass singing ever can be. Frederic's Gavotte is ill served by Olheim's swallowed tone and lack of agility.

As Philine, Sembrich pupil Josephine Antoine has plenty of agility, shaking off the actress' vapid attacks of coloratura with ease. 'Je suis Titania' is tiny in volume but pinpoint in accuracy (even in the treacherous staccato leaps), and the silvery glitter of her tone suits Thomas' Polonaise (though one remembers how Callas turned tinsel into zircon in her recording). Tenor Charles Hackett accomplishes a greater feat in his portrayal of Wilhelm Meister ("I always got stuck with *Mignon*,"[20] bewailed Richard Crooks, tenor of the Bori and Stevens broadcasts, of this thankless role). Hackett phrases elegantly throughout and provides just the sophisticated nuance which the opera requires for palatability. His 'Adieu Mignon! courage!'—highlighted by some ravishing mezza voce—provides the first moment of genuine sentiment of the afternoon. Hackett makes no big thing of the aria but turns it into a moment of affecting intimacy. In the final act the square outlines of 'Elle ne croyait pas' become poetic effusions in Hackett's throat: how skillfully he charts his way through the simple architecture of the piece, now pulling back, now pushing on, deftly preparing the firmly voiced climaxes of 'Ah! printemps!' Few tenors know how to paint a mood of quiet exaltation such as Hackett later achieves in his final apostrophe to Mignon.

The season's second broadcast of *Mignon* is a mirror image of the earlier performance, this time with a superbly idiomatic heroine. Though Pelletier is again at the helm of the Metropolitan forces, the ambiance has been purposely altered. When the Juilliard Foundation money was alloted to the desperate opera company in 1935, one of the conditions negotiated by John Erskine, president of the Juilliard School, was the establishment of a supplementary spring season to provide opportunities for young American singers ("occasionally aided by an experienced artist").[21] The prices were to be "popular," though the singers were not. Thus a four-week supplementary season, after the spring tour, was launched in May 1936. The radio audience heard three of these performances; the casts indicate how much the original intent of the season had been diluted. Castagna and Armand Tokatyan head the *Carmen* slate, though the Micaela (Natalie Bodanskaya, later called Bodanya) and Escamillo (Joseph Royer) were new to the Met. The comprimarios were all Met familiars. A week later *The Bartered Bride* was offered, the English translation supposedly providing more justification for the American portrayers of Czech folk customs; John Gurney, George Rasely, and Wilfred Engelman were all debutants who would remain with the senior company for several seasons, while Mario Chamlee and Louis d'Angelo were the "occasional" experienced artists. The Met balanced newcomers Rosa Tentoni (Aida), Royer, and Gurney with veterans Castagna, Rayner, and Cordon in Verdi's opera.

NBC was anxious to include the supplementary season in its series. (Never mind that they asked for the matinee starting time to be postponed until 2:30 so as not to conflict with the "National Farm and Home Hour," since daylight saving time would be in effect.)[22] At the end of four weeks, Ziegler was forced to report to "Eddie" a loss of $16,300 on the "Popular Season. . . . If we had not stopped when we did, but had [run] an additional week the season's loss would have exceeded the $25,000" of Juilliard financing.[23] But Bliss and Cravath were "delighted" with the supplementary season, and NBC remained excited about the next season's prospects. Vice-President Tuthill wrote to Ziegler:

In view of the fact that there seems to be considerable interest in the popular or supplementary season, which might logically lead to our finding a sponsor for broadcasting these performances, we would like to suggest that the agreement be worded as to grant us, in addition to the twenty performances to which we are entitled, ten additional performances . . . during the Supplementary Season.[24]

But the 1936–37 supplementary season remained at four weeks, and NBC had to be satisfied with four broadcasts: the entire enterprise concluded on 29 May with *Il Trovatore*, the performance notable as marking the transition from the mezzo to the soprano ranks for Rose Bampton. Her Leonora was buttressed by Castagna, Morelli, Gurney, and Arthur Carron.

From this second and final supplementary season three performances are preserved, two of them of substantial interest. In the 15 May broadcast of *Mignon* Jennie Tourel made her Metropolitan debut. Though not destined to become a Met "regular," her impact on the American musical scene would prove to be greater than that of many steady Met tenants. She came to the company with minimum advance promotion, hence her assignment to the popular-priced performances. Described by the broadcast announcer (not the ubiquitous Milton Cross) as the "young Canadian mezzo soprano" (she was touching thirty-seven years), Tourel had sung small roles with Mary Garden's Chicago Opera in 1930 and had been a leading artist of the Opéra Comique in Paris since 1933. Of Russian heritage, the soprano had studied in France, and (in contrast to Swarthout's tepid manner) she laces her performance with abundant Gallic esprit. A companion in French style is Léon Rothier whose pitch lapses and laborious line betray the heavy weight of too many years. But Armenian tenor Armand Tokatyan (Italian trained and a Met veteran since 1923) contributes a stylish Meister, and Antoine duplicates her Philine.

In the opening scene Tourel immediately establishes the changeability of Mignon's character: the darting rhythms of her refusal to dance contrast with the flowing melodic line of 'O Vierge, mon seul espoir.' In the recitative preceding her first-act aria one hears the occasionally unsettled quality of her low voice, but 'Connais-tu le pays' overflows with delicious *portamenti* and beautifully arched phrases ('C'est là que je voudrais vivre'). In her duet with Lothario she fairly prances, and unlike other Met Mignons, she even includes a little cadenza, hinting at her future Rossini speciality. Despite the excellence of her first act, one is unprepared for the searing heat of Tourel's portrayal in the second scene of act two. Tourel takes all the high options, including several high B-flats and a high C, singing with passion yet with perfect vocal and musical control. The audience bursts into applause at the abandon of her cry 'Dieu! je deviens folle de rage et de douleur!' Neither Swarthout nor Stevens (later on, in her 1943 broadcast under Beecham) comes near to matching the eloquence of Tourel in this scene, surely one of the great performances of the Metropolitan broadcasts. Tourel follows this with some touching phrases in the duet 'As-tu souffert?' Part of Tourel's uniqueness is her ability to sing intervals with exactitude; she clearly differentiates between the major and minor thirds of the duet, thereby producing a subtle and sustained pathos. Elsewhere her handling of chromatic or dissonant intervals constantly heightens the poignance of her delivery—unlike many opera singers, she doesn't need to resort to overt dramatic distortion to make her points. One is struck by the aptness of the voice for Mignon, particularly in its distinctive colorations: the sadness implicit in the mournful timbre of her low voice, the contrast of the honeyed tones of her upper voice, and the tart

Mignon
15 May 1937
Mignon
Jennie Tourel
Philine
Josephine Antoine
Wilhelm
Armand Tokatyan
Lothario
Léon Rothier
Conductor
Wilfred Pelletier

pungency of the middle range. Tourel closes the final trio with a high B, and the audience response is so enthusiastic that the announcer assures us "Miss Tourel must be very happy today for the fine ovation she's been given at her debut," adding with some amazement "here she comes again—people are really standing in the aisles and boxes applauding."

At her Metropolitan debut Tourel was already a magnificent artist, yet the peculiar repertory which would have been necessary for Tourel to attain prima donna status in opera never developed for her at the Metropolitan. During her four seasons at the Met (from 1936 through 1947) Lily Djanel and Risë Stevens sang the *Carmen* and remaining *Mignon* broadcasts. One additional broadcast in 1944 as Adalgisa completed her broadcast career. In it she showed how deftly she could handle this assignment, even as the effort confirmed how inappropriate and wasteful the demands of the big mezzo repertoire were for her.

A repeat (8 May 1937) of the previous season's English *Bartered Bride* replicates the cast with the exception of the leading soprano role of Marie, where debutante Muriel Dickson is replaced by Hilda Burke, veteran of two seasons with the regular company. The repeat is deserved, for the endearing work is given a capable performance, and the English translation by "Graham Jones" is quite intelligible. Lucielle Browning's Ludmila is mushy, while American Chamlee and Naples-born D'Angelo are exemplary in their idiomatic delivery. That the text should prove eminently singable is no surprise, for the translation is by Madeleine Marshall, author of the bible of American diction, but the juxtaposition of modern Americanisms ('Shucks' and 'What the heck') against the flavor of Czech rhythms and customs is a jarring note. Is full plot comprehension worth 'I know a honey with lots of money, I know a daisy, she'll drive you crazy'?

Pelletier's contribution, too, is equivocal; the generally fine ensemble is obtained at the expense of the comic spirit and élan with which the score abounds—possibly the prosaic tempo of the marriage contract duet is rooted in the desire to make intelligible the English translation. Returning to the Met after an absence of seven seasons, American tenor Mario Chamlee is an excellent Jenek (now converted to Hans by Miss Marshall). His easy assurance is contagious, and he fills the role with firmly centered tone of pleasing quality. The expansive line and tonal amplitude of his second-act aria confirm that Cavaradossi (his 1920 Met debut) and the Duke of Mantua had mutated into the Lohengrin and Walther of his seasons with the San Francisco Opera. (The Metropolitan stocked its roster with a superior vintage of American tenors in the thirties: Crooks, Kullman, Hackett, and among the finest of any nationality, Chamlee.) Hilda Burke, too, is unexpectedly fine, displaying a healthy lyric soprano of lovely quality—no soubrette intrusions for her in a role favored by the likes of Emmy Destinn and Elisabeth Rethberg.

As the matchless marriage broker, Louis d'Angelo demonstrates how well he knows his way around the Met stage which he first trod as Wagner in a 1917 *Faust* with Farrar and Caruso. His bass-baritone is rock solid in tone, though it lacks chiaroscuro; he never misses a comic point, but avoids the temptation of slapstick overplaying. 'Money makes the world go round' is delightfully broad (yet deft), but his first-act description of Vasek could be a bit more unctuous. In the hands of debutant George Rasely, the stuttering Vasek is merely a conventional buffoon, played for laughs. And Rasely gets them. Fortunately, he pulls back enough for the third-act 'I—I am nearly frantic,' but never inches near the humane conception of Jon Vickers ("I'm going to make you weep for him"[25]) when, forty years later, the Czech

The Bartered Bride
8 May 1937

Marie (Marenka)
Hilda Burke

Hans (Jenek)
Mario Chamlee

Wenzel (Vasek)
George Rasely

Kezal (Kecal)
Louis D'Angelo

Conductor
Wilfred Pelletier

Mario Chamlee as the Duke of Mantua in *Rigoletto*. Photography by Mishkin.

opera was next heard by the radio audience. The four-decade wait is inexplicable, as even this modest performance demonstrates.

The vein of opera in English was further mined in this spring season, but this time the ore was from American earth. Spurred by the twin prongs of the Juilliard Foundation money (American singers and American opera), the Metropolitan continued its tradition of premieres of native works. The subject matter of Walter Damrosch's *The Man Without a Country* was uniquely American as well. Edward Everett Hale's story of an American exile early in the nineteenth century had long intrigued conductor-composer Damrosch, whose Met associations went back to the very beginnings of the company when, while still in his twenties, he served as conductor during the German opera seasons of the 1880s. In 1912 the Met had produced his *Cyrano de Bergerac* with Frances Alda, Pasquale Amato, and Riccardo Martin. Since then he had become familiar to millions as the champion of music for the mass radio audience, and had served as music counselor for NBC. Thus the broadcast of his newest opera on 22 May 1937 was not unexpected. Though the Damrosch aura today has dissipated (his conducting was only serviceable, and the music appreciation racket has left a general disillusionment in its wake), at the time of the opera's premiere he was very much the grand old man of the music world—in 1935 the Metropolitan itself had honored him with a gala tribute to celebrate his fiftieth anniversary as a conductor.

The seventy-five-year-old Damrosch had conducted the opera's premiere, but Pelletier took over the remaining performances, including the broadcast. In the title role was English tenor Arthur Carron, but the other singing and speaking parts were largely filled by native singers, including Joseph Royer (Aaron Burr), John Gurney, George Rasely, and Donald Dickson. Appearing as Mary Rutledge was an unheralded debutante from St. Louis, a soprano whose name and fame would long outlast the Damrosch opus—Helen Traubel.

The part had been written with Traubel in mind. According to the soprano, Damrosch, conducting a concert in St. Louis with the then unknown Traubel as soloist, had told her "I did not know there was such a voice as yours in the world." Though his new opera had no female voice in it, Damrosch asserted "I shall go back to New York and rewrite the whole work—if you will consent to sing the lead in it."[26] Kolodin would have it that Damrosch "settled for"[27] Traubel after having failed to interest half a dozen better-known sopranos. Whatever the genesis of the role, Traubel was the clear winner in terms of critical response which, even so, was overly kind to the septuagenarian composer. Damrosch's reliance on spoken dialogue in the manner of an opéra comique prescribed set musical forms rather than dynamic continuity; the result was a work overladen with genre pieces. Sailor choruses in a Gilbert and Sullivan manner abound, and nineteenth-century salon songs of sentiment—solos for the sailors—crowd the opening of the final act at precisely the point where the drama should crystallize. The story line carried a built-in dramatic straitjacket since antihero Lieutenant of Marines Philip Nolan's fate is to wander from ship to ship, apart from all former friends ('something like the Flying Dutchman,' as one character puts it), in return for having supported Aaron Burr in his projected invasion of Mexico. Librettist Arthur Guiterman attempted to evade the problem with the reentrance of Mary Rutledge on board ship, a feat comparable in bizarrerie to conservative papa Germont's sudden appearance at Flora's gambling party in *Traviata*. Moreover, Damrosch seems unable to solve the problem of fusing melodic outpourings with continuity of orchestral texture—the latter is invariably

The Man Without a Country
22 May 1937

Mary
Helen Traubel
Philip
Arthur Carron
Aaron Burr
Joseph Royer
Morgan
John Gurney
Conductor
Wilfred Pelletier

merely supportive and does little musically to augment the expression of the text. He favors solo wind figurations to blend the spoken dialogue into the *melodrama* form. When the composer's eclectic palette turns from the simulation of sailors' ditties and four-square patriotic songs (he gives the piccolo a real workout in act three), it is his Wagnerian heritage which looms largest. The noble breadth of Wotan's Farewell hovers over Burr's act-one address, as he summons images of the Mississippi's expanses, and the aria 'On to California' (impressively declaimed by Joseph Royer with a voice of George London-like opulence). The imposing prelude to the second act relies upon the sonorities of a hero's Rhine Journey, while the low brass and wind tangles of Alberich's netherland underlie the despair of Nolan's final lament for 'My own, my native land.' Knowing so well the gamut of operatic convention, Damrosch does not neglect to close the second act with a full-scale, sombre largo concertato after Nolan's sentence is pronounced (*Tosca*-like drums accompany his departure from the court-martial). Damrosch pens a few moving passages: the duet for Mary and Nolan in act one has a sturdy grandeur to it, and Mary's apotheosis has some gloriously expansive lines for Traubel to exploit. The soprano summed up the work as "fairly good though far from great."[28]

Both Traubel and tenor Arthur Carron offer some excellent vocalism; a sense of belief in their characters makes their scenes quite persuasive. The burly English tenor (Traubel insists her only memory of the occasion is "that my tenor was a man much smaller than I"[29]—only Melchior would remedy that) had won the "Metropolitan Auditions of the Air" in 1936 and made his debut as Canio in the first spring season. He repeated the role with the main company the following year and continued to sing leading dramatic parts at the Met for a decade. Years of singing opera in English at Sadlers Wells and Covent Garden accounts for the intelligibility and beauty of his diction, while the clarion brightness and security of his robust tenor make for an attractive man without a country.

In the opening act Traubel lightly deploys her mellow instrument until Mary's warning to Philip of treason calls forth a steady column of impressive tone, all of a color throughout the entire range. Even in this debut season, a hint of pull on a few top tones as well as a curious delayed attack (as though the density of voice requires time to move it into place) mark her singing. In most of the second act Mary is forced to hide behind a pillar, but the third act is hers. When Traubel reaches the big moments of the final act, her tonal splendor frees itself; the high tessitura is fully conquered and the topmost notes are lovely. In her address to Commodore Decatur the great voice reveals itself as Mary convincingly pleads for Nolan. It is a powerful moment, eclipsed only by Traubel's soaring phrases in the closing measures of the opera after Nolan's death. Her final high B is perfectly floated ('Dream, dream' she adjures) while the undulating Wagnerian string figurations suggest her future domain.

Though the two spring seasons brought several major voices to the fore, the project was not renewed—money was still a problem. But the remedy was already at hand. Wagner had become box office.

René Maison as Lohengrin.

CHAPTER ELEVEN

1936–40
The German Wing

Over the hundred years of the Metropolitan chronicle, several periods are recognized as benchmarks of performance history.

The elegant vocalism of the De Reszkes, Melba, Eames, Nordica, Sembrich, and Plançon turned the Mauve Decade into a golden age of vocal mastery. The aureate throat of Caruso and the personal magnetism of Farrar blazoned the idea of 'opera star' into America's consciousness in the first decades of the twentieth century. Similarly, the brief period of Flagstad and Melchior's joint supremacy in the Wagner operas during the mid and late 1930s marks a concurrence of artists and repertory which finds no equal within memory. Nor was the supremacy confined to the Nordic duo, for although they were the first of their kind, the Wagnerian ranks swelled with worthy contenders: Lawrence, Lehmann and Rethberg, Branzell and Thorborg, Schorr, Hofmann and List (and hope for the forties burgeoned with the late entry of Traubel and Kipnis). Rather than the isolated fragments of studio recordings of earlier ages, a cluster of complete live performances from 1936 through 1940 preserves the indisputable splendor of the modern age of Wagner singing.

During the first two years of opera broadcasts, the weekday afternoon Wagner series had provided the luxury of complete *Ring* cycles, but two long decades would elapse before the tetralogy would be aired again. The only other opportunity for the radio audience to penetrate Wagner's complex mythology at its genesis was the 3 April 1937 broadcast from Boston of *Das Rheingold*. Bodanzky's lovingly laid out E-flat major flow leads us into a masterful reading of the prologue to the *Ring*. In this tangled world of gnomes, giants, and gods it is the latter who appropriately scale the heights of vocalism and characterization. Schorr and Branzell are commanding monarchs with maximum vocal splendor, but René Maison's incandescent Loge truly animates the performance. His full-throated vocalism with its curiously Tauber-like coloration never falters, sending shafts of light into the dark-hued sonority of his colleagues. More important, he slips in and out of the chameleon poses of the god of fire with utmost ease: 'Steal the ring,' he suggests to Wotan in bitter accents, or he covers his tone to taunt the aging gods deprived of Freia's golden apples. Now he overmatches Alberich in oily craft as he transforms him from dragon to toad; now he whispers insidiously to Fasolt to regain the ring from brother Fafner; and finally, as

Das Rheingold
3 April 1937

Freia
Dorothee Manski
Fricka
Karin Branzell
Erda
Doris Doe
Loge
René Maison
Wotan
Friedrich Schorr
Alberich
Eduard Habich
Mime
Karl Laufkoetter
Conductor
Artur Bodanzky

145

the gods march over the rainbow bridge on their way to their doom, he transforms his cynical musings into the clarion tones of a Heldentenor in response to the Rhinemaidens' lament.

The *Rheingold* Wotan offers Schorr fewer opportunities to employ his noble song than the rest of the trilogy, and truth to tell, the high Fs and G-flats of the role are negotiated with evident strain. But he is exceptionally big-and-bright-toned in his responses to Fasolt (Norman Cordon's first effort; the ringing resonance of his forward placement contrasts with List's throaty Teutonic weight). More than Schorr, Karin Branzell as the complaining consort of Wotan reaches Maison's stature. What spouse could harbor regret as Branzell, in alluring tones, soothes the troubled Wotan after the loss of the ring? The opening scene, too, is an endless outpouring of rich song by her seamless voice; to be a convincing shrew (and she is) and maintain that current of legato is not only oxymoronic but awesome. She surprises by turning delightfully coquettish when Fricka imagines the gold of the Rhine adorning her person and cajoles Wotan into seeking it. Her softly voiced and poignant cries of 'Wehe' at the gods' loss of youth are the finest moments of this convincing musico-dramatic portrait.

Beside these deities the Erda of Doris Doe is small change, indeed. Though vocally secure and of fittingly sombre timbre, her vocal size turns the earth mother into a minigoddess. Nor does Huehn's acceptable Donner or Clemens' nasal Froh enhance the aura of the gods. Laufkoetter and Habich as Mime and Alberich are experienced character singers who make their points with conviction, the baritone in fact contributing his finest broadcast. By the time Habich reaches the all-important curse which haunts the remainder of the cycle, his tone has become rather threadbare, but his horrible shriek as the ring is torn from his finger and his wild laughter are first-rank opera trivia. Throughout the lengthy single act, Bodanzky maintains a well-integrated conception, notable for the sense of spontaneous interplay between the disparate characters of the upper and under worlds.

Though no complete *Ring* would be broadcast until 1950–51, the 1936–37 season also included *Walküre* and *Siegfried*. No record remains of the former opera (Lehmann, Lawrence, Thorborg, Melchior, Schorr, List) but *Siegfried* may be heard in excellent sound. On this occasion the radio audience first heard the *Siegfried* Brünnhilde of Flagstad, and of even greater importance, the aircheck preserves Melchior's youthful Siegfried (no trace remains of the earlier airings of 1932 and 1933). A temporary cooling of their personal relationship prevented the pairing of Flagstad and Melchior in the 1938 *Siegfried*, the last broadcast of the opera until after Melchior's departure from the Met.

On the 30 January 1937 broadcast Laufkoetter, Habich, and List are the familiar inhabitants of the nether world while Schorr's Wotan seeks wisdom from a new Erda, the Swedish contralto, Kerstin Thorborg. She was destined to become a worthy and longtime tenant in the Wagnerian galaxy of the Metropolitan. Thorborg is no wooly-voiced quaker but the possessor of a bright-edged instrument which retains color throughout the entire range. For her climactic top voice she barters an occasional glimmer of unfocused tone in the lower middle range. Though insufficiently cavernous in timbre for the timeless earth goddess, her Erda suffers no lack of authority. Laufkoetter, too, is a knowing Mime, avoiding the extremes of whining complaint but sufficiently unctuous upon demand. List makes a rather too cultivated Fafner—his dragon neither spits venom nor belches forth ugly tone. The well-oiled machinery of Bodanzky's orchestra moves effortlessly through the difficult

Siegfried
30 January 1937
Brünnhilde
Kirsten Flagstad
Forest Bird
Stella Andreva
Erda
Kerstin Thorborg
Siegfried
Lauritz Melchior
Mime
Karl Laufkoetter
Wanderer
Friedrich Schorr
Alberich
Eduard Habich
Fafner
Emanuel List
Conductor
Artur Bodanzky

score; the low brass are wonderfully sonorous in the atmospheric prelude to act two, a justly scaled and paced reading by the conductor which contrasts with the energy and rhythmic directness of the prelude to the final act.

As the Wanderer, Schorr is at the peak of his form. No previous broadcast has fully revealed the tonal splendor which he summons on this occasion. When he enters to pose his three questions to Mime, the breadth and sweetness of his tone pierce the gloom of the dwarf's world—a brighter tonal sheen is particularly apparent in his naming of Valhalla as the home of the gods. In previous broadcasts the magnificence of Schorr's organ has been partially dimmed by a slight dullness of timbre, but throughout this performance the tonal glint is ravishing. Nor does his vocal strength wane in the Wanderer's peroration to Erda in act three; the high Fs are full and free (*pace* Witherspoon) and the dark low voice is vibrantly resonant. In the most stentorian moments Thorborg and Schorr never abandon the ways of song. The ensuing colloquy of Melchior and Schorr is even more thrilling—like two giants spurred on in vocal combat, they send out ever-increasing waves of tone.

The role of Siegfried may well have been Melchior's finest achievement. One anticipates his vocal mastery, but the development of character throughout the opera is equally riveting (by now the stereotype of Melchior as a disinterested or at best casual interpreter surely must be discarded). The youthful brashness of Siegfried is marvelously captured in the staccato recitatives with Mime in act one, while his unrestrained energy and high spirit enliven the Forging Song. Melchior is a little slow to hit his stride, and the top squeeze looms more prominently than usual in the opening episodes; but soon the tenor ranges over the angular phrases with ease and a cumulative brio. Only Melchior has been able to conquer the difficulties of the piece so as to be able to convey the youth's exhilaration. What a contrast is the awakening of sentiment in Siegfried during the Forest Murmurs scene as his thoughts turn to his unknown father and mother—delicacy of tone and variety of color (including a particularly lovely series of head tones) abound. Nowhere is Melchior's sensitivity more manifest than in this introspective scene. No baritonal mix clouds his boyish inquiries to the Forest Bird (Stella Andreva with an avian timbre, but technically rather sticky). Melchior's accuracy of pitch and attack in the fleet passages is striking—he flashes up to the top voice with the easy brilliance of a silver trumpet. After killing the dragon, new veiled colors of sorrow suggest his loneliness. As he approaches Brünnhilde's rock, he first brings into play his baritonal sonority and suggests the growing maturity of the hero: the boy's innocence disappears as he pursues a manly quest. In the discovery scene his conception reaches an appropriate climax; 'Erwache!' is the command of a mature and determined man, and as he kisses the sleeping woman, he voices 'sterben' in a climactic rush of tone. Then, with noble declamation, he calms Brünnhilde's terror. Melchior's Siegfried is a hero worthy of his prize.

No composer has built into the initial appearance of an operatic heroine a greater expectancy than we feel for the sleeping Brünnhilde. As if to compensate for the brevity of the role, Wagner strewed the part with vocal challenges that have intimidated even the best of dramatic sopranos. One can imagine the excitement of the radio audience as it awaited the first 'Heil dir' from the still-fresh throat of Flagstad—I felt it myself on first hearing these records. She abjures grandiloquence; no sense of gesture impels her greeting, but rather the naturalness of awakening to an everyday dawn. 'Heil dir, Sonne!' is quite light-toned, lovely, almost virginal, and followed by a slightly broader 'Heil dir, Licht!'; a hint of slumber coddles the tones of

Lauritz Melchior as Siegfried.

'Lang war mein Schlaf.' That first high C is child's play. The tone is kept buoyant throughout the entire scene, for no heavy resonances weight it down—and the legato is clean. The sounds are not warmly sensuous—she addresses Siegfried more as a companion than with the ecstasy due a lover—but her ascent into the upper voice is amazing for ease and fullness of tone. Soon her singing becomes more intimate. As she speaks of Sieglinde the conception is especially lovely, for the ease of her vocal production (in spite of abundant size) allows a girlish charm to surface. She offers Italian bel canto filtered by a Norse reticence (perhaps after all she could have sung Norma—but then again, her trills are no more than half-shakes). Flagstad shows little terror at Melchior's embrace and moves naturally to accept him as a 'treasure of the world' in a flow of gentle legato and a light, glancing high C. Until the very end the reading is unusually youthful in concept, tonal color, and weight; only when hero and bride join voices does her voice expand into a broad column of tone, and the high Bs ring out brilliantly before the two move in unison down to the concluding C. *Sun* critic W. H. Henderson's comparison of Flagstad with Nellie Melba for freedom of production and liberality of voice does not seem at all bizarre on this afternoon.

Almost two years later (10 December 1938), Flagstad sang her only other *Siegfried* broadcast. Schorr is the lone cast holdover. Erich Witte (Mime), Adolf Vogel (Alberich), and Carl Hartmann (Siegfried) are names of little repute or longevity in the Wagner chronicles of the Met, while Kaskas (Erda) and Cordon (Fafner), though longer in years, are modest in distinction. On paper the performance doesn't seem calculated to sustain the legend of Wagner performance of the prewar years. This cynicism was perhaps shared by those anonymous recorders for the future since only the final scene (beginning at Flagstad's entrance) has come to light.

Two days after the broadcast, Flagstad would celebrate the twenty-fifth anniversary of her Norwegian debut with a gala *Götterdämmerung* at the Metropolitan, again partnered by Hartmann. According to Edwin McArthur, Flagstad's accompanist and conductor in embryo, Melchior's absence was specifically prescribed by the prima donna—a minor tiff over "phony" publicity had grown into a tempest which would eventually abate.[1] Hartmann proves to be a capable representative of the guttural school of Heldentenor; at least his instrument has adequate heft and top. Flagstad remains a monumental figure, yet the contrast to her 1937 portrayal is marked. Now the colors of autumn have overspread the vernal freshness of two years earlier. This Brünnhilde has slept longer, and the vocal gears shift more slowly. The darker tonal mix (chalumeau-oboe) of the later years is the dominant timbre throughout the entire scene—it is immediately offered in her tonally dense 'Heil dir, Sonne!' The density serves well the weary sadness of Brünnhilde's regret for her lost vocation, and many will prefer the noble laying out of rich tone to the easy flow of the earlier portrayal. Certainly her rebuff of Siegfried's attempted embrace is dramatically more apt. Yet the bane of workmanlike effort mixes curiously with her more overt involvement. The middle low voice is not quite so steady in the long 'Ewig' phrases, and a few quick top tones are more acrid than yet heard from Flagstad's throat. Of course, even with momentary blemishes Flagstad is still nonpareil.

We can trace the Flagstad career during the years between these two portrayals in a series of broadcasts as Elsa, Kundry, and Isolde.

Flagstad portrayed Elsa in two consecutive broadcast seasons, the first on 27 March 1937. The princess of Brabant requires youthful song, and happily, we find Flagstad in comparable vocal form to the first *Siegfried* Brünnhilde (two months

Siegfried
10 December 1938

Brünnhilde
Kirsten Flagstad

Forest Bird
Natalie Bodanya

Erda
Anna Kaskas

Siegfried
Carl Hartmann

Mime
Erich Witte

Wanderer
Friedrich Schorr

Alberich
Adolf Vogel

Fafner
Norman Cordon

Conductor
Artur Bodanzky

Lohengrin
27 March 1937
Elsa
Kirsten Flagstad
Ortrud
Karin Branzell
Lohengrin
René Maison
Telramund
Julius Huehn
King Henry
Ludwig Hofmann
Conductor
Maurice Abravanel

before this Elsa); that is, her tones are completely unfettered throughout the entire range, and the resonances are kept as high as possible considering the natural density of the voice. The English horn timbre is banished in favor of a blend of the clarino register of the clarinet and oboe. Flagstad's voice inevitably calls forth instrumental similes, not only because of its unique timbre, but also because of her approach to song—essentially a classic ideal wherein the word governs neither individual rhythms nor phrase shapes. Hence her special aptitude for the Wagner operas. There her voice becomes part of the complex orchestral texture, and her vocal amplitude enables her to achieve the composer's ideal of endless melody or motivic interplay between voice and instruments. Such an approach inevitably is less overtly dramatic, and the realization of character is distanced, sometimes to positive effect, as in the great heroic roles whose larger-than-life quality is thereby enhanced (though this is by no means the only way to play them).

In the more lifelike roles of the early romantic operas, however, her classical reticence, in combination with sheer weight of voice, can be a drawback. Purely as vocalism this Elsa is wondrous to the ear, but it is deficient in convincing characterization. In the dream aria her tone is full, yet gentle, and she pulls back delightfully for 'Mein Aug' ist zugefallen, ich sank in süssen Schlaf,' but she is certainly not *schwärmerisch* (as Wagner marked 'Er soll mein Streiter sein'); hers is no dreamlike musing—she confidently expects her knight to appear. Flagstad mounts easily to the top A-flats and seems equally unconcerned about Elsa's plight. But her plea to the king takes on a lovely bright coloration (as though wakened to life) and her capitulation to Lohengrin ('Dir geb' ich alles, was ich bin') is heartfelt enough. She is more convincing in the second act where, though 'Euch Lüften' is not truly *piano*, a slight laziness in the legato serves well enough as substitute, and 'Wollt Kühlung nun gewähren' provokes admirable and liquid spin in her tone. 'Du Ärmste kannst wohl,' with its easy flow and marked feeling, is the loveliest of moments, and she is equally fine as the crowning phrases of 'Es gibt ein Glück' approach—by now the soprano seems more fully engaged in the drama, as well she might when confronting the magisterial Ortrud of Karin Branzell.

The Swedish contralto's portrayal is the jewel of the afternoon, for Branzell excels in every facet of operatic art. The instrument itself is of the richest coloration, splendid in size but with none of the register breaks which mar the efforts of so many big-voiced mezzos—and her technique is impeccable. Much of this may have been nature's gift. Not so her ability to portray character by voice alone while maintaining musical integrity. The lofty intent of her artistry is most evident when the diabolical Ortrud invokes the gods for vengeance. Usually 'Entweihte Götter!' with its blazing top notes, is converted into a display piece—Branzell gives us the vocal excitement but somehow manages not to wrench it out of the drama's context. But then, her entire performance is full of memorable moments: the marcato top tones of 'Gib hier mir Macht' are precisely struck and contrast with the *subito piano* at 'mein Seherauge' (how she maintains Ortrud's intensity even in the quietest moments); her two cries of 'Elsa' when she first attracts her attention might have been written 'Wehe,' so full of woe are they; she tells Elsa 'O, du bist glücklich' in the loveliest of tones and with an expressive *portamento*. Everywhere she gives Flagstad lessons in legato by a lava flow of tone. Surely no one has negotiated the full-voiced turn and jagged sixteenth-note rhythm of 'das Leben nur' with her exactitude. And Flagstad does take on new life in this scene, joining Branzell in pouring out tones of notable energy and amplitude.

The two vocal giants are heard again a year later in the *Lohengrin* broadcast of 19 February 1938, but this time only the courtyard scene is preserved. American baritone Julius Huehn is Telramund in both performances. Part of the Juilliard connection, Huehn was being groomed as the Schorr alternative, and he quickly advanced from the *Lohengrin* Herald of his debut season to center stage as Ortrud's malleable spouse. The voice is a splendid one, darkly rich and fruity but laced with a glint of bright metal. At least that is the voice heard in the 1937 performance where the burly tone seems just right for Telramund. A year later the voice has further darkened (too soon), but the dramatic profile is more sharply etched, both in the pointing up of individual words and in overall conception. If anything, Branzell, too, is more immersed in her role—her anger is acerbic ('kleinstes Glied entrissen nur'), her top voice totally unconstrained. Thus the scene for Telramund and Ortrud registers a step-up in dramatic temperature from the previous year. Branzell reaches a performance peak in 'O, du bist glücklich'; she fills her tone with yearning and caps the passage with a marvelously dark and full-toned high A-sharp. In 'Euch Lüften' Flagstad introduces more *Luftpausen* ('in—Liebe') to expressive effect. She seldom attempts a *pianissimo* dynamic throughout the entire scene (in 1937 there were frequent "attempts") and the overall vocal coloration is now darker; her approach to 'Es gibt ein Glück' holds less tenderness. But the Flagstad voice in itself is as free and impressive as remembered.

In 1938 Flagstad came to the bridal chamber with Melchior, but the 1937 performance offers the rare opportunity to hear René Maison in another Wagner role. During these years the Belgian tenor fought a defensive battle against overly high tessitura; on occasion he feels obliged to substitute declamation for the prescribed legato (in the Farewell to the Swan). That debit cannot negate his sensitive musicianship and ability to characterize with the voice. His vocal timbre is exceptionally attractive on this occasion (if only one can remember not to expect the volume and generous pacing of Melchior, Maison seems a splendid Wagnerian). He has plenty of voice to quell the raging Ortrud and Elsa at the end of act two (the women simulate a Teutonic *Gioconda* duet in their outpourings of angry tone). Maison makes 'In deiner Hand' a heartfelt plea, though his built-in sob becomes annoying, and he does have difficulty in controlling his mezza voce in the higher range ('Heil dir'). At his best in the tender intimacy of the bridal chamber duet, his manner infects Flagstad, who responds with a much gentler voicing of Elsa's music. But he obviously feels so much more than she as they alternately exclaim 'Fühl' ich so süss mich entbrennen'—he overtly caresses, she hardly fondles, the text. But her tone is as lovely and virginal as ever it can be ('Ist dies nur Liebe?') until the excitement of discovery propels her to a superb high B ('Wie deine Art?'). 'In fernem Land' becomes a genuine narrative as Maison begins almost casually in soft, mysterious tones which gradually grow in size; a songlike arch (the top As are there) and Helden power provide an imposing climax as Lohengrin names Parsifal his father. Though not perfect vocally, the conception sustains both interest and regard. And by this time in the performance the reprise of the swan song can be (and is) neatly vocalized.

Arnold Gabor's Heerrufer begins without sufficient heraldic ring, but improves. Ludwig Hofmann is properly monarchical, commanding in manner with plenty of sizable black tone and skill in declamation (though Abravanel's plodding tempo for the act-one prayer makes heavy going even for Hofmann). Overall the orchestral playing has more rough edges than usual (ragged attacks in the low strings and overemphasis in marcato passages) under Abravanel's vigorous leadership. He

Lohengrin
19 February 1938
Elsa
Kirsten Flagstad
Ortrud
Karin Branzell
Lohengrin
Lauritz Melchior
Telramund
Julius Huehn
King Henry
Ludwig Hofmann
Conductor
Maurice Abravanel

takes the act-three prelude at a pace a few notches beyond *sehr lebhaft*. Soon enough Abravanel will move on to (for him) more fertile symphonic fields (plus Broadway excursions) and his duties will pass to one who will have considerably greater impact on opera at the Metropolitan—Erich Leinsdorf.

In the meantime Bodanzky remained in control of the German wing, and Flagstad continued to attract sold-out houses. At the end of the 1938 tour the company returned to New York for three Wagner performances during Easter week. Flagstad and Melchior heroically appeared in two *Parsifals* and *Tristan* in the space of seventy-two hours. Though the radio season had ended a month earlier, both the Good Friday matinee of *Parsifal* on 15 April and the *Tristan* matinee of 16 April were broadcast.

Earlier in the season Elsa's curiosity had cost Flagstad the son of Parsifal, but now it is the guileless fool himself who resists the temptation of her Kundry. The *Parsifal* recording preserves the only "live" memento of Flagstad and Melchior in these roles; in fact, the 1938 airing is the only Met broadcast of the liturgical drama over a two-decade span (1933–1952). The audio quality is decidedly inferior, but these noisy, worn grooves contain a performance never to be equaled in later broadcast history (at least as regards the focal pair). Bodanzky's penchant for movement is a boon to this opera; his pacing and the easy fluidity of the orchestral playing suggest the everlasting rather than the interminable. (Leinsdorf conducted act two to enable Bodansky to rest; he had unexpectedly been assigned the 13 April *Parsifal* when Bodanzky's doctor advised him not to conduct. Leinsdorf recounts that the opera had been "rehearsed a bit more than the general repertoire,"[2] as is evident in the Good Friday broadcast.)

Our three peerless Wagnerians (Flagstad, Melchior, and Schorr) are at the peak of their vocal form, Gabor provides a sturdy, uncaricatured Klingsor, and Cordon is properly sepulchral as the entombed Titurel. Only List as Gurnemanz disappoints. His vocal weight is always impressive, but for much of the performance each weary tone seems wrenched by force from his throat—legato and line are in short supply. Fortunately when he reaches the Good Friday spell, he achieves a respectable tonal steadiness and line to complement his rich timbre.

The relatively low tessitura of Amfortas serves the aging Schorr well, and his several scenes are impeccably done. The serenity of his initial appearance gives way to a passionate outpouring of perfectly focused tone as he seeks relief in God's mercy—his cries of 'Erbarmen!' are heart-rending in their unique union of beauty and feeling. Though Schorr does not overtly parade the suffering of the wounded Amfortas in realistic fashion, when the Grail is revealed in act one he miraculously contrives to entwine vocal sweetness with bodily pain in a manner suggestively masochistic.

In temperament and physique, nature would seem to have intended neither Flagstad for the hag-turned-temptress nor Melchior for the spritely, guileless fool. Too much restraint, indeed, veils Flagstad's depiction of the wild, possessed Kundry of the early scenes. Beyond a slight hollowness of tone, she makes little attempt to modify her healthy sound or place it at the service of character portrayal—she *will* sing, and few if any evidences of terror or misery are wrenched from her. Kundry's prescribed cries are modestly polite. Even when Klingsor compels her to entrap Parsifal (as she had long before seduced Amfortas), Flagstad is too much in control of her tone, and thus of herself. One must admire the refulgent timbre of her middle and low voice as she bewails her part in the deception, but thus far this has not been the

Parsifal
15 April 1938

Kundry
Kirsten Flagstad

Parsifal
Lauritz Melchior

Amfortas
Friedrich Schorr

Gurnemanz
Emanuel List

Titurel
Norman Cordon

Conductor
Artur Bodanzky
Erich Leinsdorf

most reassuring introduction to a great Kundry. The second-act temptress is the auditory bulk of the role, however, and though that assignment, too, is unlikely for this most heroic of Wagnerian goddesses, Flagstad has a surprise in store for us. The first notes which Parsifal hears are suffused with a soft, girlish glow, like the ravishing warmth of a low flute, while the phrases are languorously spun out in an easy, natural flow. 'Ich sah das Kind' is a fascinating web of subtly varied lines and gently flowing tone. This is a Flagstad almost never encountered; she has left off her architectonic manner—where she is wont to manipulate her magnificent instrument like a mighty pipe organ, pulling out stops in block fashion in response to some grand schema—in favor of a seductive fluency of tone and line. And thus, though Parsifal himself may resist, Flagstad conquers the role. Her wordplay is also uncharacteristically expressive, particularly in the phrases preceding the kiss. 'Amfortas! die Wunde!' cries Melchior in powerful tones, the dark baritonal timbre which he employs throughout most of the role mixed momentarily with a thrust of bright color. The vocal squeeze in his production provides a built-in semblance of pain which is most effective in this scene. Kundry's pleas become increasingly urgent, and now Flagstad gradually returns to a more heroic mold, her voice gaining in power and thrust. Unlike most soprano interpreters of the role, she has all the solidity of tone in the lower mezzo range (where so much of the role lies), but in contrast to struggling mezzo Kundrys (who must rely on realistic shrieks for the high B-flats and Bs which pepper the end of act two), Flagstad repeatedly strikes these notes like clarion bells. All the wild exultation of Kundry's outbursts comes over. As Kundry recalls her laughter at the Saviour ('und lachte'), the fearsome intervallic leap is dead center on the mark; the moment is dramatically chilling while her vocal prowess thrills, as does the powerful shaft of tone on the final high B when Kundry calls on Klingsor to claim Parsifal.

Melchior is magnificent as he seizes the spear and vanquishes Klingsor. He remains nobly eloquent in the last act (beginning the narration of his wanderings in tones almost as dark as List's), and thereafter he constantly varies timbre and mood. His tones turn cloudy as he baptizes Kundry, but they brim with poetic wonder as he views nature's beauty during the Good Friday Spell. And now Schorr and Melchior provide the capstone of the performance. Again Schorr eschews wrenching despair in favor of sincerity as he pleads for death in tones so firm, so richly colored, so bound in peerless legato, that only Melchior's noble response could suffice. The tenor's great bursts of steady tone bring the opera to an ecstatic close.

Less than twenty-four hours later, Flagstad was again on stage summoning Tristan to her, scheming so that the two reluctant lovers might never reach Cornwall's coast. The craze for Wagner-cum-Flagstad reached its height in the multiple broadcasts of *Tristan* from 1937 through 1939, when the Flagstad Isolde was aired no less than five times during three seasons. She was partnered by Melchior on all occasions but was served alternately by Thorborg, Wettergren, and Branzell, while Huehn and Hofmann gave way to Herbert Janssen and List in the later years. Three of these performances remain to us; the first, dating from 2 January 1937, is complete except for the act-one prelude (and the usual Met cuts).

Though the 1935 Isolde prepares one for the gentle repose of Flagstad's conception, even so her first-act Isolde seems disconcertingly detached in this later broadcast. Perhaps she is not in quite as prime vocal condition, for the column of breath is less steady, especially in *piano* passages where the tone is rather white and colorless. The broad leaps of the curse are firmly delivered, however, though her demand for vengeance ('Rache für Morold') is curiously subdued. Throughout, one

Tristan und Isolde
2 January 1937

Isolde
Kirsten Flagstad
Brangäne
Kerstin Thorborg
Tristan
Lauritz Melchior
Kurvenal
Julius Huehn
Marke
Ludwig Hofmann
Conductor
Artur Bodanzky

regrets the absence of the written *portamenti*—those which are applied are quite graceless. After this disappointing first act, the lovely tonal color and shapely phrasing of act two are particularly welcome. And how she rides the tremendous climax just before Tristan arrives ('dass hell sie dorten leuchte')! But it is Bodanzky alone who provides the requisite agitation when Isolde impatiently demands that the signal for Tristan be given. In the love duet Flagstad's phrases become increasingly heartfelt (one notes her pause before 'Liebe' at the beginning of 'O sink' hernieder')—she is now more a match for the matchless Melchior, whose performance is entirely sentient. More than ever one is impressed by his musicality, the accuracy of dynamics, his plastic sense of phrase in response to dramatic intent.

Both Thorborg and Hofmann are his worthy colleagues in all these matters. In this first of her eight broadcast Brangänes, Thorborg's voice is at its most plangent; her solid, rich tones, full of commitment as she shares Isolde's predicament in act one, are appropriately pregnant in the warning of act two. Hofmann makes melodic song of Marke's monologue, the sympathetic quality of his tone and legato removing any feeling of longwindedness. No wonder Melchior is moved to respond with a depth of feeling notable even for him. Huehn is a pedestrian Kurvenal in the opening act. Though he contributes some lovely soft phrases as he tends the wounded Tristan, a certain vocal crudity intrudes—the difference between Schorr's inner sympathy and Huehn's overt voicing of 'der wonnige Mann' defines the distance the young American must travel before he becomes a worthy partner to his senior colleagues. Rather it is Hofmann's bass which takes on the typical Schorr tonal sweetness at Tristan's death, and Flagstad (in spite of what appears to be an underpitch concluding 'Lust') conjures a Liebestod this time more expressively shaped in word and tone. We can sense the play of her imagination ('die so wundervoll und leise') as well as the poise of her vocalism.

Pursuing the Flagstad Isolde in time, we turn again to the postseason performances of 1938 when the matinee Tristan followed hard upon the previous day's broadcast of *Parsifal*. Undaunted by the marathon of three performances in four days, Flagstad offers up her finest Isolde broadcast of the 1930s. From her very first phrase one senses a greater degree of involvement. 'Sag', wo sind wir?' she asks in wonder and an uncharacteristic anger invades 'Nimmermehr! Nicht heut', noch morgen' as Isolde assures Brangäne she will never set foot on Cornwall. Throughout the opening scene, more rhythmic impulse invades the interrogative phrases, and when Brangäne brings Tristan's refusal, Flagstad's voice is momentarily sheathed in steel. Simple repetitions of phrase are heightened by a step-up in energy ('auf stolzem Schiff'— 'von hohem Bord'). Expressive effects which previously were merely granted a nodding acquaintance are now fully acknowledged: the intimate *piano* of 'Für tiefstes Weh' remains, but the commitment is deeper; the vowels of 'Der Tod nun sag' ihr Dank!' are more beautifully colored. She is in her most resplendent vocal form, the tone a shade more dense (now the girlish whiteness has given way to a ravishing, womanly timbre) while the legato flow has swelled. In the second act the entire Frau Minne section is set forth in broad phrases of impressive weight and burnished color. But the most treasurable gain occurs in the love duet where, at last, Flagstad's echoing phrases move in the same trancelike languor which informs Melchior's phrasing ('löse von der Welt mich los!'—'heil'ger Dämmrung'). She harnesses the unvaried motoric pace of her syllabic delivery so that not only the text but also the intent of 'Lass mich sterben' and 'Nie erwachen' is conveyed. And Melchior is everywhere her equal in tonal beauty and expressive nuance. His response to King Marke

Tristan und Isolde
16 April 1938
Isolde
Kirsten Flagstad
Brangäne
Karin Branzell
Tristan
Lauritz Melchior
Kurvenal
Julius Huehn
Marke
Emanuel List
Conductor
Artur Bodanzky

('das kannst du nie erfahren') is a model of Wagnerian song declamation, simply delivered but carefully shaped to heighten its import. Whatever his stage presence and acting abilities, he is the peerless actor with the voice (for the radio audience always a prime merit). In the final act (as Melchior, too, nears the end of his third performance in four days) his vocal stamina is undiminished. Among tenors, he alone has fully succeeded in turning Tristan's ravings into full-voiced, meaningful song, thrillingly surmounting Bodanzky's turbulent orchestral mass ('O Treue! Hehre, holde Treue!'); he angrily hurls out 'verflucht sei, furchtbarer Trank!' to excellent dramatic effect.

The two principals are given keen support, for Huehn is much improved as Kurvenal. He has left off bluster in favor of well-focused tone, frequently colored to match the text; his self-possession permits a full portrait of the loyal friend. Branzell maintains her customary vocal beauty and augments the intimate detail of her portrayal. Fortunately, List has one of his better days; his burly sound has improved in steadiness and legato, but he cannot convey Marke's infinite sorrow as did Hofmann. When the old king wallows in pain ('warum mir diese Schmach?'), List's indulgence is convincing.

The following season (1938–39) again brought twin performances of *Tristan* to the airwaves. Once more it is the postseason performance (8 April 1939) which is preserved with most of the familiar interpreters in place. The German ranks are now swelled by a new baritone and one worthy of high rank in the Wagner hierarchy of the Met. Herbert Janssen's broadcast debut had occurred in the 18 February *Tristan*, and he had sung Wolfram in the *Tannhäuser* broadcast from Boston on 25 March (neither performance is preserved). Better we had made Janssen's acquaintance as the songful Wolfram (also the role of his house debut on 28 January 1939), for the straightforward vocal ways of Tristan's burly servant allow little play for Janssen's best qualities. His authoritative style is immediately apparent. For a decade and a half the German baritone had been a figure at the Berlin State Opera and at Covent Garden; a frequent visitor to Bayreuth (under Toscanini) and Paris (with Furtwängler), he had played Kurvenal to Melchior's very first Tristan in Barcelona, so the meeting on the Met stage was the renewal of a long acquaintance.

The Metropolitan stage would be home to him for fourteen seasons. Steane assures us that the voice had considerable ring and power in the theatre, but in the radio performance Kurvenal's vigorous passages are often rather opaque—the vigor is all in the throat rather than in the projected tone. In *forte* passages the core of the voice eludes the listener. But the promise for future broadcasts is revealed at the opening of the third act—here Janssen comes into his own. In just a few quiet phrases we know this is a special artist: 'erschien zuvor die Ärztin nicht' is marked *zart* by Wagner, and Janssen's tender voicing is in the finest lieder-singing tradition; then he makes a crescendo to a *subito piano* (marked *dolce*) on the final word of 'die einz'ge, die uns hilft' and all Kurvenal's love for his unconscious master is laid bare. When Tristan first wakes, Janssen's affecting timbre at last acquires its full, fruity resonance, a fitting complement to the lovely head tones which he saves for Kurvenal's desolation as Tristan collapses.

The third act holds a number of such reflective moments. Best of all is Melchior's 'Wie sie selig' where Bodanzky achieves a chamber-music intimacy that enables the tenor to build a heartfelt 'Wie schön bist du.' (Would that Bodanzky had achieved a similar mood in the opera's prelude—for once we have it on tape—but the beginning is more *belebt* than *zart*, and thus the required impetus at the climax must

Tristan und Isolde
8 April 1939

Isolde
Kirsten Flagstad
Brangäne
Kerstin Thorborg
Tristan
Lauritz Melchior
Kurvenal
Herbert Janssen
Marke
Emanuel List
Conductor
Artur Bodanzky

be excessive; yearning is converted into a demand.) This time Melchior further expands his range of color and expression in Tristan's delirium—his wounded knight pushes madness as he curses the potion. In the combination of lyric beauty and vocal acting Thorborg measures up to the tenor. She is wonderfully conspiratorial as she cautions the impatiently waiting Isolde in act two, and the firmly voiced warning is Thorborg at her vocal best.

Flagstad has regressed to a more detached interpretive stance. One cannot fail to lament the limited role which agogic or even stress accents play in her phrasing; of course, when she does employ them, as at 'jammerte,' they are all the more effective. The restraint of her first act still rankles until one recalls Henderson's words about Toscanini's first act as "unexpectedly subdued, and while musically finished, [it] seemed to promise a want of vital emotion. . . . But it became evident that the distinguished conductor conceived the first act in a mood of restrained intensity and reserved the outpouring of thrilling passion for the second."[3] Perhaps that is Flagstad's intent as well. The soprano is again in superb voice—but then, when was she not? The easy flow of liquid tone, the accuracy of attack at all volume levels, astound, and if word illumination is limited, a new feeling of generalized seductiveness clothes her first-act encounter with Tristan; 'Nun lass uns Sühne trinken!' is positively wily in feminine suggestiveness.

But unlike Toscanini's second act, this one does not blaze. The magic of the love potion seems to have been distilled in both soprano and tenor by the time they reach the love duet, though their tonal splendor is still potent. Melchior's most impressive moment is again his invitation to Isolde at the act's end, to which Flagstad never seems to find quite the right mood in response, leaving it to Bodanzky and the Metropolitan wind choir to convey Wagner's intent. Her Liebestod may be her best attempt, however, for Isolde's inner repose is perfectly realized. One notes the extended crescendo of 'Wie er leuchtet' and the gentlest attack on 'sind es Wellen sanfter Lüfte?' and is grateful for the lovely downward *portamento* (oh, rarity) which closes 'süsser Atem sanft entweht.'

The Wagner craze of the thirties extended to *Die Meistersinger*, the only work to which Flagstad and Melchior did not lend their aura. Of course, Schorr's mellow artistry was sufficient reason for the two broadcasts of 1939 (4 May with Rethberg and 2 December.) In the latter broadcast the new and the old converged as Bodanzky's unexpected death in November had propelled young Erich Leinsdorf to the helm of the Metropolitan's Wagner fleet just in time to conduct the aging Schorr's final broadcast of Hans Sachs. Leinsdorf had already earned a place at the Met as an occasional stand-in for Bodanzky and had made his broadcast debut conducting the Boston *Tannhäuser* in March 1939.

The 2 December *Meistersinger* is the first of Leinsdorf's string of seven broadcasts in 1939–40. The airing coincided with the opera's seasonal premiere, and thus Leinsdorf's baptismal effort with the work, though he was no stranger to it—he had prepared the opera for Toscanini at Salzburg in 1936 and for Reiner in San Francisco in 1937. The Salzburg performance held echoes for Leinsdorf both propitious (the young American tenor Charles Kullman sang his initial Walther) and portentous (Schorr had been scheduled for Sachs but Toscanini "disliked everything the singer did,"[4] and the great baritone, unwilling to change his celebrated interpretation, withdrew on request). Leinsdorf had been at the piano for these troubled rehearsals, a fact which, in his words, caused his relations with Schorr in New York to be "marked by lack of ease."[5] Leinsdorf offers no personal evaluation of Schorr's Sachs, contenting

Die Meistersinger von Nürnberg
2 December 1939

Eva
Irene Jessner

Magdalene
Karin Branzell

Walther
Charles Kullman

David
Karl Laufkoetter

Hans Sachs
Friedrich Schorr

Beckmesser
Walter Olitzki

Pogner
Emanuel List

Conductor
Erich Leinsdorf

himself with the observation that established singers at the Met were "set in their ways—as I had noticed with Schorr in Salzburg—and some of them having waited long years for the opportunity, were bitter and intransigent and very difficult to handle."[6] Having to cope with these established singers made the Met "a tough soil for conductors."[7] That soil would never quite become terra firma for Leinsdorf. He felt that growth often was inhibited, and over the next five decades, he would be uprooted more than once, usually of his own volition.

But on this Saturday in 1939, as he took upon himself all of Bodanzky's assignments plus his own modest number, the opportunity seemed without parallel for a twenty-seven-year-old conductor. And he must have felt quite ready for it. The jaunty spring of the opening chords of the Vorspiel gives the clue to Leinsdorf's precise but, in his early career at any rate, fluent readings. Excess has no place in his interpretive vocabulary, but the reins, while firmly collected, are held lightly enough to allow a good measured trot, even a canter when needed. But he is a three-gaited conductor— the rack and certainly the Bodanzky gallop seemed to him ill judged in the showring of the Metropolitan.

The polyphonic strands of the prelude may not be quite individually etched, but Leinsdorf lets us know that we have a comedy before us—a young man's spritely step will lead us on. And plenty of passion rises from the pit as Walther courts Eva in the church. The orchestra has a delightful glitter to it in the opening music of the second act, and the frenzy of the apprentice riot is well managed. Leinsdorf shapes the third-act prelude most expressively, lingering over the long phrases of the low strings in a manner which perhaps had prompted Ziegler's warning of the year before that "We in America do not go for slow tempi."[8] Even Ziegler could not cavil about Leinsdorf's mobile treatment of the rhythms of the various guilds in the last scene where, as the apprentices mingle with the girls, he allows a *Rosenkavalier* lilt to invade the waltz theme.

As for the still-young American tenor, Kullman is a delight, entirely at home with the German language and style, ardent and impetuous in manner and tone in his scenes with Eva. The low voice has surprising depth and the top range is full and firm. For once 'Am stillen Herd' and 'Fanget an!' are free from labor and set forth with a youthful sweetness. He brings the character to life, delivering the rapid dialogue of the second act with clarity and a sense of its meaning, full of disdain and anger as he decries the masters' rules until his anguished cry of 'das Herz mir stockt' betrays his bursting heart. The tutoring scene with Schorr is a joy. In their give-and-take of song we sense that not only the young man's lied but also his character grows as Schorr takes him gently on. Best of all is the pleasure shown by the teacher as he learns from the youth. Kullman differentiates the final Prize Song from its predecessors by dynamic shading (dolce at the start—*sehr feurig* at the end) and loving textual nuances; though his resources are fully extended, he meets the challenge.

Upon hearing Irene Jessner in Europe, Johnson had recognized her as "a good *utilité* and an excellent cover for the *jugendlich* roles,"[9] but she seems even less than that here. Her timbre is the typical German lyric sound with a welcome Lemnitz-like glow, and she enters fully into Eva's changing moods—she is well routined in that way. But Eva's rapid dialogue (fully half of the role) sounds a constant gobble, the tone frequently breathy, even squawky—she registers more like a worn comprimario than a "good *utilité*." Her sustained singing is an improvement. She summons a Lehmannesque urgency for an adequate delivery of 'O Sachs! Mein Freund!' and leads the quintet with firm tone; but she doesn't make it *seem* the most important

Charles Kullman as Walther in *Die Meistersinger von Nürnberg*.

moment of her life, and she lacks the trill which should illuminate her final word. Laufkoetter (David) also knows the idiomatic manner, but his song is more often a bleat; List is fearsomely foggy in tone as Pogner, and Walter Olitzki has mistaken Beckmesser for Alberich, playing for comic effects in the nastiest of tones but rewarded by the audience with applause as he leaves Sachs' shop (perhaps they were glad to see him go). Only Branzell excels. Her Magdalene is marvelously meddlesome, full of spirit, occasionally broadly comic; but she never forgets to sing her part.

This is not exactly the caliber of crew to accompany Schorr in his last season as Hans Sachs—but then, the numerous cuts in his role may have been intended to ease the passage for the aging baritone. Otherwise, only the final page and a few glancing top tones would indicate a career's end is in sight (when *Meistersinger* next rolls around, Janssen—in this performance a fine Kothner—will play Sachs). But Schorr will remain a few more seasons and we are heartened by that knowledge, for on this afternoon plenty of bright metal still sustains his voice. Every time he enters into the worn lists of the mastersingers in act one, his voice shines through. And his artistry is undiminished; how he landscapes the successive phrase units for meaning and cumulative effect in the 'Flieder' monologue. He sounds young enough for Eva (certainly this one) as she suggests he enter the contest for her hand. 'Jerum!' is rock steady. The peak of his performance (perhaps of his career) is always the 'Wahn' monolog, its message doubly meaningful in these first days of the German invasions and the start of the Second World War; the colors may be a bit less varied in the soft passages, but the legato and projection remain potent. All the old sweetness of tone warms his wise advice to Walther ('Gedenkt des schönen Traums am Morgen!'). In his perfect union of word and tone Schorr has mastered what Beckmesser could not understand: 'sollt' passen Ton und Wort.'

Leinsdorf's next effort two weeks later was a more familiar chore, for he had a string of *Tannhäuser* performances under his baton. One has doubts about the rather plodding opening to the overture (were ever the notes of the pilgrims' hymn more detached?), and Leinsdorf's bacchantes are singularly dispirited in their levity, though the thematic entries of their music are clearly presented. Soon, however, the rather spacious proportions of Leinsdorf's musical architecture become clear and satisfying in their overall relationships (he effectively saves his fervor for the closing passages of the Bacchanal), and en route one can savor the articulation and nuances of individual phrases—his Hymn to Venus is particularly shapely. A nice languor wraps the siren calls but the flame of Leinsdorf's passion seldom burns at white heat. Dissection is dear to him and the introduction to the third act comes out piecemeal— the hint of pedantry stains it.

Three portrayals new to us hold the chief interest of the afternoon. Herbert Janssen would sing many a Wolfram on the airwaves (this is the second of six); on the other hand, soprano Rose Pauly and tenor Eyvind Laholm are heard in their only broadcast. For the previous two seasons the Czech soprano, habitué of the stages of Vienna, Salzburg, Dresden, and Berlin, and one of Strauss' favorite interpreters, had astounded the Met public with her tempestuous Elektra. Venus was the first of only three Wagner appearances during her final Met season. A knowing manner sustains her darkly colored but tart timbre and she is adept at suggesting the sensuous charm of Venus. One can sense the mind at work in the concentrated intent of her phrases, but her capricious vocal technique betrays her: pitch can sag, tonal quality become pinched, a quaver interfere in sustained song, and the low voice lose character. Other stages would continue to welcome her for nearly two more decades.

Tannhäuser
16 December 1939
Elisabeth
Kirsten Flagstad
Venus
Rose Pauly
Tannhäuser
Eyvind Laholm
Wolfram
Herbert Janssen
Landgrave
Emanuel List
Conductor
Erich Leinsdorf

Eyvind Laholm (born Edwin Johnson in Eau Claire, Wisconsin—Cross informs us he "changed his name . . . so as not to confuse us" with the former leading tenor and now general manager of the Metropolitan) is dismissed by Kolodin as singing in "an effortful, throaty manner,"[10] and dismissed literally by the Metropolitan after this single season. Yet the broadcast evidence suggests he might have been useful to them (undoubtedly we welcome serviceability more today when we no longer have the standard of Melchior daily before us). Laholm has bad luck with a few exposed top tones, and he sometimes slithers over the vocal line rather than cleanly carving it. His Hymn to Venus is definitely constricted. But he does not bark nor has he a bleat. In fact, quite the contrary, for a welcome lyrical cast graces his work ("my ideal is to sing Wagner in the Italian manner,"[11] he told an *Opera News* interviewer). Of the second act, only the end is documented and Laholm is not very winning in it. But one can tell that he is undaunted by the high tessitura. (A good deal of the second act on the tape I heard is a splice from the Flagstad-Melchior broadcast of 1936.) Laholm evidently has both pluck and stamina (why not?—he had been heavyweight champion of the U. S. Navy during World War I) for he delivers the Rome Narrative with lovely tone and absolute security. The concept is straightforward, but the voice is free and quite impressive—his many appearances in German houses and at Covent Garden are not belied. Even Cross acknowledges that Laholm has "so well acquitted himself in the closing act."

It is Janssen, however, who most nearly matches the vocal and artistic standard of "the glorious artist from the fiords of Norway," Madame Flagstad. As soon as Wolfram greets his lost friend, Janssen's individual timbre and sensitive stance speak quality. In the song contest his recitative verges toward song, his song retains the dominance of the word, and the case for ideal love is well served. His third act is even better. His musings as he watches the grieving Elisabeth are a highlight; the voice is incredibly lovely and the style perfection. Leinsdorf by now may have recalled Ziegler's admonition, for the Evening Star moves at a good clip. Janssen doesn't try for (and probably doesn't command) the contrasting vocal effects of a Tibbett, but the naturalness of feeling and delivery seem entirely apt (though the final phrase is abrupt). List is his usual self, deeply resonant and occasionally stodgy in manner.

Though we are denied Flagstad's entrance music, we can hear her defense of the regressive knight. Her tone is unexpectedly plaintive, the mass suppressed in favor of tender regret. The restraint causes an occasional flutter in the evenness of her column of breath, but she surmounts the final ensemble of the act with a finely pointed laser beam of tone. This time her prayer is cast in the monumental mode, the tone entirely chalumeau-like, its lively lustre compensating for a certain stolidity in the concept; gone now are most of the subtle gradations of volume and color that were so affecting in the 1936 broadcast. But the control is absolute. It is a very measured salvation which Leinsdorf provides at the opera's close—angels and pilgrims, like their opposites of the Venusberg, know more of resignation than exaltation.

Leinsdorf may have assumed Bodanzky's repertory, but coronation was with-held in the face of a gathering storm fomented by insurgent artists. Between his broadcasts of *Orfeo* on 20 January 1940 and *Lohengrin* on 27 January the notorious "old boat" controversy was given full play in the New York papers. Melchior had con-fided to a *Herald Tribune* reporter that, in spite of Leinsdorf's talent, the Met needed a more experienced conductor to replace Bodanzky. Johnson added fuel to the fire by lashing out in print at the "old boats" (i.e. Melchior) who "objected to a young man of unorthodox attainments"[12] (Leinsdorf's paraphrase). Melchior had dug himself into a hole, perhaps with Flagstad's approval, for she was engaged in a hard-knuckle campaign to launch her American accompanist, Edwin McArthur, as a conductor of Wagner at the Metropolitan. Melchior attempted to placate Leinsdorf privately, and on 29 January a public rapprochement was achieved. But Leinsdorf's opinion of Melchior (as evident in his autobiography) remained sour thereafter, and the tenor's penchant for hasty, ill-judged action would bring about a huffy termination to his lengthy Met career a decade later.

The *Tribune* story broke on 25 January, but the events appear to have had little effect on Leinsdorf's poise on the podium. In matters of orchestral nuance and over-all interpretation his *Lohengrin* broadcast of 27 January is one of the most well conceived of the period's Wagner performances. (The vocal performance is another matter.) While happily free from the Bodanzky accelerando, Leinsdorf maintains dynamic impulse throughout the opera. In such simple moments as the recitative-like chords which punctuate King Henry's pronouncements or the interplay between chorus and trumpets as the swan is sighted, the easy precision and modest (not overblown) architecture of Leinsdorf's conception is revealed early on. We hear it again in the apt tempo for the king's prayer and in the gentle chordal triplets of the brass accompaniment to the big ensemble, and the judicious pacing of the act-one finale eliminates any hint of scramble. Leinsdorf's control is complete, but his hand is light enough to allow an unobtrusive takeoff in the closing bars of the act.

Both the second- and third-act preludes are persuasive: the long lines of the former are surely guided, while the mix of vigor and containment in the whirlwind introduction to the final act can be taken (as the future will reveal) as a talisman of the Leinsdorf manner; particularly winning is the light articulation of the rhythmic middle section. And, unlike the later Leinsdorf, he allows moments like the postlude to the Elsa-Ortrud scene to bloom expansively without harm to the overall shape. The young Leinsdorf's avoidance of fustian trappings in favor of a more discreet dynamic (precision, meaningful articulation, subtle gradations) would seem to promise well for the new decade of Wagner at the Metropolitan. And Leinsdorf took considerable (and deserved) pride in having restored the many annoying cuts in *Lohengrin*[13] (though a few remain in this performance).

The afternoon offers one of those legendary casts (Rethberg, Thorborg, Melchior, List) with two American baritones of more than average promise, Julius Huehn and Leonard Warren. But legends usually carry a quantity of myth in their make-up. Whether because of the disharmony back stage or, more likely, the attrition of age, this performance is vocally no match for those of previous seasons. Thorborg is always a provocative artist, but the suspicion lingers that she may be over-parted as the far-ranging and raging Ortrud. The soprano coloration of her instrument stands in strong contrast to Branzell: her top is decidedly slimmer and, at least on this afternoon, shorter (the G-sharps, As and A-sharps which pepper the closing moments of the opera are close to shrieks). But her word play is imaginative, her intimate plotting with Telramund wonderfully collusive, and 'Entweihte Götter!' is fierce enough to summon any god—all in all, the work of a dedicated performer. Elsewhere the shadow of age too often haunts the performance. List can still nobly shape 'Gott allein' (act one) but he is woefully wobbly and effortful in the final act. The still-young Huehn is a bit less impressive this time, his vocal sheen a shade duller, though still darkly potent, and now the interpretation has ricocheted from the dramatic to the purely musical. Warren, in his second season (he had already moved into star

Lohengrin
27 January 1940
Elsa
Elisabeth Rethberg
Ortrud
Kerstin Thorborg
Lohengrin
Lauritz Melchior
Telramund
Julius Huehn
Herald
Leonard Warren
King Henry
Emanuel List
Conductor
Erich Leinsdorf

territory with the Count in *Trovatore* and Valentin in *Faust*), commands attention as the Herald with his big, bright tones. Mercifully, no hint of woof intrudes as yet, though the top E-flats do not have the brilliant ring one knows is there.

Rethberg's Elsa arouses sorrow rather than mere regret for an ignoble performance (it is far from that), for she has tarried so long on the heights of vocal perfection that the descent could be deep and precipitous. It was, in fact, not nearly so precipitous as legend would have it—numerous broadcasts of the late 1930s testify to the ongoing bounty of her portrayals. But in 1940 that incredible core of stable, radiant tone could no longer be summoned at will. That it could be summoned on occasion is a boon to all for whom memory permits patience.

On at least two counts the appearances of a beloved artist in decline cannot be a mere catalog of debits. With any luck at all, at some point in the performance some flash of tonal splendor will return, some unique turn of phrase will shape itself, some interpretive insight founded on years of experience will illuminate character, all in a way not to be duplicated by any other artist. Then too, having repeatedly heard the same artist over a period of years, one finds in later life that time's orbit expands; the longtime listener does not live in the past but rather benefits from carrying the memory of treasured performances into the future. Thus memory nurtures many an artist in this chronicle, and so it does with Rethberg on this Saturday afternoon.

In a good deal of Elsa's dream Rethberg skirts the underside of the pitch; in midrange her tones are tremulous and the upper notes are effortful. Her plea for another sounding of the Herald provides a brief thrust of bright tone, and at the end of the act she sails along with spirit. 'Euch Lüften' is quite lovely, though the tendency to flat in the middle range (A–C) remains. Her responses to Ortrud are far more involved dramatically than Flagstad's contained rejoinders; but the high *forte*s are acidulous. She is close to her old self as she comforts Ortrud, and later in the angry confrontation with Ortrud the old thrusts of excitement, capped by a solid high B-flat, penetrate. In the bridal duet the familiar silvery thread of honeyed tone works its magic once again until her dramatic involvement (as Elsa insistently presses her questions) sours it. Rethberg certainly can't be accused of placidity, for she becomes overly emotional in the final moments of the duet (again, a far cry from Flagstad's concept) until the quiet beauty of 'Allewiger, erbarm' dich mein!' reminds us of the best Rethberg sound.

Melchior's case is quite a different matter. The aid of memory need not be called into play for almost another decade, but this is far from his finest afternoon. Perhaps the unhappy events of the past several days have made melancholy the Dane, for his tones have seldom seemed so veiled or his top voice so effortful as on this unhappy afternoon. Leinsdorf's opinion of Melchior survived for decades; "an approximate resemblance to the composer's wishes"[14] is his summation of Melchior's art, and as if to prove him right, one of the few documented Melchior gaffes occurs in act three as Lohengrin determines to reveal his name; in the phrase 'nun muss ich künden' just before 'In fernem Land' he fails to hold 'nun' for three beats and thus moves two beats ahead of the orchestra for two measures.

But the tenor has some fine moments, notably a few broadly declaimed passages in act one and the conclusion of act two, where 'Heil dir' is superbly laid out in noble tones. In the bridal duet he shows a greater than usual predilection for covered tones, and his top voice is often constricted. But he still knows the difference between *feurig* and *zärtlich*. Though Melchior presses the pace of the Narrative, it retains sufficient grandeur in declamation and architectural scope (but the

'Gral' A-naturals are far from liberated tones). The Farewell to the Swan has a lovely legato, he gives 'Kommt er dann heim' a bright Nordic ring, and his moving *Leb'wohl*s have an Otello-like intensity. In short, the afternoon is an uneven affair for all but newcomers Warren and Leinsdorf.

After *Tristan, Walküre* is the Wagner opera most frequently aired during the thirties (nine broadcasts during the first nine radio seasons); while Melchior and Schorr dominate the male roles of all the Wagner operas, the female roles offer a fascinating succession of prime interpreters (as noted with regard to the multiple broadcasts of *Tannhäuser*). *Walküre* offers the exciting prospect of soprano pairings in the same opera. No sequence of pairings is more intriguing than the succession of *Walküre* broadcasts near the end of the decade which offered Flagstad as Sieglinde, Lawrence as Brünnhilde (18 December 1937), then the role reversal on 17 February 1940, and finally the Sieglinde of Lotte Lehmann in company with Lawrence's Brünnhilde (30 March 1940).

Unfortunately, the recording of the 1937 *Walküre* is one of the worst sound documentations yet encountered. Moreover, it contains only snippets of the first act, though the remainder of the opera is complete. Bodanzky's opening storm music may be the fastest-moving weather pattern in meteorological opera lore—the storm motive fairly lurches into its transformation as Siegfried enters. This Sieglinde is evidently accustomed to finding strange men on her hearth, and Flagstad's few phrases are suspiciously broad-toned and stolid. But it would be unfair to speculate on the rest of the first act; one must be content to recall her thrilling portrayal of two years earlier. The harsh sonics of these records, however, do allow us to gain some idea of the remainder of her portrayal (recall that only act one of the 1935 debut is preserved). The Sieglinde who enters with Siegmund as they flee from her husband is frantic with fear and humiliation. The soprano actually modifies her sturdy tone (for a very few notes) to a realistic expression of shame. More important, one almost never hears a Sieglinde so easily surmount the orchestral tumult. And Flagstad proves immensely moving throughout the scene; 'Wo bist du, Siegmund?' she cries in overtly plaintive accents, and just before Sieglinde faints, she withdraws all color from her tone. Yet she cannot entirely suppress her architectonic manner: how intriguing to hear her repeated short cries punctuated by quick orchestral chords— they suggest the alternation of soloist and tutti in a concerto rather than cries of panic wrung from a human throat. Mr. Cross salutes this "glorious Norwegian" during the curtain calls and we fix upon "our auburn-haired Brünnhilde," Marjorie Lawrence.

"The lovely Australian soprano" makes a stunning entrance with the battle cry: her attack is firm, her trills well articulated, the high B excellent, and the treacherous octave leaps (not swoops as so often heard) are as clear and clean as mountain air. All the uncontained joy of the warrior maid is suggested in her knifelike thrusts of brilliantly colored tone. Later in the act the vocal edge is more finely honed and her tone takes on a gleaming warmth, but always the Lawrence voice remains a curiously sensual instrument. Left alone to lament Wotan's order to destroy the Wälsung, Lawrence manages to project the depth of her sympathy into her low voice which, considering the brilliance of the upper register, is remarkably secure. When ultimately she faces Wotan's ire, the simplicity of 'Hier bin ich, Vater' is most affecting; the low-lying lines of 'War es so schmählich' begin with deep-toned emotion before mounting with utmost ease into her radiantly shining top. Phrasing and word play urgently convey Brünnhilde's desperate plea for protection on her lonely rock (Lawrence well knows the balm of an occasional *portamento*, too). In the climactic

Die Walküre
18 December 1937
Sieglinde
Kirsten Flagstad
Brünnhilde
Marjorie Lawrence
Fricka
Kerstin Thorborg
Siegmund
Lauritz Melchior
Wotan
Friedrich Schorr
Hunding
Ludwig Hofmann
Conductor
Artur Bodanzky

encounter of the two heroines earlier in the act Lawrence's bright, cutting instrument ('Fort denn, eile') contrasts with Flagstad's broadsword of golden tone at 'O hehrstes Wunder,' and here Flagstad renounces her customary textual clarity in favor of immensity and continuity of tone.

In their scene the Valkyries produce a maelstrom of harsh tone, or so the poor sonics indicate—perhaps this is what listening on those small radio sets was really like during the 1930s. One can venture that it was actually a pretty good crew (Votipka, for one, leads off with some excellent vocalism). Thorborg makes Fricka's lengthy scene more than a mere harangue—she gives it plenty of vocal thrust, but her interpretive sincerity predominates. Of Siegmund we have only Melchior's broadly paced, nobly intoned questioning of Brünnhilde. The contrast between his fervent denunciation of Wotan's retreat and his reticent farewell to Sieglinde again shows the thoughtful vocal actor. In case the tenor's longevity be forgotten, Cross informs us that "I've been on the air over fifteen years myself and Mr. Melchior . . . was on the air before that. . . . The late Guglielmo Marconi asked him to take part with Madame Melba in the first broadcast from . . . England way back in 1920." And Melchior would have yet another decade in opera ahead of him plus a long coda in films.

Unfortunately Schorr is not at his best and has trouble at both extremes of range: the low notes are now and then gravelly, while an inordinate number of top tones are wooden. Nor is there the consummate flow of legato we have come to expect. But even on an off day he can rage without lumbering (we get equal proportions of rage and studied narrative from Wotan in *Walküre*), and when he leaves off castigating his favorite daughter and recalls their soon-to-be forbidden communion ('selige Lust') once again we succumb to the spell of the inimitable mastersinger. He casts it again during the Farewell when Wotan decrees that only one freer than he shall win Brünnhilde as bride; and yet again, when he quietly intones 'so küsst er die Gottheit von dir.' This is perfection of Wagnerian song-declamation, pure in tone, well colored, and meaningfully interpreted. But, truth to tell, it is Wagner's orchestra that has to carry more than its share of the magic in the long Farewell on this afternoon.

Fortunately there will be other Schorr Wotans, but when we next hear *Walküre*, young Huehn, having completed his apprenticeship, has ascended to full Heldenbariton status. Godlike in size (six feet four), the onetime riveter in a Pittsburg steel mill had forged an impressive record at the Metropolitan since his debut as the *Lohengrin* Herald in 1935. Only thirty years old at the time of the 1940 *Walküre* broadcast (his third Wotan at the Metropolitan), the ascent had been carefully charted (including coaching with Schorr) and he was ready for the rarefied air of Valhalla.

Huehn is impressive throughout the afternoon. The vibrant depth of his lower range is particularly effective when Wotan contends with his wife over Siegmund's fate and later as he rages at his disobedient daughter. The vocal pith is all there, but the temperament remains a touch bland when Wotan's anguish must be fully projected; his rages do not tower, but they at least loom. The text is well and meaningfully articulated (Huehn's parents were German-born and spoke German in the home). His top voice remains of a piece with the richly hued low voice, freely produced, reliable, and with a welcome shine to it. Perhaps because the voice has risen during the performance, the lower voice becomes unexpectedly short and a little dry in the third-act scene with the penitent Brünnhilde; nor can he supply liquid legato to oil the chromatically descending chords as Wotan tells her of the sleep to come. But Huehn's Farewell is beautifully sung and surprisingly tender, his emotive mezza voce

Die Walküre
17 February 1940
Sieglinde
Marjorie Lawrence
Brünnhilde
Kirsten Flagstad
Fricka
Karin Branzell
Siegmund
Lauritz Melchior
Wotan
Julius Huehn
Hunding
Emanuel List
Conductor
Erich Leinsdorf

skillfully blending into full voice as he kisses Brünnhilde's eyes and lips in farewell. Almost all of Huehn's career fell under the shadow of Schorr's greatness and thus ultimate renown was denied him, but what a welcome figure he would have been in the Heldenbariton wasteland of the sixties and seventies.

Before curtain time Cross has informed the radio audience that "we are to have this great treat this afternoon of hearing [*Walküre*] sung in its entirety, that is without any of the usual cuts." Again Leinsdorf is to be thanked for his crusade to restore the Bodanzky cuts. Not only did Leinsdorf's *Walküre* differ from his predecessor's in length but also in tone. One senses it in the opening music of the opera. Unlike Bodanzky's, his is a slow-moving storm and not particularly violent—a clear example of climate control on the part of the punctilious Leinsdorf. But orchestral punctuation is effectively used to highlight any dramatic moment on stage, and the motivic play throughout the opera is well shaped and individualized; he is, however, prone to linger over the slower themes, and the brass Hunding chords are drained of weight and thus of import. Oddly enough, the closing portion of the first act is as precipitous as any Bodanzky reading, but the orchestral painting of the scene where Sieglinde prepares her husband's draught dallies to the point of dismemberment. On the other hand, the interrogation of Brünnhilde in act two and the orchestral conclusion of the opera are most effective in their measured pacing—the subdued orchestral manner which follows Wotan's 'letztem Kuss' catches and enhances the tenderness of the moment.

Surely Leinsdorf must have been grossly tried by the interminable length of Melchior's heroic 'Wälse' pair in act one, but probably nothing as splendid has ever issued from a Heldentenor's throat. Indeed, on this afternoon Melchior seems intent on displaying his virtuosity. In the first-act narrative the rapid declamation of the long-breathed phrases positively glitters, while the final lines of 'Winterstürme' are stretched into broad arcs of fervor. The list could go on and on: his accurate (and legato) tracing of the arpeggiated chord lines ('wonnige') in his best silver-trumpet manner; the broad approach to the cries of 'Nothung'; the unfaltering ascent of his magisterial greeting to Valhalla as he rejects Brünnhilde's plan to convey him to the land of heroes. There in Valhalla Melchior, the artist if not the man, surely belongs.

Branzell, too, is superb in every way, from the precise placement of her phrases for maximum musical expression and dramatic impact to the easy splendor with which she soars through the mezzo stratosphere at the conclusion of Fricka's scene. Even List is in fine vocal fettle as Hunding.

How does the role reversal serve our prima donnas in the 1940 broadcast? During their Met careers both Lawrence and Flagstad appeared far more often as the warrior maid than the wayward wife, and with good reason. Lawrence is not quite able to submerge her aggressive personality within the pathetic compass of Sieglinde's woe. She is rather straightforward in the opening scene; her tone is overly bright, the legato imperfect, and a slight hoarseness masks her lower voice. A hint of undue command charges 'O merke wohl' as she begins 'Der Männer Sippe'; she is unfailingly responsive to the text in the narrative, but her natural ebullience catapults her (with splendid tone) into the climax, rather than allowing it to flower of itself. A radiant glow of color dominates 'Du bist der Lenz,' though word caress is in short supply until, in a lovely moment, she recognizes Siegmund as brother. By the end of the act she is in full control of her vocal resources (the coloration in moments of calm is especially winning), and as she names Siegmund, she provides the closest possible approximation of an *e* vowel on the high G that one is ever likely to hear. Her second

Marjorie Lawrence as Sieglinde in *Die Walküre*.

act continues on a high level. Now the low voice is richly colored in legato phrases of considerable emotional impact while the thrusts of agitated terror are compelling in fervor. What a fine vocal actress she proves herself in the fleeting moods of Sieglinde's hallucinations! In act three her appeal to Brünnhilde to let her die is equally fine, but 'O hehrstes Wunder' is a shade disappointing (some skittish tone intrudes), and the expected grandeur fails to materialize.

Flagstad does not disappoint in 'Fort denn, eile,' but Leinsdorf's momentum is a mite inhibiting. She doesn't quite capture the pathos of Brünnhilde's plight in her long dialogue with Wotan—the episode comes off more as a match between equals, with Flagstad pleading her case like an experienced trial lawyer who fully expects to win. When she does hone down her instrument to a *piano* dynamic, her tone sounds oddly pinched and unsupported (as Brünnhilde tells her father that she had divined his true wish in protecting Siegmund), but her softly intoned invocation of the future Wälsung which Sieglinde carries is most lovely. The final moments of the scene are made for Flagstad's equipment, and she traverses the wide intervals with complete assurance, just as at the end of the second act (when Brünnhilde determines to save Siegmund) rhythmic squareness and the accuracy of her stalwart tones energize the moment. But the security of her battle cry conveys little joy in Brünnhilde's vocation (still, the wonderful, broad downward *portamento* on 'Heiaha!' is a treat). By this stage in her career the lower voice has taken on a unique opulence, the metal of its bronze core sheathed with an enveloping luster. Is there anything nobler in all opera than the sound of Flagstad matching the horns of Wagner's orchestra when Brünnhilde tells Siegmund of his fate? She imbues the somber moment with profound significance. When Flagstad is hailed as the "first lady of Wagnerian opera," as Mr. Cross does at the opera's end, such moments confirm the claim.

How odd that in the five *Walküre* broadcasts of Flagstad's major Metropolitan sojourn this is her only portrayal of Brünnhilde. Lawrence is heard on three occasions, the last of them on 30 March during the 1940 tour performances in Boston. All the Wagnerian stalwarts are on hand, but in varying condition. Thorborg offers her customary vocal and dramatic potency and List is appropriately menacing, but both Melchior and Schorr perform at less than par. Melchior is clearly indisposed, for he cannot control his soft singing in act two (the 'Geliebte!' which he addresses to the prostrate Sieglinde falters noticeably), nor are the questions to Brünnhilde bound with his customary linear tension. His sound is excessively baritonal and covered throughout, and little light illumines the high notes. But even so, the first-act narrative is very fine, and the 'Wälse' pair are, if possible, even more elongated—he does have a stout throat. As for Schorr, age again sits heavily upon him (though he is only two years older than his tenor colleague), and he concentrates on projecting a solid and darkly colored lower and middle range (where he can be certain of vocal security) rather than essaying his well-remembered mezza voce, most precious of his many assets. The curtain on the high range has now descended to D-flat. After such a catalog of demerits one might think that little auditory pleasure remains; not so, for the vocal authority and the interpretive depth are still rewarding, and a good deal of the old tonal sheen returns in act three. He has plenty of voice to deal with the recalcitrant sisters (one of whom is decidedly weak), and though the old sweetness remains in short supply, the Brünnhilde-Wotan colloquy and the Farewell retain a not insignificant measure of their former glory.

Lawrence again proves her aptitude for the *Walküre* Brünnhilde. Though she cannot quite convey the mood of ceremonial solemnity which Flagstad provided in

Die Walküre
30 March 1940

Sieglinde
Lotte Lehmann
Brünnhilde
Marjorie Lawrence
Fricka
Kerstin Thorborg
Siegmund
Lauritz Melchior
Wotan
Friedrich Schorr
Hunding
Emanuel List
Conductor
Erich Leinsdorf

the interrogation scene with Siegmund, the exuberant battle cry coupled with the emotional fullness of the scene with her father establish an impressively wide polarity of characterization and vocal skill. This time her placement is a little unsettled in the lower reaches of 'War es so schmählich,' but soon she is in her best form, pouring out long lines of radiant tone replete with tenderness and sorrow. She has an unusual ability to reveal deep personal involvement without dismembering the musical content. And she owns a very beautiful instrument.

Excessive emotionalism is a charge with which detractors of Lotte Lehmann are wont to reproach her. The predominant remembrance which many Americans have of Lehmann stems from lieder recitals in the very last years of a long career (I recall a 1945 recital—a somber but affecting affair). In these recitals vocal shortcomings could be at least partially obscured by extrovert interpretations. From the very beginning of that career in Hamburg in 1909, the German soprano had professed her preference for communication over control. In 1938 she wrote, "Of course one knows singers who keep an exact control of themselves even in matters of vocal technique, and notice every deviation. But I give myself to my part with all my soul. I cannot think of technical matters while I sing, because I live what I sing so completely that there is no room left for anything else."[15] She admitted her autobiography was perhaps premature, but the thirty-year passage had already been dotted with memorable triumphs. From 1914 to 1938 she was the idol of the public at the Vienna Opera. She conquered London in 1924 and continued to hold it captive for a dozen years. A number of Strauss premieres were her happy lot (the Composer in the revised *Ariadne*, the Dyer's Wife in *Die Frau ohne Schatten* and the Dresden premiere of *Intermezzo*); Salzburg, Berlin, Paris, all knew her vivid creations. But it was not until 1930 that America first heard her (the Chicago Opera, of course). Thus she came belatedly to the Met in 1934 as a veteran of a quarter century of international acclaim.

Lehmann's Metropolitan career was a checkered thing. She never felt quite at home there. But though her Met performances were few (fifty-four appearances in six roles in New York with fifteen more on tour), she was already a cult figure for the American public at the time of the 1940 *Walküre* broadcast. If nothing else, the 1935 recording of *Walküre*, act one, with Melchior and Bruno Walter had seen to that. No matter how familiar, the amazing vibrancy of her vocal timbre always astonishes. Add to that the immediacy of her interpretive manner—a kind of perpetual breathless ardor—and one feels at a Lehmann performance as though propelled bodily on stage as participant. The security of being merely an auditor is denied one, a not unwelcome loss of distance to be prized as much for its feel of danger as its rarity.

On this Saturday afternoon all the beloved Lehmannisms are on parade: the onomatopoeic emphases ('Schächer ihm schenkten' is almost a snarl as she describes the wretches at her wedding); the meshing of textual rhythms with the musical phrase ('Gäste kamen und Gäste gingen'); the infusion of sudden mood changes into the tone ('Traurig sass ich'—here the *au* vowel is a cry of pain); the exalted wonder as she recalls Wotan's entrance into the feast at 'ein Fremder trat da herein.' Her way is the lieder singer's immersion in the text—amplified to the dimensions of the opera house and the realism of the stage. Often her breathless manner exactly mirrors the *Steigerung* of the Wagnerian *melos* (as in the sequence of short phrases which propels the end of 'Du bist der Lenz'). Occasionally one feels the dramatic gesture is excessive—when Sieglinde recognizes Siegfried's face as her own 'Doch nein' crackles with perhaps inordinate surprise, but you surely know that Sieglinde has not thought of it before this moment. "To portray a rôle means to transform oneself into the being whom one represents, to become completely the personality of this rôle,"[16] Lehmann wrote in her analyses of her stage lives. Her gift of transformation is nowhere more enthralling than in Sieglinde's brief scene in act two. One can hear in her voice the exhaustion and half stumble of her steps as she enters crying 'Weiter, weiter.' As she moves from expressing her love for Siegmund to absolute terror ('Hunding erwachte') one feels she enters a hypnotic state before she collapses, calling 'Wo bist du?' to the distracted Siegmund. Yet in all this hyperrealism she prudently places each phrase within an overall musical design—the terror has been carefully crafted. Best of all, though she shares the 1888 birth year with Schorr, she is in excellent vocal form throughout the performance. The voice is stable over the entire range with almost all of the top tones well anchored and only occasionally pushed sharp in pitch. Leinsdorf drives the third-act Brünnhilde-Sieglinde exchange at maximum speed, which perhaps diminishes its apotheosic impact but is mercifully kind to Lehmann's overextended resources.

In the several pairings of the *Walküre* heroines Lehmann's Sieglinde is unrivaled; she has grasped the full significance of Sieglinde's role in the trilogy: "The characters of the *Ring* are drawn superdimensionally. The humanly simplest, the nearest to our own feeling seems to me Sieglinde. Although the daughter of Wotan and so having blood half human, half divine, she is close to the earth and humanly convincing."[17] Lehmann's belief in living what she sings is singularly suited to Sieglinde's agitated condition—she removes all stylized affect from Sieglinde and transforms her into the most lifelike of operatic characterizations. As Wotan's other daughter (the *Walküre* Brünnhilde), Marjorie Lawrence, too, reveals her affinity for a role in which her personal and vocal gifts are ideally mated. (For the record, the blazing turbulence of Leider and Kappel's third-act encounter in the 1934 broadcast is not equaled by any of these later pairings.)

And what of Flagstad? A wonder of the world will remain just that no matter how much a particular perspective alters the view. It is more in the totality of her Wagnerian endeavors that her greatness remains paramount. After all, we have the evidence of the box office to confirm her appeal—they say she saved the Met. Flagstad's plentiful sound which filled the farthest corners of the big old house, the unaffected sincerity of her musical style, and the lack of artifice in her dramatic presence had given the Wagner operas a new authenticity.

The Boston *Walküre* is the final Wagner broadcast in the decade of the thirties. Two reflections suggest themselves when considering this unequaled cluster of golden-age Wagner performances. The first concerns the state of the vocal art. The Olympian character of these voices, both as natural and as cultivated instruments, is astounding. From Norway, Sweden, Germany, Australia, and Denmark came vocal gods—as though a Darwinian process of natural selection had formed them in response to the massive orchestral challenge posed by Wagner. But beyond size, it was the mastery of all phases of the vocal art (always excepting agility, for which there seemed no need) which preserved that generation of audiences from the puny, disfigured representations of Wagner so often suffered by later generations. And as if that were not enough, as heard repeatedly in the live broadcasts, these singers were invariably in prime vocal estate—they seemed virtually immune from indisposition so that the radio audience knew few cancellations and, better yet, endured few "show-must-go-on" struggles.

These broadcasts are notable also for depth of character portrayal, for interpretive finesse. Each phrase is given a life of its own, rather than being swabbed with an all-purpose brush. In part it may have been due to the relatively limited number of Wagnerian roles available to them which they repeated many times a season the world over. These artists kept within their *Fach* (that was a way to stay vocally healthy, too). The specter of routine was surely often lurking among the Wagnerian landscapes, but it rarely seems to have enveloped these singers. Their complete identification with a role, their natural give-and-take in response to other characters, the wide range of affective nuance they have ready to hand, all allied with immensely healthy instruments, distinguishes their efforts from modern performance.

As noted earlier, the lacuna in the Wagner broadcast pantheon is a full complement of Lehmann performances. She appeared in only four Wagner broadcasts: Elizabeth and Elsa in 1934 and 1935 and two later Sieglindes (no Eva, although she sang it at the house). As partial balm she has left us two accounts of her most celebrated portrayal, the Marschallin. Strauss' *Der Rosenkavalier* was first broadcast on 5 February 1938 and offered again on 7 January 1939 with Lehmann, List, and Bodanzky the major constants.

The 1939 airing is by far the more satisfying, though the presence of Thorborg as the cavalier in 1938 is an inviting prospect, perhaps more so on paper than in actuality. The full swath of her tone is often welcome, as in the 'heut oder morgen' episode or the presentation of the rose, which she delivers with a confident nobility. What is seldom conveyed is the volatility and impetuosity of the seventeen-year-old Octavian, caught up in youthful passion for a pair of strong-willed ladies. One can forgo some lack of characterization in return for her lovely tracing of the second-act 'Mit Ihren Augen voller Tränen'; unfortunately, all the scenes with Sophie are deflated by the amateurish style, colorless tone, and schoolgirl German of the American soprano, Susanne Fisher. An even greater trial is the Singer of Nicholas Massue (in both broadcasts); perhaps management's intent was to exemplify the most provincial of Italian tenors, in which case his success is only too patent. Massue is repeatedly defeated by the high tessitura of Strauss' Italian conceit.

Vienna-born Emanuel List was the Metropolitan's ranking Baron Ochs, which he sang fifty-five times in New York (plus twenty appearances on tour) during his sixteen seasons with the company. In 1938 the big voice is rather unsettled, and thus the rapid chatter of act one often bumps along in unwieldy fashion. He is more in his element in the nouveau-riche Faninal abode, though again he can't easily travel the skimming paths of Strauss' waltz melodies as Ochs nurses his wound. Can any Ochs hope to win our sympathy by deploying all those aspirates in the oft-repeated 'Mi-hit mir?' The top tone of 'einen andern Schick' is an inaudible falsetto, but List has the low notes, even if the final one ends in a bobble. Throughout, the boor is too much Hofmannsthal and too little Strauss. Of course, Bodanzky is no help as he races along in businesslike fashion with insufficient gemütlichkeit. All in all, the performance is disaffecting, lacking in the charm that is the starting point for a good *Rosenkavalier*.

Lehmann, too, seems affected by the pervasive mood. She appears to be out of sorts in her straightforward first phrases ('Du bist mein Bub') and on through some rather shrewish moments where the familiar timbre turns squawky. Her predilection for talking the text (often her greatest asset) becomes near caricature in the scene before Ochs' arrival, her hard glottal attacks tending toward an unpleasant gobble. Ochs' leave-taking has a beneficial effect, and more of the Lehmann magic settles in. When she recalls young Resi, the memory of her youth brings a lighter tonal manner with many lovely touches—the play of color and meaningful textual nuances of 'alles

Der Rosenkavalier
5 February 1938

Marschallin
Lotte Lehmann
Sophie
Susanne Fisher
Octavian
Kerstin Thorborg
Baron Ochs
Emanuel List
Faninal
Friedrich Schorr
Conductor
Artur Bodanzky

zergeht wie Dunst und Traum' are most affecting. She evokes a marvelous intimacy in the monologue (the stopping of the clocks is delivered in a conspiratorial whisper). But often the ultimate shaping of long phrases simply escapes her ('ein Geschöpf des Vaters'), and the overall absence of soft, gentle tone is particularly regrettable as she gives Mahomet the silver rose. Still, the characterful details of her portrayal satisfy: in act three, the tight-lipped 'Find' sie scharmant' betrays an underlying cattiness as the older woman first looks over her budding rival; with what fierce sternness she dismisses Ochs; her address to Sophie is entirely charming and not the least bit overstated. Unfortunately, the trio is rather harsh in tone and manner (all three participants are at fault), and Octavian and Sophie deliver a mechanistic 'dream' duet. Thus the transcendent close of the opera lacks the magic built in by Strauss, and as a final injury, the spell is completely snapped by the poor ensemble of Fisher (and Thorborg, to a lesser degree) in the final ascending phrase.

The 1939 performance is a much happier occasion. Bodanzky has loosed the reins just enough to allow sentiment to ride in tandem with momentum, and List is in more grateful voice, his fat, jolly tone conveying how pleased the Baron is with himself as lover (both past and present). And List is kinder to Strauss' waltz turns, too, though he can't resist the audible hiccup as he descends to his final low E. In the smaller vignettes Doris Doe is delightfully insinuating as she reads Mariandel's letter, her partner Karl Laufkoetter proves an appropriately slippery spy, and Arnold Gabor's caricature of the Notary is genuinely funny. More important, German-born Marita Farell is a first-rate Sophie, tracing the high-flying lines with ease and a lovely, silvery sound that has more tonal body than most ingénues can offer. For once Sophie comes off as something more than a silly goose, especially as Farell's spunky spirit holds the Baron at bay—maybe Octavian did see something there that we who cherish the Marschallin have missed.

The new Octavian, American mezzo soprano Risë Stevens, is indeed a perceptive performer. Her house debut had occurred in the broadcast *Mignon* three weeks earlier. In 1935 Johnson had offered her a debut as Orfeo in the ill-fated spring seasons, explaining that ballet dancers would enact the roles on stage while she sang from the pit. Stevens, with the forthright manner which would be characteristic of her career, responded, "That's not for me. I want to be up there on the stage."[18] As Stevens recalled in her retirement, Johnson laughed, and her teacher (Madame Schoen-René of the Juilliard School) later confirmed the twenty-two-year-old mezzo's good judgment: "You're going to be prepared when you join the Met"—and she was. Thus Stevens avoided the blot of back-door entry to the Met via 'the Juilliard connection' and, after a few years of European experience (Prague and Vienna), returned to America a polished artist at age twenty-five. She would remain a Met favorite for twenty-three consecutive seasons, leaving fifty house Octavians (plus twenty-four on tour) as indisputable evidence of her artistic merit.

Her distinction is immediately apparent in the first phrases heard by the radio audience; musical phrasing and expressive word-painting are enhanced by her peculiar timbre. The strong line of 'Wie du warst! Wie du bist!' followed by a lovely soft high tone at 'Das weiss niemand'; the expansive surge of 'Selig bin ich'; the sudden lightening of 'Du' as the bewildered youth loses himself in the wonder of his love ('aber das Ich vergeht in dem Du')—the blending of every word and tone in Octavian's verbal embrace of the Marschallin bespeaks the authentic stage artist. The plucky assurance of the young mezzo springs out delightfully in the rhythmic bounce of 'Hier bin ich der Herr,' but when the Marschallin teaches him that all things are

Der Rosenkavalier
7 January 1939
Marschallin
Lotte Lehmann
Sophie
Marita Farell
Octavian
Risë Stevens
Baron Ochs
Emanuel List
Faninal
Friedrich Schorr
Conductor
Artur Bodanzky

short-lived dreams, Stevens' vibrant outpouring of tone conveys the pain and passion of the unhappy lover. In contrast to the swiftly changing colors and nuances of act one, Stevens settles for a single tonal dynamic in her straightforward presentation of the rose. When Sophie mentions his pet name 'Quinquin,' it is a delight to hear the characteristic deep laugh of her speaking voice (which the radio audience will come to know so well over five decades). Again the interpretation flowers, moving from her sarcastic chiding of Ochs ('heut wie morgen') on to the easy tonal flow of the duet with Sophie and back to the brisk manner in which Octavian informs the Baron of Sophie's change of intent. One might cavil with her overly caricatured playing of Mariandel in the seduction scene—she cannot find a middle ground between the nasality of 'I trink' kein Wein' and her natural singing voice for the longer phrases ('Es is ja eh'). (Thorborg is preferable here in her restraint, finding just the dosage of parody without stepping out of character.) Stevens plays it for laughs (though seeming oddly without a sense of humor). In the final scene, which Bodanzky paces with an apt sense of its aura, all three ladies shine. Lehmann launches the trio superbly (with too many breaths, of course), and Farell and Stevens are vocally assured; in the duet they add a touch of ardor to music which is often handled too gingerly.

Lehmann's Marschallin is a representative sample of her mature artistry. Every phrase bears the stamp of her authority and interpretive insight, all delivered with a unique combination of spontaneity and belief. There are vocal shortcomings. In the opening scene some of the rapid conversation is a near cackle (though perfectly paced and enunciated); but she soon finds a goodly measure of her old tonal beauty ('Ich bin auch jetzt noch nicht ganz wohl') and is able to lighten the voice without loss of quality as she receives the silver rose from Ochs. The monologue is vividly done. Both vocally (a perfect legato at 'Ach, du bist wieder da') and interpretively it is more charming and more pointed in meaning than in the earlier broadcast. Many lovely touches animate the farewell with Octavian: 'Er soll mich lassen' is softly voiced (as though she already feels the pain of parting); the pacing of 'ob ich in' Prater fahr' bespeaks an easy-gaited drive; 'da drin ist die silberne Ros'n' (*mezzoforte*, not *piano*) is delightfully supple, but devoid of special import—she saves that for her last line ('Der Herr Graf weiss ohnehin'). Count Octavian will understand, she tells us, conveying a multiplicity of meanings in these few final words. Possibly 'die Zeit' already sits too heavily on this Marschallin; one cannot deny that some of the womanly charm of the great lady is lost in the absence of consistent tonal softness and subtle modulation of dynamics and vocal flow. More important, the highly charged nature of the interpretation makes the Marschallin a very commanding figure; one wonders how Octavian had the courage to approach her in the first place. We can admire, but still question, the extreme bitterness of Lehmann's appraisal of Ochs ('Da geht er hin'), the overtly tragic reading of the entire 'Heut oder morgen' passage—when she cries that everything dissolves 'zwischen den Fingern' one feels that most of what the Marschallin can ever know and love has already passed through them. 'Die Zeit' is for this Marschallin (as perhaps for Lehmann herself) not just a 'sonderbar' thing but an enemy. But she can still wear the public mask and wrap her private fears in gentle tones as she asks Sophie 'So schnell hat Sie ihn gar so lieb?' Beyond all cavil, Lehmann had in her voice the sound of that "heavenly hurt" which Emily Dickinson knew:

> We can find no scar,
> But internal difference,
> Where the Meanings are.

Risë Stevens as Octavian in *Der Rosenkavalier*. Photography by Annemarie Heinrich.

Lotte Lehmann as the Marschallin in *Der Rosenkavalier*.

Lehmann reveals all the meanings of the Marschallin, even though a few scars as well are exposed.

In this *Rosenkavalier* the juxtaposition of old and new artistic generations is particularly striking: Lehmann in her last broadcast of the Marschallin, Stevens in her first broadcast as Octavian. The radio audience knew Lehmann only at the end of a long and exceptionally distinguished career, but it would have the pleasure of hearing the entire span of Stevens' (and many other young artists') progress over the next quarter century; the overview of a long career is one of the greatest rewards which the opera broadcasts offer.

Lehmann continued to sing the Marschallin in New York until her farewell performance on 23 February 1945 (she returned to the house the following year for a brief excerpt from *Walküre* to honor Melchior at his twentieth anniversary concert). Even then she was still trying to defeat the scourge of time—the farewell opera appearance had required some chicanery on her part and was achieved with the unlikely connivance of George Szell. The conductor wrote to Frank St. Leger (Met musical secretary) that he had seen Lehmann "the other day. She said that after all she is sorry to just quit singing opera without any further ado [she had not been a company member in 1943–44] and at the end of our conversation she decided that she would like to sing the Marschallin again, if I would make a little change in the third and fourth bar of the Terzetto." Szell, a taskmaster of legendary severity, capitulated with grace: "This change is so negligible that I had no hesitation in agreeing to it—so if you will she can sing it. I think it would be a wonderful thing to have her in one or two performances."[19] St. Leger replied, "we are glad to know that perhaps something may be worked out";[20] but a nationwide broadcast was a bit more of a risk, and the radio public heard the last of Lehmann's Marschallin in 1939.

A greater lament is the absence from the Metropolitan annals of Lehmann's renowned portrayal of *Fidelio*. When Beethoven's only opera returned to the Met repertory in the mid thirties, the honor went to Flagstad rather than Lehmann, although the latter had sung it repeatedly in Vienna and Salzburg under Franz Schalk, Clemens Krauss, and Toscanini. Kolodin would have us believe that Edward Johnson felt Lehmann could no longer negotiate the vocal hurdles of Leonora's great aria,[21] but the new general manager gives the lie to that and indicates that Bodanzky was the negative factor. Writing from Florence in July 1935, Johnson noted that "Bodanzky still thinks that we are doing Holländer and does not seem enthusiastic about Fidelio, especially with Lottie Lehman [*sic*]. On the contrary I think Lehman is magnificent in the part. . . . At the Opera I heard Rosen Kavalier [*sic*] with Lottie Lehman, in fine voice."[22] When both the *Dutchman* and the hoped-for Flagstad *Norma* were scratched from the 1935–36 season, *Fidelio* became a Flagstad vehicle and remained so for the next half-decade. The broadcast of that season is not preserved, but we have a tape with fine sonic quality of her second broadcast *Fidelio* (31 December 1938).

The performance (and the opera itself) is defaced by the infamous Bodanzky recitatives which the conductor had composed to replace much of the spoken dialogue. Not only was this far removed from Beethoven's intent, but it lessened the impact of Beethoven's original *melodrama* (spoken dialogue over instrumental accompaniment) which accompanies Leonore and Rocco's descent into the dungeon. The only virtue of the Bodanzky additions lies in the opportunity to hear Flagstad's way with (pseudo) classical recitative; there she displays a keen sense of the union of mood and tone, more so, in fact, than she does in formal song. Actually, one of her most expressive moments in the entire performance is a bit of spoken dialogue

Fidelio
31 December 1938
Leonore
Kirsten Flagstad
Marzelline
Marita Farell
Florestan
René Maison
Jacquino
Karl Laufkoetter
Pizarro
Friedrich Schorr
Rocco
Emanuel List
Fernando
Arnold Gabor
Conductor
Artur Bodanzky

('Gott, wer kann das ertragen?') as she views her wasted husband in chains. Another gratifying addition to the catalog of Flagstad's virtues is her feel for classical phraseology—she is adept at varying tonal weight at both arsic and thetic points. In particular, we hear this in her expert shaping of the phrases of the act-one trio (plenty of pliant tone here) and the dungeon duet with Rocco. Flagstad was acutely conscious of the stylistic difference between Beethoven and her customary Wagner roles: "They are two completely different ways of singing. You must be more refined, more careful in performing Beethoven, to obtain the proper blending of voices in the ensembles, such as the wonderful canon quartet in the first scene."[23] And Flagstad does begin the quartet with a sense of vocal freedom and lightly floated tone (which retains its color) while she sustains the loveliest legato yet heard from her.

But refinement and care need not result in bloodless boredom. Flagstad's vocal solidity veers close to stolidity too often during the afternoon. The 'Abscheulicher' scene is disappointing in its sameness of manner. Beethoven has taken his cue from the great accompanied recitatives of opera seria, which were notable for the swift alternation of contrasting passions—his scene is a splendid opportunity for the gifted singing actress. But Flagstad is neither horror-struck at hearing Pizarro's monstrous plan to murder the prisoner nor sufficiently pathetic in the ensuing 'Des Mitleids Ruf'; she does provide her own brand of expressivity at 'so leuchtet mir ein Farbenbogen' (but it is not quite a rainbow we hear in the tone) and 'der blickt so still' is appropriately tranquil (the lower middle voice radiates the warmth which only she can provide). But the even level of expression robs the aria ('Komm Hoffnung') of its own aura of calm. Sometimes the voice seems insufficiently supported in the softer phrases and, while the marked *portamenti* are observed, they become overly weighted as they near the resting note. The upward scales are occasionally labored (yet distinct), but the treacherous high B poses no problem and the octave intervals are wonderfully secure. Again, no sense of exaltation animates the concluding agitato section as Leonore places her faith in God's help. In the finale to the act her voice gains in color and the portrayal grows more sympathetic; the concluding phrases of the act-two duet with Rocco are very lovely indeed. Her thrusting vocal manner is perfect for the confrontation with Pizarro, and in the angular phrases of 'O namenlose Freude!' both soprano and tenor avoid the jog trot which often mars this supreme moment (Flagstad and René Maison actually sing the intervals and yet manage to convey adequate elation). Flagstad loved the role of Leonora: "Nothing surpasses *Fidelio* in music, nothing!" she wrote, and noted that "it brings out the best in the sincere artist."[24] Unfortunately, not on this Saturday afternoon.

Maison is in representative form and makes a convincing Florestan. List sings Rocco as well as anything he has undertaken in these years, and Marita Farell is always in the picture as Marzelline (though perhaps too slight of tone in the ensembles). It is a pleasure to hear Schorr in such consistently fine form as the evil Pizarro. Of course, he was not born to be a villain and cannot make overmuch of 'Ha! welch ein Augenblick!' His spoken dialogue before the aria is marvelously snarly but as soon as he sings his first phrase that beauty of tone *will* shine through. He is better suited to cajoling Rocco into the crime, and there both men are at their best. Schorr gives 'Dann werd' ich schnell, vermummt mich in den Kerker schleichen' a snakelike profile, not by means of Gothic horror accents but entirely as a musical expression. And in the dungeon quartet Schorr refuses to turn Pizarro into a caricature, but relies instead on the impact of his commanding tone and manner.

Schorr and List, Flagstad and Lehmann, and Bodanzky sustain the integrity of the German wing in these adjuncts to the Wagner vogue of the 1930s, a German wing that, just as Witherspoon had written, was "probably the strongest in the world." Could it be that he was also correct in his view of the "lamentably weak" Italian wing of the Metropolitan?

Giovanni Martinelli as Otello.

CHAPTER TWELVE

1937-40
The Italian Wing

In 1935 Witherspoon had directed his strongest censure at Martinelli, but it was the grand old tenor who, two years later and in his twenty-fifth consecutive season, would provide one of the indelible portrayals of Metropolitan annals.

Benchmarks of operatic characterization dot Met history. We have marked some of them already in Lehmann's Marschallin, Flagstad's Isolde, Schorr's Hans Sachs; Martinelli's Otello is another. The opera had not been heard at the Metropolitan since 1913 when Leo Slezak, Antonio Scotti or Pasquale Amato, and Frances Alda had played out the version of the Shakespearean tragedy which Boito fashioned for the aged Verdi. The composer's sizable repertory had been doled out to the radio audience rather meagerly in the first years of the broadcasts. The popular *Aida, Traviata, Trovatore*, and *Rigoletto* were offered with some regularity, but only *Simon Boccanegra* and a single *La Forza del Destino* had given a hint of the vast riches of the Verdi catalog. *Macbeth* and *Ernani* from the early period, *Ballo in Maschera, Vespri Siciliani*, and the supreme works of his maturity, *Don Carlo, Otello*, and *Falstaff*, were strangers to the Met repertory of the 1930s. Martinelli, Tibbett, and Rethberg had ensured the success of the austere *Boccanegra*, and they would do the same for the overtly romantic *Otello*. Over four consecutive seasons, Martinelli's tormented Moor and Tibbett's suave Iago enthralled radio audiences. We hear them first on the broadcast of 12 February 1938.

Martinelli's Otello is worthy of its repute. From the unflagging muscularity of the opening 'Esultate!' through his superbly paced delivery of the monologues, his is a monumental piece of work. He is in excellent vocal form, the upper octave brightly colored and firmly gathered, the lower octave deficient in color and lyric flow but harboring a shadowy burr well suited to the grief which overtakes Otello. Though Martinelli cannot suggest mood changes by acute dynamic variation or tonal coloration, his mastery of legato and his singular ability to give meaningful shape to every phrase are near full compensation. He begins the first-act love duet with almost baritonal depth, thereby making doubly effective the closing measures where the treacherous high A-flats of 'Venere splende' are splendidly sustained by a seemingly endless flow of pointed, glistening tones, as clean and incisive as though etched by the finest Spanish scimitar. Where most tenors settle for a garbled text at this point in an effort to conquer the tessitura, Martinelli easily shapes the consonants of 'splende'—

Otello
12 February 1938
Desdemona
Elisabeth Rethberg
Otello
Giovanni Martinelli
Iago
Lawrence Tibbett
Lodovico
Nicola Moscona
Conductor
Ettore Panizza

179

it is a peerless moment, the kind that makes a Martinelli performance unforgettable. The monologues of the successive acts are equally memorable. Panizza sets too deliberate a pace for Otello's farewell to past joys, and momentum is lost (the *pesante* chords are absurdly ritarded), but Martinelli is ever the noble sufferer, never excessively overwrought; this Moor has some fiber left in him yet. Both tenor and baritone have plenty of voice for the vengeance duet.

The emotional climax of the performance is reached in the third act, and here Rethberg and Martinelli respond vividly in their dramatic confrontations. The soprano, rather dull in tone and manner to this point in the opera, suddenly comes to life, giving a lovely shape and tonal gloss to 'Dio ti giocondi.' Martinelli immediately betters her by the suavity, perfect legato, and extension of his response ('Grazie, madonna'). Otello's three demands for 'il fazzoletto' rise to the *terribile* which Verdi demanded. Rethberg fills 'Esterrefatta fisso' with genuine emotion and is vocally admirable (though she cannot quite settle her voice at the *piano* dynamic in the lower A to C range). Martinelli subtly suggests the irony of 'Datemi ancor l'eburnea mano, vo' fare ammenda,' and then moves quickly to an outsized denunciation of this vile harlot before dissolving into a truly stifled and ugly 'la sposa d'Otello' (*voce soffocata*, Verdi marked it). The tenor knows well that the heart of 'Dio! mi potevi' lies in the dull monotone of the lengthy succession of repeated A-flats and E-flats, and unlike some Otellos who mangle the monologue in a misguided search for variety, he employs a raised pitch only once (at 'd'angoscie'). An easier flow of gentler tone would be welcome at the transition to cantabile ('Ma, o pianto'), but the conclusion, with its ringing B-flat, is searing. In the final monologue, as Otello awaits death, Panizza (rather addicted to slow tempos throughout) adopts a genuine adagio pace which Martinelli is able to sustain, thus providing a more majestic close than usual. Of course, the tenor is a master of the anguished cry ('Ah morta'), but he effectively returns to noble song as Otello recalls the kisses of the act-one love duet.

If Martinelli's aristocratic art is sometimes deficient in tonal blandishment, Tibbett provides both qualities in full measure. The role of Iago seems made for him, and he takes advantage of its myriad opportunities for technical and dramatic subtleties. He is no burly bully—actually, except for the Credo and vengeance duet, Verdi's villain is quite an elegant fellow. (On this performance tape, I suggest the Credo derives from another performance where Tibbett was not quite at his best.) Tibbett is the most musicianly of singers, and his characterization is already filled out. In the opening address to Roderigo, usually a rather pedestrian moment, Tibbett weaves back and forth between the fluctuating moods of the text. In the drinking song he again is the vocal spendthrift, every resonant tone pinpointed onto the twisting chromatic phrases—his Iago makes a very jaunty drinking companion. He turns another face to Otello as he explains Cassio's drunkenness in ravishing mezza voce ('Avessi io prima'). His command of the *piano* dynamic and *portamento* gets a full workout, notably at 'è il Duce del nostro Duce' in his act-two scene with Cassio and when he taunts Otello before describing Cassio's dream. And he vividly conjures up the "dream" by insinuating and subtly controlled tone. How quietly he reminds Otello of the handkerchief before Otello dismisses him in act three! With what finesse he plays on Cassio for the benefit of the eavesdropping Otello; what man would not believe in a friend who addressed him with the tonal balm Tibbett pours into 'O Capitano'? Why would not Cassio willingly parade his love for Bianca when Tibbett's sly banter mirrors the elegant dance rhythms of the orchestra? Tibbett follows Hamlet's advice, delivering Iago's venom "trippingly on the tongue," and then he conjures up the spider's web ('Questa è una ragna') which finally entraps the lover, even as Verdi's Falstaffian phrases flit along. Tibbett's Iago is a continuous stream of virtuoso musical and dramatic effects—vocal witchery.

Rethberg startles with some decidedly acidulous tone as she enters with the children in act two, but soon she settles to an adequately voiced duet and quartet, gains markedly both in vocal control and dramatic fervor in the third act, and finally comes into her own in the Willow Song. 'Povera Barbara' is as honey-toned a phrase as ever fell from her lips, and the final 'Salce' trio is immaculately poised. One can quibble about the excessively open final *e* and *o* vowels and the annoying (and unmarked) fermate on the penultimate note of each 'ghirlanda,' but this is vintage Rethberg. The Ave Maria is not so successful (though the final ascending 'Ave' to a *piano* A-flat is neatly done). The prayer is a treacherous piece for sopranos, anchored as it is in the *passaggio*; is there a soprano who can sing the sustained 'prega' both dolcissimo and on pitch?—not even Rethberg, at this stage of her career. Panizza commits his own sins with the gigantic allargando chords preceding 'Per noi tu prega,' and he decimates the 'bacio' theme by anticipating the crescendi instead of allowing them to flower on their own (he echoes his error—on a grander scale—in the massive third-act ensemble). The taut rhythmic drive of the first-act storm music is welcome, however, and he sends the 'fire' chorus along at a good clip. In the lesser roles, Nicola Moscona is a solid Lodovico, but it takes a better tenor than Massue to make Cassio seem in Otello's league, either as lover or governor. How nice to hear Votipka at some length! She conducts a strong line in the third-act ensemble, and her fine tone and dramatic involvement sustain the vehemence generated by Desdemona's strangulation and provide a foil for Rethberg's delicate farewell.

Johnson capitalized on the success of the revival by choosing it for the opening night of the following season, keeping the cast intact with one exception: Rethberg was replaced by a debutante soprano, Maria Caniglia, still in the first decade of her long and honorable career. Two weeks later (3 December 1938) she was given the broadcast as well. Evidently great things were expected of her, for she was assigned the season's first performances of Aida, Tosca, Mistress Ford, and Amelia (*Boccanegra*), all within a three-week period. The search for the successor to Ponselle (Cigna had departed after two seasons) and an alternative to Rethberg continued. Johnson was intent on building up the Italian repertory of the Met and had begun with *Otello*. He believed that "a repertory is made from the artists that are available: it cannot be a cast-iron mold from which available artists will emerge. My first obligation is to secure the right people in the right places, and after three years I am only just beginning to demonstrate a well-balanced company."[1]

Johnson had heard Caniglia as Desdemona at the Florence Maggio Musicale the previous year. As the succession of her roles indicates, the soprano possessed an indisputable Verdi voice, and her credentials in this area were fortified by her Salzburg appearances as Mistress Ford under Toscanini. To her broadcast Desdemona Caniglia brought the overt manner of the Italian stages of the 1930s, a welcome if slightly wearing bounty. Her vocal timbre is highly individual, carrying its own authority (too much so for Shakespeare's Desdemona, though perhaps not excessive for Verdi's), and almost brazenly opulent in the lower part of the voice. Sometimes her phrasing suffers from shortness of breath—often the final note of a phrase is unsupported and abruptly released (as in the love duet). On the other hand, she knows how to dilate a line (in contrast to Rethberg's linear conduction) and how to fill it with vivid tone. Her *pianissimi* are curiously white, yet they haunt the memory.

Otello
3 December 1938

Desdemona
Maria Caniglia
Otello
Giovanni Martinelli
Iago
Lawrence Tibbett
Lodovico
Nicola Moscona
Conductor
Ettore Panizza

The top voice can turn hard and flatten out at key moments (the final phrase of her entrance with her ladies); Serafin, in warning her away from Butterfly and Elvira, had told her "You have a top, but it is not your glory."[2] Still, the timbre, legato, and musico-dramatic cohesion of 'D'un uom che geme' are worth the price of her defects, especially when solidified by our first taste of her fruity *voce di petto* ('ho peccato'). The entire quartet enjoys unusual vitality, Martinelli spinning his line, Votipka and Tibbett alert, and Caniglia's instrument by now taking on its full lustre. Her third act is less successful. In agitated moments she turns squally and the voice becomes tremulous ('A terra! sì, nel livido fango'); at this moment Rethberg summoned pathos through the beauty of her voice and style, while Caniglia's emotion overheats an already emotion-laden episode. The earlier 'Esterrefatta fisso' has a fine declamatory ring to it, and genuine horror stains her *forte* 'una Furia.' Thus, the fourth-act arias are all the more surprising for their tender feeling and even pace. The rising arcs of the Willow Song are well sculpted; the string of *Salce*s are secure and brushed with telling *portamenti*. The legato, pure tone, and distension of the concluding 'Io per amarlo e per morir,' the perfectly modulated diction of the 'Ave Maria' (on a well-settled series of low E-flats), and the tragic manner of 'Son perduta! ei tradito!' bespeak the qualities which would make her the reigning spinto soprano of the Italian opera houses for almost two decades. But New York would hear her no more, for the sounds of September guns in Europe would prevent her return.

Yet another artist made his house debut that afternoon as Cassio, and it is he who will strengthen the Italian wing and remain for a quarter century of memorable vignettes on the Metropolitan stage. Though character cameos would soon become his lot, Alessio de Paolis had sung leading roles in Italy, and in his style if not his vocal quality one discerns the assured command of a major artist. One hears it in the rhythmic stride of 'Questa del pampino' in the drinking scene, and later, when Verdi skillfully allows the clear-cut scheme of the drinking scene to disintegrate as Cassio becomes drunk, De Paolis' firm off-beat phrases point up the warring rhythms between chorus and principals. Thus the tenor gives Cassio the stature essential to his focal role in the drama. And, at this point in his career, the voice is of adequate size with a secure top.

Beyond Caniglia and De Paolis, Tibbett's altered approach to Iago focuses attention in this second broadcast *Otello*. A year earlier vocal subtlety was the keystone of his performance, particularly in his extensive use of mezza voce and his rhythmic dexterity. His current Iago is still a masterly portrayal (and he is in splendid vocal form), but the elegant virtuoso has been replaced by the powerhouse baritone. From the first, a blacker villian exposes himself. The vocal color is darker, menace is laid onto the tone, a slurred legato may be suggestively employed. Gone is Iago as the charming comrade for appearance' sake. Most of the marvelous *piano* effects have been upgraded a notch or two, and insinuation has been superceded by certainty. The Credo is stunning in its vocal magnitude, a snarl of villainy, and one notes an uncharacteristic (for Tibbett) predilection for raised pitch accents for dramatic effect. Yet the delicious swing he gives to 'Il mio pensiero è vago' as he questions Otello about Cassio's acquaintance with Desdemona in Venice, is a welcome reminder of his earlier artful manner, as is his beautiful tone and legato when he repeats Otello's 'Che ascondo in cor.' In the dream sequence he points up the text much more vividly, and as a result, the legato and mezza voce suffer; even so, the blend of the sinister with his *piano* tone fascinates.

Has not the overall character of the opera been slightly coarsened? Panizza's fast tempi, for instance, allow only the broadest of interpretive gestures. The storm opening has undeniable brio, but the 'Vittoria' ensemble becomes a rat race for brass and chorus, and there are some decidedly ragged orchestral moments in the Credo. Yet Panizza's pace for the Ave Maria is so flaccid one wonders if Desdemona will suffocate from natural causes. One welcome improvement occurs in 'Ora e per sempre addio,' where Panizza adopts Martinelli's fleeter tempo. Unlike Tibbett, the tenor has lowered the intensity of this first soliloquy—the torment has turned inward, and thus the frenzy of the later moments is doubly effective. The tenor provides a tremendous climax as he vaults to the high B-flat. The apex of Martinelli's performance remains the third-act soliloquy where he turns the long, drawn-out lines of Verdi's music into bands of anguish.

The following season (on 24 February 1940) produced yet another *Otello* (with Rethberg rejoining her colleagues); this has been selected as the fourth in the series of Metropolitan Opera Historic Broadcast recordings. (The Appendix contains a complete list of historic recordings issued by the Met from 1976 to 1990.) In some ways the selection is unfortunate, for the two earlier broadcasts capture better portrayals by Martinelli and Tibbett.

Age finally has alloyed the tensile strength of the fifty-five-year-old tenor. He gets off to a slow start, and the signs of strain which mar the opening 'Esultate!' recur occasionally throughout the performance, causing a nonresonant, wooden tone (as in the opening of the love duet) and a gravitational pull on his high register. Nothing can rob Martinelli of his linear perception, however ('E tu m'amavi'), and the sustained close to the duet is again remarkable. He can no longer rage with quite the old gusto ('Sì, pel ciel'), and he is sometimes hard put to prevent the notes in the *passaggio* from disintegrating. When he begins to resort to a number of raised pitches in the repeated note recitation of 'Dio! mi potevi,' one fears a noble interpretation is being vulgarized. But compensation is at hand. For loss of stentorian power he substitutes greater sensitivity as he begins 'Ma, o pianto'; he even manages a dolce climax at 'l'anima acqueto.' And the remarkable breath control is unimpaired. Best of all is 'Niun mi tema,' sung with a more modulated tone than before. Here, in the simple directness of Martinelli's singing, Otello regains his lost nobility—no dramatic posing, no vocal mugging mars the soliloquy, and the tenor has one moment of vocal splendor left for his trumpeted 'Oh! Gloria!'

Not age but wear and tear begins to creep into Tibbett's singing about this time. Of course, he is still the great singing actor with plenty of vocal goods to deliver, but like a bit of rust first appearing on a broad expanse of fine metal, one can spot the signs of incipient decay. In place of the remembered perfect legato, he introduces a slight puff of breath between consonant and vowel on many notes at the higher dynamic level, and the upper range can turn slightly cavernous. Thus a certain squareness penetrates the musical thought; a built-in quaver for dramatic intensification is often introduced. But all these are sometime things. Many extraordinary moments remain, including the sure thrust of the drinking song and the magical mezza voce of Cassio's dream (where the dolcissimo high E of 'sogno' is held forever, as if to show he can still command the quieter effects). And there are a few improvements. Each note in the downward chromatic runs of the drinking song is both distinct and legato; Iago's whispered advice to Otello ('Temete, signor, la gelosia') is more pregnant with meaning than before, and he fills the end of the Credo ('la Morte') with rich, menacing tone. In overall musical and dramatic manner Tibbett achieves a better balance between the elegant virtuosity of the first broadcast and the

Otello
24 February 1940
Desdemona
Elisabeth Rethberg
Otello
Giovanni Martinelli
Iago
Lawrence Tibbett
Lodovico
Nicola Moscona
Conductor
Ettore Panizza

baritonal power of the second, but neither aspect is quite as fine in itself.

Other positive elements in this historic recording stand out. Panizza has found the interpretive *mode juste.* The rhythmic drive of the opening storm music and the fleetness of the fire chorus are harnessed for greater impact than gained by the pell-mell dash of the earlier broadcasts. He now allows a graceful background to contrast with Iago's machinations in act three. (In key moments of the later acts, however, the string ensemble abandons precision.) Moscona's Lodovico has improved in legato and rich tone, while Votipka is absolutely splendid in the final act; her voice seems to take on a more solid core. Not so De Paolis; though still excellent in act one, he falters badly on a few high phrases as Tibbett parades him before the gullible Moor in act three. Character roles are clearly to be his full measure in the future.

The major gain is in Rethberg's Desdemona. She gives one of the finest performances of her late career, and the reassurance as to her vocal estate comes early on: she forbears lunging at the top notes ('ai soavi abbracciamenti'); her difficulties with the *passaggio* are minimal, and the old silver sheen threads her tones. The most difficult phrases (the descending 't'allieti il core' in the quartet and the ascending 'del mio dolor' which leads into the large concertato of act three) are well managed. Acts three and four show many exquisite effects: 'io prego il cielo' and 'Quel Sol sereno e vivido' are spun out deliciously; the Willow Song is vocally poised throughout, and while some of the Ave Maria poses a problem, it is more secure than the 1937 effort. Her overall performance holds more nuance, too, and thus her characterization is stronger. Though she tells us nothing of Desdemona's gentle nature as she matter-of-factly enters with the children in act two, she pinpoints the sorrowful moment of mystification at Otello's doubting her chastity ('la sento e non l'intendo') and is fully involved after Otello throws her to the ground before all the court. She is both strong in her challenge to her murdering husband and lovely in her defense of her innocence, even summoning an uncharacteristically realistic gasp of breath as she dies. Rethberg is certainly no mere shadow of her former vocal self on this afternoon, and to the pleasure of the moment may be added the deep satisfaction of recognition and remembrance.

When this sequence of *Otello* broadcasts ends in January 1941, yet another Desdemona (Stella Roman) makes the journey from Venice to Cyprus to be greeted by the familiar company of the earlier broadcasts. Overall, this is not an afternoon for great singing, since Martinelli's weakening vocal capacity prevents him from trumpeting Otello's frenzy and woe in the old way. We are approaching the point where Iago's 'Ecco il Leone!' over the prone Otello is not merely a stage device. But the tenor is still the artist, ever trying to communicate; and that he still can do, especially in his moving delivery of the third- and fourth-act soliloquies. With Tibbett, the case is more complicated. A "throat ailment" had caused him to cancel all operatic and concert engagements for the four months previous to his return to the Met in early January 1941. Perhaps he returned too soon, for there is no mistaking the dull, veiled tone, the slightly insecure attack, or the reliance on slurs instead of legato throughout the first act. The voice has become unwieldy, and the rhythmic and tonal point of the drinking song is considerably diminished. Of necessity, the familiar suavity gives way to more obvious dramatic effects in the big moments of act two. Nevertheless, the entire episode surrounding 'Era la notte' retains a good measure of distinction. If a little less reliable, he still can summon his haunting mezza voce for 'movea, nell'abbandono del sogno' (but not for 'quasi baciando'). No one can equal him in this kind of moment. If some of the finesse is gone, he works hard at new ways

Otello
18 January 1941
Desdemona
Stella Roman
Otello
Giovanni Martinelli
Iago
Lawrence Tibbett
Lodovico
Nicola Moscona
Conductor
Ettore Panizza

to convey the same meaning and steadily improves throughout the performance until his generally fine third act inspires hope for a full recovery. Decline there may be, but no fall seems imminent.

Romanian soprano Stella Roman had been scheduled for the opening night of the season in *Ballo in Maschera*, but conditions in Europe had prevented her flight from Lisbon on the Clipper. She finally arrived by ship to make her debut as Aida on New Year's Day 1941 and to sing her first Metropolitan Desdemona on the 18 January broadcast. She carried with her a half-dozen years' experience in the opera houses of Italy (Rome and La Scala, including the Empress in the Italian premiere of *Die Frau ohne Schatten*), Germany, Spain, and South America. Her training had included study in Milan with Baldassare Tedeschi and Ericlea Darclée (the first Tosca). Hers would become a familiar voice to the radio public, perhaps a shade more familiar than warranted, since she proves a puzzling singer in her debut broadcast.

The voice is a fine spinto with a strikingly piquant timbre (rather Muzio-like), richly colored at the higher dynamic levels and capable of spinning lovely *pianissimi* throughout the entire range. These are formidable gifts for any singer, but the soprano too often negates them by an odd, pointillistic treatment of line. Virtually every note suffers an initial attack followed by a partial float—it becomes wearing throughout an entire afternoon and is subversive to the cantabile at critical points in the opera ('Dio, ti giocondi,' or when Desdemona leads the third-act ensemble). She produces a number of fine effects: a *piano* high B-flat which concludes her act-two entry; ringing climaxes as Desdemona proclaims her innocence at the close of her scene with Otello; a lengthy and beautifully spun out A-flat at the end of the Ave Maria (one can suffer a lot for that alone); and the dramatic thrust of her final 'Son perduta!' (followed by a commanding, chesty 'ei tradito!'). She is obviously a singer of temperament, and where an isolated effect is everything, Roman can supply it readily enough. When she leaves off her pointillistic manner to sing a legato phrase ('Muoio innocente') one realizes what a beautiful singer she might be. But, alas, the wait was overlong and Desdemona is dead within the measure. Actually, the fourth-act arias are quite well done, but the suspicion grows that her breath support is erratic, preventing her from sustaining long tones or from joining her various telling effects into a cohesive whole. One can always hope debut nerves are the culprit.

Roman is yet another in that line of dramatic sopranos with which the management sought to fill the void created by Ponselle's abandonment of the soprano repertory and eventual retirement from opera. Roman would remain throughout the decade, longer than the much admired but transitory triumvirate of Dusolina Giannini, Cigna, and Caniglia. Although it seemed unlikely at the time, the hallowed mantle of Ponselle would settle eventually on the shoulders of Zinka Milanov, though it rested there rather precariously for the first dozen years of her American career. But when a singer dominates a repertory for almost three decades, a slow start is more than offset by a strong finish.

Ponselle's farewell occurred in April 1937, and that summer Johnson, Ziegler, and Bodanzky journeyed to Prague in search of new talent. A little-known Yugoslav soprano caught their attention. Milanov was just entering upon an international career after ten years of singing Italian and German opera (in her native Croatian) in Yugoslavia. Engagements at Prague followed, and in 1937 she was called to Vienna to replace an indisposed Aida. Fortune favored her, and the *Aida* conductor, Bruno Walter, recommended her to Toscanini, who then engaged her for the 1937 Salzburg Verdi Requiem. With these few sterling credentials appliquéd to her provincial experience, the Metropolitan beckoned. She made her debut as the *Trovatore* Leonora in mid-December 1937. It was a fortunate choice, for Milanov had another tie with the Metropolitan: she had been the only pupil of Milka Ternina, a legendary soprano at the Metropolitan at the turn of the century. With Ternina she had prepared Leonora.

There was yet another link with the past when *Trovatore* was broadcast on 8 January 1938: Martinelli's first Met Manrico had been under Toscanini in his famous restudy of the work in 1914. With Castagna and Bonelli in the cast, the afternoon promised a good deal. But it was a promise often unfulfilled on the harsh, shallow-toned tape. Lazzari is a sturdy Ferrando, the monochromatic blackness of his bass capably mirroring the dark horrors detailed in the opening narrative. Castagna is decidedly off form, her tones often white, the top pinched and frequently under or above pitch (an entire half-tone flat in Azucena's final cry) with too much unsupported tone in the middle range—for once her Hippodrome birthing seems credible. Bonelli provides the most secure vocalism of the afternoon (some of his scenes are not preserved).

At one time Martinelli must have been an ideal troubadour, but now both the offstage serenade and 'Ah sì, ben mio' are decidedly short on vocal charm, though the latter boasts some striking examples of his control of breath and line. Distance affects more than the heart, for he manages to sound more attractive in his remote tower during the Miserere. Elsewhere he is appropriately all virile tone and rhythmic impulse, capping 'Di quella pira' (transposed) with a pair of secure, trumpeted top tones. And he is superb in his fiery denunciation of the poisoned Leonora. The final scene of the opera is the most satisfying; this Manrico seems to have saved all his tenderness for foster-mother Azucena, and Castagna summons enough of her familiar vocal velvet in the middle and low voice for an affecting 'Ai nostri monti.' Conductor Gennaro Papi does little to abet the sensitive work of the two artists here or elsewhere, and the orchestra sounds incredibly bored with the whole affair (in 'Ah sì, ben mio' the flabby winds make no attempt to link up the vocal phrases).

Enough of debutante Milanov's performance is preserved to give a fair view of her first season's efforts (though the act-one 'Tacea la notte' has patently been pieced into the tape from another performance—it is clearly vintage Milanov and the Inez is not the listed Votipka. Occasionally these performance tapes are like a put-together antique—the material is all old and related, but the parts never saw the light of day at the same time.) Already one can recognize the singular nature of her equipment in the trio, which she closes with a brilliant, if rather hectic, high D-flat. From the first, a tendency to hurl herself against the music in agitated moments is apparent. The habit is sometimes mistakenly called 'temperament'; exciting it may be for the auditor, but the singer takes her chances with such an approach. Here it works, and the quick passages in unison with Martinelli are well cut. The most extensive excerpts are from the final act. For a few minutes, an aura of golden-age singing hangs in the air as Milanov moves with dazzling assurance through the pitfalls of 'D'amor sull'ali' (the tessitura is "tremendous,"[3] to use Milanov's word).

Her hearty chest tone leaps out at us in the introductory 'Timor di me?'—weightier than in her later years, and an effective foil for the finely floated phrases which follow. Many superb touches in the aria command attention: excellent trills, each one clearly articulated with no loss of tonal fullness; the suave descending scale of 'conforta'; unforced top tones near the end of the aria ('le pene'); a brilliant cadenza securely executed over the entire range. Inescapably in the ear is the sound

Il Trovatore
8 January 1938

Leonora
Zinka Milanov
Azucena
Bruna Castagna
Manrico
Giovanni Martinelli
Di Luna
Richard Bonelli
Ferrando
Virgilio Lazzari
Conductor
Gennaro Papi

of her later recording of this aria; we miss the extended arch of the long phrases (they are lovely here, nevertheless), and there are none of those *subito piano* tones which later make one hold one's breath.

Lovely *piano* moments peep through, but she seems not yet to have exploited their magical suspension to the full. Then, abruptly, the magic turns sour with a quick release of the aria's final tone after a dreadful bobble. Excellence suddenly becomes "erratic," a term which would haunt Milanov for a decade. Sometimes she narrows the tone into a honed brilliance with a knifelike point (unlike the rich sonority of her later career), while at other times her tone seems so full that it flies around in her mouth as if seeking escape. She handles the Miserere confidently, never coarsening her tone to manage the low tessitura. The sound of youth is in the voice and hints of the Ponselle manner in the vowel formation, smooth flow of legato, and density of sound. But prodigality is both her glory and her curse, for when she puts excessive pressure on final top tones they fly sharp (especially obvious at the repeat of 'Prima che d'altri vivere,' where she is doubled by the winds). The conclusion of the opera is marred by this momentary but critical failing.

Thus a slight cliffhanger aspect worries itself into her performance; it is a reflection of the Milanov persona—"Half child, half woman—entirely prima donna,"[4] *Opera News* called her a few years later. Language was a problem (as late as 1939 she told a reporter "I am learning Italian as fast as I can").[5] She had just worked off twenty-five pounds in six months (the requirement was a clause in her Met contract) for she was "a big girl,"[6] as she described herself. Her beautiful face would often be downcast during these early years—"The Metropolitan treated me so badly."[7] Most artists, by the time they have earned a Metropolitan engagement, have at call a large acquaintance of fellow singers from the international circuit, but Milanov had no such backlog to give her assurance. "I did not know the language and had no money and knew not a soul to talk to and advise me. . . . Maestro Papi did not believe in me, giving me a hard time."[8] Could all these uncertainties prevent the conquest which her natural abilities warranted?

Papi was again at the helm for her first broadcast of Aida on 26 February, and her uneasiness was certainly not diminished when Martinelli collapsed (an attack of indigestion) during 'Celeste Aida.' A year later Milanov again sang the broadcast Aida (4 February 1939), and this time her tenor remained constant, though he was the inconstant Beniamino Gigli, returning to the scene of his crime against company solidarity for the first time since he had refused a salary cut seven years earlier. Fortunately, Milanov this time had the reassuring hand of Panizza to guide her. We have only the extended soprano-tenor duets of the third and fourth acts, but what souvenirs they are of this rare encounter, the only Metropolitan pairing of these two mercurial artists!

Clearly, the day was meant to belong to Gigli. Though tradition calls for the final curtain bow to go to the title role, it is Gigli rather than newcomer Milanov at the end of the third act who last comes forth to receive what Mr. Cross calls "a royal reception." And though he deserves a general's welcome for his Radames, it is Milanov whose Aida is in the true regal line. The tenor's resources are better mated with lyric roles, but he captures the martial thrust of 'Pur ti riveggo,' and supplies plenty of the rapture (*con trasporto*) required by Verdi. Milanov begins in somewhat flurried fashion, but 'Là tra foreste vergine' is not only lovely in tone but surprisingly seductive in manner (as is her later questioning of Radames). Attempts at realistic character portrayal are a rarity in performances by the mature Milanov, and they are

Aida
4 February 1939
Aida
Zinka Milanov
Amneris
Bruna Castagna
Radames
Beniamino Gigli
Amonasro
Carlo Tagliabue
Ramfis
Ezio Pinza
Conductor
Ettore Panizza

welcome, indeed. Another unexpected pleasure is the mellow quality of her low voice when not utilizing the *voce di petto* (which she seldom does on this occasion). The reprise of 'Là tra foreste' at the *mezzo forte* level is exquisite, and she does not disappoint as she vaults to a sustained *piano* B-flat to close the episode. Gigli recklessly launches 'Sì: fuggiam da queste mura,' giving not even a nod to the alternating dynamics marked in his phrases, but no sense of vocal strain obtrudes as Panizza hurries both artists along the path of betrayal. Milanov now directs her full battery on Verdi's charged vocal line, and Gigli recognizes he must contend with an authentic competitor. With the unison 'Vieni meco' we enter the bullring. The splendid outpouring of tone obliterates a few messy releases, and the audience breaks in with eager applause. The excitement is palpable, one of those old-fashioned moments that makes the auditor a willing conspirator. Italian baritone Carlo Tagliabue joins them for a trio which sustains the fervent pitch before Gigli thrusts out his pointedly secure (and happily brief) 'Io resto a te.'

Milanov has all the requisite *morendo* for the tomb duet. Gigli does, too; but then, he must be Gigli and cloy his already honeyed tone with indulgent sobs. Milanov's 'Vedi? di morte l'angelo' is somewhat short on serenity; Panizza likes to keep things moving until he suddenly applies the brakes to the final four bars (they are fully twice as slow as the opening tempo), thereby enabling Milanov to produce some ravishing dolcissimo effects. She continues to spin bewitching tone throughout 'O terra addio'—the old house can have heard no more beautiful phrase than 'volano al raggio dell'eterno dì' (perhaps Panizza, too, was mesmerized, for he long delays bringing in the orchestra as she reaches the tonic note). Unlike most tenors, Gigli is able to manipulate his tone around the serpentine phrases of the duet (where Milanov oddly neglects to sing her first interjection). Though their tone is glorious in the unison repeat, the singers do not achieve quite the intimacy of this most tranquil of opera finales—to Castagna is left the task of restoring peace.

Gigli was soon off to Europe, never to return to the Metropolitan, but Milanov remained. She sang yet another *Trovatore* broadcast (1939) and the following season introduced perhaps her most celebrated portrayal: Gioconda. The broadcast of 30 December 1939 was also her house debut in the role, one of those historic occasions for which we doubly prize the preserved recording. In this case, sonic quality is more than acceptable. Deficient as the opera may be in verisimilitude, compensation comes in the multiple opportunities for full-throated song afforded the six principals.

The lower end of the vocal spectrum is rather shortchanged since Kaskas offers an unimaginative, wooden-toned 'Voce di donna,' while Moscona's bass dries up as it descends, and he is not able to stabilize the open vowel sounds on sustained notes. Carlo Morelli, in his fifth and final Met season, surprises with a well-sung Barnaba, though he lacks the built-in bite necessary for a nasty villain (his baritone is more De Luca than Ruffo). Thus, 'O monumento!' with its architectural scope and declamatory manner, is less satisfying than the lyrical moments, where his pleasant timbre and easy musicality count for more. Castagna is excellent throughout. With her warm, velvety tones she manages to make Laura's overly frenetic music fall agreeably on the ear. Martinelli's Enzo is not always so agreeable. The mood-painting of 'Cielo e mar!' requires a suave lyricism which he cannot supply (though his clear articulation of the turn that closes the aria must be admired). I like best the way he swings onto the main melody of the first-act duet; he fills it with precise rhythmic play and accents (unlike Gigli's spewing out of careless stresses in similar moments of the

La Gioconda
30 December 1939

Gioconda
Zinka Milanov
Laura
Bruna Castagna
La Cieca
Anna Kaskas
Enzo
Giovanni Martinelli
Barnaba
Carlo Morelli
Alvise
Nicola Moscona
Conductor
Ettore Panizza

Zinka Milanov as La Gioconda.

4 February *Aida*). For most of the afternoon plenty of metal still lingers in the voice, and he does manage to capture the lyricism of the middle section of his duet with Laura. The entire duet is well shaped by Panizza, who evades the customary rush, allowing the music to breathe comfortably. He conducts a fluent Dance of the Hours in spite of repeatedly pushing the climactic two-note slurs outside the frame of the phrase, and a blatant fluff which mars the unison celli melody.

Since the revival was the season's first *Gioconda*, Kolodin is able to cite this specific performance. He admires Castagna's Laura but laments that Martinelli's prince of Santafior is but a "dim likeness" of his earlier portrayal, while Moscona's and Morelli's tones are "dull."[9] Yet Morelli comes over the air with a vibrant, heady timbre, and one can find plenty to admire in Martinelli's effort (the word choice here is intended). More curious is Kolodin's summation of Milanov's Gioconda as "erratic," though often "greatly promising," for it is she who provides most of the vocal glamour of the afternoon. It is difficult to imagine a more satisfying portrayal of the Venetian streetsinger; she has everything the role requires, and no gaffes warrant damning her with a single descriptive "erratic." Milanov in her first Metropolitan decade warrants more careful evaluation. Fortunately, her abundant broadcasts offer the opportunity.

From the moment of her entrance, the Milanov voice contains a caress unlike anything earlier heard from her ('Madre adorata'). In fact, all the episodes with mother Cieca call forth a particular warmth of manner and tone quite unusual at any time in the Milanov chronicle. Throughout the opera her voice is perfectly focused, the middle and low registers wonderfully mixed and seamless (she rarely even hints at a chest tone at this stage of her career); her top voice rings out with great security, never splintering or growing harsh at the *forte* dynamic. Milanov-watchers wait for the "Milanov moment," and none is more keenly anticipated than the high B-flat of 'Ah! come t'amo!' as Gioconda leaves the stage in act one. On this afternoon she vaults to the upper octave (one has heard a more perfect attack from her) and offers a genuine (and lengthy) *messa di voce*—later on she will be content with the crescendo and omit the delectable diminuendo which she executes in this performance. In these early performances Milanov seems more deeply involved in conveying the dramatic plight of her heroines than in later years. While her desire to communicate is laudable, it occasionally causes her to overburden her instrument. When Gioconda overhears Barnaba's betrayal of Laura and learns of Enzo's reawakened love for Laura, the soprano cannot find the balance between exterior agitation and vocal composure. Vocal overfreighting occurs again at the end of act two, where she throws herself completely into the struggle for Enzo's love. She verges on losing control in these moments, and one wishes she would scale down her vocal assault. (Those *fuggi*s sound like hiccups.) But how magnificently she rides Gioconda's wide-ranging lines!

Her final act is masterful. Everything is finely controlled and well shaped. The phrases of 'Suicidio!' are artfully molded, *forte*s and *piano*s well scaled, a faultless demonstration of her ability to *filar il tuono*. She introduces only a pittance of chest mixture into the final 'dentro l'avel,' avoiding the baritonal splendor of later years— perhaps that is why the audience does not give her the ovation she deserves (or was there something in her stage deportment which inhibited belief?). In her exchanges with Enzo and Laura a youthful fragility steals into her voice—these light, deft touches are quite foreign to her more typical grand manner—and her recall of the Rosary theme is perfectly poised and polished. The intimacy and restraint of this scene are quite extraordinary. In later years, Milanov saves her most beautiful tones for the coloratura passages when she toys with Barnaba, but here again she is caught up in the drama and prefers to show the terror behind them. If all Milanov's endeavor merited only "promising," one can only wonder what fulfillment might be.

Though in her third Met season, the *Gioconda* broadcast was only the twelfth house performance by Milanov. She was sparingly used ("Mr. Johnson was a big prima donna and not nice to me . . . he did not like my frankness"),[10] but the war and Rethberg's approaching retirement would change all that.

Finding greater public favor as a prima donna during these prewar years was the American soprano Grace Moore who, in contrast to Milanov's lonely struggle for recognition, had been touched by Hollywood's fantastic wand with its guarantee of widespread celebrity. (While Milanov had been told to lose weight, when Moore signed her initial 1928 contract Gatti added a clause "calling for more weight because I was still skinny" from Broadway musical revues.)[11] Notoriety was nothing new to the operatic milieu. In the early decades of the century the exploits of the beauteous Lina Cavalieri, Geraldine Farrar, and Mary Garden had filled the tabloids and the minds of the susceptible opera public. The allure of Farrar and Garden was such that they appeared in a number of films, silent though they were. For a few brief years in the mid thirties a flicker of that glamour settled on the shoulders of a new breed of Metropolitan singer as the limelight of the movie star lent its brassy glitter to the opera stage. For an artist who combined physical attraction with vocal skill, the lure of Hollywood and the movies was strong. Tibbett and Martini demonstrated the polarity of access, the baritone bringing his acknowledged stature in opera to Hollywood and gaining an even larger public, the tenor earning his public through films and thereby keeping open the back door to the opera stage where he longed to tread.

The Hollywood operetta flourished almost as soon as sound came in—Tibbett appeared in *The Rogue Song* as early as 1930—but it was not until 1933 that the vogue for the film musical moved into high gear. Jeanette MacDonald became the ultimate Hollywood prima donna, appearing in *The Merry Widow* (1933) and going on for a decade of popular operettas with baritone Nelson Eddy. Though MacDonald was not an operatic product, filmland soon cast about for the genuine article and found it in Grace Moore (already on the Hollywood scene as Jenny Lind in 1930); her 1933 film, the immensely successful *One Night of Love*, became the prototype for future musicals. Moore made four other films (including *New Moon* with Tibbett) and was voted one of the ten biggest moneymakers in movies. The studios scoured the operatic stage for other likely candidates and discovered the diminutive Lily Pons (two films in 1935 and 1936) and Gladys Swarthout (several films from 1936 to 1939). Svelte good looks were the passport to Hollywood for all these singers—their artistic accomplishments varied. Their stay was not overlong and they all made the return trip to the opera house, some allowing the facade of "stardom" to substitute for characterization in their performances, but all with greater earning power. Top dollar was the wages of cinematic dalliance for Moore and Swarthout, and Pons' aura, too, was further burnished. But by the end of the decade the box office for musicals with opera stars declined, and a new style of musical with Broadway overtones occupied Hollywood. (Risë Stevens in *The Chocolate Soldier* brought up the tail end of the species.)

While the radio broadcast must be acknowledged as the principal agent for the democratization of opera, the musical film of the 1930s deserves a friendly nod as well. The new public it created may or may not have surged into the opera house, but the singers themselves became household names. Unfortunately, their new-found celebrity sometimes had a deleterious effect on their operatic careers, not only in allowing their film image to influence, even violate, their operatic characterizations but, as noted earlier, in so greatly increasing the demand for their concert and radio appearances (where the real money was) that they often reduced their opera appearances to a minimum.

But at least one opera star actually grew in artistic quality following her film successes, and she was the pick of the lot. Grace Moore would seem to have been following her natural bent in moving on to Hollywood, for the Broadway musical had been her home during the 1920s (she was the star of *The Music Box Revue*), and her early Met career (1927–1932) was a mere detour in this passage. But her film stardom brought about a return to the Met in 1935–36 for a single season after a three year absence. Johnson had heard her debut at Covent Garden during the summer of 1935 and wrote to Ziegler that she "was greeted by a packed house and most enthusiastic audience" (the outreach of *One Night of Love* was international). "The quality of her voice pleased, particularly certain phrases in pianissimo and her acting was quiet and sympathetic"—Johnson himself seems sympathetic to her before applying the coup de grâce: "She sang toward the public consistantly and was always herself. In short she was not changed much from that with which you are already familiar." But to be "always herself" was evidently just what the public wanted, for with an eye to the box office, Johnson continued, "I think she might draw us good houses for two performances provided you can have her at a very low figure. Try out Mr. Coppicus [Moore's manager] on the price. I did not mention Metropolitan to her."[12] The two performances of *Bohème* included the broadcast of 14 March 1936 (with Kullman, Morelli, Pinza).

Johnson's attitude toward Moore reflected the common evaluation of her at this point in her career. She was the American princess of café society, combining a worldly acquisitiveness with a disarming naiveté, as Johnson could not resist recounting. "Miss Moore gave a large party at Claridge's and . . . the Prince of Wales was on her right. The Princess Alice asked to go back-stage and Grace was so flustered she did not understand to whom she was being presented, forgot to curtsy and shook the Princess' hand lustily instead. All London's smart set was present." In this Jamesian incident much of Moore's appeal is exposed—she was "always herself."

Absent from the Met again the following season, Moore returned in 1937, one is tempted to say for good, for (though she was already far beyond the age of consent) the next decade would be her period of artistic maturity. The *Bohème* broadcast of 15 January 1938 gives a fair picture of her manner in this period of transition. The voice is a healthy one, a good-sized lyric with plenty of fiber throughout the entire range, but notably puissant at the top. Its chief glory is a highly individual timbre which gleams with a diamondlike hardness, but at the same time is sensuously suggestive. Few subtleties, either musical or in characterization, are encountered in her Mimi, although one might think differently as she begins the entrance aria, for a nice delicacy wraps 'mio nome è Lucia,' she observes all the written *portamenti*, and manages both the consonants and closed vowel sound on the high A of 'primavere.' But she makes no attempt to capture the rapture that overtakes Mimi between 'e in cielo' (which comes out 'e vita') and the quietly expansive 'ma quando vien lo sgelo.' In fact, the difference between her idiomatic rendering of the first half of the aria and the conclusion is so marked that one suspects Moore has suddenly lost interest in the

La Bohème
15 January 1938
Mimi
Grace Moore
Musetta
Muriel Dickson
Rodolfo
Bruno Landi
Marcello
Carlo Tagliabue
Colline
Ezio Pinza
Conductor
Gennaro Papi

whole affair. The duet is taken down a half step. Bruno Landi, her Rodolfo, is occasionally effete in musical effects and not overly robust in the *slancio* moments (Moore
can, and does, swamp him in the climaxes), but nevertheless he is idiomatic in style
and very much into the role. Her 'curioso' is not at all playful, and she and Papi dis-
agree on the rallentando of 'Vi starò vicina' (his is more molto than hers). But then,
Papi often seems out of touch with his stage performers throughout the afternoon.
Moore's little indiscrepancies pepper the role: in the duet with Marcello she omits 'lo
so'; in the quartet she holds 'vita' three beats instead of one; she anticipates 'Era buio'
in her death scene; there are occasional slips in diction, with a particularly noticeable
habit of turning the Italian *a* and open *o* into an American *uh*, which changes her
Rodolfo into Rodulfo—in one instance, Pinza's forceful Colline emerges as
'Collini.'

But to merely catalog her obvious lapses betrays the substance of a Moore performance. If one compares her Mimi to the raucous-toned and uncouth Musetta of
Scots soprano Muriel Dickson, Moore emerges a near paragon. Her voice is at its
most beautiful in the final two acts. She easily surmounts the climaxes of the
encounter with Marcello, lets her joyous top in the 'Addio' compensate for minimal
sentiment, proves in the death scene that she can lovingly shape a phrase ('Lascia
ch'io guardi'), and employs chest discreetly to suggest her love is 'as grand as the
ocean.' Throughout the entire 'Sono andati' duet her voice wears a most captivating
tonal sheen. If she chooses to sound as though Mimi merely dozes off at the end
rather than suggesting her weakening unto death, it is all part of her general willingness to get on with the business at hand.

Gender divides the performance into two distinct styles—the two confected
girls are partnered by three idiomatic Italians. In his debut season at the Met, Carlo
Tagliabue shows why he will go on to be one of the great artists of the Italian lyric
stage during the next several decades. His warm baritone makes for an unusually
sympathetic Marcello. The top voice can ring out forcefully, but more important for
the fourth-act duet with Rodolfo, he is capable of some fine *piano* effects. Though the
radio audience would hear him as Amonasro and Enrico Ashton, Italy's entry into the
war prevented his return after only two Met seasons. Pinza sings 'Vecchia zimarra'
with an extremely covered tone, his quick vibrato rather obtrusive, the tonal spin not
quite as fluent as usual; but in his gentle voicing of the word 'tranquilli' he provides
the heartfelt moment which one suspects Moore can never summon.

If Miss Moore's seamstress has insufficient pathos, she might be expected to
find a more complementary image in the bewitching, venal, volatile Manon, which
she essays in the broadcast of 13 January 1940. Command of the French repertory
had passed to Montreal-born Wilfred Pelletier, since 1921 a coach and assistant
conductor at the Metropolitan and since 1935 in charge of the "Auditions of the Air."
An early assistantship with Pierre Monteux had fortified his aptitude for French style,
but not sufficiently to give a distinctive profile to his work on the podium. He leads a
sprightly performance, emphasizing pace (from which the inn and gambling scenes
profit) at the expense of nuance. During this period the Metropolitan attempted to
replicate a French manner (as opposed to the international—read Italian—mode
which became the norm in later decades) with a nucleus of French stylists which
included Pons, Sayão, Lawrence, Maison, Crooks, Brownlee, Thomas, Jobin, and old
Rothier. Typical performances were the broadcasts of *Roméo* (25 December 1937)
with Sayão, Crooks, and Brownlee; *Carmen* (19 March 1938) with Castagna, Maison,
and Brownlee; *Louise* (28 January 1939) with Moore and Maison; and *Manon* (25

Manon
13 January 1940

Manon
Grace Moore
Des Grieux
Richard Crooks
Lescaut
John Brownlee
Count
Nicola Moscona
Conductor
Wilfred Pelletier

February 1939) with Sayão, Kiepura, Brownlee, and Rothier.

Grace Moore had earned a place in this group by her repeated performances at the Opéra Comique and by a friendship with that peerless interpreter of French opera, Mary Garden. The association was manifest in the tall jewelled cane which Moore carried in the Cours la Reine scene (well, at least she carried it in Europe—the Metropolitan always omitted the scene during these years). Massenet's beloved Sibyl Sanderson first had given the cane to Garden who, in what might seem an unlikely show of confidence, had passed it on to Moore. While the gesture in itself could not sustain Moore in the great line of Manons, she proves it was not merely a whim on Garden's part. Her first act is well vocalized (though short on characterization), and one must admire the accuracy of pitch and exact execution of the *acciaccaturas* in 'Voyons, Manon.' Greater delicacy of tone plays over 'Adieu, notre petite table'; she fails to observe the crescendo at the end of each phrase, but perhaps bestows as much pathos as a table deserves. Her French has flavor, even if generosity of spirit causes her to extend the nasal sounds to near neighbors (most noticeably in 'J'en suis à mon premier voyage!'). She is very fine in the Saint-Sulpice scene, skillfully maintaining the legato flow of Massenet's serpentine phrases and molding them into a delicious continuity. Her honeyed tone, with its sensuous point, and her sinuous *portamenti* make the seduction seem entirely plausible. She chooses to be selective in the gambling scene, omitting both the final top tone of the trio and the entire ascending scale with which most sopranos delight to conclude the Gavotte (the latter transferred from the Cours la Reine to the gambling milieu). But the Gavotte is otherwise deftly done, musically neat, though not particularly alive to the text (no alteration of sentiment at 'Le coeur, hélas!'). The final scene is tonally lovely—what a beautiful voice she owns! But nothing short of a natural disaster could bring this Manon to the grave, for Moore is simply too healthy in manner to suggest Manon's debility. That she could, if she would, is evident in a few isolated phrases: 'Écoute-moi!' which leads into 'N'est'ce plus ma main?' in act three, and a brief moment before Manon's arrest, where her quietly shimmering tone achieves just the right pathos.

More adept at characterization are De Paolis (who carries the sound of the aged roué Guillot in his voice and converts it into active evil as he accuses Manon in the gambling den), Cehanovsky as an urbane Brétigny, and Brownlee as the blustering cousin Lescaut (his vocalism is anything but ingratiating in its absence of legato, but it improves as the afternoon goes on). Moscona's Italianate tone and manner are a startling intrusion into the quite adequate French "feel" of the performance. In the heavy accents of 'Épouse quelque brave fille' one hears age and dignity but little elegance—evidently the trait has skipped a generation, for the young Des Grieux of Richard Crooks has it in abundance. His portrayal of the Chevalier is distinguished in every way, superbly vocalized in now manly, now dulcet tones, vividly characterized, and above all, musically refined. The vitality and thrust of his vocalism are often startling. How forcefully he conveys the ardor of the young lover at the Amiens inn, but how bewitching are the vocal demitints with which he establishes an intimacy with Manon—no country maid could resist the charming, insinuating lilt which he gives to 'Nous vivrons à Paris.' In the letter scene he shapes phrase after phrase with just proportion (though his high tenor timbre is a mite disconcerting in the spoken dialogue). In many of Crooks' recordings one hears an excessive nasality take over the core of the voice, but in 'Le rêve' the mixture is perfectly balanced for utmost suavity. Variances of vocal weight lend subtlety to the recitative phrases before 'Ah! fuyez' ('C'est le moment suprême!' is imbued with tragic significance). In the aria

Richard Crooks as Faust.

Helen Jepson as Marguerite in *Faust*.

itself, the disdain and anger he finds in the middle section are particularly convincing, and the full-voiced climaxes ring out. His stentorian repetitions of 'Sphinx étonnant' in the gambling den remind us that his European career included performances of Lohengrin and Walther von Stolzing. The last act again offers opportunity to show off his impressive control of half-voice (unlike most tenors he maintains the mood of 'rêve charmant').

Moore's hearty Manon, no matter how fine, ultimately places in greater relief the finished artistry of Crooks as the Chevalier. If Moore was reaping the rewards of film stardom, Crooks was by this time the idol of the airwaves with his broadcasts for the "Voice of Firestone." From the evidence of this performance, radio was a more salubrious environment for the opera singer.

Crooks was joined by the Metropolitan's other personality blonde, Helen Jepson, in two broadcasts of *Faust* during the 1939–40 season. The double feature was the result of NBC's airing of tour performances in Boston and Cleveland (during the 1937–1940 seasons NBC had maintained the broadcasts as a sustaining program without commercial sponsorship, so the tour decision was entirely theirs). In Met performances of these years *Faust* is shorn of the Nuit de Walpurgis, and the church scene precedes the return of Valentin. Conductor Pelletier is better at keeping the traffic moving than enhancing mood with subtle nuance. The cast, virtually identical for both performances, includes Pinza as Méphistophélès and Leonard Warren as Valentin (Helen Olheim replaces Lucielle Browning as Siebel in Boston). Jepson provides the favored naiveté for Marguerite, singing in a clear but colorless manner throughout—she is in slightly better voice on 16 March, though greater vivacity brightens the Boston Jewel Song on 6 April. The body of her middle range is an asset to the ballad and garden-scene duets, and she has a nice upward scale to launch the Jewel Song. No difficulties disturb her fluent vocalism, but one can only wonder what Faust saw in this Marguerite—he got the worst of a bad bargain. Her earthbound repetition of Crooks' ravishing 'O nuit d'amour' holds no ecstatic longing, neither she nor Pelletier brings any sense of terror to the church scene, and the lovely sounds she forms as she recalls past joys evoke no pathos. Dependable she certainly is (not an unwelcome quality in a repertory house), for her two performances virtually replicate one another.

Browning and Olheim are work-a-day Siebels; the former has a pleasant mezzo coloration, whereas Olheim betrays an unpleasant quaver and a tendency to sharp at the top. Of the women, only Votipka shines in what may have been her best role. She and Pinza animate the garden quartet with their flavorful personalities and (especially in Boston) she begins the ensemble with the tone and line of a major artist—which, of course, she was.

But on both occasions it is the gentlemen who provide the vocal glamour and strong characterizations. Pinza and Warren are at polar career points, the bass basking in the surety of a quarter century on the stages of La Scala and the Metropolitan and showing it in the unmitigated nonchalance of his portrayal; the baritone just beginning to assume major roles at the Met, his vibrant tones fairly bursting the rather square seams he sometimes imposes on Valentin's phrases. Mrs. Peltz hit the mark when, in 1942, she observed that Warren "takes his art without levity."[13] Winner of the 1938 "Auditions of the Air," his Radio City Music Hall chorus background (only a few arias, no complete roles, in his repertory) was buttressed by Italian study before his 1939 debut as Paolo in *Simon Boccanegra*. In the broadcast of that year his superbly resonant instrument more than held its own among the grand sonorities

Faust
16 March 1940
Marguerite
Helen Jepson
Siebel
Lucielle Browning
Faust
Richard Crooks
Valentin
Leonard Warren
Méphistophélès
Ezio Pinza
Conductor
Wilfred Pelletier

Faust
6 April 1940
Marguerite
Helen Jepson
Siebel
Helen Olheim
Faust
Richard Crooks
Valentin
Leonard Warren
Méphistophélès
Ezio Pinza
Conductor
Wilfred Pelletier

of Tibbett, Pinza, and Martinelli—for once, the malicious Paolo was a credible rival for the powerful Doge. Mrs. Peltz noted his "stern, handsome features, brooding eyes, dignified build, quiet, serious demeanor"—time would be needed to develop flexibility in characterization. In his Valentin, one can sense some interpretive growth in the few weeks between the two broadcasts. In the second broadcast he does narrow his tone at the approach of death (though his command of half-voice is not yet sure), but more often the burly tone still robs the line of French elegance. As sheer vocalism the aria is splendid each time, the phrasing noble, the rich tones mounting with absolute ease to the top Gs. He follows the brightly colored 'chercher la gloire' with a well-modulated covered tone which suggests the mezza voce to come. Of course, the climax is as big as one could wish (or bigger). Of more moment is the increased suavity of the Boston aria; he manages to easily float his tone and introduces a few subtleties (a sudden *piano* on the second 'toujours'). All this aids his characterization—now something of love for Marguerite invades the tone itself. The rapid growth which will propel Warren into the star baritone orbit is already apparent.

When all three gentlemen come together for the duel trio, the performance blazes with excitement. But Pinza lends an incredible vivacity to the entire performance. He bothers little with malevolence of tone or vocal asides. His devil is all extrovert charm, exceedingly jocular with the bourgeois, but showing a practical streak as he urges Faust to get on with his wooing in the garden scene. He roars at full-voice through the Calf of Gold aria, preens outrageously with Dame Marthe Schwertlein, irrepressibly plays the show-off for most of the afternoon, content with merely crystal-clear articulation of text, full tone, and matchless legato as he calls down the darkness of night to aid in the seduction of Marguerite. The serenade under her window is the high point of the Pinza exhibition. Unlike most basses, he can sing it without a trace of self-consciousness, conducting Gounod's sinuous line with accuracy and no break in continuity. It is a stunning bit of virtuosity, and for once the three octave laughter is genuinely mocking. One notes in both performances how he never quite reaches the high F in his act-one entrance. In the Boston performance the Calf of Gold is taken at an even faster pace; one can hear a few aspirants in the brief fioriture, and since Pelletier slows down the Serenade a shade, Pinza has to work a little harder to maintain the requisite panache—but he does. In general, the Boston Méphisto is clothed in a bit more dignity. 'O nuit' takes on some gravity, and the entire scene in Faust's studio has a more serious cast.

Crooks, in particular, lets us know that we are dealing with issues of life and death. The tenor is in excellent form on both afternoons, but the palm goes to the Boston portrayal where, in the opening scene, his attack is cleaner and the phrasing keener edged (on 16 March the aged scholar hardly seems world weary); but the rhythmic vitality and vigor of tone as Crooks summons the devil are surprising on both occasions—in the sequential rise of the 'à moi' phrases it is especially impressive. Thus, the contrast to his sweetly lyrical garden scene is all the greater. Crooks' 'Salut! demeure' is exceedingly adroit, and he fills the nuanced phrases with the right mix of longing and ardor (on 16 March a bit of scooping negates the sense of 'chaste et pure,' but the 6 April phrases are unsullied). His finest moment is the reprise of the opening section, all dreamy ecstasy and capped by a mezza voce high B (is that falsetto?) to sustain the mood (true, the descent has a mite of insecurity to it). He manages to create an incredible intimacy in the duets—on 6 April, in particular, the magical blending from mezza voce on through various dynamics to full-voice and back again ('O nuit d'amour') provides the climax of a memorable portrayal.

Crooks and Jepson sang the *Traviata* broadcast from Cleveland the following Saturday afternoon and so ended their opera broadcast careers (though both appeared with the company through 1943). The lamentable absence of Crooks was made somewhat palatable by his frequent commercial broadcasts throughout the forties.

Jepson's career ended abruptly. Certain parallels with Moore may be noted: both sopranos had naturally healthy instruments, their blonde beauty made them media favorites (though Moore's film career was without parallel), both had somehow managed to gain the interest and approval of Mary Garden, and in the late thirties the Metropolitan promoted them in a series of French roles for which their charismatic aura seemed appropriate: Moore as Manon and Louise, Jepson as Thaïs and Mélisande. But the similarities were only skin-deep, for Moore's temperament was the genuine article, while Jepson was singularly short on vocal and stage personality. A throat ailment cut short Jepson's career, but Moore's diligence paid off in a series of new triumphs in the 1940s.

Lily Pons, too, had followed her heart to Hollywood in the 1930s, but she did not tarry long; her innate chic and notes in alt seemed to need only her own astute promotion to maintain the image of "opera star." No opera was better calculated to exhibit the petite soprano's charms than Delibes' *Lakmé*, a flower of nineteenth-century French exoticism as fragile as the datura blossom whose poison the unhappy heroine consumes at the opera's close. Of course, science has taught us (and Delibes knew it as well) that the datura is not deadly at all—and neither is the opera, though modern critics have almost pummeled it to death.

Before Pons made it her specialty, the Met had known few Lakmés. Patti had sung it in a special season in 1890, but the first Met Lakmé (1892) was Marie Van Zandt (she had created it at the Opéra Comique), followed by Marcella Sembrich (1906) and Maria Barrientos (1917). Revived for Pons in her second Met season, her portrayal would keep the opera in the repertory for the next dozen years (lapsing only in 1937–38). Two early broadcasts featured distinguished casts (Swarthout, Thill or Martinelli, De Luca, Rothier). But the radio public waited until 6 January 1940 for a repeat, and now the casting, like Pons in person, was decidedly lightweight: only Pinza matched the Nilikantha of Edouard de Reszke or Marcel Journet in those early Met performances. The bass moves with ease from devil to Brahman priest, but unfortunately this is one of Pinza's off days. The voice is oddly unreliable (particularly at the top), though the contrast between the half-voice and full-voice phrases of his second-act aria is telling. Tokatyan makes a brave effort at Gerald's music and is often effective in lyrical passages. He is well matched in vocal weight with Pons, but while the soprano gives a graceful turn to the fleet chains of melody which permeate Delibes' score, Tokatyan too often sends them on motorically. Focus on Lakmé and her Bell Song has rendered the role of Gerald nondescript (for the public), but as the opera proceeds and Gerald's character becomes more feckless, Delibes has quixotically increased the vocal demands. Tokatyan falters in these more dramatic moments (the duet, 'Dans la forêt,' and the ardent, high-flying phrases which close the second and third acts). In the quieter moments (the opening scenes of act three, for instance) his vocal finesse proves gratifying.

The remaining roles are modestly cast. Cehanovsky's Frederic is a nice effort, a reminder that he capably filled non-comprimario parts in the first decades of his career (but in major roles, that perpetual nasal resonance becomes an annoyance).

Lakmé
6 January 1940

Lakmé
Lily Pons

Mallika
Irra Petina

Gerald
Armand Tokatyan

Frederic
George Cehanovsky

Nilakantha
Ezio Pinza

Conductor
Wilfred Pelletier

Irra Petina, who brightens many a performance with her comic gift, is a negligible Mallika; in any case, Pelletier flies through her duet with Lakmé at such a pace that the charm of the episode evaporates. The English party is properly prim but occasionally vocally sticky in the quintet, where Delibes amusingly crossbred his operetta manner with the esprit of the *Carmen* quintet. In general, Pelletier has a feel for the fineness of Delibes' orchestral fabric—this is one of his better labors.

And now for the diva herself. No doubt about it, she is bewitching in this part. In these surroundings her vocal security and elegant phrasing shine. Except for the Bell Song, the part is devoid of coloratura pyrotechnics, and the aria itself relies on nimble staccati and a pair of high Es rather than intricate roulades. Pons has them ready to hand. The spirited staccati of 'Où tinte la clochette' startle with their dash, and the long concluding E (and its approach) are dead center on. Even more gratifying is the sure control and tonal loveliness of her cantabile; by underlining the contrast between the several moods of the aria she gives it substance. It is her graceful cantilena, in fact, which proves so satisfying throughout the afternoon. 'C'est le dieu de la jeunesse' is elegantly phrased, and despite her slight resources, she achieves dynamic contrasts: in 'Pourquoi dans les grands bois?' the modulation between lightly floated song and a few brilliantly pointed phrases is carefully planned; in act three she utilizes a pallid, childlike tone as she watches over the wounded Gerald. In short, she actually works at turning Lakmé into a person. The image of Lakmé must have appealed to Pons as a conceit which even her public could accept as a satisfying substitute for Pons, the diva. In any case, her vocal security on this broadcast heralds a welcome period of more agreeable listening for the radio audience.

A month later Pons again offered her most familiar part, Lucia, the seventh of her fourteen radio portrayals of the Scottish maid. In 1938 an authentic Italian aura had adhered to the *Lucia* broadcast when Galliano Masini, Carlo Tagliabue, and Pinza had surrounded the soprano, but the 1940 cast is very much business as usual.

Jagel's constricted tenor seems more than ever ill suited to bel canto opera. He blasts away for two acts, and just when one has given up all hope, his throat seems to open up for the double aria of the final scene, where a more modulated tone enables him to realize his intelligent conception (that sturdy throat does him good service in the climaxes of 'Tu che a Dio'). Lazzari achieves no such transformation and is as worn and tired in announcing Lucia's plight as when he began. Massue again proves an unattractive bridegroom. Only Bonelli has intact the resources and craft of the major artist, and he makes of the cipher, Enrico Ashton, an impressive figure. By refusing to smudge the dotted rhythms, he imparts architectural scope to the workaday aria of the first act, and his cadenza is superb. Papi takes the cabaletta at such a pace that even Bonelli can do little but dash along with him to a splendid top G. He refuses to huff his way through 'Se tradirmi' and allows the villainous Ashton a moment of expressive sympathy as he leads his distraught sister to the wedding ceremony. The ill-rehearsed state of repertory opera in the Johnson regime is all too evident in the wayward sextet where Jagel and Bonelli, both fine musicians, can't get together on their dotted rhythms, and Papi's function seems merely to keep orchestra and singers together on the principal beats. It may be "one of the greatest numbers in opera," as Cross confides, but one would never know it from this performance.

Amidst the wreckage, Pons remains serenely confident of her star status. She sings the double arias of the first act with the same surface charm and facility with which she invested, say, Benedict's 'Lo! Hear the Gentle Lark' in her concert appear-

Lucia di Lammermoor
3 February 1940
Lucia
Lily Pons
Edgardo
Frederick Jagel
Enrico Ashton
Richard Bonelli
Raimondo
Virgilio Lazzari
Conductor
Gennaro Papi

Lily Pons as Lakmé.

ances. The tone has less float than in her French roles, for she focuses the sound as far forward as possible—a shade further and it would be unpleasantly white. But it does provide a pointed brilliance at key moments. As the opera proceeds, Pons becomes more involved in the drama. She nicely expresses her sorrow at Edgardo's leaving, etches 'Verranno a te' with a sure bel canto line, and becomes quite emphatic in her resistance to Ashton in the second act—the scene of the siblings unexpectedly comes alive. With the mad scene the Pons persona returns center stage. There may be no tragic aura to 'Alfin son tua,' but as compensation she offers unfailing security in the passages in alt. The *b*'s begin to accumulate, the trills are still sketchy, and the Fs are long and true. With the delicious ingenuousness he often displays in these early broadcasts, Cross interrupts the scene to tell us that "our nightingale . . . is in glorious voice, and in just a moment she will continue her melodious raving." She is, and she does. You can be sure that no stage blood stains this Lucia's "beautiful grayish white negligee . . . her loose golden hair flowing down her back. . . . Well, I wish you could see her bowing, her arms across her breast, and bowing to the floor." *Opera News* assured us (in 1939) that "the Metropolitan does not recognize the star system"[14] but Mr. Cross knows better. Jagel is "the faithful member of the Metropolitan" who has "filled in so many times when other tenors have been indisposed that we began to nickname him the Metropolitan Minuteman," but Miss Pons must be hailed as the "petite and chic star of opera, concert, radio, and motion pictures."

The next week the radio audience had the unexpected pleasure of hearing both the singing and speaking voice of the veteran Giuseppe de Luca who, at the age of sixty-four, returned to the Met in February 1940 for five performances. During the second intermission of the broadcast *Bohème* on 10 February, De Luca spoke to the radio audience from his dressing room, noting that he had eagerly looked forward to his return "for I have come to love this opera house." The reception accorded him "has been a surprise and has touched my heart. I did not know I had so many friends, and such staunch friends," he averred, and went on to pay tribute to the "loyalty and understanding and affection of the American musical public." Where the loyalty of the management was lodged during the five-year period in which, after twenty years of devoted service, he had been banished from the house, he did not ask. But the truth was that his heart had been heavy at his dismissal in 1935. Johnson had heard him in London shortly thereafter ("he had an ovation here in the Barber with Lily Pons and Pinza") and informed Ziegler that "De Luca feels very hurt at the treatment accorded him and I have done all I could to soften the situation."[15] It took five years before concern solidified into Metropolitan performances.

De Luca's generosity of spirit and undiluted optimism were still apparent in his Marcello in the 1940 broadcast. He had been before the public prior to the turn of the century and had created Sharpless in the world premiere of *Butterfly* in 1904 and Michonnet in *Adriana Lecouvreur* two years earlier. As Cross reminds us, De Luca had "appeared many times with Caruso." Yet he still had something precious to give. In the opening 'Questo Mar Rosso' the familiar sweet resonance brings a smile to our lips which widens as he reaches a comfortable high F on 'Faraon.' Tokatyan and De Luca toss back and forth their dialogue with insouciance, and the easy interplay increases when Pinza and Cehanovsky arrive. The baritone has plenty of voice for the big moments in act three; it may not ring as consistently as one remembers, but his quietly sympathetic 'Che far dunque?' in response to Rodolfo's tale of Mimi's illness tells us the artistry is undiminished. Nor does he falter in the fourth-act duet (F-sharp and all). The particular benefaction of his singing lies in his unique ability to main-

La Bohème
10 February 1940
Mimi
Bidú Sayão
Musetta
Annamary Dickey
Rodolfo
Armand Tokatyan
Marcello
Giuseppe de Luca
Colline
Ezio Pinza
Conductor
Gennaro Papi

tain a conversational manner while exploring the musical character of each phrase. He knows how to couple the rhythm of the word with the musical line. That he is eager in old age is evident in his two anticipatory entries ('Chi è là?' at Benoit's entrance, which he quickly repeats with a different inflection, and 'Ci ho gusto davver' in act four), and in the quartet he steps on the lovers' music by unashamedly playing to the audience (and they love it). He is reluctant to leave the scene (not only on this afternoon), and he clearly fancies himself the star of the occasion.

Tokatyan is in his best form, not short of *slancio*, his top voice reliable (firm, but sharp, on the high B of the narrative), though his open tone eventually begins to wear. D'Angelo's Benoit is free from overplaying, and Cehanovsky's Schaunard is well made. Annamary Dickey plays Musetta in rather colorless fashion, but she has the virtue of pleasant tone quality in the upper regions, a rarity in most of her kind. Pinza's well-modulated 'Vecchia zimarra' again provides the most affecting moment of the afternoon, which says something unkind about Sayão, whose Mimi is one of her most celebrated roles. From the moment of her entry into Rodolfo's garret and life, an unattractive nasality in the lower octave obtrudes, and it remains throughout most of the afternoon; the blend of registers seems out of order, and she relies on chest voice too frequently. The result is that Mimi is robbed of her gentle nature (she is, after all, far more Puccini than Mürger). In fact, the characterization is resolutely without sentiment—perhaps Sayão gauged that her lovely, fragile person was sufficient in itself (in the opera house, it well may have been, for the *Opera News* photos of her as Mimi are enchanting). The upper voice begins to work at the end of 'Mi chiamano Mimi,' and she ends the duet with a lovely high B. But little of her customary fine-spun tone graces act three ('O mia vita' is an exception); some parts of the scene with Marcello are downright shrewish, and while the 'Addio' has some spin, chest tone is laid on and pitch becomes suspect (as it does in the opening moments of 'Sono andati?' in act four). Only in Mimi's recall of the episodes of her meeting with Rodolfo does her tonal poise and gentle pathos conjure up the familiar Sayão magic. But for us, as for Mimi, 'è tardi,' and one is left with the unwelcome bewilderment which settles on the opera devotee when a beloved artist disappoints.

In the case of another much-loved artist, momentary bewilderment deepens into enigma. American soprano Rose Bampton never aroused sufficient public adulation to achieve cult status, but she engendered a deep affection among many who remember the rich mezzo tones of her early career. By the spring season of 1937 she had transformed herself into a dramatic soprano. The radio audience had ample opportunity to judge the wisdom of that elevation during the decade of the forties, beginning with two matinee Aidas in January and March 1940. With virtually identical casts of Bampton, Arthur Carron, and the young Warren, these were very much fledgling performances, with only Castagna (and Pinza in March, when he replaced Moscona) to remind us of earlier glories. And in the preserved broadcast of 2 March, it is the veterans Pinza and Castagna who deliver the finished goods. One need only place the four brief phrases wherein Ramfis instructs Amneris to pray to Isis beside most of the afternoon's efforts to know the difference between the essentials of Italian operatic art and their counterfeit (Gurney's amateurish King of Egypt, for example). The beauty of Pinza's quietly resonant tone, the accuracy of pitch, the evenness of scale in the octave-and-a-half descent on 'Iside legge,' and his warm *pianissimo* on the succeeding 'ogni mistero degli umani' are potent reminders that Pinza shared all his vocal wealth with his audience no matter how small the role. Castagna, too, is in excellent form, barring three or four top As and B-flats in the

Aida
2 March 1940

Aida
Rose Bampton

Amneris
Bruna Castagna

Radames
Arthur Carron

Amonasro
Leonard Warren

Ramfis
Ezio Pinza

Conductor
Ettore Panizza

judgment scene (they are decidedly flat). But her Amneris remains a classic portrayal. Her tones glow seductively as she invites Radames' love, they drip warmth as she entices Aida (what a neat turn on 'vivrai felice!'), and even in the animated cantabile of 'Ah! tu dei vivere' in act four, she traces Verdi's sinuous line without crushing her velvety sonority. Most welcome is her restraint as she awaits the judgment on Radames, thereby heightening the rhythmic vigor and individual shaping of the climactic phrases ('Sacerdoti: compiste un delitto!').

The thunderous blast of Warren's 'Suo padre' at Amonasro's entrance must have quelled the entire Egyptian army, but his appeal to the King ('Ma tu, Re') is deficient in balm to merit mercy, and wooly tone muffles the clarity of faster passages ('Fa cor'). In the Nile scene duet the individual vowel sounds lose definition in his cavernous resonance, but some lovely covered tone surfaces at 'e amor, tutto tu avrai.' He rises to the dramatic climax of the scene, though neither he nor Bampton has quite divined the arch of that supreme moment in Verdi where, at the cost of love, Aida succumbs to Amonasro's plea for country. The welcome spectre of Toscanini hangs over the performance in Panizza's tightly reined ensemble scene (the 'guerra' finale of the first act), but he is less successful in coloring the atmosphere of the Nile scene.

Carron provides more of the afternoon's subtleties, though the often throaty quality of his tenor is a drawback. At least one can respect the intimacy he tries to achieve in the Nile duet. His rhythms are not quite tight enough to sound the full valor of 'Pur ti riveggo,' but then Panizza is overly tepid at this moment; even so, he throws Carron rather precipitously into 'Sì: fuggiam,' and the tenor is hard-pressed to deliver. Carron has the stentorian A for 'Io resto a te,' and better yet, he offers some lovely tone and phrasing in act four, surpassing even Castagna in drawing the line of 'ma puro il mio pensiero.' He sustains the mood of 'O terra addio' better than many a dramatic tenor. Cross burnishes Carron's image for the radio audience with tales of family life: "His charming little daughter Barbara is listening in their New York home. . . . I hope she is enjoying Daddy"; no generation is neglected, for "Mr. Carron hopes that his mother is hearing him back home in England." Cross, ever the Met family man, echoes "We hope so, too."

Cross also tells us that a few weeks before the 2 March broadcast Bampton had been pressed into service as Amneris when three principals were indisposed. The search for the appropriate niche for Bampton had led her initially into Verdi (the *Trovatore* Leonora), on to Mozart (Donna Anna), and she tarried briefly in the French corner (Alceste) before settling finally on the metier of the second half of her Met career, the lighter Wagner heroines. In that versatility lay both the promise and the problem of her career. Her musical sincerity, the ample size and range of the voice, her affecting stage presence—these were as indisputable as her lack of an individual vocal thumbprint in the soprano category. Oddly enough, as her Aida demonstrates, she had enough surface temperament for the overtly dramatic moments; when Aida is agitated, Bampton is at her best. The contrasts of 'Ritorna vincitor!' are clearly delineated, and she accentuates the rising phrases of 'L'insana parola' with telling crescendos; the entire piece has an unexpected full-blooded energy. Bampton more than holds her own in the second-act confrontation with Castagna. She easily rides the big ensembles of the triumphal scene where, more than once, her top tones have a startling cutting edge which adds dramatic impact. But, notwithstanding the velvety warmth of 'Numi, pietà' (it lies in the center of her old contralto terrain), the voice tends to lose color and spin in quieter moments. This proves fatal to 'O patria

Metropolitan
OPERA HOUSE
GRAND OPERA SEASON 1939-1940
EDWARD JOHNSON General Manager
EDWARD ZIEGLER Assistant General Manager
EARLE R. LEWIS Assistant General Manager

SATURDAY AFTERNOON, MARCH 2, 1940, AT 2 O'CLOCK

A I D A

Opera in Four Acts (Seven Scenes)
(In Italian)

Book by A. Ghislanzoni

MUSIC by GIUSEPPE VERDI

The King	John Gurney
Amneris	Bruna Castagna
Aida	Rose Bampton
Radames	Arthur Carron
Ramfis	Ezio Pinza
Amonasro	Leonard Warren
A Messenger	Lodovico Oliviero
A Priestess	Thelma Votipka

ACT I, Scene 2—"Temple Dance" by Corps de Ballet
ACT II, Scene 1—"Negro Dance" by Ballet Group.
ACT II, Scene 2—"Triumphal Dance" by Ruthanna Boris, Soloist; Grant Mouradoff, Premier Danseur, and entire Corps de Ballet.

Choreography by Boris Romanoff.

Conductor	Ettore Panizza
Chorus Master	Fausto Cleva
Stage Director	Desire Defrere

POSITIVELY NO ENCORES ALLOWED

The Management requests the audience to abstain from applause at the fall of the curtain so long as the music continues.

Correct Librettos for Sale in the Lobby

KNABE PIANO USED EXCLUSIVELY

Program Continued on Next Page

Program for the broadcast of *Aida* on 2 March 1940.

mia,' where only supreme vocal poise can conjure up the tranquil beauty of Aida's faraway homeland. Her rendition is merely a lesson well learned—incandescence eludes her. She adopts an inordinately fast tempo for the aria, and the cruelly exposed high C is both loud and brief. Her concluding high A, however, is very lovely, and 'Là tra foreste vergini' is well sustained. At the end of the act, Cross informs us that Bampton is wearing costumes "fashioned after authentic costumes which she and her husband, Wilfred Pelletier, found in the British Museum in London," a welcome effort, though the eradication of her pervasive American *r* would have provided greater authenticity for the radio audience. The tomb scene seals her performance. Her vocalism is absolutely solid, but too often the tone turns brittle, and no gentle float elevates all those vaulting phrases so carefully marked *dolcissimo* by Verdi. The aura evaporates along with the air in the tomb. One desperately recalls the inherent taste of her portrayal, its musical rectitude (those perfect, tight syncopations in the act-one trio) and her overall vocal security; but the performance of this "charming American artist greatly admired by aspiring students of concert and opera" remains earthbound. Clearly, the future well-being of the Italian wing rested on other shoulders.

Ettore Panizza. Photography by Luis Richelme.

Kerstin Thorborg as Orfeo in *Orfeo ed Euridice.*

CHAPTER THIRTEEN

1939–40
New Repertory

In addition to the steady diet of old favorites like *Bohème* and *Aida*, at the end of the decade radio listeners were treated to several operas new to them.

Unable to extend the repertory with costly and chancy twentieth-century premieres, Johnson backed into the eighteenth century, settling on Gluck's *Orfeo ed Euridice*, the first Met staging since the celebrated Toscanini performances a quarter century earlier. He began with an abortive ballet-dancers-on-stage-singers-in-the-pit presentation in the 1936 spring season. When Herbert Graf came on board, the Met mounted a new production in 1938 (the premiere of 26 November opened the broadcast season with Thorborg, Jessner, Morel, and Farell under Bodanzky's baton). The radio audience next heard the opera on 20 January 1940, with Thorborg again as the hero, Leinsdorf in the pit, and Farell now promoted to Amor. The occasion also provided the first opportunity for the radio audience to hear a new soprano who would become a treasured member of the company, Jarmila Novotna.

Leinsdorf achieves a welcome balance of classical repose and vibrant impulse, the latter essential to animate the intentionally static dramaturgy of the work. Conceived as a series of stage tableaus in the eighteenth-century French manner, the musical gestures must be sufficiently vivid if the "beautiful simplicity" which Gluck sought is not to pall. Leinsdorf's efforts were especially valuable for the radio audience, which was deprived of the choreographed elements of the production—he succeeds in bringing the drama to life. In fact, if there is any fault, it is his tendency to hurry the soloists in their arias; as a result, the primary vocal moments lose some impact. Thorborg had made a name for herself in the role of Orfeo in both Vienna (with Bruno Walter) and Salzburg; the majestic interpreter of Wagnerian parts did not hesitate to name Orfeo her favorite role, and with good reason. The part requires fullness of tone in the lowest range of the contralto voice, and though even Thorborg cannot fully meet the demand, her timbre and vocal size are ideal for the part. As the opera opens, the three cries of 'Euridice' unveil Thorborg's beautiful core of focused tone. One might wish for more variety of dynamics as the afternoon progresses, but her style and noble purpose are everywhere a boon. Only some unexpected sharping at the end of the second-act scene by the river Styx mars her performance. Her straightforward 'Che farò senza Euridice' is no exercise in self-pity; this Orfeo seems intent on maintaining dignity, while still adequately sounding his

Orfeo ed Euridice
20 January 1940
Orfeo
Kerstin Thorborg
Euridice
Jarmila Novotna
Amor
Marita Farell
Conductor
Erich Leinsdorf

grief at his loss. I like best Thorborg's serene and long-lined 'Che puro ciel!' where Leinsdorf conspires to realize the ethereal beauty of Gluck's orchestral pictorialisms. Farell's Amor is merely serviceable, but Novotna makes an impressive figure of a heroine who is little more than a cipher in most performances.

Novotna was an artist of wide experience when she came to the Metropolitan. After study with Emmy Destinn (the Fanciulla in the 1910 world premiere of Puccini's opera at the Met) and an early beginning in her native Prague, she matured in Italy before achieving stardom in Berlin. When Hitler rose to power, she moved on to even greater popularity in Vienna. Lehár wrote his opera *Giuditta* (1934) for her, and Toscanini engaged her for his Salzburg *Zauberflöte*. She fled Vienna after the Nazi invasion and came to America in 1939 at the request of Toscanini for *Traviata* at the New York World's Fair. But Toscanini, refusing to perform in the available facilities, took her instead to Edward Johnson (who had heard her in Vienna during the summer of 1935). The result was a Met debut on 5 January 1940 in *La Bohème*.

In addition to her professionalism, Novotna had other assets: a face and figure of aristocratic beauty, skill as an actress (she was a protégée of Germany's greatest theatrical talent, Max Reinhardt), and sensitive musicianship. The voice itself was ample in range, though somewhat slight and not capable of great color variation. But the voice's basic pastel hue held its own distinction, like the amber sheen of a fine Chardonnay. Euridice offers little opportunity for vocal display (Violetta and Manon would soon provide that opportunity), but Novotna manages to convey the anguish of the despairing wife upon whom Orfeo must not look and adds a touch of spirit to the lovers' impassioned dialogue. Her tone resides a little too far back in the throat, which makes for a slightly fixed sound, but it is lovely nonetheless. When she comes to the supreme moment of the opera, we know as much from her timing of the silences as from her affective delivery that death is upon her; she possesses that subtle aura of quietude before a climactic moment which only the great vocal actresses recognize and turn to advantage.

Fifteen years would elapse before *Orfeo* would again appear on the broadcasts, but Johnson offered two other master operas in the 1939–40 season which would have far greater currency, though they, too, had been neglected for years. A decade earlier Chaliapin had bid farewell to the Metropolitan, and with him had gone Mussorgsky's psychological drama of the corruption of power, *Boris Godunov*. The Russian basso's czar stands as one of the mighty creations of operatic history, so perhaps the reluctance of management to challenge memory is understandable. Pinza, however, displayed no such timidity. As early as 1935 Johnson wrote of an encounter with the basso in London where Pinza "asked about his repertoire . . . and why he couldn't do Boris. You tell him,"[1] Johnson taunted Ziegler. Johnson gives us the flavor of Pinza, the man, as he arrived for rehearsal at Covent Garden with Rethberg (she looking "radiantly happy") in a "beautiful large blue automobile . . . Pinza very smart in a new spring suit, dark blue shirt and collar to match with tie and socks of the same hue. . . . Don Giovanni in person!" Could the natural life force of Don Juan be transformed into the melancholy, tormented Russian czar? The Metropolitan performed *Boris* in Italian (though Chaliapin had sung his role in Russian), so language was no barrier to Pinza's assumption. But Pinza had to wait another five years before his wish would be granted.

At the end of the thirties Pinza entered a period of authentic stardom. Méphisto and Don Giovanni had long been his own, and now he would secure his status with two other star vehicles, Mozart's Figaro and Boris. The latter opera was not new to

Boris Godunov
9 December 1939

Marina
Kerstin Thorborg
Dimitri
Charles Kullman
Schouisky
Alessio de Paolis
Rangoni
Leonard Warren
Boris
Ezio Pinza
Pimen
Nicola Moscona
Varlaam
Norman Cordon
Conductor
Ettore Panizza

him, for he had sung Pimen to Chaliapin's final Boris (a "real inspiration,"[2] Pinza called him) in 1929.

On the broadcast of 9 December 1939, not only was the language Italian but the orchestration was Rimsky-Korsakov's brilliant transformation of the Mussorgsky score. Thus we are already several steps removed from the composer's intent, and the performance cannot be considered idiomatic. The order of scenes is also altered, but then Mussorgsky himself was inconclusive on this point (his several versions of the opera offer alternative solutions). But the management's choice does indicate a point of view which governs the performing version of the Johnson era. The gripping scene at St. Basil's Cathedral (from Mussorgsky's first version), where the Simpleton accuses Boris, is omitted; the Polish scenes are included (they were absent from the Chaliapin performances); and the act-one coronation and Pimen scenes are reversed, as are the act-four death of Boris and Forest of Kromy scenes. While the love music in the Polish scene is predominantly Italianate in style, the bulk of the opera is far removed from the warmth of Mediterranean melody. But Pinza is unable to resist converting Mussorgsky's unique song-speech ("the melody that partakes of life," the composer called it) into pure lyricism. How could he do anything else when it had been his musical lifeblood? And the strong tonic accents of Italian (particularly in the imposing choral passages) are antithetic to the sonorous flow of Russian. Thus the sombre melancholy of the score is considerably diluted. Panizza magnifies this in his approach; from the first orchestral measures it is evident that mood will retreat in favor of Italian fervor. The climaxes of his reading could be at home in veristic opera (amazing how the choral scenes of *Turandot* spring to mind when hearing *Boris* in Italian).

Does all this add up to a bad performance? Not at all. Inappropriate, yes; but actually, Panizza's firm hand, plus adequate rehearsal (necessitated by the opera's long absence from the repertory), makes for one of the best ensemble performances of the period—the large cast remained intact for a half-dozen performances, a rarity at the time. Much of the impact of the opera depends on the realization of the many vignettes with which Mussorgsky peopled the opera, and no weak link strains the Met chain. Cehanovsky's Tchelkaloff is superb in announcing Boris' reluctance to assume the throne (and he succeeds through some musical sleight of hand in making Italian take on the feel of his native Russian), Doris Doe's hearty Innkeeper delivers a well-focused folksong, and Cordon is an assured Varlaam (though Panizza's orderly accompaniment in the Siege of Kazan doesn't help him convey the raucous flavor of the tale); Kaskas (the Old Nurse), Petina (an excellent Fyodor), and Farell (Xenia) are all on the mark, while De Paolis' voice and art seem tailor-made for the wily Schouisky. Moscona provides a most sympathetic Pimen; his instrument seems more pliable than heretofore, the timbre more appealing. Though Moscona makes no effort to suggest the weariness of the aged chronicler, he offers a sensitive musical reading.

Kullman is remarkably successful as the false Dimitri, not only singing with resolute tone but achieving the unlikely feat of making the renegade monk an attractive, even forceful character. He seldom sang the role (the Kromy pronouncements call for a more stentorian effort, but his tone is particularly winning elsewhere). Kullman and Thorborg make the most of the love scene, he wonderfully ardent and she in her best vocal form, retaining a round core of tone even in the jagged rhythms of the Polish folk dances. Better yet, she actually sounds seductive in the love duet; her seldom-heard *pianissimo* caps a beautiful high-lying phrase near the end of the duet. Opera managers tend to prize versatility more than the public does; too often a pleasing mediocrity is the result. But, whether portraying the classic Orfeo or her string of Wagnerian dynamos, Thorborg always contributes a musico-dramatic portrait of integrity—Marina is one of the finest of them. Warren (heard here in only his second broadcast) is a strong-voiced, dark-hued Rangoni. He deploys a smooth legato and pulls out a change of vocal color to assure Marina she need not be too scrupulous in her seduction of Dimitri as long as the church's needs are served.

Both focal points of the drama command respect. The chorus of the Russian people has been well prepared (by Fausto Cleva!) and is a potent force throughout the afternoon—more successful in the energetic moments of conflict and celebration than in mystic mood. Appropriately, the climax of their efforts is reached in the Kromy scene where Panizza coordinates the diverse choral elements to thrilling effect. Pinza is most impressive in the coronation scene where, his voice typically resonant and firm, he envelops 'O triste cor' in somber beauty and moves to a superb vocal climax (though he discloses little melancholy en route). Vocal splendor again dominates the "power" monologue—the Czar's dignity is preserved, but Pinza gives us no premonition of the ensuing breakdown. The overtly dramatic moments are more successful; he is marvelously threatening as he demands confirmation of the true Dimitri's death from Schouisky. While his inborn penchant for song robs the clock scene of pathological subtlety, it is very assured in its exterior trappings. In the final scene Pinza again makes little attempt to depict vocally the torment of the czar, now weary unto death. He counsels young Fyodor in vibrant tones as though it is Boris' nobility which he chooses to convey, and when Boris adjures the czarevitch to defend the church and protect Xenia, Pinza's haunting mezza voce is put to good use. But by now his constant emphasis on volume results in some rough vocal edges. He takes a very quiet, lyrical approach to death, devoid of theatrical gestures, a welcome antidote to the gasping realism of other interpreters. Nevertheless, the all-important moment is deficient in terror and pathos. When, in strong, firm tones, Pinza asks for the monk's robe as death is upon him, we know that this czar goes to the cloister clothed in his dignity, and unrepentant.

If the crown of Holy Russia sat somewhat uneasily on Pinza's head, a greater conquest awaited him in what was perhaps the major event of the Johnson years, the revival of Mozart's *Le Nozze di Figaro.*

The history of Mozart operas at the Metropolitan is a record of changing taste. Not surprisingly, *Don Giovanni*, upon which the romantic excesses of the nineteenth century could most readily be grafted, was a relative constant during the early years of the Met. It appeared in the Met's very first season (1883) and frequently during the next quarter century. After a lapse of twenty-two years came the 1929 revival with Pinza, and thereafter the opera was seldom out of the repertory. At the other extreme, both *Die Entführung aus dem Serail* and *Idomeneo* were the Cinderellas of the Mozart canon, their contrasting beauties waiting patiently for the acceptance of a broader spectrum of dramaturgical aesthetics. Not until 1946 would *The Abduction* appear, and *Idomeneo* lay dormant until 1982. *Così Fan Tutte's* moral ambiguity prevented Victorian and Edwardian audiences from approving its charms—is it coincidence that the Roaring Twenties saw the first performances of *Così* at the Met? But the serious decades of the thirties and forties banished *Così* until the 1951 revival. Both *Die Zauberflöte* and *Le Nozze di Figaro* had enjoyed early popularity at the Met, the singspiel appearing as early as 1899 (in the guise of *Il Flauto Magico*) and frequently thereafter until 1916 when (except for the single season of 1926) it passed out of the repertory. Mozart's greatest opera buffa was heard even earlier (1893) but faded sooner (1917). Until the Johnson revival in 1940, it had not been enjoyed for twenty-two seasons.

When one looks over the casts of the early *Figaro* performances (Eames, Nordica, Sigrid Arnoldson, Ancona, and Edouard de Reszke in 1893; Eames, Sembrich, Farrar, Didur, and Scotti in 1908–09, with Mahler conducting; and Matzenauer, Hempel, Farrar, De Luca, and Didur in 1917–18) one can only wonder at its failure to gain a foothold. Of course, Mozart's creations are inherently theatrical and require thorough ensemble preparation (both musical and dramatic) to make their full effect; opera house practices during earlier times were not conducive to this end. In the forties, the requirement of an ensemble of stars fully coordinated through numerous rehearsals must have given management even greater pause. Nevertheless, Johnson accepted the challenge in 1940 with *Le Nozze di Figaro* and again in 1942 with *The Magic Flute*.

Establishment of the Mozart operas in the repertory was Johnson's most enduring legacy for the Metropolitan audience and the radio public. Johnson's interest in *Figaro* was engaged when he heard the work in Florence in 1937. He wrote to Ziegler:

> Nozze di Figaro was a great success for Bruno Walter and gave Dr. Graf a splendid opportunity to prove his worth. In the beautiful eighteenth century theatre "La Pergola", all the grace and charm of this Mozartean chef-d'oeure [*sic*] was presented to a well disposed and enthusiastic public.[3]

Would the New York audience be as well disposed, especially in the cavernous recesses of the Metropolitan? Johnson did all he could to ensure an enthusiastic response. Though he did not have the venerable Walter, Herbert Graf was already on hand (he probably spurred Johnson on), and the general manager was able to assemble a cast to rival the legendary ensembles of earlier years: Rethberg, Sayão, Stevens, Pinza, and Brownlee in the premiere on 20 February 1940. Conductor Panizza's credentials for the work were impressive (Covent Garden in 1906 with Destinn, Maggie Teyte as Cherubino, and Scotti; La Scala in the 1920s with Favero, Supervia, and Stabile). His ideas on Mozart were less reassuring. For Panizza, Mozart "does not plumb the depths of emotion in his operas. . . . He expresses sentiment rather than passion."[4] He did advocate a reduced string component for the revival: ten first violins, ten seconds, six violas, four cellos, four double basses "and a piano for the recitatives modified to produce a tone resembling that of a clavi-cembalo." He had the orchestra pit raised to its maximum height "so that the light scoring may reach the audience distinctly."[5] What Panizza was after was "perfect clarity of execution," which he regarded as "the most difficult task in conducting Mozart."

The broadcast of 9 March was the third presentation of the opera but "perfect clarity," let alone subtle nuances of execution, was still in the future. Panizza drives the overture hard, and throughout the opera contrasting motives are seldom well enough articulated to give the requisite profile to Mozart's singing-allegro style. The prestissimo which concludes the second-act finale turns into a mad dash, and too often the ensembles seem to be aimlessly wandering in self-propelled movement. Mozart's winds, with their now graceful, now laughing, commentary on the stage action, neither sing nor frolic in this performance. What Panizza (and Graf, certainly) does provide is a swiftly paced, animated traversal of the score, never allowing the comic thread to snap between numbers. One feels a lively sense of events actually

Le Nozze di Figaro
9 March 1940

Countess
Elisabeth Rethberg

Susanna
Bidú Sayão

Cherubino
Jarmila Novotna

Almaviva
John Brownlee

Figaro
Ezio Pinza

Dr. Bartolo
Virgilio Lazzari

Conductor
Ettore Panizza

happening at any given moment, a precious commodity for any opera, but particularly felicitous in comedy—and that sense is largely due to the singers' commitment.

An almost legendary repute has accrued to the Mozart portrayals of this cast, and in a few cases the réclame is warranted; in several others, it proves mythic. Brownlee's elegance of manner and knowledge of Mozart style are oft cited as the natural heritage of his Glyndebourne performances as Don Giovanni and Don Alfonso. If Mozart style is merely the avoidance of excess and fidelity to the printed page, he qualifies. But not only is the tone monotonously wooden most of the time, but the near absence of legato is death to the sensuous curve of Mozart's music. Even in *recitativo secco* he is a slave to the mechanical alternation of eighth and sixteenth notes—contrast Pinza's handling of recitative, where the natural rhythm of the word governs the shape of the phrase while both clarity and legato are preserved. In the second-act confrontation with his countess, Brownlee's bluster smacks of an English country squire rather than a Spanish nobleman. And he lacks the vocal suavity to successfully woo Susanna ('Crudel! perchè'). A bit of character penetrates his opening recitative in act three, and later he takes on a broader manner, darkening his tone appropriately in the big aria; but the concluding triplets are poorly articulated and the high F-sharp ends in a squeak. (He concludes the aria on the upper-octave tonic—is that Glyndebourne authenticity?). Perhaps his success depended more on his being the perfect foil for Pinza's Figaro.

An even greater disappointment is the Susanna of Bidú Sayão, one of the most celebrated of all Mozart portrayals. Unlike Brownlee, the vocal and dramatic resources are all there; it is the use made of them that causes pain. If Brownlee is squarely pinned to the note, too often Sayão can't seem to find it. Sometimes her tone is suspiciously under the pitch (even in 'Deh vieni, non tardar'), but more important, she is constantly animating her character either by singing outside the note in agitated moments or interpolating little squeaks or squeals. The extraneous effects soon become tiresome. One wouldn't want to deny she is a vivid presence throughout the opera, often delightfully spunky—her manner is ideally suited to 'Venite, inginocchiatevi,' the action aria where Susanna dresses Cherubino in girl's clothes. Here Sayão's crisp bite is welcome, and she shows her sensitivity when adjusting Cherubino's neckline—her tone color changes as Susanna ponders each alteration ('più alto'). But compare Sayão and Novotna (who soon replaced Stevens as Cherubino in many of the Met performances) in the duettino which precedes Cherubino's exit via the window: Sayão does it all staccatissimo, while Novotna conveys the excitement of the moment without condescending to mere chirping. Yet, but a moment later, how deliciously spiteful is Sayão's challenge as she awaits the tyrant Count ('venga poi lo smargiasso'), and when she makes her unexpected reentry from the cabinet, she suddenly offers all the wondrous purity of her tone, and one is conquered anew. The duet with the Count is lovely, too, but the huffs, the note ambiguity, and the excessive nasality return in large order during the sextet. Too much is sacrificed for dramatic impact throughout her performance, nowhere more so than in the fourth-act finale where the repeated near-E-flats are as harsh to our ears as the accompanying cuffs she delivers to Figaro's. Only beautiful vocalism will do for the letter duet and 'Deh vieni,' and here Sayão does not disappoint. Panizza takes the aria at an abysmally slow pace, and Sayão must frequently break the phrases in half, but a good deal of finely spun tone is doled out (especially on the overly long fermata at the climax). Finally, yet another demerit must be marked against the cherishable soprano. Sayão is the only artist of the cast to consistently ignore the unwritten appoggiaturas which are integral to eighteenth-century style. (She does add a pair of them in the accompanied recitative which precedes 'Deh vieni'). Pinza and Rethberg are models of rectitude in this matter in both recitatives and set forms, Brownlee knows their value in the recitatives, and the other cast members sometimes do and sometimes don't. In short, the development of a Mozart style for the entire ensemble, both historically oriented and dramatically alive, remains in the future.

The shorter roles are well cast. D'Angelo makes a stout-voiced gardener, Petina is a delightful Marcellina, De Paolis is at home with the insidious Basilio, and Marita Farell plays an enchanting Barbarina, who sings the pin aria as though it were the focal point of the opera. Only Lazzari falters as a weary, unhumorous Bartolo.

Rethberg's assumption of the Contessa comes near the end of her career. In two short years all would be over. Expectation is thus hedged with reservations; once these are acknowledged, we can be gratified for the many positive aspects of her portrayal. She is in her best late-career form: the tremulousness and flatting in her mid voice are seldom obtrusive, and her approach to the top is well modulated. 'Porgi, amor' (the introduction nicely shaped by Panizza) is quite lovely—in it she sounds a note of real sorrow for her lost love. Throughout the afternoon she manages to find a perfect equilibrium between public playfulness and her private pathos (Albanese tells us that Rethberg did not flirt with Cherubino but treated him as a child and was "the grand lady every moment"[6]). Often she reveals an unexpected sense of humor: when noisy Cherubino, secluded in her cabinet, betrays himself, she utters 'Io non intesi niente' with just the right vocal deadpan. And she is adept at inflecting recitative: when Pinza denies having seen the ladies' note, she murmurs 'Nol conosci?' in genuine disbelief. The grand manner of the opera seria permeates her handling of the great accompanied recitative leading into 'Dove sono' (how she expands 'Prima amata'). In the aria she fines down her tone to a silvery thread, points up the drama of the middle section, and manages it all with honor and the sensitivity of a great artist—there are no false moves here.

It may be no accident that the two entirely satisfying artists of the afternoon (Novotna and Pinza) participated in the 1937 Salzburg performances under Bruno Walter. Novotna is a complete mistress of the style, eagerly entering into the fun in her recitatives and singing Cherubino's two arias with absolute assurance. How nice to hear the ascending phrases of 'Non so più' executed without effort! One may prefer the deeper tone of a mezzo in this boy's music, but Novotna's lovely vocal color and classic line (with its exquisite *portamento* at the reprise of 'Voi che sapete') go far to demolish prejudice. Pinza's Figaro is a joy from start to finish, his vibrant personality and robust tone commanding attention and belief whenever he appears. As noted earlier, his fluent recitative is a marvel, and the arias are thoughtfully planned for maximum musical and dramatic effect. He grasps and points up the significance of 'Se vuol ballare' which, along with the Count's third-act vengeance aria, is one of the twin fulcrums of the drama; plenty of menace marks the introductory recitative, but Pinza chooses to begin the aria with delicate grace, saving his bitterness for the middle section (the falsetto Fs remind us that baritones used to sing the role). 'Non più andrai' has a nonchalant gait, while his bright tone and crisp diction are perfectly mated with 'Aprite un po' quegl'occhi.' In the latter he avoids burlesque and even reveals a modicum of hurt at Susanna's supposed betrayal. His instinctive musicianship is never more apparent than in his treatment of the repetitions of 'il resto nol dico,' which he delivers with instrumental accuracy and at a lower dynamic level than the antecedent phrases—Pinza knows when the governance of the word must give way to make a purely musical point, and in this case Mozart's genius humorously but insidiously drives the meaning home. When Pinza sings Mozart, the architectural landscape (the procedures and phrase constructions of the Viennese classic school) is clearly charted. And finally, when he voices 'Tutto è tranquillo e placido' with resonant, warm tone (and how it differs from his delivery of Méphisto's invocation of the night in *Faust*), he enables Mozart's sublime humanity to force farce momentarily into the wings.

Elisabeth Rethberg. Photography by Fernand de Gueldre.

Ezio Pinza as Figaro in *Le Nozze di Figaro*.

CHAPTER FOURTEEN

Interlude
Mortgage and Marriage

Time has confirmed that the revival of Mozart's *Figaro* was the artistic event of the 1939–40 season, but two extra musical events of 1940 were of long-range importance to the Metropolitan, and oddly enough, *Le Nozze di Figaro* played its part in each of them.

The premiere of *Le Nozze di Figaro* served as an Opera Guild benefit for a new fund drive to enable the Metropolitan to purchase the opera house from its "beneficent landlord,"[1] the Metropolitan Opera and Real Estate Company. The beneficent landlords were actually the descendants or estates of the original box-holders who had owned the property since the disastrous fire which gutted the house in 1892. The artistic enterprise, known as the Metropolitan Opera Association, merely produced opera in the rent-free property at Broadway and Thirty-ninth Street (rent-free, that is, in exchange for those all-important boxes which ensured social standing). No longer able (or now unwilling) to sustain by means of annual assessments the costs of taxes, maintenance, and mortgage payments, the Real Estate Company informed the Association of its intent to sell the property and liquidate. The Association, in turn, organized a massive campaign to raise one million dollars (half to enable them to exercise the option to purchase the house, the remainder for improvements and operating capital).

Once again the radio audience was asked to play its part in supporting the Metropolitan "in a crisis that is by far the most serious of any in its history."[2] During an intermission of the *Lohengrin* broadcast of 27 January, Mrs. Belmont, Lucrezia Bori, and David Sarnoff (chairman of the board of directors of NBC) launched the appeal by asking a contribution of one dollar from each radio listener. A week later, at the end of the *Lucia* broadcast, Milton Cross noted that the Metropolitan served "the whole American people," and he felt sure that in these days "when art and culture and all we prize most dearly in our modern civilization seem to be hanging in the balance" all listeners would "want to have a part in helping the Metropolitan." And they did want to help. To a boilermaker from the Coulee Dam, the broadcasts meant "the enchantment of magnificent music magnificently performed" bringing "utter restfulness and rejuvenation" to his world of "dirt and noise, of sweat and weariness."[3] A southern listener wrote from a larger perspective, citing the broadcasts as "an inspiration to neighborly feelings, between other peoples and ourselves and thus an international influence for peace and good will."[4]

The artists of the Metropolitan, too, were pressed into service during broadcast intermissions. Even the long absent De Luca, touched by the loyalty of his public, felt sure the radio audience would "show this same loyalty to the Metropolitan Opera Company—one of the greatest in all the world . . . the pride of your nation." All the effort paid off. The radio audience contributed $372,000 toward the total of $1,057,679, a larger share than that of any other segment of the Metropolitan public.[5]

The largesse of the radio audience helped to bring about another nonmusical happening in 1940, the return of commercial sponsorship to the broadcasts. When the 1940–41 season opened on 7 December 1940 (the opera was our friend *Figaro*, the hit of the previous season), the occasion celebrated not only the nuptials of Susanna and Figaro but the marriage of opera and oil, a union destined to be the longest and happiest in the history of broadcasting.

Of the previous nine seasons, only three had enjoyed commercial sponsorship. Since 1937 the opera had been a sustaining program, dependent on the good graces of the network for continuance. That NBC was concerned about the relationship is evident in its negotiations with the Metropolitan in the summer of 1939. The network felt that the broadcasts "might be more readily salable if our network stations were permitted to secure local sponsors. . . ."[6] In addition to allowing local stations to benefit financially, the network felt the "variety of experience stories . . . might considerably widen the type of commercial sponsor who could logically and profitably take over the commercial sponsorship of the opera on a national scale." But the Metropolitan's concern to control its public image was strong—the 1940 agreement prevented NBC from commercial broadcast "unless the sponsor and the product to be advertised . . . are satisfactory to Metropolitan, but Metropolitan agrees not to unreasonably withhold its approval of any sponsor or product."[7] Reason prevailed, and the Texas Company (later Texaco, Inc.) came on board for the opening *Figaro* broadcast of the 1940–41 season.

For W. S. S. Rodgers, president of the Texas Company, there was nothing new in the merger: "American business has long acted on the policy of success through service to the greatest number."[8] Their previous commitments had been the "Fire Chief Show" (begun in 1932 with Ed Wynn) and the "Texaco Star Theatre," which featured stage and screen personalities. Now grand opera was to be "no longer the privilege of a few. Through radio, the American people have been enabled to make it their own." The company officials were particularly impressed by the fact that "financial contributions to the opera's support last year came from music lovers all over the country and in every walk of life." The Met had become "the people's opera." What was good for the people was evidently good for business. "In the long run, the success of any business enterprise can be measured by its contribution to a better life for all the people."

Initially the gain to the Met was more in security than in dollars. In 1938 NBC had reduced the honorarium from $100,000 to $90,000;[9] in 1939 the total decreased to $80,000.[10] The 1940 agreement with NBC provided for an increase from $75,000 to $85,000, plus any additional copyright fees or artists' wage increases caused by the new arrangement, should a commercial sponsor be found for the 1940–41 season. (Options could extend the agreement through 1944–45.) Especially commendable was the Texas Company's decision to utilize only two of the more than twenty minutes of advertising time authorized by the National Association of Broadcasters. It would be enough "to win a high level of good will by associating the name 'Texaco' with that of 'Metropolitan Opera' only at the highest artistic level, even to the extent of eliminating all discussion of company products by direct 'commercials.' "[11] That association was so potent that only a half-dozen years later the ultimate in popular recognition came in a New Yorker magazine cartoon: an urbane matron, whose car is being serviced at a Texaco gas station, enthusiastically remarks to a mystified attendant, "I said it's so grand of you to bring us those Metropolitan broadcasts."[12]

NBC's concern over its relationship with the Metropolitan extended to areas other than commercial sponsorship. Again the main bone of contention was the troublesome Metropolitan franchise. The whole business had become decidedly messy and was affecting relations with artists. NBC wanted the Met itself to collect the franchise charges since the franchise is "a natural consideration granted to you by the artist in exchange for your employment agreements for appearances at the Opera."[13] The network wished to have the present franchise provision eliminated from the new agreement with the Met and replaced with a provision whereby "the Metropolitan consents to our buying or selling the services of Metropolitan artists for radio programs for the broadcast by us or others so long as the broadcasts do not take place at times which would conflict with the artists' appearances at the Opera." NBC cited a long list of grievances against the Metropolitan concerning artists who were exempt from the franchise (ten were permissible exemptions, but Ziegler had sent NBC a list of fifteen artist exemptions for the 1939 season). Tibbett's radio concert appearances were especially lucrative for the network, yet his agent, Arthur Judson (president of Columbia Concerts Corporation) had informed NBC that Tibbett had no obligation for franchise payments "except during the exact time [the actual week] when he is appearing at the Metropolitan."[14] NBC asked rebates from the Met on commercial appearances by Sayão, Meisle, Gigli, and John Carter. To drive home the absurdity of the situation NBC cited baritone Carlo Morelli, with whom it found itself in the position of "having to attempt a collection directly from an artist who apparently has no present active management and who probably never considered the possibility of a franchise charge and whose broadcast fee we do not know."[15] The network wanted to wash its hands of the whole matter, since collecting the franchise for the Met from artists under managements other than NBC was "not only difficult but distasteful and creates a very unsatisfactory artist relationship which, in our opinion, cannot help react unfavorably to the Metropolitan as well as to us."[16] The conflict was finally resolved by the elimination of the franchise from the 1940s agreement.

The franchise concept belonged to another era; it died of natural causes, but the demise of the franchise arrangement made the opera broadcasts themselves less attractive to the commercial networks. A valuable bargaining chip was lost; a crack in the dike was opened which would weaken the relationship with NBC until a few years later the pioneer union of opera and NBC would be severed. (The Met broadcasts were aired on NBC's Blue Network which, at the urging of the FCC, was sold in 1943 to the American Broadcasting System, later called ABC.)

A more positive (and, for the radio audience, rewarding) addition to the 1940 agreement was the provision granting NBC the right to broadcast all "road booking opera performances"[17] for which it could obtain the consent of the sponsoring committee in the tour city. The happy result was the addition of a number of tour broadcasts before the contract expired in 1945. Approval from local officials was not always forthcoming: B. M. Grunewald informed Ziegler that the New Orleans performance of *Carmen* could not be broadcast because he was "inclined to believe that ... it will affect sale of tickets."[18] Thus we have no aircheck of Castagna's Carmen.

An even greater boon for future generations was NBC gaining the right to make off-the-line recordings of the broadcasts, to be used "only for reference or for file purposes, or for delayed broadcasts . . . not later than the seventh day after the opera is performed".[19]

The Texas Company, beneficent as it was (and is), could not help but keep one eye on public response. With the concurrence of the Metropolitan Board, the oil company, "realizing that the opera audience [in 1940] was of limited musical experience," included as one of its four policy objectives the right "to prevail upon the Metropolitan management to present on Saturday afternoons a carefully calculated percentage of the so-called 'popular' operas."[20] At the end of their first season the sponsor informed Mr. Johnson that the week following the *Tristan* broadcast "the number of listeners [*sic*] letters dropped to exactly one-half of the number ordinarily received which, of course may mean that Tristan is a little long, and hard to take as a radio performance unless you are a true opera lover."[21] NBC's survey (taken at season's end), however, reported that *Tristan* ranked first as "the opera most enjoyed."[22] *Tristan*, though absent in 1941–42 (Flagstad was gone and the opera was not in the repertory), was heard thereafter by the radio audience in every season of the Johnson regime. Obviously, the Texas Company's remarks were only wistful longings, rather than undue pressure. Their principal aim remained inviolate, and it was high-minded. Geraldine Souvaine, producer of the broadcasts, noted that a four-hour opera carried only one and a half minutes of sponsor identification. In addition, company policy dictated that the intermission features should "complement and not detract or digress from the music itself."[23] With so openhanded a marriage contract, the prospects for a lasting union could not be other than favorable.

Salvatore Baccaloni as Dr. Dulcamara in *L'Elisir d'Amore*. Photography by Louis Mélançon.

CHAPTER FIFTEEN

1940–43
Comic Relief

Most of the original participants in *Le Nozze di Figaro* are again on hand for the first Texas Company broadcast on 7 December 1940.

Pinza's Figaro is still dominant. He sets the contrasts in Figaro's music and character into even greater relief; 'Se vuol ballare' and its introductory recitative are played at a lower key, but the concluding section has greater bitter bite. Sometimes the conception has relaxed a little, with a welcome gain in refinement—in the previous season's performance the slightly madcap quality (as in 'Non più andrai') ensured a lively theatricality but was less satisfying on the musical side. On the other hand, in the act-two scene with the Countess, Pinza seems bent on showing how fast he can deliver *secco* recitative. This time the basso makes 'Aprite un po' quegl'occhi' more than a buffa piece as his anger at Susanna's betrayal boils over into genuine torment in the final pages of the aria. Brownlee is in better vocal form on this afternoon and sings with some suavity (or so it seems until one hears him pitted against the cellolike play of Pinza on a single line like 'Mente, il ceffo, io già non mento' in the second-act finale).

Novotna and Rethberg are much the same. In moments of agitated recitative a slightly strangled quality invades Novotna's instrument (the native language of an artist inevitably leaves its imprint on voice production), but her arias are models of equilibrium between the demands of music and theatre. Though 'Dove sono' may have been tonally more focused a few months earlier, Rethberg still shows her artistic mettle as she momentarily adopts a seria stance to protest her innocence to her husband or rounds off a phrase with a diminuendo in the letter duet. Panizza is now willing and able to give a sharper profile to the contrasting movements of the second-act finale. He holds the reins a little less taut, and the resultant flexibility occasionally allows the grace and humor of Mozart's orchestration to mate with the stage gestures. Petina must be singled out for providing some of the best singing of the afternoon as she begins the humorous sextet (though in it George Rasely as the notary oversings his part and throws the ensemble out of kilter).

Two fresh ingredients, both new to the radio audience, both nurtured on sunny Mediterranean shores, have been added to the mix. The Metropolitan careers of basso Salvatore Baccaloni and soprano Licia Albanese will extend into the 1960s, and the radio audience will have many opportunities to hear them in a wide range of roles.

Le Nozze di Figaro
7 December 1940

Countess
Elisabeth Rethberg
Susanna
Licia Albanese
Cherubino
Jarmila Novotna
Almaviva
John Brownlee
Figaro
Ezio Pinza
Dr. Bartolo
Salvatore Baccaloni
Conductor
Ettore Panizza

No artist of these decades came to be held in greater affection by the public than Albanese. And how well she merits regard. An exquisite lyric artist in the line of Farrar, Alda, and Bori, over the three decades of her American career she would create a series of heroines distinguished by fidelity to the composer's intent and made vivid by her rare power to communicate. Her introduction to the radio public as a soubrette was incongruous—her debut vehicle in the 1939-40 season had been as Madama Butterfly. The results are paradoxical. Unlike Sayão, Albanese sings the notes and rhythms with pinpoint accuracy, but on this occasion she shows insufficient inclination to spin tone in the captivating manner of the Brazilian soprano. The fleet pace of much of Susanna's music seems to necessitate a production which sometimes results in tone both small and rather brittle. On the other hand, she delivers the recitative with utmost clarity and telling understanding. (Questioned as to Albanese's unlikely casting as a soubrette when the historic recording of this performance was released in 1974, Mrs. Belmont defended the choice, noting that one could understand her every word.)[1] To hear Albanese utter a simple 'Bravo' or 'Guarda un po',' or propel the double consonant in 'capello' is to hear diction with a music of its own. 'Venite, inginocchiatevi' is as delightfully crisp and dry as unbuttered toast, and in the ensuing duet with Cherubino her staccati are more reasonable than Sayão's. But she is almost as chary with the appoggiatura as her sister soprano.

When, in the final acts of the opera, Mozart and Da Ponte turn Susanna from a manipulative minx into a girl in love, we begin to gain some hint of Albanese's true quality. In her duets with the Count and Countess she conducts the line with a cameo-like fragility reminiscent of Bori (the tonal acidity is not unlike, also). One notices how she rides over the crest of a phrase and then gently eases its cadence. Finally, 'Deh vieni' is a magical moment, traced with infinite care, as delicate as a drypoint etching but warmed by the breath of desire as she lingers lovingly over 'ai piaceri d'amor qui tutto adesca.' Unlike Sayão, Albanese takes most of the phrases in a single breath and marks the arch of them with the slightest expansion of volume and pace.

One can regard Albanese's Susanna as the logical descendant of the old commedia dell'arte Colombina—brittle in manner and tone, not much different from the typical Italian soubrette of the period—at least until Mozart's leavening transforms the sly servant into the warmly human woman of the final act. Though the aural result is occasionally trying, critics of the time responded enthusiastically to this very performance. Virgil Thomson admired Albanese's Susanna, and Olin Downes thought she captured the essence of the character and was in fact better suited to Susanna than to "grander parts."[2] So much for critical clairvoyance. A few weeks later in the season the broadcast of Butterfly would set the matter straight.

Baccaloni makes his actual New York debut on this Saturday afternoon—the same cast had appeared in the work in Philadelphia a few days earlier. A veteran artist with a European career of almost two decades in both serious and buffa parts, he had participated in many of the famous Toscanini nights at La Scala during the late 1920s and was a member of the Glyndebourne Mozart ensemble a decade later. Luckily, his voice was still in prime estate. The first herald of Baccaloni's presence on the Metropolitan stage was not his rotund bass but, quite appropriately, the laughter of the audience as he made his entrance. Unfortunately, Baccaloni is not in his best voice in the aria (spread tones of limited volume mar the conclusion), but one appreciates the lightness of the patter at 'Se tutto il codice' and the variety of dynamics throughout the reading; most welcome is his ability to maintain interest by means of narrative skill. His delivery of recitative is clear and characterful, and one relishes how the purposeful technique of an experienced artist motivates Baccaloni's deft thrust in the third-act sextet where his 'Suo padre' somehow manages to encompass equal parts of stupefaction and pride.

This broadcast of *Figaro* was the first of the historical recordings released by the Metropolitan in return for financial contributions to the opera company. Whatever one thinks of the performance, Wanda Horowitz's judgment is on record. She appeared during an intermission of 1974 to promote sales in an effort "to help ease the present financial crisis of this opera house." Evidently no effort was too great, for citing Panizza as the musician whom Toscanini had chosen to conduct *Figaro* at La Scala in 1929, she opined, "In a way I feel the spirit of my father hovers over this marvelous, memorable performance." Was she hedging her bet when she added, "No matter what the problems, including the performances that did not satisfy Toscanini, he always said, 'We must not let opera die'."? No argument there.

With Baccaloni at hand, the Metropolitan continued to mine the buffa genre with more than usual frequency. *Don Pasquale, La Fille du Régiment*, and *L'Elisir d'Amore* (along with the more familiar *Barbiere*) followed in short order. Just two weeks after his debut in *Figaro*, Baccaloni offered his first Metropolitan Pasquale; once again, the event was broadcast.

Donizetti's *Don Pasquale* offers Baccaloni the opportunity to add a human dimension to the masterful buffa technique already demonstrated. Happily, on this occasion the voice is as big and fat as the man himself. From the first, Baccaloni's singing is full-toned, accurate, and surprisingly straightforward, an impression solidified by the musicality of 'Ah, un foco insolito.' His finest singing occurs in the act-three duet with Malatesta. One is often surprised by the brightness and deftness of his upper voice (in fact, he seems to skirt the lowest notes of the role). Delightfully menacing in the 'bada ben' (which often comes out 'bahada ben') of the act-two quartet, he reverses the coin and captures the pathos of 'È finita Don Pasquale' in the final act. The visual virtuosity of Baccaloni's portrayal may be denied the radio audience, but Donizetti's musical gestures are so graphic that the portrayal strikes home; still, the biggest laughs of the afternoon come during the silent pause when he opens the lover's note to the newly wedded Sofronia.

Francesco Valentino (born Francis Dinhaupt and called Frank) is an apt partner for Pasquale's trials. The Milan-trained baritone had pursued a European career (Parma debut in 1927, La Scala and Glyndebourne in the late thirties) before his Met debut in *Lucia* a few days before the broadcast *Pasquale*. He would become a Metropolitan regular. In vocal terms, Valentino is an Italianate Brownlee (via the Bronx and Denver, of course), and his Italian style and (more pertinently) buffa manner, serve him well on this afternoon. The voice is dry but the high notes are all there. He handles the fast patter and roulades of the genre better than most sonorous baritones, though Papi's mad scramble in the allegro of the act-one duet turns his triplets into a slide (even Sayão is a bit hard-pressed here). The role of Ernesto should suit Nino Martini's slight voice and pleasing person, but his voice sits consistently on his throat, and the resulting tone is flat in both pitch and resonance. His deficiency lays a serious liability on the performance since the tenor of the buffa operas supplies most of the genre's romance. Without an elegant and graceful delivery of his music, the whole affair becomes excessively brittle (Papi, too, contributes to this, though he has the forces well under control). The final act is a trial for any tenor (even with both the Serenata and Notturno transposed down), and Martini is no exception. Yet his

Don Pasquale
21 December 1940

Norina
Bidú Sayão
Ernesto
Nino Martini
Malatesta
Francesco Valentino
Pasquale
Salvatore Baccaloni
Conductor
Gennaro Papi

best singing of the afternoon comes in the nocturnal duet with Sayão, where she obligingly takes some of the high-flying phrases which Donizetti assigned to the tenor.

Sayão is near perfection in this assignment, full of high spirits but never overplaying. She is in her best silvery voice and delivers the coloratura, which the composer sprinkled throughout Norina's music, with unfailing accuracy and lovely, focused tone. She knows the exact shape of every phrase ('Pronta io son' is marvelously grand), and how she fills the embellishments with liquid tone! Her Sofronia is charmingly demure (and outrageously funny as she shudders through 'un uomo, fuggiamo' while Baccaloni fairly bursts with fatuous self-satisfaction in the background). The transformation into the cruel wife presses her resources at first, but she captures a mock grand style as she summons the servants in commanding fashion—there are no vocal squeaks this time. 'Via caro sposino' is the capstone of her portrayal, the ultimate in charm and tonal loveliness. This performance was the first of only seven Sayão Norinas in the New York house; it is a portrayal to be treasured.

Baccaloni was again on hand the following Saturday afternoon (28 December 1940) when the Metropolitan presented a revival of another Donizetti gem, *La Fille du Régiment*, as a new vehicle for Lily Pons. Only two Metropolitan Maries had preceded her: Sembrich, at the beginning of the century, and Frieda Hempel (as *Figlia*, since the opera was then given in Italian), at the end of World War I. In 1940 all Europe was again engulfed in conflict and France was occupied by the Nazis. When, at the opera's conclusion, Miss Pons advances to the front of the stage dressed in regimental uniform and waving the French flag, Donizetti's pert comedy undergoes a patriotic metamorphosis as the audience rises to its feet. Mr. Cross recounts to the radio audience the "thrilling closing scene. . . . Lily Pons as Marie waving aloft the French Napoleonic tricolors of her twenty-first regiment, and the orchestra and chorus singing those strains of the Marseillaise." An aura of sentiment has accrued to this performance, heightened in memory by the image of the petite Pons as the plucky vivandiere uttering mild epithets ('Morbleu'), "currycombing one of the dappled wooden horses in its stall," and playing at soldier rather like a grown-up Shirley Temple (remember *The Little Colonel*). Even her most vehement detractors accept Pons' regimental daughter as the pinnacle of her career.

The broadcast captures the actual premiere of the new production, and perhaps the press of rehearsals (which she normally avoided at the Met) took its toll on Pons' slim resources, for she is not in her finest form. For much of the afternoon the brilliant point of the voice is absent, the cantilena (especially in the lower reaches of 'Il faut partir') is slightly tremulous, and there is a hint of instability lurking in the unfamiliar patterns of staccati (add even a slight catch in a high C at the end of the second act—and the Pons high notes were always reliable). But there are a few deft coloratura flourishes along the way, the sentiment is affecting in her farewell to camplife, both tone and feeling are firmly projected in the pathetic 'Par le rang et par l'opulence,' and her comic touch is sure (she opens the lesson scene in hooty tones and ends it with wild roulades like an overtightly wound-up Olympia). Even unseen, the Pons charm comes through. She is no hoyden tomboy, but the spoiled darling of the troops, and when they return to save her from wealth and decorum, she delivers an assured 'Salut à la France!' (with a lengthy cadenza cum flute). Now the familiar brilliant tone reasserts itself, her staccati firm up (the aspirants more ghastly than ever), and the long high D restores confidence.

La Fille du Régiment
28 December 1940

Marie
Lily Pons
Marquise
Irra Petina
Tonio
Raoul Jobin
Sulpice
Salvatore Baccaloni
Conductor
Gennaro Papi

The version of the opera which the Met elected (was Papi or Pons the determinant?) is a hybrid. Though sung in the original French, the layout is that of the Italian version which Donizetti prepared for Milan, with sung recitatives replacing the spoken dialogue. Curiously, the composer disemboweled the tenor role in his revision, so Raoul Jobin, new to the Met roster, has no string of high Cs during the first finale nor a go at Tonio's aria in the next act (the Met revival divided the original two-act opera into three acts). All this is regrettable, for Jobin is a very creditable Tonio with his idiomatic French (Canadian-born, he trained at the Paris Conservatory and was a member of both the Opéra Comique and the Opéra). His entry to the Met was via the "Metropolitan Auditions of the Air," though curiously not as a winner but snatched for a debut as Des Grieux before the contest was over. He is vocally ardent in the love duet (with Pons appropriately coy). Both he and Pons have the rhythmic éclat for 'De cet aveu si tendre,' and he delivers some of the afternoon's best vocalism in his plea for Marie's hand ('Ah! mes amis').

The comic roles are in good hands, though generally as much buffa as *bouffe*: Irra Petina (also shorn of her opening aria) doesn't caricature the Marquise; the Duchess of Crakentorp is mercifully played straight and silent by Maria Savage (no star turn by an aged diva, but rather the walk-on of a veteran chorister); and Louis d'Angelo's droll Hortensius displays the good manners of fine comic portraiture. Baccaloni's manners are another matter. His Sulpice is broadly played and trumpeted out in gruff (and highly resonant) tones that could quell an entire French army. But what a lovable old walrus he is, all bluster and big heart, dwarfing Pons not only in avoirdupois but, unfortunately, in volume as well; even Cross calls him "an old friend of ours, by now" (he had been with the company all of three weeks). Papi has the new production well enough in hand, except for some zigzagging between male chorus and orchestra in the drill music which closes the first scene. More important, the *bouffe* high point of the score is muffed—the trio, 'Tous les trois réunis,' is sadly deficient in panache: Pons is inaudible, Baccaloni gives insufficient point to his threats, and only Jobin is on the mark. One cannot deny the enthusiasm of the audience at the opera's curtain. The Met would keep the work in repertory for three seasons, though the radio audience would wait three decades for another hearing of this delicious French hors d'oeuvre.

While Donizetti's comic operas were only intermittent visitors to the Met stage, Rossini's *Barbiere* was a long-time tenant and returned again on 1 March 1941. In this musically shop-worn presentation the Metropolitan seems intent on proving the commonplace that familiarity breeds contempt; not much of the deft elegance of Rossini's score survives the rough-and-tumble antics of the Met crew. Of course, Papi's too lenient hand is an easy target, but the license of Metropolitan stage direction must share the blame.

Two ingredients are new to the radio public: the Italian-American Josephine Tuminia as Rosina, and our friend Baccaloni as Bartolo. While the soprano provides the slimmest of vocal goods rather neatly packaged, the basso's portrayal is larded with an embarrassment of vocal and comic riches. The audience's delight in the Baccaloni persona is obvious, as is his mastery of the buffa idiom, but Bartolo seems to heighten Baccaloni's worst propensities. The most outrageous of his extramusical offenses is the insertion of a reverberant 'Mamma mia' in the climactic pause of Pinza's 'La calunnia.' Nor is he in prime vocal condition. Even he must quail before the challenge Rossini posed in 'A un dottor della mia sorte' (though the allegro section is violently truncated). Typical of the afternoon's high jinks are the noisy sound

Il Barbiere di Siviglia
1 March 1941
Rosina
Josephine Tuminia
Almaviva
Bruno Landi
Figaro
John Charles Thomas
Basilio
Ezio Pinza
Dr. Bartolo
Salvatore Baccaloni
Conductor
Gennaro Papi

effects of the cast as Rosina begins 'Freddo ed immobile'; hence the requisite effect of the traditional "freezing" of the action in a buffa finale is entirely nullified. Pinza's articulation of the theme in suavely covered tones finally restores order. He delivers a well-planned 'Calunnia,' is his usual skillful self in the rapid fire of the recitatives, but badly smudges the turns in the 'Buona sera' phrases. John Charles Thomas doesn't even bother with them. Figaro may be a 'barbiere di qualità,' but this tonsorialist is no master of Rossini's fioriture—the lack wreaks considerable damage on his entrance aria and the duet with Rosina. He, too, is somewhat out of vocal form, for he avoids some of the expected high-note interpolations and muffs the final high G of the aria. His playing to the audience turns the clown into a buffoon (the gasp for breath in the middle of his spelling out of R-O-S-I- -N-A, as Tuminia holds the long note, is just one of his repellent tricks). In spite of it all, he is still a vocal spendthrift, full of spirit, sometimes vocally nimble, and when Figaro gives his address to Almaviva, able to dominate the Rossini orchestral crescendo. Petina's servant knows her place and keeps her comedy within acceptable bounds in her aria.

Of course, the lovers are well behaved. Landi's vocal finesse in the old *tenore di grazia* manner restores some integrity to the Rossini vocal line. His first-act arias are models of tone and style, though the suspicion of crooning hovers. Miss Tuminia's best effort is her assured tossing off of Proch's Theme and Variations in the lesson scene: her trill is adequate, flashing staccati are obviously her forte, and in the well-sung (and obligatory) cadenza with flute she manages to summon a decent fullness of tone. Elsewhere she is rather nondescript, sometimes suggesting a good student. Her lower voice is pallid and the very top turns metallic, but like most good students, she is always well intentioned and occasionally pumps some life into Rosina by injecting a bit of girlish pertness into her recitative.

Of more interest than Tuminia's performance itself is management's decision to place her before the radio audience, which, up to this time, has been largely spared the lesser lights of the Metropolitan roster. The advance of the Juilliard contingent was a warning sign, but Tuminia heralds the arrival of the provincial singer to Saturday afternoon at the Met. She came via appearances with her hometown San Francisco Opera and stints in Bologna, Lugano, Belgrade, Caracas, Puerto Rico, and Cincinnati. Her qualifications for a Met contract may be judged by the length of her Met career: four performances. She was not the first of her ilk and would be far from the last; future broadcasts would feature other nonluminaries such as Hilde Reggiani, Norina Greco, and Florence Kirk in parts formerly associated with Pons, Rethberg, and Milanov. Was it only the war, causing limited access to mature artists of international reputation, which allowed the shadow of provincialism to spread across certain Metropolitan performances? Or was it the inevitable result of the democratization of opera which had become a watchword of the Johnson regime about this time? Or was it simply bad judgment on the part of management or a deterioration in standards? The shrinking market of top-rank artists, a salable slogan, management myopia—all were contributing factors.

The Johnson regime dared to serve up its free-for-all *Barbiere* to the radio audience only one more time. In the tour performance broadcast from Cleveland on 10 April 1943, the buffa roles remain in the hands of Petina, Baccaloni, and Pinza, but several new elements are of interest. Foremost is the work of the conductor, Frank St. Leger. St. Leger was an odd figure on the operatic scene, a genuine man of the theatre whose career lacked a consistent upward curve. Onetime accompanist and conductor for Melba, longtime friend and accompanist for tenor Edward Johnson, a fixture at the Chicago Opera before its demise, director of the American Opera Company and the Central City Opera Festivals in Colorado, he would conduct rarely at the Met. The *Barbiere* broadcast is actually his final conducting assignment at the Met—impelled by the increasing debility of Edward Ziegler, Johnson named St. Leger musical secretary of the company. As assistant manager in charge of casting, repertory, and budget, St. Leger would be of critical importance throughout the remaining decade of the Johnson regime, so the chance to gauge his artistic character is intriguing. The report is decidedly favorable; the future factotum of the Metropolitan leads a far more disciplined performance than that cited previously. Of course, he cannot control all the silly business on stage (though he did serve as stage director for productions elsewhere), but the pell-mell musical scramble of the 1941 offering is rubbed away (with some loss of Rossini panache in the second-act finale, where the energy level drops). More important, he demonstrates a sure grasp of Rossini's musical construct, its action-oriented, graphic character within a framework of classical rhetoric. One hears his comprehension in the overture—in the strongly drawn line of the andante and in the distinctive profile given to the complementary motives of the allegro. Throughout the afternoon, his perception animates the music and creates its own drama even when the singers let him down. And some of them do.

New to their broadcast roles are Nino Martini and John Brownlee. Neither can be counted an improvement on his predecessor. Martini offers a nicely shaped 'Ecco ridente' and demonstrates a welcome use of head voice, which is new to him. By the time he reaches the Serenata, the old pitch problems return, and later on, his approximations of Rossini fioriture are painful (even St. Leger's accommodating tempi in the first-act duet, for instance, cannot save him). Brownlee is more accurate, but his barber, in tone and style, so reeks of beef-and-kidney pie that his virtues seem negligible. He delivers the notes, but all the mad fun of the factotum is missing. And vocally he is overmatched by the demands of the role (the end of the aria is a near disaster). Utilizing a very forward placement in an attempt to gain brilliance, the result is a markedly shallow tone—one always feels as though he is singing into a bullhorn. Pinza, too, is in poor form; in the calumny aria his voice sounds worn and lacks its customary resonance. Must even the gods suffer the iniquities of oncoming age? Or is it merely an off afternoon? Fortunately, some familiar virility of tone returns in the final act. On the other hand, Baccaloni is in better voice, and on better behavior, too.

More pleasant to consider are two other new players. The role of Fiorello, the Count's servant who musters the first-act musicians, is minuscule in length, but young Mack Harrell commands our attention with his resonant tone, idiomatic diction, and sense of phrase. The 1939 "Met Auditions" winner reveals his skill as a lieder recitalist with a subtle application of varied tonal weights in his few phrases—even in small packages, distinction is welcome.

Bidú Sayão is herself a diminutive package, but her impact on this performance is immense. Could any Rosina excel Sayão's portrayal in this broadcast? She plays her not as a coloratura plaything but as a young lady with a mind of her own who can charm or scheme or be bored or petulant or bewitching as necessary to gain her ends. She turns every moment of song, every word of recitative, to account and makes Rosina a vivid personality. And how fluently she sings the music, her tone constantly pure and lovely, the fioriture not only accurate but given a musical life of their own— every phrase is knowingly shaped. She is able to convey the grand musical gesture as

Il Barbiere di Siviglia
10 April 1943
Rosina
Bidú Sayão
Almaviva
Nino Martini
Figaro
John Brownlee
Basilio
Ezio Pinza
Dr. Bartolo
Salvatore Baccaloni
Conductor
Frank St. Leger

easily as though her resources were unlimited (the opening of 'Dunque io son' is a prime example). In the lesson scene she stays with Rossini (at least his *Semiramide*) and her 'Bel raggio' shows her mastery of bel canto: in the opening section the cantilena is firm and the drama intense; later her coloratura, while perhaps not quite the ultimate in brilliance during rapid passage work, is nevertheless on a high level; the top voice is a constant joy as she offers tones of limpid float or pointed brilliance at will. A well-coordinated ensemble performance remains the ultimate delight for opera lovers, but lacking that, all resistance crumbles before the star performer who achieves a perfect union of voice and technical skill, musical thought and dramatic believability. Sayão is just such a complete operatic artist on this afternoon.

The previous season Sayão had offered yet another of her buffa charmers to the radio public when, on 3 January 1942, the radio audience was first introduced to Donizetti's *L'Elisir d'Amore*. During the century's first two decades the opera had served as a vehicle for Caruso, who was attracted to the work by the gratifying cantilena of 'Una furtiva lagrima' and, perhaps even more, by the opportunity to display his comedic talents as the bumptious Nemorino. In the early 1930s Gigli had shown greater affinity for the aria than the antics, and in 1932–33 Nemorino served as a debut vehicle for Tito Schipa, whose refined artistry turned the rustic Nemorino into the suavest of country gentlemen. Early on, Sembrich and Hempel had spurned Caruso for Scotti's Belcore, while the later performances featured De Luca with Pinza as an unlikely elixir pusher.

In 1942 the Metropolitan is less generous. Landi is a Nemorino of the Schipa mold in terms of refined musicianship but without the latter's honeyed tone, and Valentino is certainly no match for Scotti or De Luca. Baccaloni fully measures up as the quack doctor. His clarity of diction delights, and he actually *sings* a good deal of 'Udite, o rustici.' But by the time he arrives at the third act (the Met's predilection for intermissions converts Donizetti's second scene of act one into act two) his manner has worsened—both he and Sayão wring every bit of insinuation out of the little barcarole ('Io son ricco, tu sei bella'). When Nemorino buys his second bottle of elixir, Landi desperately tries to maintain a meaningful characterization, but Baccaloni engages in some outlandish vocal mugging. Valentino stands at the opposite pole, always musically correct and reasonably adept in fioriture, but owning a vocal method which puts a straitjacket on Donizetti's beguiling lines. Panizza's overall approach to the score is quite straightforward, too. The set instrumental pieces lack panache, but he does know when to give the singers their head—in 'Chiedi all'aura lusinghiera' his phrases have plenty of breathing room, so Sayão spins exquisite tones and Landi executes diminuendi to their hearts' content. In the opening 'Quanto è bella' Landi summons surprising brio and fullness of tone. Though he feels the heady effect of Dulcamara's alcoholic elixir, the tenor avoids burlesque in 'Esulti pur la barbara,' and his manly outburst at Adina's proposed marriage to Belcore ('Adina, credemi') is full in tone and feeling. By the time of the final act, however, one realizes he lacks more than the 'venti scudi' to purchase the elixir, for he is short on vocal capital as well. Yet how carefully he sculpts 'Una furtiva lagrima,' keeping the entire first verse within the most intimate frame to maximize his climaxes in the second stanza. Still, his mastery of style cannot quite negate the tenorino curse.

Sayão, too, has an instrument of minimal size, but her tone is so firmly collected, and its silvery brightness so highly polished, that questions of volume become superfluous (at least in her bel canto repertory, where the orchestral forces

L'Elisir d'Amore
3 January 1942
Adina
Bidú Sayão
Nemorino
Bruno Landi
Belcore
Francesco Valentino
Dulcamara
Salvatore Baccaloni
Conductor
Ettore Panizza

do not work against her). She shows us Adina's spunk right from the beginning as she mimics cruel Isolde, and technically the aria is entirely on the mark. Sayão never allows her buffa heroines to linger overlong in the soubrette mold. When Donizetti's magical cantilena creeps to the fore and sentiment becomes warm and human, both Sayão and Landi recognize the moment (as in the middle section of the first-act finale) and make the most of it. On the other hand, when Sayão is up against the crafty Baccaloni, she matches him in buffa wiles. Their duet ('Quanto amore!') is the ensemble highlight of the afternoon as they pull and push the buffa musical fragments into a mosaic of comic style. Adina is ill used by the composer in the final scene of the opera—any soprano who has to follow the big tenor aria knows the odds are against her. Here again, Sayão triumphs. As she tells Nemorino that she has repurchased his army enlistment papers ('Prendi, per me sei libero'), her tone overflows with love and tenderness—all the ornaments and divisions are worked seamlessly into the vocal line. When her love triumphs, she assumes command in an accompanied recitative touched with grandeur and then tackles the ungrateful fireworks of the cabaletta with aplomb. Even up against a Gigli or a Schipa in this "tenor opera," the decision might still have been in her favor.

When a world is at war, the stock of comedy rises. The Metropolitan recognized as much and had at hand a master buffo in Baccaloni. He is the constant element in all these performances and was in large measure the raison d'être for this unusual concentration of buffa offerings in the Met repertory. But it is Miss Sayão's adorable creations which linger longest in the memory. With Baccaloni, you almost had to be there.

To una Governante
Sincerely Licia
Albanese

Licia Albanese as Cio-Cio-San in *Madama Butterfly*.

CHAPTER SIXTEEN

1940–42
Italian Lyricism and French Tang

Though the confections of the buffa repertory please the palate, tragedy remains the staple of any opera diet. Encouraged by the success of the *Otello* revival, Johnson reintroduced another Verdi work which had not been heard at the Metropolitan for a quarter century, this time venturing not a mature masterwork but an opera from the equivocal middle period of Verdi's long creativity: *Un Ballo in Maschera.*

The previous revival in 1913 had featured an all-star cast headed by Caruso and Destinn with Margarete Matzenauer as Ulrica, Hempel as Oscar, and Amato, De Segurola, and Rothier, all under the baton of the man who reportedly acknowledged only the stars in heaven—Arturo Toscanini. The maestro's onetime surrogate, Panizza, is on hand this time, and the cast holds at least a pair of prospective luminaries. But the overall lineup lacks depth. Still, the broadcast of 14 December 1940 shows the Metropolitan at its current best.

Castagna is probably the finest Ulrica of any Met *Ballo* for the next four decades. She meets the minimum (but oft ignored) qualification of Verdi's clairvoyant, the ability to sing Verdi's awkward two-tier aria smoothly in both the high and low registers without signaling a shift of gears in transit. Oddly enough, she avoids the low Gs which conclude her aria in favor of a debilitating leading tone a third above, thereby neutralizing the sepulchral mood. Moscona and Cordon are adequately conspiratorial. Stella Andreva has the requisite point and glitter for Oscar's dashing couplets plus an appealing childlike tonal shine which adds believability to her portrayal of the young page. She is invariably on target in her staccati and rhythmically alert, but without those life-giving trills 'Di che fulgor' loses a good deal of its luster.

That commodity is inadequately supplied by Panizza in this jewel of an opera, Verdi's most convincing assimilation of the elegant French manner. Panizza's well-tooled precision is welcome, but too businesslike to propel the swiftly moving dialectic of the first act; he does better with the love duet (which has a momentum of its own). Happily, he has in the focal roles three artists who, in varying degrees, master the considerable challenges of Amelia, Riccardo, and Renato. In contrast to earlier Met versions, the new production is set in Sweden, but Italian names are retained; yet

Un Ballo in Maschera
14 December 1940

Amelia
Zinka Milanov
Oscar
Stella Andreva
Ulrica
Bruna Castagna
Riccardo
Jussi Bjoerling
Renato
Alexander Sved
Conductor
Ettore Panizza

235

evidently no king sits on Sweden's throne since Oscar announces ('s'avanza il Conte') the Count of Warwick, Governor of Boston in colonial times, as originally dictated by nineteenth-century Italian censorship.

New to the airwaves is baritone Alexander Sved, who made his debut as Renato on the opening night of the season two weeks before the broadcast. Like a number of Metropolitan artists of this period, the thirty-four year old Hungarian had suffered a difficult wartime voyage in order to meet his Metropolitan commitments. A pupil of two Italian baritone gods of Metropolitan history (Sammarco and Ruffo), Sved reveals in his broadcast debut some of Ruffo's tonal amplitude, though not his burnished timbre and smooth legato. But *robusto* he undeniably is, and vendettas are still well served in opera by such a voice. Then too, he was a veteran of opera houses in Vienna, Rome, Milan, Bayreuth, Salzburg, and South America, so he was weighted not only with volume but assurance. In the opening aria he enjoys hurling his burly tone into the wide spaces of the Metropolitan—and why not? for he is one of the few singers who could make its old timbers resonate in return. One takes almost guilty pleasure in the plummy rumble of his baritone as he adds an unpublished cadenza (by Verdi) which he inherited from Serafin. "It rises to a B flat and is immensely effective,"[1] Sved modestly confided—and so it is. Unfortunately, he is equally fond of the emphatic baritone "huff" with consequent damage to the Verdi line. 'Eri tu' is musically more satisfying, begun rather quietly and sustained with less vibrato; he rides easily over the tops of phrases, but the 'dolcezze' are indeed 'perdute.' Unlike most baritones, sheer weight of voice enables him to turn the Meyerbeerian square-ness of the conspirators' scene ('Dunque l'onta') to account.

Sved's middle-European colleague, Zinka Milanov, is heard by default. The opening night was to have belonged to debutante Stella Roman, but (unlike Sved) she could not reach America in time. The honor fell to Milanov at a time when little honor was accorded her (this is her only opening night of the Johnson regime). Verdi's Amelia is consumed by perpetual agitation, and the interpreter must keep her emotional flaying within bounds, a task at which Milanov is only intermittently successful. At this point in her career she has not developed an adequate sense of repose in her singing; she soars with wonderful abandon, but not always in the right places. Her act-one prayer ('Consentimi, o Signore'), for all its fervent expression, takes too much to heart Verdi's marking of *con molto vita.* But her second act is superb. What splendid bursts of vibrant tone she unleashes in the aria on the heath! Both the hallucinatory midsection (no squally tone here) and the stratospheric closing moments are well managed. She mounts fearlessly up to a vibrant high C before attacking the plunging cadenza with zesty assurance. If to be "erratic" is to sharp on an octave leap in the opening recitative, briefly lose perfect focus in mid-voice at the very close of the aria, and overshoot the climactic 't'amo' in the love duet, then one might so name Milanov. But again, the weight of the evidence is on the plus side.

Both Milanov and Jussi Bjoerling possess glorious instruments, and their unrestrained youthful plenitude of voice gives an impassioned thrust and vitality to the love duet; honor aside, these two voices deserve to love one another. Her control in the frenetic trio which follows is unexpectedly sure; the high syncopations are firm in rhythm and tone. And, no matter how often encountered, a Milanov crescendo on a high note thrills. Unfortunately, Amelia's tender plea to be allowed to see her son for the last time is played for superficial emotion, and the soprano fails to evoke the immense sadness which Verdi limned. The singer who takes her cue from mere textual sense and ignores the composer's deepening of affect too often shortchanges opera's power. But again, the tonal splendor of Milanov's concluding moments demolishes reserve.

The young Milanov and Bjoerling (at twenty-nine, five years her junior) have decades of Metropolitan appearances ahead of them, yet this performance is their only pairing in the broadcast series. It is also Bjoerling's only preserved Riccardo and his broadcast debut (though he is in his third season with the company). In spite of his youth, the Swedish tenor is a veteran professional. A member of a family male quartet since age eight (they toured the States from 1919 to 1921), he had made his official stage debut as Don Ottavio at age nineteen with the Swedish Royal Opera. The European stages (Prague, Paris, Vienna, London) quickly welcomed him, while his early recordings soon made him familiar to the American public. Thus, his radio debut was not the unexpected thunderbolt of his Scandinavian colleague, Kirsten Flagstad, though his aural brilliance was similarly notable.

The stylistic and technical demands of Riccardo represent an almost unique challenge for tenors in Italian opera. Without elegance of phrasing and deft rhythmic play, the character and his music lose distinction. If a tenor cultivates these niceties, too often the choice is dictated by necessity, the invention stemming from a lack of the more salable commodities of tonal beauty and vocal pith. When all these attributes unite in a single artist, he is clearly favored by the gods (as are we). Jussi Bjoerling is such an artist. His gifts include a vocal timbre of singular radiance in the middle and upper range, while the lower notes are touched by a modestly rich baritonal coloration. Lyricism is his native habitat, but when expedient, his plangent timbre gives him the thrust of far more stentorian voices. Indeed, at Riccardo's first entrance it is the clarion force of his delivery which commands attention—no dramatic reticence here (though the apathy of his stage deportment was often lamented). Of particular interest is the security and accuracy of the upward intervallic leaps which are so prominent in his first aria—the upper tone is always the more brilliant, thereby conferring an unexpected elation on the hearer. Of the role's several test moments, the scene in Ulrica's den offers the subtlest challenge; here Bjoerling does not quite give us all the rhythmic and dynamic variety one hopes for (no suggestion of undulation in the fisherman's song, nor does he entirely capture Verdi's ironic mixture of humor and terror in the quintet). But he is as generous with his vocal riches as Riccardo with his pardons, and musically impeccable to boot. For all the splendor of the love duet, minute holes in Bjoerling's legato are exposed in the quieter episodes. Again he provides plenty of drama (when merely declaiming on a single note) as he exacts the promise from Renato to safeguard Amelia's identity, and he is fully involved in the trio which closes the act. At last the tenor offers us his mastery of quiet, lyrical lines in the lengthy recitative preceding 'Ma se m'è forza perderti' (perfect legato now), but disappointment follows since the aria itself is cut— we have to be content with the wonderfully expansive way he delivers the recall of the climactic phrase as the scene closes. At the masked ball the spectrum of Bjoerling's abilities widens: all baritonal resonance departs in favor of a more heady tone, attempts at mezza voce are made, the play of dynamics is greater. And the glorious arch of phrase ('quell'angelo tu sei!') remains.

When we hear *Ballo* again in the next season, the Swedish monarch has already departed and will not return until the war is over. Only Castagna and Panizza remain in pivotal roles, and Roman has her lost opportunity with Amelia. Of special note is the appearance of old Martinelli as the ebullient count-king. In an earlier revival of *Ballo*, Martinelli had taken over a pair of Caruso's Riccardos, last appearing in the role

Un Ballo in Maschera
28 February 1942

Amelia
Stella Roman
Oscar
Josephine Antoine
Ulrica
Bruna Castagna
Riccardo
Giovanni Martinelli
Renato
Richard Bonelli
Conductor
Ettore Panizza

at the Met on 5 February 1916 when he was virtually Bjoerling's age (thirty). Twenty-six years later (28 February 1942), the fifty-six-year-old veteran leaves off the weighty robes of the Moor (his only other role this season) for the light-hearted Riccardo. No doubt the change was dictated by the tenor shortage caused by the war.

This time Oscar sings 's'avanza il Re' (one would like to think it a complement to Martinelli's royal status), but with the memory of Bjoerling still in our ears, it is more a case of 'the king is dead, long live the king.' No matter how earnest his effort—and Martinelli never abandons his artistic integrity—the role of Riccardo demands a nimble vocal manner which his long sojourn in heroic roles renders impossible. He provides a few object lessons in Italian style (the shape of the final phrase of recitative before 'La rivedrà' is exactly right—actually, the aria itself is no embarrassment to a heroic tenor, for here Martinelli successfully fines down his tone). His best effort comes at the beginning of the quintet: his tones are light, the rhythms exact, and he catches the scherzo feel of the moment. But soon it is all too evident that the years have tarnished the metal of his voice; only at the climactic 'M'ami, Amelia' in act two does the remembered steel shine again. He can still imagine a lover's part, for he begins 'Non sai tu' with quiet tenderness and shapes some of the bigger phrases with care; but overall, the love duet is pretty rough sledding, and he settles for a low E instead of the final top C. When the third act opens, Martinelli has not yet recovered from the stringent demands of act two; perversely, he does sing the aria ('Ma se m'è forza'), but it is a cry of pain rather foreign to Riccardo's nature (still, the tenor offers a splendid high A at its close). The covered tone of his quiet farewell as death approaches is effective, but one can't help being glad the afternoon is over—for other reasons as well.

There is little in the performance to admire. Panizza consistently chooses tempi that rob the work of its essential panache. Roman is in incredibly bad form, unable to retain focus throughout most of her instrument. Virtually her only effective moment is the ascent to the high C in the second-act aria, though the voice does gain luster in the final scene. Her performance is distressingly provincial in style, as well. Oscar's airs are better served by Antoine, though she, too, begins with a quaver, and her cantilena is no match for her staccati. She knows her purpose in the quintet, however. Cordon and Moscona make heavy-handed conspirators (their irony is vocally lugubrious), and Castagna's admirable art seems in decline. Her vocal alignment is out of kilter: the top voice has shortened since last we heard her, the mid voice occasionally rasps, and the mix in chest voice is unbalanced toward blatant, harsh tone (she does take the low G this time). It seems even Castagna will not escape the dreaded mezzo disease of a hole in the middle voice. At least Ulrica's final prophecy gives her a strong finish. Bonelli provides the only satisfying moments of the afternoon, though he, too, is less effective than in his earlier broadcasts. The very bottom of the voice is dryer, and some firmness has departed. But overall, his warm, manly tone is a tonic—he alone seems capable of lining Verdi's melodic curves with a suitable legato. He has no mezza voce for the second half of 'Eri tu,' but the splendor of his top voice at 'brillava d'amor' makes for a stirring conclusion and gains him the largest applause of what has been a dismal afternoon.

Such are the vicissitudes of opera in a repertory house; last year's feast becomes this year's leftovers. How well Verdi was served during the early years of the war may be better gauged by the treatment afforded several of the operas which constituted the daily bread of the company: *Trovatore, Traviata*, and *Aida*.

Before Bjoerling's wartime departure, he offers us one more portrayal—

Jussi Bjoerling as Manrico in *Il Trovatore*.

Manrico in *Il Trovatore*, yet another virtuoso challenge for a tenor. In the broadcast of 11 January 1941 only Castagna's gypsy is familiar; Valentino and Moscona offer their first broadcast Di Luna and Ferrando under a conductor new to the house, Ferruccio Calusio. In one of the most demanding roles of the Italian repertory Johnson introduces Norina Greco, Italian-born and Brooklyn-bred, whose experience was limited to the touring San Carlo troupe (the provincial American version), the Cincinnati Zoo Company, and appearances in Rio in the summer of 1940. Again it was Roman's delayed arrival which brought Greco to the Metropolitan as substitute in the *Trovatore* revival a month before the broadcast. The *Trovatore* lineup reveals the increasingly schizoid nature of many Met performances during the war years.

    Moscona sends the opera off on an even keel with Ferrando's bizarre narrative, clearly articulating its disjunct figurations; he observes Verdi's *leggierissimo* marking in the fleet stretta, thereby magnifying the sense of horror. Calusio's hand on the choral and orchestral elements lends a neat precision to the scene. Greco makes a positive first impression with her idiomatic timbre, its darkly hued steel suggesting a youthful Hina Spani or Giannini (with a similar lack of float in the voice). The cadenza to 'Tacea la notte' is rather curious, and one suspects a tendency to sharp on sustained tones, but her staccati are accurate and pleasing in the cabaletta (taken at a genuine

Il Trovatore
11 January 1941

Leonora
Norina Greco

Azucena
Bruna Castagna

Manrico
Jussi Bjoerling

Di Luna
Francesco Valentino

Ferrando
Nicola Moscona

Conductor
Ferruccio Calusio

allegro giusto). And she has the high D-flat at the end of the trio. But her moments in the convent scene are badly flawed by pitch lapses, and fright seems to overtake her in the tricky little duet of the marriage scene. Oddly enough, the challenge of 'D'amor sull' ali rosee' calls forth some of her best work; the voice takes on a modest velvet sheen, and she commands a nice pathos without, however, providing the ultimate *espansione* for Verdi's vaulting melodies (and, unfortunately, flatting badly on the final note). The Miserere falters, what with Greco lacking the requisite power in the low range and Bjoerling's tower evidently in a very distant castle, so remote is his sound. The remainder of the opera shows Greco in improved vocal form (the descending coloratura phrases of her duet with Di Luna are very fine), and she is alive to the dramatic situation in her final moments, though insufficiently ethereal in the heavenly ascent of 'Prima che d'altri vivere.' Perhaps the *Aida* broadcast of next year will clarify the double image left by her Leonora.

Valentino's Di Luna, on the other hand, is all of a piece. One is grateful for the lack of excess or gaucherie, but the vocal quality is so consistently hard-driven that monotony is the end result. He has the breath and top voice for 'Il balen' but no mezza voce, so the poetry of the aria is nullified—after all, the Count is an aristocrat, and all those *dolcissimo* and *pianissimo* markings which Verdi penned are intended to leaven his stock villainy. But the Bellini-like cantilena goes unrealized; Valentino makes a frontal assault where bel canto seduction is required. And at times in the fourth-act duet with Leonora, he turns up the breath pressure until his quick vibrato approaches a gobble.

Happily, Castagna is in much finer vocal shape than in her earlier Azucena. One may quibble with an occasional bit of crude chest tone, but she is in full command of all the big moments. Nor is the portrayal devoid of musical niceties or subtleties of character: how deftly she manages Verdi's springing line in 'Condotta ell'era in ceppi'; what a velvet caress she gives to 'Giorni poveri,' as maternal tenderness conquers her mad quest for vengeance. Her top voice is splendidly free throughout the afternoon—even the final high B (as Azucena reveals the full tragedy to Di Luna) is a tone, not a scream. Throughout the entire final scene her vocalism is chaste, the tone spun out with easy warmth; she evokes a quiet pathos which contrasts vividly with Azucena's raging in earlier scenes.

The young Bjoerling is not quite so well matched with Manrico as with Riccardo. The *robusto* episodes of the role require almost more vocal brawn than he can muster, but he doesn't stint. He hurls himself into 'Di quella pira' with wild abandon, not neglecting to clearly articulate the repetitive sixteenth-note figures; not only are the high Cs brilliant (they are really high Cs) but he expands the climactic phrase with a fermata on the ensuing B. He is nearly overwhelmed by the furious exchanges of the act-one trio, and he cannot match Martinelli's muscular assault on Leonora in the final scene ('Parlar non vuoi'), although he offers a lively rhythmic impulse in return. In the more ingratiating moments of the score he reveals his special assets. One treasures the easy lift of the voice as Bjoerling moves up the sequential phrases of the act-one serenade and rounds them off with an unbroken final phrase—here is a minstrel who can actually sing. A heroic quality invades some of the quieter moments: in 'Mal reggendo' the tenor seems intent on strong, straightforward projection rather than the melting lyricism which he can command. Even so, all the scenes with his "mother" are on the highest level. And 'Ah sì, ben mio' is magical, delivered with a lovely head voice until he allows just the right touch of sunny brilliance to penetrate the climactic phrase—then he pieces into the cadenza a startling 'la morte' (*forte*) in the upper range. Bjoerling matches Castagna in the reposeful phrases of the final act, where his soothing recitative preceding 'Si la stanchezza' is a model of expressive lyricism.

Calusio's controlled energy would seem to be a usable commodity for the Met; later in the season he conducts *Cavalleria* and *Pagliacci* (Roman and Jagel, Greco and Martinelli), but after this season he will be heard no more at the Met. Greco's Met career is twice as long, for she returns for a second season; the regrettable absentee is Bjoerling, who will remain in war-torn Europe for the next four years. Over a seven-year span since his 1938 debut, the radio audience will have had only two opportunities to hear the tenor in his youthful prime.

Aida was the final Verdi broadcast of the 1940–41 season. Management certainly provided Roman every opportunity to prove herself during her initial season: Desdemona, Santuzza, and now, Aida. More than anything, the role requires perfect vocal control, the very quality in which Roman is deficient. She does possess plenty of temperament (though more often it converts into the emotional crudity one associates with the provincial opera house) and a repertory of vocal tricks which can serve at any given moment. But it is no accident that the great Aida of the previous generation was, not Ponselle, but Rethberg, a singer who managed tone with the precision of an instrumentalist. Roman turns 'Ritorna vincitor!' into a vocal battleground with idiosyncratic pauses, accelerandi, scoops, and register changes. 'Numi, pietà' lacks the simplicity of a sincere prayer, and to make matters worse, Panizza elongates the episode unto insipidity. The soprano can easily be heard over the ensemble in act two, and 'O patria mia' shows her know-how (the recitative is well formed and the climax of the first stanza is taken in a nice long-breathed phrase). The ascent to the high C is well managed but held so long that the tone turns blatant—and the descent is crudely achieved. Her best moment occurs in the seduction duet with Radames where her timbre and vowel coloration recall Muzio; she is a convincing temptress. But her tomb scene completely misses the mark. Willful rhythms and tonal vagaries destroy serenity until Martinelli rescues the mood by showing us the noble Verdi line. The tenor finds it even in 'Celeste Aida,' though by now the *voce fissa* is much in evidence; often one feels that only sheer willpower makes possible the upward climb of the aria's phrases. Martinelli's fixed vocal manner obtains throughout much of the performance, but he can still trot out the bouncy rhythms of his act-three entrance with aplomb, and 'Io resto a te' is as solid as remembered.

Pinza (barring an uncomfortable high F on 'morte') remains the high priest of basses. When he and Martinelli briefly join voices in the temple scene, the veristic shadow which hangs over so much of Metropolitan Verdi style mercifully recedes. Castagna's vocally full-blown princess is as vivid as ever—a woman in love rather than a vengeful shrew. Her voice is in prime condition, and when she serves up so much superior vocalism, one needn't mind a few aspirants in the opening scene or the quarter-tone-flat high B-flat near the opera's end. Warren, of course, offers us the healthiest of instruments, and he has sharpened his characterization. The climaxes are splendid and, better yet, have taken on a more meaningful shape ('Dei Faraoni tu sei la schiava!'). He chooses not to thunder out 'pensa a che un popolo,' effectively shading it for a gain in poignancy.

Thus, the performance is a mix of individual excellence and the commonplace, with Panizza contributing to the latter. The dances of the temple scene all but disintegrate. Nor is there anything very triumphant about his second act with its tired orchestral and choral passages; this terrain has been covered too often, and only the

Aida
22 March 1941

Aida
Stella Roman

Amneris
Bruna Castagna

Radames
Giovanni Martinelli

Amonasro
Leonard Warren

Ramfis
Ezio Pinza

Conductor
Ettore Panizza

Stella Roman as Aida. Photography by Reale, Roma.

conductor could have energized these forces. The curse of a repertory performance lies upon the whole affair.

A year later (21 February 1942), the well-being of Verdi's Africans is even more precarious in the hands of a conductor new to the Met podium, Paul Breisach. Years in the German network of opera houses had provided experience which qualified him more for supervising the development of young American artists (a Johnson priority in these war years) than for his occasional conducting chores. He eventually joined the line of succession (St. Leger—Breisach—Max Rudolf) in Ziegler's old post, now converted to musical secretary. His deliberate pace does not find favor with the *Aida* cast, and coordination between stage and pit is frequently askew. The lineup, except for Castagna, is entirely new, clear down to the minor roles: Votipka (Priestess), John Dudley (Messenger), Lansing Hatfield (a solid, if slightly underpowered, monarch), while Moscona dispenses the expected quantity of priestly tone but not the noble song of Pinza.

Stalwart John Charles Thomas provides the only star turn of the afternoon as a strong-voiced Amonasro. He adopts a more forward placement than usual in order to give more bite to his tone and counterfeit ferocity—his climaxes are thrilling. The affable John Charles as villain is a bit anomalous, however, for despite his attempts to disguise those genial, plump sounds, a trace of his radio personality (like Freia's eye) shines through—the menace is synthetic. As Radames, Jagel returns to the role of his 1927 debut, and it suits him far better than the puerile Alfredo or the jaunty Rodolfo; Radames himself is deficient in charm, and Jagel's sturdy tone serves him well. Yet too often his careful musicianship is defeated by his effortful production—though his singing preserves the warrior's honor, the aura of the hero eludes him. (But he had been the true hero of that *Aida* broadcast in 1938 when Martinelli suffered his attack of indigestion in the middle of 'Celeste Aida,' and Minuteman Jagel, hearing the broadcast at home, was able to respond to management's call and be on stage minutes after Martinelli's collapse.)

The young Greco does not retain even professional honor in the Nile scene, nervousness frequently driving her tones sharp (the persistent lack of control oddly does not touch her easy high C). Thomas and Greco provide some raw excitement in their confrontation, but more often she seems out of her vocal depth. Breisach brings the affair to a sorry conclusion in the tomb scene where the ragged ensemble little suggests the perfect union of two souls blissfully ascending to heaven.

Verdi is somewhat better served in the *Traviata* which opens the 1941–42 broadcast season on 29 November, an occasion notable for the debut of a tenor who would remain active on the American musical scene for the next three decades. Jan Peerce was already in his late thirties when the Metropolitan beckoned. His operatic career had been limited to a few performances with regional companies until his San Francisco Duke of Mantua a month or so before his Met debut. He was entirely at home before the public, however, with a backlog of experience uniquely American. For eight years he had been doing four-a-day at New York's Radio City Music Hall (whose Roxy rechristened Jacob Perelmuth as Jan Peerce), and he had profited from that most valuable career assist, a weekly radio program (NBC's "Music Hall of the Air"). Though an operatic novice, Peerce owned a full complement of assurance which never deserted him, even in the trying circumstances of his debut. Gennaro Papi, with whom he had rehearsed, died a few hours before the matinee; Peerce went on stage to find Panizza in the pit—his colleagues, fearing to upset him, did not tell him of Papi's death until the second act.

Aida
21 February 1942
Aida
Norina Greco
Amneris
Bruna Castagna
Radames
Frederick Jagel
Amonasro
John Charles Thomas
Ramfis
Nicola Moscona
Conductor
Paul Breisach

La Traviata
29 November 1941
Violetta
Jarmila Novotna
Alfredo
Jan Peerce
Germont
Lawrence Tibbett
Conductor
Ettore Panizza

Assurance proves to be the hallmark of the Peerce artistic persona, and it is most welcome in the tonal and musical security of his portrayal, though its less agreeable counterpart is a deficiency in imagination. Of positive note are the neatness of the turns in the Brindisi, the boldness of his dialogue in the gambling scene, and the overall reliability of his tightly collected sound. The monochromatic color of the voice robs the opening phrases of 'Un dì felice' of atmosphere, and unhappily, Peerce interpolates a strained high B on 'croce' in the offstage phrases of 'Sempre libera.' The confrontation scene at Flora's party shows Peerce's talent at full strength: he sustains the high tessitura with firm tone and dramatic fervor, and in his denunciation of Violetta ('Ogni suo aver tal femmina') he sustains the line to the high As without loss of quality or volume; in the tortured phrases of 'A sì! che feci!' he articulates the quick rhythms without mutilating the structural design, giving meaning to the utterance without tearing it to tatters. Evidence of the change in conductors surfaces in act four: a slight tempo altercation mars his entrance (Peerce prefers a faster pace for the agitated recitatives). In the duet itself he sustains a lovely line but cannot muster the *dolcissimo a mezza voce* which Verdi ordered—still, Alfredo's descending phrases in the second half of the duet are tellingly delivered. At the first of the two rapid phrases of 'de' corsi affanni,' soprano and tenor are both caught off guard and enter late; the moment is badly smudged, and their ensemble to the end of the duet is somewhat uncertain. The offense is slight, a minor blemish on a thoroughly professional debut.

Heard with Peerce is the aristocratic Violetta of Jarmila Novotna in her single broadcast *Traviata*. Introduced to the radio public as Euridice and Cherubino, the Metropolitan now sought to certify Novotna's right to the diva status (as Manon and Violetta) which her beauty and stage manner warranted. The question of innate vocal resources is more moot.

Olin Downes wrote a long panegyric on Novotna's Violetta when first heard in New York in 1940; yet after 1943, Novotna sang *Traviata* only once (and that for a student audience). Short-lived though it was for the American public, on this occasion it is a well-sung, dramatically cogent Violetta. Though denied her glamorous stage person, the radio audience could not doubt her elegance as she introduces the Brindisi ('Miei cari, sedete') and gracefully articulates the toast (marred though it is by Panizza's immense ritards at each return of the opening theme). While Panizza's treatment of the dance music conveys the brittle atmosphere of the party scene, he allows 'Ah fors'è lui' to plod—to Novotna's detriment; still, her phrases are neatly laid out. 'Sempre libera' is transposed down, but the soprano securely negotiates its florid demands without any retreat before the high Bs (heartening evidence of her vocal prowess before a narrowing of range increased her preoccupation with trouser roles in the latter stages of her Met career). Her slender voice may occasionally lack the requisite *espansione* for her role ('A quell'amore' and 'Amami, Alfredo'), yet she offers moments of genuine abandon (her full-blooded cry of 'Ah! preferirò morir' in act two is splendid). Everywhere her musical sensitivity operates; one notes the rhythmic vitality of 'Non sapete,' the cameo-like delicacy of 'Dite alla giovine' (this flower could easily be crushed). The same delicacy mitigates the impact of 'Morrò.' Her letter reading is a shade businesslike, and in the aria she breathes after each motivic unit. The dramatic demands of the final acts cause some color loss to her attractive timbre—pitch may turn to the underside in 'Parigi, o cara,' and 'Se una pudica vergine' is less than transfigured (though she contrives a grand outburst at 'Ah! gran Dio'). Nature, having been bountiful in so many ways, did shortchange her after all.

But then, so much remains to command admiration and affection.

On the other hand, nature's largesse to Lawrence Tibbett was seemingly unlimited. Only the man himself could thwart nature's intent, and that sad moment has arrived. At Germont's entry one is shocked at Tibbett's cavernous, lifeless tone. Throughout the act the struggle goes on as he strives to summon his old nobility of phrase. But the voice will not flow: he lags behind in intervallic leaps, and nearly everything is labored, indeed almost grotesque. The duet with Violetta seems interminable. Only when chastising his son at Flora's party ('Dov'è mio figlio?') does the grandeur of his style momentarily overcome his precarious vocal condition. One can only wonder what the future holds for this greatest of American vocal artists.

If Tibbett's star was in decline, the career of another American luminary was acquiring new luster. Grace Moore had earned more than her share of public favor, but critical acclaim seemed beyond her grasp. Her assault on the regard of connoisseurs and critics began anew with her portrayal of Charpentier's Parisian working girl, Louise (the initial performance had been broadcast on 28 January 1939). Encouraged by her reception, she sought new conquests; Charpentier had coached her as Louise, why not a repeat performance with another twentieth-century work whose composer remained among the living? Italo Montemezzi's *L'Amore dei Tre Re* had enjoyed a fabulous success in Italy and had remained fairly constant in the Metropolitan repertory since its 1914 premiere. Inspired by Sem Benelli's incandescent text of illicit love which culminated in death by strangulation and poison in medieval Italy, Montemezzi had provided a brilliantly colored score which some contemporary critics considered "the greatest lyric drama that has come out of Italy since Verdi."[2] The work offered vivid musical and dramatic opportunities for four magnetic personalities, and the Metropolitan had supplied them in abundance over the years: Bori, Muzio, Ponselle, had conveyed the passion and ice of the beautiful Fiora, beloved of both her noble but irresolute husband, Manfredo (Pasquale Amato, Danise, Tibbett), and the prince Avito, whose febrile ardor had been variously communicated by Ferrari-Fontana, Caruso, Martinelli, and Gigli. The pivotal role of Archibaldo, the blind king who strangles Fiora upon discovering her betrayal of his son, passed from Adamo Didur and Pasero to Pinza, whose superb portrayal is preserved in the first broadcast of the opera on 15 February 1941.

The presence of the composer in the pit lends further distinction to the broadcast. The war had brought Montemezzi to residence in California, thus permitting the Metropolitan a historic (though not necessarily definitive) reading of the opera. History is further served by the inclusion of a new prelude to the short third act; the prelude continues the rhythmic patterns which closed act two (where Archibaldo carries out the dead Fiora) and then proceeds to gather together the main themes of the opera. The composer felt it improved "the proportions of the last act as a whole."[3]

Fortunately, the performance is a worthy one, though as so often happens when composers stir their own brew, it is dramatically less highly charged and propulsive than is desirable. As Manfredo, Bonelli may not evoke maximum sympathy (he is less convincing in his grief than when he fervently pleads for his wife's love), but his vocalism is wonderfully secure. As always, his voice rings forth in vibrant, manly tones. Avito requires a tenor of more tensile strength than Kullman has on call (the climax of the second-act love duet is undermanned), and initially his portrayal seems too languid. But Kullman's tiresome built-in vocal sob (not merely an effect but seemingly part of his vocal technique) eventually disappears, and none too soon.

L'Amore dei Tre Re
15 February 1941

Fiora
Grace Moore
Avito
Charles Kullman
Manfredo
Richard Bonelli
Archibaldo
Ezio Pinza
Conductor
Italo Montemezzi

Nevertheless, the American tenor is at the top of his form, his vocal color gains in appeal as the opera progresses, and his musical instincts are compelling enough to override any limitations. Few tenors shape a phrase for maximum impact as well as Kullman does in the final pages of the love duet and in Avito's third-act lament. This may be the tenor's finest broadcast portrayal.

With Pinza one has no reservations. From his first entrance his powerful vocalism and textual clarity are riveting. Here is a mighty king whose blindness seems a mere inconvenience (and perhaps this ultimately limits our sympathetic response to the tortured Archibaldo). Though Pinza cannot fully shelter his vitality, he is in complete command of the many moods of his character: one notes the prideful remembrance of his youthful conquest ('Italia, Italia'); the hollow hurt in his voice as he falsely tells Manfredo that Fiora sleeps ('Dorma'); the ferocity of his scene with Fiora, which gradually gives way to solemn quiet as, after he chokes her, he whispers 'Silenzio'—surely stage whispers have never resonated more.

The old king and the faithless princess represent the magnetic poles of the drama. Critics have been mesmerized by the role of Fiora, granting her, like Mélisande, an aura of mystery and fascination seemingly beyond what text and music contain. Some even hang on her a symbolism as large as conquered Italy itself. Miss Moore probably never went so far in her conception as to consider herself either conquered or a nation divided, but a Fiora must at least manage in stage manner and vocal address to make credible her fatal allure. Moore achieves the goal in good part due to the sensual quality of her voice (her stage movement was considered quite stiff and artificial). And evidently her work with the composer brought results, for the music is impressively sung in the big moments and quite evocative in some of the more intimate scenes. In the first-act duet the reediness of her middle and low voice suggests a curious (and oxymoronic) intense languor—'Dammi le labbra' has the flush of suppressed passion, and when, at the climax, shafts of light in her upper voice come into play, the seductiveness of the scene is well realized. In general, she is more convincing at pouring out passion than in the moments of psychological complexity: her colloquy with her departing husband, so simply set by Montemezzi, has sufficient weight of voice but little subtlety of word play—some of the magic is missing. But there is no lack of involvement in the big love duet with Avito, or in the confrontation with Archibaldo; Moore brings plenty of dramatic excitement and full-throated vocalism to both episodes.

With the success of Louise and Fiora, the soprano seemed to have gained the authentic aura of a prima donna. Why not play a real diva on stage just as she had often done in films? Moore felt ready for Tosca. And less than a year (December 1941) after the L'Amore broadcast, she carried cane and bouquet into the Met's church of Sant'Andrea della Valle; a few weeks later (7 February 1942), her Roman diva sang over the airwaves. Unbelievable as it seems, this was the first time the Metropolitan offered Puccini's opera to the radio public, though the opera had been in the repertory for five of the eleven broadcast seasons.

It was precisely the absence of a Tosca with the right voice and adequate stage magnetism during the previous decade (aspirants included the unlikely Jessner and the intriguing Lehmann, as well as Caniglia and Giannini who would seem to have had legitimate claims) which caused the eclipse of an opera that had been nourished on the vivid portrayals of Ternina, Farrar, Destinn, Muzio, and Jeritza. That Tosca regained its popularity after a decade of near neglect may be partially attributed to Moore and her need for another vehicle to display what Max de Schauensee, most

Tosca
7 February 1942

Tosca
Grace Moore
Cavaradossi
Frederick Jagel
Scarpia
Alexander Sved
Sacristan
Salvatore Baccaloni
Conductor
Ettore Panizza

astute of vocal critics and Opera Quiz veteran, aptly called her "erotic voice and expanding personality."[4] Mr. Cross seems as surprised as any of us at *Tosca*'s absence from the airwaves, informing "those who are fond of the music of Puccini" that "today we're in for a special treat"; he assures us that "a glamorous cast has been assembled." In Cross' hierarchy, Jagel has now moved up to "brilliant," Alexander Sved is merely "the noted Hungarian baritone," while Miss Moore is "world-famous"—no need to go into the how and why of it.

Panizza, however, is the one who generates a good deal of the glamour on this afternoon, for he offers one of his most convincing interpretations. He gives a sharp profile to each of the swiftly changing elements in Puccini's score and skillfully negotiates the transitions for maximum continuity. The propulsive thrust of his work makes for a gripping second act, more so, in fact, in the pit than on stage; and how he spirits those choir boys along! In his first Metropolitan Sacristan, Baccaloni leaves off his buffa tricks and is content with character portrayal, playing to Cavaradossi and Scarpia rather than trying for center stage. The role may be minuscule, but his voice is large and the character full. De Paolis, too, offers a formidable portrait in his few moments as the spying police agent; his is surely the predestined Spoletta voice.

Jagel comes as close as ever he can to earning Cross' epithet. True, the ending of 'Recondita armonia' suffers from his usual leathery tone, but one cannot fault his vocal behavior. He refrains from tenorizing in the cliché phrases (no spitting out 'Il Console della spenta repubblica romana'), but he is not so self-effacing as to deny himself a brace of solidly trumpeted high B-flats on 'Vittoria!' Best of all is his affecting work in the third act, where the now well-oiled voice takes on a genuinely lyric cast. How sensitively he lays out the introductory phrases of the aria on a single repeated note; he executes diminuendi at the ends of phrases and yet remains effective in the big-voiced climaxes. No wonder the audience response is so enthusiastic. This is certainly Jagel's finest broadcast effort to date. Listening to how skillfully he makes his way in and out of lyric and spinto phrases in 'O dolci mani,' one wonders if he has reached a new stage of vocal command. In any case, this is a far cry from the raw-voiced performances of half a dozen years earlier.

Sved is a curiosity. The instrument is indeed formidable, and his sheer weight of voice is a boon in surmounting the Te Deum ensemble and in badgering Tosca in the seduction scene. But there is something overripe, almost obscene, about the fruity resonance which rolls out with so little subtlety. Still, menace is a good portion of Scarpia, and one might as well enjoy him. He does modify his vocal stance in the direction of greater suavity as he greets Tosca in act one. But he really is a vocal yo-yo: after opening the second act with shaky tones and insecure top ('Ha più forte') he regains control for an impressive dialogue with Tosca and wraps menace in an insinuating legato as he sings 'Già, mi dicon venal.'

The afternoon's Tosca requires a dual notice. One will find no listing of Votipka as a Metropolitan Tosca, but Moore supposedly exercised a prima donna's prerogative by having the comprimaria sing the offstage cantata in the second act. For once Dame Rumor is made an honest woman, for the Votipka vocal thumbprint is clearly recognizable as she engagingly takes the high C before Scarpia terminates her. One hopes Moore was generous.

As for the diva herself, her performance must be counted a disappointment. She has a genuine Tosca voice, but though the broadcast is her fourth Met Tosca, Moore does not seem to have the music comfortably in her voice, nor has she assimilated the text to enable it to flow in idiomatic and meaningful fashion. The *accenti* simply are not in place, neither in the expansive moments of song nor, more important, in the parlando which is so essential a component of the Puccini style. The inadequacy of her parlando dulls the first-act duet, and she is oddly ill at ease in the all-important confrontation with Scarpia in the second act. 'Vissi d'arte' becomes a jogging contest, for Moore is consistently ahead of the orchestra (though she offers some lovely tones, and the climax, over which she mercifully does not linger, is firm enough). I suspect she was not in good vocal condition on this afternoon, and when the aural bloom is off the Moore rose, not enough artistic aroma remains to compensate. From her first entrance the voice has a thicker density than usual, and by the end of the opera a slight hoarseness creeps in; pitch tends to the underside, and she wisely confines herself to a lighter half-voice for a good deal of the final duet. But Grace Moore was nothing if not game, and she has her telling moments: that arched test phrase in act one (following 'Non la sospiri') is no embarrassment, her first act exit climaxes make their effect, and if she plunged the knife into Scarpia as resolutely as she recounts it to Cavaradossi, the afternoon was not without its satisfactions for her.

Tosca
8 April 1944
Tosca
Grace Moore
Cavaradossi
Charles Kullman
Scarpia
Alexander Sved
Sacristan
Gerhard Pechner
Conductor
Cesare Sodero

One is tempted to plunge ahead a few seasons (to the broadcast of 8 April 1944) in hopes of gaining a more equitable appraisal of Moore's Tosca. Sved, Cehanovsky, and De Paolis are again on the scene, with Kullman at the canvas, all under the baton of Cesare Sodero (new to the company in 1942). One must begin with the maestro, for he casts the opera in a totally different light from Panizza's full-throttle mode. Sodero harnesses the momentum (the second act moves at an almost leisurely pace), points up the detail within phrases, and substitutes lyric flow for violence. The conception is finely conceived and rigidly adhered to from beginning to end. The odd result is that the restrained pace becomes an entity in itself, its relentless progress making the violence more appalling and the pathos more affecting: Sodero takes the shabbiness out of the shocker, and makes it work.

Far from fighting Sodero's temperance, the singers revel in it. Sved (after some initial spreading at his entrance) fills out his second-act characterization with musical and textual nuances which make his Scarpia more than a force of nature. Kullman may be a shade off his best vocal form. He is a rather disinterested painter in act one (though obligingly altering the text for his 'bionda Floria'—Moore insisted on showing her own blonde locks in spite of the brunette specified in 'Recondita armonia'), and Cavaradossi's rebellious outbursts upon hearing the news of the victory at Marengo are small-bore trumpeting. But his third act is wonderfully poetic in sound and feel: he pleads intimately with the jailer, he sings 'E lucevan' almost to himself, quietly reflecting on his remembered moments with Tosca, and although he does not always successfully maintain mezza voce at the *passaggio*, he refuses to belt even the climactic phrases. In 'O dolci mani' Sodero lets him linger to his heart's content, and here the delicate half-voice is in working order. Gerhard Pechner's Sacristan is well conceived for character, not comedy, and he really sings the role.

The diva herself is in splendid vocal form, the instrument suitably pliant and the color as vibrant as ever. Of course, she will say 'dona' for 'Quella donna!' and commit other minor musical or textual crimes, but she is very much at home in the role now and never rebels against Sodero's pacing (they had been at it together for two seasons). On her best behavior, she chooses to sing the offstage cantata, skittering up to the high C so as not to waste a good one (and several of those are offered when she is on stage where her public knows to whom they belong). On this afternoon her phrasing is more artful (as at the end of the act-one duet); she spins lovely arcs of sound and uses textual nuance to capture Tosca's changing moods (warmly caressing 'No, no' as she denies having betrayed her lover). 'Vissi d'arte' satisfies from start to finish; she stays with Sodero throughout and the climax is both secure and brilliantly colored. In the third act the 'knife' phrase again rings out superbly (though she *will* continue to jump to the upper octave at its close when she could easily manage the low B), and the unison declamation with Cavaradossi is measured and firm. At the end she stays in character with some delightfully delicate whispered instructions as Cavaradossi marches off to his fate. Hers is still a Tosca voice, and now Moore is almost a Roman diva as well as a former Hollywood star.

A stage personality such as Moore's seemed essential in order to restore *Tosca* to public favor during the early forties, but the more genuine and long-lasting stimulus for the Puccini renascence rested in a more delicate throat. In February 1940 Licia Albanese had climbed the hill overlooking Nagasaki harbor and stepped over the bridge to Pinkerton's dwelling and into the hearts of the Metropolitan public. They would be constant to her for twenty-six seasons.

For the first two decades of *Madama Butterfly* at the Met, the theatrical witchery of Farrar and the refulgent voices of Destinn and Florence Easton had made *Butterfly* integral to the repertory. By the thirties the opera's potency weakened, and though such estimable artists as Müller and Rethberg donned Cio-Cio-San's kimonos, the right mix of Italianate passion and delicate charm (both vocal and visual) escaped them. Thereafter, a train of nondescript heroines (Burke, Fisher, Somigli) had even less success. As if to confirm this appraisal, the radio public had not heard a Metropolitan Cio-Cio-San until the 25 January 1941 broadcast with Albanese.

The soprano had prepared the role with her teacher, Giuseppina Baldassare Tedeschi, a popular Cio-Cio-San in Italy at the beginning of the century, and since 1935 Albanese had been singing it at Italy's leading theatres. Following her La Scala debut in 1935, she had been heard in Paris and London (the Coronation performances of *Falstaff* and *Turandot*). It was Gigli who brought her to the attention of Edward Johnson—the tenor had selected Albanese for his Mimi in their 1938 complete recording of *Bohème*. At twenty-six, diminutive in stature, with a sure command of stage technique and mastery of the traditional vocal and textual nuances of Italian opera, the soprano was an increasingly rare phenomenon—a singer thoroughly schooled in the ways of the lyric stage.

The voice is not large—indeed, for such a part as Butterfly it is slightly undersized—but the difference is more than made up in the know-how, as is immediately apparent at Butterfly's entrance. Here the voice is very tightly collected in the manner then favored by Italian lyric sopranos, and it has a slight edge to it—clearly, warmth has been sacrificed for projection and brilliance. (Albanese maintained, "I always sing lightly [in the first act] for I am a young Geisha girl, still inexperienced and naive.")[5] Within this framework the voice opens up amazingly above the *passaggio* without separating itself from the character of the lower voice—the high D-flat is very brilliant and rock solid. Having presented her top card, the soprano proceeds to devote herself to the opposite pole of the Puccini spectrum: the treatment of text both for the creation of character and as a vehicle for musical expression. All the intimate bits of parlando are clearly articulated and tellingly varied to suit Butterfly's changing moods. Nowadays some decry these childlike nuances and pseudo-Orientalisms, but Albanese makes them sound so spontaneous and natural (barring a pair of pinched *picciol*s) that artifice seems remote. When Butterfly tells Pinkerton that she has abandoned her religion, we get our first hint of Albanese's extraordinary

Madama Butterfly
25 January 1941
Cio-Cio-San
Licia Albanese
Suzuki
Lucielle Browning
Pinkerton
Armand Tokatyan
Sharpless
John Brownlee
Conductor
Gennaro Papi

ability to convey depth of feeling. The love duet reveals yet another Albanese forte—her grasp of the characteristic shape of a Puccini phrase: sometimes she poses a subtle interplay of rhythm and dynamics that culminates in a moment when the tone seems to hang suspended, until a gentle diminuendo carries it back to conscious movement; at other times her tone rides triumphantly over the climax of a broadly arched phrase, even as the rhythmic energy of her diction propels the music vigorously forward. Albanese accomplishes these telling moments within the limits of her lyric instrument by charting the most careful gradation of tone, rhythm, and timbre, and by a masterly use of *portamento*. A prime example is the sequence at 'Dolce notte!' in the love duet, which is laid out as precisely as an eighteenth-century garden until she reaches 'O quant'occhi,' which she spins out to exquisite effect.

In the second act the Albanese voice takes on greater warmth; all the childlike tonal point is left behind along with Butterfly's innocence—only hope remains. No one could doubt this Butterfly's belief in her husband's return, for Albanese lives the narrative of 'Un bel dì,' capturing every nuance without exaggeration; the transition from delicate parlando ('Chi sarà?') to jet flight ('per non morire') reveals the fullness of her craft. No portion of the opera is more endearing than Albanese's letter scene with Sharpless (Brownlee is persuasive here, too): her pallid tone at 'Non mi rammenta più!' and the rhythmic thrust of 'mi ha scordata?' in turn capture the gentle disbelief and then the despair of the forsaken wife. The long narration leading to 'Morta!' is harder for the Albanese voice to sustain in terms of volume and ferocity, but the sighting of the ship is so on target rhythmically, the text trumpeted out with such vigor, that we share fully in Butterfly's exaltation. In the flower duet Albanese molds a genuine *messa di voce* on the high B-flat before descending with the loveliest *portamento* to the octave below (the ensemble is faulty since Browning fails to grasp the contour of Puccini's lines). Perhaps no moment better illustrates Albanese's understanding of Puccini's rhetoric than her final phrases in act two: what a vivid contrast she achieves by musical means alone, first suggesting in dancing rhythms Butterfly's glee at the thwarting of Yamadori and then, in a mesmerizing change of mood, embracing Butterfly's reverential inner calm as she requests her wedding robe.

In the final act Albanese subtly prepares the tragic moments: the easy float of the lullaby (ending with a gentle high B), the dignified calm of 'non ditemi nulla' (how warm the vocal timbre has become), the quiet and distinct but legato declamation of 'Tutto è morto per me! Tutto è finito!' (she makes music of the single reiterated note)—all these contrast with the outpouring of straightforward tone in the farewell to her child. She has plenty of voice left for the aria, and no miscalculations in the act mar the genuinely tragic portrayal. Albanese will become one of the favorite artists of the Saturday afternoon broadcasts not only because of her vocal gifts but because of her ability to act with the voice—though unseen, her heroines become visible to the invisible audience.

Albanese was thus well launched on an American career which, unlike her departed compatriots Cigna, Favero, and Caniglia, would be long-lasting. But she came perilously close to having to forfeit her Metropolitan habitat, even as her sister sopranos had, due to the vicissitudes of travel during the great war. A few months before her Butterfly broadcast, she found herself unable to leave Italy to fulfill her Metropolitan commitments; all steamship reservations were exhausted. From Milan she cabled a frantic call for help to the Met. She needed American dollars "in order to obtain visa Spain and Portugal and have possibility leaving. . . . Impossible obtain currency."[6] The Met was to send the sum by cable to Banca Commerciale, Milan,

"otherwise will also lose place on plane Rome to Lisbon and clipper to New York."
She arrived in time to offer the Metropolitan public her Butterfly during the first
week of the season and to open the Texaco broadcast era two days later in *Le Nozze di
Figaro*. And it was well that the soprano could appear in the broadcast *Butterfly*, for
there is little of comparable worth on that afternoon. Browning and Brownlee offer
pedestrian readings, while Tokatyan (though rather winning in the first act) is deficient in the forceful moments of act three and always thin at the top. It is De Paolis
who ranks as primo tenore with his pungent, well-sung Goro.

In some operatic portrayals artist and role seem perfectly mated—witness
Albanese's Butterfly. Too often, however, the fit is ill: the composer is not well served
nor do the considerable gifts of the singer show to best advantage. Yet no mezzo of
swarthy good looks and tawny vocal hue could be expected to forgo a run at Carmen,
and if the article could be stamped "made in Hollywood," its currency would
undoubtedly be inflated. Thus, for a few years Gladys Swarthout brought her
Valentina costumes to the Met stage and played at being the gypsy. The costumer
knew her customer; she judged that Swarthout "possesses an inborn good taste and
we understood each other perfectly."[7] In contrast to Ponselle's fiery ardor as Carmen,
Valentina knew that "Miss Swarthout gave an image of tender and lovely femininity
which led me to follow her type and personality." And so did Miss Swarthout in her
impersonation, no matter how remote it might be from the gypsy of Bizet, let alone
Mérimée.

Not that her portrayal (as heard in the broadcast of 15 March 1941) is without its
virtues. Not often is the first act so well sung—the deep color of the voice is most
appealing in both arias, and the sung recitatives are full of playful point. And her
taunts of José are tastefully spunky. So far, so good. Pelletier creates too sedate an
ambience for the Gypsy Song, and Swarthout cannot counteract it with rhythmic
impulse. From the opening prelude of the final act on through the death struggle
outside the bullring, the conductor keeps to a businesslike gait and eventually the
dramatic sap congeals. But not before we hear a fine quintet, fleet and well
disciplined in the expert hands of Votipka, Olheim, De Paolis, Cehanovsky, and
Swarthout—she inflects 'Je suis amoureuse' with amusement rather than heavy-
breathed ardor, and it is a deft touch. (A prime asset of the performance is its crew of
secondary principals: the two men are adept at ridicule, and Votipka's pinpoint
attack serves Bizet well at critical points).

But as far as Swarthout's Carmen goes, the game is up. She musters neither
insinuation in her vocal dance for José nor disdain as Carmen tries to keep him from
returning to his base. Yes, the voice is always beguiling—that's the problem; no ugly
or contemptuous effects in the interest of the drama shall disfigure it. She can be
playful ('Bel officier') but even there she stops just short of the dynamic gesture. It is
Kullman, in excellent voice, who convincingly carries the dramatic burden in their
scenes together. Though he enters the tavern with the least boastful of dragoon
songs, his Flower Song has sufficient ardor without muscling the music—he saves the
breast-beating for the final moments of the opera and manages even that with fine
tone and surprising vocal heft. His voice filled with regret and longing, Kullman
makes credible José's need to kill Carmen—a fine performance from the American
tenor. Swarthout is equally in earnest, but in the card scene her intonation is suspect
at the break, and she fails to make us sense the inevitability of death (but, oh, the
color is right). As José confronts her with his knife, though her vocalism is wonderfully free, this Carmen is no free spirit; she can neither dare nor spit venom nor, cer-

Carmen
15 March 1941
Carmen
Gladys Swarthout
Micaela
Licia Albanese
Don José
Charles Kullman
Escamillo
Leonard Warren
Conductor
Wilfred Pelletier

Gladys Swarthout as Carmen.

tainly, ever hate. But her voice is as polished and lovely as her Valentina gowns—
pretty as a picture she must have been.

The most vivid moments of the afternoon are provided by Micaela, for
Albanese makes a miniature drama of the aria. No coy ingénue she, but a peasant girl
courageous enough to find her way through the mountains to her lost love. As she
begins, her quick vibrato takes a moment or two to settle, but the thrusting ascents of
the middle section are vibrant with energy, and she makes a superb climax at
'Seigneur, Vous me protègerez.' The reprise is full of lovely *portamenti* as she overlaps
the phrases one to another. She caps it all with a stunning high B-flat, as all Micaelas
were wont to do then (and who would wish to be without such a B-flat as this one).
Her plea to José is vocally assured and equally charged with excitement. In act one,
both Albanese and Kullman make a lyric feast of the duet—how skillfully she
executes the sinuous lines and stepwise ascents through the *passaggio!* Management is
prodigal to place such a singer in this role, but Albanese turned Micaela into a star
vehicle during her early Met career. Warren is not quite so much the fully formed
artist as his soprano colleague, but he, too, radiates a star quality as the Toreador.
Like most baritones he is better in the higher reaches of the aria (and better there
than most baritones). Sometimes his big sound gets in the way of French fleetness,

but he fills out the refrain splendidly (and he is sensitive enough to lead into it with a finely grained diminuendo). A little more swagger would be welcome in his mountain meeting with José, but the fourth-act miniature duet is suavely lyrical in feel and tone.

Carmen had been staple fare throughout Metropolitan history, but now Johnson sought to cultivate a more novel French territory in a genre beyond the ken of the American public. Encouraged perhaps by the response to *Le Nozze di Figaro*, Johnson again reached into the eighteenth century, back to the *tragédie lyrique* of Christoph Willibald Gluck.

The thread of Gluck performances at the Metropolitan was a slim one. Johnson's earlier revival of *Orfeo* had occurred after a hiatus of two decades, though the opera had often been in the repertory during the company's first three decades. Beyond that, there was only the unlucky oblation of *Iphigenia auf Tauris* (reworked from the original French by Richard Strauss and given in German under Bodanzky's care in 1916) and, earlier on, a more authentic mounting by Toscanini and company (including Caruso) of *Armide*. In spite of the French tragedy's pride of place on opening night in 1910, it survived only two seasons. Undaunted by this thorny history, Johnson and his cohort in the revival of classic opera, stage director Herbert Graf, chose *Alceste* in the French revision (with cuts) which the cosmopolite composer had constructed from his Italian "reform" opera. The tragic heroines of French classical drama demand an interpreter of authoritative presence, commanding vocal means, and elevated artistic perception. Such a one was the revered Olive Fremstad as the 1910 Armide. Johnson recognized the challenge and believed he had met it when he engaged the foremost dramatic interpreter of the Opéra in Paris, Germaine Lubin, for her Metropolitan debut. But Madame Lubin was destined never to reach the Met stage. Just a few weeks before the premiere, Lubin's letter arrived from Paris (mailed eighty days earlier and bearing "the imprint of the Vichy post office").[8] France was now occupied by the Germans and it was impossible for her to leave the country. By a quirk of fate, Lubin's youthful rival at the Opéra had become a regular in the Metropolitan stable—at the premiere the role of Alceste fell to Marjorie Lawrence. Lawrence was scheduled for the broadcast of 8 March 1941 but had to cancel; the choice fell a step further to her surrogate, Rose Bampton, who had already sung one of the earlier performances.

The young American soprano met the test well, and the broadcast offers perhaps her finest portrayal. She had the stage assets of height and presence, her artistic intent was honorable, and the role lay in the favored portion of her vocal range. One might conjecture whether her overtly emotive portrayal was not a notch beyond the figures of Greek tragedy as purified by Racine and idealized by Gluck. She may depart from the "beautiful simplicity" which Gluck prescribed, but there is no faulting her involvement in Alceste's plight. And her voice has the chaste yet warm color of glowing marble. The first climax of the opera, where Alceste resolves to sacrifice herself to save her dying husband, pushes her to the full extent of her vocal resources; some shrillness intrudes. Nor are the angular contours of 'Divinités du Styx!' (as Alceste defies the gods) favored territory for Bampton; she doesn't know how to use the language to declaim the many repeated notes of the aria with sufficient intensity—one feels the gods might overwhelm this Alceste. But Bampton is at her best in the second act. There she captures Alceste's sorrow, pouring out streams of warm, vibrant tone, and when she tells Admetus the secret of her sacrifice, it is lovingly told. At the act's conclusion she delivers the resolute phrases of 'Ah, malgré

Alceste
8 March 1941

Alceste
Rose Bampton
Admète
René Maison
High Priest
Leonard Warren
Conductor
Ettore Panizza

moi' quite effectively. Again, as the final act opens, Bampton's ability to delineate the quickly shifting moods of the *recitativo accompagnato* impresses; she has progressed from the warmly emotional woman of act one to a noble and tragic heroine. As Alceste approaches death ('Ah! divinités implacables'), Bampton handily combines serenity with strength.

But it is the Admète (to use the French nomenclature) who better defines the Gluck *melos*. René Maison is in his best vocal form on this afternoon; the heroic ring of his voice with its burnished bronze coloration is as welcome as his command of declamation. He brings the lyric recitative to life, all sparks and pointed animation yet never disjointed. Maison drenches his tones in sorrow as he learns of his wife's sacrifice, an overt sorrow made palatable only by the manly make-up of the voice. And it is Maison who maintains the dramatic tension in the denouement when Panizza allows it to falter. Warren is equally robust as the High Priest, and the bright timbre of his upper voice pleases in the French piece. Yet Cehanovsky has the better manner as he broadly declaims the phrases of the Herald in fine style. Panizza wears an earnest face and, having recently conducted the opera in Buenos Aires, is at home with the score, but his abode is not quite that of Gluck. Too often the music meanders (especially the ballet portions) where a crisper rhythmic stimulus is needed.

Johnson's high-minded purpose in this revival is thus somewhat blunted, and Gluck's masterpiece quickly passed from the repertory. Berlioz had written of *Alceste* that "where music has reached the level of poetic elevation, one must feel sorry for the performers entrusted with the realization of the composer's thought. Talent is no longer sufficient for this crushing task, one must have sheer genius."[9] No doubt Bampton had abundant talent. For genius, one must wait another decade when the opera will be the vehicle for Flagstad's Metropolitan farewell.

Kirsten Flagstad as Brünnhilde in *Die Walküre*.

CHAPTER SEVENTEEN

1940–41
Auf Wiedersehen

Alceste would in truth be Flagstad's second Met farewell, for the war, the occupation of Norway, and the peculiar status of her husband during and after the conflict combined to prevent her return to the Metropolitan after the 1940–41 season. Before leaving, however, she offered three more portrayals to the radio audience.

Leinsdorf had weathered the storm of singer opposition and was again at the helm for the *Tannhäuser* broadcast of 4 January 1941. Is there an increased sense of well-being in his reading of the overture and Bacchanal? He adopts an easier gait which allows greater expressivity throughout (less *détaché* in the wind chords, more warmth in the strings); now the despair of the pilgrims is enlivened by a smidgen of hope. The Venusberg music, too, is less angular, while an almost chamberlike delicacy lends charm to the most seductive of the Venus themes. The conductor remains a master of scale: the ascent to a truly vibrant climax in the Bacchanal is complemented by the calculated release of tension in the transition to the call of the sirens. Leinsdorf's way with a score is not unlike that of the jockey whose finely tuned sense of restraint and release guides his mount to the finish line—not always a winner, but ever well calculated. Thus, the usual tangle of string roulades in the introduction to 'Dich, teure Halle' is avoided, and the closing ensembles of act two contain some perfectly gauged accelerandi; on the other hand, languor invades the somber opening of act three.

At the climactic moments Melchior almost gets away from him, for the tenor, like the thoroughbred he is, runs with the tempo when subject to Venus recall. But all the notes of Melchior's hymn to the goddess of love are securely in place. His Tannhäuser is an errant Tristan in fullness of voice, yet he maintains a glittering head resonance throughout the first scene, turning it into a marvel of bravura display capped by a stunning high A. One might well ask what man would want to escape from such a Venus as Kerstin Thorborg. No harridan she, no used-up Wagnerian soprano banished (as most interpreters of Venus have been) to the caverns of the Venusberg as penance for too rashly spending vocal resources in combat with Wagner's orchestra. Her warm, steady tones entice even when she upbraids. She eschews seductive kitsch in favor of full-throated splendor, and it matters not if the final high tone falls just short of the mark, for she and Melchior have made their con-

Tannhäuser
4 January 1941
Elisabeth
Kirsten Flagstad
Venus
Kerstin Thorborg
Tannhäuser
Lauritz Melchior
Wolfram
Herbert Janssen
Landgrave
Emanuel List
Conductor
Erich Leinsdorf

257

flict real. Released from erotic bondage, Melchior's silvery trumpet is muffled as he shamefully tells Elisabeth of those 'dark, distant regions' of his past; then he triumphantly sounds the 'wonder' that has made him return. In top vocal form throughout the afternoon, he never retreats before the notorious tessitura of the role; at the opera's end, his Rome Narrative is a tour de force of technical mastery, of word-motivated mood and color changes.

List, too, is in better than average vocal condition, leaving off his impressive vocal weightlifting in favor of song. Janssen again proves the ideal Wolfram. One looks not to him for breadth of phrase or sustained line (occasionally sustained tones are simply abandoned); his 'Abendstern' can disappoint—he refuses to turn it into a vocal vehicle, and some of the otherworldly calm of the moment is forfeited. But here and elsewhere the velvet sheath on his timbre pleases, his liederlike nuances charm, and in the tone itself and the feel of his phrasing the full nature of Wolfram's character is revealed. Affection penetrates his tone at his rediscovery of Tannhäuser in act one (and here he shows us that melodic sweep is not foreign to him). His carefully modulated progression from thoughtful narration to lyricism transforms Wolfram's stodgy contest effort into poetic song.

An aura of distinction envelops the entire performance, and nowhere more so than in Flagstad's portrayal. Her vocalism is incredibly fresh, and more surprisingly, so is her characterization of Elisabeth. For once she has shed even the suggestion of the heroic in both tone and manner. The perfect scaling of her instrument to Elisabeth's music and nature fully compensates for the remembered magisterial plotting of the entrance aria's final phrases (though this time the flight to the high B is not quite pristine). She is equally adept at detail: *portamenti* are judicious, and she deftly introduces a suggestion of regret in the two or three notes of 'zog aus dir' as she remembers her knight's earlier departure. Her phrasing has never been more flexible, her revelation of self more open, her spirit more capable of quick-silver changes of feeling, than in the second-act scene with Tannhäuser. One would have to return to her earliest performances to match the girlish tone and delicacy of her singing as she seeks and captures the maidenly innocence of Elisabeth. Some alchemy has allowed silver to penetrate the characteristic bronze metal of her instrument, and even at the softest dynamic the voice is perfectly poised. This easy flow of gentle tone in combination with deep feeling is far from a constant feature of Flagstad's art. The Prayer of the last act contains many lovely effects (the upward *portamenti* over the intervals of the fifth and sixth are special), and the vocalism is impeccable. On this afternoon Flagstad's characteristic instrumental timbre and execution recede in favor of human emotion and womanly song, a transformation almost as miraculous as the newly green leaves on the pope's staff.

When next we meet Flagstad a month later (8 February 1941) she has left off the reticence of the Thuringian maiden to counterfeit the wrath of the proud Irish princess, a woman not wasting away for love but rather willing to meet death head on. In truth, it is a rather aloof Isolde who reclines on her couch aboard Tristan's ship on this Saturday afternoon. Nor does the voice seem in its finest estate. During the first half of the opera, the lower octave has not quite its customary enveloping warmth; occasionally the legato is a little sticky, and she substitutes a nasal resonance for the remembered unstopped bulk of tone, a technique often resorted to by lesser sopranos but never before necessary to Flagstad. The top, too, is a little slow to respond with its wonted freedom. But early on (by the time she reaches the narrative), the lava flow of the upper voice returns in all its splendor. An awesome density

Tristan und Isolde
8 February 1941
Isolde
Kirsten Flagstad
Brangäne
Kerstin Thorborg
Tristan
Lauritz Melchior
Kurvenal
Julius Huehn
Marke
Alexander Kipnis
Conductor
Erich Leinsdorf

and security enwrap the big pronouncements ('Fluch dir . . . Rache!')—Isolde's battle with Tristan is waged with a vocal broadsword. Yet slight evidences of indisposition remain. The intervallic leaps, whose wonderful precision is always one of her glories, are smudged now and then, the second glancing high C is noticeably thin, and the closed vowels in 'O sink' hernieder' ('lebe' and 'liebe') are perilously weighted to the flat side. One becomes uneasy that this final Isolde for the radio public will fall below the standard which she alone has provided. Of course, these are blemishes on an aural Athena, but a goddess even slightly defiled is more cause for dismay then mere human error.

The characterization, too, seems less full. The Isolde aflame with love as she awaits Tristan in act two is little different from the pensive princess first met on board ship. Modifications of volume are few (no *piano* at 'Zu schweigen hatt' ich gelernt' as prescribed not only by Wagner but by the text); too often the meaningful melding of word and tone is ignored. But when she chooses, Flagstad offers plenty to admire, as when she recounts with wonder how Tristan's look made her drop the sword of revenge while he was under her care—here one feels the change in character, and she confirms it by an insinuating color change at 'Sühne.' And who could equal the masterly blend of tone, color, and shapely phrase as she invites Tristan to drink the potion ('das schenkte mir . . . zu sühnen alle Schuld'); or after the potion, the flood of gorgeous tone at 'Treuloser Holder!'; or in the second-act love duet, the quiet, trombone-like richness of 'öder Pracht schimmernd dort zu leben'; or the perfection of the wide intervals of 'Tag und Tod' later in the scene. Now, in mid-opera, the vocal mechanism is fully primed, the musical ideas flow, and dramatic meaning deepens. The final scene of the opera is incredibly lovely, her Liebestod perfect in conception and execution, an ideal realized.

Though Flagstad's Isolde will never again be heard on the Metropolitan broadcasts, Melchior has yet another decade with the company. On this afternoon his knight is as convincing as remembered—Tristan's honor is always in good hands with him. Again in the love duet the disparity between Melchior and Flagstad in the approach to song surfaces: Melchior, with his quick attack and disjunct declamation in narrative (not in song), contrasts with the delayed tonal attack of Flagstad and her slightly labored legato where each note becomes an objective in itself. The blend and way of going (she always a fraction late, he always ahead) is less than satisfying in those few phrases *a due* ('sehnend verlangter Liebestod'). In a few passages in the third-act delirium Melchior almost merges the dotted-quarter and eighth rhythms into quarter notes (is this the evidence of musical error which haunts his reputation?—surely the recitative-like layout of these moments plus dramatic circumstance make this latitude acceptable; and even a memory bobble happens to the best of them). And how believable he is, in both his darkly colored, debilitated wanderings and in the outbursts of joy which he trumpets forth.

Thorborg and Huehn operate on an equally high level. She, ever the mistress of voice and interpretation, becomes the character; nothing is merely applied, and vocally she is in best estate. I like very much the fresh opulence of Huehn's baritone. He has gained in subtlety, never barks, and moves easily back and forth between a tender mezza voce (mirroring his concern for the dying Tristan) and virile tones of reassurance and hope. It is Leinsdorf who lacks some of the vigor for Cornwall's paean—he has that tendency to edge extremes of mood toward an equalizing center. But in his hands the opera's prelude describes no abstract, timeless longing but an urgent sense of present need. The lengthy brass passages of act one (as Isolde awaits

Tristan) have impressive breadth, and the ebb and flow of the second-act love music is modeled with a control that is anything but pedantic.

A welcome addition to the Met's Wagner wing is young Emery Darcy, destined in the future to sing a few major roles but too long relegated to the confidant or messenger category. Doing double duty as the Steersman and Melot, he is no puny tenor—he owns Wagnerian baritonal underpinnings and sound musical instincts as well. Of greater moment for the Met's well-being is the advent of one of the greatest artists of the prewar period, Alexander Kipnis. Already at the mid-century mark in age, for more than two decades the Russian bass had been a favorite on the stages of Berlin and Chicago, Buenos Aires and London, Salzburg and Bayreuth. Like so many of his generation, he fled from the Nazis to Vienna in 1933 and finally to the United States, joining the Metropolitan for the 1939–40 season. In King Marke's monologue he shows most of the qualities that made his artistry so distinctive. Few voices are as ebon-hued, but those that are have nothing like Kipnis' open core, his songlike flow of rich tone. In spite of his intent ("I considered that most of Marke's monologue was an intimate reproach to Tristan")[1] we hear only one or two attempts ('Da kinderlos') at that unique silken sweetness which his records of Wolf and Brahms songs had taught us to expect. The emphasis is oddly upon anger rather than sorrow ('beschleiche' is almost a sneer, and 'Warum mir diese Schmach?' becomes a real question more than a lament). Vitality in the phrasing as well as the tone energizes the narrative sufficiently to avoid ennui.

We meet Kipnis again two weeks later (22 February 1941) in the broadcast of *Fidelio*. The earthy Rocco provides greater opportunity for his abilities, and he delivers a full portrait. His 'Gold' aria (cut at the Met since the days of Mahler but restored at Kipnis' insistence) is more agile than one has a right to expect from so massive a voice, and the singer turns this singspiel commonplace into artistic gold with lovely, deft vocal and theatrical touches. He moves with conviction from full-flavored yet restrained song in the trio to broadly limned dread in the duet with Pizarro ('Der kaum mehr lebt'). In the first-act finale how craftily he inserts his asides ('den Finger auf dem Munde' is deliciously tripped off his tongue) into his strong declamation and song! But he does not overstate the grotesquerie of the dungeon *melodrama* and duet—the superb sonority of his instrument by itself generates awe.

Few weak links enfeeble this performance. Laufkoetter (Jacquino) may not be quite pleasant tonally (though idiomatic), but Marita Farell is an exquisite Marzelline, her crystalline tone achieving surprising fullness at the climax of her aria, which she closes with a delightfully demure *subito piano*. We also have the boon of Janssen's Minister. The role is really too low for him, but who else could imbue 'Es sucht der Bruder seine Brüder' with so much humanity, and his tone and delivery are as just as the judgment he pronounces. Huehn is not so successful with Pizarro. The voice is in fine fettle, but he is musically too well behaved to incarnate evil—vengeance and murder seem beyond his ken. Nor does Maison suggest the usually weak-unto-death prisoner. He offers suffering on a grander level, taking to heart Florestan's adjuration 'Ich murre nicht' ('I'll not complain'). His lengthy scene is strong in tone and interpretive insight with every significant word and change of mood subtly marked. Nor is he defeated by the tessitura of the closing section. Both he and Flagstad successfully avoid the frenzied disorder of 'O namenlose Freude!' without curtailing its joyous abandon.

In this, as in every other aspect of the performance, it is the conductor who makes all good things possible. The broadcast marks Bruno Walter's second appear-

Fidelio
22 February 1941

Leonore
Kirsten Flagstad
Marzelline
Marita Farell
Florestan
René Maison
Jacquino
Karl Laufkoetter
Pizarro
Julius Huehn
Rocco
Alexander Kipnis
Fernando
Herbert Janssen
Conductor
Bruno Walter

ance at the Metropolitan. A week earlier, at the premiere of *Fidelio*, the Metropolitan public had given him one of the most extended ovations in the history of the house (after the *Leonore* Overture Number 3, played as usual following the dungeon scene). This afternoon's performance tells us why: he creates drama without counterfeiting it. Time is for him a blessing; he lovingly shapes the quiet phrases until grandeur accumulates, and the clarity and poise of thematic development lead triumphantly to the overture's joyous conclusion. Detractors of the practice of inserting the overture when its drama has already been played out on stage need not worry when it is in Walter's care. His is no twice-told tale but a spacious remembrance and ennoblement.

More important for the opera itself is Walter's sure hand in shaping every element of the performance. A fine sense of proportion governs the opening of act one (preceded by the *Fidelio* Overture, kept within a classical aesthetic to blend readily into the singspiel opening scene): each orchestral motive, each chord, has its appropriate place in the web of symphonic play; at the same time, each element supports and guides the action—the result is a speaking musicality. To his mastery of the late eighteenth century's narrative dramatic style, Walter adds romantic overtones from the early nineteenth century; the introduction to the canon quartet is a gratifying union of repose and sublimity. Nor does he straitjacket his singers so that they are walking on eggs of caution; in the shadowy duet of Rocco and Pizarro it is Walter who drives the menace of the villain home. Of course, he loves to linger—Flagstad may wish to move on in 'Komm, Hoffnung,' but Walter's horns want to sing (one bobble there), and after all, she needn't be anxious about those long phrases. Walter's well-known reverence for the prisoners' release to sunlight shows in his beautiful pacing of the choral ensemble. Even Maison survives Walter's predilection for slow tempi in 'In des Lebens Frühlingstagen.' Oddly, Walter chooses to emphasize classical restraint in the emotional trio in the dungeon, but it works; nor does he see any need to whip up the pace before Flagstad's climactic outcry 'Töt' erst sein Weib!'—but then, Flagstad's 'Zurück!' has sufficient impact to quell any miscreant.

Flagstad is in superb form throughout the entire afternoon. How expertly she hones the mass of her instrument to suit Beethoven's chiseled melodic lines! In the first-act trio her voice is flexible, the legato easy, the tone narrow with no loss of color—'für hohen Lohn kann Liebe' is as lovely as any phrase she ever uttered. She still ignores the contrasted dynamics of 'Abscheulicher!' and 'Des Mitleids Ruf' (though Walter well prepares the adagio), but 'so leuchtet mir ein Farbenbogen' is gentle enough and tonally resplendent, while the ensuing phrases are nicely tranquil. In the aria the ascending scale is even and unrushed, wearing its high B like a crown. Walter's calm turns 'Lass den letzten Stern' into a prayer, and Flagstad captures the *dolce* of 'die Liebe wird's erreichen' and even some of the agitated resolution at the aria's close (though the final high B is rather colorless). Whether it is Walter's doing or merely her own response to him, the aria's contrasts are clearer and the emotional impact of the aria better realized (though written evidence survives that Walter was not satisfied with her portrayal).[2] Her spoken recitatives (the Bodanzky profanation aborted at last) are a little lifeless compared to the natural play of most of her colleagues—those in act two, however, are more convincing ('O nein, es ist nur so kalt'). She provides some memorable moments in the act-one finale: her joyous 'Noch heute'; the strong shafts of tone as she anticipates going to the prisoner's cell 'this very day'; her tentativeness at 'Ich bin es nur noch nicht gewohnt' as she contemplates preparing the grave; the poised etching of motives in the concluding ensemble—throughout it all, the voice rings as clear as crystal. She wraps the entire dungeon scene in classical composure (no Lehmannisms here) and draws Beethoven's melodic profile with exemplary care; the cumulative result is moving on its own terms. In the final scene of jubilation her long, sustained B-flat, so deftly colored and perfectly placed, hangs over the ensemble like a protective shield, and her quiet voicing of 'O Gott! O welch ein Augenblick!' (as she sets Florestan free) fairly glows. Memory long will dwell on these marks of her greatness.

Not by chance were all three of these final performances selected for inclusion in the dozen or so historic Metropolitan broadcast recordings. If the *Tristan* of 8 February is a shade below her best, one should note that she had performed Isolde on 4 February (in Philadelphia) and Elisabeth on 6 February, as well as rehearsed for the revival of *Fidelio* scheduled for 14 February (which, incidentally, was preceded by a *Walküre* on 12 February). No soprano would attempt such a marathon today. At season's end she returned to her husband in Norway, and although Huehn, who took her to the plane, assured us that she would return,[3] she was never again heard during the remaining nine years of Johnson's tenure. In view of her impact on the house and its public, one is astonished to remember that, thus far, her own tenure at the Metropolitan consisted of only seven seasons—but when every performance is a banner event, the aura quickly accumulates.

Flagstad was the indisputable monarch of the Met during this period—not only in her artistry, but at the box office, a rare combination. Who could take her place in the decade of the forties? Johnson had his candidates, just as Gatti had Galli-Curci and Jeritza and Gigli after Caruso's death. But Bruno Walter, more than any individual singer, proved the most meaningful harbinger of the next decade.

The first half of the twentieth century, unlike recent times, was an age when all the great conductors were as comfortable in the pit as center stage in the symphonic arena. Indeed, the opera house had been, if not mother, at least midwife to most of them. Walter's career was typical. At seventeen he began as a coach at Cologne's Municipal Opera, before long moving to the podium of opera houses in Hamburg, Breslau, and Berlin. In those days all paths led to Vienna, where the presence of Gustav Mahler was a strong lure for the twenty-five-year-old Walter, and in 1901 Walter began a decade as assistant conductor under Mahler at the opera. Both the operatic and symphonic international scene (New York, London, Leipzig, Amsterdam, Salzburg, even Moscow) claimed him during the twenties and thirties. But still there were permanent ties to the opera house: he served as director of the Berlin Charlottenburg Opera for four years and finally returned to the Vienna State Opera as its director in 1936, eagerly championing the Mozart operas and fostering the reassessment of the neglected middle-period Verdi works. But again, it was the same unhappy story—the Anschluss drove him from the city of dreams to the land of refuge where the NBC Symphony, and eventually the Metropolitan, awaited him. At the time of his debut, the sixty-five-year-old Walter already enjoyed an almost mystical veneration among associates and public. It was partly the man, noble and beatific, but these qualities resonated in his music-making, too, and made him much loved by the Metropolitan public. Fortunately for the Met, other maestros of similar ability, if less blissful mien and manner, would follow during the next decade or so and provide a quality of musical leadership seldom duplicated in earlier or later times.

Bruno Walter.

Helen Traubel as Isolde in *Tristan und Isolde*. Photography by Alfredo Valente.

CHAPTER EIGHTEEN

1941–44
Wagner While at War

Their initial season of sponsorship pleased the Texas Company. They had read about 30,000 letters from broadcast listeners of which 3,884 contained "expressions of preference for certain operas."[1] Of the 287 different operas that were requested, the oil company sent the Met a list of the 87 preferred works for their consideration.

Carmen led the list with 867 requests, with *Aida, Traviata*, and *Faust* not far behind. The Italian repertory (*Bohème, Butterfly*, and *Lucia* included) dominated the top ten with only *Tristan* and *Lohengrin* in the running (*Manon* tied with the latter for tenth place). Surprisingly, *Götterdämmerung* beat out *Walküre* by a nose (thirteenth and fourteenth, respectively), while the fragile *Lakmé* (nineteenth place) was squeezed in between *Tannhäuser* and the entire *Nibelungen Ring* (222 votes). And somewhere out there in radioland breathed a longing for the esoteric, for tied in sixty-sixth place were *Sadko, Tiefland, Le Prophète*, and *Amelia Goes to the Ball*. Not surprisingly, W. L. Kallman of the Texas Company concluded that "the preference of the radio listener is for operas containing arias that the listener had heard frequently enough to make them familiar to him."[2] The Texas Company, faithful now and forever, offered its sponsorship for a second season, and the Met hastened to assure NBC that it approved the Texas Company "and its products"[3] for commercial sponsorship of the 1941–42 season.

Arias, familiar or not, demand singers, and now the void left by Flagstad's departure confronted Johnson. The manager might well have felt he had the situation under control with Marjorie Lawrence in his pocket. But it was not only acts of war but acts of God which oppressed him, for the Australian diva, whose forthright vitality was a cornerstone of her appeal, fell victim to polio during the summer of 1941. Paralysis would make it impossible for her ever again to stride on stage and joyously fling Brünnhilde's battle cry into the house or to ride Grane into Siegmund's funeral pyre. Eventually her courage would earn her a return, brief but exalted, to the Metropolitan stage. In the meantime, the war meant that Johnson must look close to home for help.

Helen Traubel, like Flagstad, was a late bloomer. But unlike her Norwegian colleague, who had sung in opera for twenty years before coming to the Met as a Wagner heroine, Traubel had no stage experience prior to creating Mary Rutledge in

1937. When, two years later, she returned to the house for her second debut (28 December 1939) she knew only one Wagner role, Sieglinde, with Elisabeth in *Tannhäuser* in the works. She sang only these two roles during the next two seasons. With Flagstad and Lawrence on hand, Johnson had not been eager to give her opportunity in spite of growing critical acclaim from concert appearances. Their relationship was not overly cordial—that "little, very dapper Canadian with his bouncing gait, immaculate clothes, and probing eyes"[4] was how she summed him up. But now Johnson needed a Brünnhilde and an Isolde, and he knew only one place to find them. For Traubel, already in her early forties when Flagstad departed, it was now or never to spend some of her vocal capital.

Happily, her baptism in the heroic Wagner roles occurred on the broadcast of 6 December 1941 when she sang her first Brünnhilde in *Die Walküre*. But her story was not the only drama of the afternoon. Lehmann had been scheduled for Sieglinde but was indisposed, and the shortage of Wagnerian sopranos being acute, Johnson was forced to call upon a twenty-three-year-old soprano who had never appeared on any stage. Born in Sweden of music theatre parents but raised in America from age five, Astrid Varnay had begun vocal study with her mother only four years earlier. Her luck (and her misfortune, a few might say) was to have all the big Wagner parts in hand at this critical point. "I have always accepted responsibility,"[5] she said at the end of her first eventful season, and she proved it by going on without a single stage rehearsal to be heard by a public of millions. If the occasion turned out to be not quite a repeat of the Flagstad story, fate was generous at quickening the drama of the afternoon: the radio audience heard Traubel in her first Wagner broadcast in conjunction with the debut of an unheralded soprano—two artists who would dominate the Wagner repertory in America for the next decade and a half.

The performance is also notable for Schorr's final Wagner broadcast—but, alas, not for his vocalism. Time's toll seems excessive upon his wooden tones and telescoped range (everything above middle C betrays strain), and the mere effort to produce tone decimates his legato line. Only in the tender handling of a few phrases in the Farewell do we find a semblance of the remembered Schorr; thus do aging artists kiss away their godhead. The following season a single appearance as the *Siegfried* Wanderer (not broadcast) would bring his farewell to the house he had long served with such distinction. Unfortunately, memory is little better served by a career coda in his appearance as the Sprecher in the broadcast of *The Magic Flute* a month after the *Walküre* airing.

Melchior remains in prime condition. One marvels as he moves from stippled declamation to lyrical sweep in 'Winterstürme,' or thunders out the pair of *Wälse*s at impossible length, or responds to Brünnhilde's invitation to Valhalla in tones now somber with sorrow, now brightly colored with pride and love. Familiarity has not dulled either his or our response.

But Melchior did long for relief from the incessant run of Wagner roles to which his supremacy had condemned him. In the summer of 1941 he pressed the Metropolitan for other opportunities. His manager informed him they "cannot at this time give you Italian roles because this will affect the reduced guarantees to the Italian tenors and would be just as unfair as if they would take Wagnerian roles from you to give to Italian tenors."[6] And so management's impenetrable logic denied Melchior (and us) Bajazzo (so Melchior called Pagliaccio) and Otello.

But our main concern on this afternoon is with the ladies. With the young Varnay, we immediately sense that we are in the presence of a vibrant theatrical

Die Walküre
6 December 1941

Sieglinde
Astrid Varnay
Brünnhilde
Helen Traubel
Fricka
Kerstin Thorborg
Siegmund
Lauritz Melchior
Wotan
Friedrich Schorr
Hunding
Alexander Kipnis
Conductor
Erich Leinsdorf

force—Lehmannesque in vitality but less mannered in detail. Interpretively, she is already a mature artist: character portrayal, command of diction, and word significance—these seem remarkable in so young and inexperienced a singer. She is not in full command of her voice—the lower range is sometimes breathy and without core ("I had trouble with low notes. . . . I was in the soprano line and worked hard for my low notes,"[7] she confessed decades later); some of 'Der Männer Sippe' suffers from diffuse tone in the lower octave. But the voice is striking in color, dense, slightly metallic, but without hardness. And the middle and top of the voice are very fine, both in ease of production and in size and timbre, the very top taking on a rather bright ring without losing mass; in short, a genuine dramatic instrument, well suited to her theatrical temperament. And what excitement she generates! The climax of her narrative is full of abandon (and splendid vocally)—Melchior seems to reply in kind. Seldom has he been so enraptured as in this response (Leinsdorf, too, for once seems propelled beyond objectivity, though elsewhere he is more contained). The entire conclusion to the act is one of the most fervent to be heard in the broadcast series, and Varnay appears to be the generating force.

Traubel, even this early in her Met career, was more of a known quantity. Yet one is astonished by the splendor of her achievement in her first heroic portrayal. In contrast to Varnay's, Traubel's voice, as broad as it is velvety warm, is under perfect control, seamless in timbre and quality from top to bottom. The very top tones are amazingly secure and free for a voice of this size—she approaches them fearlessly. Nor does she need to resort to ugly chest tone, for the lower voice is equally full and warmly colored. The Metropolitan has known few instruments of this quality. One recalls that Traubel's studio recordings, no matter how impressive tonally, often give off an impression of stolidity. No hint of that on this Saturday afternoon: the battle cry, for instance, is a shout of uninhibited joy, with the octave upward *portamenti* easy and accurate. Traubel plays a more realistic warrior maid than the idealized Walküre of Flagstad, but she is not deficient in the more sensitive moments (when Brünn-hilde must tell Siegmund of his fate, she caresses the *m* in 'Sieh' auf mich' with soft warmth). No barriers of reticence distance her interpretation; warmth occupies the tone itself—if Flagstad's instrument encompasses the woodwinds, Traubel's surely is akin to the French horn. Her resolve to save Siegmund is thrilling in its decisiveness, and how nimbly she moves over the angular vocal terrain of this moment. When she pleads with Wotan for protection in her isolation, the voice gleams throughout its entire range, and again the top notes are thrown out with abandon. Traubel's song is secure, beautiful, and exciting—only now is it apparent how much vocal capital she has accumulated, and that she can spend it without reducing the basis.

How to reconcile Leinsdorf's harsh judgment of Traubel? He claims that she brought only "biological attributes" with her; "otherwise she had not talent and not even ambition."[8] Lazy, perhaps, she was, though she did master all the Wagner heroines—no small achievement. And it may have been lack of ambition that made her content for almost two decades to remain in St. Louis, sheltering a voice perhaps without equal in America. (Leinsdorf was not alone in his censure. I well remember a professor of mine—an avid Flagstadite—dismissing Traubel as "bovine." Of course, this was at the time when Flagstad's return to the house was being hotly disputed.) Undoubtedly Traubel's stage deportment was less than inspired. But it is no sin to love to laugh, which she did, and when, near the end of her career, she found out she could make money at it (with much less effort than as a Wagner heroine), she would take the easy way out. But even Leinsdorf (who could not forgive her reluctance to sing Wagner uncut) acknowledged she had "a beautiful voice that soared easily over any kind of orchestral surge yet could be full of sweetness and lyricism."[9] Those are "biological attributes" any opera singer might covet.

The years ahead would lead Traubel and Varnay along widely disparate paths, but in the meantime the Metropolitan claimed them both, and their careers touched in unusual ways. Varnay's sense of responsibility and the Metropolitan's need collided again, less than a week after her debut, when she undertook the *Walküre* Brünnhilde for an indisposed Traubel. When Varnay next appeared, it was as Elsa on 9 January 1942; she repeated the role the following week in the *Lohengrin* broadcast of 17 January.

Lohengrin
17 January 1942
Elsa
Astrid Varnay
Ortrud
Kerstin Thorborg
Lohengrin
Lauritz Melchior
Telramund
Herbert Janssen
Herald
Leonard Warren
King Henry
Norman Cordon
Conductor
Erich Leinsdorf

New also to the airwaves in their roles are Cordon (King Henry) and Janssen (Telramund). Cordon is deficient on several counts: volume is merely adequate, and he is short at both ends of the range. Janssen seems an unlikely candidate for the wretched Telramund, yet not only is he vocally impressive, he manages to make "Mr. Ortrud" interesting. Though he can (and does) hurl out Telramund's complaints with ample baritonal brawn, his varied declamation animates the dramatic exchanges with the king. By following Wagner's dynamic markings (the suggestive *piano* at 'geheimnisvoll den Geist'), he finds a few lyrical moments which awaken our sympathy: sorrow inhabits his 'Der junge Tag darf hier uns nicht,' and we believe he knows the pain of lost peace ('wo mein Gewissen Ruhe wieder fänd'!' marked *schmerzlich* by Wagner). This Telramund makes clear his antagonism toward his wife. Thus, in place of the usual browbeaten, groveling baritone bawling gruff tone, Janssen gives the husband a three-dimensional fullness. Janssen's voice, too, is in excellent condition, as is Leonard Warren's (again the Herald), though one notes a contrast between the former's authentic German style and Warren's slightly over-blown pronouncements—but undoubtedly Warren's imposing sonority is suitably heraldic.

Neither Thorborg nor Melchior rival their past performances. Nevertheless, Thorborg cannot help communicating and, with Varnay, makes the second-act encounter come alive. But an echo of a quaver invades her soft singing, 'Entweihte Götter!' is less than the climactic moment it can be, and the high tessitura of the opera's close causes some outright screaming on her part. Yet, as always, there is a good deal to admire in her work. Melchior manages the big moments with his customary security and brilliance (though not without signs of effort), and he is ever attentive to word and situation. The tenor is probably in vocal trouble at the opera's close; never has he relied so heavily on realistic characterization at the expense of tonal security as in his farewell to Elsa. The signs are present earlier, too, for his usually pliant mezza voce refuses to work; all the softer moments (including the first-act Farewell to the Swan) are oddly veiled. And, a rarity for Melchior, poor intonation mars the quieter moments of the bridal duet (and he *will* nudge Leinsdorf on in this music).

To turn from old friends to new is, for once, more agreeable. One misses in Varnay the virginal purity of tone of the ideal Elsa (a Tiana Lemnitz, Elisabeth Grümmer, even Rethberg). Thus, neither the dream nor 'Euch Lüften' are models of tonal purity—the voice is ill suited in its physical make-up for lengthy abstract apostrophes. But from the first, Varnay has her voice well under control, and it gains in tonal blandishment as the opera progresses. Even in the entrance aria one can admire the gentle mood and manner of 'mein Aug' ist zugefallen, ich sank in süssen Schlaf!' and the phrasing of 'Euch Lüften' is entirely winning. As soon as the merest

Kerstin Thorborg as Ortrud in *Lohengrin*.

hint of dramatic involvement appears, she seizes upon it and her voice and person spring to life (I like the leap from her dream world to reality as she pleads with the king for yet one more summons of her knight). When she assures Ortrud 'Es gibt ein Glück,' she voices no idle promise of hope sweetened by honeyed tone but a statement of absolute truth; her accents and tone convey complete conviction (but Leinsdorf won't allow her belief to flower in the postlude to the scene). Elsa's outbursts against Ortrud at the end of the second act are authoritative and thrilling in their full-throated ring. In the bridal scene duet, Varnay's musical instincts are exactly right; the voice blooms as she skillfully shapes each phrase and finally takes flight in the closing moments. She convinces us that she is, after all, an Elsa, though she herself denied it ("I was not an Elsa sound, really")[10]—but that was three decades later when the Brünnhilde *Fach* had been both won and lost.

We have two more opportunities to test her own judgment. When *Lohengrin* is aired a year later (2 January 1943) and again in 1945, Sved and Harrell replace Janssen and Warren, but the other principals are constant. The 1943 matinee is a splendid offering with the principals in top form. Only Cordon is no match for these vocal monarchs, though it is one of his better efforts; and the choral episodes, so prominent in this ceremonial piece, are not up to standard, their precision clearly victimized by routine. With the sound of Janssen's distinctive characterization in memory, Sved's Telramund initially shocks. In the opening moments he is a very stagey villain, all trilled *rr*'s and shuddering tone, the declamation excessively broad and overwrought—has Sved anticipated Anna Russell's advice to Wagnerian singers to make an effective entrance by startling the audience with a blast of sound? At least he dominates the scene. Fortunately, the voice gains in steadiness, and though he cannot modify his tone to suit Telramund's few reflective moments, he is undoubtedly an effective knave; his sheer weight of voice and intensity of manner make for some thrilling climaxes. But one need only hear the clean, manly sound of Mack Harrell, happily moving up in the opera world, to be reminded that sensitivity and musical integrity are more cherishable than monumental tone. With relief, one notes that Thorborg's vocal condition is greatly improved. She pours out reams of finely molded phrases, her invocation to profane gods this time a full-throated assault and the tessitura of Ortrud's ragings at the opera's close all but conquered.

Opera lore would have it that hard usage in her first season robbed Varnay's young voice of early bloom. Not so. Of virginal bloom there was little enough from the beginning, but more important, in her second season the voice has become a more estimable instrument in every way. From the first she supplies not only greater authority in the dream narrative, but a full, well-focused sound. As she proceeds through the opera, the baser metal of her instrument is tempered to what is (for her type of voice) a pleasing purity. She even tries a *pianissimo* high A ('Mein Erlöser' in act one)—it comes out thin and ineffectual, but by the end of the second act her quietest moments have a suitable sheen. The low voice, too, is steadier and has sufficient body. In both the scene with Ortrud and the bridal duet her richly flowing sound enhances her deepened expressivity. I like the conversational manner which she and Melchior adopt in the middle section of the duet (some might call it careless on Melchior's part, but it is within the zones).

Disappointment at several earlier Melchior efforts might cause one to despair of hearing a Lohengrin worthy of himself; this performance may be as close as we come. Close enough, for the plenitude of his tone, vibrant, variously colored, and firm, is astonishing even for this most heroic of tenors. Is he too heroic?—after all, Lohengrin is a symbol of such sanctity that lyric tenors are often suggestively pure in much of his music. And even on his best days at this stage of his career (and this is surely one of them), Melchior seems to have lost a portion of lyrical flow at the quieter levels. But both swan episodes are at least satisfactory, and who would wish to sacrifice the overpowering brilliance of 'Heil dir, Elsa! Nun, lass vor Gott uns gehen!' at the end of act two—no single Melchior phrase can exceed its splendor on this afternoon. But the voice is impressive from start to finish, and many moments deserve praise (for instance, the surety of his stepwise ascent to high A at 'hoch über alle Frau'n,' a cause for wonder merely as a physical feat). But then Melchior, unlike Sved, can alter mood in a trice by timbre or volume variance or word inflection, as he does when he turns from his second-act confrontation with Telramund to exclaim 'Elsa! wie seh' ich sie erbeben!'

Leinsdorf, at the helm in 1943, has yet another go at the opera two years later with exactly the same cast (one realizes that the Met was a real company in those days, with singers in residence for lengthy periods and continuous seasons). In spite of his constant campaign to eliminate cuts, plenty of them disfigure all these *Lohengrin* performances. This was only one of the reasons Leinsdorf consistently sought to "end this tortuous affiliation with the Metropolitan Opera"[11] (the specific cause for this bit of hyperbole was a tour performance of *Lohengrin* in which Varnay lost her voice and Thorborg got a nosebleed on stage). Though he was no bad penny, he did keep turning up: in 1945 he was back from the army (preceded by an even briefer sojourn with the Cleveland Orchestra) and still persona grata at the Met. The *Lohengrin* broadcast of 24 February 1945, however, would be his last before a prolonged absence of a dozen years.

According to Cross, *Lohengrin* held the stage at the Met for more consecutive seasons than any other opera and held second place (after *Aida*) in number of performances. From his precurtain remarks we learn that the house is at capacity with hundreds of standees ("as I came into the opera house I saw a line that stretched clear around the block"). Noting that many world-famous singers have appeared in *Lohengrin*, Cross assures us that "the cast today will more than uphold the great traditions of the past."

Consistency was (and is) one of Leinsdorf's many virtues, so this *Lohengrin* holds few surprises. Most of the variances are minimal: Cordon's sound is somewhat woolier; Sved's manner is less frenetic, his interpretation gaining in fullness through dynamic variety and genuine anguish ('mein' Ehr' ist hin!'); Thorborg is very much herself but less happy in the tessitura; Harrell has grown more stalwart, his tone unblemished, and he manages to escape the straitjacket of heraldom by his natural inflections. Overall, Melchior's knight is a notch below the 1943 Lohengrin. Vibrant he is, especially in the final act, perhaps overly heroic, but what can a tenor do with all those Brabantines eternally hailing him as 'Held von Brabant.' He simply will not be harnessed by Leinsdorf, too frequently moving a fraction ahead of the beat and taking little liberties with the rhythms (and there are a few ungainly scoops to top tones). But when he is good, he is very, very good.

The only real surprise of the afternoon is Varnay (substituting for an indisposed Traubel), for again she has grown immeasurably, both in vocal control and in subtlety of interpretation. The increase in delicacy and tenderness of sound and manner is quite remarkable. Where did all these new colors, these bewitching diminuendi and *portamenti*, come from—one would never have thought them possible with her instrument. Her Elsa sounds youthful (Varnay is only twenty-six), and the bloom which nature had denied her she herself has cultivated. Now her artistic sensibilities, her shapely phrasing and poignant word treatment, find a willing accomplice in her responsive voice. Moreover, she has plenty of sound for the big moments, so for once we hear an Elsa who is able to bring the disparate aspects of the role into balance. The full-throated vocalism provided by Varnay (and an aroused Melchior) in the bridal duet is all the more effective for the refinement of Varnay's portrayal in the earlier scenes.

During these years our young Wagner heroine fares well enough. What of her mature counterpart? Traubel had sung her first Brünnhilde in December 1941, and a year later the radio public heard her in another Wagner portrayal. Unlike her Brünnhilde, Traubel's Elisabeth had been buttressed by several years' performances before the radio audience was introduced to her on 19 December 1942. The broadcast holds another novelty; Leinsdorf is not shepherding the Met's Wagner. Fate, with its customary irony, has twined a pair of tart tendrils into the fabric of the occasion: George Szell, who had coached Flagstad in Prague for her initial Met appearances, now guides her successor as Elisabeth; and, in 1946, it would be Szell who would dislodge Leinsdorf from his shaky perch with the Cleveland Orchestra. In Cleveland Szell found the home he had been searching for all his life. Budapest-born, he came out of

Tannhäuser
19 December 1942
Elisabeth
Helen Traubel
Venus
Kerstin Thorborg
Tannhäuser
Lauritz Melchior
Wolfram
Herbert Janssen
Landgrave
Alexander Kipnis
Conductor
George Szell

the German provincial opera houses (Darmstadt and Düsseldorf), moved on to Berlin, and then enjoyed a decade or so as musical director of the Prague German Theatre before the Nazis drove him to democratic soil. American recognition took awhile (Toscanini again came to the rescue with guest engagements in 1941). On 9 December 1942 Szell made his Met debut with *Salome*; a week later came his second appearance with the broadcast *Tannhäuser*.

As Szell moves from the pilgrims' plaint to the sirens' call, a new Wagnerian terrain is unveiled. When Traubel finishes 'Dich, teure Halle' we can only exclaim (as the soprano must have) "Phew!" The thrusting energy of Szell's accompaniment, its heady pace, is as astonishing as the precise articulation and dynamic variety are welcome. These are not exactly the qualities to complement Traubel's gifts, and one suspects that she is unwillingly swept along by Szell's autocratic beat. When she is allowed to catch her breath ('Aus mir entfloh der Frieden') the ebb and flow of her wonderfully warm tones evoke a sympathetic mood until Szell adds *molto* to Wagner's *più mosso* (but how he evokes the bursting joy of Elisabeth at Tannhäuser's return). No wonder the soprano's high B is merely a glancing blow (and slightly flat, at that). Yet one never feels that Szell's highly charged music-making puts poise at risk—it is not self-propelled à la Bodanzky. Those convoluted string passages (when Tannhäuser first greets Elisabeth) are a whirlwind of controlled virtuosity; the brief chords, so articulate and precise, which intercept recitative-like dialogue, speak a command to the singers; even the rapid duet phrases which end the lovers' scene are deftly and lightly done by both singers and orchestra—the pace is fleet, but nuance is not neglected. Everywhere graces may be admired: the clarinet sings with Traubel as she greets Tannhäuser; the entries of soloists and chorus in the act-two ensemble are well defined and their continuity well preserved; the "plodding" motives which introduce the Rome Narrative are evocatively shaped; in the reprise of the Bacchanal music (as Venus reappears) each motive is immaculate in rhythmic design, yet pulsating with life—the list is a long one. So well rehearsed a performance gives us an inkling of the rewards which the hegemony of Szell and a few equals will bring in the next few years of the Johnson regime.

Yet Szell has not tamed Melchior's penchant for anticipation. Though the Hymn to Venus which profanes the hall of song has never been so swift, Melchior manages to outpace Szell—and with rather messy results. Nor is the tenor in his best voice on this afternoon. But by the time of the second-act finale he is undaunted by his lofty task, and later the Rome Narrative is compelling not only for its interpretive fervor but for his now secure, richly colored vocalism. Janssen is again a moving Wolfram, never more resplendent tonally, and this time Szell's ritard forces him to take time for an effective close to the Evening Star aria. Kipnis pours out his near-overripe tone, introduces broad *portamenti*, and grasps center stage when sentencing Tannhäuser—it is a wonderfully succulent turn, and one feels the only thing missing is the sound of a balalaika.

Beginning with the second-act duet, Traubel's vocalism is an unalloyed joy, warm and seamless, her legato almost without equal, the top voice opulent and secure. Interpretively, too, she paints some lovely effects, playing with the feel of the line and mood quite adeptly in the scene with Tannhäuser. She doesn't try for girlish innocence, is rather too assured for the hesitant Elisabeth (those *Heinrich*s are really imperious), and in the quieter episodes merely allows vocal balm to speak for itself (as it does, most effectively). She does offer a delicious moment with her uncle where she fines down her tone and suggests a gentle femininity. Traubel is at her best in her defense of Tannhäuser; here one realizes that she excels when she has time to caress the consonants and let the long lines form themselves into broad parabolas of sound—and she never loses quality when surmounting any orchestral surge. The third-act prayer is less satisfying. She observes all the dynamic markings (with a full complement of crescendos and diminuendos), and the tone is as solid and luscious as one could desire, but she fails to create the mood of inmost sorrow which makes credible Elisabeth's impending death (nuanceful wind solos, sculpted by Szell, help, however).

Leinsdorf was still on the roster this season—as yet, neither Cleveland nor the U.S. Army had called him to service. He is again in the pit for the *Walküre* broadcast of 27 February 1943; here Traubel seems more in her element as the hearty warrior-maid. Again, the absolutely pristine condition of her voice is most impressive. How happy she seems in her battle cry with those triumphant high Bs, and how soothing is her middle and low voice in her sympathetic colloquy with Wotan! Brünnhilde's invitation to Siegmund to accompany her to Valhalla is noble in tone and dignified in manner until she resolves to shield him from Hunding and blazes into the upper octave of her voice—no dearth of excitement blunts the Traubel Brünnhilde. In the final confrontation with Wotan, she pours out wave after wave of splendid, richly colored tone—true, color is uniform (because the voice is seamless, or because the imagination is unplumbing?) and subtlety of word hue is sacrificed; but the emotional involvement is real. To hear the wide-ranging phrases of 'War es so schmäh-lich' traversed by an instrument so constant, so unmanufactured, is in itself deeply satisfying. Her finest effects come when she suddenly lightens her tone (as when Brünnhilde tells Wotan she merely did what she knew he truly wished) and the lyrical moment astounds with its sweet warmth. And then there is her staying power—at opera's end she is as fresh and potent of voice as in her opening volley.

In contrast, Bampton is a bit overmatched by Sieglinde, her third Met performance and first broadcast of the role which she would perform most often during her Met career. The decision evidently had been made that the lighter Wagner heroines were her *Fach*, for the 1942–43 season also brought her first house performances of Elisabeth, Elsa, and Kundry. Obviously Traubel's substance and Varnay's aptitude were not considered sufficient to fill the Flagstad void. The legacy of Bampton's mezzo days comes to her aid as a Wagner heroine. The warmth of her low and middle voice compensates for a certain slenderness and discontinuity of voice and manner in the exultant measures which close 'Der Männer Sippe.' She cannot spin voluminous arcs of tone to sound the ecstasy of 'Du bist der Lenz,' but she can provide some lovely, intimate moments, both vocally and interpretively, in the recognition scene where her gentle manner is a welcome change from more assertive Sieglindes. In act two her characterization of the distraught runaway is quite affecting, and surprisingly, she summons enough vocal heft for the grand pronouncements of act three—not earth-shattering, but not ear-shattering, either.

List, in good voice, is a sufficiently sinister Hunding to cow any Sieglinde (let alone Bampton's mild soul), his lethargic legato almost Fafner-like in gloomy menace. Melchior is at his most baritonal in the early scenes, strikingly heroic in recounting his attempt to save the tortured maiden. One admires again his commitment—he never stands outside the role. Some of the excessive staccato declamation of 'Winterstürme' is abandoned in favor of line, but Leinsdorf does not allow the seasons duet to surge and crest (to both Melchior's and Bampton's detriment); obviously, the conductor prefers to husband the sense of release until the final

Die Walküre
27 February 1943
Sieglinde
Rose Bampton
Brünnhilde
Helen Traubel
Fricka
Karin Branzell
Siegmund
Lauritz Melchior
Wotan
Julius Huehn
Hunding
Emanuel List
Conductor
Erich Leinsdorf

Emanuel List as Hunding in *Die Walküre*.

orchestral peroration of act one (and it is a fine effect). The Brünnhilde-Siegmund episode of act two suffers from a similar containment and lack of tension on Leinsdorf's part, though Melchior's farewell to Sieglinde is apt in its quiet dignity.

The husband and wife team of Wotan and Fricka is well served by the authority of Branzell and the prime vocal condition of Huehn. The baritone, too, has gained a goodly authoritative manner, and his sound is darker and richer in timbre. Huehn's ability to sustain a singing line is his finest asset; the low voice has plenty of resonance so he never needs to bark or pepper his declamation with huffs and puffs, and the top voice remains full and easy. As he moves through the role one senses a certain reserve which prevents him from going the limit, either when raging to Brünnhilde over his earthly troubles (he is better at cowing his warrior daughters in act three) or in summoning the emotional tension for the farewell to Brünnhilde—to the magical moment of the descending chromatic orchestra chords (delineating sleep), Huehn adds no crown of legato curve. Yet his mezza voce at 'Zum letzten Mal' is effective, and many a phrase is set forth with breadth and resonant tone.

Branzell, who would announce her retirement at the end of the next season, is heard in the final broadcast of her twenty consecutive Met seasons. No sign of imminent farewell betrays itself in her portrayal. Yes, the low voice may be a bit less plangent, the legato a mite decomposed, but the inferiority is only to her former self. Where all had once been velvety grandeur, now a slight Clara Butt hootiness invades her tone as she tries for the old volume and grand manner. She is never overparted or vanquished by the role, however, and the voice solidifies as her scene progresses. Her final dignified plea owns all the old assets, and her exit phrase to Brünnhilde is wonderfully sonorous and nobly declaimed. Francis Robinson, that unrivaled purveyor of Met tattle, confirms that Branzell chose to end her Met career (though, as often happens there will be a brief coda) because she was "annoyed and hurt, as well she might have been, that she hadn't been given what she felt was her proper share of the Saturday afternoon broadcasts."[12] For long now, appearances on the broadcasts had been as eagerly coveted as seasonal firsts and new roles. While exposure to radio's larger audience brought increased financial return in concert and radio engagements, for the mature artist like Branzell, the opera broadcasts also provided reassurance of undiminished public appeal and continued favor with management.

Just now it is Thorborg who expropriates Branzell's portion. But the tangled skein of departing Olympians and emerging tyros goes on: appearing as one of the lowly band of warrior sisters in act three is a young American mezzo who, in a few years, would be heard as a broadcast Fricka. Not long thereafter, our Schwertleite would scale further heights as the *Walküre* Brünnhilde, but the steep ascent would be long and difficult for Margaret Harshaw, the 1942 winner of the "Metropolitan Auditions of the Air."

No Wagnerian soprano could claim hegemony without donning Isolde's royal robes. Having secured the *Walküre* and *Götterdämmerung* Brünnhildes, Traubel was now deemed ready for Isolde. After a season's lapse (the first in over two decades), *Tristan* was revived early in the 1942–43 season. In what would turn out to be an age of American Isoldes, Traubel was the first American soprano to portray Isolde since the fabled Lillian Nordica at the turn of the century. It was a role which Flagstad had made uniquely her own, so the stakes were high.

In contrast to the rapture which greeted Flagstad's Isolde in 1935, the critics were slightly patronizing toward Traubel's debut portrayal on 4 December 1942. The radio public had not long to wait in order to form its own judgment. On 6 February Traubel brought the first of ten consecutive Isoldes (one more than Flagstad) to the airwaves. No tentativeness impairs the soprano's opening phrases as Isolde wakens from her reverie; the contrasted inflections of anger, confusion, and wonder are realistically set forth. The ring of 'Nimmermehr! Nicht heut'' is tremendously exciting; 'Mir erkoren' is suitably portentous; the dynamic markings of each line are assiduously observed and the meaning searched. Isolde's narrative blazes when necessary (the entire 'Fluch dir' passage is amazingly massive in sound, a truly glorious outpouring of tone), but the emotions are well contrasted: Isolde's ironic query, 'wie dünkt Euch die zur Eh'?'; the mournful cast of 'Der Mutter Rat gemahnt mich recht' (marked *düster* by Wagner); the *subito piano* at 'Ruh' in der Not'—all these bespeak not merely the carefully prepared artist but the communicative one. She just misses the melting tenderness of 'er sah mir in die Augen' (though she tells with emotion how she allowed the sword to fall from her hand), and her low voice lacks the play of color by which Flagstad's wind timbre illuminated moments like 'Ungeminnt den hehrsten Mann.' Actually, Traubel's low voice on this occasion is not quite as firm and blended to the upper register as usual. She alters a few words here and there and makes a brief false entry at 'mein Herr,' so perhaps she is not yet fully at home with her assignment. Yet the voice is generally superb at all dynamic levels, caressing the

Tristan und Isolde
6 February 1943
Isolde
Helen Traubel
Brangäne
Kerstin Thorborg
Tristan
Lauritz Melchior
Kurvenal
Julius Huehn
Marke
Alexander Kipnis
Conductor
Erich Leinsdorf

ear in the quiet moments ('ein süsser Sühnetrank') and capable of playfully teasing Tristan in act one.

In the love duet of act two both Traubel and Melchior are rather distant in manner until they settle into a melting intimacy at 'Barg im Busen'; Thorborg's poised, dark warning is the perfect complement. With Melchior in fine voice and on his best behavior, the performance overall may be the most beautifully vocalized of the entire *Tristan* series. Nor does Huehn let us down in that regard with his sympathetic tone and liederlike sensitivity in act three. He has grown in interpretation—such beautiful head tones are not often within the ken of a Kurvenal. Then there is Kipnis to complete the quintet of sovereign vocalists. King Marke is his finest effort to date, reverberant in tone and feeling; he avoids entirely the languors inherent in his scene. Kipnis, like all these singers, has a command of both *forte* and *piano* and finds plenty of opportunity to employ the contrast. Neither he nor Melchior is frightened by a *portamento*; unlike Isoldes of old, Traubel rarely honors them. And her Liebestod is less than the sum of its parts. She does not seek the transfigured calm which Flagstad projects in this moment, but rather chooses to animate the successive phrases, thereby achieving some lovely effects: the delicate *piano* shade of 'seht ihr's, Freunde?' is most winning, and one can admire the play of rhythm, line, and dynamics throughout her reading—but the mood dissipates. During the climactic phrases Traubel seems more propelled than in command. If the overall effect is too piecemeal, that lovely floated final note is worth remembering.

The spate of Wagner performances of the first half of the 1940s ends with a less than distinguished *Tannhäuser* on 5 February 1944. Gone is the élan of Szell's interpretation of the previous year. In 1944 Szell had his hands full with a complete *Ring*, *Boris*, *Rosenkavalier*, and *Salome*, so the *Tannhäuser* chore fell to the routinier, Paul Breisach. The methodical overture signals a humdrum afternoon, and Breisach's meandering account of the penitent's pilgrimage at the opening of the third act confirms it. Melchior is never lacking in fervor and is generally in fine form, still able to cope with the tessitura at the end of the second act. The intensity of his declamation and the extraordinary climaxes in the Rome Narrative convey all the bitterness and frenzy of the tormented knight. Kipnis, too, performs at the highest level, his incredibly rich tone vivified by a theatrical (not bogus) reading of the Landgrave's rather prosaic moments.

Varnay is Elisabeth—not one of her best efforts. In fact, with the warmth of Traubel's instrument still in our ears, Varnay's biting tones come as a shock. From the first the voice sounds walled in, the metallic timbre much in evidence. She blunts the rapture of Elisabeth's greeting with acidulous tone (though the climax opens out nicely); the duet is better, as her instrument gains in poise and her phrasing in breadth, yet no suggestion of youthful innocence escapes her twenty-five-year-old throat. But what a moving moment she makes of 'Heinrich, what have you done to me?'—precisely because here her interpretive bounty is matched by vocal ease. The rest of the act is quite effective (she knows how to plead in musical accents). Elisabeth's Prayer is even more disappointing than 'Dich, teure Halle,' however dutiful her effort; the voice's tendency to be sluggish in moving to the core of the note is particularly annoying in this piece—each individual note seems squeezed from her throat, though again the ascent to the climax is impressive (and I do like her flamboyant upward *portamenti* earlier on).

With this afternoon's broadcast we bid farewell to Julius Huehn. Very shortly he will be off to military service, and though he would return after the war for a single

Tannhäuser
5 February 1944
Elisabeth
Astrid Varnay
Venus
Marjorie Lawrence
Tannhäuser
Lauritz Melchior
Wolfram
Julius Huehn
Landgrave
Alexander Kipnis
Conductor
Paul Breisach

season, this admirable artist is to be heard no more by the radio audience. As with Varnay, his Wolfram is not one of his finest efforts: some glimpse of vocal indisposition surfaces by the end of the afternoon (temporary or an omen for the future, one cannot say), and the Evening Star is lacking in poise. After all his Wotans, the mezza voce of the piece does not come easily (Wagnerian cantilena demands a Tibbett, a Bonelli, at least a Janssen). What is most striking about his portrayal is the gain in subtlety and musicality over the years. As a burly-voiced young giant (age twenty-four) when he began his ten-year Met career, he had been more interested in bluster than tonal or musical refinement. On this afternoon Wolfram's Address in act two is all gentleness and devotion to Wagner's intent. His was a path, though regrettably short, well worth traversing with so much honor.

Yet another broadcast farewell gives cause for greater regret. Marjorie Lawrence, after an absence of two years as she fought to conquer the effects of polio, had returned to the Met as Venus the previous season. In spite of her inability to walk, Venus proved a practical stage assignment since the goddess remains on her couch for most of her scene. In the broadcast Lawrence gives a superb reading of the role. The built-in eroticism in the silvery timbre of her middle and upper voice had served her well as Salome and is a potent weapon for Venus as well. What a pleasure it is to hear the high-lying phrases of Venus produced without strain! The voice itself is as fresh and lovely as remembered (the very lowest notes still lacking a bit in color and steadiness), and the overall effect is quite girlishly sensuous in the quiet moments, yet grandly imperious when Venus upbraids Tannhäuser (no splintered tone for this seductress). Unlike most mezzos, she upgrades the role, giving it star quality. The Met rewarded her a month later with a single Isolde (and another on tour), well received by public and press. Not even her vocal prowess and heroic spirit, however, could seduce the Met management into further occupation for this uniquely gifted artist.

Flagstad, Lawrence, Branzell, and Schorr had departed. Would new recruits Janssen and Kipnis, Traubel, Varnay, and Thorborg, with Melchior as constant fulcrum, keep the scales tipped in favor of Wagner? Indubitably, yes—though fair weight for money down was less certain overall.

Risë Stevens as Mignon.

CHAPTER NINETEEN

1941-44
Allies—France Sustained by Britain

When the United States entered the war in 1917, Wagner had been banished from the boards at the Metropolitan. How different is the chronicle of the four war years in the 1940s when German opera remained as a cornerstone of the repertory—was there now a greater maturity in this generation of opera management and public, in spite of the even greater threat which Nazi Germany represented to Western civilization? Not in every case. *Butterfly* suffered a worse fate; subject matter intervened, for the American naval lieutenant's callous treatment of the innocent Japanese geisha could not be swallowed. *Meistersinger*, too, with its glorification of German art, was avoided until 1945. But the rest of Wagner was offered pretty much as in prewar years.

Of course, the Wagnerian wing was so deep in vocal riches that the quality of the company would have been irreparably marred if the Wagner operas had been terminated. Then, too, the absence of German singers among the Wagnerian group undoubtedly helped. Those who were of German background (Lehmann, Janssen) had fled from the Nazis in the 1930s, or were long-time residents of America (Rethberg, List); the other stellar Wagnerians were not German: Branzell, Thorborg, Schorr, Huehn and Melchior.

Flagstad, who returned to Norway, was a special case. Could there be Wagner after Flagstad? The Americans, Traubel, Varnay, and Bampton, provided the answer in resounding fashion, while the singular gifts of Kipnis added a compensatory boon to the male ranks. But it was Melchior who was indispensable throughout all these years. The more troublesome question for the future might well be "could there be Wagner after Melchior?" Four decades later it remains the unanswered question.

A more practical reason for a sound attitude toward wartime musical censorship might lie in the fact that Italy was America's ally in 1917 but was a member of the Axis in the forties. Eliminate both German and Italian opera, and only the shades of Oscar Hammerstein and Mary Garden could possibly have mounted a palatable opera season.

At the beginning of the war, French opera at the Metropolitan was not quite moribund, though the surviving relic had little of the genuine article's puissant fragrance. The probability of resuscitation was greatly enhanced by the coming of a conductor who, though as English as any mad dog, was a devotee of French music and, more pertinent, a recognized exponent of French style. Sir Thomas Beecham remains today a figure of enormous appeal, sui generis in what was an age of charismatic conductors. He was as adroit on the podium as he was trenchant in wit, which is saying a good deal. A large private fortune (Beecham's Pills) enabled him to launch himself in the music world of Britain at the beginning of the century (he founded numerous orchestras, including the London Philharmonic), but only his ability sustained a distinguished musical career over six decades. Beecham's entrepreneurial gift embraced opera, as well: he founded the progenitor of the British National Opera; he introduced many of the Strauss works as well as other little-played operas, including a number from the rich vein of Russian opera. For a few brief years during the war, Beecham lingered in America and the Met again became the beneficiary of Europe's distress. Though with the company for only three seasons, his imprint was strong, for he conducted fifty-eight performances of nine operas.

The conductorial florescence at the Met more often nurtured the through-composed, symphonic operas of the German school, and later Verdi, where the astral light shines most brightly on the podium. Sir Thomas, too, could not resist their allure (*Tristan, Falstaff*). But it was French opera, waif of the modern-age repertory, which profited most from his stewardship, with *Carmen, Faust* and *Le Coq d'Or* (Frenchified from the Russian) in his charge during the 1941–42 season, and *Manon, Louise, Mignon*, and *Hoffmann* in the ensuing years. The broadcast legacy is particularly provident here, for airchecks survive of all the French offerings (*Coq d'Or*, his New York debut opera, was not broadcast). The season's initial performance of *Carmen*, aired on 24 January 1942, marked Beecham's second appearance at the Metropolitan.

Carmen, too, can be a conductor's opera, and Sir Thomas' gifts were precisely attuned to the rhythmic esprit and vibrant orchestral coloration of Bizet's score. For two decades the hands of Hasselmans, Papi, and Pelletier had shaped Met *Carmen*s in indifferent fashion. Beecham is a tonic. The panache of the bullring music in the prelude is no surprise, but one takes heart on hearing the Toreador theme robbed of vulgarity while retaining its insouciance. Too often the local-color episodes which begin the opera are perfunctorily played, but Beecham allows nothing to lag; indeed, the orchestra is occasionally hard put to keep up with him. A breath of life touches every episode: the Morales-Micaela flirtation seems believable in its conversational ambiance (Arthur Kent is a capital Morales, attractive in tone, neat in manner); these cigarette girls do not languish—even the smoke from Beecham's violins floats rapidly down; the arsic airiness that buoys the initial notes of the Gypsy Song phrases reveals one secret of Beecham's elegant style. More comes to light in the unforced flow of the entr'actes, and the Mozartian delicacy of the third-act entr'acte (for Bizet *is* nineteenth-century Mozart) is carried over into the gypsy march in the mountains— nothing grubby about these smugglers. A rather sedately paced quintet retains a scherzo quality, and Beecham the dramatist gives an ironic twist to the wind 'Eh bien?' in the midsection. The delicate precision of the wind treatment extends to the singers—Frasquita and Mercedes are made to purl their sixteenth-note flourishes in the card scene with fastidious exactitude. Excerpts from *L'Arlésienne* are interpolated for the ballet; though the dancers are unseen, Beecham's graphic shaping of each

Carmen
24 January 1942
Carmen
Lily Djanel
Micaela
Licia Albanese
Don José
Charles Kullman
Escamillo
Leonard Warren
Conductor
Sir Thomas Beecham

phrase provides an aural mirror for their movement (although a few ensemble warts blemish one of the dances).

Throughout the opera sentimentality is abjured; will sentiment be allowed? In the major set pieces Beecham encourages individual expression, following each artist with utmost care—he is a benevolent despot, a conductor who actually listens to his singers.

Even with the ebullient Beecham in command, *Carmen* must have a stage personality of equal élan. Farrar and Jeritza easily had qualified early in the century, but approval had eluded Ponselle, while Bourskaya and Wettergren were ciphers, and neither Castagna's vocal opulence nor Swarthout's discreet glamour had made for a memorable gypsy. No obvious candidate was on the scene (in the wings, perhaps—the Stevens Carmen was four years in the offing). In the meantime Frank St. Leger, knowing in the ways of the theater and now musical secretary of the Met, offered a solution in the person of Lily Djanel. A few months before the *Carmen* broadcast he wrote Beecham:

> Madame Djanael [*sic*] has been in to see us and she is a very interesting personality. Here is an artist who is truly French and very chic. I am personally of the opinion that she will be a great asset to the Company. . . . Her vivacity and her enthusiasm are so infectious that in these days of more sombre personalities she may click.[1]

St. Leger knew his commodities, but he was also a realist. "I believe we should gamble on her," he concluded. The gamble was on the voice.

Djanel proved sufficiently interesting to remain the Met's Carmen for five seasons. Though Cross, too, described her as "the French lyric soprano," she was Belgian-born and called herself a *demi caractère* (lirico spinto). Paris-trained she was, and a veteran of a dozen years of Carmen performances (five of them—1935 to 1940—at the Paris Opéra and Comique). But occupied Paris was no longer home to her, and after South American engagements, she turned to the Met, making her debut in the broadcast *Carmen*. A decidedly wayward Habanera sets the odds against her. The voice, rather slender and slightly acidulous, flutters unduly and is sharp in the big moments; moreover, the aria is pulled badly out of shape by an overabundance of interpretive business. She injects a hint of the devil-at-work into the final verse, however, and the ensuing exchange with José is vivid. By the time she reaches the Seguidilla, the voice has settled, its timbre honed to an almond-tinted glow, and the volatility of the character is tellingly projected. Madame Djanel is, after all, the product of the French lyric theatre where the word commands and style reigns. When she utters 'Pourquoi?' to Zuniga in the tavern, or admits 'Je suis amoureuse,' the inflection is so *juste* that we succumb. When she dances for José her *la la*'s are incredibly jolly (a Carmen confident of her charms, she doesn't have to sell herself), and though her upbraiding of her recalcitrant lover is lacking in weight, it has plenty of bite (she and Beecham are momentarily out of sync in the 'ta-ra-ta-ta' bit). When she takes the high option at 'La liberté,' she affirms her claim as soprano, but the low-lying card scene (conveniently taken at a fast tempo by Beecham) is warm enough in tone. No vocal tricks cheapen her final act—she is content to let style and language convey the dignity of Carmen's resistance. Overall, the St. Leger gamble (one must resist the temptation to call it legerdemain) has paid off. Is Djanel a memorable Carmen?—probably not. But she is "very interesting."

The qualities which Djanel has in abundance are just what Warren lacks; his

Lily Djanel as Carmen. Photography by Bruno of Hollywood.

Toreador is stolid in inflection but bright in song, full of force but without swagger. His occasional attempts at head tone bespeak the conscientious, if unfinished, artist. Albanese's Micaela, on the other hand, is fully realized. The phrases of the duet are exquisitely molded by both conductor and soprano. Beecham would linger even more in the aria, but Albanese takes it on to a thrilling climax with a genuine *messa di voce* to lead back into the reprise. The afternoon's longest applause is hers. Kullman seems too effete for the violence-prone soldier and renegade; his timbre lacks virility, and he is most comfortable in the light, lyrical recall of his mother. Nevertheless, a tenor who begins the Flower Song at a *piano* dynamic deserves honor—he makes the aria more of a narrative than a solo display. His intelligence aids him in the final moments of act three and in the last act, where fervor and dramatic and musical honesty combine to overbalance a built-in simper in the voice.

The Met *Carmen* changes little over the next several years. Eventually the baton passes back to Pelletier, Jobin becomes the dominant José, Sved and Valentino play Toreador as Warren moves on to better things. Of the next four broadcasts, only one (27 March 1943) is available to us. We hear a more restrained Beecham on this occasion—the hint of the pell-mell is gone from the first act, and hardly a touch of frenzy penetrates the Gypsy Song until the orchestral peroration. Even in this tour performance (Chicago), Beecham manages to keep the orchestral and choral forces on point (Sir Thomas' third-act smugglers obviously enjoy their work with little thought of danger), and he mixes sensuousness and dash equitably in the ballet music. Unlike Beecham, Djanel has trouble recapturing the *juste milieu* of her earlier performance. For a good deal of the opera, *femme fatale* seems emblazoned on her chest; insinuation recedes in favor of broader vocal and dramatic gestures, and now chest tone is often employed to cope with the low tessitura. Yet she is vocally more secure (both the Gypsy Song and the card scene are well controlled), and the finesse of Djanel and Jobin in the recitatives is pleasing. When Don José faces her, knife in hand, Djanel again summons the remembered restraint and strength that lend Carmen dignity in death.

With Warren the pattern of reversals continues, for he shows a perceptible gain in suavity and esprit, both in vocalism and expression. Perhaps some of Beecham's sophistication has begun to rub off. Now Warren knows enough to be gruff to José, to taunt Carmen—elementary, but missing heretofore. 'Si tu m'aimes' is nicely covered, and his line is elegant. Call it an artistic ripening for the American baritone. Albanese continues to provide the major vocal pleasure of these performances. The soprano was so at home in the verismo idiom that critics are apt to forget how secure was her vocal grounding: all those delicious diminuendi and downward *portamenti*, her liquid legato, the skillful transition through the *passaggio* in those ascending phrases which sorely try so many sopranos—these are no ordinary gifts. And in the duet she can suggest the ingénue without loss of timbre. Albanese sang six broadcast Micaelas, and of the three which are preserved, this is the finest (the commercial record of the complete Reiner *Carmen* made in the early fifties does not capture quite all the charm and vocal skill of the house performances from the forties).

Of the new participants, Lorenzo Alvary's thick, Hungarian-tinged French contrasts with Jobin's native speech in their scenes together, though Alvary has the vocal weight and know-how for Zuniga. As Morales, Mack Harrell is oddly ill at ease—he misses his first entrance, but then this is his first and only Met Morales—a tour duty perhaps. Yet to hear him expand a phrase like 'Que cherchez-vous, la belle?' is to make one long to hear his Valentin. Jobin, too, knows how to shape a phrase with elegance ('Parle-moi de ma mère'). His voice loses color in its lower octave, and the Flower Song is rather bleak-toned and businesslike—not enough romance here to tempt Carmen—but his climaxes are always well focused (the end of act three is quite thrilling). When he combines stylistic acuity, command of language, and forceful expression, as in the final act, the impact is far from negligible.

Jobin and Kullman were stalwarts of the Met's French wing at this time, and they alternate in the *Faust* broadcasts under Beecham's direction. Major scenes of the 14 March 1942 *Faust* have been preserved, though the sound is below par for this period. Kullman contributes a dreamy 'Salut! demeure' with a perfect blend of ardor and refinement, his timbre well suited to the moment and the high B absolutely secure. Beecham's penchant for leisurely tempi throughout the opera works well here.

Carmen
27 March 1943

Carmen
Lily Djanel
Micaela
Licia Albanese
Don José
Raoul Jobin
Escamillo
Leonard Warren
Conductor
Sir Thomas Beecham

Faust
14 March 1942

Marguerite
Licia Albanese
Siebel
Lucielle Browning
Faust
Charles Kullman
Valentin
Leonard Warren
Méphistophélès
Norman Cordon
Conductor
Sir Thomas Beecham

With *Butterfly* banished for the duration of the war, a new star vehicle was needed for Albanese; Marguerite was this season's choice. For several years she would be the Met's prime Marguerite (four broadcasts and the opening night of the 1944-45 season). On this afternoon she is not entirely happy in the role. The Marguerite who spins and wonders has little of the ingénue charm of her first-act Micaela. The recitatives which interrupt her musing come to life, but the line of the ballad is sticky, as though the French gets in her way—all those *n's* in the nasal vowels are intrusive. The Jewel Song is decidedly cut-rate at Beecham's slow tempo, with no attempt at a trill (but a ringing conclusion). Things improve markedly thereafter. Albanese captures a good deal of the calm awe of 'O silence,' and tenor and soprano purvey the gentle romance of the duet. When Albanese reaches the more dramatic moments of the score, she is on even firmer ground: the apostrophe at her window is highly charged and superbly vocalized, while the drama of the church scene is vividly conveyed in accents of fear and supplication. Best of all is the finale of the opera where the gentle, liquid tone which eluded her in the garden scene now anoints the memory of her first meeting with Faust—she utters 'Non, non' with resigned contentment, the lyric phrases spin deliciously, and the martial rhythms and soaring phrases of the trio ring out triumphantly.

Beecham's second act is rather disjointed; now the tempi languish, now accelerandi invade; but the bourgeois accents of the 'Roi de Thulé' introduction are effective, and he does strike fire as Faust presses Marguerite. His control of line and dramatic pace at the end of the church scene (and, above all, in the closing phrases of the opera) elevates Gounod's music a notch or two.

Votipka's work in the garden scene is full of character, its humor as deft as Cordon's is heavy-handed. Cordon does have the dark vocal menace for Méphisto's invocation to the night. Though wedded to merely unloading tone, his is a stout voice, as is apparent in the church scene where the vocal quality and legato have merit. Still, to find Cordon in this star assignment seems unexpected, and it decidedly was. In one of the more bizarre episodes of operatic annals, Pinza (scheduled for this broadcast) found himself interned on Ellis Island as an enemy alien. Two days earlier FBI agents had entered his house "through the back door without ringing the bell,"[2] searched the house and arrested him. He was accused of receiving and sending secret messages, wearing a swastika ring, being a personal friend of Mussolini, and organizing a collection of gold for the Italian government in 1935. Only the final charge (it turned out to be the contribution of a gold ring at the time of Italy's invasion of Ethiopia) had any basis in fact, but Pinza was not acquitted until a second hearing (with the aid of Mayor La Guardia and personal character witnesses Votipka and Wilfred Engelman). He was released on 4 June. Regular visits to a parole officer were required until his unconditional release in February 1944. Pinza attributed the whole debacle to "the fierce jealousy of a fellow bass."[3] Engelman and assistant conductor Giacomo Spadoni sealed Pinza's acquittal with their letter stating that "on several occasions of recent date we have heard an American bass state that he personally is responsible for exposing to the FBI Ezio Pinza's political conversation"; the American claimed he "never had an opportunity to sing because Ezio Pinza was the first basso of the Metropolitan."[4] And so he was and would remain, until the Broadway stage lured him away five years later. Fortunately, many broadcasts lay in Pinza's future, even though the most ridiculous of the charges against him had been that he sent "coded messages from the stage of the Metropolitan Opera House during the Saturday-matinee broadcasts"[5] through changes of tempo in his singing. Pinza was never one to go against a conductor's beat, and the whole affair proved to be a contretemps, but it was a painful episode for the basso.

When *Faust* was next heard (30 January 1943), Pinza was back in devils' garb, as magnetic and self-assured as ever. Beecham's conducting was far from satanic, but the same adjectives apply (and this time we have a complete performance for confirmation). In spite of most critics' incipient mockery of Gounod's opera, Beecham placed it among the dozen operas that are "the quintessence of lyrical charm and beauty."[6] He readily admitted that Gounod's was not Goethe's *Faust* ("frankly, music does not wed itself happily to philosophy, ethics or political subjects") but championed it for remaining within "the wise and prescribed orbit of the true composer" in that "it makes an appeal to nothing but the sense of beauty in sound."[7] Sir Thomas always did have a penchant for the hyperbolic. Often present in his speech, occasionally it infected his music-making, and there, too, it was something to cherish, as is evident in this performance.

Beecham makes the disparate elements of the prelude and prologue cohere with an easy fluency. Throughout the opera he never confuses charm with triviality, and if he lingers overlong in sensuous sound, he provides a counterbalance in the enormous élan of the more animated episodes. He is aided in this by the muscular vocalism of his three male principals—the close of the Faust-Méphisto encounter is positively rousing. Jobin's authority and security are positive attributes in the discursive pages of the score (an excellent first act, with many vivid touches) but less salutary in the romantic heart of the opera. Seldom has 'Salut! demeure' received such modest applause. He has little of Kullman's ardor in the duets, though 'O nuit d'amour' is nicely shaped and colored. The prison scene profits by a more ingratiating tone color in the middle voice than Jobin usually commands, and he evidently believes in Marguerite's plight. Of course, he must contend with vocal giants throughout the opera. Pinza has seldom been in better form vocally, and a bit of the brittle ostentation of earlier performances has worn away. Plenty of aplomb and brio remain, however: he is the vocal spendthrift in 'Le veau d'or,' and Votipka and he enjoy to the hilt their byplay in the garden scene. Unexpectedly, his suave Serenade falters in the second verse as he and Beecham part company; seemingly unhappy with the tempo, the bass makes a false entrance and loses the beat again at 'Ne donne un baiser.' But there are no Chaliapin grotesqueries; Pinza is a rather subdued tormentor of Marguerite in church and retains his dignity in the final scene. Though the portrayal is grandly conceived, this devil would rather sing than caricature.

Albanese's Marguerite, too, is more fully realized. In the two or three phrases of her meeting with Faust in the Kermesse she signals a greater refinement: her tone and manner are all youthful delicacy, and the self-possession in these few lines conjures character to an amazing degree. The promise is kept in the garden scene where the voice flows gently in the ballad; how astutely she manages to suggest Marguerite's boredom (a daring conceit, lest the audience take it to heart), coming to life in Marguerite's asides. The Jewel Song is quite lively and playful now (still no trill—but then Marguerite-epitomy Fanny Heldy had none, and Melba was still singing Marguerite back then—and the dynamic stresses are more Italianate than French). Albanese's way is ever to convert any display piece into a dramatic situation, though in this case, when glitter is abjured, the essential artifice of the genre is slighted. She fills the duets with gracefully arched phrases and delightful demitints of liquid tone, including a vault to a *pianissimo* high A in the 'O silence! O bonheur!' section, one of the loveliest phrases ever to come from Albanese's throat. Beecham all

Faust
30 January 1943

Marguerite
Licia Albanese

Siebel
Lucielle Browning

Faust
Raoul Jobin

Valentin
John Charles Thomas

Méphistophélès
Ezio Pinza

Conductor
Sir Thomas Beecham

John Charles Thomas as Athanaël in *Thaïs*.

but lets the scene wither—languid comes dangerously close to lethargic. At Marguerite's window the soprano evokes the grand style in phrase and tone, while in church and prison her Marguerite takes on tragic stature, the melodic memories enchantingly recalled in contrast to the assured vigor of 'Anges purs' as she summons heaven's aid.

Singing his first Metropolitan Valentin on this afternoon is John Charles Thomas—it will be the last opportunity his enormous public will have to hear him in opera over the airwaves. A single Valentin in February (plus a tour performance in April) closes a Metropolitan career which numbered only thirty-five performances in New York and eighteen on tour over a period of ten years. He came late to the company, and his immense popularity in the concert halls and on radio shows limited his operatic appearances. Only fifty-one years old at his Met leave-taking, Thomas would continue to sing on the popular media for years to come.

Certainly no call to retirement is sounded in his singing on this afternoon. And he is on his best behavior, endeavoring to meld his expansive vocalism and command of French style into a convincing entity. The familiar outpouring of tone and breadth of phrase are modified here and there to produce unexpected subtleties (the quiet close and loving caress to 'Reste là sur mon coeur' just before the aria). The image of radio popularizer and homespun cutup recedes, though he cannot resist a final show of vocal bravado by interpolating a superb high A-flat at the aria's close. Thomas proclaims a noble defense as he crosses the devil, and here Beecham energizes the drama most effectively. The brief scene with Siebel, where Valentin learns of Marguerite's disgrace, strikes fire, and Pinza and Thomas meet on equal ground in the trio. The death scene is finely conceived as Thomas offers vocal grandeur free from realistic strangulation, thereby heightening the menace of the curse—a noble exit for the baritone, but lamentably too soon.

Two weeks earlier Beecham had applied his knowing way to Massenet, the boulevardier whose image Romain Rolland fancied every Frenchman carried in his inner heart. If one could look into Beecham's heart, the likeness undoubtedly would be that of Sir Thomas himself, but he was in tune with the sophisticated sensibility of this most prolific of late nineteenth century French opera composers. Though their matter is more often ingratiating than profound, Massenet's operas are nevertheless apt fodder for conductors: their orchestration is invariably masterful in deployment and coloration, and Beecham's temperament readily responds to their tangy theatricality. In the *Manon* performance of 16 January 1943, even he cannot resist the temptation (Massenet always courted temptation) to inflate a few of the orchestral effects to near-Wagnerian proportions, but for the most part his way with the score complements, or rather enhances, the composer's efforts. Though he might have cosseted Sayão's Manon a bit more judiciously, she, too, profits from Beecham's adroit treatment of the score, and this time she has in Kullman a Des Grieux more in line with her own proclivities. With De Paolis and Cehanovsky to the manner born as aged roué and willful seducer, a trio of musically accurate chatterers (Greer, Stellman, and Browning), and Moscona at his best as the stern but elegant Comte des Grieux, the components for a satisfying performance are at hand. Brownlee easily conveys the good-fellow bluster of soldier Lescaut, but his open, monochromatic tone and disjunct line again weary the ear.

Though Kullman disappoints in the big moments of the Saint-Sulpice scene, elsewhere his Des Grieux has the welcome musical manners of a Chevalier and the fervor of a youth in love. That touch of treacle in his voice does no disservice to

Manon
16 January 1943

Manon
Bidú Sayão
Des Grieux
Charles Kullman
Lescaut
John Brownlee
Count
Nicola Moscona
Conductor
Sir Thomas Beecham

Massenet's hot-house phrases. I like particularly his meeting with Manon; how well he conveys the open manner of the earnest seminarian, the sudden intoxication of discovery—one really believes when he cries 'Je ne suis plus mon maître.' In his hands the simplicity of 'Le rêve' charms; on the other hand, one wonders if the 'petite table' should generate the excess of passion which Sayão pours into the slight proportions of the aria (one cannot deny the bracing theatricality of her delivery). Kullman's vocalism unexpectedly turns throaty later in the opera, and his normally dulcet tone returns only when he succors Manon on the road to Le Havre.

If one occasionally questions the wisdom of Sayão's vocal prodigality (at the end of the Saint-Sulpice scene and in the closing ensemble of the Hôtel Transylvanie) one can only praise the completeness of her characterization and the manifold charms of her singing. No singer could be more captivating in the inn scene: the childlike giddiness of the entrance aria spills forth in tones of mint silver; 'Voyons, Manon' (sans simper) is no demure reverie but the musing of a fifteen-year-old who already knows what she wants; one relishes the sly cunning with which she suggests confiscating Guillot's coach. Equally triumphant (though entirely different) is her Cours la Reine scene (shorn of its opening and the ballet): 'Je marche sur tous les chemins' has brilliance and precision (would that the wind flourishes were equally apt), and she offers as a bonus the *fabliau* which Massenet, ever the compliant servitor of women, added for one of his Manons. Here Sayão's tart staccati are amazingly accurate and as adamantine as Manon's little heart. The piece adds little to the opera, however, and we are glad to hear the Gavotte in the gambling scene, ambling along in Beecham's sedate tempo and superbly controlled by the soprano despite ineffectual support from a sickly-toned male chorus. Subtle word play animates her moving declamation of 'Ces murs silencieux,' while the seduction scene alternately reveals Manon's insistent allure and exposes the vocal mannerisms which Sayão must adopt to achieve dramatic ends ('UH-Oui! je fus coupable!'). But what a generous spirit lives within that slim body! Heart and soul are expended in this performance, so when Manon expires (with some of Sayão's most delicate vocal effects), we fully share Des Grieux's regret.

The *Manon* performance is the best of Beecham thus far, the full palette of Massenet's skillful orchestration well cultivated, superbly paced, bracing in its passion, and savory where only confection is to hand. An even greater challenge is Beecham's next charge, Charpentier's *Louise*, heard on the broadcast of 20 February 1943. Surviving its fin de siècle birth (thanks to the city of Paris as midwife) and carrying the burden of social comment, this stepchild of the French repertory required all of Beecham's wiles to make a coherent whole of its disparate parts.

Staring him in the face is that trifling arpeggiated motive which opens the opera; Beecham gives it a more stately cast than usual, with a disjunct articulation, but the relief is only momentary as the thematic cell spreads cancerlike throughout the entire piece, intruding at every likely, or unlikely, moment. But Beecham is undaunted, reveling in the passages of sentiment, whipping up the waltz tunes with intoxicating abandon (after all, Paris, three-quarter time, and free love make a heady vintage, though the wine may be only cheap champagne), and smartly serving up the blatant tinsel of the Coronation of the Muse of Montmartre. Not for nothing was he the veteran of all those Lollipops concerts. He nourishes the symphonic continuity of the score and savors every orchestral nuance until one is willing to ignore sage judgment ("unwholesome" and "opportunist . . . something Puccinian unredeemed by Puccini's musical genius" is Andrew Porter's evaluation of the opera)[8] and

Louise
20 February 1943
Louise
Grace Moore
Mother
Doris Doe
Julien
Raoul Jobin
Father
Ezio Pinza
Conductor
Sir Thomas Beecham

succumb to Virgil Thomson's contemporary assessment of this Met revival as "a pretty poignant piece of musical theatre."⁹

And a good deal may be admired in the performance, though it falls short of distinction. The full complement of Met secondary singers admirably disport themselves as people of the Paris streets: Cehanovsky, Alvary, Garris, Gurney (a firm-voiced but characterless Ragpicker) are joined by the Philosopher of Walter Cassel, now in his first Met season and soon to move into major roles. De Paolis is an unlikely Noctambulist, only partially successful in broadening his tone to comply with his role as 'le Plaisir de Paris' but more in his element as the King of Fools. Of the occupants of the atelier (Olheim, Stellman, Browning, Petina, Kaskas, et al.), Votipka is the most suggestive as she spins some lovely tones in Camille's arietta.

Though these vignettes of Parisian life are essential to Charpentier's evocation of the lure of the City of Light, the opera demands a quartet of forceful singing actors. Doris Doe's Mother is a weak link in the family group. While she suggests the weary bitterness of the Mother, too often it is called forth by worn tone which issues from poorly blended registers. When Louise's mother interrupts the revelry of Montmartre to beg Louise to return to her ill father, one of the dramatic climaxes of the opera is muted—Doe is outmatched by the role. Nor, in the vituperative final scenes, does she muster the command necessary to qualify as the villain of the piece. With Pinza the case is almost the reverse. When he enters in act one, who could believe this vibrant-toned male to be a poor Paris workman—he seems outsized in sensuous sound and vocal thrust for the part. But his sincerity will out, and a few poignant words, movingly uttered by him as the act ends, prepare us for his triumph in act four. There his torment at Louise's defection is quietly conveyed in tones undeniably beautiful but governed by inner sorrow. The voice, so Italianate in act one, is now more collected; though a few phrases are high for him, he doesn't dodge them. The honey gloss of his tone serves the Lullaby well, and he is both mighty and broken as he alternately rages and pleads when his daughter hears again the call of Paris.

As Julien, Jobin has authority and style on his side. He begins with some strangled phrases, but his is an assured portrayal, strong and believable as he woos Louise in act two ('Si tu m'aimes, Louise'), making little effect in the Serenade, but at his best in the love duet of act three.

And what of Miss Moore, heard in her most famous role? As Louise, one had expected to witness her artistic coming of age (a late arrival, for she was now in her early forties), but ultimately a sense of disappointment settles. The part had long been in her repertory, and multiple performances before Parisian audiences could have garnered an authentic manner. The conception had been polished by both Charpentier and Mary Garden, and the 1938 film version of director Abel Gance (Georges Thill as Julien) had solidified Moore in the public mind as the real article. On this Saturday afternoon, however, she plays with a heavy hand. From her first entrance one feels this Louise is a determined woman; her conception holds little of the midinette awakening to life. Early on, an overlay of coarseness warps her interpretation, and it thickens as the performance progresses. Vocally, she is not quite free in act one (in fact, everyone seems undervocalized at the start of this matinee), though the firmness of her middle voice stands her in good stead in declamatory phrases. When she utters 'mon bien-aimé!' in response to Julien's tempting in the second act, she could be naming her nemesis rather than her lover. (Perhaps this is a dramatic subtlety of her conception, but Moore was not given to that sort of thing.)

No self-immersion of remembrance informs the opening of 'Depuis le jour' (down a half tone), but she is not deficient in rapture, soon abetted by Beecham's propulsive surge. She appears (needlessly) to be ill at ease about meeting the vocal challenges; a slight hoarseness invades the middle voice. Her start-and-stop method ruptures the mood of the aria and dissipates the artful amalgam of remembered passion which Charpentier contrived for this moment. In earlier days, the erotic sheen of her voice alone would have carried the day, but now the top has a harder edge, and she mixes an overabundance of chest into the lower tones. Yet ecstasy lurks in the air, and she manages some brilliant moments. Grace Moore was not one to be easily downed, and the rest of the act finds her gaining her best form. The voice takes on a lovelier glow, and she gives herself to the music, singing with tremendous exuberance and vibrant tone—how well suited is she by temperament to this expansive, uncomplicated rapture! She rekindles it in the final moments of the opera: we believe her when she cries 'libre,' as she captures the frenetic abandon of the waltz melody and calls 'Paris, Paris' in intoxicating tones. De Schauensee, always an astute observer, called her the most "plausible"[10] Louise the Metropolitan had known (and he had heard Farrar and Bori at the Met, as well as Garden, the most celebrated Louise of all).

Miss Moore was intent on conquering more of the French repertory. In a note to Edward Johnson a few months after the *Louise* broadcast, she recalled that Frank St. Leger had recommended *Thaïs* as an appropriate vehicle for her peculiar talents. With her characteristic humility she reminded "Eddie" that the current year was her twentieth anniversary "as a star" (the early date refers to Broadway, not the Met). She assured him that "nothing in the world would give me more personal happiness, or I am sure be of more nation-wide interest" than that she should open the next Metropolitan season. With an equal dash of coquetry and patriotism, she opined that "in these days of Progressive America . . . it would be a wonderful thing if your 'little Tennessee prima donna' could, after these many years of being a Metropolitan star, have the honor on this momentous anniversary of participating in a Metropolitan opening," adding an unintentionally prophetic close: "before it is too late!"[11] Neither *Thaïs* nor an opening night would ever be hers at the Met. For his ninth opening (1943–44) Johnson eluded all prima donna ire by offering the unlikely *Boris Godunov* with Pinza in the place of honor.

Another star of stage, screen, and radio was more successful than Moore in garnering opening nights. Lily Pons had opened the current season (1942–43) as *La Fille du Régiment*, and four years later her Lakmé would decorate the opening night boards. (In the forties, bonbons, though short of spectacle and musical substance, were considered adequate fare for first nighters.)

Lakmé was a favorite Pons vehicle during these years and was savored by the radio public in both the 1941–42 and 1942–43 seasons. Whether at Pons' or Beecham's injunction, his command of the French repertory did not extend to either *La Fille* or *Lakmé*. The routinier evidently would suffice for a Pons outing at the Met—St. Leger did her opening night honors as well as the *Lucia* which opened the 1942 broadcast season. Pelletier, as he had in 1940 and 1941, husbanded the *Lakmé* of 9 January 1943. One cannot expect the distinction of a Beecham, but when material and man are well mated, a knowledgeable routinier will do, as Pelletier proves on this occasion: he propels Delibes' salon melodies along before their delicate blooms can wither, and he grasps the gestural impulses of each brief ballet segment.

With Delibes, one cannot always sense when he passes from divertissement to drama—they have so much in common. Of course, this is made-to-order ware for

Lakmé
9 January 1943

Lakmé
Lily Pons
Mallika
Helen Olheim
Gerald
Jacques Gerard
Frederic
Mack Harrell
Nilakantha
Norman Cordon
Conductor
Wilfred Pelletier

Pons which, in large part, explains why her Lakmé is a satisfactory creation even without the pleasing visual rewards of her person. She is not in top vocal form on this afternoon, however. The middle and low portions of the voice initially sound quite decimated, the tone so fragile that the afternoon ahead seems long and perilous. (A month earlier Pons had to cancel her first Lakmé, resulting in the infamous debut of Marie Wilkins. A current contestant in the "Auditions of the Air," Wilkins saved the night for the management, but the Met standard was further sullied.) Pons may well have been suffering from a lingering indisposition at the time of the broadcast—the tendency to flat is more pronounced than usual. Nevertheless, Pons understands the style and deftly animates the little twists and turns of the duet with Mallika (how different from the lugubrious renditions of better coloratura sopranos of a later age). Olheim, however, is a complete cipher and their ensemble is atrocious.

The Bell Song was always a reliable Pons war-horse and remains so, even on this occasion: the bells chime in brilliant little spurts of energy, the staccati are neat and jolly. And she is not content merely to walk through this piece but seems quite intent on conveying the drama of the Hindu maiden's plight. The top notes are secure, and enough of the old brilliance remains to provoke some of the most enthusiastic applause of these early broadcasts. Perhaps reassured, she begins to spend her vocal capital a bit recklessly as she applies pressure to the lower octave, to the advantage of characterization. By the third act she pays the price, and we hear some uncharacteristic acidulous, even abrasive, Pons tones.

Cordon, on the other hand, offers some of his finest singing, making a capital menace of Nilakantha. Still, he is unable to modify his solid instrument to impart pathos to the second-act aria. The English contingent fares well: Frances Greer has some lovely brief moments as Ellen, the forward point of her timbre especially apt for French opera. By means of elegant singing, excellent French, and dramatic involvement, Mack Harrell succeeds in elevating Gerald's friend, Frederic, to major-role status. The hero of the afternoon (and he proves worthy of the epithet) is the French-Canadian tenor, Jacques Gerard, new to the Met. A protégé of Pelletier, Gerard came to the Met after schooling in France and fifteen years with the provincial and major French houses (debut at Liège in 1927, the Opéra Comique in the early thirties). Gerard had even partnered Pons in Lakmé in that never-never land of operatic history, her pre-Met days in the French provinces (La Baule Casino, 1928). Kolodin does Gerard a disservice (one must beware of such curt dismissals throughout his Metropolitan bible) when, lamenting the company practice of presenting unprepared and untried young artists on its hallowed boards, he mentions Gerard in a list that includes the aforementioned Marie Wilkins.[12] The facts of Gerard's career belie that judgment and, happily, so does his broadcast debut.

His voice, not overlarge, is entirely rooted in the French language. Unlike Harrell, who successfully grafts his French onto a central sound, Gerard's instrument is inseparable in timbre and technique from his native tongue. Often ill suited to the idioms of other nations, a voice grounded in French technique can make vivid and charming what had seemed merely artificial or cloying or palatable only in the salon. Even a distanced passion takes on life under its sway. Why?—because the language conditions a linear approach, and Delibes' melodies thrive under it. (Pons, too, and even Harrell, often limn their phrases with this fine-tipped brush.) Gerard's diction is clear throughout the entire range, the nasals almost overemphatic but lending color, and the tone quality is surprisingly youthful (his pictures in Opera News suggest a middle-aged bourgeois), a bit shallow but never unpleasant, though there is no velvet on the tone. Surprisingly, he is more than up to the larger aspects of this seemingly ungrateful role. In the climaxes of the opera, Gerard's stout high B-flats, a lively rhythmic sense, and an ardent manner make Gerald more sufferable than he deserves. (A favorite picture from the old *Victor Book of the Opera* strays into the mind—Martinelli and De Luca playing unlikely British soldiers. What could Martinelli possibly have made of this feckless hero?)

Kolodin asks, "Who remembers Gerard et al.?" In Gerard's case, very few, for he never sang on the broadcasts again, though he remained at the Met for four seasons singing a few performances each year of Hoffmann, Wilhelm Meister, Don José, and Roméo. Pons, of course, would endure for another dozen seasons.

The *Lakmé* of Pelletier-Pons-Gerard is briskly dispatched, but sentiment is in short supply. Some may well think French opera is best set forth as a cool *glace*, but Beecham serviced a wider palate as he continued to dominate the French repertory in the 1943–44 season. Even without Pons in his orbit, the show-biz spectrum of operadom seemed inordinately Beecham's lot this season. The Met's current media event was the baptism by fire of "the baby of the Met" (the description is from Milton Cross in the broadcast *Mignon* of 25 December 1943), and Sir Thomas was the chosen anointer. In February eighteen-year-old Patrice Munsel (born and bred in Spokane, Washington) won the "Auditions of the Air" and a Met contract, though she had appeared on no opera stage and her first professional appearance with orchestra (the Utah State Orchestra) preceded her Met debut by only a few months. Concert manager Sol Hurok's promotional machine was already hard at work image-making; only a splashy Met debut would serve, no matter how ill served was the debutante by the hype. Of course, the press smelled Talley-bait, and Munsel (and the management) was cruelly castigated at her first appearance as Philine. Three weeks later (the broadcast), with several more Met performances under her belt, the soprano showed a bit more of the mettle that would keep her a member of the company for fifteen consecutive seasons—the route would hold many valleys until her saucy stage manner and personal charm found a proper outlet.

That Munsel's training (several years with private teachers and coaches in New York) had been solid is evident in her broadcast debut: her recitatives have a respectable French élan, and, for the most part, her skimming of Philine's frivolous music reeks of self-assurance. The middle voice has a hearty color and her theatrical zest is evident (natural stage laughter is not an easy thing to counterfeit, and Munsel exhibits a very knowing manner as she taunts Mignon in her boudoir). Her staccati can become glassy as they ascend and the timbre turn overbrilliant, reaching into stridency at the very top. But she brings off a few delightful coloratura flights ('Qui m'aime' in act one), and the top E-flats and Fs in alt are definitely real. It is the Polonaise which betrays the novice. She does understand (or expert coaching has conveyed it) the rhetoric of the piece, matching the rhythms and accents of the music to the text quite convincingly, and the timbre is apt for this brilliant display piece. But by the midpoint one senses a loss of momentum, and care intrudes (those octave leaps have proved a nuisance for many a more experienced coloratura). The public is on her side and she gets a big hand. Still, exploitation (on the part of management) and youthful presumption have contrived to skew perspective—her future seems uncertain.

The *Mignon* revival was planned as an all-American effort on stage, but the indisposition of newcomer Donald Dame forced De Paolis into service. As the out-of-work actor Laerte, De Paolis' decadent tone only adds to our delight in his elegant,

Mignon
25 December 1943
Mignon
Risë Stevens
Philine
Patrice Munsel
Wilhelm
James Melton
Lothario
Norman Cordon
Conductor
Sir Thomas Beecham

pointed characterization. Cordon's sturdy tone does the reverse for the weary, demented Lotario. The second-act duet with Mignon is well sung, but he lacks a winning mezza voce for the Lullaby. Gurney is devoid of character as the menacing Jarno, while Browning's healthy voice adds assurance to the trouser role of Frederic (though the gavotte, which should be self-propelling, labors under the weight of her instrument).

Beecham had more than Munsel to contend with in this revival. Tenor James Melton was yet another media product, having progressed from the Roxy Gang and the Revelers Quartet on early radio to a few Hollywood films in the mid thirties. The Texas Company, sponsor of the Met broadcasts, provided Melton with his own radio show, and the tall, dark, and Georgia-born tenor gained public favor. At the time of his Met debut he was no novice like Munsel, for a number of appearances with the Cincinnati, St. Louis, and Chicago opera companies had preceded his first Met appearances (1942) as Tamino in an English version of *The Magic Flute.* One finds in his operatic appearances a self-satisfaction with Melton as Melton that disallows character portrayal; no musical subtlety is offered as compensation. The self-confidence is welcome enough, since an innate brashness does lend a bit of dash to his portrayal of Meister. 'Adieu, Mignon' has an easy gait, but French elegance and dulcet tone are foreign to him. For the most part the voice itself is solid (though it owns a pronounced nasal twang), but the very top is precarious. He ends the second act with an effortful near–B-flat. 'Elle ne croyait pas' (with exceptionally broad *portamenti*) is a more sympathetic effort, but a Metropolitan career of eight seasons would not seem predicated by this afternoon's performance.

Risë Stevens, too, had recently made the trek to Hollywood to star opposite Nelson Eddy in a musical version of Molnár's *The Guardsman.* But Stevens is the complete opera professional, as was evident in her broadcast debut as Mignon five years earlier. A brief souvenir of that debut performance (the duet from act three, 'Je suis heureuse') is a cherishable thing. In the recitative one is struck by the unique, sensuous color of the voice, her generous feeling for text (subtle word treatment illuminates a delightful sequence on a repeated note), and the dramatic thrust of her recognition of Wilhelm Meister. She radiates charm in the duet proper, though not quite matching the elegance of Crooks: one notes a tendency to a blatant 'woi' sound among her vowels, a slight lurch in leaping to top notes, a not quite perfect coordination between tone and breath in the middle low voice—all minor blemishes on a beautifully formed talent.

In the intervening five years the radio public has heard her Octavian and Dalila (1941). On this Christmas afternoon she delivers a wooly-toned rebuff to Jarno at her entrance, but the little prayer to the Virgin confirms her expertise in shaping a line. Stevens turns the familiar 'Connais-tu le pays?' into a modest dramatic narrative, effectively combating its static stance with tonal and textual inflections; one notices that the voice is a bit more fixed, the mid low tone straighter than in her initial appearances. Beecham is intent on making the aria into a miniature tone poem at a distressingly slow tempo, but more than most conductors, he conjures up Italy's aura. Stevens, with her modest-sized instrument, must resort to little extraneous sounds to sustain the line of the aria—one hopes the mannerism will not become a permanent stopgap. But one needn't cavil at her lovely portrayal. How well the divertissement pieces of the opera suit her vocal gifts and manner: the swallow duet is charmingly animated, the airiness in her mid to upper voice most ingratiating as she and Meister plan her future, and she is content to make a playful jest of the Styrienne,

Mignon
17 December 1938

Mignon
Risë Stevens
Wilhelm
Richard Crooks
Conductor
Wilfred Pelletier

giving it a tomboy cast. And she imbues the recitatives in the boudoir with significance. Hers is the theatrical personality, ever alive to the dramatic moment. When suicide invades Thomas' confection, Stevens is more than generous vocally; for the most part she spends her capital to good purpose (the mid and low voice have a delectable color), but she can't avoid a few effortful moments where the top is overblown. Though 'Je suis heureuse' is less pliant than in 1938 (her tones are darker in color and a little leaden), the prayer reaffirms the beauty of her singular timbre.

To conclude the opera, Beecham has brought along a finale new to America, but it merely reinforces the divertissement nature of the work and further embellishes the artifice of Philine. Beecham has to put up with scratchy winds in the overture, and the ensemble is catch-as-catch-can in the choral-soloists finale to act one. In *Mignon* he has been served up a decidedly mixed bag of soloists, but he escapes unharmed and, undaunted, shoulders the mutilated carcass of *Les Contes d'Hoffmann.* The broadcast of *Hoffmann* on 26 February 1944 is probably the most satisfying of all Beecham's Metropolitan ventures. This time he has a cast capable of realizing the polyglot wonders of Offenbach's masterwork—and for once the Metropolitan is able to offer the all but impossible: an entire act with authentic French stylists (Djanel, Jobin, and Singher).

During this period of his career Jobin was singing with atypical conviction; the *Hoffmann* broadcast is the apex of his American years. All that was staid and ordinary in manner and vocalism has vanished. In the Kleinzach narrative his crisply articulated French gives an uncommonly sharp profile to the disjunct musical angles of the legend; when he falls in love with Spalanzani's doll he fills the expansive phrases with tone, not exactly velvet-covered, but strong and vibrant, and the parlante passages are lively and charming. He turns the little Bacchic song in Giulietta's lair into a delightful character piece. Jobin never falters in the high-flying climaxes of the second act, and indeed, at the close of the Epilogue, he summons an almost Wagnerian breadth of sound and phrase to cap a superb performance.

Jobin is the axis around which Offenbach's weird crew revolves, and there are more of them than usual since the roles are not grouped in the normal way: Pinza sings only two of the villains (Harrell gets the opera off to a stylish start as Lindorf, his tonal focus singularly apt for French opera); De Paolis leaves Andrès and Cochenille to Oliviero, for he prefers to mix the master, Spalanzani, with the customary Pitichinaccio and Franz; and each of the leading ladies has her own interpreter. The lesser roles are well filled. We finally hear Donald Dame's sweet and clear tenor and characterful artistry as the student Nathaniel; Moscona, in excellent vocal form, makes a commanding father to Antonia; Harshaw sings the Mother's Voice, while Browning, though her warm voice lacks point and turns breathy in the lower regions, is an able enough Nicklausse. Pinza has a feeble moment or two at the end of Coppelius' 'J'ai des yeux' (now fifty-two, the basso is a little slower to start than of yore), but elsewhere his tones are wonderfully firm. His Dr. Miracle is Méphisto without the sugarcoating. Superbly ironic in declamation, he dispenses seductive tone as he tempts Antonia to sing (again, his mezza voce nearly collapses at one point). The male trio (Jobin, Pinza, Moscona) is dramatically telling, with Beecham the driving force—a rousing rendition. De Paolis still has plenty of tone to dispense as Franz, whose lengthy scene (for once) is not quite as much of a trial for the radio listener.

Of the women, Munsel alone disappoints. Oddly, the press had assaulted her Philine and praised her Olympia when first heard. Now, a few months later, the voice

Les Contes d'Hoffmann
26 February 1944

Olympia
Patrice Munsel
Giulietta, Muse
Lily Djanel
Antonia
Jarmila Novotna
Hoffmann
Raoul Jobin
Dappertutto
Martial Singher
Lindorf
Mack Harrell
Coppelius, Dr. Miracle
Ezio Pinza
Conductor
Sir Thomas Beecham

Raoul Jobin as Don José in *Carmen*.

already sounds in disrepair: the brilliance of the middle and upper voice is clouded, and pitch is not entirely reliable. By now the young soprano has a dozen Met appearances as Olympia, Philine, and Gilda to her (one cannot quite say) credit; clearly, too much too soon. Youthful resilience aids her in the cadenza of the doll song, and a bright high E-flat is the genuine article. Djanel, too, is a mite shrill and tremulous as she begins the Barcarolle, but one cannot mistake the fascination which this Giulietta exerts. The voice soon settles—it has an abundance of that adamantine sensuousness which gives French (or Belgian) artists their peculiar charm. What a fine temptress she makes—Giulietta is so often a travesty in *Hoffmann* productions, yet this courtesan is not only believable but hypnotic in vocal color and style. She and Jobin, ever abetted by Sir Thomas' surging orchestral forces, bring the 'Extase' duet to a frenzied climax. In the Epilogue Djanel returns as the Muse to comfort Hoffman in languorous spoken tones suggestive of immense experience.

Most interpreters of Antonia, the gentle sister of the heroines, are content to meet the considerable vocal demands of this grateful lyric role. Jarmila Novotna does this most ably (it may be her finest broadcast in purely vocal terms), but she also manages to create a character of great appeal. She accomplishes this without extraneous effects, relying entirely on that singular, musk-tinged timbre which so well suggests Antonia's sorrow and debilitated state, all the while infusing her shapely phrases with longing. A subtle artistry is at work here. And the tessitura of the role (in part, because she doesn't attempt the final C-sharp or trill) causes no concern; Novotna's voice fairly flowers on this afternoon. When Antonia gives in to temptation, the soprano captures the frenzy of the moment, and Beecham paces the demonic trio (as the girl responds to her Mother's voice) with skill, now rushing onward, now applying the brakes to make the next assault even more telling—a thrilling close to Novotna's fully realized portrayal.

Contributing to the high quality of the performance is newcomer Martial Singher, who had made his house debut as Dappertutto a few months earlier. His stylistic surety and sculpted diction create a telling mood in the recitatives preceding 'Scintille diamant.' Singher eschews velvet in favor of a timbre whose hard surface contains glinting lights of suggestive color—the knife and the caress are wonderfully wedded in Singher's delivery of the aria. He executes the leaps to the isolated top tones fearlessly; en route to the final high G, time is suspended as he masterfully controls the repeated notes of 'Beau diamant, scintille!' Singher is a mesmeric artist whose unique qualities the Met will have difficulty in displaying to full advantage over the years. For a decade the Paris Opéra had featured him in roles as diverse as Iago, Telramund, the Flying Dutchman, and in French operas from Rameau to Milhaud (Thomas' Hamlet was a particular triumph). All these would be denied him in New York, though a few roles (Amfortas, Mozart's Count Almaviva) which he had often sung in Buenos Aires would fill out the usual French fare of the Met.

When, in his second season, Singher undertakes Pelléas (the jewel in his crown) Sir Thomas is no longer on hand to guide the French repertory. Beecham's three-year tenure, though too short for any lasting residue of French style to accrue, remains a boon of the war years. Under his baton the orchestral and choral forces of the Met achieved a too rare precision and clear-cut personality (one hears it particularly in the Prologue of *Hoffmann*); his own quixotic personality is ever alert to moments of individual character (the gaggle of detached notes by the winds at the opening of the first act which captures the fantastic humor of the opera, for instance). Above all, Beecham's distinction lay in his inimitable panache and his sensitivity to sensuous sound, the former ever keeping alive the drama, the latter feeding his willingness to indulge a gifted singer's way with a phrase, or to exploit an orchestral color for its own sake (one recalls the sforzando on a single orchestral chord in the final act of *Manon* or, in the opera's prelude, the folly of the flute flourishes in contrast to the passion of Des Grieux' Sphinx theme—the entire prelude has the directness of a bracing dash of water in the face). How skillfully he paced the diverse elements leading to Méphisto's Serenade in *Faust* so that the drama was kept in focus; with what vigor he called the Kermesse dances to life—this was no namby-pamby crowd, but a lively mix of fair-goers. It was his particular gift not only to vivify masterworks, but to add musical muscle-tone to the slighter creations of a Gounod or a Massenet without forgetting to serve up their sweetmeats for our enjoyment. No need to say farewell quite yet, as we will later taste the delights of his mercurial *Falstaff*.

Eleanor Steber as Countess Almaviva in *Le Nozze di Figaro*.

CHAPTER TWENTY

1941–50
Mozart Renascence

With the advent of Beecham, Walter, and Szell, the Metropolitan might well be considered a conductors' house, although as long as the stage direction and production aspects failed to keep pace with the musical command, the familiar designation of "singers' house" retained sufficient force (when the vicissitudes of war permitted). These conductors did not leave mere calling cards; if one admits Leinsdorf to their distinguished company, Walter, Beecham, Szell, Emil Cooper, and Fritz Busch conducted fully half of the broadcasts in the five-year period from 1941 through 1946. Add to this an additional quarter of the broadcasts under Cesare Sodero, a sensitive purveyor of the popular Italian repertory, and the Met could be said to be enjoying a golden age of musical leadership.

The advantages of superior command are nowhere more essential and beneficial than in the ensemble operas of Mozart. Johnson, flush with the triumph of *Figaro*, now championed another Mozart work whose Metropolitan career was almost as spotty. *Il Flauto Magico* had been introduced to New York audiences at the turn of the century, but it appeared in the repertory (reverting to *Die Zauberflöte* a few years later) only nine seasons during the next four decades; since 1917 it had been heard only during the 1926–27 season. Fabled casts, such as Sembrich, Eames, Ternina (First Lady), Dippel, and Plançon (1900) or Hempel, Destinn, Homer (Third Lady), Slezak, and Goritz under Alfred Hertz (1912–13), had worked no permanent magic.

No such stellar assemblage appears on stage in the 1941–42 revival; the star is in the pit. In the broadcast of 10 January 1942 Bruno Walter savors the humanity of the piece, preferring restraint to brilliance and nurturing warmth and depth of feeling wherever possible. The broadly paced adagio of the overture and the stately fugal treatment forecast the benignity which Walter sheds over the entire score. Occasionally he may relish one of Mozart's melodies (Tamino's flute summoning the animals) to the point of near-extinction, but at that exact moment he picks it up and wafts it on its way. In fact, he consistently marshals a natural flow, a sense that the stage events are actually in process: the pace of the act-one finale is wonderfully apt; both the architecture and expression of the chorale prelude episode with the two guards are effortlessly conveyed. How lovingly he shapes Mozart's mediating instrumental phrases in the arias—Kullman well knows how to mold the contours of the portrait aria, but Walter's orchestra sings even more. And his shaping hand is all the more

The Magic Flute
10 January 1942
Pamina
Jarmila Novotna
Queen
Rosa Bok
First Lady
Eleanor Steber
Tamino
Charles Kullman
Papageno
John Brownlee
Speaker
Friedrich Schorr
Sarastro
Alexander Kipnis
Conductor
Bruno Walter

299

needful since, in this production, we hear 'O dearest angel, light and fair' instead of 'Dies Bildnis ist bezaubernd schön.' The language of Ruth and Thomas Martin is rather prosaic and the alliance of meaning and tone inevitably not exact; but the translation is not offensive. "Opera in English" was a lively topic during these years (*Opera News* is full of articles pro and con), and the extensive spoken dialogue of *Die Zauberflöte* argued logically for the vernacular, particularly since the management was eager to give Mozart's singspiel a good send-off with its new audience. To this end *Opera News* even published a special issue devoted entirely to the work.

The hard sell worked, for the opera remained in the repertory for five consecutive seasons under Walter's paternal hand and was not long absent thereafter. Yet all is not quite trim on this Saturday afternoon. Walter is less successful in consistently providing ensemble cohesion on stage (the first-act quintet of Tamino, Papageno, and the Queen's ladies has its wayward moments, and the trio of Genii lacks precision). The overall level of singing seldom rises above respectability and occasionally sinks below it. Rosa Bok's Queen of the Night falls into the latter category: the middle voice is not unpleasant, if occasionally tremulous, but her pyrotechnics are decidedly tepid, though the notes are there (thin at the top). Of course, the same can be said of most Queens. Novotna, in a role that would seem a natural for her, gives an equivocal portrayal of Pamina. Nurtured by Salzburg and Vienna, she is well at home in the style, and her diction in the spoken dialogue is charming and comprehensible (unlike a few of her foreign colleagues—quite a number of *not a vord*s are heard; and even Novotna is less successful when singing). But her pitch is oddly unsettled in the duet with Papageno, and she has not the heft to uphold her part in the all-important trio with Tamino and Sarastro (one of the noblest pages of the score). (The 10 January 1942 broadcast of the *Flute* is not included in the *Preliminary List of Audio Documentation* of the Rodgers and Hammerstein Archives. On the tape under discussion, several interpolations from the 26 December 1942 broadcast are introduced—the voice of Pinza is unmistakable in a portion of this trio.) With an assist from Walter's nimble tempo, Novotna's aria is cleanly managed, not quite ravishing tonally, but with a subtle sounding of Pamina's sorrow. Brownlee's bird-catcher must have newly escaped from the British music halls—the flavor of it is unsettling. His diction is brazenly clear, but every note is punched out, and his spoken dialogue, in contrast to Kullman's neat conversational manner, is oddly artificial. Fortunately, the conception relaxes somewhat as the opera proceeds; he eases his stentorian speech and even sings 'A sweetheart or a maiden' with a becoming lilt.

From Kipnis we expect something more, and he doesn't disappoint. He manages to remove the squareness from Sarastro's hymnlike solos (which can seem interminable from most sincere basses). The lows try him a bit now and then, but usually his tone rolls out in a splendid ground swell of humanity. He is not afraid to unbend when counseling Pamina—this Sarastro is no bore. Of course, his accent is thick, and those sweeping *portamenti* in 'O Isis and Osiris' would be more at home on the Volga than the Danube. Overall, it is Kullman who offers the finest portrayal, solid in vocalism, sweet or pseudoheroic as the need may be (though his cries for help at his entrance seem unmotivated). Best of all, he captures the expressive dignity of Mozart's evolving German style in the scene with the Speaker. Kullman is a secure Mozart stylist. His companion as Sprecher is Friedrich Schorr, in his final broadcast appearance. Tonal fortitude he supplies, and a convincing manner, but his accent is ungainly (rolled *rr*'s, "wisdom" inevitably becomes "weesdom") and overall his singing betrays effort.

At the other end of the spectrum we make the acquaintance of an artist destined to serve Mozart and the Met more than well. Eleanor Steber, West Virginian graduate of the New England Conservatory, winner of the 1940 "Metropolitan Auditions of the Air," is the genuine homegrown article, exuding confidence and owning a built-in zest for life. Her timbre—silvery, of diamond-like clarity—is distinctive and shimmeringly beautiful in the manner of the best German lyric sopranos (the heritage was there). In addition, the voice has sufficient point to promise future growth. At first, the German *Fach* seemed her natural hearth (debut as Sophie, follow-ups in smaller roles: the Forest Bird, Woglinde, a *Parsifal* Flowermaiden), and indeed, her finest efforts would almost always bear a Teutonic tinge. But it is in Mozart, with its union of southern warmth and northern clarity, that her special gifts would register most strongly. Now in her second season, she lends a bit of quality to an otherwise nondescript trio of Ladies (later she would sing Pamina). Occasionally Steber overmouths the English text (in truth, hers is not an attractive speaking voice) but often a delightful touch of phrasing or burst of spirit denotes the superior musician, and the mid and upper voice have a heavenly sheen.

Evidently work remains to be done if worthy Mozart is to find a home at the Met. Within the year, the *Flute* was again on the airwaves (26 December 1942) with Pinza, Antoine, and Cordon joining Kullman, Brownlee, Novotna, and Steber in the key roles. A half-dozen more playings have lent a greater surety to the overall operation—one senses it in the contrapuntal overture, where the dramatic character of the repeated notes of the fugal entries is new. Further confirmation comes in the dynamic treatment of Tamino's entry music—now Kullman conveys the prince's desperation. Walter takes great care with the Queen's Ladies (no caterwauling cats for him), and he adds an element of charm to Papageno's songs (not that Brownlee responds in kind—the fantasy of the part simply eludes him, but fortunately, his dialogue is a trace sprightlier). Kullman wears a happy combination of manliness and musicality, though his tone is a bit less well oiled.

John Garris' Monostatos is an improvement over Laufkoetter's nasal nastiness, and Cordon provides solid tone as the Speaker, but no softening curves convey the humanity which Schorr suggested. Pinza supplies that quality aplenty. Sarastro's song is heartfelt, and though the language is not English ('Thou art bidden' comes out 'Thou art beeden'), Pinza's music is Mozart. Everywhere Walter's sure-handed oversight is evident (even Brownlee sings a euphonious duet with Pamina). By the end of the first act, a first-rate performance would seem in the making. Indeed, Pinza's solos in the second act are of the highest order, rolling out in rich organlike tones, both the highs and lows on call; they contrast curiously with his spoken lines, which are delivered in a light, conversational manner. Little in the remainder of the act is of this calibre. A disastrous sequence of numbers occurs in which Antoine is the principal malefactor. Antoine's act-one aria had a measure of anger, abetted by her straightforward declamation (the high F is avoided). But the vengeance aria, even though taken down a whole step, is a catastrophe. Evidently propelled by fear, Antoine moves consistently ahead of the orchestra in the agile sections; a loose caboose, she sends staccati ricocheting every which way around Walter's beat. Preceded by a scrambling, cackling trio of the three Ladies and followed by Novotna's careful 'Ah, I feel it,' the well-being of the afternoon dissipates. Throughout much of the opera, Novotna produces effortful sounds in the upper regions, and unhappy in the exposed high tessitura and foreign language, her phrasing becomes angular. The aria, in particular, has little of the intense concentration of grief which only complete

The Magic Flute
26 December 1942

Pamina
Jarmila Novotna
Queen
Josephine Antoine
First Lady
Eleanor Steber
Tamino
Charles Kullman
Papageno
John Brownlee
Speaker
Norman Cordon
Sarastro
Ezio Pinza
Conductor
Bruno Walter

vocal repose can convey; it is left to Walter's searching postlude to make Mozart's case. Still, Novotna's refinement and chaste manner, even when she is unable to provide an aural complement, has its satisfactions. (Though Novotna would continue to sing Pamina at the Met as long as Walter was at the helm, the broadcasts of 1944 and 1945—both conducted by Walter—would fall to newcomer Nadine Conner.) By now the tensile thread of the performance is broken; even the trio of Novotna, Kullman, and Pinza seems unsettled, and we welcome Brownlee's sure-fire turn with Papagena (radio debutante Lillian Raymondi). Pinza again pulls his weight as he reaffirms that light has vanquished darkness, but too much gloom remains.

Far more rewarding is the Walter *Don Giovanni* broadcast of 7 March 1942. A cast of exceptional musicality and nearly uniform strength aids Walter in his Beethovenesque reading of Mozart's bequest to nineteenth-century romanticism. How much the validity of that conception depended on Walter's sensitive hand may be gauged from the broadcast of the following year (3 April 1943) when, though Walter had continued to conduct the New York performances, Breisach (whose normal function was to shepherd the Met's flock of singers through the makeshift Sunday night concerts) undertook the tour performance in Chicago. In Breisach's hands the demonic turns turgid and the benign, utilitarian. Constants (both in the cast and in quality) are Pinza, Novotna, Sayão, Harrell, and Cordon, with Bampton or Milanov, Kipnis or Baccaloni, Kullman or Melton the variants.

In the 1942 broadcast Walter's imprint on the overture is unmistakable, the somber seriousness of the andante giving way to the churning drama of the molto allegro. Some of this remains under Breisach, but in the quieter moments, Walter's leavening nuances are lamentably absent. Under Walter, Kipnis sings the first of only two Met appearances as Leporello, offering a delectable antidote to the steady train of priestlike portrayals which form the bulk of his radio legacy. He abjures buffa tricks, retaining only an unexpectedly deft patter, the common property of the Italian buffa trade. With Cordon an uncommonly dark-toned and secure Commandant, Mozart's score is weighted with black sonorities this afternoon. Pinza, too, chooses on occasion to color his voice to the nether side—a wonderful example occurs as he regretfully agrees to the duel ('Misero! . . . se vuoi morir'), an interpretive touch significantly abandoned in the Breisach performance. Walter's stately pace in the ghostly trio also allows Pinza some of his most affecting, expansive phrasing as Don Giovanni sees the life ebb away from the old man—a transfiguring Mozart moment doubly enhanced by Pinza and Walter, but again deficient in Breisach's reading. Kipnis, too, is imaginative in his characterization; one relishes the delicious vulgarity ('Pare un libro stampato!') of this most patrician of basses as he prepares to enlighten Elvira—his insinuating mezza voce as he moves into the catalog aria is a treat. We know this is a trial run for Kipnis and Walter when they can't quite settle the tempo of the aria; but seldom has the andante section been sung with such security and breadth of phrasing and easy command of both highs and lows. Not so for Baccaloni, who sustains a dismal high D at the aria's climax. But Baccaloni is nevertheless in superior voice on this first hearing of one of his most renowned characterizations. He takes the aria at a faster clip than Kipnis and adds a genuine narrative quality to the telling, his patter on the button, and overly indulgent only in the succession of *qual che fa*s which close the aria.

At times Kipnis and Pinza play at games in the *secco* recitative—they pepper the air with their rapid exchange of banter. Curiously, Baccaloni and Pinza adopt a more reasonable gait, pointing up key words to the advantage of the drama. But how

Don Giovanni
7 March 1942

Donna Anna
Rose Bampton
Donna Elvira
Jarmila Novotna
Zerlina
Bidú Sayão
Don Ottavio
Charles Kullman
Don Giovanni
Ezio Pinza
Leporello
Alexander Kipnis
Masetto
Mack Harrell
Commandant
Norman Cordon
Conductor
Bruno Walter

Don Giovanni
3 April 1943

Donna Anna
Zinka Milanov
Donna Elvira
Jarmila Novotna
Zerlina
Bidú Sayão
Don Ottavio
James Melton
Don Giovanni
Ezio Pinza
Leporello
Salvatore Baccaloni
Masetto
Mack Harrell
Commandant
Norman Cordon
Conductor
Paul Breisach

grandly Kipnis summons the maskers to the ball; not even Spanish grandees could resist such a command. (Baccaloni, too, abjures the clown in these moments.) Oddly, it is Kipnis who plays the fool when counterfeiting Giovanni in order to deceive Elvira: he caricatures Pinza's covered tone and even offers a naughty fast vibrato bleat on 'Sempre.' Baccaloni keeps his mimicry within the zones this time. Leporello's patter aria shows off the Italian's virtuosity, while Kipnis' flexible vocal and dramatic manner is equally attractive (the waning phrases of Leporello's escape are neatly gauged). Harrell offers a serviceable Masetto, though he can't resist overdoing the traditional crybaby stance as he uncovers his bruises to Zerlina.

On both occasions, Pinza is entirely at ease as the seducer and in fine voice (barring a few moments in the later performance where control of his mezza voce eludes him; by this time in his career the upper Ds and Es are precarious). His tempting of Zerlina is a magical moment—tone and manner are equally seductive, but he avoids overplaying the transition into 'Là ci darem' (Pinza consistently adds both an agogic and stress accent to 'Là,' thereby making sense of the text and augmenting Mozart's meaning as well). In 1943 he carries his ardor a step further in the recitative, approaching a caricature of himself. No one in memory has brought off the Serenade as well as Pinza on these afternoons; perhaps it is the utter confidence he feels in his ability to charm which enables us to share his pleasure. But he leaves off the easy manner when awaiting his sepulchral supper guest. Now the celebrated Pinza energy verges on mania. Of course, Walter's orchestral probing provides the perfect complement, for he emphasizes the ominous chromatic wandering of the string figures and brings home the horror of the cosmic moment when Giovanni takes the hand of the Commandant.

In like fashion, Walter's shaping of orchestral units abets Kullman's straightforward 'Dalla sua pace'; the conductor translates each varied topic into an appropriate musical gesture while the singer freely shapes his own phrases. Walter's tempo for 'Il mio tesoro' is a genuine andante grazioso (no showcase tactics here), and Kullman feels the sentiment of the piece ('asciugar') and conveys it, though he takes three breaths in the trial phrase. (Surprisingly, Melton needs only one breath, and his fioriture are a shade neater.) Kullman's timbre is a bit cloudy, but all in all, the aria is an easy amble for both singer and conductor. That whimper which ever lurks in Kullman's timbre surfaces in his final pleas to Anna, perhaps enough to make her favorably recall Don Giovanni's forceful assault (the Hoffmanesque solution to Anna's dilemma would not be out of place in Walter's romantic projection of the opera). In 1943 Milanov and Melton are oddly paired (what must she have thought!). Melton is aided by the low tessitura of the role and well sustains the line of Ottavio's arias, but both tone color and dynamics are unvaried. He has obviously been well schooled in the music, but Kullman's tender manner and musical grace are far more winning.

In view of her difficulties in *The Magic Flute* during this same period, Novotna's excellent pair of Donna Elviras is doubly welcome. Elvira's showpiece, 'Mi tradì,' is cut in these Met performances, and that challenge avoided, Novotna proves a complete mistress of the part, both vocally and dramatically. She turns the *secco* recitative to expressive account (as when she recounts her sufferings under Don Giovanni), and yet she is willing to exploit the bizarre element in Elvira as well. Her finest vocal moments occur in the 1943 'Ah, fuggi il traditor,' which she delivers with splendid tone, and in the beautifully sculpted phrases with which she opens the ensuing quartet—how cleverly she outlines the components of a Mozart phrase and makes clear the architectural plan of a sequence of phrases. An acute musical intelligence guides her deft traversal of the descending sixteenths at 'palpitar' in the 1943 sextet; and yet, the tortured ambivalence of Elvira is laid bare.

In the 1943 performance it is the singers who take charge, making statements which reinforce their characters both as vocalists and personages in the drama; whereas in 1942 Walter always joins and abets them in this effort, Breisach merely acquiesces. (On the debit side, Walter is not always assertive enough—at least for a repertory house—to corral his forces to a precise gait in the ensembles.) At projecting character, Sayão, in particular, is a past mistress, especially in those parts where a wheedling charm is central. Her performance varies not one iota on these two afternoons, and why should it? Need perfection be altered? One might wish for less nasality in the opening duet with Pinza, but what a delicious flow she gives to the phrase 'ma può burlarmi ancor' (1943). Nor does she overplay the soubrette. 'Batti, batti' is one of her finest efforts, and Walter's charming trills and detached sixteenth-note motives enhance the spirit of the aria. (The admirable Steane, in *The Grand Tradition* (p. 314), specifically cites the 1942 'Batti' as an example of Sayão's irritating habit of "interposing little sounds, whether for pathos or emphasis and of leaving the note in the interests of 'character.'" While these mannerisms do detract in certain Sayão performances, I find no hint of them on this occasion and only an insignificant pair of huffs in the 1943 rendering.) Again, the 1943 'Vedrai, carino' represents Sayão's vocalism at its silvery best.

If one cannot be so wholehearted in praising Bampton's Donna Anna, it is not for lack of effort on her part; Bampton is at the peak of her form here and gives an estimable performance. That it is not necessarily one to treasure is due to conditions beyond her control. Nature did not provide her with quite the characterful instrument (the vocal thumbprint) for maximum effect; then too, Donna Anna is so great a challenge. Nevertheless, she offers a thoughtful, carefully plotted reading of the role. More than that, Anna's plight has captured her imagination. All the accompanied recitatives (where the eighteenth-century seria heroine must show her mettle) are rendered with splendid dramatic verve. Yet throughout the afternoon her tone is consistently lovely, though never quite refulgent because of its inherent whiteness, a residue of her soprano conversion. (Novotna's voice has a similar white tincture, but somehow she shades more effectively, and then, this coloration can be more serviceable for a lyric than a dramatic soprano.) In this performance Bampton gives off a warmth of feeling quite unusual; her Anna is worthy of a man's devotion. The quartet is an exemplary effort by all: Bampton and Novotna match one another in musical sensibility and vocal control, Pinza relishes the long lines and mimes vocally the contrasting gestures of his part, while Walter allows the piece to lovingly unfold. The mask trio is a similarly treasurable effort. Anna's two great scenes are well done by Bampton: 'Or sai chi l'onore' is particularly impressive (the accompanied recitative vivid in the extreme) and 'Non mi dir,' in the opposite corner, is notable for its affecting musicality. Oh yes, she has no trill, and the fioriture are negotiated cagily rather than with confidence.

To cap the 1943 performance, we have Milanov's only broadcast of a Mozart role. Its uniqueness lies not only in its rarity. Of these artists, only Pinza (Kipnis, too?) would seem so beneficently equipped by nature to fulfill the demands of the opera. What differentiates bass from soprano? Pinza is weighted with inner confidence and wears it with jaunty pride; Milanov has yet to develop an inner security to match her temperament. Thus an afternoon of superbly grand singing by her once again ends

Bidú Sayão as Zerlina in *Don Giovanni*.

Rose Bampton as Donna Anna in *Don Giovanni*.

with a momentary, but disfiguring, blemish.

When Anna first enters, Milanov, in her excitability, occasionally overshoots the mark vocally, but her discovery of her dead father is a heartrending, gripping episode. Will she ever again be so passionately involved, so varied in vocal and dramatic effects, now flashing out, now retreating into sorrowful diminuendi, the vocal color astonishingly rich? She even faints convincingly. (This is a far cry from the Milanov of later years who, to convey Santuzza's anguish, would shift the stole on her shoulder.) And so it goes throughout the afternoon. Without Walter to aid her, Milanov still supplies all the drama necessary, the tone spilling out of her mouth as though it must seek release. Where is the Mozartean restraint? one might ask—there she goes, straying outside the interpretive zones again. But Anna is the inheritor of the grand seria tradition where, though the classical affect may be static, the vocal gestures are flamboyant. Breisach provides only lymphatic support in the vengeance aria, while Milanov enjoys her first high A so much that she is a shade late in reentering; she later repeats a phrase ending that should be altered. But overall, the thrill of her vocalism is undeniable. She spins great webs of silvery tone as she enters in the finale; her control is sure, the tone ravishing in the mask trio with the top voice well focused, her scales perfectly realized. The voice is well knit throughout its entire range and at all dynamic levels. She takes the first phrase of 'Non mi dir' in one breath; the turns are excellent and executed in a silky legato. All is going famously (she must always be on guard against sharping but is on firm ground this time) and she makes a brave start to the allegretto section—a shade late in starting the fioriture, but the mode of execution is apt. Now she grows a mite skittish, slights the last few notes of a downward scale, and the game is up: she makes a false entrance (thinking she should join the orchestra in the motive which she should sing two measures later). Seemingly face to face with disaster, she pulls herself together for a strong close.

Like many performances of the Johnson era, the two broadcasts contain vivid dramatic characterizations created through vocal means by artists of individuality and commitment. These artists achieve their ends even when the conductor is merely a routinier (as in the 1943 *Giovanni*); but of equal importance, when a conductor with the stature of Walter or Beecham is in command, the maestro does not inhibit the artistic verity of his singers by imposing a straitjacket on their impulses and insights. He nurtures and augments the portrayals at the same time that he shapes and codifies the performance with his own overall conception. It was a partnership between stage and pit that, within a decade or two, would become increasingly rare.

Le Nozze di Figaro, in 1940 the seminal opera of the Mozart revival, remained the jewel in the Met's Mozart diadem throughout the decade. After three Panizza airings, the radio public enjoyed five more performances before the Johnson era ended in 1950. The sequence has particular merit as one of Johnson's few attempts to sustain an ensemble of singers over many years, a departure from the rampant change of cast which was the common practice of the time.

One critical change there was, necessitated by the absence of Rethberg, who had sung every Contessa in New York during the first three years of the run. Without doubt one of the authentic luminaries of the twenties and thirties, Rethberg's star was no longer in ascendance. At the close of the 1941–42 season, she settled for retirement at the relatively early age of forty-eight. Johnson had accorded her the opening night of her final season (more likely the honor was for Mozart and the successful *Figaro* production). But her season (her twentieth with the company) also included her assault on the *Siegfried* Brünnhilde, a role far removed from her natural habitat. Though the tonal fallout from a few late broadcasts bruises memory, Rethberg is one of the artists for whom the preservation of live performances substantially enlarges our concept. This is true both in terms of repertory and in the animated nature of her stage portrayals, which contrasts with some of her studio recordings, where admittedly her vocal form is often more pristine. A few decades after her retirement Rethberg commented, "What I loved about my work was the *Tonerlebnis*, the experience of producing sound. . . . It made me happy, as if detached from all earthly concerns, just floating away, almost as if I had given birth to music."[1] That pretty well sums up the Rethberg most record collectors remember. Her live broadcasts are both something less and something more.

By 1942 Panizza, too, was gone. The precariousness of ocean travel during the war caused him to forgo the Metropolitan, thereby setting *Figaro* off on new paths as the opera passed through the hands of Bruno Walter (29 January 1944), Fritz Busch (15 March 1947 and 8 January 1949), and Fritz Reiner (11 February 1950) during the remainder of the decade. With the cast a near-constant "control," each conductor's way with the score commands attention.

Having shaped the Metropolitan's *Giovanni* and *Magic Flute*, Walter naturally assumed leadership of Mozart's other "recognized" masterwork for the 1942–43 season. Though he conducted all performances (except the student matinee), the work was not broadcast during the regular season. The company returned from an abbreviated tour for postseason performances in New York, and Walter being no longer available, the work fell into the hands of Breisach for the broadcast of 17 April 1943. Again, it is the familiar tale of the *Giovanni* sequence: surrogates cannot replicate their master's intent. This may be particularly true in the case of Walter, where "inspiration" often played a dominant role in establishing the tone of a performance. Breisach's overture has all the energy but too little of the jauntiness of Mozart's high-spirited romp; in the act-two finale he settles into tempi that negate forward movement, and contrarily, he fails to recognize those momentary slackenings of pace which Mozart cleverly plotted so that the action might be regalvanized and propelled along its frantic way.

Fortunately, he cannot greatly inhibit the artists on stage, most of them old hands by now. Pinza is as dynamic as usual and in superb voice. One never tires of praising him. Amid all the clatter of the opening duet he manages to wrap 'Sì, mio core, o è più bello' in liquid tone and shapely form. His *secco* recitatives are closer to heightened speech than was the rapid patter he loosed on Giovanni. 'Non più andrai' becomes a natural (though one-sided) conversation with the reluctant Cherubino. In the final act he whips up his indignation at the treachery of women to near frenzy (at such a moment he is the ultimate crowd-pleaser). De Paolis matches him in stage mastery, and Baccaloni's patter is expertly deployed in 'La vendetta.' The portly basso is well partnered by Herta Glaz (new to the cast), who suggests the fuddy-duddy Marcellina without descending to low clowning and sings well into the bargain.

Novotna's imprint on the role of Cherubino continues unchallenged and remains so throughout the entire sequence of five performances. (Novotna wrote me that she could not "recall that [her] interpretation of Cherubino was in any way changed under the different conductors. Maybe the tempo was [a] little different."[2] Though one can hear altered nuances in her readings of Cherubino's music, the soprano held to a higher code than conductorial meddling when she added: "It is and was Mozart's music which was our guide.") In her two arias, so often delivered with cast-iron uniformity of affect (the one impetuous, the other saccharine), she finds

Le Nozze di Figaro
17 April 1943
Countess
Eleanor Steber
Susanna
Bidú Sayão
Cherubino
Jarmila Novotna
Almaviva
John Brownlee
Figaro
Ezio Pinza
Dr. Bartolo
Salvatore Baccaloni
Conductor
Paul Breisach

subtle distinctions of movement and dynamics to show us both Cherubino's volatility and her own artistic niceness. Once again Sayão's portrayal is a paradox. How beautifully she sings her aria in the final act; free from pretense, she offers only a command of voice and expression fully in the service of Mozart. When she dresses Cherubino, the duality comes to the fore. In the first half of the aria (taken at a leisurely tempo—Walter's legacy, for sure), she tries for too much authority and the tone becomes stringy and nasal; to the last half she brings a lighter touch and is utterly captivating. She is marvelously knowing when she makes her unexpected entrance from the Countess' dressing room, but at other times her excessive exuberance (yes, the characterization is vivid and appetizingly spunky) causes too much tonal fallout—the chirps and sputters annoy.

Brownlee is marginally better than before (a bit of legato mercifully intrudes in one line of recitative), but his performance remains ordinary and lacking in suavity, particularly in the duet with Susanna (the entire piece is singularly devoid of humor and charm on this occasion). Brownlee's four other portrayals of the Count require little comment. An occasional gain in nuance and liquid tone is counterbalanced by increased pomposity (in 1947, where he consistently lags behind Busch's beat). The high F-sharp of the aria grows more perilous each time, soon turning into a seemingly obligatory crack and finally settling to F-natural in Reiner's 1950 reading. Oddly, in the latter Brownlee gives his best portayal, the sound more pleasant to the ear—by then his hegemony had been interrupted by several Counts assigned to another baritone.

Brownlee has a new consort in 1943. If anything could inspire him to keep his vows (and to better his singing) surely it is the artistry of Eleanor Steber. Walter was her amanuensis. Having guided her through many outings as the First Lady in his *Magic Flute* performances, Walter, upon Rethberg's withdrawal, recommended Steber for this difficult assignment. The change could not have been more dramatic: the aging, waning prima donna gives way to the rising, pristine-voiced youth, providing her with the pivotal opportunity of her career. Gone would be the *Ring* Rhinemaiden, the *Parsifal* Flowermaid, and quite soon, the First Lady. Even Sophie would be abandoned in favor of Violetta, Eva, and a string of Mozart heroines. By the time of the broadcast of 17 April 1943, the twenty-seven-year-old soprano had behind her a Met Violetta and Marguerite and a half-dozen performances of the Countess, and thus the assurance of her broadcast portrayal is not surprising. What remains a matter for wonder is the complete poise of her vocalism from start to finish. Most sopranos find opening cold with 'Porgi, amor' a trial. Not so Steber on this April afternoon (nor in the ensuing four performances up to 1950). Thoroughly composed, she wafts the gentlest, slenderest thread of tone onto the ether, yet there is nothing anemic or uncommunicative about it. It is a most virginal sound; no unchaste thought ever could have disturbed the heart of such a countess—yet to a modern listener the silvery timbre carries a hint of Salome's eroticism within itself. Was it Walter who guided Steber to such a poignant close in the aria, enabling her to suggest Rosina's conflicting moods in the final two phrases: the first, expressing the hope of regaining her husband's love, sung in an emphatic manner; the second, sounding the sorrow of resignation, in softest tones? Seldom does an artist capture the psychology as well as the beauty of Mozart's heroine. A second cause for joy is a Met singer actually salting the score with abundant appoggiaturas (perhaps too many, for a few occur in rather unexpected places). They add greatly to the deftness of her portrayal.

Neither the long phrases nor the high-lying tessitura of 'Dove sono' daunt Steber—her voice is all of a piece, capable of a wide range of dynamics, the top notably firm and colorful. Best of all, she closes with a neat trill. 'Dove sono' is a vocal and interpretive trial by fire, and the young soprano, whose control of the Mozartean line is both supple and steadfast, emerges not only unscathed but triumphant. In the letter duet Sayão's firm tones and matter-of-fact manner (she is the servant, after all) contrast with the float of Steber's voice as she plays with the dynamics and introduces slight hesitations in the line—a charming, if not quite stylistically unified, performance by the two sopranos.

A year later Steber's virginal pose recedes. This Countess has matured over the summer. We hear it in a greater breadth of tone and phrase (in 'Porgi, amor' the climactic A-flat is a firm *forte*, not the *mezzo forte* followed by a diminuendo of the year before). But the voice is as lovely as ever, or more so, since the palette she draws upon is greater and her emotional response has deepened—rebellion against her husband is more intense (her 'Fermatevi!' is quite insistent). In Walter's 'Dove sono' (29 January 1944) Steber is no longer merely spinning tone—she summons an outburst of tone and shame at the close of the recitative as she laments having to contrive with one of her servants. Busch (1947 and 1949) evidently curtails her appoggiaturas. And the random ones are well away: this time, neither Brownlee nor Steber is allowed to temper resolve with appoggiaturas in the pair of *Giudizios* as they confront one another in the second-act finale. By 1949 Steber's lovely voice has a welcome strength and darker coloration, the word treatment is more varied, the manner grander—we seem to hear an Elsa waiting in the wings. Throughout all these performances Steber's work remains on the highest level, deepening in affect and gathering strength, yet vocally impeccable. During the forties, her Mozart singing is a herald of the emerging Viennese Mozart manner. She is as subtle as any Viennese in handling tone and word, vocally as able to cast a glinting shimmer upon Mozart's phrases, but she never abuses the whispered inflection and is happily untouched by cloying affectation.

A particular treat in all of the *Figaro* broadcasts is the delightful byplay of the three ladies (well, two and a *travestimento*) in the privacy of the Countess' boudoir. And Walter adds to the intimacy of the scene (and elsewhere throughout the opera) with his gemütlichkeit. Actually, he launders all the commedia dell'arte spirit out of the opera (except with Pinza, whose vibrant manner and crisp diction can never be entirely tamed). Walter conducts a more introspective 'Non so più' ('parlo d'amor sognando' is the clue), and Cherubino seems a shade less callow—but he has lost some of his charming impetuosity. Sayão's dressing vignette (formerly so full of command and near-spite) is given a legato line: the 'restate fermoli' phrase and its orchestral repetitions are broadened noticeably and the final eight measures are heavily braked. Walter's Mozart must sing, sing. Sayão in particular benefits, for the edges of her conception are softened, yet sufficient comic temper remains. (When Steber, years later in a Singers' Roundtable discussion of scene stealing, refers to "dear Bidú," one rather knows what she means.)[3] On the other hand, Sayão's fourth-act aria is more mannered and a shade under her best this time.

Pinza's portrayal, too, is touched by Walter's creed. Judging from the suavity of 'Non più andrai,' it must be a very disciplined army to which Cherubino is sentenced. In 'Aprite un po' ' one notes again Walter's penchant for singling out a phrase and its orchestral repetitions ('Il resto, il resto nol dico') for the "expressive" treatment; the forward thrust of the piece is impaired.

Le Nozze di Figaro
29 January 1944

Countess
Eleanor Steber
Susanna
Bidú Sayão
Cherubino
Jarmila Novotna
Almaviva
John Brownlee
Figaro
Ezio Pinza
Dr. Bartolo
Salvatore Baccaloni
Conductor
Bruno Walter

But these are mere descriptive tallies—in Walter's hands Mozart's *Figaro* at last receives his due at the Metropolitan. In the overture he opens up a new world of music-making. The orchestra is clearly on its mettle, and the merely fleet gives way with consummate ease to the "singing allegro" (as in the bassoon transition)—plenty of bubbling vitality here. The singers, too, place their trust in him—in their opening duet Pinza and Sayão's two-note slurs fit neatly into Walter's control. All *topice* are knitted into the total fabric, yet their expressive and dramatic intent is clear. From the conversational swing of the string theme against Pinza's counting as the curtain goes up (and this time the bass really observes Mozart's *piano* and *forte* contrasts in 'Se vuol ballare') to the lilt of the wedding march and fandango, through the twilight of the garden scene finale where the gentle portent of Walter's staccati causes us to hold our breaths in anticipation of the Countess' forgiving benediction—everything intrigues. There is nothing perfunctory in the performance; yes, the "pin" aria is a shade overwrought, but Walter cares about even the smallest thing.

After a half-dozen fruitful years there came a lengthy hiatus in Walter's Met sojourn. Nothing seemed more logical than to assign *Figaro* to the maestro who abetted the Mozart revival in a series of celebrated performances (and recordings) at Glyndebourne in the mid thirties. In this case, logic proved an unreliable guide.

In 1945 Fritz Busch came to the Metropolitan as custodian of the Wagner wing; Cologne, Stuttgart, Bayreuth, and Dresden (*Generalmusikdirektor* at the latter) had affirmed his stature in German opera. Yet he had been a principal in the revival of middle Verdi in Germany in the early 1930s as well. Busch fled his homeland in 1937 (a non-Jew, but a rabid anti-Nazi), and by 1940 found succor at the Colon in Buenos Aires, and later in the States. Sad to report, on this afternoon (15 March 1947), he is no aid to Mozart. In his hands *Figaro* has sunk to a mere repertory standard, and sometimes below that.

The overture is brilliant enough if one accepts a field marshal manner. The pace is rousing and the playing has point and accuracy, but the warning is clear—no sinuous curves are in prospect this afternoon. Moreover, Busch cannot seem to control the ensemble either on stage or between stage and pit. Perhaps the introduction of a new soprano in the pivotal role of Susanna has thrown things out of kilter. Until her debut as Susanna a month before the broadcast, Swedish soprano Hjördis Schymberg, well known to record collectors as a frequent partner of Bjoerling, had sung all her roles in Swedish (a single *Così* in 1940 was the exception), which may account for some of the performance's instability.

Even Pinza seems a bit distraught, anticipating by a beat his second count ('dieci') in the opening scene, and both soprano and bass frequently part company with the orchestra in the many eighth-note pickups of their duet. Pinza has plenty of voice (this is his last *Figaro* broadcast) but is rather huffy in manner and not in his usual good humor. A little wow invades the sustained notes of 'Se vuol ballare,' and one feels that bass and conductor don't quite trust one another. Busch brings 'Non più andrai' back to a military spit-and-polish tempo, and Novotna, too, recaptures the extrovert Cherubino in her arias. Admittedly, the orchestra often performs with well-oiled efficiency for Busch, and several well-judged tempi are effective: in the finale the opening terzetto is broadly paced, and the deliberate andante con moto at Susanna's unexpected appearance creates a delicious suspense. (Again Pinza enters a beat too soon with 'Nol conosco'—these are unheard-of missteps for this artist).

Lorenzo Alvary, the new gardener, makes his mark as an imaginative character actor, and Mimi Benzell, Queen of the Night in her 1945 debut, proves to be a per-

Le Nozze di Figaro
15 March 1947

Countess
Eleanor Steber

Susanna
Hjördis Schymberg

Cherubino
Jarmila Novotna

Almaviva
John Brownlee

Figaro
Ezio Pinza

Dr. Bartolo
Salvatore Baccaloni

Conductor
Fritz Busch

fect soubrette Barbarina. Happily, the progressive mania of the ensemble finale (Da Ponte prescribed "strepitoso, arcistrepitoso, strepitosissimo") is well captured by Busch in the closing sections of the act. Pinza may be a bit inhibited by Busch's reluctant tempo in 'Aprite un po',' but he draws the piece along and makes it work for him once again. The concluding finale is slipshod: Pinza wants ahead, Brownlee is consistently lagging, and Busch must have retired to his dressing room in dismay.

Not all of this can be laid upon a new element in the ensemble—and, for a fact, Schymberg is one of the more stable elements of the performance. Stable, but not much more than that. Her tone is well focused (but alarmingly straight) and she knows her way around the role—her staccato-like delivery of the "leap" duet is excellent. But her timbre is monochromatic, and only one color in the voice tends to make a character one-dimensional as well. Beginning with the big finale, one's hopes for Schymberg's success rise. The voice takes on a fullness, and she needs no extraneous chirps in the patter to make her points. (Up to this time, one has regretted the absence of Sayão's dynamic presence.) Schymberg's vocal tin acquires a patina of silver (plate) in the duet with the Count, and she takes the *piano* B-flat in the letter duet very nicely. Throughout the afternoon the Swedish soprano's Italian has served well enough, but wonder of wonders, she muffs the opening text of 'Deh vieni,' keeps remarking on 'del rose' rather than 'di rose,' and all but loses her placement in attempting a diminuendo in the final phrase. The total effect of a decent and straightforward (but insufficiently seductive) rendering is marred. Two Gildas and two Susannas were the sum of her Met career.

Busch, however, has another try at *Figaro* in the broadcast of 8 January 1949. This time Sayão is back, but her consort is new (Italo Tajo), as are Curzio (Leslie Chabay), Barbarina (Anne Bollinger, not quite idiomatic but lovely of voice) and Marcellina (Claramae Turner). The Met was well stocked with serviceable Marcellinas this decade, and Turner is at the top of the list, unafraid to deliver her asides at a *piano* dynamic and able to portray character while maintaining vocal poise. The California mezzo had made her mark elsewhere as Menotti's *Medium*, and movie-goers remember her work in *Carousel* in the 1950s, but her short Met career would offer few challenges. Vocal poise has all but departed from Baccaloni by 1949 (and it is no momentary indisposition, for in the 1950 broadcast the voice is a mere shadow of its former self—nothing but a windy hollow on sustained tones). Sayão, on the other hand, remains in complete control of her resources. 'Venite, inginocchiatevi' has a full measure of unforced charm (though she invents a new melodic line for one phrase and avoids the high Cs in the finale—both uncharacteristic of a Sayão performance). Another revealing moment occurs in the boudoir where Sayão hesitates in the undressing scene with Cherubino, and Novotna softly prompts her. In the later *Figaro* performances (1950, as well) Sayão has toned down her characterization: the recitatives are tamer and any annoying mannerisms have been eliminated in the arias and ensembles. The 1949 'Crudel! perchè finora' duet is Sayão at her best, lovely in tone and just knowing enough. If 'Deh vieni' lacks a little of the vocal glow of earlier days (perhaps she is less intent on seducing this Figaro), the preceding accompanied recitative is entrancing in tone and manner.

Overall, the comic spirit lives in the 1949 *Figaro*. Busch has seen to that. The stage dialectic of the second-act finale is made audible, each change of movement and each motive given shape and impulse, and unlike his earlier effort, coordination between stage and pit is excellent. Busch has made the Met *Figaro* respectable again. The sextet is a highlight: taken at a leisurely tempo, it becomes more of a musical

Le Nozze di Figaro
8 January 1949

Countess
Eleanor Steber
Susanna
Bidú Sayão
Cherubino
Jarmila Novotna
Almaviva
John Brownlee
Figaro
Italo Tajo
Dr. Bartolo
Salvatore Baccaloni
Conductor
Fritz Busch

experience, with evidence of careful rehearsal (all the dotted rhythms are exact, yet delivered with a delightful bounce). A lighter, more transparent texture often enhances the concerted moments.

The void caused by Pinza's retirement was a serious problem for the Met, particularly in Mozart performances. An artist of Pinza's individuality can never be replaced in the sense that his exact qualities will be duplicated. It is folly to try to do so. But evidently that is what management had in mind when they hired Tajo. In this they were abetted by Busch. At age twenty Tajo had appeared in Turin as an unlikely Fafner in *L'Oro del Reno* under Busch, who then invited him to Glyndebourne for minor parts and choral service. After army duty, Tajo returned there in the summer of 1949, this time as Figaro, again under Busch's guidance. In the meantime Tajo's height and classic features, as well as his dramatic know-how, had brought fame in Italian operatic films.

Possibly this was the brand of charisma the Met needed. Two seasons, however, would prove enough of an ersatz Pinza. Not that Tajo was without merit. The voice has size and Pinza-like vibrancy, and positive evidence of musical rectitude survives in his two *Figaro* broadcasts. Best of all, he has the requisite panache for Figaro and Giovanni. But his lively personality entails some exaggerations of style, a tendency to snort and huff which tries to pass as dramatic involvement. The most offensive mannerisms are the frequent introduction of a cavernous shudder into the tone (whether an excessive vibrato that is part of his vocal production or merely an affectation, it proves tedious in the extreme), and a persistent tendency to sing slightly below the pitch. Before the afternoon is out, one has tired of Tajo. Yet one can admire the menace in the recitative before 'Se vuol ballare' and the phrasing in the aria itself (though he substitutes word sense for rhythmic accuracy in the presto section). Tajo talks, more than sings, 'Non più andrai,' but it can be done that way and it passes muster. He preens himself upon *secco* recitatives of lightning rapidity, though all around him court meaning rather than speed. Again, his built-in echo chamber and pitch problems take over in 'Aprite un po' '—still, his assured manner wins him the biggest hand of the afternoon.

A year later, in Reiner's *Figaro* broadcast, we meet a much-altered artist, and the change is all for the better. For the most part the shudder has been banished, the recits are logically paced, the arias well sung. Pitch is still an occasional problem—it reasserts itself in the fourth-act aria where the labored quaver also returns; when he must sing out, evidently he must shudder. Tajo is always the actor, and one can all but see him coaxing the audience into intimacy as he quietly tells them 'già ognuno lo sa.' The new Bing regime saw no need to utilize his talents, but twenty-five years after this broadcast, his considerable abilities as a character singer-actor brought him back to the Met for a decade of juicy cameos.

Whether or no it was Reiner who corralled Tajo's eccentric tendencies, the broadcast of 11 February 1950 everywhere bears the stamp of this formidable master. His *Figaro* stands at the opposite pole from that of Walter. Reiner's overture is the fleetest of the lot, yet he, too, manages to make the orchestra sing, and the final lengthy crescendo grows from nothing until it fairly bursts with comic energy. The opening duets have pinpoint accuracy; one knows his artists must toe the mark (even Baccaloni is rhythmically alert in his aria). Many felicities of nuance command attention: the delightful way the Marcellina-Susanna string motive flies off into space in their duet (it is the closest thing to a musical nosethumb); the deftly underlined accompaniment motives in the prelude to 'Porgi, amor'; the studied time-frame

Le Nozze di Figaro
11 February 1950

Countess
Eleanor Steber

Susanna
Bidú Sayão

Cherubino
Jarmila Novotna

Almaviva
John Brownlee

Figaro
Italo Tajo

Dr. Bartolo
Salvatore Baccaloni

Conductor
Fritz Reiner

during the Count's questioning of Figaro into which Reiner drops his musical ideas in just proportion (the big finale may best be described as a controlled madness). All of this is enhanced by the transparent texture of the orchestral fabric and the scrupulous observance of a wide range of dynamics. The performance seems to be borne on wings.

Nor is Reiner immune to the singers' prerogatives. Steber has time to make an eloquent moment of the close of 'Porgi, amor' (the best of her lot); Novotna pours out her heart in 'Voi che sapete' at a shockingly leisurely tempo—this Cherubino is the most languid of lovelorn youths. Is it his Budapest birth that permits Reiner a 'Venite, inginocchiatevi' hardly less gentle than Walter's, in turn permitting Sayão's most graceful rendering? The porcelain delicacy of Steber and Sayão in the second-act trio (delicacy, however, that like fine porcelain comes from having been fired in the kiln), the utter demureness of Sayão in the duet with the Count—everything speaks a Reiner credo that less is more. Reiner has come; can Krips—and the Viennese manner—be far behind?

Reiner deepens the expressive content of the opera in Steber's and Sayão's big arias. Steber again crowns the afternoon with her most heartfelt 'Dove sono,' and Reiner, too, knows how to feel. He makes songs of the slow interjections in her recitative, he expands beats in the aria to allow her and the music to breathe, the winds take on a mournful tone, and he holds back the final section of the aria until 'Ah! se almen' makes its poignant effect.

A few years later, Tibor Kozma, writing instructively about Reiner's gifts, described his "uncanny sense for form and proportion" and "the precarious equilibrium between an explosive, almost elemental temperament and a strong, mature, immensely disciplined intellect which exerts a constant effort to keep that temperament in check."[4] Kozma cited that effort as "the battle between the professional and the amateur within himself"—a battle the professional Reiner invariably wins. The professional is centered on music as a "craft" to be mastered; the amateur believes music to be "almost all inspiration"—he will surprise us "by performing very well with his human warmth and genuine love for music adding quite a peculiar charm to his achievements," but his performances will sometimes "refuse to yield to incantation." Kozma makes no mention of Walter, but the suspicion arises that Kozma may have held him in mind as the "amateur." Kozma was, after all, Reiner's right-hand man at the Met during these seasons. Though Kozma's case is loaded, one can test his argument in the two great *Figaro* broadcasts of this decade. No doubt, both Walter and Reiner served Mozart more than well.

"Professional craftsmen" were nothing new at the Metropolitan. That encomium was at least equally the property of George Szell, yet another entry in the master conductor Mozart sweepstakes of the 1940s.

Szell's authoritarian hand fell, not upon the warm comedy of *Figaro*, but upon *Don Giovanni*'s more trenchant crew. On 9 December 1944, Pinza, Baccaloni, Kullman, Harrell, and Sayão, familiar cohorts, are joined by Moscona, Steber, and newcomer Florence Kirk. Clearly, they will march to Szell's beat, marshaled like the insistent contrapuntal entries of his overture. The drive and machine-gun precision of the overture, the scrupulous care for dynamics, the compact, orderly ensemble of the concerted pieces, the control in the rousing *stretto* at the end of the first act—all are calling cards of the professional craftsman (and welcome they are). But Szell also provides a framework of unexpected intimacy for the Zerlina-Giovanni duet (Pinza has never been more insidiously seductive with his bewitching mezza voce). 'Metà di voi,' so often a dull interlude as Giovanni deludes Masetto, becomes an ear-enticing orchestral poem as Szell gives each orchestral figure a sprightly contour. Baccaloni reads his catalog (Cross, forever commenting between every scene, informs us of the "catholicity of that nobleman's taste in ladies") at a sedate pace, the final pages resolutely held back. Szell's broadly limned conception demands more than Baccaloni can supply and causes him real anguish on the high D—all the fun is in the orchestral accompaniment. Nor does Szell neglect to summon the breadth of manner due to the seria characters.

Yet, for all the surety and just proportions of Szell's interpretation, the feeling insinuates itself that the lifeblood of the work is seeping away. Elvira's entrance aria suggests no parody of a seria heroine in the lick and spittle of Szell's reading; if we can't laugh a little at Elvira's plight, she comes off as merely a nagging shrew. Nor is Sayão permitted to purvey all of Zerlina's charm in her arias, though she is vocally adept. No ethereal calm settles over the mask trio (the cemetery scene, on the other hand, is evocative). Steber is not allowed to convey Elvira's heartfelt anguish in 'Ah, taci, ingiusto core!' while Pinza and Baccaloni, two of the liveliest interpreters of the century, are reduced to automatons in the 'Eh via, buffone' and 'O statua' duets—but they deserve medals for their accurate patter at Szell's rapid pace. A double image of Szell will not down. Still, one can forgo a lot for the exquisite proportions and transparent texture of Szell's sextet—how subtly he sounds the changes of mood!

Overall, Pinza is a happy if less artful serenader, a little more subdued than formerly but in fine voice. Harrell's Masetto has grown up in both voice and manner. Kullman tries to shape a few phrases of 'Il mio tesoro,' gets behind, and struggles in the fioriture; not one of his better efforts. Kolodin chastised the management for bringing forth Florence Kirk as the most demanding of Mozart heroines (her Met debut occurred as Anna the week previous to the broadcast). But Kirk was no novice in the role, having sung it in Buenos Aires and under Beecham in Mexico City. Appearances as Maria Boccanegra and Fiora in Rio, Minnie in San Francisco, a triumph as Lady Macbeth with the New Opera Company in New York, and the soprano solos in Beethoven's *Missa Solemnis* under Toscanini all indicate adequate qualifications for the Met stage. At her entrance she proffers a thrust of dramatic soprano steel (though a bit overheated). Temperament she has, as shown in Anna's accompanied recitative, and a spacious delivery which serves the vengeance aria well (some shrillness invades the upper voice). There is nothing dishonorable about her fioriture in the trio or in 'Non mi dir' (quite clean, in the latter), but it lacks bravura. Decorous is the word for her 'Non mi dir'—everything in place but somewhat like looking through the wrong end of the telescope. Though Kirk would remain at the Met for four seasons, she was offered few opportunities, and the radio public hears no more from her.

Luckily, Steber would continue to add to her gallery of Mozart heroines for years to come. The broadcast offers only her second Met Donna Elvira, but already it attains a high level of distinction. If it is not quite at the level of her Contessa, that is because Elvira's angular lines and belligerent manner provide less opportunity to exploit her mastery of serene melody. A few squeaky moments intrude early on. Nor does she as yet project the full measure of Elvira's willful, desperate nature so as to dominate the opera—and a shrewd, individualistic Elvira can do just that, though Anna is today considered the plum role, even as Zerlina was so regarded in the

Don Giovanni
9 December 1944

Donna Anna
Florence Kirk
Donna Elvira
Eleanor Steber
Zerlina
Bidú Sayão
Don Ottavio
Charles Kullman
Don Giovanni
Ezio Pinza
Leporello
Salvatore Baccaloni
Masetto
Mack Harrell
Commandant
Nicola Moscona
Conductor
George Szell

Salvatore Baccaloni as Leporello in *Don Giovanni*.

nineteenth century (at least when Patti held sway). But of Steber's vocalism and musicianship there can be nothing but praise. By the time she reaches 'Ah, fuggi' the voice is well oiled, and she opens the quartet in commanding seria fashion. 'Never trust this evil man' is for Steber a warning of danger (Novotna infused it with the melancholy of personal regret). Steber launches the sextet most affectingly, makes music of Elvira's distraught pleas to the supping Giovanni. Fortunately, 'Mi tradì' has been restored for her, and with good reason. She is mighty in the accompanied recitative, her vengeful cries giving way to pathetic torment (and Szell fully cooperates in establishing the moods). He moves the aria at a good clip, but Steber is equal to it, not a note of the intricate roulades out of place (the major ones executed in one breath), the tessitura easily encompassed, and all done without a loss of tonal gloss. And when Mozart turns to the minor mode, Steber, not loath to inject a bit of drama into the old-fashioned display piece, captures Elvira's torment.

No comparable feat of vocalism illuminates the *Don Giovanni* broadcast of 6 December 1947. Both Szell and Walter having departed, the opera was assigned to Busch, but illness compelled him to relinquish it to Max Rudolf. Though well versed in the ways of opera theatre, on this occasion Rudolf (who later on would prove his great value to the company as an administrator) is little more than a caretaker. The Szell straitjacket has been loosened, but the reins which provide a sense of purposeful drama have been dropped as well. Rudolf holds the piece together (no catastrophic moments), but too many phrases, too many whole arias or ensembles, turn limp—to the detriment of the singers.

The male contingent of earlier broadcasts is nearly intact. Kullman's tone is headier (though his runs are largely sham), while Baccaloni's vocal condition has deteriorated to the point that the catalog aria is an embarrassment. Alvary is the new Masetto, more plebeian in manner and vocal quality than Harrell, thereby making clear to us Zerlina's preference for Giovanni—a good characterization. As for Pinza (this is his last broadcast), nothing can dim his vibrant manner, though age has thickened his tone. All attempts to utilize the fondly remembered mezza voce in the upper half of the voice founder ('Là ci darem' is sung *mezzo forte* to *forte*), pitch problems invade the Serenade, and the vocal velvet is worn. As in every performance, Pinza never stops trying to give full value to his audience, and the champagne aria has the old brio. Still, it is a lame exit for the grand basso.

Alongside the fifty-seven-year-old Pinza we hear the solid, mature bass of twenty-five-year-old Jerome Hines as the Commandant. His tones have some of Pinza's remembered vibrancy. In spite of his youth, Hines had several years of professional opera appearances under his belt in San Francisco, New Orleans (Méphisto), and Central City (Osmin). Though his debut was as the insignificant Sergeant in *Boris*, the Met recognized his mettle and had given him a Méphisto the week before this broadcast. In keeping with his six-foot-six frame, Hines' vocal stature in the supper scene makes Giovanni's vanquishment credible.

Giovanni's female adversaries, too, are new to our ears. Californian Nadine Conner (an experienced Met veteran) offers a regulation soubrette reading of Zerlina—no distracting mannerisms, but deficient in charm and tonal glow. Her arias are dutiful but dull, and she fails to share with us Zerlina's invitation to intimacy (which should make us fall in love with her). Massachusetts-born Polyna Stoska is more successful. Though again shorn of her big aria, Stoska's Elvira demonstrates the professional skill earned by four years at the Deutsche Oper in Berlin (Elsa, Sieglinde, Elisabeth, Contessa, Pamina, and Elvira) and triumphs as the *Ariadne* Composer with

Don Giovanni
6 December 1947

Donna Anna
Regina Resnik

Donna Elvira
Polyna Stoska

Zerlina
Nadine Conner

Don Ottavio
Charles Kullman

Don Giovanni
Ezio Pinza

Leporello
Salvatore Baccaloni

Masetto
Lorenzo Alvary

Commandant
Jerome Hines

Conductor
Max Rudolf

the New York City Center company. She had just won the Donaldson award as "the best musical supporting artist on Broadway" for her gripping portrayal of Mrs. Maurrant in the long-running Kurt Weill *Street Scene*. As heard on this afternoon, the voice has size, a distinctive coloration (though rather lacking in sensuousness—there is little vibrato), and is solid throughout its range. Her fioriture in the act-one arias and mask trio are on the mark, and while some of the pathos Mozart allows Elvira is not fully plumbed, her tones take on increased warmth as the opera progresses. She does treat us to a delicious pair of downward *portamenti* ('pietà!' in the sextet) as prescribed by Mozart.

Of even greater interest is the Donna Anna of Regina Resnik. Her Metropolitan career would extend over three decades, two-thirds in the mezzo soprano realm. The prospect of a change of category seems remote indeed on hearing her repulse Giovanni as the opera opens. Throughout the afternoon she proves herself a genuine seria heroine of resplendent tone and commanding manner.

The big emotions, the grand manner seem native to Resnik. When she finishes her dramatic recitative and aria in act one, we are ready to place her at the top of our Anna hierarchy. The voice is beautiful, fruity, and without a hint of vocal inhibition (those top As are all there, though hindsight suggests they are her ultimate top with full retention of timbre). She skillfully molds the long phrases of the mask trio with liquid scales ascending easily to the high B-flat. The excellent rapid runs in the sextet offer hope for a first-rank 'Non mi dir,' graveyard of many a Donna Anna. The recitative is superb, full of meaning and admitting a perfect high B-flat on 'Abbastanza' (and for once we hear the word itself). In the aria her turns are beautifully integrated into the phrase line, and though there is a slight wobble in the first few phrases, her overall rendition bids to cap a triumphant afternoon—but some strange things occur in the fioriture. What she sings is fully adequate, but she omits a full measure (the high B-flat staccati with the descending run), thus ruining the architecture of Mozart's sequence. Resnik recovers for a strong conclusion and one can only wonder at the lapse. Unlike Milanov in similar circumstances, Resnik handles it with perfect aplomb, almost as though the omissions were planned. More likely, Resnik's throat simply told her the tessitura was too much for her, and her intellect (abundantly furnished) quickly sought an out. But is it, even at this early stage of her career, a presage of the future?

Johnson's winning streak of Mozart revivals prompted him to try his luck with yet another, a work which had never been performed in the history of the house. Over the centuries *Die Entführung aus dem Serail* had proven resistant to resuscitation, either in terms of popular response or theatrical credibility. Written a decade before *Die Zauberflöte*, Mozart had filled the embryonic German singspiel with a musical baggage seemingly too heavy for the slight framework of the genre. Though the young Mozart had assured his complaining emperor that the opera contained exactly as many notes as needed, no man of the theatre could agree with him. In addition to the staging problems imposed by its outsized musical forms, the piece requires the kind of vocal virtuosity which was in decidedly short supply during the Johnson era. Though the demands of the tenor role are far from negligible, successful performance of the opera depends upon a disparate pair: Osmin, overseer of the Turkish pasha's harem and one of the most vivid characters in Mozart's varied flock ("coarse, irascible, infinitely comical as a spiteful friend of women and wine, but infinitely dangerous"[5]—a tall order for any operatic bass); and the heroine, Constanza, to whom Mozart entrusted three glorious arias demanding on the one hand a command

The Abduction from the Seraglio
18 January 1947

Constanza
Eleanor Steber
Blonda
Pierrette Alarie
Belmonte
Charles Kullman
Pedrillo
John Garris
Osmin
Dezso Ernster
Conductor
Emil Cooper

of pathos and on the other, coloratura flights of heroic dimensions. This time Johnson faced major-league hurdles. Yet the work is so full of transcendent music strongly rooted in human sentiments and abundant comic situations graphically realized in sound that the gamble was worth it.

Several of those hurdles were not cannily approached nor cleanly cleared, and Johnson was left almost prone upon the managerial track. The irrevocable misstep was to assign the work to Emil Cooper, a conductor of considerable eminence who, in appropriate repertory, contributed to the "conductors' decade" at the Met. One would never know it from the *Abduction* performance (though the conductor had guided a dozen performances at the Central City Festival just prior to the Met premiere). Cooper bulldozes his way through the score, crushing the lively spirit of the comic episodes and robbing the Janissaries' jingles of local-color charm. His earthbound tempi inhibit the singers in the arias of sentiment; and where they must soar, he plods. Thus the revival is hamstrung from the outset.

A second Johnson decision has more justification. Like *The Magic Flute*, *The Abduction from the Seraglio* is performed in the English translation of Ruth and Thomas Martin. Since spoken dialogue is an integral feature of the singspiel genre (though its extent is frequently curtailed in this production), introducing the work to Met audiences in English should have contributed to public acceptance.

Problems are evident in the casting, as well. Blonda, the sprightly seconda donna, is assigned to Canadian Pierrette Alarie, pert in appearance, but shrill of voice on this occasion, and her lover, Pedrillo, falls to tenor John Garris, honorable of voice and frequently intelligible, though in a German-tinged accent. The servant pair are comic foils for Osmin, and on this afternoon, the match is unevenly weighted on the side of the Turk. Kullman is the logical choice for Belmonte, the young Spanish nobleman who seeks to rescue his beloved Constanza (she had been captured by pirates) from the clutches of the Pasha, the latter a speaking part played with a surfeit of resonant dignity by William Hargrave. For most of the opera Kullman is not in his best form; though conscientious in matters of style and superbly clear in diction, the top voice is tight, and the fioriture (what little is retained of Mozart's tortuous roulades) clumsy. The virtuoso aria ('Ich baue ganz'—'I build my faith') is truncated and entirely bereft of coloratura. To Belmonte falls one of Mozart's most delightful arias ('O wie ängstlich'—'Oh how anxious'), and Kullman works well at it but is ulti- mately defeated by Cooper, who so belabors the delectable orchestral painting of Belmonte's heartbeats that one fears this hero will suffer cardiac arrest before the final curtain.

Hungarian Dezso Ernster possesses a striking bass organ, wonderfully black, big and brawny, and of that density which middle-European basses seem to acquire merely from their proximity to the Black Forest. In vocal terms alone his resonant tones suggest a formidable adversary. Ernster's career had been interrupted when he was confined to a concentration camp during the Nazi occupation of Hungary. Before that he had a backlog of twenty years' experience in Berlin (with Walter), Bayreuth (Toscanini), Vienna, and Graz, with South American experience just preceding his Met debut as King Marke in 1946. In vocal majesty and personal temperament Ernster is more at home with somber assignments. He lacks the deft touch of the comic "natural," and more important for this production, his English is so heavily accented that he is almost completely unintelligible both in speech and song. Thus, Johnson's effort is severely blunted in this focal portrayal. Ernster, how- ever, does churn up some towering Osminic rages.

No reservations need be expressed about our Constanza. By 1947 regarded as America's prime Mozartean, Steber has a field day in this virtuoso role. Undoubtedly she profited from her performances in the Central City run. Normally assigned to a slighter voice which can negotiate the pyrotechnics with ease, Constanza spends a good deal of time bewailing her fate, doing most of it in the middle vocal range. With her healthy lyric soprano, Steber is able to sustain Constanza's darker moods; a vivacious personality herself, Steber lamented the heroine's lack of a sense of humor, noting that Constanza "insists on her sorrows at all times . . . is hopelessly romantic . . . a symbol of fidelity."[6]

From the first Steber is in full command of the music (the up and down repetitions of a half scale in the uppermost voice at the conclusion of 'Ach, ich liebte'—Ah, in loving' are the only technical blemish of the afternoon). In the recitative preceding 'Traurigkeit' she conjures a tragic-sentimental mood before lading the aria with broad arcs of tonal splendor; what strength she summons, and yet how feminine she remains! She has the vocal size and metal to make the initial pronouncements of 'Martern aller Arten' ('Tortures unabating') formidable, and she never falters either in clarity of coloratura or purity of tone in the upper regions. The concluding ascending and descending scales are fired off with brio, exactitude, and the determination of an Amazon.

The Abduction received only three New York performances (this was the third). Critics at the premiere were equivocal; Thomson, in particular, quibbled about the level of vocalism. Sometimes later performances, preserved in airchecks, can alter harsh judgments occasioned more by the arduous preparation for a premiere than the innate ability of the artists. In Steber's case, her performance in the broadcast can only be described as a triumph. Yet, overall, Johnson's attempt to resuscitate Mozart's Turkish opera for American audiences must be accounted a failure; thirty-four years would elapse before the Met would try again.

Thus the path of Mozart opera at the Metropolitan during the forties was not free of artistic debris. Mere repertory performances of masterpieces like *Don Giovanni*, *Le Nozze di Figaro* and *The Magic Flute* are often less gratifying than routine offerings of lesser works—we know too well what might have been. Even world-famous maestros proved no guarantee of complete satisfaction, though there was always plenty to admire in the individual components of any performance by a Walter, Busch, Szell, or Reiner. When their interpretations passed into caretakers' hands, blight quickly set in. Singing, too, was variable. *Figaro* fared best in the vocal area. Pinza, Steber, Sayão, Novotna (and to a lesser extent Baccaloni, De Paolis, and Petina) invariably served Mozart well. Don Giovanni's *donna*s were more of a problem. Novotna and Steber could turn Elvira into a winner, but Anna was always a toss of the coin. With the Queen of the Night, there was not even a coin to toss. Age, too, took its toll, and artists (Baccaloni, Rethberg, Kullman) were continued too long in parts for which they had once been well qualified. Two artists consistently gave unalloyed pleasure in many broadcasts: Pinza and Steber were the shining lights of the Met Mozart revival. Though eighteenth-century performance practice (appoggiaturas, ornamentation) remained largely a closed book, the overall stylistic approach moved (with occasional balks) to a higher level than Panizza had provided when he launched the series.

Most important, the repeated presentations of these operas forced them upon the public's consciousness, created a genuine love for their musical subtleties, and fostered such deep and affectionate acquaintance with Mozart's lifelike characters that we could never again bear to lose sight of Pamina and Papageno, the Countess and Figaro, Zerlina and Don Giovanni and their cohorts. Happily, in the future lay even broader acceptance of the Mozart canon: in a few years *Così Fan Tutte* would grace the repertory and, after far too long a wait, would come the revelation of yet another aspect of Mozart's genius—the opere serie, *Idomeneo* and *La Clemenza di Tito*.

In the forties Johnson tuned our ears and primed our hearts, and Mozart found permanent refuge at the Metropolitan.

746

Lily Pons.

CHAPTER TWENTY-ONE

Intermission

Broadcasting "live" means dead time between acts. Air time must be filled, and the home listener could not drop into Sherry's or order a quick pick-me-up at the foyer bar and thus make palatable the several twenty- to thirty-minute breaks of most operas. Over the years the solutions were many, and eventually the intermission features became, for most radio auditors, a cherishable part of Saturday afternoons at the Met.

In the early broadcast days intermissions were considered merely a nuisance, a time to be idled away catch-as-catch-can, even as the ticket holders did in the house. All of the old friends of the Met intermissions (the Opera Quiz, the Goldovsky analysis, the Singers' Roundtable) were later adoptions. It was the Texas Company which, beginning in 1940, brought about the change—they and the Souvaines, Henry and the redoubtable Geraldine, foster parents of these favored children and a few bastards along the way as well.

Since few complete operas were broadcast during the first couple of seasons, an organized pattern of entertainment would have been as much a hindrance as a benefit. Milton Cross did it all (well, almost all). When *Opera News* made known the pattern of the future in 1940, Mrs. Peltz felt it necessary to reassure broadcast devotees that "the scholarly observations of Milton Cross to which the intermissions have largely been devoted in the past will not be lost."[1] Cross would continue in "his valuable capacity as commentator and announcer; the story will be told in his words and the vivid description of scenery and costumes will be as usual entrusted to him." Years later Cross still fondly remembered the early days when all of the intermission pie belonged to him. In an unusual burst of ego, he admitted he liked it that way; he was proud of his ability to ad lib around an emergency.

Though Cross was alone at the helm from 1937 to 1940, he had been ably supported in the earlier seasons. Some deemed composer-critic Deems Taylor's comments an intrusion in 1931–32, so Cross went on alone the next season. John B. Kennedy arrived with the American Tobacco sponsorship in 1933–34. But the boon of commercial sponsorship evidently had compounded the problem of how to fill the intermissions to the satisfaction of the invisible audience. The radio public was far from happy, as an irate listener from North Carolina makes clear.

The Chapel Hill resident wrote directly to Miss Bori, noting with some asperity that last year the soprano had called upon radio listeners "to help . . . save the opera."

> Some of us wonder if we helped save it to provide an advertising medium for Luck [*sic*] Strike cigarettes. . . . I realize that with radio organized as it is in this country we have to have the advertising or we would not have the music. I try to be reasonable about it and not complain—if the advertiser is reasonable. Probably we are a bit spoiled by having had opera for two years as a sustaining program; probably the very call on us to help gave a feeling of vested interest in it as it was being given then.
>
> But even taking all these things into consideration, I think few people objected to its becoming a sponsored program. Indeed I felt a thrill of pleased surprise that enough people listened to opera to attract the attention of a great advertiser. I naively supposed that the American Tobacco Company would reason that since the program had apparently built up a great audience as it was being run for the last two years their best tactics would be to preserve its spirit as completely as possible.

It is the intermission commentary that annoys our critic. Her ear-witness account continues:

> The first broadcast or so was not bad, though we could have well spared Mr. Kennedy's highpowered discourse in favor of more detailed account of the story. But last Saturday was really too much! [The broadcast was Meyerbeer's *L'Africaine* on 14 January 1934.] A regular variety show: rebroadcasts from Hawaii, interesting enough in their place but totally out of place between acts of the opera; more of Mr. Kennedy's big figures about the value of the fiddles in the orchestra; a little badly played string ensemble interlude; more and ever more of the roundness and tightness and smoothness of Luckies till Mr. Cross could only have a minute or two in which to breathlessly tell us the barest outline of the story, and in one case actually had to tell about the act after it had been performed.
>
> . . . Personally I liked the plan two years ago when Mr. Taylor would quietly tell us that so-and-so had entered and the like. Last year it was quite satisfactory when Mr. Cross had time to give almost the entire libretto, indicate the action and describe the setting and the costumes. . . . We need that much. We certainly needed it last Saturday when the opera was relatively unfamiliar.[2]

Our tart correspondent concluded by placing her faith in the beloved Bori: "I somehow felt that you might be able to do something." And Miss Bori tried. She sped the letter on to John Royal, vice-president of NBC, who in his response to the complainant also contributes to the lore of early opera broadcasts: "Regarding the case you mention about the variety show—the interlude by a small orchestra was due to a mechanical failure. The steam curtain at the Metropolitan Opera caused our microphones to get out of order, and it was necessary for the engineers to send the program back to the studios while repairs were made."[3]

On two points consumer interest paid off, as Royal makes clear:

> Regarding the rebroadcast from Hawaii,—it was an endeavor to show that the great opera broadcasts are heard all over the world by means of short wave, and we regret that you did not like it. In this case there was quite a difference of opinion. Many enjoyed it very much and others, like yourself, were not pleased. It was thought advisable that where there were so many who did not like such a feature, to eliminate it in the future.
>
> We agree with you about there not being quite enough time to tell about the opera, and last week we went on fifteen minutes earlier than usual, and in the future we intend opening the program from ten to fifteen

minutes earlier than we had originally planned, in order to get more of the
story explained by Mr. Cross.[4]

These were the happy-go-lucky radio days when time schedules did not dictate
programming.

Geraldine Farrar arrived as intermission commentator in 1934. The diva had
never played a supporting role in her entire life and did not intend to start now. Farrar
was given a free hand to "turn back to some of opera's most colorful pages and bring
to the listeners the pictures of past and present glories."[5] She wrote all her own
material and even illustrated the opera themes by singing them herself, confining
them to one octave (lower to middle B-flat) since, to continue her own words, "only
the vibrations in this range were those easily handled by the engineer without blasts
and gurgles."[6] The soprano strove to introduce a more intimate note into the
intermissions. On one occasion it was her "sad duty to announce . . . the death of the

Geraldine Farrar as Elisabeth in *Tannhäuser*.

greatly beloved Marcella Sembrich [the favored debutante of the Metropolitan's opening season in 1883 and a revered artist until her retirement a quarter century later]. . . . I noted her passing with reference to the *Marriage of Figaro* of my earlier recollections, when, with Eames and Scotti, we shared the triumph of an almost perfect revival under Mahler."[7] These are hallowed names. But so are Bori, Pons (23 February 1935), Martinelli (2 March), and Ponselle (18 January), all of whom joined Farrar in the intermissions for "thumb-nail sketches." Usually the prospective guest attended a rehearsal in the Rockefeller Plaza office of Bertha Brainard, NBC program manager, the day before the broadcast. Other intermission guests of the 1934–35 season included Mary Garden (16 February), Helen Jepson, and Myrtle Leonard (8 February).[8] Conductor Vincenzo Bellezza, however, was informed by Miss Brainard that, despite an earlier invitation, "eminent conductors" could not be included "due to the limited time accorded between the acts for these interviews."[9]

But Mr. Kennedy's "high-powered discourse" returned in 1935 until RCA sponsorship lodged author Marcia Davenport at Mr. Cross' side the following season. When commercial backing ceased during the next three years, Cross again did all the talking, but most of the words came from the NBC Script Division. Lawrence Abbott, annotator for the NBC Symphony Orchestra broadcasts and assistant to NBC music counsel Walter Damrosch, was the man with the pen. He had Cross open by describing "the interior of the Metropolitan, the crowds standing in line to buy tickets, and the arrival of the audience."[10] Abbott knew the value of a personal note as well as Miss Farrar, though he preferred the common touch. "Mr. Hugh Brown," Cross would say, "wearing a silk hat as usual, is taking tickets at the main door."[11] Abbott's style was purposely colloquial—"spoken English, not the 'king's English' . . . so it would sound natural when read by Milton Cross." He sought a middle ground between the "lavender and old lace type of listener who loves opera, but who prefers to have the more lurid details of the plot glossed over" and "more sophisticated listeners." It was Abbott who gave us the familiar "the first voice you hear will be. . . ." Even in the thirties there were occasional guest speakers, but more often Abbott would write up a catchall on a topic related to the broadcast opera: *Lucia*, for instance, prompted a discussion of composers' operas set in foreign lands. Such is the prosy way of music annotators, even today.

Unlike Abbott, Cross was loath to depart from his customary patrician style. Initially he pronounced the characters in the language of the opera, but listeners "resented Des-day´-mo-na" so that he was "practically compelled to revert to the English norm,"[12] at least for Shakespearean characters. Although armed with stacks of background material on both the opera and singers, in the supreme moment of trial (26 February 1938, when Martinelli collapsed midway through 'Celeste Aida'), the valiant Cross was spurned. Jagel was sent for, and NBC chose to fill the twenty-six-minute delay with music from its Radio City Studios.[13] But the homely elements of the episode did not go unreported: Martinelli confessed he had overeaten, and Jagel reported he was just leaving with his two sons for the Sportsmen's Show in Grand Central Palace when the Met management collared him.[14]

But in other crises, intermission time was more welcome to the management. In both the 1933 "Save the Met" campaign and the 1940 effort to purchase the opera house, NBC offered the company intermission time to solicit the radio audience. Once the Souvaines (to their regret) interrupted the opera's overture in order "to emphasize the importance of the current fund drive." They didn't try that again— "The audience rose up in arms,"[15] Geri admitted. More conventional tactics were the norm. On the *Walküre* broadcast in 1940 the impressive lineup of New York Mayor Fiorello La Guardia, Kirsten Flagstad, and Lauritz Melchior played pitchmen. Melchior noted the changed complexion of opera, which formerly had been enjoyed by only "a few people in a few big cities. . . . Now it belongs to all of you everywhere." He pleaded for one dollar from each listener to save the great institution of the Metropolitan, "perhaps the greatest" in the world, a world which "must have a place so the beauty and education of grand opera can be continued." The war in Europe was already in its sixth month, and Melchior argued that "America must take over the fight for all that is left of things which can make life beautiful."[16]

Flagstad's comments hold more interest; she spoke at length of her own career. After noting that her Metropolitan debut had occurred on a Saturday afternoon broadcast, she recalled

> the fortunate set of circumstances that brought me to America. I had sung on a number of European stages but I had a home and family in Norway and wanted to be with them. I remember that I refused an offer to go to Berlin. But then something happened which seemed to me a miracle. I was asked to sing at the Metropolitan Opera in New York. Such an offer means much to an artist. Of course, you must be proud of your great Metropolitan Opera, but maybe in America you take it for granted because you can turn on your radio each week and hear it without effort or expense. Sometimes we do not appreciate the true value of those things we get free. But I assure you that the name Metropolitan is a magic one throughout the world. I am very grateful to the Metropolitan for bringing me here since it has introduced me to a large and understanding public for which I have much respect and affection.[17]

Before the decade was over the reciprocal gratitude of the management to the artist who, more than any other, had kept it solvent in the late thirties would be severely tested. But in 1940 the soprano was concerned that the opera might "have to close its doors." Before she concluded her appeal she spoke of the music of Wagner:

> To me Wagner's music is the most inspiring in all opera. It is at the top of the ladder. In my singing career I had to climb the ladder to reach it. I sang in many operettas and light operas before I was ready to understand and interpret those wonderful characters of Wagner's imagination. . . . When I first heard *Die Walküre* I found parts of it beautiful yet it all seemed very mysterious and bewildering. It was only when I came to know it better that I found it no longer mysterious but full of great beauty and tenderness and nobility. Perhaps you have found the same thing, or perhaps there are some of you who have heard this opera only once or twice and still find parts of it strange. To those of you may I say you have a wonderful experience before you, for no matter how many times you hear this music you will always find new beauty in it.

Especially, one might add, if Madame Flagstad was in the cast—the Wagner operas seemed more viable with her on hand.

The casual manner of the 1930 intermissions ended in 1940 when the Texas Company hired Henry Souvaine, prominent producer of radio programs, to develop and oversee an organized series of intermission features.

Opera News, in its announcement of the new intermission format, all but caused Souvaine's three feature categories to be stillborn when it christened them "intimacy, information, and inspiration."[18] Mrs. Belmont and Miss Bori were to oversee the Metropolitan Opera Guild At Home where backstage "experts" would help in "bringing the radio listeners as intimately as possible into the comradeship of the opera staff and the Guild family."[19] By the next season intimacy had been rejected in favor of a more democratic Meeting of the Air with Guild officers and famous guests. In 1942 collectivism was abandoned for the all-embracing Metropolitan Opera Column of the Air; the emphasis had shifted to "the human side" of opera and its stars.

If the Guild's efforts at "intimacy" proved elusive, "inspiration" was firmly nailed down as a series of talks under the rubric Our American Way. On 7 December 1940 former president Herbert Hoover launched the series, which was under the auspices of the National Council of Women. The tone was high. University presidents evidently towered in the inspirational realm—Robert Hutchins of Chicago and Nicholas Murray Butler of Columbia were on the docket. But artists like playwright Robert Sherwood had something to offer, too, in promoting "confidence in the American system" and illustrating "the advantages and privileges to be enjoyed in a democracy as contrasted with the stifling forces unleashed under foreign ideologies."[20] Clearly the specter of war was haunting the American airwaves. For the 1941–42 season, the third or "extra" intermission soft-pedaled ideology in order to explore Music in America, the musical history of a different city each week.

But with America's involvement in war, the patriotic emphasis returned in 1942 with Guild sponsorship of the Opera Victory Rally, which highlighted speakers from the United Nations. The Rally remained a feature until victory was achieved: "The Road to Lasting Peace" was the topic for the 1943–44 season, "The Fight For Peace" served for the following year. During these years one might hear Tibbett narrate a "Red Cross Newsreel," or Raymond Swing, the news analyst, speak on "A Citizen of the World at Peace." Geraldine Souvaine recounts how Mrs. Roosevelt came to speak on the Victory Rally during the war years, refused script or rehearsal, arrived fifteen minutes before her appearance, asked Henry Souvaine the scheduled topic and desired length of her talk. Twelve and a half minutes were allotted, and Mrs. Roosevelt closed her eyes and spoke "with continuity and meaning" for exactly twelve and a half minutes.[21]

But the enduring legacy of the Souvaine tutelage was the Opera Quiz, still going strong a half century after its inception in 1940. Initially Cross conducted the quizzing of the experts from the fields of opera, music criticism, or literature (even "the sophisticated layman" could qualify as an expert). The aim was to "provide the information requested by members of the radio audience."[22] Gladys Swarthout, Lawrence Tibbett, and New York Times critic Olin Downes were the baptismal experts on 7 December 1940. Before long Downes assumed the post of quizmaster, presiding until his retirement in 1948. Downes' manner was short on the urbanity associated with his son, later quizmaster Edward Downes, as one can hear in a 1947 quiz.[23] By then the quiz had gained such favor that an occasional doubleheader was programmed, as occurred on the 20 December broadcast. Regular quiz experts on hand were Deems Taylor, Robert Bagar, and Sigmund Spaeth. With a liberal number of Sure 'nuffs Downes certifies their answers. "Now this is a humdinger, so watch out," he warns them, asking them to identify opera librettists from a one sentence description: "My uncle was the father-in-law of the composer" is the query (Downes notes it "just bamboozles me as I look at it")—"Halévy to Delibes" is the answer. His manner surprises if one has read Downes' rather turgid criticism. Geri Souvaine recounts how, when the experts were unable to name Lohengrin's father, Downes opined "I guess it was an immaculate conception."[24] When Opera News recorded Downes' death in 1955, the obituary noted that he "freely admitted the superior knowledge of the authorities across the table,"[25] and Mrs. Peltz cited his "burly personality and honest, homely mind"—how clearly they came through on the 1947 quiz.

Cross introduced the 1947 quiz as "our game of operatic questions and answers"—along with intimacy and inspiration, the founding principle of "information" has been abandoned. Entertainment has become the watchword. Yet Texas Company functionary Harold V. Milligan, who served as editor of the quiz, reported that the most frequent question submitted concerned the desirability or undesirability of opera in English (a much hotter topic in the forties than today). Other favorite questions were of the "name three operas mentioning . . ." type: bells, flowers, trees, and death agents were exceedingly popular. But Milligan was always on the lookout for questions concerning the music itself—these were much rarer.[26] The flow of listeners' questions increased relentlessly until, by the end of the fifties, it reached ten thousand a year.

During the forties the lineup of quiz experts broadened to include Huntington Watts, Boris Goldovsky, George Marek, Robert Lawrence, and most delightful raconteur of all, the Philadelphia *Evening Bulletin* critic Max de Schauensee. Occasionally a ringer was brought in: on a 1945 quiz Basil O'Connor (Chairman of the American National Red Cross) officiated as guest quizmaster; on 29 November 1948 a very young Leonard Bernstein made an isolated appearance as guest expert. Artists of the company were sometimes included (John Charles Thomas in 1948, Tibbett in 1949—baritone parity there, though Thomas was out and Tibbett, just barely, in), and on the Christmas Eve matinee of that year, Mary Garden, on a lecture tour of the United States from her home in Scotland, joined in the game. By now the delightful editor of *Opera News*, Mrs. Peltz, had added pith and elegance to the quiz with semiregular appearances.

Souvaine's other two programs (the intimacy-inspiration duo) had nothing like the longevity of the quiz, and in 1945 a new regimen began. A pleasant lunch with Frank St. Leger and Eddie Johnson encouraged Henry Souvaine to pursue a project he had in mind. On 24 October 1945 Souvaine notified St. Leger that "nice progress in some conversations with Boris Goldovsky" would soon lead to a "sound and articulate plan."[27] Opera News on the Air, the long-running first intermission of each opera broadcast—a virtual Goldovsky sinecure—was suggested to Geraldine Souvaine when she recalled a 1930s reception at the America-Italy Society at which Tullio Serafin analyzed *Don Giovanni* at the piano while Ponselle and Pinza provided vocal illustrations. Geri came to consider the musical analysis "the commercial for the broadcast."[28] Eventually the program was planned in committee (four Guild members, two representatives of the Metropolitan Opera management, and five members of Souvaine associates).[29] As enunciated by Souvaine, the programs were guided by "the sound and proven fundamental rule that 'education' per se, stripped of 'entertainment' or 'enthusiasm' or a lively curiosity for the little-known, is pedagogy and, as such, is limited in appeal to an earnest though infinitesimal minority."[30] In her mind it was the "careful nurturing—educating step by step"—which has led to acceptance "even enthusiasm" for operas (such as *Rosenkavalier, Così Fan Tutte, Manon Lescaut*) which in 1940 had appealed to only a small minority. (Undoubtedly the operas themselves—and the opportunity to hear them repeatedly—were of equal importance, to give Strauss and Mozart and Puccini their due.)

Current broadcast devotees, used to the Goldovsky monologues on the opera of the week, would have been surprised at the early format of Opera News on the Air. During his first season, master of ceremonies Goldovsky was assisted by guests ranging from Patrice Munsel to Reverend Robert Gannon (president of Fordham University), from Lucrezia Bori to pianist Alec Templeton. In later seasons, Maria Jeritza and stage director Dino Yannopoulos, critic de Schauensee and Robert Merrill were paired, while theatre director Margaret Webster did a single on a *Walküre* broadcast in 1947. The venerable De Luca and Teresa Helburn, Rose Bampton and Ralph Bellamy, Novotna and Crooks, Martinelli, Albanese, Paul Althouse (*Elektra*), Branzell and Margarete Matzenauer (a frequent guest), all played to the Goldovsky personality.

The parade of retired divas before the microphone went on and on in the fifties with Garden, Marjorie Lawrence, and Ponselle. Ponselle's appearance in 1954 was a novelty—the first intermission ever presented on tape. The production team had traveled to Stevenson, Maryland, to record her interview. Before discussing the afternoon's opera (*Norma*) Ponselle told Goldovsky she had asked for only one role during her Met career—Adriana Lecouvreur. "I had studied it thoroughly. I thought it would be a good part for me and a successful production for the house. Then somebody came up with a box-office report from 1908 when the work had last been done in New York by Caruso and Cavalieri. . . . For some reason it had not been a financial success. So they refused me. This was one of the real disappointments of my career."[31] So disappointed she was that Ponselle retired soon after and "made a new life for myself." As heard in the 1954 interview, the early Goldovsky delivery is not nearly so theatrical as it came to be. In fact, he sounds curiously detached and matter-of-fact, his staid but rapid-fire delivery contrasting with Ponselle's vivacious, natural responses. (Goldovsky recently recalled that numerous takes were required for that interview due to Ponselle's nervousness—which may account for his cool manner, while editing provided the Ponselle spontaneity.)

All the features (except the quiz, scrupulously advertised as unrehearsed and ad lib), were carefully scripted, and only consummate actors (of which Goldovsky would come to be the foremost) could escape the deadly "your-turn, now my-turn" curse when reading lines. We can hear Goldovsky in his natural habitat on the first intermission of the 1947 broadcast of *Manon*, introduced by Cross as the "guiding spirit" of Opera News on the Air, "the genial and talented head of the opera department of the New England Conservatory."[32] His guests are Lawrence Tibbett ("among the illustrious great") and young coloratura soprano Pierrette Alarie, sounding just like Leslie Caron and equally charming as she delivers unbelievably well-thought-out analyses of Massenet's photographic technique ("almost like a candid-camera scene"). Tibbett's beautiful speaking voice and conversational delivery carry the day. He can't help acting as he interprets his script: "Well," he taunts the guileless Alarie, "even if I didn't know the opera, I wouldn't give odds on love to win over money where that girl is involved." He plays the modern cynic—"Convent school will never be like this," but it's "nice work" if Manon can get it. Goldovsky layers in the learning deftly enough (no wonder Geri gave him a run-of-the-show contract): "This knack of writing a vocal line that seems absolutely continuous is . . . possibly [Massenet's] most important contribution to the musical theatre." That extrovert manner can get away with almost anything, and no one has ever played the musical examples with such orchestral simulation. At the intermission's close, Alarie draws in her invisible audience, assuring them that Massenet's characters are so vivid "even the radio audience, which hears but does not see except with the inner eye of its imagination" knows Manon and Des Grieux well.

In the previously cited apologia that she sent to Rudolf Bing, Geraldine Souvaine wrote of the "impressive amount of operatic information and lore—never before in print and not available in books"—which the intermission features revealed to the radio audience. Her claim was valid, particularly after the war's end in 1945; now the old format of the third intermission required an overhaul. According to the Texas Company ads, Opera Roundtable was initially designed for "a brilliant group of critics, artists and musical personalities" to focus on the opera of the following week "or some similarly interesting subject." In its early years guests like stage director Herbert Graf might appear, but more often the guest personalities were merely a reshuffling of the familiar quiz participants. By 1948 the Texas Company ad promised that each third intermission "will be different—but in character with this entire afternoon of fine musical entertainment." Thus, one might hear chairman of the board of directors George A. Sloan tout "The Metropolitan Family," or Howard Hanson cover "Twenty-five Years of Music Education." On 11 November 1950 a bit of the old patriotism returned as "The Metropolitan Welcomes the United Nations on Armistice Day" brought U.N. representatives Warren Austin, Carlos P. Romulo, and Nazrollah Entezam to the microphones.

At times special occasions prompted a departure from the routine. When premieres were offered, flexibility was required, but even here the Souvaines held the reins firmly. When Bernard Rogers' *The Warrior* was first aired on 11 January 1947 the "apostolic thinking"[33] of the Met management was for Goldovsky to do an analysis; he ended up commenting on *Hansel and Gretel* (the afternoon's opera partner). Henry Souvaine reasoned that, since Opera News on the Air followed *The Warrior*, even a Goldovsky could not concoct a radio analysis that would "carry conviction or artistic integrity" from just studying "a black and white score." (The apostolic thinking seems more in the naive Souvaine mind on this and other issues of the education versus entertainment tussle.) The solution Souvaine proposed was palatable enough: Cross could give "some important generalizations about the type of opera and what Corwin and Rogers have to say about it"; he would then introduce the composer, to give his short personal view of the music, and Edward Johnson, to cover "the essentials from the standpoint of both the Metropolitan management and the listener." All this would produce "the desired impressions" in the radio auditors "directly before" the premiere, "setting their minds as tolerant, intelligent listeners."

Even if this be media manipulation (not merely an invention of the television age), to create "tolerant, intelligent listeners" was a modest goal and one that the intermission features often enough abetted.

Zinka Milanov as Norma.

CHAPTER TWENTY-TWO

1942-45
The Italian Wing While at War

While Mozart and Wagner were the natural province of the master conductors, and the evocative orchestrations of the late nineteenth century French school were sufficient to induce a Francophile like Beecham to shepherd them, Italian fare, especially of the bread-and-butter variety, was less tempting to the virtuoso conductor. Happily, in a few years Toscanini's broadcasts with the NBC Symphony would reaffirm their merit so as to make them worthy of even the most revered maestro's care.

Early in the century Toscanini's concentrated light had shone on the Met's Italian offerings, and Serafin had provided comparable quality in the twenties and early thirties. Around these polestars, Moranzoni and Panizza had maintained a worthy standard, but in recent years the more popular operas had been farmed out to a Papi, a Calusio, a Cimara. Pons' appearances, for instance, were fair game for lesser hands: over the years Lakmé fell to Pelletier, Marie and Gilda to Papi, Rosina and Lucia to Bellezza and Papi. When Pons opened the broadcast season of 1942–43 as Lucia, St. Leger was on the podium, just as he had been for her opening night a few days earlier as *La Fille du Régiment*.

A clue to this mating of unequals (of star power only) may be gleaned from a bit of correspondence for Pons' first appearance the following season. In response to St. Leger's letter expressing the hope that Pons could return to New York previous to the rehearsal of 22 November, Pons cabled "Cannot be at rehearsal November 22nd as am singing concert Denver on 19th. However will be at stage rehearsal November 24th."[1] The first *Lucia* of the season was scheduled for 25 November. Of course, Pons, like Melchior, sang a repertory so circumscribed that rehearsals seemed a walk-through nuisance. Unlike Melchior, Pons' actual performances could reflect a similar lack of involvement (with the character, certainly not with the character as Pons).

The *Lucia* broadcast of 28 November 1942 was the first of only two St. Leger broadcasts (the *Barbiere* previously cited is the other), though he would remain at the house for a decade in critical administrative posts. As a conductor, St. Leger's instincts (as in the *Barbiere*) are sound. He almost succeeds in removing the cobwebs from the perfunctory opening scene. Valentino's able but dry voice and humorless bluster suit Ashton's old-fashioned melodramatics, and he is in excellent voice. From the spirited hunting tune of the introduction on through Ashton's cabaletta, St.

Lucia di Lammermoor
28 November 1942

Lucia
Lily Pons
Edgardo
Jan Peerce
Enrico Ashton
Francesco Valentino
Raimondo
Nicola Moscona
Conductor
Frank St. Leger

333

Leger speeds the work along—chorus and baritone are hard put to keep up. The effect on Pons is salutary. St. Leger's momentum forces her to forgo posturing, and in the first act she delivers some of her finest vocalism in many a season. In top vocal form, her virtuosity in the double aria creates genuine excitement—Pons often can sing "prettily," but on this occasion the apt word is "brilliantly." Even with her slight resources she is able to spin tone ('Verranno a te') rather than merely articulate the notes in a phrase.

In act two St. Leger shows he is not indifferent to the nuanced line of Donizetti's bel canto ('Soffriva nel pianto')—his strings weave and spin, too ('Il pallor funesto'). But these are not Pons' most effective moments (low tessitura and tragic emotion are her natural enemies), and the scene is soon eviscerated; ensemble imprecision between soprano and baritone (the fruit of insufficient rehearsal) proliferates. St. Leger makes more of the sextet than many a conductor, allowing the final concerted section unusual breadth and charting a grand buildup to Donizetti's version of Rossini's godlike cymbal crash. The conductor's tempo modifications may disturb purists, but they make for strong drama. Peerce's articulation of the dotted rhythms in the principal theme is a plus, but Pons' aspirated two-note phrases detract. St. Leger captures the frenetic quality of the ensuing denouement, but he must drag everyone along by the scruff of their vocal necks—the edges are ragged indeed. The afternoon's watchword is clear: spirit, rather than precision.

Moscona offers a pumped-up account of Bidebent's narration of Lucy's crime—long on resonant tone and somber vocal accents but short on horror and pathos. Now comes the main business of the afternoon, Pons' stepped-up version of the mad scene. The cantilena of 'Il dolce suono' is pallid-toned and somewhat breathy (could this be a dramatic choice to indicate Lucia's weakened state?—Pons does offer a shade more characterization than usual throughout the afternoon). As she begins the second section, Pons' tones and manner suggest a heroine barely into adolescence. But again the top voice is brilliant and the cadenza flashes out importantly. Her recall of the 'Verranno a te' theme, now in the stratosphere, is impressively focused, but one must accept the untidy (really nonexistent) trills of 'Spargi d'amaro pianto' in return for a pair of secure high Fs.

Exactly a year after his debut, Peerce makes his second broadcast appearance in the role which he would sing most frequently at the Met. His Edgardo is a very serious young man indeed. Peerce projects a welcome dignity as he recounts the unhappy fate of his forefathers ('Sulla tomba') or bids farewell to earth ('Fra poco a me ricovero'). His feisty defiance at the wedding ceremony and anger at Lucia's supposed perfidy are almost blatantly thrown out; Peerce is nothing if not committed, as full-toned as he is full-hearted. And, of course, he is musically exact, rhythmically alive, and expansive of phrase at appropriate moments (the recitatives which begin his final scene). The line of 'Verranno a te' is exemplary, and the repeated ascents of 'bell'alma innamorata' are readily conquered. Quite a catalog of merits; but the pressurized production, the unvaried volume and timbre (warm enough in itself), and above all, the lack of nuance within the phrase all belie the bel canto style. (How welcome is his bit of mezza voce at the end of 'Verranno'!). Too often one admires, but remains uninvolved. Still, his noble phrasing of the opening of 'Tu che a Dio spiegasti l'ali' stays in the memory.

As noted, St. Leger did not have an active conducting career at the Met. Pons had added to her 1943 cable to him: "Regret your administrative duties will prevent you conducting, but am happy with choice of Sodero." And well she might have been, for Cesare Sodero was the management's inspired response to Panizza's abdication as principal conductor of the Italian wing. In 1942, the Met entrusted Sodero with the repertory staples (*Aida, Bohème, Traviata, Tosca, Trovatore, Cavalleria Rusticana* and *Pagliacci*) which for too long had felt only the cursory embrace of routine.

Diminutive in stature, his credentials, too, seemed minisized when placed up against the illustrious achievements of the celebrity conductors on the roster. On the face of it, his was a journeyman record. Born in Naples, the twenty-year-old cellist came to America in 1906 and went into the pit of Hammerstein's Manhattan Theatre as a soldier in its notorious war with the Metropolitan. Baton assignments with the Henry Savage and Philadelphia Grand Opera companies finally came along. Even the brand of the Hippodrome was upon him. Of longer duration were his early years conducting for the Edison Phonograph company and, of greater interest, his involvement (1925 on) with radio opera, plus innumerable symphonic concerts for NBC and the Mutual Network. Top the record off with nine years (1933–42) as leader of the Mendelssohn Glee Club, and Sodero would seem no more than a last-minute substitute for the reluctant Panizza, holed up in Argentina.

But Sodero had grown up in the opera house. His father was a member of the San Carlo orchestra in Naples; on one occasion, when he was only two, forgetful parents had left him overnight sleeping cozily among the kettledrums in the San Carlo pit. His Metropolitan performances soon confirmed that he was a man completely at home on the podium as well. Suckled at Italian opera's fount and tempered by extensive, if rather commonplace, experience, Sodero nurtured a musical sensitivity far removed from the complaisant routine of a Papi or Calusio. Could it survive and thrive under the constraints of the Metropolitan's meager rehearsal allotment? The popular Italian operas were seldom out of repertory, and only unusual circumstances would allow even moderate restudy of a work such as *Traviata*.

The 5 December 1942 broadcast of *Traviata* provided just such a circumstance. On that afternoon Albanese sang her first Violetta on any stage. (She had withdrawn in favor of Novotna from a non-Met *Traviata* in Newark a year earlier.) The mating of conductor and soprano is apt, for Sodero provides a framework of chamber music intimacy which allows Albanese's sentient interpretation to flower. Tibbett and Kullman are in their familiar places as Germont *père et fils*, along with the full complement of the Met's best comprimarios: Votipka, De Paolis, Cehanovsky, and D'Angelo. Sodero is everywhere indulgent to his singers: tempos are always on the slow side, ritards are abundant, and broad *fermati* and *portamenti* abound. Yet, nowhere is there any sense of musical violation—the overall effect is one of exquisite charm and finely tuned sensibility.

The first-act prelude tells the tale with its caress of string tone, scrupulous attention to dynamics, and controlled intensity of line, all expressive of careful, loving preparation, yet redolent with emotion. Surely one's maiden aunt could rub shoulders with the demimondaine companions of Violetta without fear of contamination, so elegant and well behaved is Sodero's party music. Kullman has never been sweeter-toned. The role suits his resources perfectly, and he makes a real love song of the aria, aided by Sodero's genuine andante rather than the usual bumptious trot. Nor is Kullman deficient in fervor; he rides the climax of the denunciation effectively. Unhappily, Tibbett is in his worst vocal estate, and his performance must be counted the nadir of his broadcast career. To hear an artist labor so, ever trying to oil his recalcitrant vocal mechanism but to so little effect, is more than distressing. Each note seems an effort, and the upper part of the voice is hollow and weary. As soon as

La Traviata
5 December 1942

Violetta
Licia Albanese

Alfredo
Charles Kullman

Germont
Lawrence Tibbett

Conductor
Cesare Sodero

one imagines a bit of tonal life creeping back into the sound ('Bella voi siete'), a more wretched patch displaces hope ('Piangi'). The aria is marginally better, and at last a bit of the old majesty invades 'Se la voce dell'onor.' The audience savors the past and gives him a big hand. Yet one feels that an era has ended.

But the tale is not quite over. A year or two later a pair of *Traviata* broadcasts (1 January 1944 and 17 February 1945), with Sodero still comfortable in the pit, show a marked improvement. In 1944 Tibbett has more tone at his command and an almost serviceable legato. It is still obviously an aged voice (though Tibbett is only forty-eight), and he sinks below pitch in 'Pura siccome un angelo,' but the top opens up a bit and he risks a few mezza voce effects with reasonable success. The following year's Germont is better still. A solid core of tone is at his command: he lingers on a few resonant top tones (a fine high G-flat to launch the cadenza in the aria), and the old buzz has displaced the recent hollow ache. Of course, the old Tibbett mastery can never be fully reclaimed, but one feels his honor has been restored.

Albanese commands unrestrained admiration during this series of *Traviata* broadcasts. We rejoice that the airwaves captured her very first portrayal of this many-faceted Verdi heroine. According to *Opera News*, Albanese "thought that Violetta was much too difficult a part for her when she first heard *La Traviata* in Milan."[2] For the next two decades she would dominate the role at the Metropolitan (eighty-seven performances in the house and on tour). Of the fourteen broadcasts of *Traviata* from this debut performance to her final broadcast Violetta in 1959, Albanese sang ten (Sayão, Steber, Tebaldi, and De los Angeles were each allotted a single broadcast). Seldom has the interpretation of a single artist so penetrated the consciousness of so large a public (among female singers Flagstad's nine and Traubel's ten Isoldes, Stevens' eleven Carmens, and Pons' fourteen Lucias are similar totals).

At its first hearing, Albanese already offers a fully rounded characterization, sure in intent and execution. A momentary tempo miscalculation in 'Un dì felice' and a slight memory lapse in the introduction to 'Parigi, o cara' only serve to underline her otherwise complete musical and dramatic authority throughout the afternoon. The clarity and succulence of her diction are a familiar boon: Violetta's entrance phrases are bracing, the command to her guests ('Miei cari, sedete') a firm and expansive bidding. The Brindisi is rather carefully turned, but the alternating *piano* phrases (the dynamic distinction is seldom made) are welcome. As Albanese leads into the duet, Violetta's mandated laugh is natural and warm (she should give lessons in laughter to prima donnas whose cackles are laughable in themselves). The frivolous decorations of 'Un dì felice' are neatly done, the entire duet a feast of finely spun tone with Sodero allowing both singers plenty of time for affective niceties.

The recitatives which begin Violetta's solo scena reveal Albanese's unique interplay of word and tonal nuance in the service of character, a virtue too often lacking in otherwise attractive artists. 'Gioir!' and the flourishes which precede 'Sempre libera' are converted into life-seeking thrusts of emotion; 'Ah fors'è lui' is heartfelt and tonally ravishing, marred only by a few *piano* tones, inadequately supported. Both ascending and descending scale-work in the cabaletta are excellent, and she summons a tremendous burst of energy in the second verse, reveling in Violetta's frenzied capitulation. No lyric soprano in memory has matched the security and tonal splendor of the succession of high Cs with which the aria culminates.

In the lengthy scene with the elder Germont we meet a changed Violetta. The quiet sweetness of 'O, come dolce,' the simplicity of 'Dite alla giovine' (with its per-

Licia Albanese as Violetta in *La Traviata*.

fectly controlled line), clothe this Violetta with almost virginal gentility. At this stage of her career, Albanese's vocalism is of surprising delicacy with frequent *pianissimi* in the upper range. 'Imponete' and 'Conosca il sacrifizio' are voiced with harrowing fragility. Her pallid tones take one into the heart of the character and serve as a foil for more passionate moments such as 'Non sapete,' where Violetta's terror at the prospect of giving up Alfredo becomes manifest. Nor does Albanese neglect a middle ground of expressive musicality—the expansive arch and vocal control of 'Qual figlia' in themselves convey the poignancy of renunciation.

One may miss, in this debut performance, the tragic aura of the *grande amoureuse* in 'Amami, Alfredo,' but her refusal to overstep the zones of musical rectitude offers compensation in the form of tonal and linear control— rather than a passionate spilling of tone at the climax, the young Albanese molds the entire outburst. Unlike many of her later performances, 'Alfredo, di questo core' is limned with the loveliest, most pallid thread of tone (the true *voce debolissima* that Verdi prescribed) yet full of restrained tears (*e con passione*, Verdi added); a flower has been crushed underfoot, an impression that deepens in the final act. The letter scene is not overdramatized. Every progression of feeling is minutely scaled, the *pianissimo* echo phrases are faithfully observed, and while an exquisite bloom of tone animates 'L'amore d'Alfredo,' Albanese never allows us to forget the fragile state of Violetta's physical and mental health—even the concluding series of high As are quietly attacked. Again in 'Parigi, o cara' one hears that gentle spinning of flowerlike tone which is seldom (if ever) captured in Albanese's American commercial recordings (too close miking is often the culprit). 'Prendi, quest'è l'immagine' is wonderfully integrated in form, 'Se una pudica vergine' full of exquisite shadings and diminuendi.

Finally, there comes what Budden calls the "false miracle": Albanese whispers the gentlest 'È strano,' full of wonder, almost as though she contemplates a palpable life outside her self, followed by a most skillful transition to Violetta's cry of joy. Virgil Thomson, noting that a consummate portrayal of Hamlet or Dumas' courtesan guaranteed the "coronation of stardom," decreed that in her debut Violetta, Albanese had gained the "royal crown."[3]

If the uniquely fragile, virginal quality of this performance is not often duplicated in Albanese's later career, the ensuing decades confirmed her royal hegemony in the role. During the forties Sayão was the closest competitor, Novotna soon relinquished the role, while Dorothy Kirsten sang it infrequently in New York— never on the broadcasts.

The postseason broadcast of 24 April 1943 offers a last opportunity to hear Sayão's Violetta. During the war years the radio public enjoyed broadcasts of tour and New York postseason performances, often a newly cast repeat of an opera heard earlier. Kullman is the familiar Alfredo, a shade less ardent this time and mooning to excess; a dose of the energetic huntsman (Alfredo, according to Verdi's stage directions, enters in hunting costume) would add spine to his dreamy lover. In the final acts he is oddly deficient in urgency and concern for the dying Violetta, though his singing is always pleasant.

Warren, in his first broadcast Germont, has displaced Tibbett (a familiar refrain from now on), parading a ravishing display of old-style vocalism, exploiting his command of all dynamic levels (the mezza voce by now well disciplined), with the decorative elements of the Verdi line clearly and easily negotiated. Of course, Sodero's leisurely tempi are an aid. The balm of Warren's 'Piangi' would surely comfort any Violetta, yet there is a surprising amount of tearful emotional overlay which

La Traviata
24 April 1943

Violetta
Bidú Sayão

Alfredo
Charles Kullman

Germont
Leonard Warren

Conductor
Cesare Sodero

threatens the nobility of his utterance in the duet and definitely spills over into excess in the final stanza of 'Di Provenza.' And then the suspicion arises that the flood of tone is slightly walled in, causing a rather cavernous resonance. Warren's entrance at Flora's fete has abundant dignity but little passion (Verdi marked it con dignitoso fuoco). In the final act a touch of gaucherie lingers in his phrase endings, and Germont's regret doesn't quite ring true. These few reservations cannot obscure the many excellences of his reading: his care for nuance, his complete abjuration of baritone bawling (even in the climaxes), and the easy transitions between all dynamic levels. Above all, the heady air of Verdi's tessitura is home territory for Warren.

On this afternoon Sayão, too, seems afflicted with the blight of excess bathos. Oddly enough, she is frequently more overtly emotional than Albanese. The frivolous nature of Violetta is well conveyed in the opening scene—she doesn't hesitate to point her tone acidulously in Violetta's coloratura response to Alfredo's love plea. In the scena she is more tenacious than her colleague in pursuing frivolity; the recitatives are quite markedly accented (but a delightful light touch at 'anima mia'), and a few extraneous squeaks intrude as she strives for dramatic emphasis. 'Ah fors'è lui' contains some lovely head tones, but the aria is not as well integrated in toto as Albanese's, and she pushes the interpolated high C beyond its limit. 'Sempre libera' is splendidly delivered, virtuosic in manner, the coloratura expert, and the high Cs telling (Sayão is now past the point of interpolating the E-flat as she did in 1937 and on her later commercial recording). All in all, Sayão is the more frenetic, volatile Violetta, in contrast to Albanese's more thoughtful, genteel, and potentially crushable heroine.

In the later acts an occasional soubrette touch creeps in, but lovely effects abound in the duet with Germont. 'Dite alla giovine' is genuinely tragic, devoid of mannerisms and beautifully poised (unlike the 1937 traversal, where purity of line was lost in the search for dramatic weight). Hollow despair convincingly penetrates 'Imponete.' Sometimes she inexplicably opts for a forte dynamic where Verdi prescribes piano ('Non sapete' and 'Così alla misera'), spending resources that might have been saved to give greater force to 'Amami, Alfredo.' Throughout, she more than matches Warren tear for tear. Still, Sayão's second act is immeasurably finer than her earlier broadcast. All of Violetta's moods are strongly conveyed in beautifully controlled vocalism; she understands exactly how far she may venture and remains within limits without loss of commitment.

In Sodero's hands Flora oversees a most sedate gambling table (a tea-party tempo, the acciaccature robbed of their harsh piquancy). Sayão's 'di questo core' is all shimmering silver (her most rapid vibrato) and very lovely. The 'Addio' in the final act is beautifully vocalized, though matter-of-fact—neither sufficiently dolente nor filled with realistic despair; her concluding high A (piano) is a thing to treasure, however. (This is one of the poorest tapes in terms of sound quality; there appears to be an incredible blunder where Sayão descends several beats ahead of Kullman in the unison conclusion which precedes 'Parigi, o cara.') The remainder of the act holds admirable moments—she even manages to conjure an aura of grandeur at 'Ah! gran Dio!' Only in the false resurgence of life does Sayão's insight fail her, for her up-and-down theatrics are overly spasmodic, far removed from the unearthly transfiguration which made Albanese's death scene so moving.

The 1943 Traviata remains one of Sayão's most notable performances, dramatically vivid and vocally superb. An opera company with two such sterling Violettas might well indulge in self-congratulation.

La Traviata
1 January 1944
Violetta
Licia Albanese
Alfredo
Jan Peerce
Germont
Lawrence Tibbett
Conductor
Cesare Sodero

On New Year's Day 1944, Albanese's Violetta is once again on the airwaves. The wartime holiday brings a novel rendition of the National Anthem to start the performance: Cross tells us that "forty-one singing WAVES are now appearing in the glow of the footlights, making a very attractive picture in their blue uniforms. . . . Speaking of men in uniform," Sodero is "very proud indeed of the fact that two of his sons are wearing the United States armed forces uniform"—remember, Italy is the enemy in this world war.

Sodero's intimate prelude is just as affecting as before ("it tells us," according to Cross, "of a sad story that takes place in a pleasure-loving palace"). Throughout the opera Sodero has upscaled his tempi and downgraded some major ritards without violating the chamber music delicacy of his conception; the modifications are all to the good of the drama and Verdi's score. This time Peerce has joined Albanese and Tibbett, offering unwavering vocal stability. How firmly he turns the ornaments of the Brindisi! This is no youth moonstruck by 'misterioso' love; one feels he could offer Violetta a lifetime of security (and sobriety). The aria is rhythmically alert, swabbed in broad vocal gestures with little textual or tonal variety; many will prefer Peerce's ecstatic fervor to Kullman's dreamy ardor. He dominates the denunciation scene; as anger and spite give way to remorse, Peerce pours out forceful tone like a Lilliputian *tenore di forza.* Unfortunately, without referring to the text, one often could not guess whether anger or love was his preoccupation; 'Parigi, o cara,' for instance, is wholly forthright—not a hint of Verdi's *dolcissimo a mezza voce* comforts Violetta.

Albanese is in superb vocal form, and her mastery of both dialogue and song is even more satisfying than in her debut broadcast. Now the conscious aura of the prima donna sits ever so lightly on her manner, just enough to heighten romantic projection without endangering the honesty of her portrayal. An expansive air permeates her work; one inhales it in her command of vocal climaxes, in the fervor with which she rejects, holds tenaciously to, and finally renounces love. About this time in her career, Albanese begins to wrap herself in the raiment of the tragic singing actress. The vocal and dramatic gestures are inched toward grandeur: 'L'uomo implacabile' fairly tumbles out of her mouth, 'Non sapete' is a flash of anger directed at her persecutor, 'Amami, Alfredo' is passionately extended with a bit of chest voice to heighten the drama, and the farewell aria ends with a series of overtly tragic cries of 'tutto.' Here we have the diva in her natural habitat, and quite thrilling it is. Happily, there is no lessening of Albanese's command of delicate, pathetic effects when she chooses: the tonal warmth of 'Alfredo, di questo core' is most affecting, the *debolezza* of the wakening Violetta is tellingly suggested, the letter is simply perused (and what a striking effect follows when she cries 'Ah, con tal morbo!'), and the fragile cantilena of Violetta's final moments with Alfredo are as immaculate as one could desire. Albanese's vocal control is indeed impressive.

La Traviata
17 February 1945
Violetta
Licia Albanese
Alfredo
Jan Peerce
Germont
Lawrence Tibbett
Conductor
Cesare Sodero

In the 1945 (17 February) *Traviata*, Tibbett, Peerce, and Albanese are in characteristic form: Tibbett on the mend, Peerce substantial and achieving a modicum of sympathetic concern in 'Parigi, o cara'—he modifies his breath pressure—and Albanese again displaying her complete stage command. She is the vocal spendthrift in act two, the dramatic moments ('Non sapete' and 'Morrò') scaled up yet another notch, and 'Alfredo, di questo core' dosed more with Verdi's *passione* than his *debolezza.* 'Così alla misera' and 'Imponete' are lovingly delivered, the voice at its most beautiful. For the first time her realistic coughing before 'Amami, Alfredo' seems excessive; one has the feeling that she is too personally involved, and she just avoids overextending her resources in search of the big effect. But the three repeti-

tions of 'Ah perchè venni' (now held to reasonable shape by Sodero, who has also vivified his gambling music) are magical, and the soprano maintains a haunting quietude
in 'Parigi, o cara.' In most of the last act her vocalism suggests the translucency of
finest porcelain. Only the other end of the spectrum has been enlarged to encompass a grander conception.

While Albanese was consolidating her lyric supremacy in the series of *Traviata*
broadcasts, yet another artist was laying claim to another of Verdi's most exacting
creations. Though it was only the jester's tasselled cap rather than a royal crown
which Leonard Warren donned, pride of ownership was as eagerly sought. Nine
broadcast Rigolettos are testimony to Warren's claim of possession.

Like Albanese's Violetta, Warren's first Met Rigoletto was captured on a broadcast (18 December 1943); the baritone had appeared with success in the part in
Buenos Aires the previous summer. Originally scheduled for the 27 December
Rigoletto, Warren unexpectedly fell heir to the broadcast when Tibbett was unable
to appear. To add to the burden of the event, Warren had appeared (for the first time)
as Renato in the revival of *Ballo* on the evening before the broadcast. The Verdi realm
had long been the province of Tibbett who, despite vocal uncertainties, continued to
sing Rigoletto, Falstaff, Don Carlo, and Germont as well as Scarpia and Tonio this
season. Already Warren had garnered Di Luna, Amonasro, Germont, and Don Carlo,
and his assumption of Renato, Rigoletto, and Falstaff in the 1943–44 season further
legitimized his claim to the Verdi coronet. In most cases Tibbett still gained the first
nights, but the glory was increasingly earned by Warren.

Sodero oversees a curious broadcast performance—schizophrenic, one might
call it—with Pons and Kullman picture-postcard lovers, Moscona and Kaskas down-
to-earth villains. The gentle elegance with which Sodero beguilingly swathed *Traviata*
serves *Rigoletto* less well. We get no sense of the licentious Duke of Mantua's raucous
court in the *banda* music, nor is the horror engendered by Monterone's curse caught
in the whispered choral response of the courtiers. The flaccid meandering of muted
cello and double bass eviscerates Verdi's black comedy when Sparafucile solicits
Rigoletto's trade. Sodero adheres to the score's metronome markings, however, and
the tepid nature of the performance must be laid equally to Pons and Kullman.
Sodero's deft 'Zitti' chorus and measured control of the time-honored (but illegiti-
mate) accelerando favored for 'Sì, vendetta' reaffirm his skills. His elegant accompaniment to 'La donna è mobile' holds vulgarity at bay (proving there is room for
elegance in *Rigoletto*), and his wide dynamic palette is gratifying. In the closing
moments of the opera (after the quartet) the afternoon finally comes to life as Sodero
recaptures the dramatic thrust which seemed implicit in his act-one prelude.

Contributing to the garden party atmosphere of the performance, Kullman is at
his most effete, adhering to Verdi's dynamic markings, to be sure, and entirely
musical, like the artist he is. But he offers hardly a moment of *slancio* to convince us
that this youth is the virile despoiler of women. Perhaps that is the secret of the
Duke's success with Gilda (after all, she believes him a poor student), but at least
'Questa o quella' could give some inkling of the Duke's character. Kullman does
supply a measure of the *eleganza* Verdi calls for, but he seems unduly bored by the
whole affair. He summons a modest ardor in the love duet and his suavity is welcome
in the cantabile, though he flies a bit out of vocal focus near the end. 'Parmi veder le
lagrime' is exceedingly well sung within the dolce manner Kullman cultivates
throughout the afternoon. He concludes 'La donna è mobile' with an oddly manipulated cadenza and a resounding high B (but the tessitura of the quartet pressures

Rigoletto
18 December 1943
Gilda
Lily Pons
Maddalena
Anna Kaskas
Duke
Charles Kullman
Rigoletto
Leonard Warren
Sparafucile
Nicola Moscona
Conductor
Cesare Sodero

him). In the reprise of the aria the tenor negotiates a convincing *morendo* to excellent dramatic effect.

With her childlike tone and manner, Pons is a fitting partner for Kullman. The voice is perilously shaky in the lower octave at her entrance, but soon it settles, the touch of shrillness fading. Her farewell to her father has a lovely simplicity. Occasionally she seems more disposed to play Gilda rather than Pons on this afternoon—her girlish fear at Gaultier's entrance is quite convincing. 'Caro nome' becomes an exercise in fermate on high notes, with weak low notes, neat short trills, and an excellent cadenza which houses a secure *messa di voce* before a tenacious high E. Pons' cameo-like delicacy has its charm, but the audience response is surprisingly slight (as it is for everyone throughout the afternoon). In the coda she prefers to ascend in arpeggio fashion to another (even tauter) high E rather than rely on Verdi's effective long trill. 'Tutte le feste' has some fine tone, a bit glassy now and then, but overall well controlled, and 'Lassù in cielo' is effective in its quiet resignation. Moscona and Kaskas are effective foils: the Greek bass has never sounded better and is suitably menacing, while Kaskas, though vocally coarse-grained, is dramatically apt. Osie Hawkins' curious voice hurls a potent curse.

Warren provides the adrenalin of the performance—his biting interjections at his entrance are a tonic. He exploits his easy command of head voice in 'Pari siamo' and reveals a wider range of interpretive insights than expected from earlier performances: Rigoletto's brutality, fears, and love for his daughter are well suggested by vocal coloration. The contrast between 'Ma in altr'uomo' (mezza voce) and the concluding rousing high G (no isolated, belted top tone, but an integral part of the voice) shows the range of affect in his arsenal. Only the sobs at 'il pianto!' sound a false, insincere note. If his command is not quite complete, the spectrum of his vocal skills is greater than most baritones could contemplate. His mezza voce in the scene with his daughter ravishes the ear, and the outburst of feeling as Rigoletto recalls his lost wife convinces—here Warren is well immersed in the character. But in the third act he is better at bel canto than raging against courtiers. The voice clouds up occasionally in 'Miei signori, perdono' and he pushes a few pitches sharp—the final note of the aria really gets away from him. 'Piangi, fanciulla' reaffirms his incipient greatness, while the quiet opening of 'Sì, vendetta' is most affecting. A wandering high A-flat as the act closes indicates that the conjunction of a Friday Renato and Saturday Rigoletto is a bit too much, even for the prodigious resources of a youthful Warren. But he comforts his dying daughter in richly colored tones, reassuring us that the great baritone roles of the Italian repertory have found a new sovereign.

Neither management nor Tibbett, however, were ready to acknowledge the right of succession at this early stage. When, after a hiatus of eight seasons, the Met revived *La Forza del Destino* in January 1943, it was Tibbett who sang the premiere, as he would the revivals of *Falstaff* and *Il Tabarro* over the next several years. Tibbett's Carlo was new to the Met (he had appeared in the unlikely robes of Fra Melitone in the 1926 revival with Ponselle, Martinelli, Danise, and Pinza). For the broadcast of 23 January, Pinza is still on hand to comfort Leonora with his vocal balm. Baccaloni adds another lively portrait to his buffo catalogue, replete with intrusive comic effects but commanding in manner and vocal size—it would take an abbot of Pinza's stature to quell this monk. Though Milanov and Kurt Baum were the lovers in the premiere, Roman and Jagel take over for the broadcast (the second of the five performances—no one of which replicates the cast of any of the others; the Met's casting policy in these years sometimes defies reason).

La Forza del Destino
23 January 1943

Leonora
Stella Roman

Preziosilla
Irra Petina

Don Alvaro
Frederick Jagel

Don Carlo
Lawrence Tibbett

Padre Guardiano
Ezio Pinza

Fra Melitone
Salvatore Baccaloni

Conductor
Bruno Walter

Amazingly, it is the august Bruno Walter who must cope with this capricious casting policy. During the twenties and thirties Walter had been active in the middle Verdi renascence in the Germanic countries, but he had never before conducted *La Forza*. A marvelous and unexpected *slancio* animates several scenes: in the prologue, the cumulative drive from the duet through the murder of Leonora's father engenders an excitement that carries on to the tavern scene. There Petina's slight but rhythmically alert Preziosilla is an aid. The mocking snarl in her tones as she confronts the disguised Carlo shows her acumen—she has the flair, if not the voice, for this troublesome part. Walter tellingly whips up the conclusion of the Leonora-Guardiano duet, yet coaxes an ethereal statement of the 'Madre, pietosa vergine' theme from the orchestra as the monks enter, all the more effective for its union of spin and intensity.

Not even the adroit Walter can work ordinary clay into gold. He is saddled with an impossible chorus, the male contingent consistently below the pitch in the convent scene (with a few imprecisions in the orchestra compounding the guilt), the muleteers and peasant girls equally vague in the tavern scene. The nadir is reached in the opening moments of the final act where all participants seem to be feeling their way—the entire scene lacks cohesion (and Verdi did not help matters in that regard). Nor are the principals (Pinza ever the exception) more than workaday. Jagel's timbre has taken on a heroic cast, but the quality is correspondingly more leathery. To his credit he has the stamina for the role, sings a clean, if inexpressive, line, and is mercifully free of the vulgarisms of many a *tenore di forza*. In the difficult aria he can't signal the pathos of 'Leonora mia, soccorrimi' (marked *cantabile, dolce*), but the climactic phrase is well surmounted. And he has the necessary bite (in fact, he growls like a wounded dog) for 'Ah, segnasti la tua sorte!' as he finally succumbs to Alvaro's taunts; conversely, he commands a noble manner as death claims Leonora.

Jagel and Roman make an odd couple: he musically straightforward, dependable but stolid, she overtly emotional, hurling herself at the music, cherishing the artifices of the provinces, yet often enough kindling a glow of theatrical excitement. If she is not the real thing, she offers a fair imitation. Vocally, Roman is in her best form. The prologue shows the bewitching colors of her instrument, with a Caniglia-like use of chest tone and a touch of the Milanov shimmer at the top. But the grandly arched Verdian lines of the convent scene betray her patchwork technique. This Leonora captures the heroine's despair but misses the ecstasy in the peroration of 'Madre, pietosa vergine'; the noble exaltation of Leonora's plea to God mounts step by step but never soars.

Pinza is magnificent in the lengthy duet, one of the best efforts of his later career. Barring a splintered high E (he seems as startled as we are), the fiber and strength of his instrument are undiminished and fully convey the exalted manner of the padre. Now Roman lapses into mere note-spinning. So much of Leonora's music utilizes sequential repetition of intervallic units ('Più tranquilla,' etc.), and she neglects to trace the connecting links which knit them into the grand line. Repose is entirely sacrificed to agitation. Even 'La Vergine degli angeli' fails to work its magic in her thin, unsupported tones. 'Pace, pace' fares much better. The sculptured diminuendo of the half-step 'pace' pair, the lovely timbre of the middle high range, the octave leap vaulted to theatrical purpose, a good (but interminable) high *piano* B-flat, the command of *subito piano*—all restore belief. Best of all, for 'Lieta poss'io precederti' she successfully deploys a liquid *piano* tone throughout the entire range, wafting a welcome fragility in this precious apotheosis. Such moments occur too

Stella Roman as Leonora in *La Forza del Destino*.

seldom in a Roman performance, for Roman's voice, despite the Muzio-like color play and mannerisms, remains a mosaic in which the individual pieces are perpetually in danger of dislodgment.

Roman is a case of what might have been. With Tibbett, we remember what was and search ruefully for any remaining evidence of greatness. Hope awakens as we recognize the old resonance in the tavern scene (only a few weeks before we cringed among the ruins of his 1942 Germont). The metal is still there in the battle scene, and the artist survives, too, as he brings forth his sympathetic *Boccanegra* manner to comfort the wounded Alvaro ('Amico, fidate'). He manages some effective *fortes*, as well. Jagel is strong but earthbound, yet Tibbett's empathic way allows the duet to garner a modest portion of its fabled effect. The great scene for Carlo finds Tibbett woefully lacking, however. He can still communicate (he recognizes the theatrical moment; for instance, at 'S'ei fosse il seddutore?' vocal timbre and manner are notably altered); but the climaxes of 'Urna fatale' are hard-sledding—Tibbett can only hurl his shattered instrument at the burly phrases. The cadenza (words added) is as ugly as anything to come from Tibbett's throat (mercifully, sixteen measures of high tessitura in the cabaletta have been cut). To Walter falls the task of resuscitating the drama in the recognition scene with his explosive orchestral interjections.

That a conductor should again emerge the dramatic protagonist of the next season's Verdi revival seems foreordained in the pairing of Beecham and *Falstaff.* So goodly a portion of Anglo-Saxon independence dwelt in the bosom of the cosmopolitan baronet that it made him a fit companion for Shakespeare's rogue.

Once again a pragmatic management, however, introduced a set of inhibiting factors. Operatic comedies were fair game for translation (the success of *The Magic Flute* was certification enough) and none more so than Verdi's mercurial comedy which for decades had escaped the warm embrace of the public. Since its introduction to Met audiences in 1894, just a year after the La Scala premiere, the work had appeared in only eight seasons. Where star-studded casts had failed (Eames, De Lussan, Scalchi, and Maurel; Destinn, Alda, Gay, and Scotti in 1908; Bori, Alda, Scotti, Gigli, under Serafin in 1924–25; Caniglia, Castagna, Tibbett in 1938) English translation just might triumph—or so reasoned management. Naturally, the condition for casting was intelligibility. The Met by now was well stocked with fine American artists: Steber, Harshaw, Greer, Browning, Kullman, Warren, Rasely, and Gurney are joined by the down-under pair of Brownlee and Dudley. And intelligibility is fairly served (not always the case with the American singer), but Verdi and Boito are shortchanged.

Beecham has the intricacies of the score well enough in hand—there are no mishaps (with characteristic directness Beecham told prompter Victor Trucco "You take the men and I'll look out for the women").[4] Pinpoint precision is not overabundant (the complex ensemble which ends the first act barely passes muster). English robs the score of both the fleetness and crisp consonant bite of Italian, and Beecham's tempi are often just a shade under the mark. For whatever reason, the performance lacks the full measure of intoxication which Verdi's bubbly score supplies in such abundance. The deficiency is caused in part by a lack of comic spirit in several principals. How can *Falstaff* come alive without a Quickly as wily as the old rogue himself? Harshaw, for all her solidity of vocal means (and the ease of her upper range is welcome respite from the trials of many an aged mezzo in this role), doesn't relish the earthy humor of Quickly, so neither can we. Master Ford is a character in earnest for much of the opera, but we watchers should savor his pigheadedness and enjoy his

Falstaff
11 March 1944

Alice
Eleanor Steber
Nannetta
Frances Greer
Dame Quickly
Margaret Harshaw
Fenton
Charles Kullman
Falstaff
Leonard Warren
Ford
John Brownlee
Conductor
Sir Thomas Beecham

plight; Brownlee's incessant bluster allows the poor man not an iota of charm. The baritone is in his best vocal form, however, offering abundant (and unmodulated) rancor in his monologue—tonally it is solid enough. Oddly, it is the young (and normally somewhat stolid) Warren who supplies a bit of the requisite suavity in the scene between the posturing intriguers. Verdi shortchanged Mistress Page, and Browning's neutral timbre does little to redress the account with Shakespeare.

Of the women, both Steber and Greer contribute to the festive sport, Greer by playing Anne (Nannetta) as a lively minx, her vocal timbre and manner clearly confirming her independent spirit. The same quality robs her aria of its magical repose—no 'fil d'un soffio etesio' here. But Greer has a distinctive Teyte-like vocal thumbprint that stays in the ear; perhaps only the lack of complete poise in the highest reaches negated a more prominent career. Steber doesn't project all of Alice Ford's mettlesome temperament, but she is mistress of the deft vocal touch, repeatedly turning a phrase with subtlety. And the comic spirit sits easily upon her. One senses she is enjoying the intrigue. When she delivers her final reproof to her foiled husband ('Quella mania feroce'), the upward thrust of voice and light staccati are musically exact, yet the combination of jest and earnestness is skillfully conveyed. How enchantingly the bloom rests on this voice during these early years—a pity that Beecham hurries her through the cantabile phrase which concludes Falstaff's love letter. (Beecham may be right; Falstaffians must remember that Verdi, rehearsing the cast of the Paris premiere in 1894, exclaimed "I beg you, ladies and gentlemen . . . do not lapse into sentimentality! Gaiety! Gaiety! That is the essence of Falstaff."[5]

Like Steber, Kullman has a modicum of lyric balm to offer (he is not quite yet in his dotage, as Kolodin would have it). An occasional scratchy top tone isn't enough to squelch either his ardor or our pleasure. The stopped-horn quality of his production actually abets the mood of Fenton's aria, and he lifts the difficult dolcissimo half-steps out of the *passaggio* neatly enough.

Tibbett had sung the title role in the first two performances of the revival, but this time the broadcast fell to Warren. Nature had not equipped either baritone with the ideal Falstaffian mix. (Two decades earlier Tibbett had earned his Met spurs as Ford, a more perfect mating of young artist and role.) Nevertheless, Warren's effort is impressive for a debut in the role. Most striking are the clarity and, equally important, the naturalness of his diction. So many American singers (at least through the first half of the century) are not only unintelligible but affected, casting a layer of artificiality over the language to avoid peculiarly American sounds—"can't" comes out "cahn't." At the same time the elegance they seek is dissipated by intrusive vulgarities of regional speech. Apart from an occasional excessively rolled *r*, Warren has found an agreeable middle ground.

Though too often the comic point of the role resides disproportionately in Beecham's orchestra (of course, Verdi weighted the odds on that score), Warren's brightly focused tone is an asset in the dialogue scenes. For the most part his musical subtleties are on a higher level than his characterization. When Falstaff sings (in the translation purported to be largely by Beecham) 'I have within me still the glowing ember of Indian summer,' Warren's lovely mezza voce on the high note is a welcome respite from the sham falsetto of more experienced, but vocally weary, baritones. The honor monologue is scrupulously delivered, but no amount of correctness can counterfeit the oversized self-delight of the rascal. Still, throughout the opera Warren sings in godlike tones devoid of any wooly rumble. 'Be sure you greet my charmers,' he tells Dame Quickly, and the tones and phrase are lovingly done. Then again, both oral bulk and manner disable him from rising on vocal tiptoes for 'Go, good old John.' The contraries continue: the elegance of the youthful swain is in his voice as he courts Alice, and he makes a fair try at 'Quand'ero paggio.'

Steber plays to him beautifully, and the scene goes very well (her descent into a phony chest voice at 'You love another' is an adroit touch, while Warren's cries from the basket of 'I'm stifling' are genuinely funny). In the final act Warren's Falstaff is on firmer ground. He laments the 'vile, treacherous world' with conviction, and as he describes the pleasures of wine spreading through his body, his vocalism is as light and flowing as the 'quaff of sunshine' which Falstaff salutes. If vocalism alone could win the merry wives, they should all capitulate to Warren.

Even the ebullient baronet cannot keep afloat the airy effervescence of the opera. The entire concluding Herne Oak scene, though tightly organized by Beecham, is labored, and the denouement, which should fly on the wind, is all too earthbound. Five years would pass before the merry wives would romp again on the Met stage, and only Warren from the present cast (and Verdi, too) would prosper under a conductor of more somber mien, but even slighter hand—Fritz Reiner.

Undeterred by deficiencies in his Verdi revivals, Johnson offered *La Forza del Destino* again with the same principals as the opening broadcast of the 1943-44 season. During this season Walter expanded his Metropolitan commitments, and the radio audience heard not only his *Forza, Figaro*, and *Magic Flute* but both the New York and Chicago broadcasts of *Un Ballo in Maschera*.

Perhaps profiting from the ill effects of *Forza*'s revolving-door casting, the *Ballo* cast remained virtually intact throughout the season, and the broadcast of 15 January 1944 is a well-knit, persuasive performance. Verdi, in the prelude's disjointed components, posed problems which challenge any conductor's skill; Walter not only logistically solves them but, by means of easy transitions and gentle melodic contours, draws an affecting profile for the opera—an anticipatory touch of sorrow is subtly evoked. The matchup is intriguing: how will Verdi's wedding of Italian passion with the panache of French opera fare in the hands of a German master conductor noted for philosophic gravity? Pace is apt, and Scribe's sensational theatrics, if not quite relished, are brought off with goodly flair. Of greater moment, Walter articulates the precise formalism of the score and cultivates its sparkling wit so that its classical elegance (almost unique in the Verdi canon) shines forth. Few German profundities are allowed to dull the vitality of Verdi's conception. At first Walter seems a bit cautious in the *stretta dell'introduzione* at the end of the first scene, but the energy accretion is beautifully scaled, and he is able to skirt the vulgarity of the belching brass coda. Walter's prelude to Ulrica's scene wears a mask of horror, Beethovenesque, and all the more effective for that. In the ensemble where the courtiers mock the deluded Renato, the halts and thrusts of the orchestral phrases better convey the bitter irony of the situation than do the forces on stage. Only in 'Di che fulgor' (the big ensemble which concludes the conspiracy scene) does the firm cohesion of the performance momentarily lapse, a happening of some frequency toward the end of a Walter performance. Perhaps Walter's benign manner eventually subverts the conductor's essential field marshal stance.

A first-class group of principals responds to Walter's leadership. Thorborg is the most convincing of Ulricas, primarily because she has a sizable, well-knit voice which surmounts the ungainly aspects of her music. The register fracturing which Verdi built into Ulrica's music is well bridged by Thorborg's solid middle voice, and her top

Un Ballo in Maschera
15 January 1944
Amelia
Zinka Milanov
Oscar
Frances Greer
Ulrica
Kerstin Thorborg
Riccardo
Jan Peerce
Renato
Leonard Warren
Conductor
Bruno Walter

rings out splendidly. With Thorborg, vocal amenities are always placed at the service of the drama; she is wonderfully mysterious and conspiratorial. Her theatrical know-how is particularly striking in the fruity flamboyance of her warning to Riccardo that he will die by the hand of a friend.

In Verdi's scheme, the witch's blackness is countered by the page's ebullience, a quality that Frances Greer offers in abundance. It is mostly in her manner, however, and welcome enough in that. But Oscar's vocal filigree must be as rapier sharp as her *ballata* and *canzone* are brief, and this "sweet golden-haired page" (Cross) wields only a hard-edged, even blunted, weapon. She doesn't simper, though, and holds her own in the exchange with Renato. Over most of the decade the management promoted Greer, a 1942 "Auditions" winner, but the young American soprano could never escape the Musetta curse (her debut role). She remained in the ranks of the talented ingénue for her eight Met seasons. In his radio debut, John Baker, another "Auditions" alumnus, is a forthright Silvano. Moscona and Cordon are serviceable conspirators, savoring their sardonic laughter at Renato's plight (but Cordon's cloudy 'Ve', se di notte' lacks the elegance clearly demanded by Verdi's music and marking).

The vocal honors of the afternoon fall to yet another "Auditions" winner, but one who, unlike his less fortunate (and less gifted) colleagues had been elevated early on to the principal ranks of the company. By now Warren has reached full mastery of his powers. From the first note of 'Alla vita che t'arride,' the voice's opulence is perfectly focused and the glorious upper register blooms. Better yet, Warren shakes off the hint of stolidity which often lurks in the recesses of his musical thought and is alive to the rhythmic impetus of the piece. 'Eri tu' attains an even higher level. Warren prepares us for Renato's inner hurt as he dismisses Amelia, dignity mating with wrath. In the aria he moves to cantabile immediately. Particularly fine is the transition at the end of the first section—the 'dolcezze perdute' are ever present to this sensitive husband. His vocal command is complete (those old-fashioned upward *portamenti* of a sixth are a treat) and he exudes self-assurance as he directs Sam and Tom—seldom has Verdi's hymn to vengeance been so richly intoned. One can hear a hint of a future Scarpia in Warren's cruel treatment of Amelia as he commands her to choose the assassin, and when Renato's name is drawn, Warren thunders his triumph in the brightest of tones. The entire afternoon is his triumph.

Peerce, equally self-assured, gives one of his finest performances. In the opening scene his authority and expansion of phrase convey an appropriately ceremonial manner. Throughout the opera he delivers the recitatives with unflagging spirit and tonal bite. In Ulrica's den he looses the requisite *slancio* but scarcely suggests the parodistic humor which enlarges Riccardo's character. Peerce briefly modulates his *forte* dynamic and nasal timbre to simulate a dolce phrase, but his barcarole contains little of an engaging lilt. Virtuosity in abundance Peerce dutifully supplies, but his Riccardo is devoid of wit. When Peerce introduces the obligatory (but non-Verdi) laughter into 'È scherzo od è follia,' the vocal hand is a mite heavy, but the rhythm is scrupulously observed. He is splendidly sure-throated in the grand duet (the piece really sails along under Walter's impulse—he doesn't drive it, it wings itself); Peerce never flinches at a climax and the effect is thrilling. He fills the recitative to the cabinet aria with a surfeit of rolled *r*'s and nasal tone, but the aria receives its due. Ever the conscientious musician, where he cannot offer Verdi's quintuple *piano* he alters the quality of movement to obtain a suitable effect. Straightforward his rendering of the aria (and the entire opera) may be, but it is a full-throated outpouring, and after the assassination, his noble song confirms the sincere artist.

If dependability is Peerce's virtue, Milanov makes more than a hobgoblin of consistency. Fear and agitation are the built-in mental states of Amelia throughout most of the opera, and Milanov suffers no deficiency there. 'Consentemi, o Signore' splashes out in exciting but slightly undisciplined fashion as she surmounts the ensemble with ease. Verdi's demands in the heath aria are touchstones for any soprano's aplomb, and for a while Milanov seems well on the way to success in her reading. The high *fortes* are finely honed (brilliant without turning squally), 'Deh mi reggi' is beautifully limned, and she is actively involved in the dramatic situation. But on-again, off-again becomes the order of the day: the ascent to the high C is hurried and ugly, a lovely cadenza follows, the aria close is marred by unsupported tones in the low voice. The scenario is familiar: reams of glory dissipated by a moment's insecurity. The Milanov blemishes are like a chip on a fine Titian—we continue to admire, but oh, the regret.

She manages many a ravishing phrase in the duet, but sharps fearfully on the exposed 't'amo' (yet this young Milanov really means it). Amelia finally gains some reposeful moments in the third act, and we may expect Milanov to shine here—no one can deploy a grand 'Morrò' like Milanov. Unfortunately, her low voice refuses to settle comfortably, and she flats a bit in the middle range before a splendid close. At the ball Milanov's final words of renunciation are superbly poised, and in Verdi's glowing apotheosis after the assassination she contributes some hairbreadth *pianissimi*, quite unlike her usually refulgent soft tones.

Milanov is now in her sixth Met season. Unfamiliarity with language and environment are no longer acceptable excuses (actually she seems to have achieved greater consistency in her earlier seasons). Evidently the Met's two leading dramatic sopranos of the forties have something in common after all: incertitude. The difference is that Roman's inequities are planned, Milanov's uncharted. In that difference lies hope for future greatness.

Roman and Milanov dominate the remaining popular items of the Italian repertory during the war years. Not even the war's assault on quality casting could alter the public's appetite for *Trovatore, Aida, Cavalleria* and *Pagliacci*.

Trovatore seldom has been considered a conductor's opera, but Toscanini's famous restudy of it for La Scala in 1929 suggests that care lavished on the too familiar has its rewards. And in the broadcast of 13 March 1943, it is Sodero and his orchestral and choral forces which shine the brightest. Very little on stage would do credit to even a provincial house, let alone the first opera house of the world.

Thorborg, long a treasured artist, is pressed into service as the wild gypsy. The broadcast is the first of only two Met Azucenas by the Swedish contralto. Whether at any time she was well equipped temperamentally for this assignment, her vocal state at this juncture of her career disqualifies her a priori. An Azucena may inflame the gallery with a brilliant top and a belching chest voice (Thorborg never courted the latter, and the once clarion top is now only sparingly on call), but many of Verdi's most telling phrases demand a secure middle voice. Thorborg's middle range, at least on this occasion, is frayed. 'Stride la vampa!' passes without applause (has this happened before or since to this war-horse?). Of course, her theatrical flair and artistic sensitivity provide some compensation. She makes something of the pathos of 'Giorni poveri vivea' as Azucena describes her mountain home, carefully plots the path to hallucination in the final scene, and in contrast, finds an affecting simplicity for 'Ai nostri monti' (her tones, though, are pallid by necessity rather than choice). Unlike many an Azucena she gets off a satisfactory high B as the curtain falls. But

Il Trovatore
13 March 1943
Leonora
Stella Roman
Azucena
Kerstin Thorborg
Manrico
Arthur Carron
Di Luna
Francesco Valentino
Ferrando
Nicola Moscona
Conductor
Cesare Sodero

none of this adds up to Verdi's masterful creation of the vengeance-driven mother.

Arthur Carron's Manrico deserves little comment. Either his stalwart tenor has markedly deteriorated or he is seriously indisposed—the congested nasal timbre does suggest a cold. He is audibly in difficulty as he begins 'Ah si, ben mio.' Seldom can the elegance of Verdi's cantabile have been so resolutely mangled (even though Sodero's liquid arpeggiated accompaniment offers every opportunity for a singer to show his bel canto wares). In 'Di quella pira' Sodero alone supplies the excitement, for he is not afraid to charge Verdi's insistent rhythmic figurations with cumulative energy. Sung a full tone down, the cabaletta is a poor thing in Carron's throat, the sixteenths barely articulated, the first high B-flat only gradually reaching the assigned note. Unlike Martinelli in 1938, distance does not lend fondness, for Carron off in the Miserere tower is still too close for comfort. Valentino, on the other hand, is dependable enough, but nothing more. Undaunted by the high tessitura and stylistically knowing, he gives a modest imitation of a Verdi baritone. But the tone lacks density, is juice-free; Di Luna may be a cardboard figure, but a cardboard timbre cannot fill out Verdi's music.

Sodero serves Verdi well. From the opening arpeggio coils (clean and significant without becoming ponderous), to the reinforcement of the rhetoric in the recitatives by the just placement and weight of chordal interjections, to the swing of 'Abbietta zingara' and the *leggiero* choral conclusion, Sodero converts Ferrando's scene from dutiful narrative to robust dialectic. Moscona aids him; seldom (at least in a repertory house) have singer, chorus, and orchestra achieved so rhythmically precise a performance of the scene. Throughout the afternoon Sodero's *Trovatore* looks back to the bel canto era, losing, in the fond gaze, some of the muscularity and febrility of the score. Often he is reluctant to release the ultimate degree of energy when the heady moment arrives. Still, Sodero knows that although Gutiérrez' tale is heavy with melodrama, classical proportions permeate Verdi's score.

Oddly, it is Roman who shares this understanding. Often the most peripatetic of prima donnas, she performs with a restraint, both vocal and emotional, ordained no doubt by Verdi's music (a dictum which Roman was not always wont to honor). Could it be Sodero's calming touch?—Roman ever has had the ability to spin tone but preferred to substitute vocal effects for the long line. At her entrance the gentle play of her brief arioso ('come d'aurato sogno') gives one hope—she suggests the demure convent-aimed Spanish lady. 'Tacea la notte' affirms that hope. Both Sodero and Roman form 'dolci s'udiro e flebili' to its ultimate shape, achieving both the *animando* and *espansione* demanded by Verdi (in Sodero's hands, the proportions are ever just). Roman treads carefully through the vocal spasm of the cabaletta (a clean scale passage or two a bonus) and offers a spunky high D-flat to conclude the trio. In the apotheosic phrase which caps the convent scene Roman falls short of the grandeur such a supreme Verdi moment demands, but elsewhere she holds her own. (The little duet at the Chapel of Castellor is omitted in Met performances of this era).

'D'amor sull'ali rosee' has a faulty moment or two (flat at the end of the introductory arioso, short of breath once or twice) but the vaulting 'le pene' sequences are exquisitely done. Nor does she mangle the phrases of the Miserere, a temptation few sopranos can resist. If Sodero's pace for 'Mira, di acerbe lagrime' is too tightly reined, 'Vivrà! contende il giubilo' is exactly on the mark, with plenty of momentum but never reckless; even so, the ensemble of Roman and Valentino grows a bit scrappy at the end. The soprano doesn't disappoint in the ethereal phrases which signal Leonora's death. All in all, this is Roman's finest broadcast portrayal. Is it a harbinger of a consistent performance standard for Roman so that the Italian wing (like its Teutonic kin) can claim a pair of dramatic sopranos of unquestioned merit?

Whether Roman would be the lesser half of that duo (which seems incontrovertible in the light of the final half of Milanov's career) was still in doubt at this juncture. Though a veteran of the company with five seasons to her credit, Milanov was still subject to performance contretemps. Her paradoxical early Met career gains clearer definition in the series of five performances of four roles broadcast in the period 1943-45.

On 6 March 1943 Milanov sang the third of her seven broadcast Aidas. The cast was a strong one (Castagna, Martinelli, Bonelli) but was hampered by Pelletier's matter-of-fact supervision. *Aida* was a round-robin during the war years: Breisach, Sodero, Cooper, or Pelletier might show up in the pit at any given performance. From a lethargic opening, the matinee progresses to some searing moments when the singers are self-galvanized by Verdi's theatrical pulse. Pelletier seldom gets in their way except when he takes off at a precipitate tempo and leaves them scrambling to keep up—Martinelli, never a rhythmic laggard and one who had sung his first Met Radames under Toscanini in his debut season, must have been surprised to find himself hurtled along in 'Sì: fuggiam.'

The broadcast marks Martinelli's final Radames with the Metropolitan, thirty years and 123 portrayals after first praising Destinn's 'forma divina,' rejecting Ober's advances, and repelling Amato's Ethiopian king. Few tenors convey any hint of celestial beauty to the ear in Radames' opening aria, and at his age Martinelli is certainly no exception. What is amazing, however, is the vibrant tone which enlivens his ever-taut melodic line in the aria. The upward intervals are not nearly so painful as heard from Sisyphusian tenors, and in spite of his brutal assault on the final note, the audience's memory is sufficiently stirred by the present to give him long applause. Like many an artist when age depletes vocal strength, the tenor resorts to a few ungainly raised pitches in declamation ('Nel fiero anelito'), and time turns his tone to leather as the Nile duet proceeds. But he stays with the high tessitura tenaciously; the spirit of this old warrior is always willing. And more than sincerity carries the final act: palpable emotional tension lends credibility to the scene with Castagna, and a momentary youthful flash of burnished timbre invades his tones in the quiet opening to the tomb scene. He still knows how to sculpt the opening lifts of 'O terra addio.' Since Martinelli is capable of phrasing like the soprano, the entire duet, despite a strained B-flat and the absence of *piano*, gains the transfigured composure proclaimed in Ghislanzoni's text.

Castagna offers the finest performance of the afternoon. Her voice is in prime condition, velvety and liquid, though rather chesty. In the opening scene she lays out her tone at the expense of subtle nuance, but her singing grows increasingly sensitive in later scenes. No Amneris can have counterfeited a more blandishing manner to entrap Aida's confession of love. The ensuing contrast as she castigates the slave girl is immensely effective; Castagna is all dignity and command. She paces herself effectively through the judgment scene (the pair of near–B-flats are glancing), with plenty of grandeur where needed, and denounces the priests with a riveting vocal sneer.

Bonelli is her equal in sure-throated sonority and idiomatic manner. One is reminded that, no matter how impressive Warren may be, he has not yet achieved the final fill-up of vocal focus and style that Bonelli owns. Bonelli does not offer the mood change and *piano* dynamic as he begins 'Ma tu, Re,' however. But what ringing,

Aida
6 March 1943
Aida
Zinka Milanov
Amneris
Bruna Castagna
Radames
Giovanni Martinelli
Amonasro
Richard Bonelli
Ramfis
Norman Cordon
Conductor
Wilfred Pelletier

manly tone he pours into the night air along the Nile—and, in the midst of his raging ('with savage fury' as the old scores have it), he does observe Verdi's *mezza voce* marking at 'Flutti di sangue.' Bonelli imbues the scene with some intimacy, a directness in commanding his daughter to which Milanov responds with surprisingly appealing character touches (those fragile little *Pietà*s are uncharacteristic Milanov). When Bonelli delivers the climactic phrase of the duet, one must regret that he will be heard no more on the Met airwaves. Absent in 1943–44, he returns the following year for a final season as Tonio, Amonasro, and Barnaba (in the first cast of *Gioconda*, but the broadcast goes to Warren.) Though he sang nineteen major roles with the company over twelve seasons, his house total was only 102 appearances (plus 36 on tour). Tibbett, Thomas, Warren, Weede—the field was crowded and choices had to be made, but from Bonelli's broadcast performances one feels that the scales were unjustly tipped.

Cordon's black sound has a priestly aura, and young Lansing Hatfield, unfortunately destined to have a short Met career of three seasons, makes an uncommonly fine king. Hatfield is no cavernous pontificator; his tones are solid and appealing in timbre, his manner straightforward but stylistically apt. Greer seems an unlikely priestess, a Susanna who has strayed into the catacombs.

Milanov, by this time, should be at ease in a role which critical report in future years would claim as her own. Her right of possession seems less than secure on this afternoon. 'O patria mia' again is the problem. She forms the recitative with sensitivity, flats a bit in the aria proper, and seems terrified of both stepwise ascents. Even the first move to A lacks authority, and the top C is badly below pitch—rightly, she hurries off it. The coda, with its floated soft high A, often so purely delivered by her, is a mite skittish as well. 'Ritorna vincitor!' is another story, a commanding reading not only in tonal amplitude and control but in the vivid contrasts of mood. Her anguish is genuine, and she applies abundant interpretive touches and shadings of tone (regrettably absent from the more statuesque conception of the mature Milanov). But one senses that same hand of fear resting upon her in the early release of the sustained tones in every phrase of the 'Numi, pietà' coda (in both episodes). She is a match for Castagna in their scenes together. The solo phrase springing out of the triumphal ensemble is superbly controlled from its long-spun high B-flat down through the tightly coiled conclusion, and Milanov shows no fear as she rides the ensemble with searing top tones. A chronicle of faults must include a fiercely sharp high B-flat on the exposed 'fuggiam' in the duet with Radames, but the sound of 'Là tra foreste vergini' is tempting enough. Nor can a bit of suspect pitch in the opening arioso diminish her exquisite singing of the tomb scene. Her uniquely full, floated soft tone remains a paragon for the ethereal yearning of 'O terra addio.'

The *Aida* broadcast, in sum, is a slightly scrappy performance with some high-powered vocalism to offset deficiencies. Two weeks later (20 March 1943) Madame Milanov is heard again in what is not only her first broadcast of Santuzza, but her first portrayal of the Sicilian peasant at the Metropolitan. (She had sung a single tour performance in Cleveland in 1941). Eventually Santuzza would be second only to Aida in number of Milanov Met performances, but during her first decade she appeared in it only three times in the house. The lacuna is understandable during her first seasons when Cigna and Giannini filled the part, but not with the later procession of nondescript Santuzzas (Roman, Ella Flesch, Resnik, and even Djanel).

Since Santuzza would be the role in which the "new" Milanov would return in triumph to the Met in 1951, this earliest record of her portrayal holds particular inter-

Cavalleria Rusticana
20 March 1943

Santuzza
Zinka Milanov
Lola
Anna Kaskas
Turiddu
Frederick Jagel
Alfio
Francesco Valentino
Conductor
Cesare Sodero

est. Santuzza's woes seem to have touched Milanov deeply. She is very much into the role: Milanov's volatility, her almost excessive tonal ebullience, fit well with Santuzza's personality, and the portrayal gains a dramatic credibility unusual in a Milanov reading. The verismo genre does not permit her to distance herself and recede into the grand manner as she does in more classic roles. 'Voi lo sapete' is meaningfully presented, and in the lengthy duet of Santa and Turiddu she is at her most impressive, the middle and low voice richly colored. She handles the dialogue portions with surprising effectiveness and caresses the plaintive 'No, no, Turiddu' phrases, filling the voice with vocal tears. The whole episode has just that element of nervous excitement which Santuzza's predicament allows. She reverts to a grander style (the fullest outpouring of tone and extended line) as she tells all to Alfio, and interpolates a high B to poor effect (sharp) as the scene ends. From the technical standpoint, in this scene she seems both uncertain about when to introduce chest tone and reluctant to exploit her *piano* top (that familiar octave vault is absent). But Santuzza remains one of her most successful early broadcasts.

The opera benefits immeasurably from Sodero's sure guidance. The elegiac moments (the andante sostenuto of the prelude) are sensitively drawn, but uncloyed. Yet he captures the momentum and excitement of the verismo style (more than one would expect from his finely drawn early Verdi readings) without sliding into the tawdry. For once the peasant choruses have a joyous lilt to them. No false sentimentality clots the broad-limbed melody of the intermezzo. As Turiddu begins his farewell to his mother, Sodero's strings spin a pungent tracery of fear around his words. Jagel gets badly out of line with him in the opening two phrases of the Brindisi, but otherwise the tenor is as stalwart as ever. His voice has more color, the production is less effortful than usual, and he never shies from a climax. In the final scene his Turiddu is more of a man than most as he eschews tenorial lachrymosity, content with a forthright farewell to 'mamma.' Both Kaskas and Valentino provide strong support. An uncommonly commanding Lola, Kaskas sings well, offering more chest tone than one usually hears from the Santuzza—no soubrette coyness for her. Valentino, heard for once in a role well matched to his abilities, is an excellent Alfio, ever firm-toned and appropriately playing as if with clenched fists—a manner that does not extend to his throat.

Though Milanov maintains that she was rudely treated by the management, Johnson and Ziegler must have had high hopes for her, for they considered her worthy to follow Lilli Lehmann, Ponselle, and Cigna as Norma. Lehmann deemed the role the equal of all three Brünnhildes and, of course, the redoubtable lady was seldom, if ever, wrong. During the final curtain calls of the 12 February 1944 broadcast, Cross assures us that Norma is Milanov's favorite role—she had sung it first in her native Zagreb in 1939. Undoubtedly she felt she sang it well (remember, she told Sayão "it is easy if you sing it badly"), for Cross tells us that Milanov sang five Normas in eleven days at the Teatro Colon in Buenos Aires in the summer of 1942, not an easy feat (even for the fearless Lehmann). And lack of confidence—even fear—was embedded deeply in the Milanov of these early years, as the mercurial mix of several of her broadcasts demonstrates.

Milanov sang three *Norma* broadcasts, the first two in 1944: 12 February (Castagna, Jagel, Lazzari) and 30 December (Tourel, Jagel, Cordon). On both occasions Sodero offers his singular blend of supple pacing and precision. In *Traviata* he emphasized the chamber music qualities of Verdi's most intimate opera; he found in *Trovatore* more of classical repose than most imagined could be there; but in *Norma*,

Norma
12 February 1944
Norma
Zinka Milanov
Adalgisa
Bruna Castagna
Pollione
Frederick Jagel
Oroveso
Virgilio Lazzari
Conductor
Cesare Sodero

Norma
30 December 1944
Norma
Zinka Milanov
Adalgisa
Jennie Tourel
Pollione
Frederick Jagel
Oroveso
Norman Cordon
Conductor
Cesare Sodero

paragon of bel canto style, he often chooses to replicate in the music the ferocity of the emotional turbulence on stage. The drive and agitation of the overture sound this note (more so in the second broadcast). Again, the choral and orchestral mass in the opening scene of the Druids complements the grandeur of the subject. Aiding the theatrical force of his conception is the degree of continuity he brings to the characteristic "number" layout of the opera. Master of transition and tempo flow, Sodero converts each act into a unilinear progression.

None of this detracts from the lyric splendor of Bellini's score, for Sodero never neglects an opportunity for the voice to dominate. His sensitive hand affects characterization as well. By minimizing the martial stamp of the accompanying triplet motive ('Meco all'altar di Venere'), he allows Pollione to become more the lover, less the stock tenor warrior. Jagel has the intelligence to respond. On both occasions the tenor begins quietly (although in the earlier broadcast the voice is overly thick, the top effortful). December finds him a much more attractive lover, less weighty in tone, phrasing with greater musicality—in fact, he has never sounded better. Both Lazzari and Cordon are properly authoritative as Oroveso, one of those priests whom only a Pinza could elevate to importance.

The opera belongs to the women. Castagna and Tourel, both superior artists, are poles apart in their approach to their role, as dictated by both natural equipment and national origin. Tourel makes her second (and final) broadcast appearance as the hapless junior priestess. But Adalgisa is no diminutive in vocal demands (early interpreters included many a current or future Norma—Grisi and Lilli Lehmann head the list). True, Adalgisa benefits dramatically from an air of youthful innocence, but then she must contend with Norma in those duets. Tourel is hard-pressed to meet all the demands. The unique color of her voice is an asset, for it automatically confers a touch of sensuality on the priestess who longs for the fulfillment of love. Her gentle manner also arouses our sympathy. But vocal size dictates that Tourel must always be at the full extent of her resources, and even then, she cannot quite impart that aura of time suspended which Bellini's long-limbed phrases require. In the duets Milanov's refulgent tone too often dwarfs her efforts, and of equal importance, in her softer singing Tourel's tone lacks amplitude. These are all faults of nature's chary hand, but Tourel's artistry can be telling in terms of style and subtle nuance. The moments before the second-act duet proper are particularly expressive. As one of the earliest mid-century exponents of the Rossini coloratura revival, Tourel's fioriture are the most clearly articulated of any of the singers on either afternoon—Castagna is particularly deficient in this area. But nature would be better confounded if Tourel could manage a smoother transition into the low voice. And in the 'Mira, o Norma' duet, where the two voices join in thirds and sixths, Tourel consistently enters late, an odd happenstance since the cadenza in thirds in the earlier duet is well matched and well timed. Happily, the artists avoid the mechanical motoric accent so deadly to this style and so frequently heard (and lauded) in later years. But the gulf between the two singers is greater than the fraction of a moment. Tourel's instrument is largely self-constructed through intelligence and willpower, and she moves it from note to note with care. Milanov's is a natural force that pours out in unchecked splendor and occasionally overflows its banks.

In many ways, Castagna is Milanov's identical twin, and they are a stalwart pair in the earlier broadcast. Bellini's noble melodies permit Castagna to eschew the chesty mode common to Italian opera's mezzo villains, witches, and temptresses. When her warm, velvety timbre is governed by classical restraint, her vocalism, always striking, becomes even more admirable. How beautifully she sounds the note of Adalgisa's sorrow in her opening aria! And in the first duet Castagna, the mistress of the grand vocal gesture, suggests the fragility, the weakness, of Adalgisa's position. In the big duet of the second act she still refrains from barnstorming, letting the voice flow out in liquid majesty (here Sodero, Milanov, and Castagna achieve a tenderness quite unusual in this opera). Unfortunately we are denied the all-important 'Mira, o Norma.' This is wartime, and Cross has informed the radio audience that the third intermission will begin at 4:30 to enable President Roosevelt to participate. Evidently a time miscalculation necessitates cutting into the opera at this point—the war effort's gain is our loss.

The *Norma* broadcasts represent a high point of Milanov's first Met decade. In the February 1944 airing one can cavil about a spread tone here and there, the unsettled placement of the opening phrase of 'Casta Diva' and its final note pushed sharp, a lumbering bit of coloratura, a slightly screamed high C or two in the act-two trio—all insignificant blemishes on a generally well-controlled performance. More pertinent is the lack of steel in the instrument. Norma indulges in a good deal of raging over her perfidious lover, and given Milanov's all-or-nothing temperament, she holds nothing back at these moments. The voice, so bewitching in full-throated cantabile, can grow shrewish in these moments. Indeed, in the fourth act, as Norma awaits news of and then confronts her lover, her manner, though grand, is overly stagy. Into one's thoughts flits the desecration that something comical (approaching caricature) marks Milanov's voicing of those favored operatic sentiments of anger, hatred, revenge—a series of aural Delsarte poses that raise the eyebrows of the auditor. Her voice and temperament propel her into outsized heroics. Still, in much of the February broadcast, Milanov tarries on heights that few sopranos of the last fifty years have touched. The wonderfully spacious recitative to 'Casta Diva,' the vocal poise of her scene with Clotilde, the distended vocal arc of 'Oh rimembranza,' her perfect control of *piano* phrases and crescendi throughout the duet—all these are memorable achievements. She combines tragic power with vocal splendor as she contemplates murdering her children. A worthy Norma, notwithstanding the flaws.

Even so, one is unprepared for the magnificence of her December broadcast. One can only wonder if, in the ten-month interim, some exterior event has buoyed her self-confidence. The absolute security of her performance, its authority, its vocal control, are quite amazing. No Milanov performance thus far has operated at so consistently high a level. Banish any reservations about heroics or caricature (only a few vehement moments of 'In mia man' are a shade wildly voiced). The affective states are now well corralled within zones matched to her vocal control. And those zones are more than ample. Neither her dramatic commitment nor vocal stamina flags throughout the long afternoon. The purely vocal effects are often arresting: 'Casta Diva' has a broader line, greater security, and unfailing beauty of tone; 'Ah! bello a me ritorna' is launched with full confidence; in the duets she shades her tones from *piano* to *forte* and back again with consummate ease. Milanov dominates the act-two trio, turning the opening into a long-spun band of silver. The act-three scene over the children and the duet with Adalgisa contain some of the finest phrases of her entire career. All the familiar virtues of her second Met sojourn are in evidence, yet the top is freer (the high Cs uniformly secure), the *forte* dynamic more attractive, and a silver glint illuminates a timbre which might be preferred to the bronze swath of her later years. If Milanov's portrayal lacks the subtlest revelation of Norma's inner life, the

La Gioconda
3 March 1945
Gioconda
Stella Roman
Laura
Bruna Castagna
La Cieca
Margaret Harshaw
Enzo
Frederick Jagel
Barnaba
Leonard Warren
Alvise
Nicola Moscona
Conductor
Emil Cooper

capacity to evoke the deep pathos of her plight, it owns abundant tragic grandeur—this Norma thrives on the big emotions. Milanov gives everything she has to the role and shows us the fullness of her heart.

With Milanov seemingly entering into her golden age, the large-scale operas of the Italian wing would appear to be on their surest footing since the departure of Ponselle. But when Milanov was preoccupied with the lofty affairs of Bellini's priestess, the more plebeian matter of Ponchielli's street singer (arguably Milanov's ablest portrayal) fell into the hands of Roman, who sang all the Giocondas during the 1944–45 season, including the broadcast of 3 March. Her rather girlish sound is effective juxtaposed to Harshaw, whose Cieca lacks dramatic projection but is tonally impressive. (Actually, Harshaw possesses the better Gioconda instrument, even in these early years of her Met career.) Roman displays a command of the big phrase, at least when it is anchored in the upper octave. If only the middle voice were more securely joined to the pungent, expressive tones of its higher neighbor. Her high B-flat on 'Ah! come t'amo!'—superb in color and control—rivals Milanov's (the note has come to be thought of as Zinka's own); in fact, Roman is so fond of the note, so reluctant to relinquish it, that she holds it several measures beyond its prescribed value, barely condescending to utter the final syllable an octave below. Though ineffectual in the lower range, the beautifully colored middle and brilliant top, coupled with her fervid temperament, allow her to bring the act to a telling close.

Similar moments occur in her scenes with Laura, but the final act, where any Gioconda must make her mark, exposes her deficiencies. The architectural layout of 'Suicidio!' betrays the patchwork of her voice; she wobbles in the low passages, and the baritonal close is threadbare. Despite a stunning high C in the trio and a few quietly spun phrases in her farewell to Enzo and Laura, too many of Gioconda's vocal thumbprints pass by without individuality. Thus we have half a Gioconda—the better half, true, but still only half. These performances are the only Giocondas of Roman's Met decade; the role reverts back to Milanov for the next two seasons.

Other holes in the Italian wing have not been stopped. Jagel is again the Met's journeyman *tenore robusto*. Robust he is, but without the *slancio* flavor essential to the breed. His sturdy, firm tones serve the duet with Barnaba far better than 'Cielo e mar,' for he cannot summon an ounce of reverie over nature's wonders. Jagel makes a glaring false entrance at 'L'angiol mio,' an error uncharacteristic of this secure musician—but then, his last Met Enzo was in 1928, in his second Met season. That he was called into service seventeen years later might seem to confirm the Met's problem in the tenor wing, but the fact is that all of the season's earlier Enzos had been sung by a tenor new to the Met: Richard Tucker. Johnson was evidently reluctant to open the airwaves to so inexperienced a debutant as Tucker, an omission soon to be remedied with a vengeance. Jagel is no cipher in the role's stentorian stands, and his quiet, straightforward response to Gioconda's heroic sacrifice has merit.

Moscona, too, has his moments. Though unable to make much of his aria (the fault is equally Ponchielli's) his resonant tones lend authority to Alvise's condemnation of his wife. Both Moscona and Castagna know how to legitimize the melodrama of their scene, and here Castagna can display her still-beautiful instrument to full effect. She ranges over the widely arched yet angular phrases without ever losing color or poise—once again we are denied 'Stella del marinar'—and she gives Jagel lessons in style with her artless play of word and phrase in the shipboard duet. In the largo concertato which follows the revelation of the "dead" Laura, Harshaw's healthy tones anchor the ensemble; it is clear why management assumed her to be the heir apparent to Castagna's roles. But any Castagna withdrawal seems far in the future when hearing her splendid singing on this afternoon.

The earlier acts of the opera are dominated by Warren's thundering Barnaba. The baritone proves adept at invoking the villainy and thwarted desire of the Inquisition spy. Not only is the voice under superb control (no wooliness now) but his interpretive range is measurably larger, and this in a role that can be (and most often is) played as a one-dimensional villain. Even in his opening recitative, he deploys a variety of tonal weights and colors. In the duet with Enzo, Warren offers a virtuoso display of vocal art, a blend of technical mastery and dramatic suggestion ('Buona fortuna!' is both malicious and subtle). As he dictates the letter to incriminate La Cieca, the ghost of Ruffo's menacing manner hovers. No doubt now, he is the fully matured artist, ready and willing to spend his prodigal powers. True, he can't quite counterfeit the insouciance necessary for the jaunty barcarole, a deficiency as trivial as the piece itself (the measured gait of conductor Cooper is no help). As Barnaba cringes over Gioconda's dead body, Warren brings down the curtain with a wonderfully bizarre growl; it belongs in a collection of operatic grotesqueries, a gallery which includes innumerable frenetic laughs of sopranos as they launch 'Sempre libera.'

If one could place an entire performance in that gallery, Emil Cooper's cumbersome handling of *La Gioconda* would qualify. Ponchielli's overripe score can seem either grand or bloated, but seldom stodgy; Cooper achieves the latter. He had come to the Metropolitan the previous season with more réclame than many a Met maestro. Born and trained in Russia, an intimate of Rimsky-Korsakov, Cooper had conducted the 1909 world premiere of *Zolotoy Pyetushok* (*The Golden Cockerel*). Among his more intriguing credits was his tenure as musical director for Diaghilev's celebrated company in Paris. His acquaintance with the French repertory promised to fill the gap left by Beecham's withdrawal, while his natural affinity for Russian opera could be expected to open new vistas. After his Met debut with *Pelléas*, he undertook *The Golden Cockerel, Roméo, Samson, Boris, Khovanchina*, and *Peter Grimes*. His assignments in the Italian repertory seem an anomaly, and judging from the *Gioconda* broadcast, they also seem ill advised. Melodic lines, accompaniment figures, soloistic flourishes of the winds—all are given equal and unvaried emphasis, and the already thick score becomes overburdened. We count every minute, every second, of the Dance of the Hours; Cooper's day surely holds more than twenty-four. To be legitimate (and the opera need not be disowned) *Gioconda* must blaze away, but unlike Enzo with his ship, Cooper is unwilling or unable to put the torch to it, and the old barge with her rich cargo of melody sinks under its own weight.

The outing with Cooper underlines Sodero's worth to the Metropolitan. Gratefully, we return to him in the *Trovatore* of 31 March 1945, the final Met broadcast of the war years.

Sodero had been limited by a sorry crew in the 1943 *Trovatore*; some improvement was found in a 1944 airing (Milanov, Harshaw, Baum, Warren). Still more promising is the 1945 performance where Milanov, Baum, and Warren are joined by the redoubtable Castagna.

The Czech tenor Kurt Baum was another escapee from the European conflict. A half-dozen years of opera appearances in Prague, Vienna, Salzburg, and Monte Carlo had preceded his 1939 debut with the Chicago Opera. After settling in the western hemisphere, his José, Radames, and Manrico were heard in Buenos Aires, Mexico City, and Canada. One might expect a healthy voice from a gentleman who

Il Trovatore
31 March 1945

Leonora
Zinka Milanov

Azucena
Bruna Castagna

Manrico
Kurt Baum

Di Luna
Leonard Warren

Ferrando
Nicola Moscona

Conductor
Cesare Sodero

had won the amateur heavyweight boxing championship of Czechoslovakia—to have one's nose broken in an exhibition bout with Max Schmeling is no mean recommendation for a *tenore di forza*.

Alas, the voice proves to be as muscle-bound as the body. What price must one pay for two stentorian high Cs in 'Di quella pira' (the third one turns out to be a B-natural, though Baum, unlike most modern tenors, is singing in the original key)? In any case, the price is too dear: a tight, strangled, unmodulated tone which takes on a bleat in cantabile passages, and pitch suspiciously flat a good deal of the time. The tenor is not devoid of a feeling for the architecture of Verdi's music—his denunciation of Leonora has not only size but breadth of manner. In fact, his entire fourth act arouses a flicker of hope: the voice takes on a bit of color, pitch is relatively faithful, and he conducts the line with care in the reflective duets with Azucena. Whether hope is enough to explain a Metropolitan career of twenty-two seasons is another matter.

A briefer career, but one of far greater import, comes to a close on this broadcast, the final day of the 1944–45 season. Bruna Castagna, since 1935 the stalwart mezzo of the Italian wing, will be heard no more at the Metropolitan; on the season's tour she sings only a single Maddalena in *Rigoletto* (Harshaw gains the meaty assignments). At age forty-seven, Castagna's instrument is no longer quite as resplendent in volume and tonal sheen, but that she was still very much the best of her kind (at least in America—Ebe Stignani was active in Italy) is obvious from this final hearing. Even more impressive than her vocal command is her fully developed characterization. Her Azucena is no mere crazed demon.

Fond memories of Azucena's mountain home, tender regard for her foster son, are the heart of Castagna's portrayal. How well she knows her way around the twists and turns of Azucena's music: the dotted sixteenths of 'Stride la vampa!' are neatly articulated, Verdi's dynamic shadings are carefully observed, and while she hardly ever plays to the gallery, she is alive to the built-in theatrics of the role. Not only is she willing but still able to provide that extra fill-up to a phrase at a climactic moment (a broad allargando and deep *portamento,* rather old-fashioned but delectable, at the end of the aria). The second-act *racconto* is touched with sorrow in the tone, compassion and horror skillfully intermingled. Everything is adroitly scaled until she pleads with Manrico before he flees to save Leonora from the convent—there she pulls out all the stops. Perhaps the size of the voice in the theatre cannot be accurately gauged, but the vocal thrust is obviously potent; an occasional rasp as she eases into the chest voice is the only sign of wear. Her final act is the acme of her performance; there liquid legato, quiet regret, artfully sculpted phrases ('Si la stanchezza'), all combine to produce a childlike aura, as telling as it is simple.

If artists must leave, Castagna does so honorably. She remains, today as then, an underrated artist, never having gained the acclaim which her natural instrument and cultivated style warrant. Her commercial recordings, though splendid, are few in number. In her case the legacy of the aircheck is all-important.

With the exception of Baum, all elements of this performance are on a high level. Moscona is the best of Ferrandos, a mite less scrupulous this time in rhythm, but more overtly dramatic and thereby serving the narrative well. Sodero has sharpened the dramatic focus of his concept, retaining classical control but willing to touch the crop to his forces in the home stretch of the ensembles.

As Di Luna, Warren disdains to play the heavy, preferring bel canto as love's weapon. He relishes the high tessitura of the role and breasts any orchestral sonority with ease. But 'Il balen' turns out a bit more tremulous than expected, and the notion lingers that all that suave tone and musical rectitude is just a bit self-conscious. One longs for the natural song of a Battistini or Schlusnus or, conversely, Ruffo's direct assault. But then, Warren can caress the ear as well as play the lion. His voice takes on a lovely color in the duet with Leonora, a discreet foil for Milanov's far-flung phrases. Sodero's newly propulsive manner combines with the vocal richness and idiomatic style of the two singers to provide the afternoon's climax.

Milanov, too, is at her very best. One is tempted to speak of vintage Milanov, but in her case the full flavor of the draft still lies in the future. Nevertheless, her Leonora on this afternoon is the apex of her first Metropolitan career. All her virtues and none of her frailties are on display.

Leonora's great arias can only be fully realized by the poise of voice and repose of phrase which Milanov offers on this occasion. Arioso passages are floated with the utmost delicacy ('come d'aurato sogno'); the low voice is well focused without becoming unduly baritonal for this chaste Verdi heroine; the brief trills are neatly done, and the coloratura flourishes are not only clean but full-throated (with an acceptable high D-flat at the end of the trio and a magnificent high C to close the fourth-act duet); and the three-note phrases which decorate the convent finale are *leggierissimo*, as Verdi instructed. Unlike many a Leonora, she has the vocal size and fruity middle low voice to sound the anguished lament of the Miserere. Her old bane of agitation almost never causes a suspicion of tonal overblowing.

When interviewed on a broadcast intermission twenty years after her retirement, Madame Milanov remarked truthfully: "*Trovatore* was my destiny."[6] Vocally, it offered her every opportunity to show her strengths. And more than any other of her roles, it was dramatically plausible for her, not merely from the standpoint of stage action, but also in the projection of character and mood through the voice. Leonora exists in the splendid isolation of the Spanish donna of the fifteenth century—her vocal reveries epitomize her remoteness. The built-in distance makes entirely credible Milanov's expansive phrasing and stylized expressive devices, so musically satisfying in themselves, as revelation of character. Of course, her Gioconda has dramatic credibility too, but there it is because her outsized vocal gestures complement the mock theatrics of melodrama. Verdi is not Ponchielli. His truth must be taken at face value. As the *Trovatore* Leonora, Milanov can be not only relished but believed.

After years of struggle, the great soprano may have come into her own. Odd that, after only two more seasons, the Met would no longer welcome her.

Giovanni Martinelli as Éléazar in *La Juive*. Photography by Mishkin.

CHAPTER TWENTY-THREE

Coda: Vale

Castagna's premature leave-taking at the close of the 1944–45 season removed one of the strongest pillars from the Italian wing. Mezzos, seldom Italian and never as congruous, would come and go, but none would establish the hegemony which was Castagna's for a decade. During the war years yet another reign, more central to the history of the house in longevity and stature, was also drawing to a close.

Since his debut in 1913, Martinelli's hearty personality and vibrant tenor had captivated Met audiences. Three decades later the record seemed about to be tallied—he was not engaged for the 1943–44 season. But he resurfaced a year later for two performances (Manrico, Pollione) and made a final appearance the following season (24 March 1946), singing the third act of *Bohème* with Albanese in a gala to benefit American Relief for Italy. Now in the winter of his days (age sixty), the tenor might well have wished to echo Mimi's words: 'Vorrei che eterno durasse il verno!' (Ah, that the winter might last forever!) But the time of parting could no longer be delayed.

Martinelli's final broadcast was in *Pagliacci* on 20 March 1943. Again Sodero manages to maintain the elemental sweep of the opera without allowing the brutality of the action to coarsen the music's contours; as Colombina acts out her deceit in the play-within-a-play, Sodero's elegant articulation of the minuet paradoxically compounds the tension of the drama. When Martinelli first sang Canio at the Met early in the century, his colleagues were Bori or Muzio, Scotti or Amato. Warren is in that league, singing his first Met Tonio on the broadcast (act one on the 7 March Sunday night concert had been a trial run). I doubt that either of his Italian predecessors could have sung the prologue more beautifully than Warren on this occasion. Absolute security of tone throughout the entire range (including a brilliant high A-flat), clarity of focus, a finely honed 'Un nido di memorie,' meaningful pointing of text—all mark this as one of Warren's finest efforts. And he mixes a good brew of fool and song in his scenes with Nedda.

Albanese had been scheduled as Nedda but canceled, and the management offered up Marita Farell. Her light soprano has its charms, but a Sophie or Forest Bird cannot easily migrate to the Calabrian hills. Though she makes a spirited try at characterization, and her silvery top tones have a pleasing glint, lack of projection in the lower octave nullifies Nedda's fear and scorn. Farell's slim resources dilute the

Pagliacci
20 March 1943
Nedda
Marita Farell
Canio
Giovanni Martinelli
Tonio
Leonard Warren
Silvio
Walter Cassel
Conductor
Cesare Sodero

fiery conclusion to the opera and the climaxes of the Silvio duet. Walter Cassel is an above-average Silvio, but Dudley's Serenade is not worth hearing.

Pagliacci
25 March 1944

Nedda
Licia Albanese

Canio
Raoul Jobin

Tonio
Leonard Warren

Conductor
Cesare Sodero

Oddly, no complete recording, commercial or aircheck, of Albanese's Nedda exists; two brief fragments from the broadcast of 25 March 1944, however, confirm a perfect mating of role and artist as, in the first-act scene with Tonio and the second-act finale, Albanese displays her singular combination of vocal excitement and vivid characterization. Textual rhythms supply the bite for her rejection of Tonio—what mockery she puts into 'Quanta poesia'! No wonder that her swift alternation of venom, teasing, and laughter inflames Tonio. Jobin (Canio) sings 'Sperai, tanto il delirio' better than many a clown but without quite tearing our hearts. Albanese's gavotte is on the mark, and her final confrontation with Canio thrills: the top notes are thrown out with superb abandon as though Nedda's confession of love bursts proudly from her throat. A small but telling detail is Albanese's exact integration of the rhythms of 'Non parlerò! No! A costo de la morte!' with the orchestral interjections—the effect is hair-raising.

One can only regret that Albanese could not have played Nedda with Martinelli who, even in the final stages of his career, is a memorable Canio in the 1943 broadcast. Yes, he can only offer a grey-toned 'Un tal gioco,' opening the vowels unpleasantly, and the absence of either velvet or ring in the tone is lamentable. By the time he vaults to the optional (but de rigueur) higher octave of 'a ventitrè ore,' his vocal metal is tempered to good effect and the old sheen shines again. A touch of hollow laughter before the lament sets up Canio's distress, and in the aria itself he reaffirms his mastery of line, binding the long-drawn climactic phrases with steely tone. Saving himself for the opera's final pages, 'No! Pagliaccio non son' is more declaimed than sung. But he molds a genuine cantabile for 'Sperai, tanto il delirio' with some affecting touches of characterization in the voice (the evil cast of 'Ma il vizio alberga,' the sorrow and regret in 'ed un amor ch'era febbre e follia') and a strong B-flat at the climax. 'La commedia è finita!' is quickly, emphatically uttered—no tatters, the dignified exit.

With Martinelli's retirement the last link with the Caruso era is broken. Other broadcast veterans from the Caruso period—Ponselle, De Luca (Martinelli had preceded them at the Met), Bori—had vacated the stage before him. Of nearly 900 Met performances in the house and on tour, the radio audience was privileged to hear him often as Radames, Canio, Manrico, Gabriele, Pollione, Enzo, Riccardo, and Otello. If there is a regret, it is not to have mementos of his French repertory. His Don José was second only to Radames in number of Met performances, with Canio leading Faust by only a few appearances; he appeared as Éléazar in *La Juive* an amazing 31 times. Of his Italian roles, Don Alvaro and William Tell (the Met's language was Italian, though the role's genesis is French) would surely have enlarged our regard. Martinelli's voice (or rather his manner of producing it) may not appeal to all, but his live performances are vivid testimony to his command of style, musical integrity, and sincerity of manner. A genuine *tenore di forza* is a rarity, and none of his few successors could match him for nobility of expression. "When our voices fade, and we are old, will we be forgotten?"[1] he asked many years later. The Met remembered. On 20 November 1963, the fiftieth anniversary of his house debut, the management offered a gala performance in his honor.

His winter, after all, was long (he died in 1969, age eighty-three) and often warmed by audience applause as he strode majestically to his seat on his frequent visits to the old Met.

Alexander Kipnis as Boris Godunov.

CHAPTER TWENTY-FOUR

1942-45
Maestros and Masterworks

While the self-effacing Sodero was reanimating the Italian repertory, his high-powered colleagues were marshaling the Metropolitan forces through the complex web of symphonic opera. *Boris, Tristan, Die Meistersinger, Fidelio*, and *Pelléas* all felt the imprint of the Met's eminent maestros (Szell, Beecham, Walter, and Cooper) during the final years of the war.

The glow from their endeavors was not uniformly bright. One particularly radiant occasion was the broadcast of *Boris* on 13 February 1943. Not only did George Szell offer a completely integrated, dynamic performance of this diffuse masterwork but New York audiences, as well as the radio public, heard for the first time the awesome Boris of Alexander Kipnis. His portrayal must be counted among the most memorable creations of this Metropolitan era.

Kipnis, like Chaliapin, was Russian, and his native tongue is a powerful aid, as it was for his remarkable predecessor in the 1921 revival. Then, and now, all other participants sang in Italian, a wrenching reminder of the bilingual opera not uncommon in earlier times. Kolodin reports a projected English translation was scuttled due to the high cost of retraining the chorus.[1] Szell, "thoroughly in favor of opera given in the vernacular," opined that *Boris*, having been introduced by Toscanini in the Italian wing of the company, had "at least the greater fluency in its favor" over French or German. Even if the English project could be financed, he decried the "element of uncertainty" which would "inevitably creep in. The healthy automatism of all performers, ingrained in countless rehearsals and performances would certainly be disturbed," he wrote to a fellow musician in England. The paragon autocrat was willing to "stick to our compromise solution."[2] How Pinza would have fared as an English Boris is a fearsome thought, and perhaps Kipnis would have been denied his opportunity.

Almost all of the capable participants of the 1939 broadcast are again on hand. De Paolis' Schouisky is oiled evil; on the debit side, it takes all his skill to get through the demanding tale of the murdered children. Moscona, a Pimen who seemingly has drunk at the fountain of youth, enjoys perfect vocal health with nary a suggestion of the mystery of the old monk's musings. Newcomer John Garris is also short on suggestion but strong of voice as the most straightforward of Simpletons. Szell is at fault, too, in his brusque handling of the half-step motive which should convey the

Boris Godunov
13 February 1943
Marina
Kerstin Thorborg
Dimitri
René Maison
Schouisky
Alessio de Paolis
Rangoni
Leonard Warren
Boris
Alexander Kipnis
Pimen
Nicola Moscona
Varlaam
Norman Cordon
Conductor
George Szell

hopelessness of the Simpleton's (and Russia's) fate. Cordon's vocal weight is impressive in the Siege of Kazan, but his account gives no hint of Varlaam's vulgarity (Szell again more intent on precision than ferocity). Doe makes an able enough Innkeeper, though rather overcultivated for Russian soil, while Kaskas tills more solid vocal ground in her song of the gnat and the flea (Szell has the clapping game running like clockwork). Together they make up a rather antiseptic crew of seventeenth-century Russian lowlifes. The aristocrats fare better. Farell is unexpectedly full-toned in expressing Xenia's sorrow, and Petina shines as an assertive Fyodor (her Italian, like Cehanovsky's, somehow manages to counterfeit the inflections of Mussorgsky's song-speech).

The Polish aristocrats rank even higher. Warren's song elevates the usually journeyman role of Rangoni to a prince of the church. His ability to characterize with the voice has grown since he sang Rangoni in his first season: now he can suggest the venality hiding behind the Jesuit's sanctimony (again Scarpia comes to mind). Few baritones can turn the serpentine line of Rangoni's chaste seduction of Marina as bewitchingly as Warren does on this occasion. To continue to put a Rigoletto to cameo usage is prodigal on management's part.

With Thorborg again contributing her superb portrait of Marina, the two artists confer legitimacy on the much-maligned Polish act. Szell's rhythmic élan is a boon to them; in the mazurkas his hesitations and accents intoxicate, and Thorborg, in top vocal form and ever the keen musician, stays with him every time. Indeed, Szell carves a vivid profile throughout. The insistent rhythms of the Polacca generate excitement, and he adds spice to the long, sinuous lines of the love duet. Maison, pretender to the throne but patrician artist, is a manly Dimitri, a bit short on top and relying excessively on declamation, but his unique timbre is immensely appealing. In the hands of Maison, Moscona, and Szell the scene in Pimen's cell takes on a welcome immediacy, the conductor charging the accompaniment motive with drama. This is Maison's final Met season (only a single Dimitri follows this broadcast), and his distinctive artistry is not replicated in future seasons. When Maison promises that the murderer of Dimitri will be punished, the impact of the true singing-actor is strong.

In the early scenes of the opera Szell is less convincing. As the opera opens he immediately establishes a dynamic tension; the melancholic folk content suffers, but his way leads effectively to the ensuing police brutality. Nothing drags, the chorus sings with bite and determination, and the Russian aura, already diluted by the Italian translation, is reduced one notch further by the drillmaster. The gain in linear clarity is welcome, the loss in sonorous Slavic mass (in the coronation scene), regrettable. A measure of the immensity of the Russian landscape, the endless struggles of its tortured people, is forfeit.

Slavic sonority is what Kipnis supplies in abundance. He unleashes a flood of tone, but without any of that lugubrious extra ballast which overburdens most Slavic basses. One marvels at his variety of color, ranging from the profoundly opaque to clarified, even sweet, head tones. His voicing of the coronation scene, fine as it is, is mere prelude to the tragic power he displays within the Kremlin. (Again we are denied the crucial cathedral scene.) Tender with Xenia, commanding as he teaches Fyodor his responsibilities, Kipnis knows the value of the touching vignette. But the power monologue reveals the full scope of his interpretive gifts. His range of feeling is enormous, the command of vocal technique absolute—and all without Chaliapinesquerie—yet the troubled monarch's anguish is fully exposed. (He allows himself only one bit of staginess: 'Aha! Schouisky' he squeezes out at length when the traitor enters—a marvelously theatrical coup.) By now Szell is equally persuasive, weaving the orchestral web in the clock scene for maximum effect; *Boris* normally boasts a duality of protagonists (czar and populace), but Szell's orchestra makes it a triumvirate. Kipnis brings the act to a conclusion with a moving (and songful) prayer for forgiveness. He exposes the heart of Boris even as the czar is racked with terror.

The Kromy scene is perfect fodder for Szell's genius. His musical landscape is alive with the exuberance of a people roused; no drab gray musical colors clothe these revolutionaries. As Boris faces death, Kipnis again proves his right to the czar's crown, offering a rendering superbly varied in timbre, vocal weight, and coloration. Realistic outcries judiciously interrupt the faultless legato phrases; 'I am still czar,' he majestically cries at the end—who could dissent? Yet it is Pinza who will open the following season as Boris and sing the next two broadcasts. Undoubtedly the Italian had a vocal *droit du seigneur* earned by tenure and his own enormous gifts. But for Kipnis to portray Boris on only two occasions in New York is incomprehensible. Though fifty-two years old at the time of this broadcast, Kipnis' powers are undiminished, and of equal importance, his portrayal is devoid of the caricature which, fostered by time and repetition, so often creeps into even the greatest characterizations. Once again, the preserved aircheck of a broadcast is invaluable, especially when Kipnis' Boris is captured under Szell's superbly disciplined, dramatically taut direction.

The embarrassment of riches in the wartime conducting staff necessitated a judicious allotment of prime assignments among these lords of the podium. In addition to *Boris*, Szell drew *Rosenkavalier* and several Wagnerian plums. The territory of Walter, senior in age and experience, was foreordained: Mozart, Beethoven, and middle Verdi. By this time Beecham's sweet tooth was well sated by the French repertory, and he relished more solid fare. In 1943–44 (his third and final season) he tasted the fruits of a broader repertory. In addition to broadcasts of *Mignon, Carmen, Hoffmann*, and *Faust*, he not only served up Verdi's *Falstaff* but fell heir to the departed Leinsdorf's *Tristan*. If any barnacles had accrued to "old boat" Melchior, did Beecham, known for his saltiness, attempt to remove them?

During the final years of the war, the Wagner repertory, so long monopolized by Bodanzky or Leinsdorf, was parceled out among the more peripatetic maestros. Beecham had his *Tristan*; Cooper slogged through *Parsifal*; and now-you-see-him, now-you-don't Leinsdorf returned (in 1944–45) to conduct *Tristan* and *Lohengrin*; and Szell, having triumphed early on with *Tannhäuser*, turned his penetrating gaze on *Walküre* and *Meistersinger*.

Whether due to Schorr's declining powers or management's reluctance to mount so explicit a paean to "holy" German art, *Meistersinger* had languished for five seasons until its revival in January 1945. Most of the participants in the broadcast of 10 February offered portrayals new to the airwaves (Kullman and List are the sole carryovers). Only the exigency of commercial radio marred the pleasure of the unseen audience (the broadcast began a half hour later than the house performance), for Szell oversees a performance of singular distinction. True, List settles for the Bayreuth bark in act one, but authority and heft count for something. He proves a kindly father to his daughter and establishes an appealing intimacy in their scene. Kullman is splendid throughout. One would prefer more tonal weight, but he is not deficient in lyrical warmth, musicianly manners, and most important, youthful ardor. Nor is he daunted by the rigors of the Prize Song, either in the bud or fully ripened. He makes it more a love song than a mere contest entry, and thus has the

Die Meistersinger von Nürnberg
10 February 1945

Eva
Eleanor Steber
Magdalene
Kerstin Thorborg
Walther
Charles Kullman
David
John Garris
Hans Sachs
Herbert Janssen
Beckmesser
Gerhard Pechner
Pogner
Emanuel List
Conductor
George Szell

George Szell.

reserves to bravely meet the high As head on. And no need to feign ardor with so charming an Eva as Steber. She plays the ingénue delightfully in the early scenes, deftly teasing Sachs like a knowing flirt, while Janssen subtly adds a manly burr to his half-humorous responses. (The warmth and penetration of 'Lieb' Ev'chen, machst mir blauen Dunst?' well conveys Sachs' complex emotions.) Steber can add a child-like tonal pout when crossed, yet effortlessly expands voice and heart as Eva's spirits and line ascend. Her timbre is perfect for the role, like a fount of springwater, so fresh, so clear, and her command of dynamics makes for some lovely effects (the gentlest shaft of silver at 'Dem Meistergericht,' for instance). Her soprano has plenty of thrust for the outburst in act three, with no sacrifice of color (the future dramatic soprano in embryo), and she leads the quintet with opulence and authority.

For once the second-string lovers are more than filler. Thorborg plays with self-effacing assurance, John Garris is a David with easy projection, fine rhythmic sense, and the intelligence to make the apprentice more than a stock figure in the heartwarming scenes with Sachs. The Meistersinger themselves are a worthy group (Laufkoetter now promoted from apprentice to master, though demoted in song). Kothner is only Wagner's major-domo, but Mack Harrell's bright and steady baritone shines lustrously in his every utterance. Beckmesser can be played as little more than Wagner's revenge—at least, that was the norm until recent times—and

Gerhard Pechner is thoroughly in command of the pedantic Hanslick manner. He does come up with a welcome touch of singing tone as he begins his purloined contest song. His is a virtuoso performance, but one-dimensional—somehow calling to mind the thwarted self-importance so outrageously caricatured by Herman Bing in B-films of the thirties.

Janssen is an able successor to Schorr. One expects abundant lyricism and warmth of feeling, and he doesn't disappoint in that area. His voice and art are made for the moment when Sachs, sitting under the elder tree, recalls Walther's song of spring. Like the elder's scent, his 'Flieder' monologue casts a beneficent spell. He moves from musing to action with equal assurance, expertly mapping the climaxes and wrapping all in the best Germanic legato topped by a mix of head voice that forswears strain. Once again an artist's commercial recording of a scene cannot match the eloquence of his stage portrayal. What does surprise is his command of the role's burlier moments; his voice is fully equal to all demands. 'Jerum!' bursts with energy, and in the ensuing scene with Beckmesser, his pith and humor make for an unusually extrovert Sachs. The opening of 'Wahn! Wahn!' is beautifully colored, and though the next portion may be a mite pedestrian, 'Ein Kobold' is nicely evocative, with Szell's orchestral web of wonder an immeasurable aid. We share Sachs' enthusiasm as he teaches Walther, Janssen now spending tone and exuding warmth with uncommon largesse. He never tires throughout the long afternoon, and he, too, offers a trill as the quintet is about to begin. No other broadcast so fully reveals Janssen's artistry.

Is the whole more than the sum of these excellent parts? Decidedly so, with Szell at the helm. Superbly disciplined throughout, no hint of pedantry, no reining in of spirits, mars this performance. Proportions are just, the complexities of the ensembles fully mastered. Szell moves from gait to gait with deceptive ease (especially winning is the measured transition to the second-act fracas, its well-ordered chaos, oxymoronic though it may be, simulating a convincing street brawl). The third-act prelude is lovingly conceived, the strings singing expressively and the detached dolce chords setting the scene effectively. How the orchestra shimmers and preens itself at the Nuremberg meadow! Szell's dance music is delightfully lighthearted and gives us the flavor of this joyous moment. Throughout the entire opera, Szell maintains a lyrical, deceptively unhurried flow which waxes easily to full-blooded climaxes and then almost imperceptively wanes so the grand moments never overpower the comic spirit. Excellence abounds on stage, but the dynamism of this splendid afternoon is generated in the pit.

Only half of that statement may be made for another revival of the same season. Bruno Walter, missing from the Met for a year, interrupted his "sabbatical leave of absence and vacation just for the production of *Fidelio*" on the afternoon of 17 March 1945. The occasion was the premiere of Beethoven's opera in translation, the "first time anywhere the opera has been sung in English," according to Cross. The announcer sets the stage for the occasion in his own inimitable fashion, hailing the auditorium "with its decorative scheme of red and gold" as a "brilliant sight," citing the "latecomers of what is obviously a capacity audience." Soon "the bright footlights will begin to dim slowly and the warm glow of the footlights against the great gold curtain will introduce the first notes of this afternoon's matinee performance." The years have not dimmed his sense of wonder at the "much larger audience" throughout the United States and Canada which would hear "by the magic of radio" the music "directly from the stage and broadcast by the Texas Company."

Fidelio
17 March 1945

Leonore
Regina Resnik
Marzelline
Frances Greer
Florestan
Arthur Carron
Jacquino
John Garris
Pizarro
Kenneth Schon
Rocco
Lorenzo Alvary
Fernando
Hugh Thompson
Conductor
Bruno Walter

Herbert Janssen as Hans Sachs in *Die Meistersinger von Nürnberg*.

All the wonder of this afternoon, however, is on the wrong side of the footlights. When Walter conducted the *Fidelio* performances of 1941, Maison, Kipnis, Huehn, and Janssen had surrounded Flagstad in some of her final performances before her enforced exile in Norway. Whether the absence of a Flagstad was cause and an English translation effect (the latter necessitating a predominantly American-English cast), the performance is deplorable. The prominence of spoken dialogue made the choice logical, and the memory of Walter's successful *Magic Flute* seemed to promise success. According to *Opera News*, Walter was "enthusiastic" about performing the work in the language of the audience. He had been "rigorously training the principals all of whom [except Resnik!] impersonate their roles for the first time."[3] But not even saintly Walter could turn water into wine.

To say that Frances Greer's Marzelline is the most satisfying portrayal of the afternoon tells all. Her lively stage personality makes something more than an ingénue of the jailor's daughter, though at some loss of linear purity in the classic phrases of the canon quartet. German-born John Garris takes the prize for intelligibility. Hungarian Lorenzo Alvary does almost equally well in recitative (intelligible, but cluttered with *v*'s where *w*'s are wanted); but he loses out entirely in song. Alvary's tone is insufficiently centered either to convey the hearty gruffness of Rocco or to conduct Beethoven's line in the ensembles. As the villainous Pizarro, debutant Kenneth Schon offers a bright, clear baritone of modest size but without a suggestion of the *Schrecklichkeit* which must motivate the trumpet call's deliverance. Young Hugh Thompson (Schaunard at his debut a few months earlier) is entirely beyond his depth (both in authority and range) as the deus ex machina minister.

Though new to the role, Carron has enough stage experience to make a commanding Florestan, but he wallows in self-pity, further constricting his effortful production. There is no joy for him in his hit-or-miss 'O namenlose Freude' (who can decipher the English translation of Theodore Baker at this point?). The duet, however, is a proud moment for Regina Resnik. Here her affecting timbre and mettlesome temperament confirm her right to walk the Met stage. But only a surrealist casting director could have conceived that a pair of diverse Leonoras (the bel canto *Trovatore* at her unexpected debut earlier in the season and the German *Fidelio*) were appropriate fare for a twenty-one-year-old "Auditions of the Air" winner. Undoubtedly an early bloomer (a repertory change a decade later would save her from "soon-to-fade" consequences), Resnik already laid claim at the time of her debut to a demanding repertory, including Lady Macbeth (New Opera Company) and Fidelio (with Kleiber in Mexico City).

After a throaty opening of the canon quartet, the voice comes under control and many phrases reveal her fine sense of line and emotive force. The voice has arresting size and color, and her musical instincts count for much—she knows how to control Leonore's strength of purpose and sorrowful belief in the great aria, though the overall effect is one of insufficient grandeur. An occasional wobble in the middle voice is troublesome, and 'First kill his wife!' makes little impact (her vocal resources are overtaxed in the dramatic confrontation with Pizarro). Yet her voice shines forth in the ensuing quartet, and she conveys Leonore's nobility of song and person in the final scene.

A promising Leonore surrounded by mediocrity will not a *Fidelio* make. One can only settle for what emanates from the pit; if one could turn down the vocal track, the pathos and tumult of the drama would be revealed without alloy. In the adagio of the *Fidelio* Overture, the heart already swells as the tympani strokes underline the

Regina Resnik as Leonore in *Fidelio*.

warmth and nobility of strings and horns. Throughout the opera Walter expertly controls and lovingly shapes every motivic kernel. The *Leonore* Overture Number 3 (again played after the dungeon scene) is the climax of the afternoon, brought to an energetic conclusion by Walter and, for once, no anticlimax as Beethoven takes us again through the dramatic action—we have missed it in the first go-round. Well might the audience savor the afternoon, for though the production was heralded as Walter's *Fidelio* (he receives a long standing ovation after the overture), the broadcast proved to be his only Met *Fidelio* in the decade between Flagstad's farewell and return. Breisach took over the second performance, and in the following season Szell inherited the damaged goods of the English *Fidelio*.

Apparently not even the presence of distinguished maestros could certify quality of performance during the war years. But at least the odds were higher with their participation. And the Met could occasionally assemble from its stable of contract artists a consummate cast for a particular work. *Pelléas et Mélisande* is a case in point, though a good deal of trial and error preceded the triumphant revival under Emil Cooper in 1944.

After its first presentation in 1924, the opera fared well and remained in the repertory for a dozen consecutive seasons, largely due to the prepossessing portraits of Bori and Johnson, with strong support from Rothier and Clarence Whitehill (later supplanted by Pinza). But no magic was worked in the revival of 1940 under the unlikely Leinsdorf, with Jepson, Georges Cathelat or Jobin, and Brownlee. (Mélisande was blonde, so was Miss Jepson, ergo she could play Mélisande; it's a wonder the management didn't settle on Grace Moore, but safe mediocrity came easier than blind courage.) Bidú Sayão had been on hand at the time, but though supposedly brought to the Met for Bori roles, she did not undertake Mélisande until her Chicago performances under Eugène Goossens in 1944 (rumor has it that Bori was reluctant to have Sayão perform certain of her prize roles). Perhaps Sayão herself was reluctant to play Mélisande: "In the beginning, I did not like it. I felt I was unsuited temperamentally to Mélisande."[4] So she had Eva Gauthier, the celebrated *mélodiste*, teach her the part "word for word"[5] and worked on the stage action for six months continuously. Though Mélisande cost her "many heartaches and trials," she ended by loving her. Bori had had to face the tangible Mélisande of Mary Garden; for Sayão only the myth remained. The latter may well have been the greater danger, but fortunately, what had passed in the decade since Bori's retirement had made critics and public receptive to a new look at Mélisande. Sayão, with her delicate person, vivid stage personality, and musical sensitivity, seemed made for the part (her early study with Jean de Reszke guaranteed stylistic affinity).

Martial Singher, though a veteran at the Paris Opéra, sang his very first Pelléas in the Met revival. Another experienced debutant was the well-aged Tibbett, for whom the virtuoso Italian parts were no longer safe terrain. Harshaw (Geneviève), Kipnis (Arkel—the one carryover from the 1940 revival), and the diminutive Lillian Raymondi as the child, Yniold, completed an ensemble that promised a good deal.

Pelléas had been Emil Cooper's introduction to the Met public the previous season, and with cast intact, the broadcast of 13 January 1945 is, at the least, a well-disciplined performance. Some critics found the Russian an odd choice for this most elusive of French operas, but in addition to his early Paris years with Serge Diaghilev, Cooper had shepherded Mary Garden's Mélisande in Chicago (as close to the fount as one could get). Perhaps the only hint of heritage is his affinity for the more sombre moments of the score; he revels in the atmosphere of underground grottos and murky castle chambers. A touch of heavy hand lies on the opening measures, but the interludes are well paced, and he is no novice at exploiting the suggestive tone-painting of Debussy's prismatic orchestration. The rapidly changing imagery of the cave where Pelléas and Mélisande seek the lost ring is expertly pictured, the shimmering play of light and flow of water no less evocative than the more bizarre elements of Maeterlinck's symbolism.

Equally felicitous are the emanations from the stage. There is not a weak link in the cast. One would not have envisioned the still-inexperienced Harshaw (in her third season) as mother Geneviève, but this is one of the most satisfying portrayals of her decade in the mezzo terrain. Though her vocal armor does not include the subtle gradations with which creatrix Jeanne Gerville-Réache, Gauthier, or Teyte inflected Geneviève's reading of Golaud's letter, her agreeable voice sounds right in French (it is free from any contraltoisms which are antagonistic to Debussy's musical speech), and her musicality is an asset. For once Yniold is both aurally pleasing and convincingly childlike; Raimondi is delightful as she kisses Golaud's gray-touched beard. At the other end of the generational spectrum, Kipnis has no trouble depicting the aged, nearly blind Arkel. With his retirement from opera only a year away, his tone

Pelléas et Mélisande
13 January 1945
Mélisande
Bidú Sayão
Geneviève
Margaret Harshaw
Pelléas
Martial Singher
Golaud
Lawrence Tibbett
Arkel
Alexander Kipnis
Conductor
Emil Cooper

has turned a bit wooly; the production is more laborious, but his manner suits the role and he is able to summon a full sonority for the climax of his monologue, vividly communicating the old man's need for beauty in the face of death. Even more impressive are the closing moments of the opera, his voice now rock steady, yet suggesting the immense *tristesse* of man's earthly sojourn.

Fine as these singers are, when Pelléas appears we recognize the missing ingredient in their portrayals: a command of French declamation in which clarity and elegance of utterance lend a classical distance appropriate to the fantasy world inhabited by Maeterlinck's shadowy characters. How deftly speech falls from Singher's lips! His lines glide by on a seemingly continuous arsic filament. We begin to feel the other players are too realistic, too ordinary, in their search for character. Singher can brush a key phrase with legato, and suddenly Debussy's speech becomes loaded with emotive power. The timbre is as pointed and glistening as the stalactites in the caves that Maeterlinck's characters so often frequent. The climactic love scene reveals the fullness of Singher's artistry as he allows his vocalism to flower while confessing his love (though the absence of a tenorlike head tone at 'Ah! qu'il fait beau dans les ténèbres!' hurts). With the exception of one or two notes in the fountain scene, the higher reaches of the role are not only encompassed but are handled without evident strain or change of color. Even as one admires Singher's command of the role and superior artistry, his Pelléas is circumscribed by his vocal type. That glinting, metallic timbre is seldom modified, and the darker baritone resonance fails to suggest the youth and innocence of Pelléas. Thus, the poetic naiveté which keeps Pelléas free from guilt is seldom captured.

The combination of Cooper's conducting, a baritonal Pelléas, the black sonority of Kipnis' Russian bass, even Tibbett's residual Verdi sound, combine to emphasize the sombre colors of the work. And the playing manner of the principals (Singher excepted) is rather too realistic to shelter the ambiguity of Maeterlinck's characters or to conjure the futility of their struggle. The broadcast is a tremendously exciting performance, our involvement is intense, but the enigmatic flavor of the work evaporates under pressure.

Sayão, too, contributes to the dilemma. From the first, her energetic 'Ne me touchez pas!' suggests a lady who can take care of herself—one can believe that this Mélisande really would carry out her threat to throw herself into the water. Throughout the opening scene her excitement remains at a peak. She is indeed affecting in her fear and sorrow, but she keeps no portion of Mélisande to herself. And yet, the essence of the drama is that we can never fully understand her. Again the voice's native qualities are a contributive factor: Sayão must use a chest mix and nasal resonance in the lower octave where much of Mélisande's dialogue lies. Some of Mélisande's childlike charm and intrigue are dissipated by the absence of a delicate yet spicy color in this range. These are relatively minor reservations in the face of her overall accomplishment. She is in lovely voice (the tower song is superbly sung with strong, pure tone) and is fully alive to the key phrases of the text—she makes the hidden meanings shine through. The second-act scene with Golaud shows Sayão at her finest: 'Je suis . . . je suis malade aussi,' she expressively intones, and our belief is complete. And when Mélisande momentarily turns operatic, as the doves depart and she sees Golaud's eyes in the darkness beyond the tower, Sayão is in her element. As Pelléas kisses her hair entwined in the branches, Singher conjures an unmistakable eroticism. The lovers are equally adept in their final scene together, Singher now more romantic in tone and manner, Sayão's brief replies infused with desire. Unfortunately Sayão, in the final moment before the kiss, is compelled to shriek her lines; the lovers' fear and abandon is patent, but oddly, we auditors become less involved; at this supreme moment in the drama, the players let us down—realism is no substitute for transfiguration. But a Sayão death scene is always touching, and so it is on this afternoon. Her pathos is the more affecting for its containment: with lovely tone and a sense of wonder, she takes her child into her arms—the poor child, as Arkel says, whose turn at life has come.

Tibbett provides the most compelling interpretation of the afternoon. To hear Tibbett in superior vocal form at this late point in his career (after four or five years of severe vocal distress) is a tonic. A good deal of the old ring has been recaptured, the leaden passage from note to note has disappeared. Vocally this performance is fully worthy of the great baritone of the years between the wars. Interpretively it reaches the heights trod by his Doge of Genoa. No chance to create character is overlooked: he proudly announces to Mélisande his rank as prince, then displays his psychological insight as he sings, with suggestive intent, 'Je regarde vos yeux.' When he questions Mélisande in act two, his stage command is potent: one can hear the rising tide of Golaud's emotion in Tibbett's legato, in his burnished tone, as he asks to take Mélisande's hand; he quickly moves to impressive vocal and dramatic authority as he orders her to find the lost ring. Everywhere he shows us the mind and soul of a great artist fully engaged. He presses Yniold with questions: 'Ils s'embrassent quelquefois?' he asks, and in a wonderful creative stroke, lightens and weakens his voice for 'Non?'—how Golaud hopes he is wrong. The great monologue where he punishes Mélisande is the climax of this imposing portrait—he rings a multitude of changes on her supposed "innocence." 'Et alors,' he intones, and the threat of the unknown hangs in the air; Golaud takes on the complexity and torment of a Boris at this moment. Of course, Tibbett's is a theatrical conception, but then, as noted when Pinza sang him, Maeterlinck's Golaud does not belong to the mists of Allemonde. He is real. We know him through and through—at least when Tibbett reveals him to us.

Pelléas, Szell's *Meistersinger* and *Boris*, Beecham's *Hoffmann*, and Walter's *Don Giovanni* are achievements beyond the norm of a repertory house. The Nazi threat and European war had thrust these maestros into Johnson's willing hands. Now the war years were coming to a close. With unexpected prescience, the Metropolitan closed its 1944-45 season with *Götterdämmerung*; within weeks false gods would fall in Europe and, before the opening of the fall season, in Japan. The Metropolitan had survived.

Not all the company's vicissitudes could be laid to the war. Time was the culprit which inevitably robbed the Met stage of its timeless luminaries: Rethberg, Lehmann, Schorr, Thomas, Castagna, Martinelli. Personal misfortune had claimed Lawrence and diminished Tibbett. The war itself had been both bane and boon to the company. Flagstad chose homeland and hearth, and the flow of new European artists was minimal. But Albanese, Baccaloni, Novotna, Singher, and Kipnis came and remained, artists of abundant gifts already ripened by experience. And Johnson cultivated a new generation of American singers full of promise: Steber, Traubel, Varnay, Warren, and Peerce soon established themselves in the Metropolitan firmament. Above all, the extended sojourn of several of Europe's foremost maestros ensured that the war years were not devoid of superior musical achievement.

Jarmila Novotna as Octavian in *Der Rosenkavalier*.

CHAPTER TWENTY-FIVE

1945-46
Postwar Stasis

As if to signal artistic freedom as well as national liberation, Johnson chose a Wagner opera to open the first postwar season. For the first time the radio public was invited to the festivities. Perhaps caught unawares, no enthusiast captured the opening night broadcast of *Lohengrin* on 26 November (nor the 22 December Saturday afternoon repeat)—the lapse is doubly regrettable since a new tenor and conductor added novelty to the occasion. Despite Melchior's long preeminence, opening night honors went to Swedish tenor Torsten Ralf (joined by Traubel, Thorborg, Janssen, Cordon). The great Dane had begun his flirtation with Hollywood, an activity that suited not only his extrovert personality but also his pocketbook. He returned in time for the Saturday afternoon *Lohengrin* broadcast, where Varnay and Moscona replaced Traubel and Cordon.

Though critical response was favorable, Ralf remained at the Metropolitan for only three seasons, singing broadcasts of Otello and Walther. The other newcomer (but not new to our survey) was a more potent force in the company, though his Met career covered only four seasons. Fritz Busch was another of the internationally renowned maestros who joined the Met during this decade of conductorial riches. The rather equivocal image of him drawn in the Mozart survey may now be filled in.

Tucked in between his broadcasts of *Lohengrin* and *Tristan* (the latter broadcast also unavailable) is the innocuous *Don Pasquale*, an unlikely companion to the purple profundity of Wagner's scores. But when Busch had played the Mozart pioneer at Glyndebourne, Donizetti's bonbon also figured on the bill of fare. Baccaloni and Brownlee (the Pasquale and Malatesta of the 5 January 1946 broadcast) were alumni of his Glyndebourne performances, and Sayão, Martini, and De Paolis were well anchored in their roles.

Overall, the performance is felicitous. (Martini, however, desecrates Ernesto's melodies with incessant flatting and dull tone—this would be his final Met season.) A major portion of the pleasure flows from the podium. We know at once from the capricious nuances of the cello solo which opens the potpourri overture that Busch savors the buffa spirit; the cello melody is absurdly sly in its halts and starts, the winds carry on in almost burlesque fashion, and accompaniment figures are singled out to underscore the wit of the piece. Busch resists the temptation to throw the final section into overdrive—he doesn't want Donizetti's filigree to turn brittle. Throughout

Don Pasquale
5 January 1946

Norina
Bidú Sayão

Ernesto
Nino Martini

Malatesta
John Brownlee

Pasquale
Salvatore Baccaloni

Conductor
Fritz Busch

the opera Busch shows that he knows how to mix a buffa recipe with just amounts of bravura and good humor, then add more than a dash of sentiment. Though every opportunity to turn motivic play into graphic gesture is seized with relish, Busch spins the most beguiling of melodic lines in the orchestra as the stage participants chatter away. He seems intent on weaving a more continuous web of sonority than one would have imagined possible (let alone, desirable) in this conservative genre. If his way is occasionally a bit more than Donizetti's lightweight concoction can bear, the end result pleases.

His firm hand extends to the stage, where no obvious high jinks intrude. Brownlee and Baccaloni are musically well behaved without diluting the comic nonsense of the piece. Brownlee remains Brownlee, but he is in decent vocal form and offers his best on this occasion. At least one feels his Malatesta is a man of the world, and he is one of the few baritones who can manage an acceptable facsimile of the fioriture in the coaching scene with Norina. But that same clarity is death to his recitatives, which are as lifeless as the proverbial list. Baccaloni is almost restrained (for Baccaloni), his voice showing its age but still a potent tool for the drolleries of old Pasquale. Busch's slow waltz doesn't allow the basso to turn 'Un foco insolito' away from characterization toward indulgence. Delightfully deft in his exchanges with the innocent Sofronia, as expert as ever in rapid patter, his portrayal arouses more sympathy than Donizetti's befuddled pantaloon normally garners.

Of course, only Sayão provides vocalism of real distinction, vocalism of perfect poise and point in the most intricate roulades, of bewitching grace in cantilena, always in the service of character. She is mistress of the role from first to last, and Busch's tempi offer her innumerable opportunities for characterful nuance.

Her rendition of the aria (including an excellent mid-range trill) is adorable. 'Pronta io son,' she announces, in sweeping seria style—and she does play her part to the hilt, the shyest of the shy with the unsuspecting Pasquale and outrageously funny as she accepts him. Nor does she forfeit vocal balm in her personality change. 'Via caro sposino' is no vivace under Busch, but it gives Sayão plentiful opportunity to display her vocal charm in finely spun cantilena. But back to earth we come with an abrupt thud as Martini mauls the serenade in the garden scene. What a trial is the Notturno duet (transposed down a full tone, as was the serenade) for Sayão, as she struggles to hold up the sagging tenor. Better old Pasquale should win her than this laboring Ernesto. At least Sayão has a chance to resuscitate the performance with her soothing pronouncement of the moral in Busch's gentle handling of the rondo finale.

In the old days the fragile charms of *Don Pasquale* were considered insufficient to satisfy the ravenous palate of Met audiences (or the demands of Sherry's restaurant, whose contract with the Met prescribed at least one intermission in each performance). Over the years, the opera either preceded or followed *Cavalleria* or *Pagliacci*, Victor Herbert's *Madeleine*, *La Serva Padrona*, or Bizet's *L'Arlésienne* ballet. In 1945 the Met turned to an opera that had not been heard for a quarter century, though it was one of the Met's own children.

The Metropolitan had hosted the world premiere of *Il Tabarro* in 1918, but the first of Puccini's three one-act operas had survived only two seasons. It would vanish again for another three decades after only three performances (plus a Philadelphia outing), the first of which was broadcast on 5 January 1946.

The performance, while adhering to a high standard, never quite makes a convincing case for Puccini's tidy exercise in Grand Guignol. At least in the first half, an air of caution dampens the atmosphere, an atmosphere Puccini has skillfully ground into our consciousness—the grayness of the waterfront, the sameness of life aboard Michele's barge, all of which makes Giorgetta's frustration plausible. Though Sodero captures the monotony of life along the Seine in his reading of the score, he does not fully integrate the picturesque elements of life on the docks which the composer graphically painted in his music (even though each element is carefully etched under Sodero's fine hand). After all, this is the first performance of an opera new to everyone, principals and orchestra as well as conductor. Eventually the lugubrious, unbroken rhythm of the Seine ensnares us, and when the drama of the love triangle finally becomes overt, Sodero, now on safer ground, brings off some exciting climaxes.

Not all of the inhabitants are at home on the docks. Harshaw, bright and secure of voice, is inordinately cultivated for a ragpicker; thus her dream of a little house in the country loses poignancy—perhaps Lazzari, her stevedore husband, has enough weariness for both of them. Anthony Marlowe, the song peddler, would make no sales with his quavery tenor. De Paolis, on the other hand, surprisingly firm-voiced, and in easy command of Tinca's music, is a convincing wharf rat into the bargain.

The aging barge master, Michele, offered Tibbett one final chance to take on a new role in the Italian repertory where he had triumphed so often. He fares well, since the suave cantilena of a Verdi baritone is not required. Still, for maximum effect, the role depends upon burliness of voice, and Tibbett comes up short in that regard. Nor can one deny that the sheen is off his tone. But we are spared the labored and tortuous sounds of a few years back; like Michele's cloak, Tibbett's voice is, on this occasion, a serviceable instrument. 'Resta vicino a me!' he begs Giorgetta, and Tibbett makes us feel Michele's longing as he remembers other nights, other moons. His monologue is touched with the hollowness of age, concentrated in intent and capped by a secure top note. The Saturday afternoon audience, happy enough for present probity and again remembering former greatness, breaks into the fabric to give him a brief hand.

Jagel is a capital Luigi, his leathery tenor suiting the rugged stevedore. One seldom questions Jagel's musical security and dramatic commitment, and in a role in which his native equipment is not placed at cross purposes, he is an effective performer. So he is on this afternoon. A bit more velvet would make a more convincing lover, but then Luigi is far from a sympathetic character, and Jagel's strong tones and intensity are a definite asset to the highly charged drama. He and Tibbett are telling enough in the swift denouement when Michele strangles Luigi—a clap of thunder from Sodero would have added to the chill.

In 1918 Claudia Muzio played the passionate, frustrated heroine. One can imagine the feverish pitch of her Giorgetta. Though only in her late twenties, as Fiora, Tosca, Margherita (*Mefistofele*), Desdemona, Aida, and Santuzza, the diva was already acknowledged as a formidable tragedienne. Though Manon Lescaut, Mimi, and Nedda were her favored lyric parts, the spinto repertory was home ground for her, and Giorgetta, too, is cast in that vein. Albanese's instrument is clearly lyric, and though her temperament inclined to the grander passions, she was even more adept at portraying feminine warmth and gentle charm. Giorgetta is a difficult assignment for her—in addition to lack of vocal size, she is playing against type; that she succeeds so well is a measure of her artistic acumen and the thorough manner in which she prepared all her roles.

Though tonal weight and sultry color are not abundant, pointed diction, insis-

Il Tabarro
5 January 1946
Giorgetta
Licia Albanese
Luigi
Frederick Jagel
Michele
Lawrence Tibbett
Conductor
Cesare Sodero

tent rhythms, minutely graded dynamics, and expansive phrasing turn the tide in her favor. When the unsuspecting Tinca comments on Giorgetta and Luigi's dancing, Albanese spits out 'Basta' with positive venom. As Giorgetta dreams of returning to the suburb where she and Luigi grew up ('È ben altro il mio sogno!'), her voice soars—the thrust of the top voice, its freedom and complete security, are thrilling. Left alone with her lover, 'O Luigi! Luigi!' reeks of unfulfilled desire, and she sounds the sensual lyricism of the duet with the expertise of a Puccini veteran. Sodero, too, is at his best in these surging phrases. If occasionally the word rather than the tone must carry the burden of dramatic excitement (at the expense of legato), Albanese is clever enough to make it work. When Michele tries to revive the love of former days and recalls their lost child, Albanese can momentarily allow her gifts of characterization fuller play. As she moves from brittle ill humor to lustful craving to momentary regret, the soprano brings Giorgetta to life.

Only when once again hearing Albanese on her natural hearth need one own that she excels more at conveying feminine frailty than hardness of heart. Two weeks after the *Tabarro* premiere, the radio audience, along with the New York public, heard the first Met performance of *Madama Butterfly* since its Japanese setting caused banishment after the Pearl Harbor attack. The revival might have prompted greater largesse from management. While Sodero guided all the remaining *Butterfly* performances, his illness caused the premiere to fall to Pietro Cimara, definitely a back-bencher throughout his twenty-three Met seasons—this is his broadcast debut, though he has been a member of the conducting staff since 1931. Scratchy strings and lack of poise in the opening fugal measures fortunately prove aberrational, as Cimara charts a safe course throughout the rest of the afternoon. The delicacy of the figurations which open the second act, the lyrical expanse of Yamadori's love music, the momentum of the flower duet, are welcome, whether Sodero's legacy or Cimara's way. The overly aggressive orchestra at key moments (the sighting of the ship, for example), the imprecision of attack and movement in the intermezzo (a mere run-through), the absence of tension in Puccini's final ironic comment as the curtain falls, are more likely the unwelcome consequences of circumstance.

Entirely predictable, however, is the efficient mediocrity of Melton, Browning, and Brownlee in the principal roles. Solid in tone but stolid of phrase is Browning's Suzuki, unnecessarily realistic in her froggy tone as she wakens after the night's vigil. Brownlee on this occasion summons a modicum of tonal ripeness and legato to enhance his assured consulate manner. But both he and Melton seem overly adept at affecting a Yankee twang.

The broadcast is Melton's first Met Pinkerton, and the assignment seems logical. But management had an inflated view of Melton's abilities. In June of 1944 St. Leger had written to "Jimmy" suggesting he study Lohengrin, a role the Met's casting director felt "should suit you admirably. I strongly advise you to take this seriously under consideration."[1] Melton liked Walther von Stolzing even better, writing back that he found the role very agreeable and advised "when you get around to scheduling the vehicle, I would like you to give it to me."[2] St. Leger had already told him not to "bother about the Meistersinger now, Jimmy. Get after Lohengrin." When *Meistersinger* rolled around in ensuing seasons, better heads prevailed, and Melton had to be content with the rank of lieutenant rather than knight of either Franconia or the Grail. As Pinkerton, Melton fairly reeks of self-confidence—a naval seducer needs that. He can offer no vocal balm to tempt Butterfly in the love duet, and his climaxes are always undermanned, but at least he is serviceable. Probably the

Madama Butterfly
19 January 1946

Cio-Cio-San
Licia Albanese
Suzuki
Lucielle Browning
Pinkerton
James Melton
Sharpless
John Brownlee
Conductor
Pietro Cimara

casting office counted overmuch on his being the very picture of a naval lieutenant in his regulation whites and blues.

Into this plebeian setting the Metropolitan placed the jewel of Albanese's Butterfly. Undaunted by her surroundings and rejoicing in the opportunity, after a lapse of five years, to live again the joys and sorrows of Butterfly, Albanese is in consummate form. What a fully realized portrait she provides, full of delicate character touches, yet never overplayed. And she is in complete control of her vocal resources.

Even as she begins her entrance far back in the wings, one can hear the rock solidity in the voice, a solidity fully confirmed as she vaults to a secure high D-flat. Without exaggeration, Albanese captures the childlike wonder of the fifteen-year-old bride; her sincerity as she recounts Butterfly's change of religion engages our sympathy. Her part in the love duet flows with an easy continuity, though every detail of word and phrase is lovingly etched. The voice, even when narrowed to preserve illusion, is patently warmer than in the 1940 broadcast.

Interpretively, minute *portamenti* and subtle gradations of volume and rhythm proliferate ('Vogliatemi bene' is delicacy incarnate). In such carefully nuanced settings her climaxes are immensely effective. 'Un bel dì' becomes a heartfelt narrative rather than a soprano showpiece; she even manages to make the Japanese mini-effects palatable in her exchanges with Sharpless and Goro (De Paolis at his best). Her charming mimicry of Yamadori sets off the ensuing lyric phrases, which she fills with liquid tone—what crafty juxtaposition of exquisite parlando and thrusting, full-throated arcs of phrase! Yet it is the spontaneity of this most carefully planned and executed portrayal that is ultimately so satisfying (the letter scene is a prime example). The tragedy deepens, and poignancy, which until now has been Albanese's aim, gives way to grandeur. The rhythmic sculptings of 'Abramo Lincoln' and 'Trionfa il mio amor!' become aural justifications of Butterfly's pride and integrity. In contrast, when Butterfly learns from Suzuki of Pinkerton's deceit, Albanese's quiet control conveys the forsaken wife's desolate isolation, as though she is drained of life and pride of person. Not even the cries of 'Triste madre' are played for effect; Butterfly congratulates Kate with hushed simplicity, and the full impact of the tragedy is driven home. In the final aria the soprano offers more tonal variety and dynamic gradation than in her commercial recordings of this moment, though not neglecting to provide a firmly intoned climax.

Puccini made Butterfly a test of a soprano's vocal durability and emotional control. On the occasion of the opera's return to the repertory, Albanese performs with restrained sensibility, absolute security of vocal placement, unfailing beauty of tone, and though burdened by "business as usual" surroundings, offers one of the most finished portrayals of the broadcast series.

Johnson had announced five revivals for the first postwar season, and in addition to *Tabarro, Pasquale*, and *Butterfly, Otello* and *Roméo et Juliette* returned to the boards.

The Gounod opus was favored with, to use Mrs. Peltz's canny phrase, "several novel castings," which meant Munsel and Jobin for the special preseason benefit and the broadcast, debutante Dorothy Kirsten and Gerard for the one-nighter late in the season—actually, the novelty lay more in the rarity of future repetitions of their efforts. Though an ideal Juliette (Sayão) was ready to hand, Munsel (albeit no longer a teenager) was undoubtedly closer to Juliette's age and, in the eyes of the management, warranted the assignment. (A year later not only Sayão but Gounod would

Otello
23 February 1946
Desdemona
Stella Roman
Otello
Torsten Ralf
Iago
Leonard Warren
Lodovico
Nicola Moscona
Conductor
George Szell

obtain redress, with the soprano and Bjoerling more mature, but far more satisfying, lovers.)

Verdi's *Otello* deserved, and got, better. Roman's experienced heroine is now buttressed by several new and substantial elements. Since the premiere of 23 February 1946 was broadcast, we have not only Warren's first essay of one of his prime roles but also the bow of Torsten Ralf as the Moor. The presence of George Szell on the podium adds to the sense of occasion.

The opportunity to restudy Verdi's wrenching depiction of jealousy and deceit was clearly at hand, and in Szell's clean-edged traversal of the score, we see how resolutely he grasped it. From him one expects precise modeling of the more complex passages—the turbulence of most of the first act, for example—and he does not disappoint. Equally salutary is Szell's subtle differentiation (seldom captured) between the orchestral figurations of the raging storm and the jocular winds of 'Fuoco di gioia!' or the burlesque of the drinking song. And, despite the welcome transparency, the excitement of the act is undiluted. Szell doesn't merely lay on the heavy sonorities of the Credo as though Hades were one great brass meeting ground, but points up the individual motives to amplify the varied textual points. The suavity of motivic play as Iago plants the seeds of suspicion; the insistent tumbrel tread of Szell's accompaniment to Otello's farewell to glory; the preference for grandeur rather than fustian rage in the vengeance duet; the balletic sprightliness of the Falstaffian third-act pantomime; the lift of the detached pickup as it falls on the pressed quarter-note motive in Otello's monologue of despair ('Dio! mi potevi') which, in Szell's reading, suggests not the hammer blows of fate but the incessant water drops of Chinese torture—all these bespeak Szell's aural amplification of the drama on stage, both graphic and psychological.

An unexpected boon is the emotive power of the maestro's conception: Desdemona's kindly intent is more manifest in his lovingly shaped phrases than in Roman's 'Dio ti giocondi.' Szell adroitly observes Verdi's quickened metronome marking at the first sounding of the kiss motive (both in the love duet and as Otello kisses his murdered wife), allowing it to flower only at the height of its almost too potent sequential climax and then, at the moment of Otello's death, releasing the full expressive power of the entire sequence. The perhaps too broad allargandi which Szell favors at the close of several scenes are of a piece with the overall breadth of his view of the score.

One notes almost with relief that even a Szell is not immune from the treachery of double bass players as Otello enters the bedchamber: they negotiate the first leap safely but a moment later the unison turns sour. Far grosser transgressions occur on stage. Roman is the chief culprit, her precarious vocal estate causing an abnormal amount of erratic phrasing and technical cliffhangers. Noticeably short of breath in the love duet (a chronic affliction for many sopranos in this scene), too often blowzy of tone, Roman makes a patchwork of the long Verdi lines which graphically represent Desdemona's untroubled innocence. The act-two quartet's difficult octave-and-a-half descent in unison with orchestral chords is more perilous than usual. All these mishaps cannot be redeemed by occasional ear-catching effects in the upper regions ('io prego il cielo') or dramatic outbursts (when Desdemona laments that she should cause her husband grief). Roman is more successful in leading the great ensemble and manages to carefully make her way through the Willow Song, though with some decidedly idiosyncratic vocal behavior. (Here, and in the denouement, youthful Martha Lipton reveals a dusky mezzo and budding professionalism.) Roman effectively declaims the opening of the prayer, but thereafter chews her way to a long crescendo on the high A-flat (which unfortunately provokes applause and stifles the final 'Amen.')

With the male contingent we enter another aural world (though even De Paolis' know-how cannot disguise his age-weary tones sufficiently to suggest a Cassio robust enough to provoke Otello's jealousy). Moscona's ambassador, as in all four previous broadcasts, solidly reassures Desdemona, and Kenneth Schon is an uncommonly firm-voiced Montano.

The Shakespeare-Boito-Verdi "story of misunderstanding, treachery, and tragedy" (as Cross defines the afternoon) requires epic portrayals from its two male leads. Warren comes amazingly close in his first encounter with a role that, more than any in the Verdi baritone canon, demands both thorough vocal mastery and the craft of the singing-actor. With almost a surfeit of tonal splendor, an easy command of the quieter dynamics, and most welcome of all, a newfound suppleness of phrase, he moves his performance level up yet another notch. His thorough preparation is evident in every utterance. One notes his conspiratorial tone in the exchange with Roderigo just after the curtain rises and the jauntiness of the drinking song (the sole sign of a debut occurs when he substitutes the third verse for the second with a phrase or two of different text and a few dropped notes). For once the high As of the Brindisi are accurately touched. No crude bellow mars the Credo—a moderate level from a Warren voice will do. Is he overly unctuous as he tries to prick Otello's confidence in Desdemona? Is he maybe not quite as poised over Szell's precise accompaniment as he might be in inciting 'la gelosia?' Well, it is only too evident that the vocal means are all there for a memorable 'Era la notte,' and there will be a half-dozen more Iago broadcasts by which to measure him. He proves unexpectedly adept at the patter of the pantomime episode—insouciance is not a word one thinks of with Warren, but in this case, there it is. When, with the proudest outpouring of tone, dominating the brass unison, Warren plants his foot on the fallen Otello, he leaves no doubt of his primacy in the baritone realm.

Unlike Warren, Torsten Ralf will have no lengthy opportunity to establish his credentials at the Met. Two more seasons, with yet another *Otello* and *Meistersinger* broadcast, will see him depart for his homeland, his international career over and, though only in his mid forties, death a short half-dozen years away. Like many a Scandinavian, the Wagnerian realm was a natural habitat for him, but the assets he brings to Otello are far from negligible. The tonal brightness of his 'Esultate!' is partially negated by overshooting a few pitches, and he is a bit short of heft. But the metal of the voice clangs clearly in the love duet, the sturdy bronze core wrapped in a Nordic light, as though a Bjoerling resonance were forged for maximum density. How satisfying to hear a *tenore robusto* with a free top voice! He may not achieve the Martinelli tension of line, but he has musicianly feelings. Few tenors can match his delivery of the closing phrases for pliancy and radiant coloration of secure tone. Later on we learn that the price he pays for his plangent top is a few dull notes—still a good buy.

In the later acts his tone turns a bit snarly as he tries for stentorian weight, and a high B-flat thins out. But he (and Warren, too) well withstands Szell's measured tread in the vengeance duet, gladly accepting the conductor's trade-off of apoplexy for majestic purpose. Certain nuances escape him (no *voce soffocata* at 'la sposa d'Otello') and, in general, his attempts at characterful declamation are less than convincing. He settles for open bitterness rather than hollow despair in 'Dio! mi potevi scagliar,' but when the monologue slips into song, Ralf again touches our hearts and satisfies our ears—with most Otellos, that rarely happens. Ralf is at his best in the fourth act, the questioning of Desdemona his most effective declamatory moment; here the brilliance of his tone lends heroic stature. In 'Nium mi tema' he at last fully opens Otello's despair to us (the ringing splendor of 'Oh! Gloria!' is a moment to treasure). Though not the most heartwrenching of Moors, his honesty in characterization, his musicianship, and above all, his colorful tones are assets the Met must have wished to harbor for more than three brief seasons.

Though *Rosenkavalier* had been continuously in the repertory since 1937 (and would remain there until 1947–48) no performance had been aired since the Lehmann-Bodanzky performances of 1938 and 1939. In 1943–44 the opera happily fell into Szell's receptive hands. Broadcast with virtually identical casts in both 1944 and 1946, the latter airing reveals Szell's consummate way with the complex and effervescent score. In it we find further confirmation of the depth of feeling which warmed his *Otello.* Though known as a rigid disciplinarian, musical ardor and personal sensibility were certainly not foreign to him. The latter, doused with a dose of pragmatism, is evident in his exchanges with musical secretary St. Leger dating from this period. Before the opening of the 1943–44 season, St. Leger informed the conductor of the loss of certain members of the orchestra, lamenting that "the headache of headaches has been the horn section,"[3] to which Szell responded with an uncharacteristic "let us hope for the best."[4] The "best" could no longer include the now retired Lehmann (recall that, though Szell had obligingly altered a few bars of the trio for her in 1945,[5] no *Rosenkavalier* broadcast was ventured), and when the opera returned to the airwaves on 16 February 1946, Jessner sang the second of her unlikely string of four consecutive Marschallin broadcasts.

That Jessner cannot efface the memory of Lehmann's princess may not be so damning, for it was to be almost two decades before the challenge would be fairly met in the person of Régine Crespin. The idiom is not foreign to Jessner (something that cannot be said of many a recent Marschallin). Jessner, after all, is Viennese-born, and many of the "throw-aways" of the role are deftly done. It is in the weightier moments that she is wanting. The obvious points are made, but the inner radiance of the monologues eludes her. The voice, too, is serviceable enough: sizable, quietly appealing in the middle upper range (the 'kleine Resi' phrase is lovely), and intelligently used. In many roles solid competence will serve, but the Marschallin is not one of them. Jessner's tone does not quite purl and the personality lacks definition—as the Marschallin says, it is "the how" that makes the difference.

The Marschallin's words are even more apt in regard to Novotna who, with no more vocal resources than Jessner, demonstrates "the how" in no uncertain terms. Of course, her timbre is the more affecting, but it is her manner that conquers. The exuberance of her lovemaking in act one, the questioning surprise as she confronts the Marschallin with 'Einmal . . . was war einmal,' the sense of vocal and emotional climax she achieves in the 'heut oder morgen' episode, bespeak a command of stage and personal projection beyond cavil. Still, Johnson was rather less generous a decade earlier when, in Europe, he caught Novotna in a *Rosenkavalier* with Lehmann ("in fine voice") and apprised Ziegler of "the good looking young Novotna making her debut as the Cavalier. She looked and acted exceeding well but the voice was inadequate for the role."[6] The manager evidently altered his thinking upon further acquaintance: only Novotna's Cherubino and Orlofsky were heard more frequently at the Met than her Octavian (thirty-one readings in the house and on tour). One

Der Rosenkavalier
16 February 1946

Marschallin
Irene Jessner
Sophie
Nadine Conner
Octavian
Jarmila Novotna
Baron Ochs
Emanuel List
Faninal
Walter Olitzki
Conductor
George Szell

must acknowledge that Novotna is a better wooer than warrior. When she courts Sophie (on her own) she is enchanting; we breathe the perfumed elegance of an earlier age in her wooing. Perhaps she is too ladylike in both bulk and color of tone to take on the gruff Baron, although sopranos can handle the role (Bori, after all, created the role at La Scala). Of course, it is her aristocratic manner which, in the house, carried the day; even over the air we sense it as she refuses to overplay the cheap theatrics of the tavern scene. Do we lose a little of the fun of boy playing girl when she can't alter the already light timbre of her voice to aid the disguise? But when she reappears as the embarrassed Rofrano, she is on home ground and her radiant artistry shines through.

The surprise of the performance is the Sophie of Nadine Conner. The quintessential American soprano, California-born with Gold Rush era antecedents, California-trained (USC), with pre-Met experience only with the Southern California Opera Association but carrying the assurance of six years of radio work with a raft of baritones (Eddy, Thomas, and Bonelli for "Vicks Open House"), Conner could have found no more apt fairy godfather than the California transplant, Bruno Walter. Under his baton she made her 1941 Met debut as an English-language Pamina. By 1946 she had already appeared as a broadcast Micaela, Sophie and Pamina. No one would have predicted that, unlike many another perpetual ingénue, she would remain for eighteen seasons and earn star assignments as Mimi, Violetta, and Mélisande, finally gaining a gala farewell celebration and a comparison with Bori and Ponselle (who, like Conner, "left at the height of their powers—and much too early"[7]) from Rudolf Bing, a manager little given to sentimental indulgence.

By the *Rosenkavalier* broadcast of 1946, she is well in command of her tolerable resources: purity of tone (small, but inherently round), firm musicianship, and proficient dramatic skill. Overall there remains something innocuous about the instrument and the stage personality that stamps every role with the brand of Sophie. But what a fine Sophie she is. The higher flights are easily encompassed (without the tone turning thin or metallic), and she wields a more full-bodied tone in the lower octave than most Sophies, effectively projecting aggression (innocent forwardness with Octavian, belligerence toward Ochs). The touch of wonder eludes her as she accepts the rose (no rhapsodic caress of cascading triplets), but in the final scene Conner's confident delivery leaves us with a bit more assurance than usual that Octavian is not quite the dolt he appears to be in forswearing the Marschallin. Ultimately the ladies' efforts are less than the sum of the parts, perhaps because of the sameness of timbre, with only a decibel separating Conner from Novotna, Novotna from Jessner.

In the other roles, neither De Paolis nor Glaz seems sufficiently on the mark to guarantee success for their conspiratorial efforts. Thomas Hayward, however, proves that an Irish-American tenor can more easily surmount the traps of an Italian aria (he actually articulates those arpeggiated ascents) than many a star turn by a high-priced tenor. In this, his debut season, Hayward's firm, dense tone promises more of a major career than will be realized in his dozen Met years.

List, perfectly at home in the fourth of his seven broadcast Barons, gives one of his finest performances. For once the voice is pliant from the moment of his entrance, and we are spared his lugubrious wobble; he seems as rejuvenated as Ochs at the prospect of his young, nouveau riche bride. His rich, beery sound enables him to serve up a fine brew of self-satisfaction and humor, while the sheer bulk of the voice obviates the need for overplaying the boorish aspects of the part.

List is undoubtedly aided by Szell, whose finely tuned sensibilities are again prominent. The familiar Szell hallmarks—pinpoint control of dynamics and tempi, clarity of texture, precise coordination between stage and pit—remove any Straussian bloat which can obscure the multiple charms of the score. Beyond that, the interplay between aural and graphic representation is keen (when little Mahomet brings the Marschallin's chocolate, he wears an orchestral coat of many colors). And Szell never misses the chance to allow the comic to blossom into the heartfelt when Octavian is on stage—the leave-taking in act one is blatantly romantic. After three seasons of Szell's *Rosenkavalier* the orchestra has never been more assuredly frolicsome. Yet they never grab the reins. The twinkling chromatic chords for the presentation of the rose don't just tumble down; they are judiciously landscaped. At one moment in this scene Szell's winds skirt the erotic; and then how deliciously he sends the orchestra along as the young lovers converse—Sophie's naiveté is as much in the pit as on stage. Ochs' waltz is kept to its metronome mark (slower than usually heard), but the Viennese string slides are encouraged to sprout. While Ochs' third-act exit may be a shade decorous, Szell allows a touch of ecstasy to invade the serenity of the 'Traum' duet in compensation.

The *Rosenkavalier* and *Otello* broadcasts are the last the Met radio public will hear of the formidable Szell until his isolated 1954 broadcast of *Tannhäuser*. At the close of the 1946 season, Cleveland claimed him and a legendary symphonic tenure began.

The postwar years were a time for returns as well as departures. Relief and gratitude were mingled when Jussi Bjoerling, in the garb of Mantua's Duke, again stepped onto the Met stage he had left almost five years earlier. A brief stint in a Swedish artillery regiment, appearances with the Swedish Opera, and an occasional opportunity in Italy, Norway, and Denmark had occupied him in the interim. Perhaps more important for the American public, he had continued to add to his considerable discography each year. Now that he was back, he would remain for nine consecutive seasons and a few scattered seasons thereafter. But it is discomfiting to note that, during his fifteen Met seasons, management assigned him only eleven broadcasts (plus a canceled Cavaradossi)—all the more reason to cherish each of his radio appearances.

Verdi's portrait of the Duke of Mantua is defined in explicit musical strokes; if a tenor combines elegant musical manners with a healthy instrument capable of an easy ascent into the upper regions, the ruler-rake comes alive. But the role is laden with pitfalls which have defeated many a tenor deficient in technique. The role seems most apt for the Bjoerling of the 1940s: if his character portrayal is rather generalized, it is always buttressed by a strong, often heartfelt, commitment, and his vocal resources are, as always, plentiful. He was normally generous in spending them—he certainly is on the occasion of his only broadcast *Rigoletto*.

Bjoerling puts the emphasis on elegance rather than brio in the Ballata, where Sodero's moderate tempo allows him some clear and deft *acciaccature* and a marvelously insouciant roulade at the close. Already we know we will love this Duke (that seldom happens); we certainly are captivated by his nonchalance and taken in by that bright silver trumpet Bjoerling plays above the staff. We may wonder how he could be attracted to such a frowzy-toned Countess Ceprano as Stellman presents, yet how fastidiously Bjoerling cultivates Verdi's sinuous melody as he woos her. (Tenor Richard Manning, however, is a Borsa worthy enough to serve this Duke.) Bjoerling is even more assured in his scene with Gilda (and maybe a shade less winning, for he is not really dulcet-toned in 'È il sol dell'anima'). The difficult chromatic ascents are taken in stride. Later he captures the Duke's newfound, if momentary,

Rigoletto
29 December 1945

Gilda
Bidú Sayão
Maddalena
Martha Lipton
Duke
Jussi Bjoerling
Rigoletto
Leonard Warren
Sparafucile
Norman Cordon
Conductor
Cesare Sodero

maturity as he muses alone on Gilda. The recitative is broadly sculpted and overtly dramatic. Again one might hope for more vocal caress as he begins the aria (marked *dolce*), but knowing he is no De Lucia, one must be grateful for the modest distinction he makes between declamation and reverie; and his overall manly vocalism and the lack of tenorial self-indulgence are decided assets. We value them even more in 'La donna è mobile' (in key); the aria is child's play for him. He is positively jaunty, and who wouldn't be if one had high Bs to squander as freely as Bjoerling. To hear the grace notes articulated cleanly in the quartet is a treat. True, by now we might welcome more dynamic variety from him; his reading is all pretty much *mezzo forte* and *forte*, with even the stentorian quite prominent in the final acts.

Warren is equally generous with his vocal resources. In his second of nine consecutive *Rigoletto* broadcasts he has raised all facets of his portrayal a cut, not always for the better. Palpably nastier as he taunts Monterone, and scattering extraneous vocal noises in the name of characterization, his instrument is woof-free, almost blindingly brilliant at full voice, perfectly controlled and ravishing in mezza voce ('Ma in altr'uomo'). But no mystery invades the key phrase ('Quel vecchio maledivami!') as he launches 'Pari siamo.' Perhaps Cordon's foggy, weary vocalizing of Sparafucile provides enough atmosphere (he is better on the home ground of his tavern). After a half-dozen years of increasing prominence, Warren is fully at home on the Met stage, entirely confident of his vocal mastery. But he paints with an even broader brush than Bjoerling on this matinee, content with coating the surface. He misses some of the pathos of 'Ebben, piango' as he pleads with the courtiers (the interpolated high Gs are thrilling, and the diminuendo-portamento on 'Tu taci' is model vocalism). Suddenly he gives us some quiet, thoughtful phrases as the distraught Gilda enters, and his dismissal of her tormentors is magisterial. The final half of the 'Piangi, fanciulla' duet is beautifully drawn by both Warren and Sayão; this is the most touching moment of the afternoon. I like his quiet beginning of 'Sì, vendetta'—to free Verdi's melody from brutality is a boon. But again, when Gilda's body is handed to him in a sack, he gives us neither macabre delight at his revenge nor a sense of the desperate situation. 'Ah, mio ben solo' is so beautifully and quietly vocalized that one can almost forgive his settling for the usual stagy hysterics when the tragedy of the curse comes home to him.

Sayão, always the mistress of pathetic death, is at her best in this scene. More than most who make their career on coloratura, she makes the moment ring true with some lovely vocal touches. 'Tutte le feste' is equally fine. Soubrettes and automatons have long inhabited this role, but Sayão moves beyond play-acting in these moments, and her lovely, pliant, fully rounded tones are immensely affecting. In these intimate moments one prizes the command which both Sayão and Warren have over gradations of volume at the quiet end of the spectrum.

Nevertheless, Gilda is a problematic role for Sayão. She sang it only six times at the Met (plus once on tour). At her first entrance she seems in rather poor voice and resorts to little squeaks of pressure on each note. Ultimately the tone begins to flow, though pitch is not always true. We sense her calling up all of her skill to surmount the obstacles of the coloratura *Fach*, a territory in which she scored memorably earlier in her career. She still commands some fair high D-flats, but the tone turns rather breathy, or even shrill, in the agitated moments of the love duet. 'Caro nome' (taken leisurely by Sodero) becomes an exercise in ingenuity. For the most part she is successful, with here an exquisite touch, there an artful dodge, moving very gingerly over the highest notes of her roulades and cadenza. If the virtuoso requirements of the role are a challenge, the more dramatic moments cause her greater concern. Sayão's temperament and honesty make her unwilling to falsify the requirements of the drama, even when they overextend her vocal capabilities. When Rigoletto raves for vengeance and she implores forgiveness, Gilda comes vibrantly alive, but it is rough-going for her with a few wild pitches. Nor does she stint in the trio at the tavern where Gilda surrenders herself to murder (her clipped rhythms are far more effective than the sluggish movement of Cordon and Lipton). Lipton is a trifle clumsy in the quartet as well, but Sayão holds her own with her deft, tonally secure interpolations. The broadcast holds Sayão's last Gilda at the Met. We are glad to have this souvenir of her portrayal, but it is probably best that discretion obtained in regard to further repetitions.

Though Sodero provides some exquisite accompaniments here and there, the performance bears the signs of a repertory offering insufficiently rehearsed. The orchestra is well in hand, but phrase endings in duets, releases in ensembles, even occasional feminine endings between soloist (Bjoerling) and instruments, are sometimes haphazard. Even with three such responsible musicians as Sayão, Bjoerling, and Warren, the suspicion arises that each is doing a star turn. As a result, the performance, though often brilliant, is rather hard-edged.

The Metropolitan in these days was indubitably a repertory house. Usually seven different operas were performed each week, and casts were varied as the artists' schedules demanded or the Met's limited coffers required. The system brought the opportunity to hear a variety of artists in the same role within a few months, a practice that had its rewards when the variants were worthy, but less so when, as in a *Rigoletto* later this same season, an audience heard, not Sayão, Bjoerling, and Warren, but Mimi Benzell, Bruno Landi, and Frank Valentino.

No role was fair game more than Puccini's hapless seamstress, and the Met annually paraded a string of celebrated Mimis before its New York public. On 2 March 1946 the radio audience shared management's discrimination when Stella Roman sang her first Met Mimi. If the role seems an unlikely venture for the perennial Gioconda, Aida, and Leonora, we have Olin Downes' word that her portrayal was the "most significant and communicative interpretation [of Mimi] that this stage has offered in many seasons"[8]—the inclusion of his review in the *Metropolitan Opera Annals* has given currency to his appraisal. Curiosity is whetted beyond the norm, and well enough, for otherwise the performance is standard repertory fare with Greer, Brownlee, and D'Angelo more or less adequate familiars. Greer's metallic point, in fact, enables her to suggest the brittle without the need to overplay the brazen; her Musetta is as welcome for what she does not do as for what she does. The same may be said for D'Angelo's restrained pair of buffo portraits. Brownlee is unrelievedly in the picture and in solid vocal form. Arthur Kent, returning after years of military service, unfortunately is not in good vocal shape, his once firm baritone grown wooly from disuse. His Schaunard muddies the ensemble picture at several moments. Newcomer Giacomo Vaghi completes the Bohemian quartet, portraying a Colline as savory and genuine to the aural palate as the cut of salami the philosopher orders at the Cafe Momus is to the oral. Sizable tone of appreciable warmth and a not unattractive vibrato make for an appealing coat song, though sustained tones tend to deaden.

Peerce as Rodolfo is familiar to the radio public. Not only had he sung the role in the 1945 Met broadcast, but a month before this season's offering, he had participated in the NBC Symphony broadcast to celebrate the fiftieth anniversary of the

La Bohème
2 March 1946
Mimi
Stella Roman
Musetta
Frances Greer
Rodolfo
Jan Peerce
Marcello
John Brownlee
Colline
Giacomo Vaghi
Conductor
Cesare Sodero

opera's premiere. Toscanini conducted both the 1896 and 1946 offerings, and thus the tenor's portrayal could be considered authentic Pucciniana. If so, Rodolfo is a far soberer fellow than the poet he describes in his act-one *racconto*. Peerce's virtues are not calculated to enhance the aura of romance. Not a shade of fondness invades his tone as he introduces his 'gaia fioraia' to his friends; he might as well be celebrating Napoleon's victory at Marengo. Toscanini's tutoring would seem to have aggravated Peerce's crisp attack and strenuous musical gait. He is intent on giving full value vocally, however, and does so throughout the afternoon. The narrative is taken in key (with the shortest of high Cs—a Toscanini legacy, perhaps), his tone darker but less nasal than heretofore. One is always grateful for the firmness of his musical line and the solidity of his tone, as well as tenorial continence at Mimi's death.

Sodero, too, refuses to overplay the score either by inflating orchestral sonorities to Wagnerian proportions or by dawdling in the treacly patches. In contrast to the idealized romanticism of his *Traviata*, his Bohemians are seen with clear-eyed, slice-of-life veracity. But his candid way does not prohibit suppleness of phrase or limit emotional impact—the less he wallows, the more we are inclined to weep.

Now to search out that "indelible impression" which Miss Roman made on Mr. Downes. The aural facts suggest that it was more intangible than indelible, for the diva offers the same crazy quilt of notes which has marred her spinto roles. Not only is the Puccini line ill served (she slithers rather than soars) but she lacks a prime requisite of the Puccini heroine, a "speaking attack" in parlando. Nor can she counterfeit the youth of the grisette, for the tone is too often tremulous and uncentered. In the final acts she does suggest the fragility of the ill heroine, choosing to sing virtually all of Mimi's music at a sometimes precarious, but not ineffectual, *piano* dynamic. Though the effect is too often merely skittish, a few moments are notable: the winsome pathos of her very gentle 'È finita' as she tells Marcello that Rodolfo has forsaken her; the climax of the Addio followed by a very pretty (and overlong) floated 'rancor.' Downes was particularly taken with the latter moment (it "made the action pause and the house break into applause"—as it has for every Mimi in broadcast history, some of whom have proffered a genuine *messa di voce* at this point). Both the bonnet and muff episodes profit from her fragile tone, but overall the death scene, too, is catch-as-catch-can.

For Downes "some minor technical flaws in her earlier moments" fade into insignificance for "yesterday Miss Roman was a great singer, . . . a great dramatic interpreter, a great artist with something elementally true within her revealed by gesture, action and supremely by the inherent qualities of a superb voice." Inherent, yes. Roman's timbre, particularly at softer levels, evokes considerable emotional response (as Downes says, "the voice, not under perfect control, is nonetheless a superb one in its color and emotional quality"). But even the loveliest timbre and evident sincerity of interpretation retreat before the technical inadequacies that undermine Roman's performance. According to Roman, Downes' review caused some apprehension at the Met. Years later she recalled that "the really incredible number of superlative adjectives" of the review caused "all the other sopranos who sang the part—and there were many—" to be "perfectly furious." Among the many were Moore, Sayão, Novotna, Albanese, and Kirsten—rather a formidable lineup. "There was a lot of intrigue," said Roman, "so that I wouldn't get the opportunity to sing it again."[9] In fact, Roman sang a second Mimi two weeks after the broadcast, though never thereafter in her final four years at the Met. During that period Conner, Pia Tassinari, Claudia Pinza, and Steber were added to the list of intriguers—a less challenging contingent, with only the aging Tassinari as competition for Roman. The ways of management are evidently as unfathomable as those of critics.

But the Roman-Mimi standoff was uncharacteristic. More often, critical judgment was in the negative while the Met management resolutely continued down a blind alley in its desire to mold a star.

Particularly ill served in this regard was Munsel. Pons had assumed guest status, and the Met thrust the coloratura mantle onto the comely shoulders of the youthful Spokane soprano. Having survived the challenging but non-starring roles of Philine and Olympia, the Met felt her ready for center stage, and in her second season the radio public heard her as both Lucia and the Queen in the *The Golden Cockerel.* Gilda, Rosina, and Norina were other house efforts, while her third season brought broadcasts of Juliette and Lucia. From the latter broadcast (9 March 1946), the soundness of the Met's judgment may be gauged.

The soprano is surrounded by *Lucia* regulars: Peerce, Valentino, Moscona, Oliviero, and the ever-faithful Votipka. The newly prominent Cimara wields an accommodating baton, managing to infuse the more pedestrian pages with some expressive life, but allowing the tension of the sextet to sag and not sounding the melancholy of Lucia's entry in act two or the mourners' chorus in act three. Valentino is in top form (aided by Cimara's stately larghetto in 'Cruda, funesta'), Moscona is sonorous and sympathetic, while newcomer Thomas Hayward turns the ineffectual Arturo Bucklaw into a proper tenor rival for Lucia's hand.

The afternoon belongs to Peerce in what is probably his most convincing portrayal. Donizetti's Edgardo is often in a state of bellicosity, and whether castigating the house of Ashton or denouncing the bride Lucy, Peerce's emphatic attack and pressurized vocalism are to order. Less well served are the lyrical moments. His reading gives little hint of those "melodious lamentations languishing over the strings"[10] which so captivated Madame Bovary at Rouen when the opera was in its infancy in the 1840s. Like Flaubert's fictional Edgardo, Peerce can summon "outbursts of rage," but his solid tones never suggest "mournful murmurs of infinite sweetness." Nor are the notes that "escape from his throat . . . full of sobs and kisses"—well, maybe an occasional sob, but certainly Peerce's tones do not kiss the ear as a bel canto singer's should. (But then, Flaubert's Edgar Lagardy was "more temperament than intelligence, more pomposity than poetry . . . a wonderful kind of charlatan"—Peerce was anything but that.) We have to be content with the superb breadth of line and manly tone which he lays on the duet. Following the sextet, he pumps an amazing amount of vocal energy into his muscular rejection of beleaguered Lucy. The darker resonance which he summons for the somber opening of the tomb scene is effective, and 'Fra poco a me' suffers no lack of conviction, for the phrasing is expressive though the dynamic is unvaried. And how resolutely he thrusts through the cadenza! For the opening of 'Tu che a Dio' he finds a clearer timbre; the difficult ascending phrases are sturdily surmounted, and more important, his fine musical instincts are to the fore. The tomb scene is always a virtuoso turn for this tenor, though like Emma Bovary, one still hankers after a few 'sospiri ardenti.'

Although Miss Munsel had not yet reached her majority, the broadcast was her eleventh Met Lucia. Having already sung more Met Lucias than Tetrazzini and Hempel, within a few years she would pass Barrientos and Galli-Curci, and eventually her thirty Lucias would nudge Melba's house and tour tally of thirty-one performances. Munsel's Lucia is clearly no mere byway in the Met chronicle.

Lucia di Lammermoor
9 March 1946

Lucia
Patrice Munsel
Edgardo
Jan Peerce
Enrico Ashton
Francesco Valentino
Raimondo
Nicola Moscona
Conductor
Pietro Cimara

We sense her girlish charm in the opening colloquy with Alisa—Munsel is alive to the dramatic situation—and in the fountain arias we take heart that the bite of her uncommonly brilliant and attractive timbre is still intact. Throughout the afternoon the top Ds and E-flats have more color, size, and surety than those of many a more highly regarded *soprano leggiero*. But the brief trills and downward leaps of 'Regnava nel silenzio' are smudged and effortful. By the time of the duet, the defects in her cantabile singing are blatantly apparent. With each change of vowel the tone varies in quality, steadiness, and volume; in purely vocalized cadenzas or ornaments the tone is always steadier and better focused—the text is usually more hindrance than help. The long line of 'Verranno a te' is a shaky path indeed, the voice an incessant flutter. 'Soffriva nel pianto' is fragile enough and thus dramatically credible; she manages an occasional spin of tone to good effect, only to negate it by passages of tremulous tone, even in the agitated moments. The mad scene (with modest ornamentation) has its moments, if one can be satisfied with a childlike prettiness rather than prima donna brilliance. Above all, her reading lacks the concentration, the dramatic tension, to hold the lengthy monologue together. The assurance of those glassy high E-flats is too little gain for ransom paid.

Pons is the standard by which coloratura singing of the 1940s is weighed in America (Europeans were blessed with Erna Berger and Lina Pagliughi). One can question Pons' dominance, even granted the inequity of age and experience between her and Munsel. Was Pons' singing, her art, that much worthier than Munsel's? Pons' lower octave was frequently tremulous, her aspirants were notorious, interpretation was too often a void. Yet a rehearing of her 1942 broadcast (in her best vocal form, it is true) compels attention and even admiration—sometimes for the wrong reasons. Her cantabile on that occasion is as firm as it ever can be, her attack more alert, the filigree far more articulate, than that of Munsel. Automaton she may be, musically and dramatically, but the choice is her own; it is precisely that calculated pose which her public perhaps most admired. She is Lily Pons, making every roulade, every finely spun melody, a challenge to be overcome, setting herself for each intricate phrase and bringing it off against what she hypnotizes her audience to believe are insurmountable odds. Munsel, on the other hand, displays not the slightest sign of trepidation. Appealing in person and incredibly young, with an inherently better instrument and limited, but passable, agility, she makes it all seem like child's play (in a way, of course, it was). Thus she casts no spell. Three years would pass before the Met management would see fit to exhibit her again to the radio public.

While management's discretion in regard to Munsel's continued exposure was prudent, it was needlessly chary in bringing a tenor recruit before the radio audience. Richard Tucker first appeared at the Met in the 1944–45 season as Enzo in *La Gioconda*. Though he sang all other performances, the broadcast went to old-hand Jagel. Redress occurred a year later when Tucker was granted both the *Gioconda* airing of 16 March 1946 and, a week later, the broadcast of *Traviata*.

In his radio debut Tucker is in high-powered company: Milanov, Warren, Harshaw, are in their familiar places under Cooper's baton. We might have garnered another Pinza role (he sang several Alvises this season), but he had begun to limit his appearances. The war over, the Met was free to replenish its vocal coffers at the Italian and German houses, and the search for a successor to the aging Pinza could begin. Giacomo Vaghi, a sympathetic Colline, is less imposing as the leader of the Inquisition; his voice is short at the bottom and lacks steely menace, though his knowledgeable style and warm tones in the upper range are pleasing. Harshaw, too, is ill suited to

La Gioconda
16 March 1946

Gioconda
Zinka Milanov

Laura
Risë Stevens

La Cieca
Margaret Harshaw

Enzo
Richard Tucker

Barnaba
Leonard Warren

Alvise
Giacomo Vaghi

Conductor
Emil Cooper

old Cieca, singing 'Voce di donna' in musical fashion but without a trace of contralto depth; that she manages it all without any mix of chest voice is testimony to the health of her wide-ranging soprano—but the result is decidedly unidiomatic.

Apparently intent on forcing round pegs into square holes, management offers up Risë Stevens in her only Italian dramatic mezzo portrayal. Harshaw is a mother figure, ergo she received mother assignments, and Stevens' slim silhouette qualifies her for the glamorous Laura. How to effectively utilize a mezzo of modest vocal means, sound musicianship, well-honed acting skills, and popular appeal in a house of limited repertory remained a quandary. The French repertory having fallen from fashion, only Octavian and Cherubino remained as characteristic Stevens parts. The German *Fach* (Fricka and Erda) had been early tried and (at the mezzo's insistence) soon abandoned; a run at the Italian heights was in process, with the Russian Marina just around the corner. None would prove efficacious for either the mezzo or the Met. Mignon, a perfect vehicle for her, would soon be banished, but her Dalila, in whose contralto depths many a mezzo has foundered, maintained its ground, though it pleased the eye more than the ear.

The same, or less, may be said of her Laura. As Laura's voice emerges from the persecuting babble of the crowd one is startled by the wooden, grainy texture of Stevens' voice and the angularity of her phrasing. Nor does her vocalism improve as the opera progresses. The effort to match the larger-than-life passions of Ponchielli's melodrama causes Stevens to produce a good deal of spread, hollow tone in the love duet with Enzo (the contrast is the greater for Tucker's elegant vocalism). 'Stella del marinar,' ungrateful in any case and doubly so with Cooper's choppy accompaniment, makes little effect until suddenly Stevens' innate musicality comes to her aid: at 'Scenda per questa' she eschews the cheap mezzo tonal belch and quietly conducts the long line to prayerful effect. Reserve is of no use, of course, when confronted with Milanov's fiery temperament in the beastly duet. Stevens responds in counterfeit kind, managing to spill out quite a bit of tone but decidedly living on her vocal capital. Milanov shows us the real thing here, blazing away in full-throated grandeur, the tone occasionally razor-edged (and pushed off pitch on the final note). As Laura makes her escape and Gioconda confronts Enzo, Milanov continues her assault, filling her broad phrases with reams of gorgeous tone. One feels the soprano is completely submerged in her role, giving entirely of herself emotionally and vocally. And she has it to give. When Alvise condemns Laura to death, Stevens, too, knows what is required of her and is game enough; but the results are sadly different—Ponchielli's wide-ranging, angular line is too unkind to her modest resources.

The dramatic Italian repertory was palpably a wrong turn for the normally career-wise Stevens, and the dilemma of appropriate roles remained. The answer, of course, was so obvious that evidently only Hollywood could supply it.

In the grand tradition of the thirties this last of the operatic cine-belles once again followed her heart to Hollywood to film *Going My Way* (1945) with Bing Crosby. She played a diva who is featured at the Met as—Carmen. The potency of the celluloid image was reaffirmed and, just a week after her first Laura, Stevens sang her first Met Carmen (28 December 1945—she had tried it out at the Cinncinnati Zoo Opera during the summer). Over the next decade and a half, Stevens' Carmen was a sure-fire seller; her Carmen appearances totaled seventy-five in the house plus forty-nine on tour. Hollywood had set the ball rolling, and the great American public kept it in motion for the duration of Stevens' career.

Meanwhile, other American artists had achieved their primacy without benefit of a glamour image. As Barnaba, Warren's vocalism is as brilliant as ever, hampered only by Cooper's bloodless batoning. No lively pulse mitigates the squareness of 'O monumento'; the innocuous barcarole and sailors' chorus are joyless, in spite of Warren's stalwart efforts. But Warren commands a full vocal arsenal and deploys it (shamelessly, to our delectation) as the villain of Arrigo Boito's incredible melodrama.

Milanov is absolutely endearing as the hapless Gioconda. Her belief in the character carries all before it—at least when she is in as splendid vocal form as she is on this afternoon. Barring an occasional slippage from grace (a shrill note in an agitated moment, or the B-flat of her act-one exit, this time a mite less glowing) she offers peerless vocalism. In this early decade of her Met career her tone was paradoxically both luscious and sharp-edged at one and the same moment. When she, Warren, and Tucker raise their voices in the concertato which closes the third act, one's tolerance for Ponchielli's work is mightily increased; to hear Milanov's fourth act is to capitulate completely. Her flamboyant, fruity rendition of the suicide aria is even better than the celebrated commercial recording: especially noteworthy are the skillful register mixing; the floating, dulcet voicing of the middle section; and her magnificent chest tones—somber but still quivering with life—as she descends 'fra le tenebre.' In the trio her quiet phrase of renunciation is deeply moving. If she grows a trifle blowzy in her dealings with Barnaba, the scene fairly cries out for a bit of wallow.

Nothing unkempt touches Tucker's princely portrayal. His vocalism is a model of musical sensitivity and tenorial restraint. The young (thirty-two) Tucker had not yet acquired a taste for the counterfeit mannerisms which, in later years, he presumed authenticated his Italian style. At his entrance, his clarity of attack and rhythmic brio register immediately, and if we sense a pinch of roosterism in the manner, Tucker probably felt it a psychological necessity to counter the incredible tutu-length skirt clothing his ample nether regions as the disguised sailor. Luckily, the brief raiment in no way inhibits his vocal aplomb.

Since his debut as Enzo the previous season, Tucker had added a half-dozen performances as the prince of Santafior and Alfredo before this broadcast debut. Before that, Tucker's operatic experience had been not only limited but provincial. Still, he was no stranger to the singing game. Native to New York's lower East Side, he early gravitated to the synagogues, rising from boy alto to a prominent cantorial post. Early marriage to Jan Peerce's sister and the tutelage of former Met tenor Paul Althouse whetted his appetite for an operatic career. No contract came to him from his 1942 appearance on the "Metropolitan Auditions of the Air" (the winners were Harshaw, Greer, Clifford Harvuot, and tenor Elwood Gary), but later auditions in the house proved successful. At the time of his debut, *Opera News* pictured him "with burning eyes . . . , smooth in his speech . . . self-possessed in his manner . . . well tailored and groomed" and holding "the example and success of Jan Peerce as his guiding star." (Mrs. Peltz's bright outlook on life was sometimes overly ingenuous.) Once having gained the Met, for thirty years Tucker would maintain a standard of tenor vocalism seldom equalled in the history of the Metropolitan.

'Cielo e mar' appropriately is the high point of his performance, notable for the fineness of his musical manners (the quietly intoned opening, eloquent *portamenti*, spacious pacing, and elegant shape of phrases) and the firmness of tone and freedom in the upper range. Most astonishing is the degree of tenderness he imparts to the piece, refusing even to belt out the final 'Ah, vien.' Not that Tucker is reluctant to excite his auditors, but moderation is generally paramount. He is a shade tame in the duet with Barnaba, for instance—his propulsive melody doesn't quite have the requisite swing (but neither does he bathe Enzo's 'O Laura mia!' with sobs); Cooper may be at fault, for he is deficient in rhythmic *slancio* at key points. Such elegant musicality and sweetness of tone (in the middle portion of his duet with Laura) is a rarity in the long-term Tucker canon. Only in the closing moments of the act, with his ship in flames, is Tucker roused to the fervid, emotional outpouring which he later so easily, and sometimes indiscriminately, dispensed. Like any good Italian tenor he drops a few sobs into the big concertato of act three, but they little disturb his noble conduction of line. He maintains both musical and dramatic integrity as Enzo and Laura accept Gioconda's sacrifice. A warmly colored instrument in pristine condition and a sensitive musicality which embraces the drama inherent in the music—these are attributes which seldom coexist in a tenor's bosom.

The *Traviata* broadcast of 23 March 1946 may be the finest reading of the decade. We hear Tucker in his second Metropolitan role in company with Albanese and Warren, both in spectacular form. The virtues of Sodero's sensitivity remain, while time has lessened indulgence on his part.

What a pleasure it is to hear Tucker's richly colored, manly tones and plangent top voice, all in the service of a firm legato line unfettered by exaggerated gasps and explosive wheezes. Even in the denunciation scene Tucker prefers legato to distraught overemphasis. No *dolcissimo a mezza voce* swathes 'Parigi, o cara,' but (unlike Peerce) he is able to vary his vocal weight somewhat and refrains from bawling the *con anima* descending phrases at the end of the duet. Of course, Albanese gives him lessons in elegant, idiomatic phrasing there and elsewhere in the opera. Tucker, though limited in rhythmic niceties of language and phrase in the second-act aria and betraying a tendency to sharp where excessive breath pressure is applied (the end of 'Un dì felice'), overall is a very well-behaved tenor, capable of the necessary *slancio* at key moments and yet genuinely affecting in his grief as hope fades for the dying Violetta.

Once again Warren confirms that he has all the components of vocal and dramatic art in balance. He and Albanese provide a superb demonstration of vocal artistry in their lengthy scene. How well they play off one another, making the scene dramatically vivid as well. In 'Di Provenza' Warren has forsworn the tear-drenching which marred his earlier efforts; now he concentrates on dynamic variety for expressive nuance. Still, the breadth and tonal amplitude of his castigation of Alfredo in the gambling scene is almost awesome.

From first to last Albanese is at her most beguiling. Her conception has obtained greater repose, free of any raw emotionalism or mere theatrical effect, its emotional honesty anchored by thorough vocal command. Never has the voice been more responsive to her demands, the tone now warm and vibrant, now pallid and exquisitely pellucid, always flowing in a stream of liquid beauty. Everything seems to come from an easy throat. The coloratura demands of act one are readily conquered, their dramatic intent thrillingly conveyed. In contrast, phrase after phrase ('Così alla misera' and the long-lined repetitions in the gambling scene) are spun out with a quiet nobility. She can dominate the largo concertato of the third act with full-throated vocalism, yet in both song and manner capture the ethereal beauty of Violetta's final moments with Alfredo. 'Addio del passato,' not as overtly tragic as some other Albanese readings, is a judicious balance of realistic acting and lovely vocalism, the latter exploiting a full dynamic range. Albanese, Tucker, and Warren

La Traviata
23 March 1946

Violetta
Licia Albanese

Alfredo
Richard Tucker

Germont
Leonard Warren

Conductor
Cesare Sodero

make this broadcast a feast for lovers of beautiful singing; even the concluding trio is nobly sung rather than masticated.

Clearly Albanese is at the height of her powers during this period. This was the year of the celebrated Toscanini broadcasts. In February 1946 the Toscanini *Bohème* had captured the classic refinement of her Mimi (her 1944 Met broadcast of the role is not preserved, and unlike the string of Met *Traviatas*, there would be no other Albanese Mimi broadcast until 1950). Then, in December 1946, the Toscanini *Traviata* first astonished the American public; none of the ensuing Toscanini opera broadcasts so divided admirers of his genius. I remember how eagerly I had awaited the release (in 1950) of the RCA records of the broadcast and how shocked I was at what seemed to me the rigid, harsh character of the performance. My memory of it had been quite different, even though I had in my ear, as a teenager, all the Met *Traviata* broadcasts of the early forties. Reviewing it again, I find it much more to my taste.

We can take a moment to juxtapose it against the 1946 Met broadcast. Rigidity there undoubtedly is, but also Toscanini's reading abounds in plentiful instances of the just (not necessarily the familiar) adjustment, the fluid (if minuscule) manipulation of tempo. Of course, in his interpretation one does not find the many violations of the printed score—"We artists had been putting in extra notes, dragging here, dragging there," Albanese commented; "This changed when we studied with Toscanini."[11] Many of the changes are welcome, the cleansing of tradition's clutter. But singers were undoubtedly indulgent in Verdi's day; the composer named Adelina Patti his favorite Violetta, and she was not known for self-abnegation. But Patti was a singer of utmost refinement and elegance. Perhaps Verdi valued those qualities as much or more than fidelity to the necessarily incomplete directions of the printed page. To the musician, what is not in the notation can be as important as what is.

In most cases the Toscanini tempi were considerably faster than the Met norm. Yet they conform essentially to Verdi's metronome markings in the score. De Schauensee, however, avers that Bori (she had sung Violetta with the Maestro in Busseto in 1913) recalled that Toscanini "was far less autocratic in his treatment of score and cast then" than in 1946.[12] Oddly enough, even with the sound of Sodero's graceful, one might say languid, tempi fondly lingering in the ear, Toscanini's tempi make sense if taken in the aggregate. With him one hears *Traviata* as a totality rather than a set of beloved individual numbers. The last act is entirely convincing and full of expressive nuance (Albanese is most affecting), and the gambling scene particularly gains from his agitated reading. (Peerce remarked of this scene that, ever since the Toscanini broadcast "the tempi at the Met have become faster.")[13] The atmosphere of Violetta's demimondaine world is certainly more vividly conveyed in Toscanini's first act than by Sodero. Excitement was clearly a Toscanini trademark and there is plenty of it in his *Traviata*. Yet, if the overall structure of the opera is more fully revealed under Toscanini, his reading lacks something that the Met broadcast has in abundance. One need not go so far as to agree with Virgil Thomson's judgment of the Toscanini modus operandi as "a systematic throwing away of all refinements that might interfere with his schematic rendition"[14] to regret the overemphasis upon motoric drive and energetic thrust. Even if one welcomes, as I do, Toscanini's eschewal of the traditional allargando for Violetta's three solo phrases in the gambling scene, his relentless pressure offers only a whirlwind of agitation without suggesting the inner suffering of Violetta (Verdi has, after all, marked it *da sè*). The heartrending scene between Violetta and the elder Germont is particularly

NBC Symphony
Orchestra
La Traviata
1, 8 December 1946
Violetta
Licia Albanese
Alfredo
Jan Peerce
Germont
Robert Merrill
Conductor
Arturo Toscanini

vulnerable under the Toscanini treatment. It is not so much a question of tempo as the feeling that the singers are servants of the beat—the absence of breathing space robs the piece of its humanity.

With Peerce and Merrill the insistence upon toeing the mark does not appreciably alter their practice. Albanese, however, is so much the mistress of refinements of phrasing, rhythmic subtlety in treatment of the word, and dynamic nuance that the Toscanini performance presents an incomplete picture of her Violetta (a portrayal which the Metropolitan performances of the same period more fully reveal). She obtains a full measure of excitement (and far better vocalism) in her 'Sempre libera' at Sodero's moderate tempo than at Toscanini's breakneck race. In other moments one feels the voice not to be as fluent as usual—perhaps it is the sense of occasion, the need to be on the mark with Toscanini, that inhibits. The wonder is that, even under these conditions, Albanese's Violetta is as moving as it is. The soprano recounts a revealing anecdote which the conductor told her of his first visit to an opera *(Ballo in Maschera)*: he knew the tunes from an organ grinder, and the boy Toscanini "corrected the singers mentally when they were wrong. 'I thought the organ grinder was better',"[15] the aged conductor told Albanese. An organ grinder is capable of mechanical, orderly precision, however incomplete the message; singers are only human. Undoubtedly Toscanini supplies a sturdy spine to Verdi's opera, adding a tonicity too often neglected. It hardly justifies Peerce's comment on the maestro's *Traviata*: "There's only one way—the right way."[16]

The increasing prominence of Peerce and Merrill, Tucker and Warren, affirms the rising curve of the American singer on the operatic scene. They had had illustrious forebears. The earliest had been primarily female: Minnie Hauk and Clara Louise Kellogg, Lillian Nordica and Emma Eames, Geraldine Farrar and Rosa Ponselle, all names that shine more brightly, though perhaps not less honorably, than a Riccardo Martin or a David Bispham in the operatic firmament. Though of a later vintage, the *Tosca* broadcast of 9 February 1946 united two American singers whose careers stretched back into the 1920s. Both Grace Moore and Lawrence Tibbett had earned a réclame (of disparate character) reserved for few performers. Their careers were now moving to a premature close, the one in tragedy, the other in a slow, troubling decline. Moore was killed on 25 January 1947 in an airplane crash near Copenhagen while on a concert tour. The *Tosca* broadcast was her last Metropolitan performance. Though Tibbett remained with the company until the end of the Johnson regime and appeared in major character roles on broadcasts of his final two seasons, his Scarpia broadcast was the last opportunity the radio public had to hear him in one of the charismatic roles of the Italian repertory where his fame had been so honestly garnered. Moore was forty-six years old, Tibbett not yet fifty; both should have had years of productive singing ahead of them.

With Sodero exercising his ever-judicious control, the *Tosca* broadcast maintains an overall standard of quality. Peerce offers an earnest, though unpoetic, portrait of Cavaradossi. His splendidly secure outcries of 'Vittoria!' ably suggest the revolutionary, though the ensuing song is dwarfed by the orchestra. 'Recondita armonia' is nicely spacious, the tone less pressurized than usual and thus more beguiling to the ear. Of necessity, he shortchanges the rounded Puccini climaxes of the first-act duet. 'O dolci mani' brings out the gentlemanly musician in him (though the gentleness is more in the manner than in the tone), and one must admire his measured scaling of 'E lucevan le stelle'—no misshapen lunges for him. Baccaloni dominates his few moments, though his vocalism is merely approximate. With even

Tosca
9 February 1946

Tosca
Grace Moore
Cavaradossi
Jan Peerce
Scarpia
Lawrence Tibbett
Sacristan
Salvatore Baccaloni
Conductor
Cesare Sodero

Jan Peerce as Alfredo in *La Traviata*.

fewer notes, De Paolis shares with us his delight in Spoletta's staccato malice. Sodero is ever content with Petit-Guignol, eschewing brutal strength in favor of pliant phrasing, vibrant tone, and breadth of line in the grander moments of the score. But he does not neglect to generate sufficient hubbub to prepare Scarpia's entrance.

The first act is rather tepid. Moore is vocally and dramatically recalcitrant ('Perchè chiuso?' is curiously undemanding in view of the famous Moore temperament). The voice has an uncharacteristic hoot, and she is a jot careless in rhythm, pitch, and language. Her *portamenti* turn into legato smears. She does provide an excellent climax to the duet and one knows the voice is all there, secure and colorful and without tremolo. Tibbett, too, is carrying heavy vocal baggage. The weight of tone suits the powerful police chief but the lack of legato suavity does not. He can still dominate the 'Te Deum,' however, with tone of size and adequate color. Except for the crowning peaks, Scarpia's long phrases are skillfully managed. When we meet him at dinner the voice is better lubricated, and as he writes his invitation to Tosca, his musings are pleasant to the ear. If the tone occasionally grows wooden at key moments ('Mia! Mia!' has a fine ring, though, and the final struggle is suitably big-toned), his old gift for characterization assures some effective moments: his suave, quiet suggestions to Tosca of a possible escape; the admirable pacing of 'Già, mi dicon venal.' Throughout the encounter with Tosca he is abetted by Sodero's subtle piecing together of Puccini's insidious thematic mosaic.

Moore overconcentrates on realistic delivery rather than note fidelity in her desire to moderate Cavaradossi's torture, but her efforts are effective, and the high regions of the role are bravely conquered, with the old vocal ring much in evidence. 'Assassino!' is well laid out, and she moderates her brilliant tone for some feminine cajoling of her injured lover (and slides up to a high C or two). Not too happy with Sodero's slow tempo for 'Vissi d'arte,' she still supplies plenty of beautiful tone— one hears an echo of Farrar's jewel-hard timbre in Moore's diamantine tone. Like Eames, she is unwilling to provide three climaxes at the aria's close and is content with a firm high B-flat. But she is rewarded with long applause, and no doubt she felt she had earned her paycheck with the public. A rather elocutionary 'E avanti a lui tremava tutta Roma!' puts a typical Moore cap on a resourceful second act.

The soprano throws her voice around a bit haphazardly as she describes her struggle with Scarpia, but one can relish the zest with which she recalls plunging the knife. In the duet, on the other hand, she summons some of the loveliest, relaxed vocalism ever heard from her throat, and one laments what might have been, not just in the future, but more wistfully, in the past. She departs, not only from the Castel Sant'Angelo but forever from the Met stage, with a secure, full-blooded, and surprisingly un-self-indulgent 'avanti a Dio!'

Moore had appeared in the first season of broadcast opera as Manon and Juliette (Gigli and De Luca were her partners on both occasions). There followed a hiatus of several broadcast seasons until she settled into her mature repertory of Louise, Fiora, and Tosca (retaining also her debut role of Mimi). Moore's outsized fame was the product of filmdom's flirtation with opera stars of the 1930s, and her life story had the makings of a movie (as indeed happened in the 1950s when moppet Kathryn Grayson played Moore; it was a bloodless opus—Moore was a lot of things, but never anemic). No scriptwriter could have dreamed up a more gripping finale than the plane crash in which she died. With a hint of Mayerling, a royal prince died with her— no romantic attachment, since the Swedish King had ordered the Crown Prince to escort her on her progress. A fabled life, yet according to Vincent Sheean's unkind account, Moore "lived in terror twenty-five hours a day over her own shortcomings."[17] "I appreciate Grace," Sheean claimed, though he is merciless in heaping ridicule on her musical and dramatic deficiencies and often derisive about her personal qualities. Grace Moore was an almost too easy subject to lampoon. RCA Victor record chief Charles O'Connell wrote with equal candor, but far more affection, of both her vagaries and attractions, professional and personal. Ardent Francophile Virgil Thomson appreciated her will and her way, at least enough to give her credit for what Grace called "the conscientiousness"[18] of her career. While Sheean claimed that Mary Garden "tried to teach Grace *Louise*" but "could not endure the result," Thomson, as wittily acerbic and more perceptive than Sheean, could, and did, abide it.

Neither critics nor public disputed Tibbett's supremacy as a singing-actor. Unlike Moore's, Tibbett's film triumphs, while undoubtedly expanding his public appeal, were mere incidents in a distinguished career. At long last, to that line of celebrated American prima donnas could now be added a male singer equal in ability, achievement, and fame. And like Rosa Ponselle, the first of the American-trained divas, Tibbett's background was all-American. Moore had studied to apply a French veneer, but nothing could disguise her healthy American "have-a-go" at things. Early on in their careers Moore and Tibbett had crossed paths as stars of the film, *New Moon*. Their futures were as bright as any singers' of their period, though the arcs they travelled were in different spheres: her triumphs of the thirties were largely celluloid (whether in the opera house, concert, or filmdom), while Tibbett created an unforgettable group of operatic characters and became the premier American balladeer and radio artist. In the forties their career arcs crossed in orbit, Moore's making a modest ascent with her Fiora, Louise, and Tosca, Tibbett's declining as he abused his health with alcohol and suffered inevitable vocal deterioration.

In time Tibbett became a purveyor of popular song on the "Lucky Strike Hit Parade" ("Deep in the Heart of Texas" was a perennial assignment). After the *Tosca* broadcast, his Met appearances dwindled to three or four a season. The broadcasts all went to Warren (five in 1946–47) or the debutant Merrill, with Valdengo and even Valentino taking on many of the old Tibbett vehicles. Though even the Doge's crown would pass to Warren in Tibbett's last season, the older baritone's aptitude for powerful characterization would earn him a place in operas new to the Metropolitan during his final seasons.

Grace Moore as Fiora in *L'Amore dei Tre Re.*

CHAPTER TWENTY-SIX

1946–48
Postwar Premieres

While the Johnson regime had performed valuable service in reviving the Mozart and Strauss operas during its initial decade, the Gatti specialty of American opera premieres had largely fallen victim to depression budget constraints and wartime restrictions. Undoubtedly Johnson's conservative bent made it easier to escape the challenge, and avoid the risk, of seeking out and mounting new American works.

The conditions of the Juilliard grant had required the Metropolitan to support American singers and American opera; as a consequence Damrosch's *The Man Without a Country* and Menotti's *Amelia Goes to the Ball* were mounted in the 1936–37 and 1937–38 seasons. (Pitts Sanborn denied the latter work citizenship since it was composed to Italian words and its birth was merely a matter of "geographical accident.")[1] But *Amelia* was neither a premiere nor was it broadcast. Another Menotti one-act, *The Island God*, qualified as a world premiere during the 1941–42 season, but again the radio audience had no opportunity to sample its limited charms. Greater faith, or perhaps courage, is evident in the decision to present Bernard Rogers' *The Warrior* on the broadcast of 11 January 1947; the occasion marked the work's premiere.

Rogers, who, like Hanson before him, was resident at the Eastman School, earned his Metropolitan premiere by winning the Alice M. Ditson Award. Once again it was outside money which furthered the cause of American opera at the Met. Rogers, though admitted to the veritable temple of musical conservatism, chose, in his words, to "live dangerously," to speak, unlike Menotti, in the language of the present. Not that he eschews models, predictably *Pelléas* and *Boris*, where language is treated with "scrupulous—even relentless—insight and integrity," where "action is finally unfettered."[2] In stating his intentions, the composer noted how Debussy "declaimed against 'parasitical' musical phrases which shackled the action," and he himself seeks to be "equally accomplished as portrait and landscape" artist. Rogers indeed proves relentless in his treatment of the word, but his musical landscape remains unduly barren, and his portraits owe more to their interpreters than to their creator.

Originally a radio play by Norman Corwin which recounts the Samson and Delilah tale, the opera is in one act with four divisions, each episode connected by brief musical transitions, the latter in order that the "musical fabric" should be

The Warrior
11 January 1947

Delilah
Regina Resnik

Samson
Mack Harrell

Conductor
Max Rudolf

401

unbroken. The problem is that one cannot find the continuity in the musical fabric. The orchestral score is merely a series, sometimes effective, occasionally striking, ultimately debilitating, of pseudopointillistic effects, the familiar contemporary language but without the evocative power of its better practitioners. The effect follows the word but neither joins with nor embroiders it. It is the text itself that carries our interest, and fortunately it is declaimed with magnificent clarity by Mack Harrell in the title role, Regina Resnik (Delilah), and a half-dozen male singers (especially John Garris, who takes ghoulish pleasure in putting out Samson's eyes). The work receives an exemplary performance under conductor Max Rudolf.

The action begins at the midpoint of the Saint-Saëns opera, Delilah's enticement already complete and the warrior about to be shorn. As a result, Delilah's role is truncated, too—unfortunately so, for Resnik gives us a good measure of the dramatic conviction that would sustain her in her maturity as a mezzo. (But even she cannot wash the triteness from a number of prosaic lines she is required to utter.) Rogers' treatment of the four divisions suggests the time-tried symphonic layout: a strong exposition in which the dirty deed is done; a marchlike taunting of the bound Samson; the blind hero alone in his prison at Gaza (the slow movement); and the final denouement as Samson regains his strength and topples the temple. Any romantic relationship between the principals receives short shrift. Hope momentarily rises that music may be allowed its rightful province during their brief interchange in the first scene (and the affect does deepen), but satisfaction is all too fleet. A few lovely percussion and wind effects underscore Delilah's mock lullaby. The full vocal range of both players is well exploited, but no profile emerges from their angular ascents and descents. Contemporary reviews noted the use of *Sprechstimme*, but as heard in performance, the words are either spoken or clearly pitched. The best moments of the score are the brief atmospheric preludes (what would have been considered mild dissonance for even the mid-forties ear is easily assimilated), and the monologues for Samson in prison and en route to the temple.

Harrell's voice is almost too beautiful for the burly warrior, but ever the complete artist, he dominates the performance with the kind of committed, nuanced vocalism and dramatic sincerity that the young Tibbett brought to his American creations. We share in Samson's despair even when, seeking answers ('Why is the Lord departed from his soldier for so long?'), Harrell is on his own, with no orchestral augmentation of his quest. A moment's lyricism startles ('I am weaker than the lad who holds my palsied hand'), and now the orchestra momentarily whets our starved aural palates. But the opera's close is anticlimactic, the emotional mood blunted by too-long commentary as Samson tells us what he will do. 'I'll have the last to say of what is said today,' he intones at his exit, and were it not for Harrell's exalted utterance, we would be glad of it. A single repeat performance followed the premiere. On both occasions *The Warrior* was harnessed to an English version of *Hansel and Gretel*.

Commendation must go to the selection jury for not playing it safe by offering yet another bland Hageman or Menotti concoction. The problem of *The Warrior* lies not in the idiom but in the earnest composer's willingness, nay proud desire, to forswear music's role in the scheme—that is, to amplify, to fill in the landscape, to vivify the characters. ("I have tried not to retard or interrupt the drama for purely musical effects.")[3] The jury was large and talent-laden: Edward Johnson, Douglas Moore (who would write several operas far worthier of the Met which happily found a home at the New York City Opera), and a number of the Met's conducting staff, including Max Rudolf. That they mistook the composer's professionalism and sincerity of purpose for operatic know-how signals our continued lack of clairvoyance in spotting stageworthy works.

Perseverance need not be its own reward, as was demonstrated in the new work of the following season. True, Benjamin Britten's *Peter Grimes* was heralded by a bouquet of triumphant performances following its premiere at Covent Garden in 1945. But advance praise had not earned Met berths for operas of Shostakovich, Milhaud, or Hindemith. Mr. Cross was able to describe *Grimes* for the radio audience as "one of the most talked about operas of the present day," an opera, though less than three years old, already heard in "nine different countries." But he could not commend the Metropolitan for even an American premiere—the opera had been performed by student forces at Tanglewood in 1946 under the youthful Leonard Bernstein. In fact, the Koussevitzky Foundation had awarded its first commission ($1,000) for the completion of *Grimes*. Toward the end of Britten's two-and-a-half-year residence in America (1939 to March 1942), the aging Boston Symphony conductor had frequently performed Britten's *Sinfonia da Requiem*; the young composer had informed Koussevitzky of his projected opera—hence the commission. On Britten's return to England, Montagu Slater formulated a libretto from a portion of *The Borough*, an 1810 epic poem by the Aldeburgh poet George Crabbe. The opera's setting ("a small fishing town on the East Coast") is Aldeburgh itself, which would soon become Britten's home (he was born only a few miles away) and, later on, the setting of one of Europe's acclaimed music festivals, a living memorial to Britten and his music.

All that was far in the future when the Met launched its production of *Grimes* on 12 February 1948, with Jagel, Resnik, Brownlee, and Hines under Cooper's direction. During two consecutive seasons the opera would achieve the remarkable total of twelve Metropolitan performances (eight in New York, including two broadcasts, four on tour). Though a public surfaced for the work, critical response to the opera, and particularly to the Metropolitan production, was mixed. In one of the few times when *Opera News* (a Met house organ de facto, if nominally the vehicle of the Guild) printed negative comments on the Met and its artists, the broadcast issue contained "Pro" and "Con" quotes from the New York critics:[4] Virgil Thomson, while noting that "it adds nothing to the history of the stage or the history of music," called it a "rattling good repertory melodrama" that "works." Irving Kolodin went further, deeming it a "work of great imaginative power and theatrical force," a judgment in which Douglas Watt of the *Daily News* joined. Olin Downes, the aging critic of the *Times* and quizmaster of the Met intermissions, decried its lack of lyricism and deemed the libretto "foggy and in the main melodramatic and untheatrical." Jagel was either excellent or miscast, Cooper masterful or deficient in intensity. To judge from the *Opera News* photos, the cardboard picturesqueness of Joseph Novak's sets was oddly at variance with the honest realism of Crabbe's borough.

By the time of the broadcast on 13 March 1948 (the season's fifth performance), the Met's forces and Britten's trenchant score should have been compatible. Cooper's stolid hand on the tiller, however, ensures only a steady course rather than a voyage of discovery. His interludes depict a turgid rather than free-flowing sea, with little of the "surging, relentless sea, the breakers, the cold wet spray, and the sea gulls crying" that Mr. Cross assures us are there to hear. The choral chantey 'Old Joe has gone fishing' lacks the jaunty flavor of the folk; that it provides an effective first-act climax is due to Britten's skill at integrating dramatic elements. Too often the pictorial play of Britten's orchestration eludes Cooper, even the

Peter Grimes
13 March 1948
Ellen Orford
Polyna Stoska
Mrs. Sedley
Martha Lipton
Auntie
Claramae Turner
Peter Grimes
Frederick Jagel
Balstrode
Mack Harrell
Boles
Thomas Hayward
Swallow
Jerome Hines
Conductor
Emil Cooper

opening of the second act with its echoes of *Pelléas* (the ascent to the terrace) and *Boris* (the coronation scene), which ought to be home ground for him. Like any good opera composer, Britten is not afraid to recycle the tried and true clichés of the lyric stage (the offstage chorus and organ à la *Cavalleria*, with the action proceeding as Ellen questions the bruised apprentice). We get a full dose of Britten's emotive power when he combines lyrical expansiveness and a relentless chordal drone in the introduction to the final act, though the genre music which follows (dance-hall filler and hanky-panky) is a falloff.

Jagel's Grimes meshes well with his pit leader: sturdy and honest in application, if insufficiently febrile to evoke our full response. Vocally he is in excellent shape for a tenor in his twenty-first season with the Met, and the leathery timbre is not ill mated with the seaman's weather-beaten existence. One can hear a suggestion of Peter Pears' weary, beating timbre in the quiet meandering of Jagel's 'Now the Great Bear'—but the fantasy of the episode eludes him. The tenor carefully sustains the long recitatives on a single note, admirable as tenorizing but no aid to character. Nor is he adept at spontaneously inflecting the text (the rest of the splendid American cast is). Britten's masterly soliloquies when Grimes, alone in his hut, dreams of marrying Ellen and, later on, raves in desperation as the villagers shout his name from a distance—in these peaks of the score Jagel's honorable intent and solid craft, considerable as they are, keep us at arm's length from the eerie core of the crazed seaman. Not unexpectedly, Jagel sang only four of the twelve performances in the opera's two-year run, the role soon passing to the young American tenor Brian Sullivan.

The opera is well stuffed with other fine American artists. Jerome Hines (Swallow, the lawyer), though only in his second season, sings with the assurance of a veteran in tones secure and vivid. He is apt in characterization, too. Claramae Turner (Auntie) and Martha Lipton (Mrs. Sedley) are able enough, though the latter is too slight of nether tone to make the gossip's 'murder most foul' the catalyst it should be. Thomas Hayward's resonant tenor qualifies him to lead the townsfolk in their persecution of Grimes, while Hugh Thompson makes the most of apothecary Ned Keene. Even John Garris, *aus Deutschland*, is at home as the English preacher.

Though Regina Resnik and John Brownlee had starred in the premiere, the broadcast Ellen and Balstrode are Polyna Stoska and Mack Harrell. Happy choices, indeed. Now in his eighth Met season, Harrell has only lately been coming into his own in leading roles. A lyric baritone of moderate vocal size, like the mezzo of similar cast, is usually an anomaly for a repertory house such as the Met. No matter how beautiful the instrument and gifted the artist (and Harrell qualifies on both counts), it is not a "money role" voice, to use trade argot. Thus, his is not one of the names which glitter in the Met pantheon. Only the opportunity was lacking, however, as he proves again with his beautifully articulated and subtly shaded portrayal. If the voice is a bit lightweight for the blustering sea captain (Tibbett would sing the broadcast of the following season), Harrell's vigorous rhythmic gait and bright timbre convey the virility of the man. Of course Balstrode's sympathetic nature is his to command. And how he loves the language: the speaking rhythms of a phrase like 'We live and let live and keep our hands to ourselves' come alive on his lips, and he readily turns a phrase into lyrical bloom. At the close of the opera ('In the black moment') he conveys Britten's eternal message of concern for our fellow man as effectively as could anyone.

Even as the title role passed to Sullivan, Polyna Stoska sang nine performances of Ellen, including both broadcasts. While her apprenticeship in the German houses and City Center stardom had led to both an assured debut and a broadcast Donna Elvira earlier in the season, one is not quite prepared for the magnitude of her achievement as the constant schoolmistress. She is the perfect Ellen Orford. The voice is sizable and unique in timbre, double reed rather than flute, and occasionally suggestive of a mini-Flagstad in its piquant middle register and lack of vibrato. The quality is maintained in unblemished state throughout the entire range, including both a *forte* or *piano* top. Her manner of using the voice is equally apt for Britten's quasi-instrumental lines: she threads her way up and down and over and around the composer's angular traceries with both ease and care. The exactitude of her intervallic skips is exhilarating. Despite her obvious concern for precision of vocalism and musical rectitude, the singer's portrayal is entirely empathic. Her reposeful vocal manner ideally reflects Ellen's dogged devotion to the difficult fisherman. And whenever she has a bit of recitative or spoken dialogue (urgently questioning the apprentice, or bleakly intoning 'We have no power to help him'), her sympathetic delivery shows us the skill that won her Mrs. Maurrant the Tony Award. Her combination of strength and quietude (abetted by a few lovely *piano* effects) is telling. 'Embroidery in childhood' is a difficult piece, but Stoska (after taking a moment to settle into it) makes it the musical highlight of the afternoon by her sensitive delivery (including an uncanny matching of voice with solo winds). Seldom are artist and role so perfectly matched as on this occasion.

Nearly two decades would pass before Britten's amalgam of theatricality, atmospheric music, and psychological portraiture would again be mounted. The Met remained a conservative house.

Leonard Warren as Amonasro in *Aida*.

CHAPTER TWENTY-SEVEN

1946–48
New Artists

During the seasons of 1946–48, the repertory (other than *The Warrior* and *Grimes*) is in the familiar mold. Only the first Met performance of *The Abduction from the Seraglio* adds further pith to the 1946–47 season. If novelty is wanted, one must look to the introduction of new artists, particularly Europeans now free from the constraints of war.

The Nordic countries, less ravaged by destruction and often untainted by collaboration, initially lead the influx. A freshet of new singers enlivens the *Tristan* broadcast of 30 November 1946. Sweden would seem a fertile breeding ground for tenors, for to the newly arrived Torsten Ralf and the returning Bjoerling, the 1946 season added Set Svanholm, destined to be a stalwart of the Met's Wagner wing for the next decade. Joining Svanholm in the *Tristan* broadcast is another Swede, the superb baritone Joel Berglund, who, following his debut in January 1946 as Hans Sachs, had appeared in broadcasts of *Tristan* and *Walküre*. Anchoring the male contingent is Hungarian bass Dezso Ernster (recall his Osmin), yet another victim of religious persecution, who had begun his fourteen Met seasons just ten days before this broadcast.

Thorborg had temporarily left the Met in 1946 (actually it was the other way around), and Flagstad was still persona non grata, else the Nordic strain might have been pervasive. Americans Traubel and Harshaw prove to be worthy keepers of the Wagnerian flame. Wagner at the Met, if not quite so holy as the 1930s brand, still commanded reverent address from both management and public. Melchior, now fifty-six and enjoying movie fame and fortune as an MGM cutup, was no longer solely at the Met's command (he did not appear until midseason), so Svanholm and Ralf handled the Wagner chores, with Traubel the more constant heroine.

And a very beautiful heroine she is in this, her fifth, broadcast Isolde. More alive to Isolde's changing moods, equally adept at summoning rant or warmth, prodigious of voice and, moreover, generous with it, on this afternoon Traubel is at her representative best. How fiercely she rages as the curtains part! Yet she is never lovelier in tone and manner than in recounting the moment when the wounded Tristan looked into her eyes and Isolde allowed the sword to fall from her hand. 'Fluch deinem Haupt!' is impressive in breadth and density of tone. Of course, she is satisfied with a pair of glancing high Bs—at least they should be Bs. Nor is she a chameleon in regard

Tristan und Isolde
30 November 1946
Isolde
Helen Traubel
Brangäne
Margaret Harshaw
Tristan
Set Svanholm
Kurvenal
Joel Berglund
Marke
Dezso Ernster
Conductor
Fritz Busch

407

to vocal color (but how insinuatingly she asks for the *Todestrank*). Throughout the first act Busch's hand charts a steady course, insufficiently *schmachtend* in the prelude, valuing precision over longing and settling for a businesslike efficiency where agitation and ecstasy are required. Once on land he is a changed man, lingering over the lyricism of the second-act introduction and providing a chamber-music ambiance for the colloquy of Isolde and Brangäne (Traubel and Harshaw are delightfully intimate and conspiratorial here—Traubel's *subito piano* at 'Nicht Hörnerschall tönt' fairly gleams). Busch astutely raises the temperature as Tristan arrives, then discovers unwonted sweetness in the measures preceding 'O sink' hernieder,' turning the entire episode into an oasis of love. Traubel, too, seems alive to Frau Minne's spell, that touch of lethargy in her make-up helping her find the repose which so often escapes Isoldes in these moments. Even the usual Met cuts cannot diminish the expressive sweep of Busch's third act, though the audience hacking almost vanquishes the shepherd's languid English horn solo. While a few flat tones by now blemish the final pages of Traubel's love duet (she moves so much vocal weight that she tires), her Liebestod owns both warmth and poise (the turn and little upward filigree are exquisitely done, a small thing but so often sticky in other throats).

Harshaw, too, is in splendid voice, floating her upper voice to beautiful effect (it is a rarity to hear two contiguous Isoldes, especially when the Brangäne fields more of a soprano sound than the Isolde). The budding soprano (who would sing Isolde during the Bing regime) shows more spirit than in previous portrayals and gives a lively impetus to Brangäne's phrases. 'Einsam wachend' could be more tightly knit architecturally, but it is tonally very lovely. Of the regulars, John Garris is surely the most cultivated Sailor of record; nothing lusty or casual in his way with the opening song, but it is neatly done.

Ernster, on the other hand, is the perfect King Marke in terms of character, the lugubrious emission of tone capturing Marke's weary despair. His voice is a bit recalcitrant, though superbly black in color and monumental in resonance. One fears it will be a long lament, for the emphasis is on declamation, but surprisingly, Ernster summons legato at will for certain key moments, lightens the voice beautifully at 'Der mein Wille nie zu nahen wagte,' and comes off as the genuine article, authenticating twenty years' experience on the German stage.

Svanholm and Berglund enjoyed a common inheritance. Both were baritone pupils of the legendary John Forsell (Telramund at the Met in 1909 and teacher of Bjoerling, as well). Berglund's Dutchman and Wotan were known in Vienna in the mid thirties, his Sachs in Chicago in 1938, and he was a Bayreuth Dutchman in 1942. His sumptuous bass-baritone would be heard at the Met in only four seasons before he assumed the directorship of the Stockholm Royal Opera. Of the three newcomers, his is undoubtedly the superior organ, both in quality and usage (the Met's regard for him is evident in his debut role of Sachs). While Kurvenal offers little opportunity for individuality, Berglund manages to make 'Wer Kornwalls Kron'' a good mix of character, voice, and musicianship. His true sensitivity comes into focus as watchdog over the wounded Tristan: the timbre (closer to Schorr's than any other) is richly colored throughout a wide range, solid at the bottom and bright on top—he can float a lovely head tone, too ('hilft'). Tessitura is never a problem and the vocal movement is always agile, the song firm and easy with that gleaming Nordic shine at key moments. He is, in fact, the complete artist and welcome at any time, but especially now in the void created by Schorr's retirement.

Svanholm's voice has not been blessed with the Nordic glow of a Bjoerling or

Berglund. At least, that is the critical residue to be gleaned from his recordings and reviews. At the time of his Met debut as Siegfried in November 1946, his modestly apt *physique du rôle* was admired almost as avidly as his more considerable musical attributes. Neither vocal size nor timbre were overwhelming, but there was general relief at the sight of a Wagnerian hero (and particularly the young, athletic Siegfried) of handsome profile (aided by an essential blonde wig) and recognizable waistline. Never mind that, set alongside the typically Amazonian Wagner heroine, his slight height was a drawback.

To the radio audience, questions of weight, height, and hairline were of little moment. Happily, Svanholm's aural merits were substantial. Like Melchior and many another Wagner tenor, Svanholm was an erstwhile baritone (debut as Silvio); after six years, he turned in 1936 to tenor roles (Radames, Don José, Max) and migrated to the Teutonic lands and the Wagnerian *Fach* (Vienna, Graz, Salzburg, Munich, Prague). Prevented by the war from coming to the United States in 1940, the forty-two-year-old tenor's 1946 Met debut had been preceded by appearances in San Francisco, Chicago, and Detroit.

Only two weeks after his New York debut, Svanholm was introduced to the radio public as Tristan. At first the lean sound and flatness of timbre startle (Melchior's juicy clang still saturated the ear), while the manly vigor of articulation and meaningful phraseology command respect. The manner is heroic and the tonal mass soon seems ample. Unlike his later records, no bleat invades sustained tones, and gradually the timbre begins to take on a more youthful and interesting color. The top voice is reached without strain. As act one draws to a close, a brassy chime lends a marvelous clarity to his naming 'Isolde'; the excitement resulting from the drinking of the potion swells in swordlike thrusts, and 'O Wonne voller Tücke!' is splendidly sustained.

Svanholm's rhythmic acuity better serves the ecstatic hurly-burly of the lovers' greeting in act two than does Traubel's laying on of tone, and he proves an ardent wooer. As he launches 'O sink' hernieder,' his song belies the criticism of tonal bleakness so often leveled against him—the voice has taken on a lovely sheen, head resonances enlivening the plangent timbre. Seldom does one hear the interlocking phrases of 'Barg im Busen' and 'Von deinem Zauber' sung with such warmth and linear caress—even Tristan's treacherous harmonies with Isolde are quietly and accurately blended. As the languor of the love duet crests, one hears genuine legato from a Wagner tenor, utterance noble both as vocalism and expression. Only Tristan's abject invitation to Isolde following their entrapment lacks the requisite poetry (a few ruminative moments in act three invite the same reservation). He has the stamina for the lengthy ordeal of the third act, charting the series of outbursts and relapses for variety and believability. Overall, he finds more music in these pages than most heroic tenors: 'Sterbend lag ich' is gently colored and lyrical; 'Wie sie selig' is beautifully intoned—Svanholm is not afraid to sing, even in Tristan's agony. This Tristan may be short on anguish (sheer volume may be a factor here), but he is never deficient in musical virtue.

Virtue no longer seemed much on Melchior's mind when he finally made his reentry past the midseason mark. A few days after his return as Siegfried, he sang his ninth broadcast of Lohengrin (25 January 1947). Perhaps in response to the warm critical praise elicited by the less plentifully endowed Svanholm and Ralf, Melchior is intent on overwhelming his auditors by sheer bulk of tone. The mystical purity of the Knight of the Grail is all but crushed in the onslaught of beefy tone and fiercely

Lohengrin
25 January 1947
Elsa
Helen Traubel
Ortrud
Margaret Harshaw
Lohengrin
Lauritz Melchior
Telramund
Osie Hawkins
Herald
Hugh Thompson
King Henry
Dezso Ernster
Conductor
Fritz Busch

heroic phrasing. Nor is rhythmic exactitude a merit in his eye this time (no longer will he acknowledge dotted rhythms). One so often reads of Melchior's musical carelessness as though it were a feature of his entire career; in fact, it is a late blemish. Something can be said for an easy, natural fall of phrase, and Melchior has always favored it, but now he is wont to overstep the accuracy perimeter.

Where sweetness of tone is called for, Melchior either refuses to, or no longer can, supply it—the addresses to the swan which frame the opera are a case in point. But in the initial greeting to King Henry, the tenor is in his element, his top voice shaftlike and his manner splendidly commanding. Lohengrin's warnings in the second-act finale are stoutly delivered. Here, and in the opening phrases of the third-act love duet, his reliance on murky, clouded tone (an effective occasional coloring device) is excessive. But the duet offers many rewarding moments—no tenor can equal Melchior's outburst of tone and greatness of heart when he proclaims 'Lieben sei mein stolz Gewähr!' The final narrative moves at a good clip—subtleties of color, volume, and word are mostly ignored, and the going gets a bit heavy toward the end. The swift performance-cut to the swan farewell is welcome. Though Melchior is now fifty-six, perhaps not age but boredom and atrophy have burdened the great tenor's efforts. Svanholm will sing seventeen different roles in his mere decade at the Met, while Melchior was confined to only eight portrayals over a quarter century.

Three new male colleagues assist the veteran tenor on the broadcast. Ernster is in fresher voice than for *Tristan*—abundant weight, vibrant color, and a measured royal gait commend him. Alongside Melchior and Ernster are two relative novices, neither fulfilling role requirements. Hugh Thompson's baritone doesn't carry sufficient vocal ballast for the stately pronouncements of the Herald—but he lacks little else. His easy nonchalance is a tonic in the rather pompous ceremonial moments, and the bright timbre and ease of production throughout the entire range define a most attractive lyric singer. These assets are denied the reliable Osie Hawkins. Size of voice he has, but management must have relied on bulk alone in imagining he could be a satisfactory alternate for Berglund and Janssen. In his defense, his broadcast Telramund is his debut in the role and a replacement for the oft-canceling Janssen. But he had regular assignments as Kurvenal, Amfortas, and Don Fernando (*Fidelio*) during this period (quixotically Hawkins had been assigned the *Butterfly* Bonze earlier in the week). To his credit he doesn't falter throughout the afternoon, but word and phrase are seldom significantly heightened—his performance is little more than a reading, and perhaps it actually was. Moreover, the voice sounds oddly unfinished. Pitch can become suspect, and inadequate support indicates that vocal cultivation is deficient. Hawkins had many years of valuable service to the Metropolitan ahead of him, but the Wagner Heldenbariton *Fach* was a road wrongly taken.

Traubel and Harshaw, unlike their colleagues, are again in splendid voice. Traubel is innately as ill suited to Elsa as Melchior is to Lohengrin, but this time she defies nature and, at least aurally, offers a convincing portrayal. Charm is a quality seldom associated with the hearty soprano, but she has it in her arsenal on this afternoon. Traubel is a slow starter in characterization. The dream narrative is typical Traubel (at least as revealed in many commercial recordings): dense, solid, unvaried tone of undeniable beauty, but the manner is rather somnolent—'Mein armer Bruder!' sounds like an item on a shopping list. But gradually she enters into the drama, greeting Lohengrin with a lovely and meaningful 'Mein Held, mein Retter!' 'Wie ich zu deinen Füssen liege' is perhaps not submissive enough, but tonal modification and expressive shaping of line make up the difference. The upper voice is freer than in the recent *Tristan* broadcast; a secure high B-flat caps her jubilation as Lohengrin triumphs. For 'Euch Lüften' a gossamer tone is required, but Traubel is not insensitive to the gentle mood of the moment. And, wonder of wonders, she begins to lighten her voice (without loss of color or steadiness) so that the entire sequence leading to 'Es gibt ein Glück' holds abundant ethereal, almost maidenlike, tone. The true Elsa is suddenly before us. Of course, her outbursts as she later rejects Ortrud are splendid ('Du Lästerin!'), and again she offers an exuberant high B-flat. Perhaps her loveliest vocal moment comes as she submits to Lohengrin at the close of the second act: 'Mein Retter, der mir Heil gebracht!' is radiantly clear in tone and dramatically vivid. In the opening phrases of the duet she offers a bell-like, narrow stream of sound unlike any remembered Traubel voicing—her manner is positively girlish. Is it because she is so relaxed that she badly mangles a phrase, losing both text and melody over a couple of measures as the orchestra cadences under her?—a minor blemish on a superb performance. As Elsa's demands increase, Traubel supplies the requisite excitement with a flood of substantial, handsome tone. Any reservations about Traubel's capabilities must recede in face of this lovely portrayal.

In her first Metropolitan Ortrud, Harshaw again matches Traubel in vocalism and dramatic aptitude. One would prefer a darker timbre for the malignant witch (Harshaw is by now a soprano in all but name); that reservation aside, one cannot fault either her singing or her characterization. The top Gs and A-flats are easily encompassed, and her timbre has taken on a more vivid, glinting cast. Questions of temperament arise in her later Met career, but on this occasion (no matter if it is due to thorough coaching) Harshaw is adept at pointing up the text to dramatic effect. Perhaps 'Rache Werk' is too mild an oath on Harshaw's lips and 'Entweihte Götter!' not the ultimate in demonic rage, but she commands abundant thrust and a resplendent top voice; it is almost a relief to be spared the overstressful efforts of a star turn at this moment. Harshaw can plead for Elsa's mercy in effective, sweet tones, as well. In the final pages of the score, as Ortrud's wrath spills out, most mezzos have to be content with hurling themselves at the notes and hoping for the best—Harshaw holds her own with incredible ease, a small measure of strain marring only the very close of her excellent performance. With Busch molding the orchestral fabric with admirable plasticity, the afternoon has a fair share of rewards.

While management continued to deny Melchior Otello and Canio, it allowed its new Wagnerian tenor a few forays into the Italian repertory. During Svanholm's initial season, his Radames kept company with Siegfried, Tristan, Siegmund, Walther, Lohengrin, and Parsifal, and seemed reasonably at home among his Teutonic brethren. The broadcast of *Aida* on 28 December 1946 offered yet another portrayal new to the radio audience in the Amneris of the American mezzo Blanche Thebom. With old hands Roman, Warren, Moscona, and Votipka, the performance was a somewhat polyglot but not uninteresting mix of vocal ingredients. Not even Sodero can escape the slipshod routine of the Met's triumphal scene (at least he infuses the ballet music with a bit of spirit), but his merit registers in the combination of fluidity and repose in the prelude and continues to his adept pacing of the disjunctive elements in the judgment scene.

Roman's instrument is in prime estate, but her command of it is familiarly variable. In the abstract, hers is an ideal Aida voice. Its neatly honed edge easily penetrates the choral and orchestral mass, and as Aida's line consistently vaults into isolated top notes, Roman's shimmering *pianos* and pungent *fortes* can incite operatic mania. But the afternoon is definitely manic-depressive, beginning with a shrewish

Aida
28 December 1946

Aida
Stella Roman
Amneris
Blanche Thebom
Radames
Set Svanholm
Amonasro
Leonard Warren
Ramfis
Nicola Moscona
Conductor
Cesare Sodero

'Ritorna vincitor!' (a gorgeous high B-flat eradicated by the illogical push and pull of 'Numi, pietà'). 'O patria mia' suffers similarly from the haphazard nature of her vocalism and musicality; but the audience clearly loves that stunning final A, no matter how much sliding and slurring has gone before. Moscona is secure and well mannered as Ramfis, while newcomer Philip Kinsman makes it a worthy pairing of church and state with his bright, well-placed tones (and even a Pinza-like quick vibrato).

As Amonasro, Warren simply has everything: size and beauty of voice, under perfect control, and effective characterization. He chooses to sing the role; no need to bluster his way to convey the ferocity of the Ethiopian king. Routine is routed in the confrontation of father and daughter: when Warren momentarily modifies the glorious outpouring of 'Pensa che un popolo' to caress 'vinto, straziato,' we feel genuine sympathy for his vanquished countrymen. On such minute strokes are portrayals elevated out of the ordinary.

While Svanholm cannot offer similar balm for ears or spirit, his is a worthy effort, sturdy and forthright in tone and manner. Actually, his 'Celeste Aida' is more gratifying than that of most of the Radames brethren. He acknowledges the upward *portamenti*, and the difficult close (*forte*, of course) is very well managed. He offers no Italian tonal plush—but then we are spared stylistic vulgarities. Throughout the afternoon the voice has just enough Nordic brightness (in the upper octave) to mitigate a lurking aridity of timbre, while his sincerity moderates the hint of square- ness in his phrasing. Svanholm suffers a touch of (alleged) Melchioritis in the rhythmic freedom of some of his recitatives; freedom there may be (no less in Verdi than in Wagner), but at the least it must be allied to word shape; Svanholm too often merely flattens out the verbal rhythms. The tenor unleashes unsuspected passion as the fervid lover in the Nile scene and is at his tonal best ('Dell'amor mio' is lovely in timbre) and rhythmically alert in these vibrant passages. And the top B-flats and As are perfectly respectable. In the tomb scene Roman supplies appropriate timbre and soft dynamics but mutilates the line; Svanholm has no mezza voce, but he knows the importance of sculpting Verdi's melody and does so to fine effect. The radio public will hear no more of Svanholm's Italian efforts, though Rudolf Bing allowed him Otello at the end of his Met career.

Hearing Roman and Svanholm in juxtaposition reinforces regret that natural gifts and artistic sensitivity are seldom ideally mated in an artist. Blanche Thebom's Amneris revives hope that the combination is not entirely chimeric. Pennsylvania- born, and reared in Canton, Ohio, the mezzo is a once-removed partner in the Swedish invasion (her parents were Swedish immigrants). But more than heritage qualifies her to continue the high standards of Swedish mezzos Branzell and Thor- borg. Not that she is a replica of those great ladies. Both in vocal weight and tonal depth they were rather more formidable (as Thebom's later career confirms). Like every memorable artist, her assets are her own.

A shipboard encounter (enroute to Sweden, of course) with Marian Anderson's accompanist encouraged the Canton secretary to pursue vocal studies in New York. In the early forties a few recitals and orchestral appearances (Philadelphia with Eugene Ormandy, Minneapolis with Dimitri Mitropoulos) seemed to designate her natural habitat. But a New York recital in 1944 earned rave reviews, and the Met signed her up, with no previous stage appearances, for the 1944–45 season. She would remain with the company for twenty-two seasons. Wagner seemingly had an inviolate claim on Swedish singers at the Met, and Thebom's first seasons were spent

Blanche Thebom as Amneris in *Aida*.

largely in that domain (debut in Philadelphia as Brangäne, house debut as Fricka). She was rapturously received, not only for her voice but for her acting skills (long, swirling capes were her specialty, but more important, she had studied ballet). Like many a young American artist she could not be confined to the Wagner *Fach* alone. Her broadcast debut came in her second season as Giulietta in *Les Contes d'Hoffman*; Mignon, Dalila, and Carmen were to come. She first invaded the Italian terrain as Laura in *La Gioconda*, and an occasional Azucena and Adalgisa spelled her oft-sung Amneris (eighty times in the house and on tour). Mozart (Dorabella), Mussorgsky (Marina), and Stravinsky (Baba the Turk) in the fifties further detail her versatility. The aptitude and intelligence reflected in these varied assignments mark her broadcast Amneris. Hers is a thinking woman's princess, relying less on the *accenti* and artifices of the chesty, flamboyant Italian dramatic mezzo (these may or may not have been at her beck) but still rendering full service to the role's demands. She can command a healthy, appealing chest register (free from coarseness), but she spares it abuse, choosing often an effective stage whisper in moments of inner anguish or terror. The upper octave of her voice is surprisingly voluminous in size and lustrous in sound, and she is not restrained by the recitalist's canon from unleashing it at key moments. If one must cavil, the slightest hint of dislocation in the low F–G range is troubling—the chronic mezzo disease, but here certainly under constant care and, at least at this stage of her career, negligible.

Thebom is able to voice Amneris' passionate but inner summons at the beginning of the second act in a genuine *piano*, gentle in feel but not without voluptuous overtones; each repetition grows in volume and intensity. She can be overtly dramatic, as well, and wraps up the scene with effortless, full-toned phrases ('se lottar tu puoi con me'). Most mezzos sound as if they are lifting weights at this point (and at the end of the judgment scene as well), but Thebom's free and easy top takes it in stride. She makes her presence felt in her few measures on the Nile; Amneris' love for Radames reverberates in Thebom's womanly tone and meaningful utterance as she goes to the temple to pray before her marriage. Thebom's princess is a worthy rival for Radames' love, and as a result, the judgment scene becomes something more than the usual tour de force. True, she resorts to a bit of subterfuge in the declamatory recitative (reiterated on low F), but the big phrases are fervently delivered. She rides the arch of 'la vendetta or dal ciel' with amazing ease (both times), sustaining a pair of ringing B-flats at the crests that any Italian mezzo would covet. Like most of her low-voiced sisters, Thebom has little in reserve by the time Amneris turns her curse on the 'Empia razza' of priests, but to the end, she is valiant. A brave beginning—a bright future seems assured.

While Thebom was apparently capable of ranging wide over the operatic repertory, another Metropolitan mezzo, already favorably ensconced with the public, once again was seeking to broaden her dominion. Though Risë Stevens had not quite the vocal resources of Thebom, she was equally canny and, of greater importance for her, a mistress of the craft of career management. With her assumption in 1945 of *Carmen*, she reached operatic terra firma, guided by the time-tested and still-potent stimulus of cinematic glamour. She would take another detour or two, but these were minor deviations from a career path that was otherwise sure-footed, rooted as it was in critical acclaim on the one hand (Octavian) and mass appeal on the other (Carmen). During the 1946–47 season the radio public could finally sample her gypsy wares as well as hear Octavian, Hansel, and in another assault on new territory, Marina in *Boris Godunov*.

Not only for Stevens is the 7 December 1946 broadcast of *Boris* noteworthy. The season held Tucker's only encounters with the false Dimitri. And if one is alert, one can hear the broadcast debuts of two young Americans destined to have long Met careers—Robert Merrill and the previously introduced Jerome Hines. When Tchelkaloff informs the populace of Boris' reluctance to become their czar, Merrill's plushy tones are aural balm. That he seems more concerned with vocal placement than character may be attributed to youth (of course, it was a harbinger), and if he turns the Duma clerk's lament for Russia's future into a Pucciniesque arietta, a good deal of the blame may be laid to the Met's continued use of Italian translation for its Russian repertory. Mussorgsky's song speech cannot thrive when deprived of its native air. But the beauty and security of Merrill's singing are most welcome. At twenty-nine his vocalism already sounds as mature as any baritone's has a right to be. Why the Met should have given him this thirty-measure assignment in the midst of a series of major roles, including Germont, Ashton, Escamillo, Valentin, and Amonasro, is yet another vagary of management. On the other hand, Hines, who had made his debut only two weeks earlier as the *Boris* Sergeant of the Frontier Guard, would have a healthy share of cameos like Schwarz (*Meistersinger*) and the First Philosopher in *Louise* during his early Met career. His vocal security throughout the entire range, depth of timbre, and assured manner (holding one's own against Baccaloni is a challenge even for an experienced hand) mark him for better things. They come soon enough.

Other cameos of merit are Greer's Xenia (no whining self-pitier but a wretched, bereft woman), Lipton's Nurse, and Doe's idiomatic Innkeeper. Moving a step up in the hierarchy, De Paolis (looking oddly like an American Indian chief in his *Opera News* photo) retains his built-in sound for the unctuous Schouisky. Baccaloni (even more strangely resembling Anthony Trollope with his *front bombé*) is at his very best, dominating the Lithuanian border scene with vocal size (his wobble under control) and masterful characterization (likewise free from exaggeration). To turn gross Varlaam into a sympathetic character as he struggles to read the description of the escaped monk is stage sorcery. With Moscona in capital form, making Pimen's lengthy narratives palatable, the underpinnings of the opera are uncommonly solid; and Cooper's Russian hand helps immensely.

One never quite knows what one will hear and when one will hear it in a *Boris* performance, and the Met's offering is as strange as any. In addition to the Italian translation, the Met still omits the cathedral scene, and the coronation scene follows the Pimen-Gregori episode even as Boris' death succeeds the Kromy scene. If all this magnifies the star-tsar at the expense of the Russian people, at least Pinza is worthy of it. We take our leave of him at this performance (his final broadcast is the 1947 Giovanni previously cited).

Like many a bass before him, Pinza had presented himself to the 1926 Met audience in the neutral garb of a high priest (Pontifex Maximus in Spontini's *La Vestale*), but his vocal abilities were buttressed by physical attributes which soon enough liberated him from excessive religious devotion. His uniquely colored, puissant instrument, fierce musical integrity, and power of projection (all heightened by an élan unrivaled on the operatic stage) had conferred incontestable stardom during the final decade of his operatic career. And he had achieved it without recourse to the sometimes self-indulgent theatrics of a Chaliapin. Pinza's magnetism was self-generating.

As Boris, once again he draws us in. The voice is as resonant and self-assured as

Boris Godunov
7 December 1946

Marina
Risë Stevens
Dimitri
Richard Tucker
Schouisky
Alessio de Paolis
Rangoni
Francesco Valentino
Boris
Ezio Pinza
Pimen
Nicola Moscona
Varlaam
Salvatore Baccaloni
Conductor
Emil Cooper

in its prime, with a firm command of legato and varied dynamics. On this afternoon one hears none of the wearing away of color, power, or control which have occasionally intruded on recent performances. The fruity, majestic tones of the 'Highest Power' monologue in act two convert with ease to an affecting softness in his address to his children; stern command and sympathetic tenderness make a telling contrast. When De Paolis and Pinza engage in a game of cat and mouse, they play off one another with audible pleasure. The skills of craft learned over the years inform his clock monologue, which he intones with undiminished splendor of voice.

Most notable is the artistic integrity of his portrayal. He doesn't bawl in the coronation scene. Nor does he pull out the theatrical stops for the death scene: a few suffocated tones at his entrance, then glorious declamation, the honeyed quiet of his viola stop as he instructs Fyodor to protect the church and watch over his sister, and the quiet, gasp-free death—all these testify to the probity of his art. Pinza would achieve greater fame through Broadway stardom in the next several years, but his operatic legacy—preserved in numerous broadcasts of roles both small and large, from the philosophizing Colline to the charismatic Giovanni—is a far worthier monument to his greatness.

In these Italian performances the Polish act fares rather well with its broadly flowing melodies. An Italianate tenor can do more justice to them than the usual throaty middle European or second ranker to whom the role normally falls—how fortunate that the aircheck captured this memento of Tucker's early career (he undertook the role for only four house performances and a few more on tour). Ungrateful as the role is, Tucker fills it with splendid tone and contrives a convincing characterization of the enigmatic Gregori-Dimitri. He unloads a bit of his later explosive style as the dreaming monk wakens suddenly in Pimen's cell, but the manner suits the moment this time. As he woos Marina, romance invades his tone. Everything he does has a surety to it; a touch of regality is applied when Dimitri reiterates his resolve to gain the throne. Still, in the end it is the incredible tonal splendor and rapt phrasing which win more than a Polish princess for Tucker—his ascendancy to primo tenore cannot be far off. Alas, we will not hear him again on the broadcasts for several years.

Stevens' accomplishment is equally assured; she is the professional to the nth degree, and all that can be achieved by intelligence and dramatic skill is hers. But she lacks exactly what Tucker offers in abundance: an instrument capable of responding to her demands. Of course, the role is a scratchy one with its belaboring of the quick mazurka and cracovienne dotted rhythms—these are not kind to any singer (but the memory of Thorborg and Warren in the 1943 broadcast dwarfs the efforts of Stevens and the ever-reliable Valentino). Commendably, Stevens never shrinks from the dramatic and musical demands of Marina, and she is an accomplished vocal actress. Her delivery is always purposeful; Marina's will is well conveyed. The Polish act is often belittled as an extraneous divertissement, but in little more than twenty-five minutes Mussorgsky has painted a vivid portrait of a complex woman; Stevens' portrayal is like a Renaissance portrait strongly drawn but whose vibrant colors have lost their opulence. When she gets hold of a legato phrase she makes it count. But not only is the voice light for the role, too frequently it sounds fixed, wooden in timbre, cumbersome, and obviously manipulated. The role simply doesn't offer her opportunity to display her best wares. Again it must have been the glamour of the Polish princess which prompted the undertaking, for she was well aware of its demands ("Assuming the role after the great Thorborg is a double responsibility,"[1] she told

Opera News). Astutely, she pulled it from her repertory after this season.

The Met was now ready to capitalize on the tremendous publicity which Stevens had engendered when she sang the Habanera in *Going My Way.* Djanel departed at the end of the 1945–46 season (in which Stevens had sung her first Met Carmen) and the way was clear for Stevens to begin her remarkable sequence of Carmen broadcasts.

To a large public all too familiar with bits and pieces of the Stevens Carmen, the full figure of the gypsy was finally revealed on the broadcast of 22 February 1947. In another of Johnson's commendable attempts to renew the French style at the Met, Louis Fourestier was imported to oversee the initial *Carmen* performances, but by broadcast time the baton had passed to Max Rudolf. This was Rudolf's broadcast debut, and a spirited one it is. His may be the fastest *Carmen* on record. In his motoric race, nuance is in short supply (the entr'actes are particularly lacking in suavity). The male chorus greets Carmen in shabby disarray, while the cigarette girls are singularly deficient in languor. John Baker's bright timbre and stylistic polish make him an uncommonly adroit Morales, while William Hargrave's baritone and manner convey just the degree of dull solidity to make plausible Carmen's preference for his inferior in rank. Votipka and Browning are expert card shufflers (the soprano supplying an occasional on-the-mark high note in the ensembles), and Chabay and Cehanovsky combine character portrayal with elegant musicality. And wonder of wonders, this reliable crew manages to keep pace with their conductor.

Neither Nadine Conner nor Robert Merrill is much more than a cardboard figure; their characters seem merely appliquéd to the drama. Merrill's Toreador is nevertheless opulent in tone, his voice magnificently collected, its solid core ever constant. Tonal splendor may well be enough when matched in combat against a fiery José. Then, too, his invitation to Carmen is beautifully laid out, even simulating a modicum of tenderness (a nicety that will seldom invade the later Merrill tones). However, the fourth-act duet holds no hint of intimacy, though his sound remains attractive. The same cannot be said for Conner. Her silvery, pointed tone suggests the innocent country girl of act one, but its glassy glare soon wearies the ear. The commendable clarity of her enunciation turns the arabesques of the duet with José into a mere succession of notes. One can appreciate the delicacy of her approach, though inadequate breath support causes *forte* tones to fly sharp. The latter tendency is most distressing in the aria, which is devoid of either the vocal glamour or the graces which justify its inclusion. Oddly enough, she is far better in her pleas to José to succor his dying mother—here the line is firmly drawn, the tones alive, and the chill of her message convincingly conveyed.

If Micaela and Escamillo may be treated as traditional habitués of the opéra comique, Carmen herself has no such protective sugarcoating (at least not in the latter portion of the opera). Carmen herself must be emotionally honest. The Hollywood preview and subsequent popular acclaim which pressured the Met into granting Stevens appearances as Carmen (so asserted in her autobiography) may initially have diverted the accomplished mezzo from developing a portrayal as genuine as her fervent Octavian or her beguiling Mignon. What emerges is less a characterization than a string of external vocal and dramatic effects. Sometimes these are executed with the confident know-how of the professional theatre person. Occasionally they come off as mere sham. Her Habanera signals the "hard sell." The really distressing thing is that this frontal assault results in shockingly substandard vocalism. On this occasion the Habanera is a vocal disaster: phrasing is pulled grossly

Carmen
22 February 1947
Carmen
Risë Stevens
Micaela
Nadine Conner
Don José
Ramon Vinay
Escamillo
Robert Merrill
Conductor
Max Rudolf

out of shape, pitch is often suspect, the voice is throaty, raspy, tremulous. Hope revives in the opening phrases of the Seguidilla, but this, too, soon disintegrates into nervous, brassy braying. Stevens seems unwilling to let the music speak for itself.

There are arresting moments: 'Je suis amoureuse' in the quintet is neatly pert, then repeated with intense meaning; some top tones ring out effectively. She has not the vocal size or timbre for the card aria, but she works intelligently at it (the preceding recitative is most convincing), and though the lowest notes virtually disappear, the climaxes are well sustained. And the declamatory make-up of the final scene with José enables Stevens to make her points cannily. Often she can summon abundant tone to make these isolated moments count.

In sheer number of performances, the record of the Stevens Carmen at the Metropolitan is unequaled, and her popularity in the role (and its box-office power) is unassailable. Eleven broadcasts over fourteen seasons made it one of the most familiar characterizations for the greater American public. Yet the inadequacies of her portrayal at its near-inception are blatant. With a sense of relief, we read in her autobiography Stevens' angry admission (at about this time or a year earlier) to her husband "Why kid ourselves? . . . I'm singing lousy."[2] Stevens was nothing if not perspicacious. She latched on to Viennese prima donna Vera Schwarz, whose instruction was calculated to provide a remedy. (In a recent interview Stevens acknowledged that her characterization was not fully formed until the 1952 Tyrone Guthrie staging.)

In addition to the radio premiere of Stevens' Carmen and Merrill's first major role on the broadcasts, the afternoon contained yet another novelty in the house debut of Ramon Vinay as Don José. Though Mr. Cross insists on Anglicizing him as "Ramon(d)," Vinay was born in Chile of a French father and Italian mother, spent his early years in France, and finally settled in Mexico. His remarkably virile timbre signals his baritone beginnings until, aided by René Maison, he undertook Otello in Mexico City. Along came Samson, Cavaradossi, Des Grieux (Puccini), and his New York City Opera debut as Don José in the fall of 1945. A Met debut quickly followed in 1946. With his robust physique and voice to match, Vinay was a formidable antagonist for any Carmen. His French (aided by his youthful residence in France) and alert musicality make him an impressive dragoon. Though not blessed with an easy top, he makes a virtue of it by not playing to the gallery. Surprisingly fluent in negotiating the coils of Bizet's melodies in the duet with Micaela, he formulates an acceptable quiet close without a degrading falsetto. A lustrous shine warms the dark, manly timbre—it bespeaks the tenor ambiance. His honest emotion and well-bred musical manners in his exchanges with Carmen are gratifying. When, amid the busy turmoil of the mountain retreat, Vinay utters a phrase, one is startled to attention, not only by the plangent richness of voice but by his earnest delivery, his belief in José's plight. After Micaela's plea, Vinay is mighty in the mix of anger, dignity, and vocal solidity with which he commands Carmen.

This suggestion of tragic grandeur makes less surprising his unscheduled assumption of Otello for the indisposed Ralf two months earlier. The impression is confirmed in the final act of *Carmen*; this José doesn't grovel vocally, and his full-throated top voice sings rather than sobs José's final lament.

The following year Vinay not only repeated his José (Stevens and Conner again, with Singher and Pelletier adding French authenticity), but broadcast his second Met Canio on 28 February 1948. Though the role would seem tailor-made for the Vinay persona, his success is somewhat equivocal. The commitment is there, and the solid baritonal underpinning augments command. But when he flies above the staff, gears shift and the bottom drops out of the voice; we hear the tone clearly, but it seems to have no core. With the memory of Martinelli's linear pull still in the ear, Vinay's 'Vesti la giubba' seems fitful, lacking that uninterrupted stream of tone essential to Italian melody. The climax is impressive, however (as are his dramatic instincts in the recitative), and we do feel that a strong man has been toppled. That, after all, is what the opera is about. He has other mighty moments (when demanding the name of Nedda's lover, for instance), though he drops a dram too much of bluster into 'No! Pagliaccio non son.'

Warren is the only familiar in the cast. His Tonio is not immune from bluster, either. For the first time in a Warren performance, his tendency toward the pompous tips the scale onto the downside. He offers a very dull prologue until the peerless A-flat and G startle with their brilliance: no invitation in the opening measures, the individual sections insufficiently differentiated, the voice both cavernous and not without wobble. In the scenes with Nedda he labors too often for effects (some of them are impressive, too). Everything seems overfussy and self-conscious. Still, no one can fill the tone with velvety insinuation as Warren can when cautioning Canio to bide his time. And his mannered way suits Taddeo perfectly in The Play—how many vocal tricks he trots out for our delectation! On the other hand, Hugh Thompson is straightforward and neat in Silvio's music, a bit undermanned in vocal size (not in height), and raw-toned when trying to fill out the demanding lyricism which Leoncavallo penned for his secondo baritono. (If one remembers that the premiere featured not only Victor Maurel as The Fool but Mario Ancona as Silvio, one can sympathize with management's casting problem.) With Beppe's Serenade, Leslie Chabay adds a welcome touch of elegance to the veristic imbroglio.

The afternoon contains one unmixed blessing in the Nedda of California-born Fiorenza Quartararo. Although in the third of only four Met seasons, this is her broadcast debut; unfortunately, it is also her broadcast farewell. Her idiomatic performance owes its roots to speaking Italian with her parents at home and impeccable models (on record, Muzio, and as a very young girl, some of the last performances of Ponselle and Bori). After a radio appearance (as Florence Alba) with Bing Crosby and a concert performance of the *Trovatore* Leonora at the Redlands Bowl, she was brought by a vacationing Met administrator to Bruno Walter for a hearing. A Met audition and a 1946 debut as Micaela before a student audience was the result. At twenty-three she had never before appeared on an opera stage. An eavesdropping critic (Howard Taubman of the *Times*) at the student matinee called her "the find of the season."[3] After a succession of sporadic appearances as Pamina, Desdemona, Donna Elvira, and the Countess, the radio audience finally was granted a hearing. What they heard was a healthy lyric voice, easily produced throughout the entire range and richly colored, with the inimitable Italian blend of cream and incisiveness.

She uses glancing bits of chest tone in her parlando, and she allows the language to shape the phrase. For once the Ballatella is not an effortful tug of war—the music, like the birds, takes wing (the composer marked it *passione allargando la frase e ben cantato*). Everything Quartararo does seems a natural effusion—even the pair of trills is done without self-consciousness. Her idiomatic style in the duet makes Silvio's all-American nonchalance seem mere naiveté. Here she might have extended the Leoncavallo curves a bit more, but like many an Italian soprano, she prefers thrust to lyric conduction. 'Aitalo Signor!' she cries when the lovers are discovered,

Pagliacci
28 February 1948
Nedda
Fiorenza Quartararo
Canio
Ramon Vinay
Tonio
Leonard Warren
Silvio
Hugh Thompson
Conductor
Giuseppe Antonicelli

and sounds like an Aida in the making. Though Giuseppe Antonicelli (new to the conducting staff) robs the play-within-a-play of rhythmic esprit, her smartly articulated phrases put Colombina back on point. She caps her admission of illicit love with a ringing high B. During the forties and fifties only Albanese could have delivered a portrayal of Nedda so satisfying in its vocal, musical, and dramatic totality. One brief final season and she would be heard no more. Hers was not a case of burnout, too much too soon—far from it. Perhaps she found she needed the theatre less than it needed her.

Madama Butterfly
8 February 1947

Cio-Cio-San
Regina Resnik
Suzuki
Lucielle Browning
Pinkerton
Charles Kullman
Sharpless
John Brownlee
Conductor
Cesare Sodero

The featured singer in the *Cavalleria Rusticana* which preceded *Pagliacci* was Regina Resnik, her Santuzza little aided by the distinctly minor-league Sicilians of Mario Berini and Brownlee. A year earlier (8 February 1947) Resnik had been pressed into service for the broadcast Butterfly when Albanese was indisposed. Cross tells us that "Miss Albanese had hoped to do the role until eleven o'clock this morning, but finally the doctor said no and Miss Resnik was called upon." Under the circumstances Resnik's performance is admirable.

Resnik's first (and only) Met Butterfly, however, is a Caesarean birth, drawn prematurely from the artistic womb, embryonic in characterization and, in the dramatic climaxes of the score, vocally acrid. Though (or more likely, because) the young soprano's Met assignments had included Leonora (*Trovatore*), Santuzza, Aida, Fidelio, and Tosca, she is more successful in the lighter portions of the score. Her first act is unusually girlish in timbre, weight, and manner, conveying a charming innocence (innocent, too, is she of some—not all—of the interpretive nuances of the role). As such, it is refreshingly free from mannerism, but textually and musically underinflected. With Kullman adopting a conversational posture (happily, his 'Bimba dagli occhi' is *sostenendo, dolcissimo*, as marked), the love duet is rather underpowered. But Resnik swings into high gear momentarily at 'Sì, per la vita' and occasionally imparts a welcome thrust to her phrases. Having wisely avoided the high D-flat of the entrance aria, Resnik chooses an ambivalent close for the duet, touching an insecure high B and quickly joining Pinkerton on the lower ending. She sings with more authority in the second act. The lead into 'Un bel dì' is sensitively plotted, and she eschews the grand manner—desertion and motherhood have not altered the child bride, evidently. Cio-Cio-San's narrative is intimately, lovingly told, though the initial attack is a scoop. One does notice an excessive looseness of tone in the lower octave, but often the voice has a fresh float that is quite appealing (as in the scene with Goro and Yamadori). As the more dramatic moments accumulate, her melodic line slackens, top tones turn harsh, and enchantment dissipates. The first half of the flower duet (with Browning's experienced Suzuki) is nicely fluent, but the slower 'Gettiamo a mani' is ineffective: Browning grows tremulous and Resnik's octave vault to the high B-flat is skittish. Her third-act lullaby is equally precarious, and this time Resnik omits the final (admittedly difficult) top note. Though spread, harsh tone mars the death aria, the soprano's sound theatrical instincts provide an effective close. Resnik has the potential for a fine Butterfly; it was unfair of management to have drawn it from the chrysalis too soon.

Brownlee, De Paolis, and Cehanovsky contribute sure characterizations. With more assertive stage colleagues in the lead roles, Sodero's loving and elegant traversal of Puccini's most evocative orchestral score might have impressed more. He prefers a decidedly deliberate pace for the humming chorus; the low octaves which introduce the death scene are indeed heavy with foreboding. Overall, the temperature on stage is too tepid for this *Butterfly* to capture our belief.

Albanese was forced to cancel not only her Butterfly broadcast. Kolodin reports that her long absence was due to a "throat ailment that had required surgery."[4] In a radio interview two decades later the soprano vehemently denied this. "No, no surgery . . . I needed six months' rest. This is what the artist goes through when they do too much . . . rehearsals, benefits, concerts, and then the radio program ['The Treasure Hour of Song'] every week, and then the Metropolitan." Certainly Albanese was at the height of her fame following the Toscanini broadcasts. "So much, but [it] wasn't too bad though . . . but I needed a rest; we never rest in the summer. So this time I needed a very nice, good rest in the summer."[5] Following the Butterfly cancellation Albanese hied herself to Arizona, expecting an early recovery. In mid-March her husband informed Johnson that "upon the insistence of her doctor" she would be forced to rest an additional week but was "certain" for the Boston *Bohème* at the end of the month. Though the winter had been "trying and depressing," her husband was happy to report that "news has reached me this morning that our little girl is feeling her old self again and ready to resume."[6] But a week later Albanese herself expressed her "great sorrow" at having to inform the general manager, whom she deemed "a real friend," that "fate was not with [her]." She would be unable to return for the Met tour. Her throat specialist had ordered her to rest "for an indefinite period."[7]

"She is her old self again," Gaetano Merola, general manager of the San Francisco Opera, was able to report to readers of *Opera News* in the fall of 1947.[8] And a few months later the Albanese Butterfly reappeared on the Met airwaves. In the meantime the Met had to scurry for Albanese replacements. According to Kolodin, one of the replacements was debutante Hjördis Schymberg[9] (whose broadcast Susanna has been cited previously), but the Swedish soprano had been contracted in December 1946. Much was evidently expected of Schymberg, for she had a large feature story and the cover of *Opera News* magazine for the *Rigoletto* broadcast of 1 March 1947. Her performance is paradoxical, the first half dominated by tone both acidulous and unfloated—not only is the music ill served, but the gentle trust which defines Gilda's character is totally lacking. Schymberg's long experience tells as she picks her icy way through the intricacies of 'Caro nome.' Actually a core of piquant tone within the surface hardness holds a measure of fascination in the manner of a Mercedes Capsir, Miliza Korjus, or Mady Mesplé, all of whose crisp authority has at various times commanded approval. But Schymberg is too inclined to precipitate vocal action, as when, in the epilogue to her aria, she executes an arpeggio series of distinct trills leading to the high E—the effect is startling and rather like a well-schooled Florence Foster Jenkins. Perhaps because her ordeal is over, the final scenes are far more satisfying. The uncut diamond of her tones has now been polished so the hard brilliance takes on luster sufficient to please. And she shows us Gilda's hurt and regret in 'Tutte le feste'; her combination of childlike innocence and deep pain is more than most Gildas offer. In the 'Sì, vendetta' duet she occasionally reverts to imprecision, probably the result of overzealousness, while the storm trio brings an excess of literalness, for her tone really turns squally. Clearly, Schymberg has not found the balance between vocal control and character portrayal. But again, her tone in the quartet is an appealing combination of pungency and glow, and she betrays no acrophobia, offering a secure (but brittle) E-flat and D-flat in alt.

Marred by Schymberg's second act, the performance initially seems to be another offering in the dreary repertory routine, but Sodero, in the measured mystery of his prelude, has made it clear that he is a man with a purpose. He could not

Rigoletto
1 March 1947
Gilda
Hjördis Schymberg
Maddalena
Martha Lipton
Duke
Jan Peerce
Rigoletto
Leonard Warren
Sparafucile
Giacomo Vaghi
Conductor
Cesare Sodero

know that this would be his farewell broadcast. He was in poor health, and in December 1947 he died; the Metropolitan lost a most worthy overseer of the Italian wing. On this afternoon he guides a reliable (barring Schymberg) group of artists. Lipton is small-scale for Maddalena, but her dusky color is exactly right for the seductress with a heart. She avoids vulgarizing the character, as became fashionable in the bare-bosom era later in the century. Vaghi's overripe vibrato is troublesome on the street where Rigoletto walks, but he is strong and certain on his home ground. Hawkins lacks the depth of tone to give the curse maximum impact. But Peerce and Warren elevate the performance with their splendid vocalism and convincing characterizations.

The baritone is, as usual, in superb form, and (unlike the *Pagliacci* of a year later) his portrayal is entirely free of exaggeration and self-conscious mannerisms. Seldom has he exhibited more perfect vocal control; his reliance on subdued, touching vocalism adds a dimension to Rigoletto the father. He voices 'Deh non parlare' with infinite tenderness, and in the 'Cortigiani' aria it is the heartfelt transition ('Ah! Ebben, piango') and the cantabile of 'Miei signori' which are most telling. He refuses to mangle 'Solo per me l'infamia' as Gilda confesses her guilt—the nobility of his response is far more touching. Again, when he discovers Sparafucile's duplicity, his subtle progression from disbelief to hurt is masterful—the work of an artist in full maturity.

The same may be said of Peerce. He gives the performance of his career, singing with unfaltering assurance from the moment he launches, with jaunty humor, 'Questa o quella' on through the fearless high Bs of 'La donna è mobile.' Seldom has he offered so full a characterization; the brash cockiness and expansive manner of this Duke are exhilarating. Musically, too, he is more interesting than in the past. Even the absence of sufficient dynamic and color variation cannot dull the impact of his splendid breadth of phrase or the deft touches of ornamentation which pepper his vocal line. He pours out his heart and soul in 'Parmi veder le lagrime,' and the hearty *slancio* of the love duet, the quartet, and 'La donna' is exceptional. For once the aria's overfamiliar tune is turned toward dramatic veracity.

Peerce and Warren are again the stalwarts in the *Ballo in Maschera* broadcast of 22 November 1947. The opera (and identical cast) had opened the Met season a week earlier. Since its 1940 revival, *Ballo* had rarely been out of the repertory, with the two Americans and Milanov under the stewardship of Bruno Walter ensuring a high standard of performance in the last several seasons. Unfortunately, the era of the great stopover conductors is past, and Antonicelli's pedestrian way depresses the French buoyancy with which Verdi seasoned the score. Solid experience in Italy (assistant at Turin, at La Scala 1934–37, later director of the Trieste Opera) shows in Antonicelli's correct tempi, but Verdi's dynamic rhetoric stays fallow. Thus Warren's 'Alla vita che t'arride' is cumbersome, and the stretta which closes the first scene, though well disciplined, is enlivened only by Peerce's rhythmic vitality. In the great duet the conductor is content to follow, and he must hasten to catch Warren in the trio on the heath. By now the singers have shucked the reins and are manufacturing their own excitement.

Warren is not in his best vocal estate: a little rasp intrudes in the quiet, low passages of 'Eri tu,' and he sounds weary. This has its compensations, as he doesn't bully the piece, relying on purity of line, a patrician manner, and an always vibrant top voice to carry his message. And Warren, even below form, means a high standard of vocal art.

Un Ballo in Maschera
22 November 1947

Amelia
Daniza Ilitsch
Oscar
Pierrette Alarie
Ulrica
Margaret Harshaw
Riccardo
Jan Peerce
Renato
Leonard Warren
Conductor
Giuseppe Antonicelli

Peerce has magnificent staying power in what may be Verdi's most demanding tenor role (Otello is a punishing assignment, but in a totally different way). He is properly monarchical throughout—a Swedish king (in the Met's setting) is evidently grander to Peerce than a licentious Mantuan Duke. Peerce's manner and vocalism are manifestly weightier than in *Rigoletto*—the result is more a strong dramatic characterization than a pleasing vocal portrait. The tenor never falters; both brio and breadth of line are summoned at will. But in the big moments his resources are pushed to the limit (a perpetual, all-but-audible grunt underlines a good deal of the duet). The grand recitative before he renounces Amelia, however, is delivered with splendid conviction and spacious design, and while the aria itself could be more varied tonally and musically, its straightforward cast suits Riccardo's honest renunciation. The other facets of the role are well served, too, though he does not sufficiently cherish the sensuous Verdian curve of 'La rivedrà nell'estasi'—obviously, a more businesslike than amorous king. In spite of his virtuoso efforts, Peerce can't quite shake off the shackles of Antonicelli's beat (in the fisherman's canzone, for one).

Among the new cast members, both Harshaw and Pierrette Alarie had been heard in the (unpreserved) broadcast of 1945; time evidently has not improved their portrayals. Harshaw is woefully miscast as the brooding Ulrica. She gives a laundry-list reading of 'Re dell'abisso,' completely devoid of mystery or horror. The young French-Canadian soprano (student of the beloved Elisabeth Schumann and wife of the excellent tenor, Leopold Simoneau) had won Honorable Mention in the 1945 "Auditions of the Air" (Merrill and Hayward were the winners). Though pretty in name and charming in form, Alarie is ineffectual in her recitatives and only acceptable in the arias. Her staccati are an asset in 'Volta la terrea,' as is the finely honed line she etches in the quintet. For lack of a trill, 'Di che fulgor' loses its impact, but Alarie has the right nose-thumbing jauntiness for 'Saper vorreste.' Vaghi and Alvary are dependable conspirators, if not quite sardonic enough in their chuckles.

Of major interest is the broadcast debut of soprano Daniza Ilitsch as Amelia. Early appearances with the Berlin State Opera (1936–38) and Vienna State Opera (1938–41) had given the young Yugoslav soprano experience of a high order before her war adventures in the underground. Her Met debut as Desdemona in the final week of the 1946–47 season had not disappointed. Kolodin states that her late arrival was due to Roman's unavailability for part of the season,[10] but the Met Archives reveal rather different facts. She was actually a replacement for her compatriot, Zinka Milanov. In the end it proved not to be a fair exchange. Milanov, feeling unprepared or unwilling to undertake her first career Desdemona, had requested release from her contract. On 6 February 1947 the Met obliged "with the understanding that she will make no claims on the Metropolitan for payment of performances on the following dates: [March 12 in New York and two *Otello* performances on tour] but must sing Aida on March 22 in Boston."[11] Her season's guarantee was accordingly reduced from fifteen to eleven performances. When the 1947–48 season's roster was announced, Milanov's name was missing. Thus ended the first unhappy decade of Milanov's Metropolitan career. The Boston Aida was her final Met performance until her return four years later under new manager Rudolf Bing. But perhaps love, not the Met, was the culprit—on 31 March in Washington, D.C., Milanov married her Yugoslav general and soon returned to her homeland.

That Johnson and his team considered Ilitsch an important accession is evident in her assignments for the 1947–48 season. In addition to the opening night *Ballo*, her Aida, *Trovatore* Leonora, and Gioconda were all unveiled during December.

Reportedly only twenty-eight years old at the time of her *Ballo* broadcast (her Berlin debut at age seventeen would indicate a nineteenth-century type of precocity), the soprano's entry into Ulrica's den confirms that she is the real thing. The flavor of the true dramatic soprano in voice and temperament penetrates the airwaves. Verdi's soaring 'Consentimi, o Signore' reveals no enveloping resonance à la Milanov; rather, Ilitsch's voice is in the Anita Cerquetti mold, bright of timbre in the upper octave with a healthy chest mixture. The latter can take on an unattractive Slavic snarl in agitated moments (in contemporary times, Anna Tomowa-Sintow is not unlike). Alone on the heath, Ilitsch shows her mettle: the recitative demonstrates an acute response to situation; her instincts are good (she is not afraid to begin the air quietly); though the tone is narrow on high, it has character and doesn't spread; her attack on the cadenza is accurate, and the concluding phrase is beautifully etched (like many an Amelia, the high C borders on a shriek).

In the duet Ilitsch handles Amelia's confession of love with some subtlety and refuses to aggrandize 'Oh qual soave brivido.' Though the voice refuses to bloom , it cuts with a surgeon's exquisite care. Her scrupulous observance of the dotted rhythms of 'Morrò, ma prima in grazia' engenders a stop-and-go delivery, but she has a fine feel for the piece, relishing the opportunity for a *piano* dynamic. Later in the season Ilitsch was granted the broadcast of Aida (21 February) but had to relinquish the role to novitiate Florence Kirk after the Nile scene. I well remember the actual broadcast when she came to disaster on the high C of 'O patria mia.' Few artists suffer so blatant a public breakdown as occurred. (According to the *Annals*, she was "taken ill.") She then sang a single Leonora in New York and a few tour performances (Kirk also assumed four of her scheduled Aidas on tour). Thereafter she was heard no more at the Metropolitan.

The Ilitsch saga points up the problems of management during the 1946–48 seasons in refurbishing its soprano wing. The house was cursed with single-season tenures. The door to Europe was now open, but neither Schymberg nor Ilitsch nor several other well-regarded European artists earned audience or critical favor. German Erna Schleuter failed miserably as Isolde, French Renée Mazella was an ineffectual Marguerite (broadcast of 4 January 1947), Italian Elena Dosia raised no temperatures in the *Tosca* which opened the 1947–48 broadcast season. Two who earned favor were the American Polyna Stoska, familiar to us as Donna Elvira and Ellen Orford, and the Italian Pia Tassinari, a spinto of immense experience and sterling artistry whose age alone may have prevented a longer Metropolitan association than the 1947–48 season.

That Tassinari came to the Met at all was due to the presence of another Met debutant of the 1946–47 season, her husband, Ferruccio Tagliavini. We first meet him in the broadcast of *Lucia* on 17 January 1948. Cimara, who had nursed Munsel's Lucia in the 1946 broadcast, here renews his long-standing acquaintance with Pons' bride (he first conducted it at his 1932 Met debut). Perfunctory wind solos in the prelude and slapdash ensemble of the chorus and orchestra as the curtain rises make for a precarious send-off. But Cimara catches the attention of his forces for an adequate reading (indeed, the harp solo is played with considerable élan "by Miss Whiteman," so identified by Cross).

Miss Pons is not at her best—far from it. The ear is beset by a generous portion of downside pitch throughout the afternoon and, in the early portions of the opera, more than her usual quota of tremulous tone. The brief trills which salt the melody of 'Quando rapito' are a sham, and only the (aspirated) staccati are a coloratura

Lucia di Lammermoor
17 January 1948

Lucia
Lily Pons

Edgardo
Ferruccio Tagliavini

Enrico Ashton
Robert Merrill

Raimondo
Nicola Moscona

Conductor
Pietro Cimara

Lily Pons as Lucia. Photograph taken backstage by a colleague.

soprano's worthy wares. Even the celebrated Pons notes in alt are shadows of their normally reliable selves. The diva can still etch the line of 'Verranno a te,' however. The low tessitura of her scene with brother Henry is not Pons' home ground, but at least the voice has steadied and gained in color. She returns to form in the mad scene, beginning with considerable assurance and bite in the tone, tossing off a few flourishes with the old brilliance, and almost conjuring up the fountain ghost in her time-lapse imaginings. But though the cadenza begins to sink in pitch and the final F comes in woefully flat with the orchestra, a sour effect indeed, the audience cheers long and loud. It is, after all, the most assured off-pitch singing one will probably ever hear. A few lovely flights leaven 'Spargi d'amaro pianto' before a high F that is truly an F sounds, short in duration and prudently reached. Surely there can't be many Lucias left in this fifty-year-old throat. But Pons will endure at the Met for another decade, and the radio audience will be treated to four more of her demented brides of Lammermoor.

The men fare much better. An exception is Felix Knight, whose debut as Almaviva in 1946 should have signified a superior Lord Arturo; but his raw, open sound and square phrasing disappoint. Moscona delivers one of his best performances—when he sings with such well-focused tone and characterful intent, he is the best journeyman bass around. As Ashton we hear Robert Merrill (only his third broadcast in four seasons) in a magnificent portrayal. Bountiful and beautiful sonorities are, and will continue for decades to be, his at will—they all but overwhelm the double aria which opens the opera. But what startles is the absence of that perfunctory manner which vitiates so many of his later portrayals of the major baritone roles. His sense of style and dramatic purpose are splendid on this afternoon. Merrill is musically alert as well, rhythmically alive in 'La pietade in suo favore,' and scrupulous in articulating the filigree in the second-act encounter with Pons. And to think all of this is expended on Ashton, normally a piece of vocal furniture in *Lucia* performances (when did the sextet become a vehicle for the baritone?). Based on this portrayal, Merrill would seem destined to rank with the great turn-of-the-century baritones.

Major interest devolves on Tagliavini. That he had impressed in his first few months at the house is evident when the chary Cross names him "the brilliant Italian tenor"—even Pons gains no adjective from him on this afternoon. A late starter (Tagliavini studied to be an engineer), the then twenty-six-year-old tenor first appeared in 1939 (*Bohème*) in Florence. During the war, he sang at La Scala, Venice, and Rome, and starred in five films. Mascagni, in his last years, voiced his gratitude to Tagliavini for gaining popular acceptance for *L'Amico Fritz*. Finally, engagements at the Colon in Buenos Aires brought him to the western hemisphere in the summer of 1946. Appearances in Mexico City and Chicago preceded his Met debut as Rodolfo on 10 January 1947, an occasion, according to *Opera News*, "for such rejoicing as the historic opera house had not witnessed for years."[12]

When Tagliavini enters after Pons' fountain arias, his bold egotism is a blast of fresh air off the Mediterranean sea: "I am a tenor and Italian," he tells us and he is welcome. Forthright command of his recitatives and vocal bravado in 'Sulla tomba' prepare us for his feisty stance at the marriage table. When, at 'Verranno a te,' we get the first taste of that sweet Gigli-like mezza voce (no careful weeding out of resonance, but full-throated, dulcet tones) the confection is gratifying to aural taste. After the sextet he launches 'Maledetto' with fiery energy, throwing in a few long-held notes merely to keep up membership in the tenor brotherhood. But he is perfectly well mannered both musically and dramatically throughout the afternoon. Best of all, the transition from mezza voce (which became his trademark) to full-voice is always smoothly effected; there is no hint as yet of the abasement of the mezza voce into falsetto, or the fixed full-voice of later years. The *accenti* of the tenor *scena* with which the opera closes are time-honored, but always conscientiously applied, and the flow of feeling and variety of tone and dynamic are far more gratifying than Peerce's stalwart reading. His finest moment comes when he begins 'Tu che a Dio spiegasti l'ali' ' with honeyed tones of heavenly beauty. The climaxes are well managed, too, and we are spared any vulgar histrionics as Edgardo stabs himself. Here, too, is hope: an idiomatic tenor of sense and sensibility. Or so it seems.

Among the many transitory figures of the middle forties (and even Tagliavini was fated for only modest longevity) one was destined to endure longer than almost any major female artist in the company's history. The light cast by Dorothy Kirsten's star may not have been as bright as some, but then she was spared the meteor's short path.

The soprano first entered on the operatic scene as the protégée of Grace Moore. The year before the war, the diva financed Kirsten's study in Italy with Astolfo Pescia, Gigli's teacher. "Hard cash" was "more efficacious" than mere advice in Grace's book;[13] she claims Kirsten had been "working in a dentist's office every

day and scrubbing the floors of that office three times each week for the extra over-
time pay." (*Opera News* wrote that Kirsten was a secretary with the Jersey Bell Telephone Company for five years). After columnist Dinty Moore (who had heard her
sing on radio) brought her to Moore's attention, Kirsten made her debut as Poussette
in *Manon* with the Chicago Civic Opera, moving up to Nedda, Micaela, and Musetta in
her second season. A contract with the New York City Opera gave her a home base
for appearances in San Francisco, New Orleans, Mexico City, and Montreal. Her
successful Metropolitan Opera debut as Mimi occurred on 1 December 1945, the
beginning of a three decade association with the company.

With her attractive blonde looks and Moore's image in the background, the
Metropolitan management felt Kirsten the natural heir to the late diva's special
repertory: Louise came in 1947–48, Fiora a year later, with Tosca just a few years
down the road. Like her benefactress, Kirsten would eventually make the trek to
Hollywood (*The Great Caruso* in 1951). But even her glamour was insufficient to keep
Louise and *Amore dei Tre Re* afloat for long.

Kirsten avowed that she "had resolved not to sing [Louise] while Grace Moore
was still alive."[14] Moore died in January 1947, and in December of that year Kirsten
became the Metropolitan's fourth Louise. The role also introduced her to the broadcast public on 10 January 1948, a rather belated introduction considering the
soprano was already in her third season with the company and had appeared as Mimi,
Violetta, Juliette, Marguerite, and Butterfly—but then the lyric field was crowded in
those days, with Sayão, Albanese, Steber, Novotna, Conner, and Moore well
ensconced in this repertory. Still, Kirsten had a brilliance to her persona which commanded attention, and she owned a self-confidence which became the hallmark of
her performances. Even so, a prima donna must seek her own niche in order to distin-
guish herself from her sisters; was it not logical that Kirsten's voice, hard-edged
beauty, and no-nonsense temperament might match up well with the fire and ice of
Fiora and the independence-seeking Parisian midinette?

Unfortunately, this time Beecham is not on the podium to help her create the
French heroine. In his place is Louis Fourestier, experienced in the French lyric
theatre, but a routinier who may have known the recipe for the sauce Charpentier
serves up but still cannot work the right mix. In his hands the opera becomes a mosaic
seen too close up. The romance of the piece is dissipated by plodding tempi, its
bourgeois framework fully exposed.

The artists on stage offer greater rewards. Jobin had served Moore well in earlier performances and, in what would prove to be his final Met broadcast, offers the
performance of his broadcast career. This time he has the tessitura under command
from the opening moment, and his spirited, well-focused singing and strong
portrayal repeatedly bring the performance to life during the first three acts.
Baritonal heft gives credence to his third-act credo ('Tout être a le droit d'être libre'),
and he has the skill to bring off the climaxes of the love duet. Abandon and commitment are not necessarily the words one applies to Jobin's underrated Met career, but
they ring true for this broadcast farewell.

Only a few of Jobin's cohorts remain from the earlier broadcast. Cehanovsky
has changed studios and is now a painter, Votipka and Stellman are still at their
sewing machines (the soprano showing a proclivity toward sharp pitch), while De
Paolis retains only the King of Fools, thereby negating Charpentier's dramatic point
that the Noctambulist's 'plaisir' is a fool's paradise. The halving was vocally
gratifying, however, for Hayward's Noctambulist offers vocalism that is in itself a

Louise
10 January 1948
Louise
Dorothy Kirsten
Mother
Margaret Harshaw
Julien
Raoul Jobin
Father
John Brownlee
Conductor
Louis Fourestier

pleasure. In fact, a step-up in the entire range of cameo parts makes quite a remarkable showing for the company. Moscona is superb as the bitter ragpicker (the adage of "no small roles" is affirmed), and sustaining the honor of the bass contingent, Jerome Hines commands attention (and was already receiving his fair share of it) in the few phrases of a philosopher—the bigness of voice and expression are quite startling in this context. Irene Jordan (a mezzo soprano here) and Martha Lipton are new sewers who have the stuff to make their mark in the future. They have a worthy model in Margaret Harshaw who has already achieved that near-impossible (at the Met) elevation from comprimario to major artist (and further heights await her). Still billed as a contralto, she offers a mother short on dour villainy but one who sings agreeably with a free-flowing, sizable instrument—plenty of color in the voice, too, before her soprano transformation bleached it out. In the last act Harshaw summons unexpected temperament to drive home the mother's declamatory statements.

John Brownlee, too, makes a fine thing of the father. The role is low in range for him, and he must change the gravity of his resonance, but that seems quite to the good, for the voice is less dry, the tone firmer, the legato more appealing. He cannot rage like Pinza nor seduce Louise with honeyed tones in the fourth-act lullaby (and here we fail to sense the bond between father and daughter which is essential to Charpentier's dramaturgy). But the role sits rightly on him; he manages a fine climax to the overlong monologue which opens the last act and carries his weight in the brawl with Louise that ends the opera.

The broadcast marked Kirsten's fourth appearance as Louise. At the premiere she was chastised for a lack of conviction and abandon (terms which were always in the critical wings throughout Kirsten's career), though her promise was approved. By the time she reaches the fourth act on this afternoon, she achieves a vocal and interpretive commitment quite complete.

The route to that gratifying end has its detours. In the opening scene Kirsten certainly brings a greater variety to the role than did Moore. There is more of the welcome way of the *diseuse* in the conversational passages—she is alive and playful in her initial exchanges with Julien. The sense of something in the bud animates these moments (we remember that, like all faithful Louises, she had made the trek to study with Charpentier). But in the scene with her father she remains either petulant or bland—one cannot catch her discontent or her receptivity to rapture. Again, as Julien pleads with her outside the atelier, her response rises little above a whimper. Kirsten's voice is perfect for the contours and content of 'Depuis le jour,' and indeed her reading is a fine achievement, garnering lengthy and vocal applause. But here Fourestier is at his worst, failing to provide the orchestral surge at midpoint in the aria which enables a soprano to soar in remembered ecstasy. On Kirsten's part, her peculiarities of vowel formation are troublesome; she virtually eliminates any approximation of closed vowel sounds in the upper octave, and the tendency to open everything extends even to a few words in the lower range: 'première' becomes 'prumière'. In the animated narrative which follows the aria Kirsten's tones turn narrow and pinched; Moore's midrange solidity was an asset in moments like this, and one remembers how at home on the boulevards the late soprano seemed as she coveted the freedom of Paris. Kirsten's tone is small for the climaxes of the love duet, and she hasn't divined the secret of phrase rhythms and varied nuance which well serve to counterfeit expansive expression. Then, quite unexpectedly, in the final moments of the duet she achieves the desired vocal thrust without harm to her delectable vocal quality. This dichotomy, the eternal problem of the lyric singer, surfaces again in the opera's last scene, but to reverse effect. Kirsten (well abetted by Brownlee and, in this instance, Fourestier) fully gives herself up to her heroine's demonic surrender to pleasure and Paris. Seldom will one find in her performances such an unreserved liberality of tone in the service of the drama. She is able to maintain vocal suavity in the waltz tune, but the all-out effort soon robs her of her capital (that beguiling, honeyed tone)—she begins to sound like any ordinary light soprano. Thus, while lauding her faithful response to character and dramatic situation, one senses something amiss. In later years, when belaboring the restraint and coolness of her interpretations, one might remember her loss of distinction under vocal stress and be grateful for her continence.

While many newcomers invaded the Met in the postwar years, there remained artists tried and true, of whom few were more highly regarded than Sayão and Bjoerling. On 1 February 1947 they joined forces in one of the most fondly remembered performances of the era. Their broadcast of *Roméo et Juliette*, long savored by private record collectors, eventually gained entry to the series of Metropolitan Opera Historic Broadcast recordings. Its repute is well merited.

Though the male chorus (one nasal tenor, in particular) disfigures its music at every turn, and Cooper's hand lies heavy on the first half of the opera, nothing can dim the lustre of the two stars. The Russian conductor had had a lengthy French sojourn, but the guiding principle of native French interpreters—'pas d'excès'—seems to have made little impression on him. Stodginess is his byword; the ritards are interminable in length and slack in pace. Happily, in the later acts, some measure of French élan invades his weary beat, and the opera gains impact.

The lesser roles are generally well taken. Only Brownlee disappoints (the Mab Ballad is really quite awful—all thetic, where it should scamper along with the lightest of touches), though he does have the bravado to take on Tybalt. Hargrave's Duke is of good vocal quality but lacks sufficient command and vocal size to dominate the banishment episode. But Thomas Hayward is a worthy foil for even this Roméo, singing with style, resonant tone, and excellent French. Kenneth Schon does well enough with Capulet, and Moscona is an able Friar Laurence, the narrower focus required by the French language limiting tonal spread and inducing a more becoming timbre than usual. The Met currently favored a soprano Stephano, and the loss in vocal contrast receives compensation in Mimi Benzell's delightful insouciance and tripping way with the graces of 'Blanche tourterelle.' Her lower voice doesn't quite settle, but the cadenza and high C are first-rate as she all but thumbs her nose at dull Gregorio.

Stellar pairs had made memorable a half-dozen opening nights in the early days of the Metropolitan from Eames and De Reszke in the premiere of *Roméo* (1891) to Melba and Jean in 1894, Eames and Albert Alvarez (1899), and Farrar's debut in 1906 (with Charles Rousselière). Even after the string of opening nights had run out, remembrance of Bori and Gigli or Galli-Curci and Johnson in the twenties quickens the pulse. The broadcasts of the thirties offered Gigli and Moore in 1932 (Georges Thill had been her partner earlier on) with Sayão and Crooks a memorable 1937 radio team. The exalted level sagged with the 1946 airing of Munsel and Jobin, but the next season set things right again when Sayão and Bjoerling sang the second of only two joint appearances in Gounod's opera. (These were, in fact, Bjoerling's only Met Roméos, while Sayão's house total was only five.)

The two artists are perfectly mated to their roles and each other. Has there ever been a Juliette so delightfully virginal in her entrance roulades and waltz? The com-

Roméo et Juliette
1 February 1947

Juliette
Bidú Sayão
Stephano
Mimi Benzell
Roméo
Jussi Bjoerling
Mercutio
John Brownlee
Friar Laurence
Nicola Moscona
Conductor
Emil Cooper

plete ingénue, yes, but with a bounding joie de vivre that makes her impetuous love entirely believable. The waltz melody floats with the utmost ease—coloratura fleet and natural, the graces (from above and below) exact but not intrusive. The mood change at 'Loin d'hiver' is exactly right—evident, but discreet (as marked, *un peu moins vite, mais très peu*). Mentor De Reszke would have been proud. And to the vocal expertise of Eames and Melba (as heard on records) Sayão adds her own dollop of charm— 'cette belle enfant,' Roméo aptly describes her. Sayão introduces a bit of coquetry into their first duet but signals the coming tragedy with her pregnant delivery of 'je l'ai vu trop tôt!' One moment on the balcony she is as assertive as her lover, the next she turns demure, filling her tones with an adorable sweetness. The remainder of the opera tests her skill at balancing her slight vocal resources against the weightier musical and dramatic demands of the role. A hint of pressure invades the wedding scene, and those annoying 'huh' anticipations intended to reinforce the more strenuous phrases mar a few moments (when the 'alouette' is rejected). But how quietly the two singers lay out the 'Nuit d'hyménée!' and the interlacing lines of 'Il faut partir' are elegantly traced. Though Sayão overblows the final note ('Adieu! toujours à toi!'), the coda is most lovingly rendered. Of course, Juliette's great air ('Amour ranime mon courage') is not included—just as well, for the soprano can turn shrewish in her despair (she does fly sharp on a few top tones in the tomb). There are always moments where character and situation are deemed of greater importance than vocal nicety in a Sayão performance (in spite of having to face Danise at home). In Juliette's final moments Sayão's still, small, shimmering phrases as the lovers commend themselves to God are unforgettably touching.

Bjoerling's range of emotion may be a shade more circumscribed, but he is an ardent lover. The glorious, radiant sound he offers upon first sighting Juliette seems to burst from his throat. He discovers her to be a Capulet, and the vocal color turns manly and his phrasing firmer ('et je l'aime'). Among the innumerable vocal felicities of the afternoon are the exquisite quick turn in 'Ange adorable' and the incredible silver-trumpet high C which closes the banishment ensemble. Roméo's aria is more a command than a reverie—this sun must surely rise—but one cannot quibble with the brilliance and surety of his vocalism. He is genuinely romantic, moreover, in 'Ô nuit divine!' and the rhapsodic close of the balcony scene is masterfully controlled and quietly done (though this Roméo belies his text—no lost dreamer he). Bjoerling's tenor is made for the opening of 'Ah! jour de deuil;' sword-blade thrusts of tone, free from any overblowing, obliterate mawkish self-pity, leaving only grandeur. As the opera progresses his indefatigable outpouring of fresh, vibrant tone (as in the bedchamber duet) astounds. Bjoerling is perhaps too detached upon discovering Juliette's body, but one can be grateful for his refusal to gulp the music—it is beautifully intoned. Roméo's final apostrophe has a noble repose, and Bjoerling's expansive delivery of 'Non, ce n'est pas le jour' puts the seal of greatness on his portrayal. Perhaps only the celebrated broadcast of *Manon Lescaut* in 1956 (where the tenor is joined by Albanese and Mitropoulos) is an achievement of equivalent stature.

In spite of the sterling performances of Sayão and Bjoerling, *Roméo et Juliette* dropped from the repertory (though the tenor remained with the company another dozen years). For two decades the opera was banished until the physical appeal (certainly not the vocal and musical aptness) of Franco Corelli was deemed sufficient to warrant a revival in the late sixties. Renewed interest in French opera (and the more agreeable Roméo of Alfredo Kraus) kept the opera afloat thereafter. *Faust* at least would retain its place (though no longer hallowed) in the Met repertory well into the sixties. Massenet fared less well, for among his many enchanting heroines only Manon enjoyed even a sporadic existence. When contemplating the graveyard of Massenet's onetime triumphs, resuscitation appeared highly unlikely. But *Werther, Thaïs, Don Quichotte, Cendrillon, Le Cid,* and *Esclarmonde* were not moribund after all; they would find modest favor again with management and audiences of the seventies and eighties.

That *Manon* held its own in the forties was largely due to the charms of Miss Sayão. They are again evident in her fifth (and final) broadcast of the convent-bred minx on 20 December 1947. Sir Thomas was no longer on hand to ensure the proper Gallic seasoning, but Fourestier was, after all, a native-born *chef-d'orchestre,* and this time the brew he mixes is agreeable enough. In a prelude of well-contrasted moods the climactic moments have sufficient sweep, and the bustling atmosphere of the inn is well captured (though Fourestier's transients are a shade more relaxed than Beecham's Amiens crowd). Fourestier has a curious propensity for allowing Massenet's more earnest thoughts to go limp (the act-two quartet, the chorus of admiring church women at Saint-Sulpice), and the gambling scene is devoid of menace, except for De Paolis' malevolence as Guillot. On the other hand, the Cours la Reine scene (now including the Gavotte, ballet, and extensive scene for the Count and Manon) is supple and lively.

Among the many voices familiar from earlier *Manon* broadcasts, Fourestier has a compatriot in Martial Singher, who converts cousin Lescaut from a mere family functionary into a delightful companion. This time 'Ne bronchez pas' is a lesson worth hearing—Singher coins a wily French Polonius capable of instructing Manon in the ways of the world. In excellent voice, Singher's sermon is not merely fatuous, but holds a modest measure of warmth, as in the hesitation just before his close. (Manon, of course, will to her own self be more than true.) The restoration of Lescaut's Cours la Reine aria ('À quoi bon l'économie') allows Singher to display both his vocal facility and suavity. His Lescaut is the complete sophisticate, and Cehanovsky's Brétigny is a worthy second (the veteran is in particularly elegant voice). Moscona plays a resonant father Des Grieux, a touch heavy on dramatic punch at the expense of finely drawn French line, but still a strong portrayal.

Kullman is again the young Des Grieux; his voice is undoubtedly less flexible (congested at the top), but the timbre remains appealing and the artistry sincere. He still can summon a burst of impetuous youth as he discovers Manon. His manly delivery of 'Le rêve' removes Massenet's kiss of effeteness (*mezzo forte* rather than *piano* is his basic dynamic), but his reverie is not the ultimate in vocal poise. Conversely, Kullman begins 'Ah! fuyez' quietly (as marked and seldom observed), and by now the voice has gained in control and color—a successful reading. Most tenors are bound to wane in face of Sayão's artful tempting in the Saint-Sulpice duet, but in the gambling den even this Des Grieux ought to be more aroused by his 'Sphinx étonnant.' Still, Kullman flares up convincingly at Guillot's condemnation of Manon, and refusing to tatter emotion as Manon is carried off to prison, his stance is decidedly effective. Act five finds him in best form, decisive in his demands, exquisitely tender as he recalls 'N'est ce plus ma main.'

If one were to retain only one Sayão performance, this might well be the choice. Though all the components of her art are familiar and beloved, on this afternoon every facet is thoroughly polished and exhibited in pristine form. If the entrance aria is a bit tamer than in earlier days (those indecorous flights of uninhibited glee are now a shade restrained), its charm is intact. 'Voyons, Manon' is near perfect in

Manon
20 December 1947

Manon
Bidú Sayão
Des Grieux
Charles Kullman
Lescaut
Martial Singher
Count
Nicola Moscona
Conductor
Louis Fourestier

manner and execution. In her solo scene in act two Sayão, from the passionate recitative on through the final 'adieu' to the table, offers a virtuoso display of vocal acting. How insinuatingly she introduces the Gavotte (unafraid to show Manon's hardness of spirit); the aria itself is free of coyness and concludes with a charmingly fluent upward scale. Saint-Sulpice fittingly houses the climax of her portrayal: the spoken recitation and evocative prayer prepare the way for the long temptation scene where her control never falters, though she attacks like a tigress, with danger in every vocal gesture. No problems today of pitch or overblowing the voice, small though her resources are and immense her intensity. 'À nous les amours' has plenty of abandon, but more striking is the pregnant inflection with which she intones 'son père'—the whole tragedy of her short life seems before us in those two words. That she should shine so brightly on this afternoon may not have been fortuitous, for Cross informs us at the opera's close that Sayão is "the little lady who promised her mother years ago to give up the operatic world if her debut was not a success," and in one of those unashamedly intimate moments seldom encountered nowadays, he owns that "her mother has been our guest here in the box all this afternoon." He drives it home: "her proud mother."

It would be well if no mothers were present on the afternoon of 27 December 1947 for the broadcast of *Trovatore*. True, for a final opportunity to hear the Bjoerling Manrico one can suffer much, and in this instance, one does. The recorded performance is considerably truncated, the recorder knowingly concentrating on Bjoerling and Warren. Roman's Leonora is shorn of both her arias, half the Miserere, and the death scene, while Ferrando's narrative (by Vaghi) and Azucena's third-act scene (by Harshaw) are also missing. Judging by the remnants of their performances, the loss is not great.

Roman is in characteristic form, scratchy and unsettled in the lower octave and perpetually agitated (but her Miserere is acceptable). The reliable Harshaw is again cruelly miscast as the wild Azucena. Neither by temperament or timbre can she counterfeit the vengeful gypsy, and without a believable Azucena, Verdi's opera is rudderless. (A month before the broadcast, Cloe Elmo had made her Metropolitan debut as Azucena; scheduled for the broadcast, Elmo canceled and we are denied what was purportedly one of the memorable portrayals of the last half century.) After an uncharacteristically tremulous 'Stride la vampa!' Harshaw recites the horrible events of her mother's execution and the incineration of the child like an efficient schoolmarm—could anyone believe that the obliging Harshaw could perform such deeds? She is better suited to the gentle mountain remembrances of the final scene, and there she and Bjoerling offer some lovely lyrical singing.

The albatross on the performance is Cooper's flaccid conducting. If there were a rudder, this ship would have no hand on the tiller. Only in the 'Mira, di acerbe lagrime' duet of the last act is there a shred of dynamism (and here he almost catapults Roman and Warren into a catatonic state with his accelerating tempo—the baritone is several times caught unawares). When the tempo is accurate (metronomically), Cooper is incapable of animating Verdi's simple but propulsive accompaniment patterns. Tempos alter in mid-aria as the singer struggles to keep alive vocally and inject some life into the drama. The brand of an ill-rehearsed production marks the performance as well: the act-one trio is ragged, the wonderful 'spezzato' chorus of the Count and his men nearly falls apart, and Roman holds her high C a full measure after Warren has correctly moved to the tonic at the close of the fourth-act duet.

Amidst all the wreckage, Warren floats the bel canto line of 'Il balen' with

Il Trovatore
27 December 1947
Leonora
Stella Roman
Azucena
Margaret Harshaw
Manrico
Jussi Bjoerling
Di Luna
Leonard Warren
Ferrando
Giacomo Vaghi
Conductor
Emil Cooper

assurance. But the saving grace of the afternoon is Bjoerling's troubadour, captured in its entirety. Most striking is the lyrical flavor of his reading in what is usually a rather strenuous vocal workout. Even Bjoerling in his only other *Trovatore* broadcast (1941) marshaled all his vocal resources for a portrayal heavy on brilliance. Not so this afternoon. Time after time he employs head resonance where we expect the more baritonal timbre and firmest breath support. His serenade is sung as sweetly as a chanson (a gratifying change from the bawling one usually hears). Moreover, he offers a number of delicate vocal effects never heard in the role (and seldom heard from Bjoerling in any role, for that matter). Several times he essays a *messa di voce*, first at the close of his angelic 'Mal reggendo' (the attempt turns virtually into falsetto) and then, more successfully, on the penultimate note of 'Ah si, ben mio,' again not perfect but quite lovely. The recitative leading into the aria may not have the tensile grandeur of Martinelli's reading, but its color and lyrical extension are equally telling. Cooper takes the aria at a snail's pace, and so cloudy is the accompaniment figuration that Bjoerling can hardly find his way; he consistently moves slightly ahead—for all that, it is beautifully done. A nonstentorian 'Di quella pira' may be refreshing, but Bjoerling's temperature (and ours) remains at normal in this heated moment (again, the high Cs are more head tones than brilliant climaxes). More appropriate is the tenor's dreamlike close to 'Riposa o madre' in the final act.

The *Trovatore* broadcast is very much a hand-to-mouth performance. It points up the ills of the Johnson regime more than most: ill-considered casting, threadbare vocalism, rehearsal-shy ensemble work, and even superior artists at the mercy of unidiomatic leadership. Happily, other broadcasts of these postwar years often enough tell another story. (Novotna, in a letter to the author, held that "rehearsals during the Johnson regime were plentiful and relaxed,"[15] including in support of the latter claim a charming photo of Walter instructing Pinza and herself in benign but intent manner at a *Giovanni* rehearsal. Of course, Novotna's Met career was centered in ensemble operas—*Figaro, Giovanni*—where adequate rehearsal was a prerequisite.) But three years after the end of the great war, the Metropolitan management has not effectively stabilized or elevated the company's performance quality. Great artists indubitably adorn the roster, but deadwood accumulates and the cluster of masterly conductors has dwindled. The Johnson regime moves to its close. Are there pages of glory still to be written?

Licia Albanese as Desdemona in *Otello*.

CHAPTER TWENTY-EIGHT

1948-49
An Upward Curve

The 1948-49 season began with promise. The Metropolitan management, reluctant bridegroom of early radio, now eagerly sought to embrace the newer technology of television. The union proved premature, but the impulse to televise the opening night *Otello* was not only courageous but modestly prophetic.

Actually, an earlier attempt at courtship had occurred in 1940 when the television industry was hardly of age. Once again, the National Broadcasting Company played the role of matchmaker. The network, for the past year, had been offering ten hours a week of television to over two thousand fans. On 10 March 1940 the network added an operatic program by Metropolitan artists: the *Carmen* Habanera (Castagna) and Micaela's aria (Albanese), Figaro's aria from *Il Barbiere* (Warren), 'Cielo e mar' (Jagel), and the *Rigoletto* quartet (Reggiani, Castagna, Jagel, and Warren). Concluding the program was an abbreviated act one of *Pagliacci*, the artists (Hilda Burke, Tokatyan, Bonelli, Cehanovsky) in Metropolitan costumes performing against "a couple of scenes on which the Calabrian town was portrayed in grisaille."[1] St. Leger conducted an orchestra of thirty-two NBC musicians, and Edward Johnson, not so reticent as the recalcitrant Gatti, acted as master of ceremonies. For *Opera News* the event "partook of the miraculous." The brilliance of the illumination and the "network of cords controlling it, gives the studio the look of some giant spider web glowing with the radiance of Judgment Day and something of the heat of Kingdom Come." Oh, Mrs. Peltz!

Though NBC continued its in-house television opera experiments, with CBS also offering capsule productions, there was a long Metropolitan hiatus. Not until the *Otello* telecast of 29 November 1948 did the company reenter the lists. The Texas Company again played guardian angel, but NBC had long forfeited its Metropolitan hegemony in favor of ABC. Two dress rehearsals provided test runs for the thirty ABC engineers who set up eight television cameras throughout the house.[2] This first complete television opera was seen as far as Boston and Washington, D.C.; an estimated 477,600 sets tuned in. Four of the cameras were utilized for introductory and intermission features: interviews with the stars and management backstage, the quiz (where the experts hopped and skipped as a piece of floor cloth was removed), interviews with celebrities (Margaret Truman, the Italian Ambassador, Mrs. Belmont, and Met Board members, as well as the opera glamour contingent from the audience—

Pons, Swarthout, and Kirsten). The Texas Company would continue the experiment of telecasting the opening night opera for two more seasons, but the venture was costly, though the estimates provided by the Met to ABC television hardly seem staggering in view of current costs.[3] (The *Otello* total of $10,886.09 included $3300 in artists' fees—Albanese $750, Vinay $700, Warren $500, Busch $500, and six "weekly" artists $600. The *Rosenkavalier* total for the following year was $12,105 with $3800 for artists' fees—Stevens $650, Steber $500, List $500, Di Stefano $500, Berger $240, and Reiner $500, plus $900 for chorus, $1920 orchestra, $3000 stage departments, and $1250 staff.) But the medium was not yet ready for live telecasts with its problems of adequate lighting and the need to integrate long shots and close-ups into a cohesive and sensible whole. The Met tried again with *Don Carlo* in 1950 and then, in a new format, offered *Carmen* (1952) and scenes from four operas (opening night, 1954) televised on closed circuit to theatres in principal cities throughout the country (I saw the latter in St. Louis). Opera audiences would have to wait a full quarter century before live telecasts of Metropolitan Opera would be available in their homes.

The cast of the televised opening night *Otello* was heard intact on the radio broadcast of 18 December 1948. Albanese, who had appeared on the initial 1940 Met telecast and had sung her first Metropolitan Desdemona for the television cameras, was joined by Vinay and Warren, by now familiar exponents of Otello and Iago. The Met's remaining maestro of rank, Fritz Busch, immediately shows his quality in the controlled energy of the storm opening, grand in scope but clear in texture, with chorus and comprimarios well disciplined. Busch captures the scherzo mood and graphic motivic play of the 'Fuoco di gioia!' chorus, shortchanging only the growing delirium and formal disintegration of the drinking episode. Throughout the opera, in fact, he nurtures the expressive lyricism of the score, a welcome counterbalance to its almost obsessive intensity. The brass do not snarl in Iago's Credo (neither does Warren) and the gain in subtlety offsets the loss in brute force. Taking his cue from the pizzicato strings, the baritone deftly offers his advice to Cassio and exploits to the full his suave legato and control of the quieter dynamics as aids in corrupting Otello. Verdi should have written his *ppppp* at 'Temete, signor, la gelosia!' for *ppp* doesn't deter Busch from covering Warren at this evocative moment. With superb control and insinuation Warren quietly intones 'che pur poco allar certezza vi conduce,' and his vocal certainty delights as he twits Cassio about Bianca. Yet while reveling in Warren's vocal command and earnest character portrayal, one can still slip into the role of mere observer as he patently displays his wares.

The entire cast is in fine fettle on this afternoon: Garris, a secure, undemonstrative Cassio, Hayward and Harvuot making every phrase count as Roderigo and Montano, the ever-dependable Moscona a courtly ambassador, and Lipton fearless in her last-act confrontation with the murderous Moor. By now Vinay is in full command of his role, having opened the first postwar La Scala season in it, and anchored the Toscanini broadcasts of December 1947. In vocal size and color he is an ideal Otello, the baritonal weight making Otello's decline doubly awesome, yet the timbre, so manly, carrying within it an emotive wrench that makes his torment and grief heartrending. Spacious phrasing ennobles the 'Esultate!' entrance. The treacherous close of the love duet is well sustained but, like most Otellos, unduly stentorian—still, he leaves no doubt of his love for Desdemona in the earlier phrases. I like his forbearance as he mimics Iago's repetitions of his questions. Then, 'Miseria mia!' bursts forth as from a wounded animal, and the high B that many an Otello

Otello
18 December 1948

Desdemona
Licia Albanese
Otello
Ramon Vinay
Iago
Leonard Warren
Lodovico
Nicola Moscona
Conductor
Fritz Busch

Ramon Vinay as Otello. Photography by Louis Mélançon.

skirts, he conquers head on. Again (is it Toscanini's coaching or the Busch overview?), he infuses the lament over past glories with dignity, avoiding self-pity. Vinay can thunder marvelously, though, and does as he names Desdemona a 'vile courtesan'; even better is his excessively polite and sardonic salute a moment before. If, in Otello's final soliloquy, his top voice clouds up in the emotional turmoil of the scene, the majesty of his portrayal speaks.

Albanese had prefaced these initial Met Desdemonas with appearances in the role with the San Francisco Opera. What one hears is a fully finished portrayal, both musically and dramatically. While the soprano was noted for her thorough (and extended) preparation for a new role, even greater care was necessary here, for the role often edges over into the spinto realm. Most critics found her admirably suited to the lengthy scene of the final act with its contrasting arias of lyrical cast (Bori commented that "Licia banked everything on the fourth act, and there she was wonderful").[4] Oddly, enough, the picture is rather different on this Saturday afternoon.

Perhaps because she has given so unsparingly of her vocal resources in the earlier acts, the fourth-act arias are not as poised vocally as one would have expected. Of course, her interpretation of the scene is more overtly dramatic than that of most sopranos—no dreamy, apathetic willow of a woman, but one distraught, living fully the tale of Barbara's woe, attentive to Verdi's frequent markings of *marcato* and *con accento*. Notwithstanding the touch of excess, entirely admirable are the naturalistic parlando asides, the lovely upward thrust of the 'Cantiamo' phrases and the skillful declamation in the opening of the Ave Maria (the latter, a deeply felt expression of faith). And no one can die more affectingly than Albanese—her final 'Addio' dissipates into nothingness.

The surprise of the afternoon is her command of the earlier acts. Phrase after phrase is laid out with expansive grandeur. The voice may not be large, but with gradation of volume, play of rhythm, pungent diction, and above all, seamless legato, she conjures a grand manner. In her first words ('Mio superbo guerrier!') Albanese reveals all her pride in her husband; she expands the line of 'Ed io t'amavo' in the love duet exactly as Martinelli (as Otello) had a decade earlier. She ascends easily to the high Bs over the women's chorus, and in the quartet negotiates with equanimity the tricky descending phrase over orchestral chords. The warm color of the voice and thoughtful phrasing (now tender, now broadly drawn) create a sympathetic character of immense self-possession. She fills 'Dio ti giocondi' with lovely arcs of sound, the voice ever poised, the top ringing out with complete security. Has any Desdemona quite realized Verdi's *con garbo*, "with elegance" (or "courtesy"), as does Albanese when Desdemona becomes playful with her distraught husband? Most sopranos forswear the critical word 'lagrime' in the giant upward leap which caps Desdemona's despair, but Albanese is faithful to the composer's demand. In this third-act scene we hear the complete singing-actress, giving unrestrainedly of voice and heart. In the scene with the Venetian ambassador she must resort to a few extraneous sobs to effectively deliver the low-lying 'A terra! sì nel livido fango' after Otello throws her to the ground, but thereafter she handily negotiates the wide-ranging phrases which introduce the concertato. Sheer weight of voice may have lessened the effect in the house, but Albanese is a memorable Desdemona. One is reminded that Toscanini, following her portrayals of Mimi and Violetta, wanted Albanese for his 1947 broadcasts of *Otello*, but the Metropolitan refused to release her from a broadcast Butterfly.[5] After seven more performances in the season's tour, the Met heard her Desdemona no more, though she pleaded for the role in 1954.

The mature Verdi was particularly well served this season. An eagerly awaited revival of *Falstaff* had its first performance on the broadcast of 26 February 1949. The anticipation centered in large part on the Met's new conductor, Fritz Reiner, although players of considerable merit frolicked on stage as well.

Reiner had made his debut conducting *Salome* earlier in the month, with sensational impact. For twenty-five years, his American repute had rested almost entirely on his symphonic work (Cincinnati and Pittsburg were home base, with many guest appearances with the Boston, New York, Philadelphia, and NBC orchestras). When he finally came to the Metropolitan, Richard Strauss saluted him: "What a blessing for opera."[6] Following an early apprenticeship conducting opera in his native Budapest, in 1914 Reiner, age twenty-five, had been named director of the Dresden Opera, home of many Strauss premieres—the Dresden premiere of *Die Frau ohne Schatten* had been under Reiner's youthful hand. America enjoyed a tantalizing foretaste of his operatic acumen during the mid thirties when he conducted the Philadelphia Orchestra in memorable performances of much of the repertory which would be his lot at the Metropolitan for the next five seasons: *Falstaff, Le Nozze di Figaro, Rosenkavalier, Tristan, Meistersinger.* Once again Johnson had succeeded in luring back to the opera house a conductor worthy to continue the long line from Mahler and Toscanini on through the recently departed Beecham, Walter, and Szell.

Reiner's constant admonition, "It must be clean,"[7] was particularly apt for Verdi's mercurial score, and remarkably clean are all the intricate ensembles. Clean, but not dry. Even in the bombastic opening scene with Falstaff, the music (except for those blatant tuttis) moves on tiptoe, with any possible lyrical shred of a motive made to sing. The orchestral commentary in the honor monologue speaks as potently as Warren. Winds whisk off, delightfully scherzolike, when we first meet the wives of Windsor; in the unflagging momentum of the nonet which closes the act the image of Falstaff swelling up to the bursting point is vivid to the imagination. When (in act three) Ford plots to marry off Nannetta, Reiner lays it out carefully so that we may be let in on the plan. Similarly, the denouement is allowed time to explain itself. And for once some light shines into the maze of the fugue—pleasure magnifies. Though this is the first of only three performances, Reiner's control is absolute; more important, he fulfills the credo he set forth at the time of the broadcast: "In opera there can be no devotion to musical problems without devotion to dramatic emphasis . . . one needs the kind of control that enables one to hold in the palm of one hand the entire action and meaning of the stage and in the other, the entire action and meaning of the music, and with both hands bring about a fusion concealing the separate doings of both in the mutual propulsion of the whole."[8]

Agreeably, the stage is peopled with artists both lively in character and capable in song. Two newcomers command attention, both from Italy's sunny shores, both singers of inestimable worth and yet neither destined to be long on the Metropolitan boards. Cloe Elmo (Dame Quickly) is just such a dramatic mezzo as had been too long absent from the American operatic stage. Mistress of the skills of character portrayal and possessor of a hearty instrument, pungent in color and with a fruity chest mix in the lower octave, Elmo is a complete delight as Verdi's bustling matchmaker. Her brash delivery dominates every dialogue, whether conniving with her lady friends or trading barbs with Sir John. Often she anchors an ensemble with a single robust interjection. She has a field day with Quickly's signature figures ('Reverenza!' and 'Povera donna!'), and recounting her encounter to her friends, Elmo fires off 'Dalle due alle tre' with deadly aim. But I like most of all the touch of affection which creeps

Falstaff
26 February 1949

Alice
Regina Resnik
Nannetta
Licia Albanese
Dame Quickly
Cloe Elmo
Fenton
Giuseppe di Stefano
Falstaff
Leonard Warren
Ford
Giuseppe Valdengo
Conductor
Fritz Reiner

Fritz Reiner.

into her voice as she describes Meg Page to the would-be lover; for a moment, when she leaves off playing the harridan, one hears a woman, and the voice takes on a luscious tone. Undeniably, it is the extrovert assurance of her comedic play which pleases overall. Expert assistance in comedy comes from De Paolis (Bardolph), Alvary (Pistol), and Leslie Chabay, a Caius who makes the Garter Inn scene skip along.

Giuseppe di Stefano presents rather a different picture. Originally intended for the church, but soon turning to the more likely arena of the stage, he studied with Luigi Montesanto (creator of Michele at the Met world premiere of *Tabarro* in 1918). Army service followed. He escaped from a German prison camp by donning women's clothes and swimming across the Fiume river to Switzerland—clearly a theatrical talent in the making. Following his debut as Des Grieux (Massenet) at Reggio Emilia in April 1946, Di Stefano leapt onto the world stages: Venice, Barcelona, Rome, La Scala in Milan. Met audiences first heard him as the Duke of Mantua in February 1948. Now in his second Met season, the twenty-seven-year-old tenor has not the well-honed skills of his experienced mezzo compatriot. What he does have is perhaps the most innately beguiling timbre of any tenor since Gigli—and a romantic stage presence to boot.

On this occasion, the rather one-dimensional role of Fenton enables Di Stefano to flaunt that dimension of his art which is most treasurable, namely, the ardent lover charming his quarry (Albanese is his Nannetta) with velvety tone and insinuating intimacy. One too often hears a tenorino Fenton (not Verdi's intent) and a wispy ingénue of a Nannetta; this assertive pair of lovers is a novelty (and certainly a rare largesse of casting). Their charm comes not from pallid coyness but from warmth of timbre and seductive savoring of language. Di Stefano fairly makes a sexual assault as he rolls 'Bocca baciata' on his lips. Of course, he lunges at a top tone or two (so does Albanese) and lumbers just a smidgen in the aria. But there is never any doubt of the lover's intent; his manner and tone are ravishing, and he makes several attempts (some more successful than others) to shade Verdi's ascending line into the difficult *passaggio* without thinning to falsetto, a rare feat for any tenor (other than the French artists of yore). Careful auditing shows a hint of overly open tone in the mid voice, harmless here, but a thing that might grow unattractive if abused. The tenor had already sung the Duke, Des Grieux (Massenet), Wilhelm Meister, Alfredo, Nemorino, and Rinuccio during his brief Met tenure and would add Rodolfo before the season ended. The career pace was fast, and perhaps a bit loose.

Nannetta had been a favored role of Albanese in her early European career. Toscanini had wanted her for his 1936 Salzburg production (an earlier contract prevented acceptance), and she sang the role in the famous Coronation season at Covent Garden with Eva Turner and Martinelli in 1937. A dozen years and myriad Violettas and Butterflys later, Albanese's soprano is no longer as well suited to the ingénue Micaela and Nannetta. All that art can do, she does, but there are no vaulting *pianissimi* here. Still, Verdi's lovers are no Shakespearean WASPS—they have been warmed by the Mediterranean sun. So Albanese and Di Stefano eagerly embrace the infrequent cantabile outbursts with which Verdi larded his operatic scherzo; they revel in their crisp exchanges, he ever with a smile in his voice and she with a playful taunt in her lovely tones. And Albanese is a lively and charming participant in the ensembles, clearly a full partner in the fun. She has a mother made to order in Resnik, who gives one of her finest soprano performances. The mother and daughter pairing is apt in both weight of voice and manner, unlike that strange union in the 1920s of

Giuseppe di Stefano as the Duke of Mantua in *Rigoletto*. Photography by Louis Mélançon.

Bori (mother) and Alda (daughter), in which the latter took such malicious delight (the cast also numbered Gigli, Scotti, Tibbett, Telva, and Didur under Serafin). Resnik ranks as a practiced comedienne, but she never abandons her musicianly garb, deftly launching 'Gaje comari di Windsor!' and adding just the right touch of coyness to her responses when Falstaff woos her. Barring a bit of wow on an occasional sustained note, the voice is at its loveliest, rich yet pliant. Nor does Lipton let the female quartet down.

About the male leads one is a bit less comfortable, though both Warren and Giuseppe Valdengo are indisputably artists of high merit. Warren is no stranger to his role, but like the fat knight's padded paunch, it sits a trifle uneasily on his sturdy frame. Unlike Falstaff in his youth, Warren is not 'sottile,' being neither slender of voice nor subtle in interpretation. With that amount of sonority ready to hand, it is difficult for him to throw anything away; he even overloads some of Falstaff's outbursts. On the other hand, he dominates by sheer vocal bulk and can thus bring the opening episode with his menials to a rousing climax. And one would not wish to forgo the strokes of mezza voce which he scatters throughout the afternoon ('rubar con garbo,' 'O amor!'). But 'V'è noto un tal, qui del paese ch'ha nome Ford?' lacks the playful insouciance which Verdi has built in—one need only hear De Paolis and Alvary toss off their lines to know what is lacking. As in 1944, Warren's monologue is short on self-confident swagger—less conscientiousness and more conspiratorial glee, please. What we hear is a great voice and a great vocalist, but not yet a great Falstaff. He grows measurably in the scene with Signor Fontana, finally coming into his own in his idiomatic and beautifully voiced jousting for the right of passage; and he trumpets 'Te lo cornifico' with triumphant assurance. Warren knows how to woo Alice with suave tones, though 'Quand'ero paggio' merely bumbles along. The pathos-touched scene back at the Garter Inn gives him his finest moment. Now the voice is fully oiled and the man is at one with the character. Of course, Verdi allows his knight to sing out here and that puts Warren in his element. He captures the knight's foolish fear as midnight strikes, and when finally brought to bay at Herne's Oak, he shows us he is very much a take-charge baritone.

Valdengo gives us the other side of the coin: less voice, more art—at least on this afternoon. The art was rooted in solid experience: a 1936 debut as Figaro in Parma, La Scala debut in 1939, then war service (oboe in an army band). After he returned to La Scala, De Luca introduced him to Toscanini, who took the young baritone under his wing for his NBC *Otello*. Perhaps not quite an Iago as yet, but well used at the City Center, San Francisco, Philadelphia, and Cincinnati Operas, he came to the Met as Tonio in December 1947. As he plays the volatile Ford, Valdengo's musicianship and intelligence are everywhere apparent, and whenever Verdi allows it room, his compact, sympathetic timbre is a boon to the ear. He shows some excessive vibrato when he first encounters Falstaff (and well he might, when pitted against Warren's formidable instrument). The vocal contrast is neat, Valdengo's viola playing against Warren's full orchestral complement (well, at least a mix of cello, brass, and occasional wind). Soon his quick vibrato merely warms his tones, and he musters a measure of virtuosity as well. The dull stupefaction of 'È sogno? o realtà' is masterly, and the voice is lovely at the middle dynamic—he can't afford to bellow. But his instrument is short at the bottom and deficient in ring at the very top; thus, the aria (the only full-scale vocal display piece in the score) is shortchanged—Valdengo cannot ride the climactic ascending phrase to triumph. The suspicion grows that the two baritones might have interchanged roles to better effect (unthinkable, of course, for the star baritone), and when Toscanini presents his NBC *Falstaff* in 1950, Valdengo will be his choice for the title role.

No minor reservations can dim the luster of the *Falstaff* broadcast. It is one of the Metropolitan's indubitable triumphs, in large part owing to Reiner's leadership. Though taciturn and forbidding in manner, Reiner was fully aware that "Opera is theatre, a show, and a good opera conductor looks above all to his showmanship."[9]

Reiner's Met career had begun a few weeks earlier on one of the most famous nights in Metropolitan history when the combination of Reiner, fellow debutante Ljuba Welitsch, and Richard Strauss' *Salome* combusted. From the broadcast of 12 March 1949, we learn more about operatic showmanship.

The matinee offered *Gianni Schicchi* as a curtain raiser, and here, too, we find much merit. New basso buffo Italo Tajo has the title role with three of our esteemed Falstaffians infusing new life into the one-act comedy: Elmo (Zita), Di Stefano (Rinuccio), and Albanese (Lauretta—this was clearly the year for the soprano to escape her familiar repertory). With De Paolis, Cehanovsky, Lazzari, Votipka, and Alvary on hand as well, the comic spirit is well served on stage. In the pit, however, Antonicelli waves a rather sedate baton. Though stage buffoonery is vividly mirrored in Puccini's graphic figurations and orchestration, Antonicelli refuses to join in the fun. Perhaps coordinating this difficult ensemble opera was enough of a challenge; indeed, during the ceremony of the new will, an otherwise well-disciplined performance begins to lose focus.

Tajo is an effective scoundrel. That overbright, brassy timbre has the sound of a rascal built in, and the voice is sizable enough to dominate any aural turmoil. Musically more precise than most buffo singers, at the close of the opera he invites audience response in heavily accented but comprehensible English. Di Stefano begins by declaiming Rinuccio's ungrateful music in rather blatant tones, but as soon as his Lauretta appears, he turns on the charm and vocal warmth. By the time of his concluding apostrophe to Florence, his melting tones and ardent manner are irresistible. Conner and Quartararo played the ingénue in the first four performances, but management prodigality offers Albanese for the broadcast. No one knows better than she how to turn a brief Puccini melody into a thing of moment, and she does so with her utterly charming 'O mio babbino caro.' As Nella, Paula Lenchner's fresh and silvery tones cap Puccini's gracefully gaited ensemble of expectant relatives. None of the numerous miscreants disappoints, but the experienced ways of Votipka and Alvary warrant particular notice, while Lazzari's weary voice makes old Simone credible. Again Cloe Elmo manages to dominate whenever old Zita mixes in the fun—what a pithy delivery she owns! When Elmo and Tajo engage in verbal jousts, the airwaves crackle.

Elmo's Metropolitan career was almost as brief as her role of Zita. After two seasons she bade farewell to the Met. To lose an artist of her quality is more than merely disappointing. When she came to the Met her career was already of major proportions: in 1935 the twenty-three-year-old mezzo had appeared in Sardinia and Turin; she soon became a regular member of La Scala and sang in Germany, Austria, Switzerland, and Hungary, as well as at all the major Italian houses. Her short Met tenure may have its roots in the initial contract negotiations. They were difficult. Upon concluding negotiations with her manager, St. Leger (the Met's administrative Figaro) concluded with an ominous warning: "It is earnestly hoped that there will be no further difficulties over the contract of this artist, otherwise the management will be compelled to make other arrangements."[10] Perhaps Miss Elmo herself finally

Gianni Schicchi
12 March 1949

Lauretta
Licia Albanese
Zita
Cloe Elmo
Rinuccio
Giuseppe di Stefano
Schicchi
Italo Tajo
Simone
Virgilio Lazzari
Conductor
Giuseppe Antonicelli

determined to make "other arrangements" in spite of her enormous success with public and press (Thomson said of her debut "The Metropolitan struck gold"). Unfortunately, of her Met assignments (including Santuzza, Ulrica, La Cieca, and Azucena) only Quickly and Zita were broadcast. While Elmo continued to sing in Europe, her achievements were overshadowed by the dominance on Italian stages of Ebe Stignani and, later, Giulietta Simionato, an embarrassment of mezzo riches for any age. Elmo eventually turned to teaching in Ankara, Turkey, and died an early death there at the age of fifty.

Soprano Welitsch made an even larger splash than Elmo. She remained twice as long as Elmo (four seasons) but not long enough to certify the expectations generated by her sensational debut as Salome. No career was more meteoric than Welitsch's Met sojourn: a blazing launching, a traversal of limited duration, and then sudden disintegration.

A red-haired Rubenesque beauty and holder of a Doctor of Philosophy degree (incredibly, in religion), Welitsch tutored at the Vienna Academy. Her native Bulgaria, Graz, Hamburg, and Berlin were early career stops. A member of the Bavarian Opera in Munich from 1943 to 1946, she was a guest in Vienna as early as 1943 (Salome under Strauss, the *Ariadne* Composer under Karl Boehm), taking up permanent residence with the Staatsoper in 1946. Recordings of Chrysothemis under Beecham and the final scene from *Salome* (Karajan) preceded her American debut. Even so, the operatic world was little prepared for the flamboyant stage manner and vocal witchery she displayed during the run of half a dozen Salomes. If ever there was justification for a candle to burn bright, it was Welitsch's Salome as heard on the broadcast of 12 March 1949.

Reiner's taut control allows no false sensationalism (Strauss has built in plenty), no noise for noise's sake (enough there already, too). But control need not vitiate excitement, and the performance, especially the orchestral reading, pulsates with vitality. The Strauss cauldron now burns low, here simmers, there seethes, but in Reiner's tending, it ever burns. What a smooth, glassy sheen he lays on the opening scene as Narraboth lustfully watches the princess! Reiner's brass blow a seductive warmth rather than a blatant assault. As Jokanaan ascends from the cistern, the orchestral melodies soar and shimmer with the same allure that Welitsch provides on stage. More than anything, it is the songlike utterance and free flow of the orchestral fabric which stays in the ear. Of course, he makes his instrument grind and fume as the prophet returns to the cistern after his encounter with Salome, and the winds belch and skitter effectively as the debauched Herod appears. Those are facets of any decent Salome performance. But Reiner's band behaves like some giant ballet dancer, capable of remaining on point no matter how gargantuan its labors. When Herod begs Salome to dance, the orchestral abandon betrays his weird condition better than Herod himself; no wonder the debased ruler is intoxicated by the rubato sway of Reiner's Dance of the Seven Veils.

No deficiencies on stage can lower the temperature of the afternoon. Young Brian Sullivan, fresh from his triumphs as Peter Grimes, is an imposing Narraboth; he lends stature to the opening scene with his budding Heldentenor sound and earnest delivery, though a bit more rapture might better explain his suicide. Thorborg, in her final broadcast, shows she still has a secure core of tone for Herodias' intermittent phrases, and authority is hers by right. Hines' weighty tones demand attention, too, in his brief appearance as the First Soldier. All the male supporting cast make an assured clatter as Nazarenes (Ernster, Darcy) or Jews (Chabay, Hayward,

Salome
12 March 1949

Salome
Ljuba Welitsch

Herodias
Kerstin Thorborg

Herod
Frederick Jagel

Narraboth
Brian Sullivan

Jokanaan
Herbert Janssen

First Nazarene
Dezso Ernster

Conductor
Fritz Reiner

De Paolis, Franke, Pechner). Though Max Lorenz (returning after an absence of thirteen years) and newcomer Berglund had sung the premiere, the broadcast Herod and Jokanaan fell to more familiar voices. Both Jagel and Janssen are experienced troupers and acquit themselves well. Jagel, a Met Herod as far back as 1934, may not uncover the full neurotic sickness of the Tetrarch, but his steady vocalism has merit. Indeed, when he begs Salome to dance and, particularly, tries to avoid surrendering the prophet, he summons some impressive sounds, creating a Herod more manly than most—too often the role falls to tenors on their last vocal legs. Jagel also contributes a few deft character touches, as when he jauntily offers wine to Salome. Janssen, on this occasion, is more of a slow starter, barking a bit as Jokanaan first encounters the siren (cistern air is undoubtedly bad for the voice). Nor is there that touch of zealotry in his tones to suggest the committed religious, now blowing hot, now cold, in fervor or rejection. But he has plenty of voice, an intent manner, and soon the voice warms ('Er ist in einem Nachen' elicits an appealing tonal glow and adept legato as the prophet pleads with Salome to seek salvation in God). And near the opera's end, as Salome prepares for her dance, Janssen delivers a few phrases of commanding vibrancy.

But the willful Salome brooks no interference, and the afternoon belongs to Welitsch. The voice is an ideal Salome voice, suggesting the child seductress with delicate, shimmering tones which never fail to penetrate the orchestral mass, or spewing forth in strong bands of steel in the highest tessitura and middle voice; often she wraps its cutting edge in a sheath of honeyed, almost Rethberg-like tone. Now and then she dabbles in a touch of brassy chest tone as Salome's degrading impulses surface. And Welitsch is mistress of Strauss' sinuous line. She whips her voice in and out and around the tortuous melodies with seemingly complete spontaneity; the utter freedom of her vocal manner is mesmerizing.

When Welitsch tempts the Baptist, her voice is like the keenest of knives etching a line on his white skin—what a strange mixture of sweet tone and bitter, animalistic clatter! Waiting for the severance of John's head, she voices 'Ich höre nichts' in grotesque tones of utter quiet; a moment later she sounds breathless with anticipation. When Salome must soar, nary a hint of a wobble intrudes, and in the final scene her voice becomes fuller, rounder, casting off any hint of cutting edge. Vocal coloration grows ever more sensuous (especially in the critical phrase which descends into chest voice) as lust and languor paradoxically coalesce. Welitsch delivers 'Ah, ich habe deinen Mund geküsst' as though in a daze—it is a weird, haunting moment. Then she moves into pure song: in the final peroration of voice and orchestra her tone and manner suggest that Salome has been cleansed—decadence, not transfigured, but certainly transformed. Strauss' eerie combination of degradation and beauty is fully forged.

A year later I heard Welitsch sing the Salome final scene with the Philadelphia Orchestra under Ormandy. She had the same glorious tonal prodigality as heard in the 1949 broadcast. I well remember her entrance at the rehearsal as well, all flaming red hair and beaming smile, with hand aloft in a comradely salute to the applauding orchestra members. Seldom, even in the theatrical world, does one encounter so dynamic a personality or such obvious relish in sharing her flamboyance with others. A half-dozen years later, hearing her Tosca at the Vienna Staatsoper, the change was startling—the voice still owned its silvery aura but was barely a third of its former size. She played in character (no Musetta self-indulgence) and concentrated on controlling that ethereal thread of argental tone. Time and trouble had tamed her.

L'Amore dei Tre Re and *Mignon* were also revived in the 1948–49 season. Both operas had long, if intermittent, histories of performance at the Metropolitan, yet both would disappear permanently from the Met repertory following these performances.

The radio audience heard its second broadcast of Montemezzi's atmospheric tragedy on 15 January 1949. Except for the durable Kullman, the participants are entirely new to the opera. Of these, Antonicelli is perhaps the most important, for his energetic baton adds a welcome propulsion and dramatic impact to the score. This time Montemezzi was in the audience rather than on the podium; perhaps he felt again as he did when, in response to his inquiry concerning the initial success of *L'Amore* at the Met in 1914, a friend had played the score in Toscanini's highly charged interpretation: "Wrong, all wrong," cried the composer. Truth to tell, little *poesia* distinguishes the current performance. Kullman still provides a measure of it in the final pages of the opera, but his voice has lost some color, become more fixed, without a compensating increase in metal for the grander moments. (Fortunately, a side effect of the loss is a decline in lachrymation.) Robert Weede comes off better as the distraught Manfredo. One cannot doubt this husband's anguish—how could Fiora not be moved by such fervid pleading? In 1941 Bonelli posed a richer, more commanding vocal timbre, but Weede never falters, phrasing with greater variety and skillfully shaping the climaxes for maximum effect. At the time, Lazzari garnered the press kudos, perhaps in tribute to his forty-year stage career. After early operetta experience in South America, the Italian basso became colleague to Caruso and an elite member of the famed Chicago troupe for twenty-five seasons. He was featured at Salzburg in the thirties, and Brussels, Paris, and Covent Garden had all been on his itinerary. Lazzari had played the blind king to Muzio, Garden, and Bori, but on this afternoon the sixty-two-year-old veteran is less than compelling over the airwaves; undoubtedly his stage manner counted for much. His gruff vocalism in itself suggests the age of the timeworn monarch, his cares and agony (more than Pinza could). But Lazzari's interpretive insights are quite ordinary. Of course, he cannot match Pinza in Archibaldo's fleeting moments of lyrical warmth or, above all, in the sonorous grandeur of 'Italia! Italia!' An honorable portrait, but not a great one.

Not quite so much may be said of Kirsten's Fiora. In the quieter moments (at the beginning of the act-two love duet), the dulcet sweetness of her upper voice pairs well with Montemezzi's lyrical lines. But her instrument is rather wooden in its lower range, and too often she fails to realize the seductive intent of Fiora's phrases. For the most part, she offers only a childlike tonal play where Moore had a built-in eroticism at her command. How businesslike Kirsten is in her dismissal of Manfredo! Then she can turn chirpy in the more agitated moments with Avito and Archibaldo. Always at her best in a high tessitura, the climax of the love duet is securely etched (but not enveloped). In the outburst just before Archibaldo strangles Fiora, Kirsten at last generates vocal and dramatic excitement, but she pushes the pitch at the very top of the voice, and the tonal quality is squeezed out—the outcome is the same as a year earlier in the broadcast of *Louise*. In future years the soprano ensured a long career by keeping within a vocal perimeter that was, after all, in line with her interpretive insights. To Kirsten's credit, however, it was her star quality that spirited the few *Amore* revivals (in San Francisco) during the next two decades (in 1961 Albanese sang a lone Fiora in Philadelphia).

Mignon had figured in the repertory even longer than *Amore*. During the second week of the Met's inaugural season, Christine Nilsson had played the gypsy waif with

L'Amore dei Tre Re
15 January 1949

Fiora
Dorothy Kirsten
Avito
Charles Kullman
Manfredo
Robert Weede
Archibaldo
Virgilio Lazzari
Conductor
Giuseppe Antonicelli

Victor Capoul and Giuseppe del Puente to succor her. Though currently identified with mezzo sopranos, the principal interpreters at the Met had been lyric sopranos; Farrar and Bori, in particular, had profited from the modest tessitura. As we have seen, in the thirties and forties the role passed from Swarthout to Tourel to Stevens.

Stevens is again the raison d'être for the present revival, with management content to surround her with workaday colleagues. Where in 1943 Beecham had breathed belief into Thomas' glossy score, the task now (4 December 1948) fell to Pelletier, who settles for a less flammable, but nevertheless fluent, reading. A responsive heart proves to be enough, after all, for in *Mignon* Thomas concocted a bourgeois delight. Melton is the only repeat from earlier broadcasts. His high notes are just as precarious, the nasal twang is even more pronounced, and while his naturalistic approach to tempo and rhythm remains nonchalant, the manner is overly casual for the French style. For most of the opera the Melton timbre simply cannot be assimilated into the musical fabric. (Hawkins' Jarno is another unsettling element.) In 'Elle ne croyait pas' (and to a lesser extent in 'Adieu Mignon!') Melton manages a reasonably relaxed tone, but here and elsewhere he too often blunts the melodic curves by precipitous movement. One could wish Garris' tenor, too, fell more easily on the ear, but he limns an idiomatic and characterful Laerte. Moscona is no epitomy of a *basse chantante* (bobbles of pitch and legato mar his cradle song, but at least he doesn't falsify the mood). He does attempt a few welcome demitint nuances in the duets with Mignon and, while not effacing the memory of the absent Pinza, may be counted an acceptable Lothario. Jean Madeira, who had made her debut only two days earlier as the *Götterdämmerung* First Norn, tries on Frederic for size—it is a bad fit. This is another of the Met's unfathomable casting blunders. In every way role and artist are mismatched. Madeira has a large voice, its most striking attribute a weighty, even ponderous, lower octave—the nearest thing to a contralto in these times. The Trebelli Gavotte lumbers along, her bumptious characterization perhaps not inapt, but her song inept in pitch and unsettled support. (One recalls the luxury of a Sofia Scalchi as Frederic in the 1883 Met premiere.) Future assignments would better serve this interesting and serious young American singer who eventually would find great favor in leading roles in Vienna.

Making her Met house debut on the broadcast is "Auditions" winner Marilyn Cotlow. Although this was her only Met season, the young soprano makes an auspicious debut in a difficult role (a far better effort than was offered by Munsel, whose tenure was fifteen seasons). In judging a Philine, one must forgo the idea of a Tetrazzini—if there were one around, no general manager could afford to cast her as Philine. Marilyn Cotlow has a tiny instrument. That said, she is the best of her kind in some time. Her coloratura (scales, staccati, trills, roulades) is exceptionally fluent, seemingly effortless. The timbre is silvery pure and her pitch excellent. Best of all, Cotlow exudes a vocal exuberance which suits the empty-headed coquette to perfection. She captures what Ernest Newman called Philine's state of "perpetual effervescence" with feathery light traceries of lovely tone. 'Je suis Titania' races along, not rocketlike because of her diminutive tone, but with plenty of élan, marred only marginally by nonstaccato (but pitch-accurate) leaps in the cadenza and a brief (and thin) high F. Was it size of voice alone that made her unfit for a Met career?

Risë Stevens' improved vocal status is the best news of the afternoon. Almost two years have passed since the *Carmen* broadcast of lamentable quality. Whatever vocal tutelage she undertook, the results are spectacular. As Mignon, she gives

Mignon
4 December 1948

Mignon
Risë Stevens
Philine
Marilyn Cotlow
Wilhelm
James Melton
Lothario
Nicola Moscona
Conductor
Wilfred Pelletier

probably her finest broadcast performance to date, with no hint of the wooden timbre or strained top which had disfigured her recent vocalism.

To hear, at her entrance, the lovely, fluent, lightly colored tone of her prayer to the Virgin is immensely reassuring. In 'Connais-tu le pays?' the Stevens voice is more soprano than mezzo, without an ounce of excessive pressure, and her reading, both in sound and conception, is entrancing. 'Légères hirondelles' is equally deft. The Styrienne calls for a more vibrant manner, and she supplies it, flashing out here and there, yet still continent. If the suicide scene by the lake is not as searing as some, her unique coloration is now much in evidence, she is untroubled by the tessitura, and her skills as a singing-actress come to the fore. The last act offers Mignon few opportunities, but Stevens' mastery of the angular phrases of 'Je suis heureuse' and her effective exploitation of tonal colors (from the low-voiced reiterations of the prayer to the eerie high A-flats—like string harmonics—in the closing trio) confirm her newfound vocal freedom. In short, a lovely performance, and what a happy occasion.

Beyond these revivals, the 1948–49 season held its usual quota of familiar elements, on several occasions offering romantic pairings that promised, at least to the eye, a higher quotient of vocal glamour than usual. Sayão and Bjoerling (*Bohème*), Steber and Di Stefano (*Traviata*), were new duos of Parisian lovers. Pons and Tagliavini found the Scottish highlands so much to their liking that they journeyed there again, dawdling overnight among the fountains and tombs of the Ravenswoods, from their matinee performance on 1 January 1949 to the actual broadcast on the second.

"Place aux games" was the order of the day—commercial radio ceded precedence of opera to the New Year's Day football marathons. *Lucia* is the only delayed airing in the history of the broadcasts (in 1955 the problem was averted by passing over the Saturday matinee *Aida* and airing the evening *Traviata*). The *Lucia* broadcast has gained a measure of notoriety as the single occasion where the studio-recording practice of tape splicing invaded the opera broadcasts. Pons had stumbled badly on the high F which ends the first section of the mad scene. The second F at the close of the scene went better, and reportedly at the suggestion of the resourceful Cross, the second was substituted for the first as well. Two high Fs for the price of one, not a bad deal for an aging coloratura. From the radio audience point of view, of course, it was one high F where two were ordered, but at least (remembering Flagstad's *Tristan* high Cs à la Schwarzkopf on records, or even the Votipka-Moore *Tosca* cantata) they were both Pons.

"The Nightingale of Provence" (Cross was singularly inventive in manufacturing sobriquets for Pons) has other problems throughout the afternoon—the pattern of the 1948 Lucia repeats itself. In the first two acts her voice is of eggshell-thin fragility, brittle and white; short trills are a squeak, long ones a blur, and the coloratura (especially in 'Quando rapito') effortful. Pitch tips to the downside more frequently than on other occasions. If Cross hadn't told us, we would never imagine that Pons likes "the emotional character of Lucia." Valentino, frayed in tone at the beginning, stentorian but hollow thereafter, is at least authoritative. The Lucy-Ashton scene is far from a thing of beauty, though Pons by now has begun to gain in steadiness and quality of tone. When mad Lucy enters we hear a different voice, calmer, warmer, fluent in scales and sure of legato. One feels reassured—evidently Miss Pons can always undergo a conversion for the mad scene. But she tires slightly at the very top as she nears the fatal F. In the second section a few upward flights are

Lucia di Lammermoor
1 January 1949
(broadcast 2 January)

Lucia
Lily Pons
Edgardo
Ferruccio Tagliavini
Enrico Ashton
Francesco Valentino
Raimondo
Jerome Hines
Conductor
Pietro Cimara

smudged, and she omits a note or two. The final F (this is the good one) is both thin and flat, but it is *there*. (The first F, as broadcast, is oddly shorter in its reincarnation.)

Cimara is a more forceful guide than many of Pons' baton men. After a precipitous start (the Normanno of Anthony Marlowe, with his Simpleton bleat left over from *Boris*, is quite incredible), Cimara does well enough by the score. The only completely satisfying vocal offering is Hines' Bidebent (he first had assumed the role two weeks earlier). Like Merrill in the *Lucia* of a year earlier, the American basso's resplendent instrument is a tonic in the midst of much vocal dross. Oh, the manner is rather square, but won't time cure that? (In Hines' case, time offered no remedy.) One mustn't shortchange Tagliavini either, for he does some very fine things. The voice remains healthy, the transition from half- to full-voice is still smooth, the style idiomatic and not unduly florid. Remembering his 1948 Edgardo, this time Tagliavini, in the more emphatic episodes, indulges in a bit more of the vocal blind staggers (all those dotted eighths and sixteenths in the denunciation scene are relentlessly punched out), and the tomb arias are washed by a few more tears. But the deterioration in style is slight, and the tenor is really in lovely vocal form. That sudden introduction of dulcetness never fails to touch the heart, and the generous measure of stout, pleasantly burred tone in the tomb scene shows the resourceful singer.

The other pairings of lovers should prove more equitable. Hard to believe that Bjoerling, who had made his debut as the Bohemian poet in 1938, offers his first and only broadcast Rodolfo a decade later. In the interim we have had Tokatyan, Jagel, Martini, Kullman, Peerce (twice), and Tagliavini. His Rodolfo is long in coming and, on this 1948 Christmas afternoon broadcast, a gift worth waiting for.

Fortunately, the entire performance sustains the holiday air. Antonicelli provides strong and sensitive leadership, his best work to date. More observant than many conductors of Puccini's explicit markings ('Soli l'inverno' moves *con anima* before the *allargando*), Antonicelli stays alive to the varied shape and dramatic intent of Puccini's motivic play. Though occasionally deficient in Toscanini-like energy, he imbues the entire performance with a free-flowing exuberance.

Antonicelli has a group of experienced (old) Bohemians at his command. There is Cehanovsky, talking the parrot narrative rather than playing the young baritone trying to make his mark; he expeditiously leaves the dying Mimi alone with her lover without milking his exit lines. And there is Moscona, who sings the coat aria most affectingly, the tones a shade cavernous for a young philosopher, but giving welcome attention to the quieter dynamic markings in his role (although he overdoes the final *addio*s). As Marcello, Valentino offers his best performance in years, sympathetic in characterization and tonally quite attractive in the big moments. He is far better at Puccini's conversational manner than at belting out bel canto arias—Valentino and Bjoerling even manage a dulcet close to the fourth-act duet. Baccaloni's pair of fools makes a play for the limelight whenever possible (when Musetta's shoe hurts, why be satisfied with Puccini's single 'Dove?' when you have four or five in your throat?), but he knows how to create a character in a moment and does make one chuckle.

Mimi Benzell is no old hand, but you wouldn't suspect it from her deftly sung Musetta. She is neither shrew nor vamp, just a good-hearted girl who knows her way around. Like many a Musetta, she is short at the bottom range, but elsewhere she reveals abundant vocal charm (staccati on the mark, pleasant tone, and an easy top). Not an earthshaking voice, but even a serviceable Musetta is hard to find—how rarely we hear a Musetta who manages both the waltz song and the fourth-act narrative and

La Bohème
25 December 1948

Mimi
Bidú Sayão
Musetta
Mimi Benzell
Rodolfo
Jussi Bjoerling
Marcello
Francesco Valentino
Colline
Nicola Moscona
Conductor
Giuseppe Antonicelli

Ferruccio Tagliavini as Edgardo in *Lucia di Lammermoor*.

prayer to equally good effect. The dreary line of would-be scene stealers seen and heard over the decades makes one wonder how Fritzi Scheff played the part at the turn of the century.

Puccini garrets are not entirely free from affliction, however, and when first we meet Mimi she seems unduly distressed. Sayão is in excellent vocal estate, but seems to have confused the first and fourth acts. 'Ove sarà?' she sobs, at the loss of her key (never mind that she, better than anyone, knows how to play the coquette), turning it into full-scale tragedy. 'Mi chiamano Mimi' passes muster in the climaxes, but is very nasal and metallic elsewhere, and overcloyed with squeaks and superfluous "huhs." When she tells of her nonodorous flowers, one might think there had been a death in the family. The duet is on a more even keel, and the little bonnet arietta at the Café Momus is better yet. Then, praise be, she comes into her cherishable own in the final two acts (could husband Danise have phoned during intermission?). A few extraneous noises are necessary to help her through the strenuous appeal to Marcello, but she is in command and the upper voice rings out. Regression sets in for the little trio (after she learns of her illness), and she covers the stage with sobs. But from the 'Addio' on to the opera's close, she is perfection itself, maintaining an ideal balance between purity of tone, musical rectitude, and emotional communication. The farewell aria is affectingly simple, her tone finely spun and most beautiful. (She must pay for a too long, but shimmering, fermata on 'rancor' by running out of breath on the final note.) The quartet is equally fine. As the dying Mimi, Sayão shows more pluck than most, but soon enough subdues her desires, content to ravish us with ethereal tone ('O come è bello e morbido') and chaste manner as she slips away.

Bjoerling operates in a more controlled emotional climate; he can never be accused of overplaying. Not that his Rodolfo is at all lackluster in song or manner. His initial phrase ('Nei cieli bigi') flows as effortlessly from his throat as wine from a bottle, and though the stock may be Swedish rather than Mediterranean, the yield is full-bodied and the bouquet flavorful. By this time in his career he takes the Racconto down a half tone. At 'Cercar che giova?' one hears what must be the only pair of insufficiently supported Bjoerling tones in existence (he wants a head tone, but the voice is not well enough oiled as yet). When he reaches 'Talor dal mio' we hear the Bjoerling we expect, and at the close he offers a long, very solid (slightly sharp) high B. The duet, too, moves down in the middle, and for this episode, Bjoerling prefers silver to gold in timbre (the freight is to the head, rather than the chest). He stands out from the Momus crowd: 'sboccia l'amor' is a pair of bursting blossoms of love. No deficiency of *slancio* in this Nordic tenor as he confides in Marcello—'Ora il tedio l'assal' would not shame a true *tenore di forza*. His anguish at Mimi's illness convinces, but he cannot quite counterfeit the intimate lover as he launches the quartet (that takes a Gigli, a Di Stefano). Bjoerling can turn matter-of-fact at such a moment, but one can relish the diminuendo ('carezze') which prepares Sayão's delicate entry. Then again, both Bjoerling and Sayão indulge in a bit of vocal grandstanding in the climactic phrase which ends the act. How easily the tenor rides up over Puccini's curves in the duet with Marcello (he never makes an issue of the *passaggio* traversal). Like a good lover, Bjoerling allows Sayão plenty of room to cast her spell in the death scene, even eschewing the stentorian bellows of 'Mimi' favored by other tenors. Rodolfo's hurt is internalized, and the more affecting for that.

A month later Sayão was scheduled for a third broadcast of her Violetta, but her indisposition offered Steber the opportunity. New also to the airwaves are the father and son of Merrill and Di Stefano. With Antonicelli in charge, Verdi's chamber opera wears a fresh face.

The conductor is a man of moderation, opting for an interpretive stance midway between his predecessor Sodero's fond sway and Toscanini's energized command. Tempos are often fleet, yet curves of phrase are preserved. Antonicelli is content to allow the largo concertato of the gambling scene to amble along, and he adds no intensity to the potent melodic line of the last-act prelude (even the *martellato* repeated notes are accommodating—this Violetta evidently will not struggle with death). Overall, his is an apt combination of *poesia* and salubrious momentum.

Standing out among the familiar comprimarios are De Paolis (too aged of voice to be at ease among Violetta's fast crowd) and Votipka, delightfully roguish as she taunts her Marquis for his inconstancy.

By now Merrill is a Germont of considerable experience. It tells in his unpressurized delivery, in the expansive folds of warm, refulgent tone with which he envelops Verdi's melodies. If his reading is not quite distinguished in musical conception, he doesn't bludgeon the line nor falsify the drama. We are allowed to hear almost all the thirty-second note figurations in 'Un dì, quando le veneri,' and only the numerous *piangi*s suffer a huff or two in what would too soon become a preferred Merrill vice. The baritone adopts a grand manner in the recitative to the aria, the latter splendidly vocalized, the graces all there, if too much to the fore. But his legato is not supple enough to round off the blunt edges of the tune. In this moment, Warren offered a restrained reading, almost a prayer for his son, while one feels Merrill may not be overly fond of his wayward child—he is thinking (if at all) of the family. Nevertheless, his song is gorgeous to the ear. Germont's abrupt intrusion at Flora's party would be even more effective with more tonal bite, but one learns soon enough that vocal coloration is not Merrill's strong suit—it is not even in his deck of vocal cards.

At this early stage of his career, the young Di Stefano should be perfectly matched to Alfredo. With his dashing appearance and winning vocal ways, expectation is high. Before the afternoon is out, expectation has turned to disappointment, disappointment to disbelief. Seldom can a major artist have given so inept a performance. From the first the voice is recalcitrant, refusing to flow. He savors the language, a welcome trait, yet too often the excessive articulation negates legato. Many a tenor slights the turns in the Brindisi, but Di Stefano barely acknowledges an acquaintance with them (all the more obvious, since Steber's turns are cleaner than usually heard). One admires the tenor's earnest manner as he begins 'Un dì felice' (the mere sound of a genuine Italian tenor voice inevitably brings a sense of well-being, no matter what its deficiencies), but pitch grows suspect, the upward scale is a mere slide, and the final F is distressingly flat. Di Stefano's obvious pleasure when Violetta accedes to his impetuous wishes restores confidence (his, and ours), but not for long. Alfredo's second-act aria exposes the unfinished artist: his tendency to flat increases, the tone is excessively open, lying baldly on the throat, and the upper notes are effortful. He well knows how to denounce the hapless Violetta at Flora's house, and I like the note of personal sorrow, even pain, which he suggests. His best effort comes as he declaims his remorse ('Ah sì! che feci!') for he takes to heart Verdi's indication (*da sè*) and makes it an intimate moment of self-abuse. But the final act is sheer disaster (the desperation more Di Stefano's than Alfredo's). He jumps in a couple beats ahead as he begins 'Parigi, o cara' (the error is terribly exposed), and it takes Antonicelli a full phrase to gain realignment. His phrases in the ensuing dialogue are not always

La Traviata
22 January 1949
Violetta
Eleanor Steber
Alfredo
Giuseppe di Stefano
Germont
Robert Merrill
Conductor
Giuseppe Antonicelli

rhythmically accurate, and he is late in entering at the cabaletta, thereby causing another Antonicelli adjustment. Papa Germont arrives just in time; by this time the runaway tenor needs a father's restraining hand. The broadcast is Di Stefano's first Met Alfredo (perhaps he went on without orchestra or stage rehearsal) and his broadcast debut as well—to have introduced him thus in our chronicle would have been too unkind; the *Falstaff* and *Schicchi* broadcasts provide a fairer picture of his abilities or, more appropriately, his potential.

Expectations of Steber as Violetta would tend to be rather moderate: one might anticipate a professional but idiomatically neutral reading, with some moments of superior vocalism. Thus far, her prominence has rested on her notable skills as a Mozartean and the musicianship that made her a sure partner in ensemble pieces like *Hoffmann* and *Falstaff*. In addition to her exquisite Mozart heroines, the radio audience also knew her as gifted in the Germanic tongue of Sophie and Eva. Neither Marguerite nor Manon (which by now she very occasionally undertook at the Met), Mimi nor Manon Lescaut (which were yet to come), were ever broadcast fare for Steber—of the old-fashioned diva roles only Tosca (in 1958) was an earned broadcast right. A few days after the *Traviata* broadcast she sang her first Met Mimi at a student matinee (Sayão had the first night—but remember those were the days when student performances often represented top Met quality; the 1948–49 student pairings were Steber-Tucker and Kirsten–Di Stefano). I recall hearing Steber as Mimi a few years later on the Met tour (she replaced Albanese, who was expecting a child). Her irrepressible vitality is all that stays in the memory—the Steber energy could not be sufficiently subdued for her to capture the mood and manner, either in song or action, of the demure seamstress. One could not weep over a Steber death scene. The qualities which made her exceptional in her own *Fach* mitigated against her in other roles (listen to her beautifully vocalized Marguerite and Butterfly in the "official" Met recordings of this period, her selection dictated primarily by contractual snarls). She was a quick learner, but versatility has its downside. I can still see her in Central City in 1951 at rehearsals for Menotti's *Amelia Goes to the Ball*, all but learning the role on stage just a few days before the premiere—of course, she was an ideal Amelia with her pouter-pigeon cheeks and Victorian big blue eyes and high spirits. Those spirits could not be kept under cover (except by Mozart). I met her once driving over the treacherous Virginia Canyon road (dirt and single lane most of the way), I clinging to the mountainside in my Ford while she, at the wheel, sailed past *allegro con brio* from the opposite direction. After a performance at the Central City Opera House, artists often sang for the mere pleasure of it late into the evening in the Teller House Gold Nugget lounge, and once Steber doffed her black lace wide-brimmed topper, the spotlight shining harshly down on her blondined head, and told the pianist, who had entered into 'Sempre libera' a half tone down: "Pitch it up a tone, honey, I sing it in the original key." She was the born Minnie, playing the demimondaine and loving every reckless minute of it. At least she might be expected to have an easy manner at Violetta's party.

How often the broadcasts give the lie to preconception. Steber's Violetta is a sensitive, idiomatic portrayal, gloriously sung from start to finish, certainly one of the finest Traviatas of broadcast history. For once the florid flourishes in Violetta's brief entrance lines are well delineated, and Steber is both charming and commanding to her party guests. Even her laughs are light and easy (the Met *Traviata* parties in those days were decorous affairs, no howling or whooping it up by a motley crew such as disfigures recent broadcasts). Her coloratura in the duet is accurate, fluent, and lovely in tone, and throughout the first act she keeps her voice on a tight rein. The pseudoseparated notes which open 'Ah fors'è lui' are done legato, and in these moments of introspection, we miss a bit of wonder, but the line leading into 'Ah quell'amor' is tellingly drawn. Throughout the afternoon Steber's phrasing and manner are those of the best Violettas (that is, they conform to Verdi's markings with tradition's imprint selectively and tastefully acknowledged). Steber has a genuine and quite wonderful trill which she doesn't hesitate to display wherever possible; a particularly long and scintillating one ends the aria. 'Sempre libera' is child's play for her, no mad reckless dash (perhaps it should be), but 'Gioir! gioir!' is frenetic enough. Short trills are cleanly articulated, the sequence of brief downward scales is clearly etched, and the high Cs are full and secure. All in all, her first act is a neat mix of vocal skill and a party mood.

In the remaining acts Steber creates a portrayal of dramatic and musical substance. The swiftly changing moods of the scene with Germont are well captured; 'Dite alla giovine' is simply phrased in ravishing tones, while 'Qual figlia' touches the heart. A splendid outburst caps 'Amami, Alfredo,' not the wild, passionate pleading which Toscanini preferred—Steber allows the music to speak for her. Antonicelli adopts a progressively broader arch for each of Violetta's three phrases in the gambling scene, the first one barely stretched, the third measurably slower. No tears touch Steber's voice in 'Alfredo, di questo core,' but how skillfully she moves from *piano* to a full-voiced leading of the ensemble.

With Annina, she is the little girl again, almost tremulous in conversation. Of course, the chest voice reading of Alfredo's letter is grainy, with no blended transition from recitative to song (but what a lovely *piano* at 'morta'). She draws the 'Addio' in firmer lines than normally heard (and very effective it is), deploying rich, full tones of exquisite color in the major section. One of her talents is clarity of attack in the upper voice (a skill prevalent among turn-of-the-century singers but seldom heard today), and she employs it to telling effect in the closing phrases of the aria. After Di Stefano's debacle in 'Parigi, o cara,' she reanchors the duet with soundly cored tone, but the exquisite calm of the moment is too difficult to recapture. Again those exhilarating trills cause astonishment as Violetta prepares to dress. 'Ma se tornando' would benefit from greater intensity, but 'Ah! Gran Dio!' has the right thrust. In the closing moments of the opera she retains a healthier tone than Verdi probably wanted—little *debolezza* here—but 'Se una pudica vergine' carries its own message in purity of tone (surprisingly, no *piano* at the top, though she has it always at her beck). This time, the transition from speaking to joyful cries is well managed. At the end of the performance Steber is as fresh vocally as when Violetta first welcomed her party guests. A few years later she would sing a broadcast Desdemona and step in as the evening's Fiordiligi a few hours later. At mid-career Steber seems a vocal Olympian; if there was a price to be paid for such largesse it was far in the future. In the meantime, her star continued bright, and she would be granted opening night honors for Johnson's final season.

Astrid Varnay as Venus in *Tannhäuser*. Photography by Sedge LeBlang.

CHAPTER TWENTY-NINE

1949–50
Curtain for Johnson

The winds of change were already wafting through the old house when Johnson opened his last season with *Der Rosenkavalier* in November 1949.

Not only were the television cameras again on hand, but Johnson was joined in the manager's box by his successor, Rudolf Bing. The newly elected manager's presence throughout the season as observer and planner for the 1950–51 season occasioned a good measure of company turmoil—particularly since new brooms are not only wont but expected to sweep clean. Kolodin contends that Met singers were so concerned about their future status with the company that they "barely bothered to execute" their current contracts[1]—quite an indictment and one that makes the season's airchecks particularly intriguing.

The *Rosenkavalier* broadcast of 3 December 1949, identical to the opening night in its make-up, tells us the old regime, far from being a lame duck, was intent on a new look. The podium vacated by Szell and Busch passed to a Straussian of even greater repute, Fritz Reiner. While the aging Emanuel List and the gallant Stevens are in their familiar parts, Steber no longer apprehensively awaits her future lover in the Faninal town house but enjoys his company in the boudoir of the Princess von Werdenberg. There she is serenaded by an Italian tenor (Di Stefano) of indisputable right to the title (only the Pavarotti appearances in the eighties were a comparable gesture of managerial prodigality). As the war years receded in memory, the wares of the German houses began to be palatable to Americans: Erna Berger appears as Sophie, perhaps the oldest debutante soubrette on record; German-born Peter Klein, as Valzacchi, is also new to the house. Finally, young American Hugh Thompson takes on Faninal, a role recently in the more august hands of Schorr and Frederick Lechner.

Reiner rightly recalls Strauss' intention to write a Mozartean opera. He emphasizes textural clarity and sprightly elegance—even Ochs' vulgarity is almost washed away by Reiner's cleansing hand. The waltzes are nonchalant rather than sentimental. Not that Reiner is unwilling to allow Strauss' magical phrases to flower at the close of the presentation of the rose, for instance; it's just that he employs no force-feeding. The tedium is deftly extracted from the first half of the inn scene (at least the radio audience hears none—they do not suffer the stage barbarities). The elaborate fugato flows like a stream over flat pebbles which barely ripple its surface,

Der Rosenkavalier
3 December 1949

Marschallin
Eleanor Steber

Sophie
Erna Berger

Octavian
Risë Stevens

Italian Singer
Giuseppe di Stefano

Baron Ochs
Emanuel List

Faninal
Hugh Thompson

Conductor
Fritz Reiner

457

the orchestra dancing along with wisps of string tone—even Ochs' horns enter on tiptoe with him. Tarantella rhythms willingly capitulate to the waltz as Reiner's whirl of gossamer sound moves toward the denouement.

Reiner has willing colleagues in his conception. Stage participants don't over-play, either. List is in surprisingly good form, occasionally short of breath but resonant and hearty of tone and never overweighting the music. The humor may be low but his delivery is aboveboard. By the end of his famous waltz scene this Ochs begins to run out of voice, but his know-how carries the day. And his command of the intricacies of the role is so confident—a characterization that has been absorbed into the glands is a treasure. When the Marschallin orders him out, his touch of genuine regret that 'all is over' arouses a bit of sympathy for the old roué.

With his well-belted aria, Di Stefano undoubtedly fulfills the parodic intent of composer and librettist, his voice solid at the top and the line reasonably legato. All in all, he makes a forthright assault on the aria's difficulties. But, in the repeat, the rascal misses his final entry and sings it two beats behind the doubling flute; no wonder the Baron's ears are offended and he breaks it off.

Klein, a Vienna veteran, makes a virtuoso Valzacchi, always hitting the mark in the brittle machinations of the Italian spy. Lipton (as Annina) and Thompson fare less well. Often inaudible, she stumbles more than once over a tricky passage and the charming "messenger" moment falls flat. Thompson, despite his fine baritone, is not up to the knotty duty of Faninal, either in dialogue or character play. An odd role, Faninal paradoxically recedes into the background when well done but sticks out like a sore digit when merely given an earnest effort, as on this occasion. Two veterans who do know how to make the most of their fleeting moments are Votipka as Sophie's duenna, and Alvary, an idiomatic Police Commissioner (and himself an Ochs of repute in many of the world's opera houses).

Steber's Marschallin is far closer to young Resi than to 'die alte Frau.' She might more profitably have waited to assume the role when her soprano had broadened into the Elsa and Donna Anna voice of several years later. Her beauty is an asset (no difficulty in believing an age of thirty-two when viewing her *Opera News* photos in the role). But it is the sound itself which seems too delicate, too light for the pregnant utterances of the Marschallin. Beyond that, much of the dialogue—that which lies in Steber's weaker middle low range—fails to penetrate the orchestral fabric, so the Marschallin's psychological insights can't make their full impact; it's rather like the aural equivalent of viewing a performance through an unlighted scrim—the charac-ter is there if only we could bring it closer to us. Still, Steber sings many a ravishing phrase and certainly conveys the elegance of the aristocratic princess. The great monologue has some telling moments: here her low voice ('Die alte Frau' section) is well collected and not excessively grainy (as it is wont to be), and she can lighten her voice delightfully for the more pensive moments. But 'Da liegt der ganze Unter-schied,' though lovely as song, is too self-consciously calculated. Much of 'Die Zeit, die ist ein sonderbar' Ding' dwells in the loveliest part of her voice—give Steber something to sing and she makes it count. The magical phrases in which the Marschallin sets forth her day's routine (the visit to old uncle Greifenklau, her ride in the Prater) well suit Steber's vocal persona, but her rendering does not quite deepen our understanding of the Marschallin's character. Similarly, the long concluding phrase in which the Marschallin directs her servant to give the silver rose to the departed Octavian is exquisite (and heroically delivered in one breath), but its signifi-cance is not really driven home. As often happens with even the finest singers, that ultimate sorcery which marks the memorable singing-actor proves elusive. The more overt actions of the third act suit Steber better. A touch of majesty here, a bit of anger there (her grudge against 'men' deepened by almost a sob) are enough and, of course, she launches the trio in wondrous fashion; very few Marschallins can provide the tonal radiance, control of breath, and nuanced line which Steber offers at this critical moment. With a final light 'Ja, ja' (devoid of artificiality) the soprano hints at what her characterization might become.

As luck would have it, Steber, in her first Marschallin, must compete with a Sophie not only thoroughly well versed in all the nuances of the role, but possessed of a vocal enchantment that cannot help but fix attention whenever she utters a note.

The Dresden-born soprano, Erna Berger, was not unfamiliar to American operatic devotees, especially as the Queen of the Night in Beecham's 1937 recording of *Die Zauberflöte*. An early protégée of Fritz Busch at the Dresden Opera, she was heard in Bayreuth and Salzburg in the early thirties before she began her tenure at the Berlin State Opera. Covent Garden, Bucharest (under Boehm), Holland (with Kleiber), Rome and Vienna (with Hans Knappertsbusch), all were favored with her coloratura skills. No mere nightingale, her lieder recitals were cherished events in the European capitals (and continued to be—I well remember an enchanting concert at the Vienna Musikverein as late as 1957 when the soprano was in her fifty-seventh year).

In spite of her extensive career, Berger's voice on this afternoon retains its honeyed core of youthful innocence, mercifully free of soubrette insipidity and without a hint of whiteness in the timbre. Eager but not coy, she shuns the simper, allowing a gentle wonder to invade her responses to Octavian's questions. No matter how dense the orchestral mass, Berger never fails to project, to communicate. And she moves into the stratosphere without loss of timbre ('Wie himmlische, nicht irdische' is perfectly poised, her tones firm and round)—only one or two very top tones scratch the perfection of her vocalism and betray her age. Her Sophie is no ninny—with feisty charm she bests her father as she refuses the match with the Baron. In the final scene Berger artfully suggests Sophie's doubt and hurt with her whispered 'nur eine Farce,' and you can hear her assumption of dignity as the trio approaches. She is clearly the leader in the final duet, suggesting a cozy delight, a savoring of her future with Octavian. The pair's final ascent is effortless—the dreamlike mood remains intact.

Stevens deserves credit for this, too, and for her reticent caresses in the duet— she doesn't interfere with Berger's lead. But, on her own, no reticence masks Octavian's emotion as he vibrantly voices his debt to the Marschallin ('Marie Theres', wie gut Sie ist'). Her Mariandel is girlishly charming, not so crass as some, yet full of amusing foolishness. The Stevens voice is slightly recalcitrant in the opening act, plentiful in size but initially quite fixed and wooden in timbre. No doubt about her ardor, however. By the time Octavian makes his resplendent entry into the Faninal house, Stevens' voice has taken on color and flows with greater ease (though the grain in her low voice cannot quite be vanquished), and the well-contrasted timbres of the young people enhance the presentation scene. The mezzo is mistress of the Teutonic bark in her angry confrontation with Ochs, but readily discards it for some charmingly deft exchanges with the distraught Sophie. Like Berger and List, Stevens has plumbed the musical and dramatic depths of her role.

Clearly, Octavian, along with Mignon, remains a commanding portrait in the Stevens gallery. Not so her Dalila, which opened the broadcast season a week earlier.

Samson et Dalila
26 November 1949

Dalila
Risë Stevens
Samson
Ramon Vinay
High Priest
Robert Merrill
Old Hebrew
Dezso Ernster
Conductor
Emil Cooper

Stevens' move into the forefront of operatic stardom is apparent in her tally of four broadcasts plus the opening night in the 1949–50 season. Carmen had become regular radio fare (this season was the fourth of her eleven airwaves gypsies). She would, in addition, have an important role in the Met's first production of Mussorgsky's *Khovanchina*.

While Marina and Laura are borderline glamour roles, Dalila was de rigueur for any modern mezzo if the seductress image were to be sustained. Evidently neither the Dalilas of earlier Metropolitan history (Gabriella Besanzoni, Margarete Matzenauer, Louise Homer, and Karin Branzell) nor their publics were troubled by an even match between vocal amplitude and a sturdy frame or generous girth. For the current management, the visual outweighed the aural. In no way could Stevens' modest mezzo be considered sufficient in tonal allure and size (particularly in the critical lower half of the voice) for Saint-Saëns' heroine. Few prima donnas have made so ineffectual an entrance as Stevens in the opening act ('Je viens célébrer la victoire'); a trio it is not, for Stevens' tones are swallowed up by the more voluminous voices of Vinay and Ernster (the Old Hebrew). Presumably the dance which followed made up for the deficiency (Stevens' new costumes—by Motley, executed by Karinska—suggest, according to *Opera News*, "barbaric splendor").[2] Cooper sets a lugubrious pace for 'Printemps qui commence'—it's a wonder that Stevens can achieve a measure of spaciousness in her dignified conduction of line. But her portrayal remains a line drawing where Saint-Saëns calls for a splash of generous color. Ever the professional, Miss Stevens' skill allows her to adequately negotiate the exposed close of the aria.

In the second act, Dalila must leave off her languorous manner and both command and seduce. Whenever Stevens' lower voice is called upon, listening pleasure declines, since the tone is quite fixed, the manner angular and cumbersome; whenever the melody moves to the upper range, the voice takes on color, beauty, even distinction. One misses a continuous legato in 'Amour! viens aider ma faiblesse!' The hollow chest voice in the exchange with the High Priest distresses—her voice sounds spent in these strenuous calls for vengeance. But she recovers in time to greet the warrior in beguiling fashion. At last, now operating in her best range and not bullying her voice, Stevens offers some lovely singing—her manner is tempting indeed. And there are effective moments of calm—Cooper has been consistently kind to her in terms of orchestral volume. But 'Mon coeur,' the heart of the opera, achieves that status only through Saint-Saëns' skill rather than Stevens' effort. She can only offer a carefully routed stream where the lava must flow—"well schooled" is the damning comment. Still, a few hooty tones aside, Stevens and Vinay provide some highly charged singing to close the act effectively. While Stevens is always in the dramatic picture, the spirit and mind ever willing, her Dalila remains a brave but ill-considered effort.

Throughout the afternoon, Cooper has been a positive force, occasionally a bit sedate (even in the Bacchanal) or failing to fully relish the composer's sensuous orchestral palette, but more often maintaining a just balance between French nicety and theatrical impact. The chorus is merely serviceable (the women less than that), but the orchestra plays well and, particularly in the introduction to the final act, has an attractive sheen. Cooper adopts an unusually stately pace for the canon duet (here Stevens is again dwarfed, this time by Merrill) which does enable the singers to well articulate the melismas—Stevens' upward scales are neatly done.

Ernster's instrument, though of impressive bulk and marvelously black in color, is variable in pitch and tonal steadiness, deficiencies which deface the lovely concluding phrase of the trio. Hawkins' calliope tones are likewise a disservice to satrap Abimelech. Merrill, on the other hand, continues his impressive series of early career broadcasts with a capital performance. Few voices are innately less French in character, and his vocal production allows no concession to the language itself, but the singing is not only glorious in tone but rhythmically acute and dramatically vivid. Of course, the High Priest is a one-dimensional role (vengeance is his only concern), but Merrill fills that dimension to the full.

As Samson, Vinay is in his element. (One could think him a Latin Vickers in individuality of timbre and musical commitment, though without quite the depth of character immersion.) His timbre is both manly and emotionally vulnerable, as well suited to Samson as to Otello. Avoiding bullish tone, Vinay is both able to meet the role's musical demands and to sustain the heroic aura which a Samson conjures up in our minds—a strong-man capable of a moving confession of love is rare, at least in the opera house. Turning the grindstone, Vinay choses not to wallow in realistic despair; his splendid declamation is a nobler alternative; one might prefer a more doleful tone, but when he reaches the brief prayer, the anguish in his tones is wrenching. In contrast, his final phrases alone are mighty enough to tumble the temple of the Philistines.

French opera at the Metropolitan continued on its wayward path a month later with the *Faust* broadcast on the last day of 1949. The absence of specialists in French style in either *Samson* or *Faust* tells the fate of Johnson's mild efforts to sustain any semblance of authenticity. For decades the decline had been creeping in, and with Johnson's departure the French operatic manner at the Metropolitan expired. Estimable French stylists such as Victoria de los Angeles, Régine Crespin, Alfredo Kraus, Pierre Monteux, and Jean Morel would still inhabit the Met, but the all-purpose singing mode which came to overlay national operatic styles became too pervasive to allow resuscitation of an authentic French manner.

On the broadcasts *Faust* had been guided by Hasselmans, Beecham, and Fourestier, with Pelletier taking periodic control during any hiatus occasioned by their absence. In the 1949 broadcast Pelletier's long acquaintance with the work guarantees a smooth reading, and he never allows the score to languish unduly (no Beechamesque dalliance in the garden-scene duets). Nor does he generate any particular musical distinction. Warren repeats one of his earliest roles—this is his first broadcast Valentin since 1942. Either he is not in best vocal form, or his years in the big baritone parts have thickened his instrument, coarsened his style, and rendered him ill fit for French opera. No wonder Marguerite finds Faust so entrancing with so somber a brother. His climaxes still thrill, and he has the command of the upper range to make the martial moments of the aria speak. But vocal overacting mars his curse and death.

Claramae Turner is a delicious Marthe, excellent in vocal control, never seeking cheap effects, yet creating a vivid character. To say that she equals, and perhaps excels, Votipka in this role is high praise. The other portrayals are all new to the radio audience. Met newcomer Denis Harbour (Wagner) sings with more of the French manner than any other cast member—but this is his only Met season. At the other end of the spectrum is Italo Tajo, whose Méphistophélès is a far distance from the elegant conduct of Marcel Journet and Pol Plançon, or even the witty panache of Pinza. His performance is one long attempt to circumvent the vocal requirements of his role: at his entrance, the long descending scale tumbles midway into laughter;

Faust
31 December 1949
Marguerite
Dorothy Kirsten
Siebel
Inge Manski
Faust
Giuseppe di Stefano
Valentin
Leonard Warren
Méphistophélès
Italo Tajo
Conductor
Wilfred Pelletier

unable to sing an acceptable sustained line for any length of time, a multitude of extraneous noises intrude—his vocal shudder is obsessive today and most wearisome. The Calf of Gold aria moves at a daredevil pace (no harm in that, although marked *allegro maestoso*) and he has a rough ride indeed. Then the presence of the ladies induces a more modest behavior—we can be grateful for that. Tajo does know how to make the brief character turns effective, but an evocative invocation to darkness is technically beyond his means. The church, like the garden, subdues his worst instincts, and later his habitual reliance on vocal grotesquerie makes for a provocative Serenade—insolence and crudity (though perhaps to a degree remote from Gounod's conception) are viable here, and Tajo's professionalism carries the day.

Signor Di Stefano's professional skills are not yet in the same league. The young tenor is naive enough to shun deception, preferring to confront head-on the difficulties of his role. As a consequence, his performance has its ups and downs. A famous "up" is the garden-scene high note in 'Salut! demeure' celebrated by Rudolf Bing in his memoirs. On hand to observe in Johnson's final season, Bing felt that Di Stefano provided the year's "most spectacular single moment" when he effected a diminuendo on Faust's high C in the garden scene. Years later, Bing (not known for sentiment) confided that he had never forgotten "the beauty of that sound."[3] The broadcast may or may not have prompted his comment, but a similar treatment of the note is there. The tenor's frontal attack on the note, open and approaching a shout, is certainly a few steps removed from beauty, but the note is solid and the diminuendo down to A-flat, though very brief, is an effect within the capabilities of few tenors. The remainder of the aria is not remarkable for poise of voice or phrase, the singing more ardent than suave (from Di Stefano's impetuosity one would think Méphisto had been overgenerous in restoring his youth). But then Di Stefano has made no attempt to counterfeit age in old Faust's study, so there is little change to effect. The lengthy duets with Marguerite find the tenor reaching maximum form. His rather bumptious stylistic manner recedes, his dulcet tones completely beguile the ear, and he deploys his ravishing mezza voce frequently and to telling effect. His technique may not be perfect, but his singing is impressive in the aggregate; few maidens could resist his courtship. And as he enters the prison where Marguerite lies, his phrases do take on the bewitching beauty which moved Mr. Bing earlier in the opera.

Faust is our first opportunity to hear Dorothy Kirsten in the staple repertory, in a role where memory recalls Melba, Eames, Farrar, Rethberg, and many a modern-day prima donna. Without quite matching the varied gifts of the above quartet, the American diva meets all the requirements of the role; she gives a lovely performance. With her finely honed instrument, its faint suggestion of nasality in the lower octave and overall silvery timbre, Kirsten is well suited to French opera. Sufficiently pointed to complement the language (though diction could be more idiomatic), her tones are blessedly free from the excessive astringency which plagues many a French soprano.

The Jewel Song has a delightful sparkle, with plenty of youthful enthusiasm at her find (is it a shade strong on aggressive greed at the expense of charm?), a full-blooded high B (almost pushed sharp), and wonder of wonders, a true trill. In recitative she relies too often on a whispered kind of gasp (it must serve to convey both Marguerite's ecstatic discovery of the jewels and her terror in church), and when in prison Marguerite's mind wanders over the past, Kirsten doesn't savor the remembrances with sufficient fondness. Though not an overly imaginative singing-

Dorothy Kirsten as Marguerite in *Faust*.

actress, she is always in the dramatic picture, and her beautiful voice and its skillful use are a joy. She conducts a better line in portions of the garden duets than Di Stefano (but oddly evokes less emotive response—one can't feel the completeness of her submission, while the tenor's ardor is never in doubt). All of the top notes in the garden and prison scenes are rendered full-voice with none of the thinning of tone which she practiced in later years. If Kirsten doesn't quite dominate the final act as a Marguerite should, she never falls below an estimable standard. No wonder in this same season Kirsten was assigned the role of Manon Lescaut in one of the few new productions of the entire Johnson tenure. The radio audience heard the Puccini opera for the first time on 10 December 1949, two weeks after its premiere.

Manon Lescaut had been absent from the Met for two decades. The opera had enjoyed remarkable popularity in the earlier part of the century after Caruso and the beauteous Lina Cavalieri had ensured initial acceptance at its premiere in 1907. At the Metropolitan's ill-fated Paris venture of 1910, the opera had provided Bori the opportunity for an unforeseen debut, which led to her long tenure as the company's lyric soprano *assoluta*. Muzio and Martinelli, Alda and Gigli, were later potent pairs. Though granted the honor of opening the 1929–30 season (Bori, Gigli, De Luca, and Serafin), the opera thereafter was ignored until Johnson, perhaps fondly remembering his own triumphs as Des Grieux in Italy and at the Met (one performance only), brought the opera again into favor. Puccini's maiden success has seldom been absent from American opera stages since the 1949 revival.

Antonicelli begins the broadcast with a fervor appropriate to the score, a score bursting with musical energy which the youthful Puccini felt no need to constrain. Its interpreters (on this occasion Kirsten, Bjoerling, Valdengo, and Baccaloni) must feel a similar impetuosity if the drama is to ring true; or better yet, they must convey that abandon without descending to crudities of style. Unfortunately, Antonicelli, after a well-knit first act, too often allows the pace to lag, the tension to slacken. The great duet, the heart of the opera, in particular fails to flame. Perhaps because of the newness of the opera to orchestra and chorus (this is the third Met performance of the run), the conductor's priority seems to be coordination rather than interpretation. The women's chorus needs constant watching, and Puccini's eighteenth-century simulations in the second act fail to convince—the "artificiality" of the madrigal lacks manneristic touches, the minuet is poorly coordinated. Nor does Antonicelli lighten the burden of hero and heroine by winging their more arduous solo moments. Bjoerling manages to overcome the deficiency; Kirsten, more often, cannot.

Puccini has merely appliquéd, however skillfully, the remaining principals to the drama, and they function capably on this afternoon. Thomas Hayward is an excellent Edmondo, capable of removing the tedium from the student levity which the opening curtain reveals. De Paolis' decadent tenor is unction itself when instructing Manon in the minuet, while Paul Franke's baritonal tenor fixes our attention in the important Lamplighter vignette. Madeira is too rough of voice for the delicate charm of the madrigal. Baccaloni, the consummate clown, is equally master of the nasty— no vocal tomfoolery mars his portrait of Geronte. He prepares us well for Geronte's vindictive accusation of Manon at the close of act two. Baccaloni and Valdengo make vivid their brief scenes together, in particular plotting their future entrapment of Manon with such relish that (with Antonicelli's telling assistance) the first act comes to a lively close. Valdengo is a boon throughout the entire afternoon. To hear a role so fully explored, so suavely delivered, the character revealed with no disservice to the music, the music flowering with no diminution in portraiture, is gratifying. And

Manon Lescaut
10 December 1949

Manon Lescaut
Dorothy Kirsten
Des Grieux
Jussi Bjoerling
Edmondo
Thomas Hayward
Lescaut
Giuseppe Valdengo
Geronte
Salvatore Baccaloni
Conductor
Giuseppe Antonicelli

vocally, the role is entirely within the capabilities of his modest baritone.

The afternoon is a triumph for Bjoerling. Perhaps no other role is so well suited to the tenor's vocal and interpretive gifts as Puccini's lovestruck Des Grieux. Though he was stiff in action on stage, one would never know it from his pointedly inflected, passionate singing. Now at the midpoint of his two decade span with the Metropolitan, musical style and vocal form are in perfect balance. He imbues 'Tra voi, belle' with the jaunty rhythms of youth and just a dash of *slancio*, well conveying the innocence and eagerness of the idealistic Chevalier. The full-throated close of 'Donna non vidi mai' marks the man altered by love, while the elegantly drawn opening lines confirm Des Grieux's virtue. Here, and in the duet before the lovers depart for Paris, textual nuances are savored, tone is varied, and above all, without the Puccini tenor's proclivity to bellow, he conveys all the young man's ardor. In their duets he (unlike Kirsten) is adept at converting mere notes into an arched phrase, his top voice now flashing out, now shining quietly (the *piano* caress he bestows on 'soffrir' at the close of the act-two duet is delectable). If 'Sempre la stessa!' is not as emotionally shattering as his later commercial recording, the climactic phrases of the act are splendid. The high resonance he chooses to employ as he awaits Manon on the dock at Le Havre (a silvery, incisive tone is the consequence) makes his lament doubly affecting. Throughout the act he disdains the vocal sob, able to suggest remorse through vocal color alone. But not even Bjoerling can quite overcome Antonicelli's methodical manner in 'Guardate, pazzo son,' and at its close (after a stentorian high B) Bjoerling capitulates and erupts into a burst of sobs completely foreign to his usual pose. That Bjoerling has supplied the emotional fervor of the afternoon is reaffirmed in the final act: he soars, he implores, railing persuasively against fate until, without a sob, he accepts Manon's death.

Kirsten is no stranger to Manon's weal and woe. Her Metropolitan appearances having been prefaced by performances in Mexico and with the New York City Center Opera, her portrayal is free of tentativeness. Her honeyed tones and girlish naiveté are most effective at Manon's entrance; 'Una fanciulla' is delightfully spun out, and her top tones are bracingly on the mark. But Manon's vanity and volatility are not much in evidence as she prepares for her miniature levy in act two; the soprano fails to articulate the text with sufficient bite and clarity. 'In quelle trine morbide,' Manon's supreme solo moment, is astonishingly matter-of-fact in contour, but how effortlessly the voice is projected, and how lovely the tones are in themselves— Kirsten seems entirely oblivious of the text's import.

By now it is clear that this Manon is a porcelain creature with a doll's feelings and tones. 'L'ora, o Tirsi' (its initial phrase aspirated) is neat but tiny-toned, the voice whitened unduly to aid negotiation, the high C slightly thin. I hear no difference between her complaisant self-appraisal ('Sarò la più bella') and her greeting of Des Grieux ('Tu? Sei tu, amore, tu'). The hypercharged phrases of the duet do not flame with passion, nor are they propelled by adequate thrusts of tone or varied rhythmic impulse. While Kirsten takes care not to unduly expand her top voice (she experiences, in fact, one perilous moment), even here the vocalism per se is consistently lovely. With childlike glee she laughs at old Geronte and subsequently begs Des Grieux's pardon most appealingly. Sadly, in Antonicelli's loose hands the frantic turmoil of the jewel gathering is dissipated as Puccini's music turns into mere bombast.

Since projection of despair is evidently not within the soprano's ken, the final two acts lack an appropriate focus. As Manon wastes away in the Louisiana desert, we hear the same doll-like silvery tones as at the inn at Amiens. (Vocal size is not a requisite for projection of the grander emotions, as Sayão repeatedly has demonstrated.) Does Manon suffer?—'Orribilmente!' Kirsten replies, but we cannot believe her. 'Sola, perduta, abbandonata,' while not devoid of pathos, lacks grandeur; so much depends on skill in parlando, and Kirsten is only moderately accomplished in the technique. The soprano is husbanding her lower octave as well, but when, in the final phrases of the aria, the voice rises, she makes a fine effect. In Manon's final moments Kirsten is inattentive to the veristic *accenti* ('Ahime' is amazingly prosaic), and we are not disposed to weep. That this very able American soprano would increasingly forswear roles which complement her considerable vocal and interpretive abilities in favor of an almost complete diet of Puccini heroines would be difficult to imagine from this initial acquaintance with her veristic competence. But those widely disseminated photos of Kirsten as Manon Lescaut are exquisite and perhaps lend credence to her choice.

Throughout this era Albanese was the paramount Puccini interpreter, and she assumed the role of Manon Lescaut later in the season. Both her Butterfly and Mimi were offered to the radio public during this final Johnson season. Like most Met *Butterfly* performances of the period, the broadcast of 18 February 1950 is undermanned; Melton and Brownlee are again on hand, evidently on the theory that Anglo-Saxon miens justify the ends. Their prosaic readings and receding ranges suggest these models should be taken out of service; indeed, this will prove to be Melton's final Met season. Melchiorre Luise's thunder is small-scale, so even Melton can rout this Bonze. De Paolis and Cehanovsky were the first broadcast portrayers of Goro and Yamadori and, before ending their careers, would rack up an unbroken string of nine and thirteen radio portraits. Even at the midpoint, the wear of age is evident on sustained tones (De Paolis really creaks), but their ability to paint character is undiminished. Thelma Altman opens the second act with a wobbly prayer, but thereafter her rather soprano-like mezzo is pleasant enough and well matched for size and warmth of tone with Albanese's voice in the flower duet (though the mezzo mars the critical moment by a delayed descent from the high tenuto).

Even more than usual any distinction in the performance falls to conductor Antonicelli and Albanese. They supply it. Antonicelli, alive to the constant fluctuations of tempo and dynamics and the subtleties of orchestral detail, manages to knit the minutiae into a continuous whole. His freely flowing phrases broaden easily into climactic gestures. Though the humming chorus is overly casual, and his treatment of the final brass theme more brisk than shattering, overall his approach mirrors Albanese's way with the score and enables the soprano to contribute a memorable performance.

That the end result will be so satisfying is not apparent at the soprano's entrance. As she climbs the harbor hill at Nagasaki, one hears some of that vocal thickening which infects a few of Albanese's commercial recordings of these mid-career years. Nuances of tone and volume are less delicate, phrase shapings are less polished, words are entities in themselves rather than laid into the line in the remembered Albanese fashion. At the entrance aria's close, a hearty breath promotes a stentorian high D-flat which ensures audience acclaim—that hint of a scream in it seems entirely foreign to her ever-reliable top notes. Ten years after her Metropolitan debut in this role, is the diva's object a grander vocal splash?

All fears are soon allayed. The voice merely needed some priming. The ascent over, Albanese settles into her familiar mold of creating character with myriad inflec-

Madama Butterfly
18 February 1950

Cio-Cio-San
Licia Albanese
Suzuki
Thelma Altman
Pinkerton
James Melton
Sharpless
John Brownlee
Conductor
Giuseppe Antonicelli

tions of word and tone. Her parlando is just as charming and natural as recollected, and how easily it erupts into song. Her tone in 'Ieri son salita' may be a touch thready, but Butterfly's confession of conversion is beautifully phrased. By the time she arrives at the love duet, Albanese's voice is fully responsive, flowing expansively, the top resplendent as usual. The balance between delicate nuance and grand manner may be tipped a little in favor of the latter (as it will be throughout the afternoon), but the sacrifice of a bit of inner quiet ('Dolce notte!') has other compensations.

In the remainder of the opera Albanese's authority is absolute. Not only is she mistress of the role's interpretive demands but her voice is completely responsive to her wishes. With liquid, gentle tones she leads us into the aria (the attack on 'Un bel dì' is oddly accented), and she provides the widest gamut of nuance as she narrates Butterfly's hopes. The climax is as firm and free as ever.

As the opera progresses, Albanese's immersion in Butterfly's fate overcomes any remnant of the diva mode. Everything rings true. Her restraint and delicacy in the letter scene are most affecting. In contrast, the sighting of the ship is almost reckless in its vocal abandon, but her voice responds splendidly to her demands. Again a sea change occurs as the girls gather flowers; Albanese's singing is all delicious composure and spontaneous curves. When Butterfly calls for her bridal vestments, the soprano invests her request with almost holy significance. In the unique manner in which Albanese combines tone and text, the lullaby all but overflows with love (does the high B sag a mite?), while her tragic power quickens the confrontation with Kate. The resignation in her voice as Butterfly accepts the inevitable ('Triste madre!') is crushing to the auditor. And she has plenty of vocal thrust to make the farewell to her child a thrilling climax to the afternoon. Once again Albanese's command of a wide range of emotional states, combined with her vocal poise, provides a portrait whose fullness is uncommon even in that age of convincing characterizations.

The Puccini resurgence, begun in the early forties, is by now in full swing; for the first time the broadcast season contains four Puccini operas. On 21 January 1950 *Tosca* is aired with Roman and Tagliavini, in new broadcast portrayals, badgered by Alexander Sved, an old hand at police brutality. It is a Janus-faced performance. Pit and stage seem to be in different worlds. Antonicelli operates within zones of musical and dramatic probity, letting the visceral theatricality of the piece speak for itself; no need to pump it up further. Rather it is the lyrical beauty of the score which receives his fondest attention—all to Puccini's gain. If no shabbiness dwells in the pit, more than enough lives on stage; Roman and Sved are bent on serving Sardou at Puccini's expense.

Is Tosca excitable, capricious, volatile?—without doubt. Pitch each of those moods up another notch or two and you have a soprano in a near-frenzy for most of the afternoon. Such is the broadcast Roman diva. Oddly enough, the voice seems more firmly anchored than in many of her Verdi portrayals; it has the right weight and a captivating color for the part. And she is certainly alive to the text—in fact, she all but devours it. Apt touches there are: her entrance *Mario*s are fearfully imperious; 'Il prezzo!' is merely a quiet response to Scarpia's 'Quanto?' and more effective than the usual snarl; her revelation of Angelotti's hiding place is a breathless, whispered rush of words, psychologically telling. But 'E avanti a lui tremava tutta Roma' is almost laughably stagy. Puccini has given his soprano a clutch of brief outbursts of tone (especially in the struggle with Scarpia), and since this is Roman's normal operational mode, she scores in these moments. More often the Puccini phrase is slighted, dissected, pummeled. Some of the intervallic leaps are unprepared and the final

Tosca
21 January 1950

Tosca
Stella Roman
Cavaradossi
Ferruccio Tagliavini
Scarpia
Alexander Sved
Sacristan
Gerhard Pechner
Conductor
Giuseppe Antonicelli

resting place is dubious. (At the close of the second act Cross informs us that Roman is wearing Muzio's "tiara of diamonds and gold leaves"—harrowing thought!) Her third act is quite wretched, the vocal and dramatic detritis strewn all over the stage. Roman does turn a profit with 'Vissi d'arte.' Though plagued by shortness of breath, she sings with strong intent and the climaxes (three) are stunning, the final one a ravishing spin of shimmering *piano* tone continuing long after the orchestral release. The audience loves it.

This was Roman's final broadcast. After a decade of also-ran status in the hierarchy of Met divas, she would not continue under the new regime. She bore no grudge: "Mr. Bing came in and had all his own group of singers. He did not need me,"[4] Roman told Lanfranco Rasponi, but she added that Johnson "knew voices and how to treat singers. His successor was another story." Since Roman made almost no commercial recordings, only the broadcasts remain of her years of prominence at the Metropolitan.

Sved, too, is on the Bing termination list. In vocal bulk the baritone is just as potent as ever, but now age sits upon his tone and a sizable wobble distorts it. No shortage of menace in his manner, though, and he is one baritone who can dominate the Te Deum. But the interpretation is too one-dimensional, though that dimension is effective. In the seduction scene he and Roman provide highly charged, elemental theatrics. It is amusing to hear how wickedly he plays the part to Roman's perpetually affronted Tosca—he offers us a vocal mustache twirl. Though hardly a hint of suavity invades his singing ('Già mi struggea' is chewed to bits), by this time in the performance a goodly measure of the remembered fruity color makes his tone quite digestible.

With Hungarian Sved, Rumanian Roman, Hungarian Alvary (Angelotti), and German Pechner on stage, a central European imprint marks the performance. In spite of a bit of odd Italian here and there, Alvary limns a vivid portrait of the escaped political prisoner (the burst of tone as he names Scarpia is impressive). Pechner is even more unidiomatic (boasting no core of Italianate tone, he must bark—often he sounds as though his voice is housed in a small-sized cistern). Still, his Sacristan is refreshingly free of comic tricks.

Clearly, anything distinctive on stage must come from Tagliavini. Cavaradossi is not a role well tailored to his gifts. The tenor must resort to his least attractive vocal production to manage the stentorian outbursts with which the role is mined. Not that he doesn't successfully negotiate them—his 'Vittoria!' (preceded by a good deal of ironic laughter) is stout enough to shame many a more robust tenor. In the denunciation of Scarpia in act one, the top B is clearly the thing—getting there is rather treacherous. 'Recondita armonia' occurs, as it does for most tenors, too early in the afternoon to be entirely free from effort, but Tagliavini's reading is beautifully laid out in phrase and justly balanced between dulcet and healthy tone. He comes into his own in the final act where Puccini has alloted the prisoner abundant ruminative moments. Once again the Gigli-like timbre conquers complaint; it is vastly appealing in the pathetic opening recitatives. Tagliavini has a way with words reiterated on a single note, and his mezza voce (subtract a couple of near-falsetto top tones) marries Puccini's mood in 'E lucevan le stelle'; he manages the transition to a plangent full-voice in excellent fashion. While Roman spews and gasps, he wraps Tosca's sweet hands in exquisitely gentle tones—a lovely Tagliavini moment in what is, overall, a *Tosca* more suited to a provincial house than the touted Metropolitan.

Tagliavini finds a happier milieu in the bel canto environment of *L'Elisir d'Amore* in the Christmas Eve broadcast matinee. His cohorts are a much more likable group as well: Sayão, Valdengo, and Baccaloni. One anticipates an idiomatic, stylistically apt performance with plenty of vocal blandishment; one is not disappointed.

Antonicelli is not as sure-footed in the opera buffa realm. He holds the reins a little too taut so that the comic spirit cannot escape in the orchestral and choral passages. Rhythms and dynamics are maintained overlong on a plateau. But he controls a well-knit performance with no mishaps and, with this quartet of principals, plenty of high humor.

No conductor could corral Baccaloni for long. Still, once past the hard sell of his elixir, he is well within the zones of acceptable buffo behavior. Antonicelli sets a modest tempo for 'Udite, o rustici,' and Baccaloni has no trouble spilling out the patter in big, black tones. He does more than a few passages à la Rex (*My Fair Lady*) Harrison, and the concluding high Es are nowhere near the pitch (mercifully the chorus comes to his aid with loud guffaws in order to cover the discrepancies). Basso and tenor play off each other delightfully in their scenes; when they come to the duets proper they are more discreet, Tagliavini ever seeking the opportunity to sustain a melodic line, Baccaloni now in full command of his brilliant patter mode. The basso is in firm, colorful voice in the second act, weaving his patter around Sayão's melody in their duet not only with expertise but with accuracy.

For once Belcore is something more than a strutting bore. Even Valdengo can make little of the sergeant's martial aria; the bottom of his voice disappears and both singing and interpretation are ordinary. But in the first-act finale he converts the love tangle into a triangle through his emphatic and characterful singing. Belcore becomes a worthy rival for Adina's hand. In fact, the finale, thanks to Valdengo and Antonicelli's expansive way, gains in emotional weight, with Sayão and Tagliavini also contributing to the heightened affect. The baritone may blur a bit of the fioriture in 'Venti scudi' (though elsewhere his florid work is, by current baritone standards, more than acceptable), but again he lifts Belcore out of the bin of stock buffa characters. Paula Lenchner, too, scores in Giannetta's few moments, revealing a bright, flavorful voice and acting with assurance.

Tagliavini is a memorable Nemorino. He strikes the right balance between appealing clown and cherishable lover. In superb vocal form, his top voice is reliable at all dynamic levels, and he overlays Donizetti's melodies with a variety of coloration that few tenors can match. His is a fully rounded portrait, terribly assured in both musical and comedic aspects. 'Quanto è bella' is a simple piece, but Tagliavini grasps its fluid rhetoric and honors the four or five rhythmic gaits within its modest compass. In the duet with Adina he shows a decent command of melisma, and though his ravishing demitints are laid on wherever possible, he is no tenorino sighing on the breeze—Tagliavini offers an abundance of full-throated vocalism with a minimum of blatant open tone. The tenor acts an amusing drunkard, the 'la la la' bursts of confidence unforced. 'Esulti pur la barbara' has just the right combination of humor and song, with a dash of *slancio*. Unlike most Nemorinos, Tagliavini can modulate his voice when entwined with Adina in thirds and sixths; in the cadenza both he and Sayão are superb. I find his part in 'Venti scudi' overly blunt in tone quality and volume, but there can be no question about 'Una furtiva lagrima'—memory calls up few finer renderings. A particular joy is the lack of affectation in his interpretation: no exaggeration, no setting up of vocal tricks (not even a head voice 'una' or swooning *portamento* to begin), no lingering on sustained tones, no undue pauses. He takes the aria at a pace a shade faster than favored by other tenors. And yet it makes a stunning

L'Elisir d'Amore
24 December 1949
Adina
Bidú Sayão
Nemorino
Ferruccio Tagliavini
Belcore
Giuseppe Valdengo
Dulcamara
Salvatore Baccaloni
Conductor
Giuseppe Antonicelli

effect, in part because it rings Nemorino's sincerity even as it demonstrates Tagliavini's vocal expertise. Where most tenors have to counterfeit the tried and true *accenti* which all lovers of bel canto expect, with Tagliavini they are truly the building blocks of his instrument and technique. I do wish he had added (after his expert cadenza) a *messa di voce* on the final dominant, but one shouldn't be gluttonous where so much vocal suavity abounds. Still no sign on this afternoon of that vocal dismemberment, that audible gear-shifting, which lay in his future.

The vocal mating of Tagliavini and Sayão is a complete joy. How seldom one hears artists of similar scale in duets—management almost never seems to consider it when casting. Interpretively, too, Sayão and Tagliavini are in the same orbit. Inevitably they find the judicious balance between comic play and musical expression. Sayão makes malicious fun of the Isolde tale, not afraid to be brittle-toned in the dotted refrain and as deft as ever in the triplet coloratura decorations. In spinning a long-limbed Donizetti phrase she is without equal ('Chiedi all'aura'). Unlike her 1942 portrayal, she adopts a pinching nasality for the little barcarole, but remember, she is up against a Baccaloni who is visually on the loose in these late Johnson stagings.

'Quanto amore!' brings out all the loveliest aspects of her art. The voice still retains a full, silvery core of tone, and she bewitchingly manipulates the melodies and roulades of the duet—no clowning now, Baccaloni or no. Does any soprano relish having to follow 'Una furtiva lagrima?' Sayão need not fear. 'Prendi, per me' is exquisitely shaded, each note etched and placed with exactitude into the phrase. Her rendering is a little heavy on pathos (perhaps stepped up a notch to make up for Donizetti having served Adina less well than Nemorino); thus it is a bit less stylistically pure than in 1942, and needlessly so, for the vocalism is equally superb. Sayão attacks the florid measures of Adina's capitulation with abandon (and a sharp tone or two). Clearly, her zest for performance is undiminished.

With such a performance in the memory it is hard to understand Bing's rejection of this most delightful artist. The new manager was noncommital about reengaging her: if the company should do *Bohème*, Bing seemed to recall promising her two performances (so he wrote Max Rudolf);[5] but Rudolf (who would become Bing's major factotum for the next half dozen or so years) fought for her. He noted that "if we offer her the two Bohèmes it would be an affront not to offer the Broadcast."[6] Thus Sayão was granted at least a radio farewell as Mimi in the broadcast of 17 March 1951 with Di Stefano, Valdengo, and Siepi. She would remain with the company for two Bing years, her allotment a paltry pair of *Bohèmes* each season and a final Manon in Boston (at that city's request) in April 1952.[7] Perhaps Bing felt her particular *Fach* best served by youth; the soprano was fifty years old at the time of her Met retirement. Judging by her broadcast Adina, her capabilities were intact and the illusion of youth in her art was paramount. No future soubrette has equaled her in certain roles. "What has been, has been,"[8] she could only comment in later years.

As the careers of longtime favorites were drawing to a close, the light of public favor refocused on new artists, of whom none shone more brightly than the charismatic Ljuba Welitch (by now, she has dropped an *s*). Curiously, her Met career would end at the same time as that of Sayão—a reminder of the inconstant glow of fame.

The soprano followed her triumph as Salome with Aida, her only Verdi venture at the Metropolitan, a portrayal heard by the radio public both in 1949 and on 11 March 1950. Three young stalwart Americans (Harshaw, Merrill, Hines) who would continue into the Bing regime (and beyond, for the men), manipulate warrior Vinay with varying degrees of success. Emil Cooper's evocative, fluid prelude arouses expectations, but he soon allows the dull glaze of repertory routine to settle over chorus and orchestra. But then, he has his hands full just keeping tabs on Welitch.

Vinay, for all his earnestness, is an unsatisfactory Radames. His vocal production is overly congested on this afternoon, the tone too often diffuse, the effort too palpable for the listener's comfort, let alone his. 'Celeste Aida' is, if possible, less heavenly than on other occasions—maybe Jean de Reszke had the right idea, after all, when he refused to sing it. Vinay pleases with an occasional interpretative touch (in the Nile scene), and he has ready to hand that mantle of nobility which enables him to be credible in the tomb scene. Even the gossamer duet phrases are kept aloft by his musicality. Merrill is an imposing Amonasro. The voice is incredibly sonorous and its timbral warmth unequaled. He is quite attentive to the musical and dramatic demands, preserving line and the *accenti*. No change of color or caress, though, as he pleads for the Ethiopian prisoners. Now in his fifth Met season, a few of the later Merrill mannerisms intrude in the duet with Aida. But there are welcome interpretive insights, too, especially the tonal coloration at 'Ei t'ama.' Hines, not yet thirty, sounds surprisingly off form, the tone less plangent, even a bit unsteady—the absence of vitality in his tone and manner is worrisome. But before the afternoon is out he recovers vocal substance, though the manner remains lugubrious. Alvary's tone is wooly, but his legato serves Verdi well enough, in spite of an occasional 'Dunqve' for 'Dunque' from this Egyptian King. Paul Franke's Messenger is aggressive and sturdy of tone.

In her third broadcast of Amneris, Harshaw is a paradox. By now eminently soprano in color and technique, though not in name, she stands entirely outside the role's theatrics. Her judgment scene is slack and ineffectual, and *passione* is in short supply as she pleads with Radames; Harshaw simply refuses to indulge in those healthy vulgarisms so dear to the dramatic mezzo and the gallery. The result is a lovely singing lesson, but no Amneris. Earlier in the opera, it's a different story, though the vocalism is the same (surprising how often Verdi has marked *grazioso* in Amneris' part). Here Harshaw sings with fine musicality and genuinely seductive charm—'Ah! vieni, amor mio' and her courting of Aida are lovely moments. Harshaw owns a beautiful instrument, and she has absorbed her coaching well; a decided upgrading of her abilities is apparent. It only remains to move her into her true *Fach*.

None could doubt that Welitch is prima donna on this afternoon, both in the literal and old-fashioned sense of the term. Beauties abound. Welitch's solid core of silvery tone conjures up remembrance of Rethberg in its combination of honey and ice (though with Welitch the proportions are reversed in favor of the latter). I doubt that any major soprano of modern times has been more willful in performance. Erratic or wildly abandoned she is not, but like an unbridled thoroughbred, she races through the score savoring none of its varied treats. No, she is rather a champion hurdler (to try another image) to whom the challenge of the course is nothing, even though the role of Aida is mined with vocal pitfalls that have worried great sopranos to distraction.

But back to those beauties. In the first-act trio she takes hold of Aida's lines and makes them soar to stunning effect. Yes, her attack is occasionally sloppy, but then most of the time no current soprano could match it. More concerned with tone and line than diction, Welitch allows little of Aida's personality to be revealed beyond what music without words can convey—in fact, Welitch's singing is essentially instru-

Aida
11 March 1950

Aida
Ljuba Welitch
Amneris
Margaret Harshaw
Radames
Ramon Vinay
Amonasro
Robert Merrill
Ramfis
Jerome Hines
Conductor
Emil Cooper

mental in conception and execution. Her syncopations in the ensemble are thus thrillingly exact. She enjoys them so much she adds an extra pair, and ends up two beats behind for three full measures, with Vinay trying to hold his own against her. Welitch has a casual way with rhythm throughout the afternoon, and Cooper has a hard time keeping up with her as she charges along.

Welitch handily rides Verdi's elevator lines in 'Ritorna vincitor!' with no loss of color or register break, but all sections of the aria are treated alike ('e l'amor mio?' provokes no mood change). Both renderings of 'Numi pietà' are lovely in tone, the first one marred by haste. 'O patria mia,' too, moves at a rapid clip and has insufficient atmosphere, but the high C is incredibly pure and easy, with even a modicum of diminuendo (and she has set up the mood in the preceding recitative where she shows she can inflect the word). Aida's appeal to her father (on reiterated tones) also makes a strong effect. Her seduction of Radames ('Là tra foreste') is insinuating enough and well controlled, though she rushes two beats ahead to the high G in the unison duet. Her vocalism, as such, is consistent and stunning in itself, but one begins to long for a few moments of repose. In the tomb 'Vedi? di morte' is lovely, though the instrumental cast and rapid pace negate the ethereal calm Verdi deserves. But 'O terra addio' is glorious, an effortless stream of pure, silvery tone.

The lights come up. "The world of make-believe gives way to reality"—the words come from Cross. Hearing Welitch's assured performance, one might wonder how long this flame could burn. She might have undertaken other Verdi roles at the Metropolitan for our delectation. To her Donna Anna, Tosca, Rosalinda, and that single notorious Musetta could have been added at least the *Ballo* heroine; her records of the arias are superb. But time was running out.

Absent Milanov, the Metropolitan felt it worthwhile to tap Varnay's potential as a Verdi spinto soprano. With Warren having attained the fullness of his vocal and interpretive powers, a revival of *Simon Boccanegra* was in order, and Varnay was called to service as Maria/Amelia.

The casting of Tucker, Valdengo, and Mihaly Székely added further potential to the revival. At the helm was the unlikely Fritz Stiedry. Unlikely, at least, in terms of his Met career thus far, which—since his 1946 debut with *Siegfried*—had included *Hänsel und Gretel, Parsifal, Die Zauberflöte*, and the ill-fated Lee Simonson-designed *Ring* cycle. The Teutonic repertory was his heritage by his Viennese birth. Early in the century, Mahler had recommended him as coach at Dresden. A conducting career in the lesser German centers (including, in 1914, the first non-Bayreuth *Parsifal* in Cassel) led to longer engagements in Berlin and Vienna, where he succeeded Felix Weingartner. In the early thirties Stiedry replaced Walter as principal conductor of the Berlin Municipal Opera. It was there, before seeking refuge from the Nazis in Russia, that he and stage director Carl Ebert presided over the Verdi renaissance; *Simon Boccanegra* was one of the Verdi operas which they brought back to the fold. A resident of the United States since 1937, he had had to struggle for recognition until, in 1946, his Met engagement brought him back upon the major musical scene. He proved himself another in that distinguished line of conductors whom Johnson brought to the company. His twelve-year tenure was longer lasting, and in some ways of greater impact, than that of some of his more celebrated colleagues.

From the beginning of his Met career Stiedry longed to realign himself with the Verdi operas. "Please accept my urgent appeal not to consider me merely as a conductor or a kind of 'specialist' of Wagner,"[9] he wrote Johnson at the close of his first season. "The surest way to make me grow tired of this composer is to have me

Simon Boccanegra
28 January 1950

Maria/Amelia
Astrid Varnay
Gabriele
Richard Tucker
Simon
Leonard Warren
Fiesco
Mihaly Székely
Paolo
Giuseppe Valdengo
Conductor
Fritz Stiedry

Ljuba Welitch as Donna Anna in *Don Giovanni*.

conduct his music exclusively." He reminded the manager that his "European reputation was founded also on my conducting of Verdi, Mozart and Strauss. I belonged to the founders of the so-called 'Verdi Renaissance.'" Three years later *Boccanegra* was his reward. The Bing years would see his oversight of *Don Carlo, Otello,* and *La Forza* as well.

He was right to put himself forward. The *Boccanegra* broadcast is one of the finest Verdi performances of the decade, for Stiedry is alive to Verdi's mobile dialectic. He does not overweight the sombre prologue, overcast as it is with conspiracy and death—the main events are yet to come, he seems to say. The fleetness of the prelude, the dynamic vitality of the string pizzicati as Paolo muses, the stealthy agitation as Pietro's forces gather, the plasticity of Paolo's 'L'atra magion vedere?'—all these brief moments of the prologue signal Stiedry's discerning response to both music and drama. Most notable, he always embraces the graphic image: he savors the trills as Amelia views the sea; the entire prelude and accompaniment to her aria are as fresh as the sea breeze Amelia enjoys. (A quite different evocation is the orchestral melancholy which accompanies Boccanegra's lonely voicing of 'Il mare! il mare!') Nor does Stiedry neglect to care for the singers' molding of word and musical phrase. Pacing and control of the contrasting moods of the council chamber scene are worthy of Verdi's inspiration (the 'Plebe! Patrizi!' ensemble receives a heartrending performance). The depth of his feeling suffuses so many moments of this remarkable score—in the end he weaves a heavenly orchestral web as Boccanegra utters his benediction on the lovers.

With a single exception the performance on stage is equally accomplished. Valdengo's superb Paolo heightens the dramatic conflict of the score. Warren, in his debut performance a decade earlier, could not match the skillful portrait which the experienced Italian baritone draws. This is luxury casting, for Valdengo was not only the Met's Figaro, Germont, Di Luna, and Ford, but Toscanini's Iago and, only two months after this *Boccanegra* broadcast, his Falstaff. He carries the aura of Iago with him to Paolo—his manner is wonderfully sinister and manipulative. As Valdengo recalls Boccanegra's curse he combines guilt, horror, and evil in a few brief utterances. In their different ways, this Paolo and Doge are equals.

As Fiesco, newcomer Mihaly Székely is a solid addition to a bass roster sadly depleted by the departures of Kipnis and Pinza. The Hungarian had frequented the stages of Budapest, Berlin, Vienna, Bergamo, and Florence before his 1947 Met debut. His impressive instrument bears both the merits and drawbacks of his Slavic heritage. 'Il lacerato spirito' has immense dignity and emotional impact, but one resents any slight bludgeoning of Italian lyricism; bulk he has in plenty, but a Pinza-like legato would make many a phrase more effective. The resonant burr of his low voice satisfies—these are healthy sounds indeed. As the opera progresses, his granitic tones and chiseled molding of phrases well suit the unforgiving Fiesco. The prologue duet with Boccanegra provides an intriguing contrast of temperaments, Székely's Christoff-like tone (conveying now the worn distress, now the sternness of the old man) pitted against Warren's now spinning, now thrusting lines. And by the time Székely reaches the closing scene, his voice has taken on a more cultivated sheen. He and the Doge finally come to an understanding, and as he learns Amelia's identity, his vocal stoniness melts, to moving effect.

At the time, Varnay's venture into the Italian repertory evoked considerable critical acclaim, even prompting some to pronounce her a worthy candidate for the sparsely populated Italian dramatic soprano ranks. The broadcast belies that judgment.

One must honor her sound musicianship and the obvious care and sincerity of her portrayal. But the opening phrases of 'Come quest'ora bruna' are shocking to the ear: how cold and spare the tone, how constrained the vowel sounds, how lacking in fluidity the phrase! Varnay's sound is devoid of blandishment. Not all Italian dramatic sopranos have the velvet of a Ponselle or a Milanov, but the more steely voiced of the breed (a Caniglia, a Giannini) have so many compensatory virtues that the lack is hardly regretted. It would be wrong, too, to deny something intriguing in the Varnay sound, but it lies more in the intent than the result. As Amelia and Gabriele voice their love, Varnay works a few intimate effects, and she knows how to expand a line. But her efforts pale as Tucker plants a veritable caress upon 'Ripara i tuoi pensieri.' Varnay is better at conveying the excitement of the moment, and both singers excel in the cabaletta. Her lower octave warms in the recognition scene, the style of 'Ah se la speme' is right, her excitement at remembering her youth expertly planned, and the final top tone well controlled (though it doesn't quite sum up the elation of discovery as Verdi intended). Throughout the duet Varnay's care for musical detail has its own rewards, and her exchanges with Warren conjure a touching father-daughter intimacy.

Amelia's *racconto* detailing her abduction is aptly dramatic, with compelling weight of voice, but occasionally hollow-toned. In the 'Patrizi' ensemble Varnay offers a more liquid tone and surprises with a perfectly lovely trill, the two tones clear, but liquid; only a downward octave *portamento* would have added to the moment. But further disappointment lies ahead. Swallowed tone and pencil-thin line will not allow the Verdi melodies to bloom (and thereby to affect us) in the second-act duet with Gabriele. A vocal quaver prevents her from placing with exactitude the all-important syncopations of the final trio—the surges of feeling in Stiedry's orchestra make up the difference.

Tucker is in superb form all afternoon. His legato line and collected tone serve the offstage Serenata well. The tenor embraces every opportunity to allow phrases (even the briefest) to flower, a predilection particularly welcome in this most austere of Verdi operas. He has a powerful command of declamation as well, as is evident in the council chamber scene and, especially, when consumed by jealousy in the recitative of the second act. The young Tucker is pushed to the limit of his vocal resources in the first section of the aria, though his voicing of 'Pietà, gran Dio' is most affecting. The cantabile of 'Cielo pietoso' should be more his province, but he is a shade spent from the turmoil of the opening section and vocally a little less secure. (Seeing Tucker in this scene twenty-three years later at the Met, I marveled at his reckless expenditure of tone in both sections—a formidable display for a tenor just short of sixty.) Tucker recovers completely for the duet with Varnay and reaches the apogee of his performance in the terzetto ('Perdon, Amelia'). Indeed, the trio marks the high point of the afternoon as all three principals expertly chart their cruelly exposed lines. Tucker is all line and rhythmic alacrity (fairly spitting out the text—acceptable in this instance), Warren elevates the mood, and Varnay has her best moments as she splendidly rides up over the arch of the climactic phrase.

On this afternoon Tucker is heard in the full bloom of his first maturity. This is the tenor that Rudolf Bing heard in his observation season when he determined that Tucker would be the house Italian tenor of his regime. Prescient he was, even taking into account some coarsening of Tucker's style over the years.

As Simon, Warren is free from any stylistic vulgarities and, once having assumed the robes of Doge, in peak form. The young Boccanegra should not have so cavernous a tone nor, as he describes the loss of his daughter, be consumed with such self-pity; yet even here Warren's vocal mastery is impressive. By the time he finds his daughter fully grown and housed with the Grimaldi, he offers some magical father phrases. 'Figlia! a tal nome' displays his perfect technical command; though excited at his discovery, he laces the piece with exquisite half-voice nuances, honoring Verdi's *dolcissimo* markings. 'Plebe! Patrizi!' is powerfully voiced, the tone a bit diffuse but the quieter moments of exceeding beauty ('Piango su voi, sul placido') and the phrasing alert to the changing moods of the text. 'E vo gridando' is perhaps the noblest Warren moment in memory, sung broadly but quietly, the legato and line expansion most expressive. It is a wrenching moment, as though the Doge's heart will break if peace does not prevail, entirely different from the powerful command of Tibbett but more than its equal in potency. Warren could use Tibbett's palette of vocal coloration to better chastize Paolo. Nevertheless, he quells the abductor by sheer vocal size and breadth of manner.

Warren has grown in character portrayal, as we discover when he reappears as the aging, weary Doge, alone and drinking the poison. Not only are the quieter phrases exquisite as he dwells on Amelia, but he acts adroitly with the voice. His command of mezza voce is made to mirror the Doge's decline; where Tibbett drained his voice of color and life, Warren is content to let beauty and control weave a spell—lovely as it is, 'Il mare! il mare!' owns a greater measure of sorrow than Warren delivers. The afternoon reaches a second climax as Fiesco and Boccanegra reconcile. The duet bursts with emotion, Stiedry allowing Székely and Warren a fluid rubato, and Warren ends with some ethereal phrases. The baritone's singing and characterization remain on this exalted plane until death claims the Doge. Fine as Warren's portrayal is, the Doge's portrait is a shade one-sided: the pastel colors of introspection overbalance the stronger hues of the bold, noble leader.

The throne of the Doge of Genoa was conclusively claimed by Warren on this occasion, but the abdicator was not yet banished from the house. Johnson called upon Tibbett, who had virtually given up all of his great Italian roles, for one last service. The manager determined to exit by introducing a work as novel as any in Metropolitan history. The Metropolitan premiere of Mussorgsky's *Khovanchina* occurred on 16 February 1950, and the second performance was broadcast on the twenty-fifth. Sung in the English translation of Rosa Newmarch by an all-American cast (Chabay the exception), the production is a final affirmation of Johnson's commitment to significant musico-dramatic works. The commitment would have been even more welcome if less intermittent.

Mussorgsky's final opera lacks the focus of *Boris*. No central character captures the audience's interest; instead, the opera functions as a historical allegory in which mysticism and fanaticism figure prominently. As Prince Ivan Khovansky and his Streltsy struggle to gain the throne of the czar in late seventeenth-century Russia, the Old Believers, firmly adhering to the tenets of Greek Orthodoxy, oppose Prince Golitsin's desire to introduce European tastes. In Dossifé, leader of the Old Believers, and his devoted follower Marfa (possessed of psychic powers and in love with Khovansky's son, Andrei), Mussorgsky created two of his most powerful characters. But the human conflicts ultimately recede before the philosophical forces which dominate the opera. In the end, Khovansky is assassinated, Golitsin exiled, Dossifé, Marfa, Andrei, and the Old Believers immolated. Peter the Great would remain to take Russia into the modern age.

From the beginning the Metropolitan's effort was compromised by the deci-

Khovanchina
25 February 1950
Marfa
Risë Stevens
Susanna
Polyna Stoska
Golitsin
Charles Kullman
Andrei
Brian Sullivan
Khovansky
Lawrence Tibbett
Shaklovity
Robert Weede
Dossifé
Jerome Hines
Conductor
Emil Cooper

sion to sing the work in translation (again the familiar dilemma of the Met with regard to Russian opera). Management also reasoned that a work of such complexity and dramatic diffuseness could only hope to find favor if heard in the vernacular. It would be decades before the Met could command a stable of singers equipped to perform Russian opera in Russian. At least Italian (the language of earlier Met Russian operas) was eschewed in favor of audience comprehension. The Met did have at hand a Russian conductor intimate with the work: Cooper had conducted *Khovanchina* in Moscow as far back as 1909 and presided at the first performance outside Russia in Paris four years later.

As is true of a good deal of Mussorgsky's output, no definitive form of the opera exists. The Met utilized the brilliant orchestration of Rimsky-Korsakov (unlike the "somewhat shortened" Shostakovich version of the next Met presentation in 1986). Rimsky had "completed" the work after the composer's death, but Cooper felt further adaptations were in order; he reinstated the scene of Marfa and Susanna and the song of Kuska in act three, and expanded the apotheosis of the finale; since Rimsky had ignored them, these sections were orchestrated by Cooper. A more serious departure was the conductor's excision of the dramatically important scene in St. Basil's square in which several plot lines are clarified: Prince Golitsin is exiled, the Streltsy (or musketeers) are pardoned by the czar, and Marfa brings Andrei back to the faith—obviously, quite a passel of events to leave up in the air.

Nevertheless, Cooper's hand in performance is a beneficent one. The lovely prelude to act one gains a gleaming translucence as Cooper paints a colorful instrumental mosaic of dawn over Moscow. In scenes of conflict (the act-two confrontation of Golitsin and Khovansky, for example), he stirs the musical pot with vigor, and the choral episodes (all important, as in *Boris*, though the entity is not personified quite so effectively) are alternately rousing (when the Old Believers triumph over heresy in act three) or haunting (the prayer for deliverance of the Streltsy). Choral precision and tonal appeal are satisfactory.

Perhaps because the opera is new to everyone on stage and in the pit, the experienced Cooper too often maintains control at the expense of buoyancy. The rhythms do not always enliven, and the graphic dramatic gestures lack ultimate profile. The opera seems to move at too deliberate and uniform a pace, a burden doubly hard upon a work of such serious intent. Of equal importance, the English translation frequently straitjackets the flow of the singers' phrases. Often a character will sing in unison with a solo wind, and the substitution of clipped English (at least as sung by most of the Americans) for the rich liaisons of the Russian language robs the singers of the musicality shown by the instrumentalists. Even in passages where lyricism is not paramount, the Mussorgsky song-speech (so prominent in the first act) is delivered more for intelligibility than flavorful nuance.

Yet this is a most admirable group of American artists who vindicate Johnson's transformation of the company during the 1940s when necessity altered the balance between native and foreign artists. Foremost is the portrayal by Jerome Hines of Dossifé. Firm and resonant of voice throughout the long afternoon, more than any of his colleagues he manages to connect song and speech in meaningful fashion. Though younger than almost anyone on stage, Hines takes command of critical scenes (interfering between Khovansky and Golitsin, for instance) and well conveys the zealotry of the Old Believers' religious leader. Perhaps never again would Hines find a major role so attuned to his musical and interpretive abilities (it is, in fact, difficult to reconcile some of his late career portrayals with this successful achievement).

More often than not his English diction is not only clear but musical to the ear. He stirs up powerful emotions ('I too have sinned') in the great scene of act three—the entire act is a succession of magnificent musical and dramatic moments. If, in the immolation scene, he doesn't risk a realistic Chaliapinesque delivery, in their own way his stern, steady tones exemplify the austerity of the Old Believers.

Non-American Leslie Chabay, too, manages simultaneously to characterize the Scrivener and articulate the text intelligibly. As the enigmatic Boyar, Shaklovity, Robert Weede (marvelously clear of diction) makes an all too infrequent broadcast appearance. In rather narrow but firmly based tones, he delivers the opera's most extended set piece—the third-act soliloquy in which Shaklovity expresses his fears and hopes for Russia's future. Weede doesn't hesitate to take advantage of the Italianate close with some vocal grandstanding—he still owns ringing high notes. The strong cast boasts two major tenors. As the vacillating aristocrat, Prince Andrei Khovansky, young Brian Sullivan's bright timbre and fervent manner are a tonic among so much low-voiced lugubriousness, though an occasional splintered high tone jars and his diction varies in clarity. With the role of Prince Golitsin, Khovansky's rival, Kullman enters upon the major character roles which would be his lot during his final Met decade. Ever the responsible artist, his tone and diction are admirable, and as he reads and comments on Regent Sophie's letter, the drama gains in intensity. His aria is only moderately effective, however. The suspicion grows that too many of the afternoon's portraits are small in scale, lacking a larger-than-life aura to fill out the vast canvas of this epic work. A thin veneer of musical politesse robs the work of elemental force.

Risë Stevens' dutiful portrait of Marfa, along with Dossifé the opera's dominant character, adds to that impression. Not that her work is not consistently admirable, but the role of the rejected lover of Andrei, seer to Prince Golitsin, and committed confidant of Dossifé, demands a voice of more heroic proportions (the old refrain). Marfa is the heart of the opera, a creature torn between desire and religious devotion, symbol of the Russian soul. Much of the role lies in the contralto domain where Stevens must manufacture tone, and she is one of those whose taut vocal production sometimes smothers Mussorgsky's musical point. Undoubtedly her box office appeal was a strong factor in casting her in this little known work.

The mezzo has some very attractive moments in the folk-song-like melodies of the lengthy act-three scene in which she strives to forget her love for the Prince. Here the tone flows, the timbre is lovely, and even the low voice speaks convincingly (and what an attractive *portamento* she provides at the close of her piece). Stevens is equally effective in the scene with old Susanna, who castigates her for her inability to forget Andrei. Containing some of the most lyrical music of the score as it does, one can understand Cooper's desire to include this scene. While Stevens ably lofts Marfa's broad singing lines, Polyna Stoska is less happy with her assignment as Susanna, seeming not to be in best form. As Emma, strenuously resistant to Andrei's advances, young soprano Anne Bollinger is largely unintelligible, but proffers some secure top tones.

Stevens is less affecting elsewhere—in fact, downright shrewish and unclear of diction in act one. Marfa's strongest scene (the prophecy of exile for Golitsin) lies well for her voice and she is properly dramatic, but here, and in the long peroration which accompanies the progress of Marfa and Andrei to the funeral pyre, more tonal heft and flow of phrase are essential. The flame of fanaticism is not fanned by her singing. One cannot, however, gainsay her serious intent (no playing to an audience), and early on in the scene she ably conveys Marfa's powerful emotion ('We all shall die').

The leader of the Khovansky faction for whom the opera is named—Khovanchina refers to the plotting of this noble family against the czar—is at best a bass-baritone role (Nicolai Ghiaurov in Chicago and Aage Haugland at the Met are later interpreters), but here it is assigned to Tibbett. Since Tibbett is no longer able to operate in the baritone stratosphere, Johnson evidently felt the old (in company longevity, not years—twenty-seven of the former, only fifty-three of the latter) singing-actor might contribute skill of character portrayal where all else is wanting. Whatever the stage portrayal, the result of the broadcast is desultory and saddening in the extreme.

In the final broadcast of his Met career (he rightly is not on Bing's retention list) Tibbett's voice is in pitiful condition. He all but gargles his way through the afternoon. One cannot even recognize the Tibbett timbre, so little core is left to the tone. Always the exemplary singer in English, as his many records and broadcasts of American operas demonstrate, his struggle to wed tone and word is so insurmountable that he is barely intelligible. Only an isolated moment or two reminds us of his greatness, as when he demands that his son leave Emma to him—here his commanding manner takes hold (but the tone remains diffuse). In the monumental confrontation between the two opposing philosophies of old Russia and Westernized Russia (personified by Khovansky and Golitsin), Tibbett's vocal troubles and Kullman's restraint minimize the immensity of the struggle. The magnificent scene (the emotional charge is augmented when Dossifé appears) calls to mind, if only in its opposition of mighty forces, the Grand Inquisitor scene in *Don Carlo*—if either scene is inadequately realized, the overall impact of the opera is seriously diluted. When Hines intervenes, he carries the day for the Old Believers. As Shaklovity prepares to assassinate Khovansky, the Prince is clothed in the ceremonial robes of the white swan, and now a brief flash of the old Tibbett virility invades his sound—the baritone falls, his operatic career all but over. I like to believe that there was in Tibbett's effortful struggle with the role, in his churning, exaggerated words, a mirror of the wild, egomaniacal, drunken Prince Khovansky—perhaps Tibbett's power of characterization was not completely dissipated, even at the end.

The production of *Khovanchina* is the final highlight of Johnson's fifteen-year tenure. It was a qualified success—certainly instructive, though ultimately more intriguing than fully evocative of the panoramic sweep of Mussorgsky's grand epic. A daring venture for Johnson, management would wait three and a half decades before embracing the challenge again.

A few days after the broadcast Johnson called on Tibbett for yet one more service, this time unforeseen. Paul Schoeffler, having replaced Janssen as Hans Sachs, was unable to appear as Scarpia in the Opera Guild's gala testimonial in honor of Johnson's retirement. Tibbett did the duty, and a pair of Khovanskys thereafter brought his career to an end. His entrance (a walk-on as Lovitzky in *Boris*) had been paltry, his exit, ignoble, but in between he had been, and remains, a giant of the American stage.

Yet another operatic career of similarly epic proportions ended with the Johnson era, not in dusky twilight like Tibbett's, but with a proverbial bang. Bing provided the bang, while Melchior had to be content with the whimper.

On the scene for observation, by midseason the new manager had begun negotiations with certain artists. Not being one of them, Melchior was affronted and

Helen Traubel as Elsa in *Lohengrin*.

allowed the hurt of neglect to fester into angry recrimination. On 2 February 1950 he announced he would sing no more at the Metropolitan. Before that, on 28 January, Traubel had made it known that *she* would not sing at the Met in 1950–51. Bing, finding rumor rampant about his plans for the 1950–51 season, on 1 February announced the return of Flagstad, at the same time soothing the wounded pride of Traubel with a season of equal prestige and equal pay. Clearly, cutting out the American soprano to provide for the politically tainted Flagstad would have been disastrous. But Melchior received no conciliatory gesture, and verbal warfare flourished.

Bing's intent was clear. Melchior must go. Wishing to leave nothing to chance, Bing felt it necessary to ask the Board president for official termination of the great tenor. Notice of the company's intention regarding reengagement was required by 11 March, and Bing wanted it on record. Since mere argument in the newspapers was insufficient protection, Bing (now preferring the shadows of manipulation) requested either Association president Charles M. Spofford or board chairman George A. Sloan to formalize the breach, to express regret at the tenor's desire to leave the Metropolitan, but to leave no room for a rapprochement.[10] And there was none.

By this time in his twenty-four-year association with the Metropolitan, the tenor's appearances had dwindled to half a dozen per year. Hollywood and radio had proved lucrative venues for the tenor's hearty amiability. At sixty years of age, combative retreat seemed both valorous and prudent.

Lauritz Melchior as Lohengrin.

Melchior's penultimate Met performance is the broadcast Lohengrin of 7 January 1950. Stiedry, back on familiar terrain, has a prime crew in Traubel, Varnay, Janssen, and Ernster. They prove that the Wagnerian incandescence of the previous decade is not yet extinguished.

Janssen is in marvelous form, perhaps the best in his broadcast history. Though his unique qualities are little served by Telramund's surly grumblings, the fifty-five-year-old baritone sings with complete vocal freedom, his top voice (which could be recalcitrant) particularly resplendent. He prefers passion to self-pity, relying on quantity of tone to convey the miscreant's anger and despair. And there are always those sensitive Janssen moments: his meaningful plea to King Henry ('sein Leben war das Kleinod meiner Ehre'); the bewitching half-voice of 'Du wilde Seherin' (marked by Wagner *mit leiser, bebender Stimme*—how often the greatest artists triumph merely by responding to the composer's wish). Yet when Telramund must rage (as when he confronts Lohengrin before the wedding), Janssen hurls his mighty mix of declamation and sustained tone with unrelenting force. Though Ernster has the true Germanic bass timbre, on this occasion he sounds weary even beyond his considerable years.

The Herald, calling card of many a young baritone whose natural habitat was Latin rather than Teutonic, serves that purpose once again for Frank Guarrera. In his second Met season, the "Met Auditions" winner reveals the cultivated musicianship and authoritative manner which would sustain him through nearly three decades at the house. Of moderate size and initially slightly dry in timbre, the voice takes on color as he warms to his assignment. When released from the dramatic straitjacket of the Heerrufer (as he was in his debut as Escamillo and the *Carmen* broadcast of 4 February 1950), his true worth was more evident.

Once again Elsa and Ortrud are a memorable pair. Both Traubel and Varnay contribute exceptionally vivid portraits. Varnay, just a few weeks before the *Boccanegra* broadcast, sings with the open throat and vibrant timbre which were too often missing in her Italian venture. This is her only broadcast Ortrud, a role which, unaccountably, she sang only five times in the house. In it she appears to have found her métier as a singing-actress of the dramatic German roles. What malevolence resides in the steely timbre of the middle and low voice, and how she puts it to use! The tone remains potent at the top, in fact, opening up to a richer sonority than she normally commands. Varnay and Janssen bring the plotting scene to life as few have, the airwaves crackling with excitement. And it is all done within the zones of musical rectitude and stern vocal discipline. Both artists not only articulate the word but convey its meaning and the meaning of the musical phrase as well. Stiedry serves them well here (as he does Wagner everywhere in the score, for that matter). Their vow (more slowly paced than usual—these artists can handle the tempo) is doubly effective coming after the surging phrases which Stiedry has shaped earlier on. Stiedry's rhythmic acuity lends buoyancy to the ceremonial scenes of act two and later turns the trite familiarity of the bridal procession sequence into charming naiveté (his dotted rhythms actually bounce). Even the spiritual stasis of the first-act prelude has musical plasticity—in Stiedry's Montsalvat the air is not so rarefied as to rob it of warmth. And he commands a stately step as well; the choral close to the second act gains by Stiedry's majestic pace. If a certain slackness of ensemble creeps into the final scene, it little blunts the probity of Stiedry's overall conception.

As oft in the decades of the thirties and forties, the two sopranos excel in the scene between Elsa and Ortrud. Again Varnay shows herself capable both of beautiful singing and of animating the melodic line by molding words to it. Her outburst to the gods is less abandoned than some (she narrows her tone a bit for the assault), but it is capped by a stunning A-sharp on 'Rache.' Traubel again achieves a beguiling vocal charm in these moments, and she seems most sympathetic to Ortrud's plight. Varnay attacks Traubel before the cathedral in steely tones of splendid thrust; Traubel responds with tones of even greater size (dramatically unlikely, but a thrilling confrontation), flatting a tad on the final B-flat. Varnay's B-flat shortly thereafter is clear and full (perhaps it gave her secret pleasure). But Traubel is fully involved in the drama, and one fails to fathom the oft-read accusation of lethargic performance. Ortrud has the last word; no Ortrud of recent memory (perhaps Marton) equals Varnay's brazen traversal of the final pages of the score.

Traubel, too, is in magnificent voice. For the dream she offers a steady column of glowing tone, this time not devoid of gentleness. She pleads sweetly for yet one more trumpet summons to her savior knight. An occasional downward pull on a few upper notes occurs (after all, the voice is of incredible density all the way up the range), but for the most part the top voice is as free and lovely as the lower octave. 'Euch Lüften' demands a silver thread of tone, and Traubel can offer only the warmth of gold—not a base metal at that. Though the B-natural which ends the love duet turns into an abrupt A, her reading of the bridal chamber duet is superbly vocalized and exposes Elsa's ever-growing curiosity and agitation. No wonder Bing wanted to keep her—and Varnay, too, though his fidelity to them both would not be overlong.

Had Melchior's career as Wagnerian monarch reached the time when abdication, for the well-being of his public, was required? This broadcast delivers an unqualified "no" to that query. His performance is uneven, yes, but the peaks have been unequaled by any tenor to follow him, and the valleys are moments more of neglect than inadequacy.

Melchior's Lohengrin is no lyrical knight. We know that it never was. More than ever, the swan farewell is no dreamy invocation, but his stout head tones are absolutely secure and unmarred by strain. Right off he offers a bright high A as an obeisance to King Henry. He *will* hurry his charge to Elsa ('Nie sollst du mich befragen!') and there are now more phrases where rhythm is casual, often due to a desire to evade a succession of sustained tones. Nor can he command the old sweet head tone at 'Ich liebe dich!' (but he counterfeits a quiet, serviceable sound). Some of the old magic returns as he reclaims Elsa from Ortrud's wiles ('Komm, lass in Freude'), and his clouded resonance makes his warning to Ortrud a meaningful thrust. The tenor can still trot out his silver trumpet on need; it shines forth as he commands Elsa to stay from Telramund. 'Heil dir, Elsa!' is a blast of tone where *piano* is called for, but the nobility of 'Nun, lass vor Gott uns gehen!' cannot be denied.

The bridal duet begins at a lower level (a frog from the river Scheldt, perhaps): Melchior's phrasing is rather choppy, the dotted rhythms are lax; some holes appear in the voice, and he seems to be tiring. But he returns to form at 'Höchstes Vertrau'n' and several cuts in the score come to his aid. 'Weh', nun ist all unser Glück dahin!' is simply and affectingly done, while his commands to the vassals to remove Telramund's body are forceful in the extreme. When he confronts the assembled court, his powerful and brightly colored tones again assert themselves. In this heroic portion of the role, Melchior reveals his better self; plenty of top voice remains, only an effortful release or two betraying stress, and his declamation is magnificent. 'In fernem Land' is declaimed more than sung, but he manages the tessitura handily.

Signs of age there are, but the make-up and quality of the voice are still characteristic. A moment to cherish is the quiet regret of 'Schon sendet nach dem Säumigen
der Gral!' and 'Mein lieber Schwan!' is finely done, filled with silver and without
strain. How well the voice holds up throughout this lengthy scene! And Melchior
proffers some touching moments (the best of them is the moving 'wollt' ich dich
anders wiedersehen!' with its lovely change of color) to offset the grand outpouring
of tone and emotion in his final 'Leb' wohl!'

Describing the final scene as the artists come before the curtain for their bows,
Cross offers prophetic words: "As Lohengrin was borne away . . . the people uttered a
wail of lamentation." And well they might. So many artists have been cited as
irreplaceable. Melchior, though too often ridiculed for what were minor infractions
and charged with laxity toward his art, may be the only singer to fully qualify for
Horatio's lament: "We shall not see his like again." With Melchior passed not only a
Heldentenor's art, but the type itself.

When the final broadcast of the Johnson regime came round on 25 March,
Johnson, in spite of the internal tug of war, offered to introduce Bing to the millions
of radio listeners. Bing, feeling the sting of the Melchior rebukes, relished the opportunity to present his case. No names would be mentioned, but Bing, with an eye to
possible libel, sent a copy of his remarks to the company lawyer.[11] Clearly, a new era
was opening at the Metropolitan.

Johnson, having paid homage to enlightenment by introducing *Manon Lescaut*
and *Khovanchina*, went out on the arm of the familiar. *La Bohème* has a generous dose of
the Johnson laissez-faire mode of operation (Lois Hunt, Brownlee, Moscona,
Pechner; Antonicelli). Its heroine and hero, however, were the stuff of legend and not
inapt symbols of the two regimes: Albanese, beloved soprano of the Johnson era who
would continue under Bing until the old house fell a decade and a half later, and
Tucker, Johnson novitiate and anchor of the Bing tenor wing for two decades.

Antonicelli knows his work and presides over a smooth performance (barring a
bit of loose coordination between the tattoo and the other onstage participants). His
is a split-personality *Bohème*, often relying on an easy fluidity, deficient in incisiveness
(the opening motivic play), with tempi little short of lazy, and expanding occasionally into symphonic breadth (the Mimi-Marcello scene, and a good deal more in act
three). Then again, he will adopt the Toscanini manner, compelling his charges to
chase after him—most often, they catch him. In his well-ordered way, he offers abundant heart and spirit.

The old hands are simply themselves. Brownlee sometimes surprises with more
legato and line than is his wont, even mustering a fine body of tone here and there,
but letting Albanese down at the tollgate and turning the unison tenuto at the close
of the duet with Tucker into a quarter-tone struggle. Moscona misses an entrance in
act one (rehearsals?) but delivers a manly coat song, welcome enough until the hearty
close robs the moment of pathos. Pechner plays Benoit more as a coy naif than a dirty
old man. In the parrot narrative Cehanovsky is simply superb, wickedly humorous
but never stepping over the musical line. Lois Hunt follows her broadcast debut as
Barbarina with an expert Musetta. Her good-hearted girl is neither a shrew nor a
harlot, and her round core of lovely tone and genial musicality are equally effective in
the waltz song and last-act prayer.

Though Albanese had been singing Mimi for more than a decade at the Met, had
recorded it with Gigli before that, and in 1946 celebrated the fiftieth anniversary of
the opera with its first conductor, this was only her second broadcast of the role and

La Bohème
25 March 1950
Mimi
Licia Albanese
Musetta
Lois Hunt
Rodolfo
Richard Tucker
Marcello
John Brownlee
Colline
Nicola Moscona
Conductor
Giuseppe Antonicelli

our first opportunity to hear this familiar portrait from the Metropolitan. Her Mimi is a most heartwarming creation, fully explored in every detail, yet another demonstration of the unique combination of refinement and expansive song which make her Puccini portrayals so memorable.

She is in fine vocal form, the voice a bit diffuse in the lower octave early on, but always supremely assured as it ascends. Does any other soprano sing the correct vowel in 'primavere' on the high A? The top tone of the duet is a far easier mark for her than for Tucker (a bit of effort from him, even though down a half tone). Albanese's interpretive breadth allows for a full portrait—her passionate confession to Marcello contrasts vividly with the delicate, even pallid, phrases she utters as Mimi returns to Rodolfo's garret. The climax of the 'Addio' is forthright and thrilling. No more lovely Albanese moment exists than her subtle expansion of the two solo phrases at the end of the quartet when Mimi wishes the winter might last forever; all the longing of the doomed seamstress for life and love is laid bare in Albanese's caress. She is at the peak of her form in the final act. 'Oh come è bello e morbido' (that seemingly simple, but tricky, utterance) is perfect in design and delivery. But then, the entire death scene is full of subtle nuances and color changes—no one slips away into stage death like Albanese. On this afternoon her interpretation lies midway between her two commercial recordings, warmer in tone and less excitable than the 1938 version, yet not quite capturing the exquisite repose of her Toscanini portrayal (the latter a portrait almost too angelic, as though greater propriety befitted the anniversary occasion). Her combination of tonal warmth and extrovert play in this 1950 broadcast is a felicitous match.

Albanese and Tucker work extremely well together. He plays the part in sportive fashion (poets need not be morose), musically and dramatically jaunty, almost cocksure in the garret scenes. His high spirits do much to enliven the afternoon, and the insouciance is complemented by marvelous vocal freedom. He is mindful of Puccini's markings, keeping 'L'amor è un caminetto' exactly in tempo, and eschewing even the hint of a tenuto on his splendid A at 'Eureka!' Can any sacrifice be greater for a tenor?

Tucker takes great delight in his own powers, and since he enjoys himself, we do, too. Everywhere his line is firm and the tone solidly collected, a tonic for the ear (everywhere except the A-flat and B which crown the Racconto—a bit of weakness mars them). He captures the humanity of 'In povertà mia lieta,' and gives 'Talor del mio forziere' a round send-off—one cannot fault his interpretation of the aria. What one does wish to modify is his excessive aspiration of the Italian consonants, both single and double (especially the latter—'freddo') which occasion an excessively jerky line. He spits them out where they must be dry—rhythmically alive, but not intrusive. When he wishes (as in much of the quartet), his Italian can be as liquid as need be, and then his song is beautiful. 'Invan, invan' he cries to Marcello, lamenting Mimi's declining health, and the line is marvelously drawn and the feeling intense. Few pairs of Bohemian lovers execute the long unison ascent and descent at the close of the quartet as securely and with such tonal beauty as Albanese and Tucker. As the opera moves toward its tragic close, Tucker catches a bad attack of pseudo-Italian sobs. It is Mimi's coughing that is supposed to reveal her presence at the tollgate, but Tucker looses a string of sobs through which even so experienced a cougher as Albanese cannot penetrate. After her death, he drenches the postlude à la Gigli—like many of its productions, the Met's *Bohème* needs a strong stage director.

That is the card which Bing intends to play.

Richard Tucker as Tamino in *The Magic Flute*. Photography by Sedge LeBlang.

CHAPTER THIRTY

Coda: Reckoning

Bohème was a safe choice for the Johnson broadcast farewell. It was representative of the normal house routine: workaday subordinates surrounding a star portrayal or two of prime stature, presided over by usually efficient, sometimes imaginative, leadership. Then too, while Johnson's championing of the Mozart and Strauss operas is oft cited, during his regime the Puccini operas regained the repertory primacy they had enjoyed in the first decades of the century. Not only did *Bohème, Butterfly,* and *Tosca* become weekly encounters at the Met, but *Il Tabarro, Schicchi,* and *Manon Lescaut* were offered as virtually new experiences for the radio public.

Acknowledged as the crowning glory of his regime is the presence of the world's great maestri for relatively long periods of time: Walter, Beecham, Szell, Busch, Reiner, Stiedry, Leinsdorf, even Panizza, Sodero, and Cooper. Unlike recent encounters, most of them came to oversee more than a single production each year. Though Martin Mayer mounts an attack on Johnson as manager, and even more virulently as man, Johnson knew singers. For every Milanov who was at odds with him there was a Steber or Sayão to remember him as ever supportive, especially when sustenance was most needed. Mayer sees Johnson's way with people (the manager knew singers were people) as mere ego, but it had its salutary effect.

Johnson is sometimes criticized for abusing young, untried talent, especially in the difficult war years. The radio public heard little of that since, unlike recent times, the broadcasts invariably got the best that was available. And Johnson brought many excellent American singers to enduring fame—Merrill, Kirsten, and Tucker were the latest in a long line. If, as Johnson asserted, the broadcasts had given the Metropolitan Opera increased stature as a national institution, subsidiary benefits for others were of equal, or perhaps greater, consequence. Without doubt, the broadcasts made and sustained careers of individual artists, increased record sales, and most important, created and nurtured an appetite for live opera which before long would foster the establishment of numerous regional companies.

On the debit side, the fundamentally conservative repertory eventually would solidify the taste of the American public on far too narrow a base. Rudolf Bing's tenure would greatly augment our knowledge of Verdi's genius, and Strauss' creativity would be seen not to have withered quite so early as we thought. But the conservative elements of Bing's repertory were tenaciously cultivated in the fifties and sixties (a seemingly endless round of *Tosca*s clotted the sound waves). Many of the facile genre operas which were so much a part of Metropolitan history (they were often broadcast favorites during the Johnson regime) would disappear not only from the airwaves, but from the Metropolitan repertory. *Lakmé* (six broadcasts), *Mignon* (eight broadcasts), *Louise* (three broadcasts), *L'Amore dei Tre Re* (two broadcasts), would depart, their charms, ever evanescent, fading from the scene with Johnson's leaving. (Recompense would come in the respectability accorded the bel canto operas as a new generation of singers cultivated agility.) As for American opera, Gatti's proselytizing was barely sustained by Johnson, and Bing was not overzealous in nurturing the American (or, for that matter, the contemporary European) composer.

The curse of the Johnson-Ziegler-St. Leger regime—lackadaisical stage direction and aged, worn scenic investiture—meant little to the radio audience. Perhaps that is why the Johnson regime is fondly remembered for the individual portraits by a long list of supreme interpreters, singers with both vocal allure and the ability to act with the voice. They created characters who live now in the imagination, even as they did when they came over the airways into the homes of millions: Flagstad's Isolde and Brünnhilde, Martinelli's Canio and Otello, Bori as Mélisande, De Luca as Marcello, Rethberg's Desdemona and Elsa, Albanese's Violetta and Butterfly, Tourel as Mignon, Sayão as Adina and Norina. Time has not erased the memory of Pinza's Figaro and Don Giovanni, Lehmann as the Marschallin, Novotna as Cherubino and Antonia, Tibbett's Boccanegra and Iago, Schorr as Sachs, Baccaloni as Pasquale, Melchior's Tristan and Siegmund, Kipnis' Marke and Boris, Stevens as Octavian and Mignon, Singher as Pelléas, Welitch as Salome. How often vocal supremacy was savored, as in Bjoerling's Roméo and Riccardo, Milanov's Gioconda and Norma, Branzell's Ortrud, Castagna's Amneris, Crooks' Faust, Warren's Germont and Rigoletto, Traubel's Isolde, Tucker's Enzo Grimaldo, Steber's Contessa and Elvira, Tagliavini's Nemorino. Nor are Pons and Moore forgotten—their aura lingers. Noteworthy artists like Hackett, Bonelli, Janssen, Kullman, Bampton, Peerce, Ralf, Thebom, Vinay, Varnay, Berger, Di Stefano, Svanholm, were eagerly welcomed on many a Saturday afternoon at the old Met.

Now the neutral reading of roles increasingly has become the norm, not only from run-of-the-mill performers, but the near-greats and the so-called superstars of the jet age. Who could have imagined that the stylistic vacuum which decimated French opera would descend upon Puccini and Verdi!

If an opaque gloss has settled upon too many of the portrayals in recent times, it goes with the cooler milieu of the new Lincoln Center house. To one who often sprinted up the dingy back stairway to standing room in the Family Circle of the old house, the deeper tones (was it merely tarnish?) of the old maroon and gold will always warm memory, in part because here trod Fremstad and Caruso and De Reszke. Though we are robbed of the opportunity to visit the old house, the broadcasts of the thirties and forties preserve the aura of a time and a place.

Set Svanholm as Lohengrin.

Notes

CHAPTER ONE

1 "Texaco's Roving Opera Reporter," Met broadcast, 29 December 1956.

2 "Fourth Annual Report of the Metropolitan Opera Guild 1938–39," *Opera News,* p. 2.

3 "10,000,000 Opera Fans," *Opera News,* 6 February 1939, pp. 15, 16.

4 "The Prize Winners Are Here!" *Opera News,* 2 December 1940, p. 7.

5 Met broadcast, 29 December 1956, op. cit.

6 Irving Kolodin, *The Metropolitan Opera 1883–1935*, 1st ed. (New York: Oxford University Press, 1936), p. 408.

7 Cedric Hart, "Those Early Opera Broadcasts," pt. 2, *Opera News*, 23 November 1942, p. 27.

8 Hart, op. cit., pt. 1, *Opera News*, 11 November 1942, p. 14.

9 C. J. Luten, "Golden Age of the Air," *Opera News*, 18 December 1976, p. 56.

10 H. B. Schaad to Edward Ziegler, 6 April 1931, Met Archives.

11 Lee de Forest, *Father of Radio* (Chicago: Wilcox and Follett Co., 1950), p. 267.

12 Ibid.

13 Ibid., p. 268.

14 Art Ronnie, "Verismo in the Air," *Opera News*, 3 December 1966, p. 7.

15 De Forest, op. cit., p. 269.

16 Ibid.

17 Met broadcast, 29 December 1956, op. cit.

18 Ibid.

19 William H. Seltsam, "The Dawn of Opera Broadcasts," *Opera News*, 10 March 1952, p. 12.

20 Met broadcast, 29 December 1956, op. cit.

CHAPTER TWO

1 NBC, Metropolitan Opera Company Agreement #1, May 1931 and 27 May 1931, Met Archives.

2 Ziegler to Giulio Gatti-Casazza, 18 May 1931, Met Archives.

3 Ziegler to Gatti, 21 May 1931, Met Archives.

4 Gatti to Ziegler, 22 May 1931, Met Archives.

5 Ziegler to Merlin Aylesworth, 25 May 1931, Met Archives.

6 Otto Kahn to NBC "for Aylesworth," enclosed in Aylesworth letter to Ziegler, 2 January 1931, Met Archives.

7 Ziegler to Aylesworth, 3 June 1931, Met Archives.

8 Martin Mayer, *The Met: One Hundred Years of Grand Opera* (New York: Simon and Schuster, 1983), p. 171.

9 Aylesworth to Ziegler, 1 June 1931, Met Archives.

10 A. Usher (NBC Advertising Department) to Met Opera, 11 December 1931, Met Archives.

11 Ziegler secretary to Usher, 15 January 1931, Met Archives.

12 NBC, Metropolitan Opera Company Agreement #2, 21 May 1931, Met Archives.

13 Ibid.

14 H. B. Schaad to Ziegler, 21 July 1931, Met Archives.

15 Ziegler to George Engles (NBC Artist Services), 26 November 1931, Met Archives.

16 Engles to Ziegler, 27 November 1931, Met Archives.

17 Ibid.

18 Frank K. Starbird (Firestone Tire & Rubber Co.) to James B. Post (NBC), 12 December 1931, Met Archives.

CHAPTER THREE

1 Ziegler to Aylesworth, 2 January 1932, Met Archives.

2 Ibid.

3 Aylesworth to Ziegler, 5 December 1932, Met Archives.

4 Ziegler to J. F. Royal (NBC), 12 January 1932, Met Archives.

5 Seltsam, op. cit., p. 13.

6 Met broadcast, 29 December 1956, op. cit.

7 Gerald Chatfield to Ziegler, 10 February 1932, Met Archives.

8 Chatfield to Phillips Carlin, 5 March 1932, Met Archives. Chatfield's airtime contradicts the listing ("act two partial, three partial") in *The Metropolitan Opera: The Radio and Television Legacy* (The Museum of Broadcasting), p. 137.

9 Met broadcast, 29 December 1956, op. cit.

10 Ziegler to Aylesworth, 19 January 1932, Met Archives.

11 Ibid.

12 Met broadcast, 29 December 1956, op. cit.

13 Horace A. Hastings to NBC, 22 April 1932, Met Archives.

14 Kolodin, *The Metropolitan Opera 1883–1966*, 4th ed. (New York: Alfred A. Knopf, 1966), p. 367.

15 Ibid., 1st ed., p. 419. Letter to Gatti, 12 April 1932.

16 Gatti to Ziegler, 11 June 1932, Met Archives.

17 The sixty-four-year-old Jeritza returned for a single benefit performance of *Die Fledermaus* in 1951.

18 Ziegler to Aylesworth, 16 April 1932, Met Archives.

19 Aylesworth to Ziegler, 18 April 1932, Met Archives.

20 Ziegler to Aylesworth, 14 January 1932, Met Archives.

21 Kolodin, op. cit., 1st ed., p. 417.

CHAPTER FOUR

1 Ibid., p. 438.

2 Ibid.

3 Paul Cravath to Ziegler, 7 October 1932, Met Archives.

4 Ziegler to Gatti, 8 July 1932, Met Archives.

5 Ibid.

6 Aylesworth to Ziegler, 1 December 1932, Met Archives.

7 Aylesworth to Ziegler, 12 December 1933, Met Archives.

8 Aylesworth to Ziegler, 1 December 1932, Met Archives.

9 Ziegler to Aylesworth, 2 December 1932, Met Archives.

10 Memo from Aylesworth, 21 February 1933, Met Archives.

11 Ibid.

12 Ziegler to John Royal (NBC), 2 March 1933, Met Archives.

13 Enclosure in above letter.

14 Mayer, op. cit., p. 179.

15 Lawrence Gilman, *New York Herald Tribune*, 17 January 1933.

16 James H. Sutcliffe, "Lady of Berlin," *Opera News*, 28 January 1967, p. 29.

17 Lanfranco Rasponi, "Tristan and Tannhaeuser turn to the Grail," *Opera News*, 31 March 1941, p. 16.

18 Ibid.

19 Gatti to Ziegler, 16 June 1932, Met Archives.

CHAPTER FIVE

1 Ziegler to Engles, 12 May 1933, Met Archives.

2 Profit and Loss Statement, 1 January 1933 to 31 May 1934, Met Archives.

3 Royal to Ziegler, 26 February 1934, Met Archives.

4 Ziegler to Engles, 12 May 1933, Met Archives.

5 NBC, Metropolitan Opera Agreement draft, 19 June 1933, Met Archives.

6 Ziegler to Engles, 12 May 1933, Met Archives.

7 Exhibit A, appended to NBC, Metropolitan Opera Company Agreement, 19 June 1933, Met Archives.

8 *Opera News*, 25 November 1940, p. 25.

9 Kolodin, op. cit., 4th ed., p. 342.

10 Robert Lawrence, "Settling a Score," *Opera News*, 10 January 1976, p. 27.

11 Erich Leinsdorf, *Cadenza* (Boston: Houghton Mifflin Company, 1976), p. 61.

12 "Artur Bodanzky 1877–1939," *Opera News*, 4 December 1939, p. 1.

13 Ziegler to Luigi Villa, 20 May 1933, Met Archives.

14 Kolodin, op. cit., 1st ed., p. 456.

15 William Ackerman (Galaxy Music Corporation) to Ziegler, 20 December 1933, Met Archives.

16 Ackerman to Ziegler, 1 March 1934, Met Archives. Ziegler to Ackerman, 2 March 1934, Met Archives.

17 Ziegler to Mark Woods (NBC), 23 February 1934, Met Archives.

18 Joseph F. Tomaselli, "Seraphic Veteran," *Opera News*, 29 April 1961, p. 19.

19 Ibid.

20 In his excellent Tibbett discography William R. Moran has identified the recording of *The Emperor Jones* as a condensed version of the opera which aired on the Packard Hour, 16 October 1934. *Lawrence Tibbett: Singing Actor*, ed. Andrew Farkas (Portland, OR: Amadeus Press, 1989).

21 Ziegler to Gatti, 31 May 1933, Met Archives.

22 Ruby Mercer, *The Tenor of His Time* (Toronto: Clarke, Irwin & Company, Limited, 1976), p. 164.

23 Ibid., p. 165.

24 Ibid.

25 "Milton Cross and His 20,000,000 Ears," *Opera News*, 1 January 1940, p. 11.

26 Milton Cross, "Forty-Year Man," *Opera News*, 5 December 1970, p. 9.

27 *Broadcast Station Directory: RCA Radiotrons* (Schenectady, NY: The Maqua Company, 1930), p. 23.

28 *Opera News*, 1 January 1940, p. 11.

29 Lillian E. Foerster, "Milton Cross, the Speaking Voice of Opera," *Opera News*, 17 April 1944, p. 9.

30 Howard Hanson to Ziegler, 19 September 1934, Met Archives.

31 Ziegler to Villa, 21 September 1934, Met Archives.

32 Johnson to Ziegler, 13 June 1935, Met Archives.

33 Mercer, op. cit., p. 165.

34 Richard Aldrich, *The New York Times*, 16 November 1922.

35 C. A. Austin (Speak-O-Phone Recording Studio, Inc.) to Lucrezia Bori, 12 March 1934, Met Archives.

36 Kolodin, op. cit., 1st ed., p. 468.

37 Royal to Ziegler, 26 February 1934, Met Archives.

38 J. B. Steane, *The Grand Tradition* (New York: Charles Scribner's Sons, 1974), p. 64.

39 Ziegler to Gatti, 13 July 1934, Met Archives.

40 Ziegler to Villa, 13 July 1934, Met Archives.

41 "Opera News on the Air," Met broadcast, 27 March 1954.

42 *New York Telegram*, 17 January 1931.

43 Michael Scott, *The Record of Singing* (New York: Holmes & Meier Publishers, Inc., 1980), p. 151.

44 Olin Downes, *The New York Times*, 28 December 1935.

45 Walter Legge, "Rosa: an eightieth birthday homage," *Opera News*, 12 March 1977, p. 15. Legge's disappointment was based on the recording of the performance of 28 April [*sic*] 1936.

CHAPTER SIX

1 Ziegler to Robert C. Patterson (NBC), 17 September 1934, Met Archives.

2 Ibid.

3 Patterson to Ziegler, 18 September 1934, Met Archives.

4 Ziegler to Patterson, 16 November 1934, Met Archives.

5 Ziegler to Patterson, 11 March 1935, Met Archives.

6 Daniel S. Tuthill (NBC) to Young & Rubicam, Inc., 15 September 1934, Met Archives.

7 Season 1934–35: Artists who have only a few performances (document), n.d., Met Archives.

8 Ziegler to David Rosenblum (NBC), 24 April 1935, Met Archives.

9 Patterson to Ziegler, 20 February 1935, Met Archives.

10 Translation in Julian Budden, *The Operas of Verdi*, vol. 2 (New York: Oxford University Press, 1979), p. 253.

11 Marguerite d'Alvarez, *Forsaken Altars* (London, 1954), p. 265.

12 Translation in Budden, op. cit., p. 281.

13 Scott, op. cit., p. 188. Kolodin, op. cit., 4th ed., pp. 401, 402.

14 Kolodin, op. cit., 4th ed., p. 384.

15 Ziegler to Gatti, 14 August 1932, Met Archives.

16 Ziegler to Johnson, 11 June 1936, Met Archives.

17 William Ashbrook, "Perspectives on an Aria," *Opera News*, 7 January 1984, p. 32.

18 Kolodin, op. cit., 4th ed., p. 384.

19 Villa to Ziegler, 14 August 1934, Met Archives.

20 Villa to Ziegler, 17 August 1934, Met Archives.

21 Gatti to Ziegler, 6 September 1934, Met Archives.

22 Ibid.

23 Villa to Ziegler, 10 September 1934, Met Archives.

24 Ziegler to Villa, 7 September 1934, Met Archives.

25 Villa to Ziegler, 10 September 1934, Met Archives.

26 Kirsten Flagstad and Louis Biancolli, *The Flagstad Manuscript* (New York: G. P. Putnam's Sons, 1952), p. 70.

27 Quoted by Francis Robinson, Met broadcast, 11 March 1961.

CHAPTER SEVEN

1 Kolodin, op. cit., 4th ed., p. 385.

2 Geraldine Farrar, *Such Sweet Compulsion* (New York: Greystone Press, 1938), p. 232.

3 Ziegler to Chatfield, 10 December 1934, Met Archives.

4 Ibid.

5 Berthold Neuer (Wm. Knabe Company) to Ziegler, 18 December 1934, Met Archives.

6 Farrar, op. cit., p. 238.

7 Royal to Gatti, 19 March 1935, Met Archives.

8 Farrar, op. cit., p. 239.

9 Eleanor R. Belmont, "A Cause to Celebrate," *Opera News*, 8 October 1960, p. 9.

CHAPTER EIGHT

1 John Erskine, *My Life in Music* (New York: Wm. Morrow & Co., 1950), p. 156.

2 Herbert Witherspoon, Memo to Metropolitan Board, n.d., Met Archives. The quotes which follow are all from this memo.

3 Mayer, op. cit., pp. 203, 204.

4 Edward Johnson to Ziegler, 13 June 1935, Met Archives.

5 Ziegler to Gatti, 13 June 1935, Met Archives.

6 Ibid.

7 Ibid.

8 Quoted in Mercer, op. cit., p. 183.

9 Ibid.

10 Ibid.

11 David Sarnoff to Cornelius Bliss, 29 April 1935, Met Archives.

12 Patterson to Sarnoff, 29 April 1935, Met Archives.

13 Ziegler to NBC. Change approved by Tuthill to Ziegler, 21 January 1936, Met Archives.

14 Memo regarding meeting of Ziegler with Tuthill, 15 August 1935, Met Archives.

15 Tuthill to Ziegler, 17 December 1935, Met Archives.

16 Engles to Ziegler, 10 September 1935, Met Archives.

17 Quoted in Mercer, ibid.

18 Ziegler to Johnson, n.d., Met Archives.

19 Johnson to Ziegler, 6 June 1935, Met Archives.

CHAPTER NINE

1 Witherspoon, op. cit.

2 Marjorie Lawrence, *Interrupted Melody* (New York: Appleton-Century-Crofts, Inc., 1949), p. 127.

3 Johnson to Ziegler, 15 June 1935, Met Archives.

4 "Wotan Comes of Age," *Opera News*, 10 February 1941, p. 4.

5 Quoted by Elizabeth Eulass, "A Milestone for Friedrich Schorr," *Opera News*, 14 February 1944, p. 14.

6 Johnson to Ziegler, 6 June 1935, Met Archives.

7 Kolodin, op. cit., 4th ed., p. 408.

CHAPTER TEN

1 Belmont, op. cit., p. 11.

2 H. M. Beville, Jr. (Chief Statistician, NBC) to Ziegler, 11 May 1936, Met Archives.

3 "Singers' Roundtable," Met broadcast, 28 March 1981.

4 Johnson to Ziegler, 13 June 1936, Met Archives. By now their correspondence had achieved greater intimacy; the "Edward"'s became "My dear Neddie" and "Eddie".

5 Met broadcast, 28 March 1981, op. cit.

6 Gordon M. Eby, "Bidú," *Opera News*, 2 January 1965, p. 11.

7 Gatti to Ziegler, 22 May 1931, Met Archives.

8 Johnson to Ziegler, 6 June 1935, Met Archives.

9 "Personality of the Week," *Opera News*, 19 October 1942, p. 5.

10 Ziegler to Tuthill, 15 August 1935, Met Archives.

11 Rasponi, *The Last Prima Donnas* (New York: Alfred A. Knopf, 1982), p. 209.

12 Ziegler to Flagstad, 22 May 1935, Met Archives.

13 Ibid.

14 Ziegler to Johnson, 9 July 1935, Met Archives.

15 Ibid.

16 Johnson to Ziegler, 13 June 1935, Met Archives.

17 "Singers' Roundtable," Met broadcast, 28 March 1981.

18 W. J. Henderson, quoted by Kolodin, op. cit., 4th ed., p. 401.

Nicola Moscona as Ferrando in *Il Trovatore*. Photography by Sedge LeBlang.

19 Licia Albanese, "Memories of Susanna," Metropolitan Opera Historic Broadcast booklet for *Le Nozze di Figaro.*

20 Mary Jane Matz, "The Voice of Crooks," *Opera News*, 9 April 1966, p. 27.

21 Erskine, op. cit., pp. 157, 158.

22 Ernest La Prade (NBC) to Met, 7 April 1936, Met Archives.

23 Ziegler to Johnson, 16 June 1936, Met Archives.

24 Tuthill to Ziegler, 21 May 1936, Met Archives.

25 Jon Vickers in "Czech Mates," *Opera News*, 2 December 1978, p. 41.

26 Helen Traubel, *St. Louis Woman* (New York: Duell, Sloan and Pearce, 1959), p. 65.

27 Kolodin, op. cit., 4th ed., p. 403.

28 Traubel, op. cit., p. 67.

29 Ibid., p. 70.

CHAPTER ELEVEN

1 Edwin McArthur, *Flagstad: A Personal Memoir* (New York: Alfred A. Knopf, 1965), p. 86.

2 Leinsdorf, op. cit., p. 73.

3 Henderson, *The New York Times*, 28 November 1909.

4 Leinsdorf, op. cit., p. 44.

5 Ibid., p. 45.

6 Ibid., p. 59.

7 Ibid.

8 Ibid., p. 98.

9 Johnson to Ziegler, 13 July 1936, Met Archives.

10 Kolodin, op. cit., 4th ed., p. 422.

11 "Wagnerian Pagliaccio," *Opera News*, 4 December 1939, p. 11.

12 Leinsdorf, op. cit., p. 99.

13 Ibid., p. 96.

14 Ibid., p. 65.

15 Lotte Lehmann, *Midway in My Song* (New York: Bobbs-Merrill Company, 1938), p. 114.

16 Lehmann, *My Many Lives* (New York: Boosey & Hawkes, Inc., 1948), p. 3.

17 Ibid., p. 96.

18 Risë Stevens interview, Met Marathon broadcast, 1 December 1984.

19 George Szell to Frank St. Leger, 6 September 1944, Met Archives.

20 St. Leger to Szell, 12 September 1944, Met Archives.

21 Kolodin, op. cit., 4th ed., p. 393.

22 Johnson to Ziegler, 5 July 1935, Met Archives.

23 Quoted by Gerald Fitzgerald, "Flagstad and Leonore," Metropolitan Opera Historic Broadcast booklet for *Fidelio*, 1978.

24 Flagstad and Biancolli, op. cit., p. 70.

CHAPTER TWELVE

1 "Mr. Johnson Presents a New Desdemona," *Opera News*, 7 November 1938, p. 1.

2 Rasponi, op. cit., p. 241.

3 Robert Jacobson, "The Most Beautiful Voice in the World," *Opera News*, 9 April 1977, p. 12.

4 "Personality of the Week," *Opera News*, 1 March 1943, p. 5.

5 "Milanov from Ternina to Toscanini," *Opera News*, 25 December 1939, p. 12.

6 Jacobson, op. cit., p. 13.

7 Ibid., p. 14.

8 Ibid.

9 Kolodin, op. cit., 4th ed., p. 423.

10 Jacobson, op. cit., p. 14.

11 Grace Moore, *You're Only Human Once* (Garden City and New York: Garden City Publishing Company, 1944), p. 124.

12 Johnson to Ziegler, 10 June 1935, Met Archives.

13 "Personality of the Week," *Opera News*, 23 November 1942, p. 5.

14 "The Broadcasting Opera Season of 1938–39," *Opera News*, 6 March 1939, p. 18.

15 Johnson to Ziegler, 6 May 1935, Met Archives.

CHAPTER THIRTEEN

1 Johnson to Ziegler, 10 May 1935, Met Archives.

2 "Ezio Pinza Discusses His Roles with Lanfranco Rasponi," *Opera News*, 8 April 1946, p. 11.

3 Johnson to Ziegler, 2 June 1937, Met Archives.

4 "Mountain Water," *Opera News*, 5 February 1940, p. 10.

5 Ibid., p. 9.

6 Albanese, op. cit.

CHAPTER FOURTEEN

1 "Metropolitan History in the Making," *Opera News*, 5 February 1940, p. 2.

2 Ibid., p. 1.

3 "The Prize Winners Are Here!" *Opera News*, 2 December 1940, p. 8.

4 Ibid., pp. 7, 8.

5 Mayer, op. cit., p. 216.

6 Tuthill to Ziegler, 2 June 1939, Met Archives.

7 NBC, Metropolitan Opera Agreement, 23 September 1940, Met Archives.

8 "Oil and Opera," *Opera News*, 9 December 1940, p. 26.

9 Memo, 1 February 1940, Met Archives.

10 Niles Trammell (NBC executive vice-president) to Ziegler, 1 June 1939, Met Archives.

11 Souvaine Associates (prepared for Rudolf Bing), *A Metropolitan Opera Broadcast Digest 1940–1959*, p. 1, Met Archives.

12 The New Yorker Magazine, Inc., 1946, drawing by P. Barlow.

13 Tuthill to Ziegler, 2 June 1939, Met Archives.

14 Ibid., p. 2.

15 Ibid., p. 3.

16 Ibid. The finale to the franchise saga came a year later when NBC informed Ziegler that it had sold the Artists Service business to four NBC executives (Morton, Tuthill, Levine and Bottorff) who would operate the new company as National Concert and Artists Corporation. Trammell to Ziegler, 2 December 1941, Met Archives.

17 NBC, Metropolitan Opera Agreement, 23 September 1940, p. 1.

18 B. M. Grunewald to Ziegler, 30 March 1939, Met Archives.

19 NBC, Metropolitan Opera Agreement, 23 September 1940, p. 2. In reality the inclusion of the aircheck provision in the agreement was recognition of common practice. On 23 March 1940 Ziegler confirmed to NBC that counsel for both RCA and the Metropolitan had approved the gift of earlier NBC opera broadcast transcriptions to the Library of Congress with the understanding they would be available "for reference only to officials of the Library and will not be available to anyone else without the written permission of the donor."

20 Souvaine Associates, op. cit., p. 2.

21 W. L. Kallman (The Texas Company) to Johnson, 18 April 1941, Met Archives.

22 M. E. C. to Met, 19 August 1941, Met Archives.

23 Souvaine Associates, op. cit., p. 2.

CHAPTER FIFTEEN

1 Met broadcast, 30 March 1974.

2 Olin Downes, *The New York Times*, 8 December 1940.

CHAPTER SIXTEEN

1 "The Metropolitan's New Cosmopolite," *Opera News*, 9 December 1940, p. 6.

2 Herbert F. Peyser, "For Deeper Enjoyment of *L'Amore dei Tre Re*," *Opera News*, 10 January 1949, p. 4.

3 Ibid., p. 6.

4 Max de Schauensee, "In and Out of the Puccini Doldrums," *Opera News*, 29 January 1945, p. 4.

5 "Licia Albanese Discusses Butterfly with Betty Van Der Bergh," *Opera News*, 8 December 1947, p. 8.

6 Albanese cable to Metropolitan Opera, 10 October 1940, Met Archives.

7 Valentina, "Designing for Opera," *Opera News*, 10 March 1941, p. 23.

8 "Names, Dates and Places," *Opera News*, 13 January 1941, p. 3.

9 "Hector Berlioz on Gluck's Alceste," adapted from the French by Maryla Friedlaender, *Opera News*, 20 January 1941, p. 12.

CHAPTER SEVENTEEN

1 Alexander Kipnis, "Memories of King Marke," Metropolitan Opera Historic Broadcast booklet for *Tristan und Isolde*, 1976.

2 Bruno Walter to Rudolf Bing, 29 November 1949, Met Archives.

3 "Personality of the Week," *Opera News*, 1 February 1943, p. 5.

CHAPTER EIGHTEEN

1 Kallman to Johnson, 18 April 1941, Met Archives.

2 Ibid.

3 Metropolitan Opera secretary to NBC, 23 May 1941, Met Archives.

4 Traubel, op. cit., p. 95.

5 "Varnay Reviews Her First Season," *Opera News*, 16 March 1942, p. 11.

6 Marks Levine (telegram copy to Ziegler) to Mrs. Lauritz Melchior, 18 July 1941, Met Archives.

7 Jacobson, "Varnay Revisited," *Opera News*, 21 December 1974, p. 25.

8 Leinsdorf, op. cit., p. 104.

9 Ibid.

10 Jacobson, op. cit., pp. 25, 26.

11 Leinsdorf, op. cit., p. 111.

12 Francis Robinson, "Daughter of the Gods," *Opera News*, 26 December 1964, p. 28.

CHAPTER NINETEEN

1 St. Leger to Sir Thomas Beecham, 28 October 1941, Met Archives.

2 Ezio Pinza with Robert Magidoff, *An Autobiography* (New York: Rinehart & Company, Inc., 1958), p. 205.

3 Ibid.

4 Ibid., p. 220.

5 Ibid., p. 216.

6 "The Question of Faust as Sir Thomas Beecham put it to the Metropolitan Opera Guild in a lecture at the Metropolitan Museum in 1942–43," *Opera News*, 25 January 1943, p. 6.

7 Ibid., p. 7.

8 Andrew Porter, *Music of Three Seasons 1974–1977* (New York: Farrar Straus Giroux, 1978), p. 546.

9 Virgil Thomson, "Free Love, Socialism, and Why Girls Leave Home," *Music Reviewed 1940–1954* (New York: Vintage Books, 1967), p. 87.

10 De Schauensee, "Louises in New York," *Opera News*, 5 January 1948, p. 10.

11 Grace Moore to Johnson, 2 June 1943, Met Archives.

12 Kolodin, op. cit., 4th ed., p. 495.

CHAPTER TWENTY

1 Ann M. Lingg, "Friendly Voice," *Opera News*, 15 February 1964, p. 12.

2 Jarmila Novotna to Paul Jackson, 23 September 1989.

3 "Singers' Roundtable," Met broadcast, 6 March 1982.

4 Tibor Kozma, "Ave atque vale—Fritz Reiner," *Opera News*, 6 April 1953, p. 6.

5 Alfred Einstein, *Mozart, His Character, His Work* (New York: Oxford University Press, 1945), pp. 458, 459.

6 "Eleanor Steber Discusses the Mozart Heroines with Lanfranco Rasponi," *Opera News*, 13 January 1947, p. 10.

CHAPTER TWENTY-ONE

1 "Intermission News," *Opera News*, 16 December 1940, p. 10.

2 H. H. to Bori, 16 January 1934, Met Archives.

3 Royal to H. H., 14 February 1934, Met Archives.

4 Ibid.

5 Farrar, op. cit., p. 232.

6 Ibid., p. 233.

7 Ibid., p. 234.

8 Chatfield to Miss Klaffky (Met secretary), 8 February 1935, Met Archives.

9 Bertha Brainard to Vincenzo Bellezza, 5 February 1935, Met Archives.

10 "Tuning in to the Plot," *Opera News*, 18 November 1940, p. 13.

11 Ibid., p. 14.

12 Milton Cross, "Opera Broadcasting," *Opera News*, 25 March 1946, p. 10.

13 "Elements and Emergencies of Operatic Announcing," *Opera News*, 2 December 1940, p. 13.

14 Ibid.

15 Geraldine Souvaine to John Gutman, 9 December 1964, Met Archives.

16 Met broadcast, 17 February 1940.

17 Ibid.

18 "Intermission News," *Opera News*, 16 December 1940, p. 10.

19 Ibid.

20 Ibid., pp. 10, 11.

21 "Lady of the Intermissions: Geraldine Souvaine," *Opera News*, 5 December 1964, p. 14.

22 "Intermission News," *Opera News*, 16 December 1940, p. 10.

23 "Opera Quiz," Met broadcast, 20 December 1947.

24 Frank Merkling, "The Spoken Word," *Opera News*, 28 November 1959, p. 15.

25 Obituary for Olin Downes, *Opera News*, 17 October 1955, p. 30.

26 Harold V. Milligan, "The Opera Quiz," *Opera News*, 10 December 1951, pp. 28, 29, 30.

27 Henry Souvaine to St. Leger, 24 October 1945, Met Archives.

28 Souvaine Associates, op. cit., p. 3.

29 Ibid.

30 Ibid., pp. 3, 4.

31 "Opera News on the Air," Met broadcast, 27 March 1954.

32 Met broadcast, 20 December 1947.

33 Henry Souvaine to Margaret Carson, 3 January 1947, Met Archives.

CHAPTER TWENTY-TWO

1 Lily Pons cable to St. Leger, 27 October 1943 in response to St. Leger to Pons, 16 October 1943, Met Archives.

2 "La Traviata," *Opera News*, 28 March 1949, p. 16.

3 Thomson, *New York Herald Tribune*, 6 December 1942.

4 "The Man Behind the Cue," *Opera News*, 6 March 1944, p. 11.

5 J(ules) H(uret), "Deux interviews—Giuseppe Verdi" in *Le Figaro*, Paris, 5 April 1894. Quoted in *Encounters with Verdi*, ed. Marcello Conati (Ithaca, NY: Cornell University Press, 1984), p. 256.

6 Zinka Milanov interview, Met Marathon broadcast, 28 November 1987.

CHAPTER TWENTY-THREE

1 "Death of a Lion," *Opera News*, 22 March 1969, p. 16. (Martinelli quote of 26 October 1967.)

CHAPTER TWENTY-FOUR

1 Kolodin, op. cit., 4th ed., p. 440.

2 George Szell, "The Baton Points at Boris: Letter to a fellow-musician in England," *Opera News*, 29 November 1943, p. 9.

3 "Names, Dates and Places," *Opera News*, 12 March 1945, p. 3.

4 "Bidú Sayão Talks of Mélisande to Huntington Watts," *Opera News*, 8 January 1945, p. 14.

5 Eby, op. cit., p. 11.

CHAPTER TWENTY-FIVE

1 St. Leger to James Melton, 2 June 1944, Met Archives.

2 Melton to St. Leger, 8 June 1944, Met Archives.

3 St. Leger to Szell, 14 September 1943, Met Archives.

4 Szell to St. Leger, 25 September 1943, Met Archives.

5 Szell to St. Leger, 6 September 1944, Met Archives.

6 Johnson to Ziegler, 5 July 1935, Met Archives.

7 "Names Dates Faces," *Opera News*, 14 April 1960, p. 3.

8 Downes, *The New York Times*, 3 March 1946.

9 Rasponi, *The Last Prima Donnas*, p. 557.

10 Gustave Flaubert, *Madame Bovary* (Paris: F. Sant'Andrea, L. Marcerou & Cie, 1921), p. 242. Author's translation.

11 Gerald Fitzgerald, "Birth of a Tradition," *Opera News*, 25 March 1957, p. 8.

12 De Schauensee, *The Collector's Verdi and Puccini* (Philadelphia and New York: J. B. Lippincott Company, 1962), p. 55.

13 Jan Peerce radio interview, 1963.

14 Thomson, "The Toscanini Case," *Music Reviewed 1940–1954*, p. 75.

15 Fitzgerald, op. cit.

16 Peerce, op. cit.

17 Vincent Sheean, "Toujours La Moore," *Opera News*, 20 December 1969, p. 15.

18 Moore, op. cit., p. 137.

CHAPTER TWENTY-SIX

1 Pitts Sanborn, *New York World Telegram*, 4 March 1938. Quoted in *Metropolitan Opera Annals* (New York: H. W. Wilson Company, 1947), p. 563.

2 Bernard Rogers, "Intentions of *The Warrior*," *Opera News*, 6 January 1947, p. 5.

3 Ibid., p. 6.

4 "The Critics on *Peter Grimes*," *Opera News*, 8 March 1948, p. 7.

CHAPTER TWENTY-SEVEN

1 "Risë Stevens Discusses Marina with Lanfranco Rasponi," *Opera News*, 2 December 1946, p. 5.

2 Risë Stevens, *Subway to the Met: Risë Stevens' Story* (Garden City, NY: Doubleday & Company, Inc., 1959), p. 139.

3 Howard Taubman, *The New York Times*, 19 January 1946.

4 Kolodin, op. cit., 4th ed., p. 473.

5 Radio interview, July 1966. Martinelli and Albanese reminisced about their combined fifty-three-year careers at the old Met.

6 Joseph Gimma to Johnson, 18 March 1947, Met Archives.

7 Albanese to Johnson, 25 March 1947, Met Archives.

8 "Summer Starlight," *Opera News*, 6 October 1947, p. 6.

9 Kolodin, op. cit., 4th ed., p. 467.

10 Ibid.

11 Document, 6 February 1947, Met Archives.

12 "Ferruccio Tagliavini," *Opera News*, 10 February 1947, p. 8.

13 Moore, op. cit., p. 140.

14 Dorothy Kirsten, "Farewell, Not Goodbye," *Opera News*, 3 January 1976, p. 12.

15 Novotna to Jackson, 23 September 1989.

CHAPTER TWENTY-EIGHT

1 "Television Tidings," *Opera News*, 25 March 1940, p. 2.

2 Foerster, "Metropolitan Video," *Opera News*, 20 December 1948, pp. 8, 29.

3 St. Leger to Harry Morgan, 23 December 1949, Met Archives.

4 Rasponi, *The Last Prima Donnas*, p. 443.

5 Gimma to Bing, 24 January 1954, Met Archives.

6 Frieda F. Rothe, "Opera News presents Fritz Reiner," *Opera News*, 21 February 1949, p. 6.

7 Quoted by Philip Hart, Reiner Obituary, *Opera News*, 14 December 1963, p. 29.

8 Rothe, op. cit., p. 7.

9 Ibid.

10 St. Leger to Andre Mertens (Columbia Concerts), 1947, Met Archives.

CHAPTER TWENTY-NINE

1 Kolodin, op. cit., 4th ed., p. 484.

2 *Opera News*, 21 October 1949, p. 21.

3 Rudolf Bing, *5000 Nights at the Opera* (Garden City, NY: Doubleday & Company, Inc., 1972), p. 191.

4 Rasponi, *The Last Prima Donnas*, p. 560.

5 Bing to Max Rudolf, 1950, Met Archives.

6 Rudolf to Bing, 1950, Met Archives.

7 Rudolf to Bing, 25 June 1951 and 27 June 1951, Met Archives.

8 Rasponi, *The Last Prima Donnas*, p. 511.

9 Fritz Stiedry to Johnson, 19 April 1947, Met Archives.

10 Bing to Charles M. Spofford, 4 March 1950, Met Archives. In a recent *Opera News* interview (7 December 1991) artistic administrator Max Rudolf asserts that he and Bing had scheduled Melchior for performances in 1950–51. On 28 January Melchior demanded a contract by 30 January; Bing refused to be coerced by the ultimatum.

11 Bing to Spofford, 31 March 1950, Met Archives.

Giuseppe de Luca, Ezio Pinza, Giovanni Martinelli, and Lucrezia Bori.

Operas and Casts
of the Broadcasts
1931–1950

Major roles in all broadcast performances from 1931–32 through 1949–50 are listed in this table. Italicized dates indicate those performances which are discussed in detail in the text. Symbols preceding the performance date are

> \>   Incomplete broadcast performance

> E   Translation from original language into English

> F   Translation from original language into French

> G   Translation from original language into German

> I   Translation from original language into Italian

The Abduction from the Seraglio (Mozart)

Date	Conductor	Constanza	Blonda	Belmonte	Pedrillo	Osmin	Pasha	Mute
E 18 Jan '47	Cooper	Steber	Alarie	Kullman	Garris	Ernster	Hargrave	Burgstaller

L'Africaine (Meyerbeer)

Date	Conductor	Sélika	Inès	Vasco	Nélusko	Don Pedro	Inquisitor	Diégo
I 19 Mar '32	Serafin	Rethberg	Morgana	Gigli	Basiola	Ludikar	Pinza	Ananian
I 13 Jan '34	Serafin	Ponselle	Morgana	Jagel	Borgioli	Lazzari	Rothier	Ananian

Aida (Verdi)

Date	Conductor	Aida	Amneris	Radames	Amonasro	Ramfis	King	Messenger
> 2 Apr '32	Serafin	Rethberg	C. Ponselle	Merli	Borgioli	Pinza	A. Anderson	Paltrinieri
27 Jan '34	Serafin	Rethberg	Branzell	Del Corso	Borgioli	Lazzari	A. Anderson	Tedesco
16 Mar '35	Panizza	Rethberg	C. Ponselle	Martinelli	Borgioli	Lazzari	D'Angelo	Paltrinieri
25 Jan '36	Panizza	Rethberg	Wettergren	Jagel	Thomas	Baromeo	D'Angelo	Windheim
30 May '36	Papi	Tentoni	Castagna	Rayner	Royer	Gurney	Cordon	Oliviero
6 Feb '37	Panizza	Cigna	Castagna	Martinelli	Morelli	Pinza	Cordon	Paltrinieri
26 Feb '38	Papi	Milanov	Castagna	*Jagel	Tagliabue	Pinza	Cordon	Paltrinieri

*In mid-'Celeste Aida' Martinelli collapsed and Jagel replaced him.

Date	Conductor	Aida	Amneris	Radames	Amonasro	Ramfis	King	Messenger
4 Feb '39	Panizza	Milanov	Castagna	Gigli	Tagliabue	Pinza	Gurney	Altglass
19 Jan '40	Panizza	Bampton	Castagna	Carron	Warren	Moscona	Gurney	Oliviero
2 Mar '40	Panizza	Bampton	Castagna	Carron	Warren	Pinza	Gurney	Oliviero
22 Mar '41	Panizza	Roman	Castagna	Martinelli	Warren	Pinza	Cordon	Oliviero
21 Feb '42	Breisach	Greco	Castagna	Jagel	Thomas	Moscona	Hatfield	Dudley
6 Mar '43	Pelletier	Milanov	Castagna	Martinelli	Bonelli	Cordon	Hatfield	Dudley
15 Dec '44	Cooper	Resnik	Thorborg	Carron	Valentino	Moscona	Whitfield	Oliviero
28 Dec '46	Sodero	Roman	Thebom	Svanholm	Warren	Moscona	Kinsman	Oliviero
21 Feb '48	Cooper	†Ilitsch	Harshaw	Baum	Warren	Moscona	Kinsman	Oliviero

†Ilitsch was replaced by Kirk for Act IV.

Date	Conductor	Aida	Amneris	Radames	Amonasro	Ramfis	King	Messenger
19 Feb '49	Cooper	Welitsch	Harshaw	Jagel	Guarrera	Hines	Kinsman	Franke
11 Mar '50	Cooper	Welitsch	Harshaw	Vinay	Merrill	Hines	Alvary	Franke

Alceste (Gluck)

Date	Conductor	Alceste	Woman	Admète	H. Priest	Oracle	Évandre	Herald
8 Mar '41	Panizza	Bampton	Farell	Maison	Warren	Kent	De Paolis	Cehanovsky

L'Amore dei Tre Re (Montemezzi)

Date	Conductor	Fiora	Avito	Manfredo	Archibaldo	Flaminio	Young Woman	Old Woman
15 Feb '41	Montemezzi	Moore	Kullman	Bonelli	Pinza	De Paolis	Stellman	Kaskas
15 Jan '49	Antonicelli	Kirsten	Kullman	Weede	Lazzari	Chabay	Lenchner	Turner

Un Ballo in Maschera (Verdi)

Date	Conductor	Amelia	Oscar	Ulrica	Riccardo	Renato	Sam	Tom
14 Dec '40	Panizza	Milanov	Andreva	Castagna	Bjoerling	Sved	Cordon	Moscona
28 Feb '42	Panizza	Roman	Antoine	Castagna	Martinelli	Bonelli	Cordon	Moscona
15 Jan '44	Walter	Milanov	Greer	Thorborg	Peerce	Warren	Cordon	Moscona
22 Apr '44	Walter	Milanov	Greer	Thorborg	Peerce	Warren	Lazzari	Moscona
8 Dec '45	Walter	Milanov	Alarie	Harshaw	Peerce	Warren	Cordon	Alvary
22 Nov '47	Antonicelli	Ilitsch	Alarie	Harshaw	Peerce	Warren	Vaghi	Alvary

The Barber of Seville (see Il Barbiere di Siviglia)

Il Barbiere di Siviglia (Rossini)

Date	Conductor	Rosina	Berta	Almaviva	Figaro	Basilio	Bartolo	Fiorello
> 23 Jan '32	Bellezza	Pons	Wakefield	Tokatyan	De Luca	Pinza	Malatesta	Gandolfi
22 Jan '38	Papi	Pons	Petina	Landi	Thomas	Pinza	Malatesta	Engelman
11 Feb '39	Papi	Sayão	Petina	Martini	Thomas	Pinza	Lazzari	Engelman
1 Mar '41	Papi	Tuminia	Petina	Landi	Thomas	Pinza	Baccaloni	Engelman
10 Apr '43	St. Leger	Sayão	Petina	Martini	Brownlee	Pinza	Baccaloni	Harrell

The Bartered Bride (Smetana)

Date	Conductor	Marenka	Ludmila	Jenek	Vasek	Kecal	Krusina	Esmeralda
G 4 Feb '33	Bodanzky	Rethberg	Manski	Laubenthal	Windheim	Hofmann	Schützendorf	Gleason
E 23 May '36	Pelletier	Dickson	Browning	Chamlee	Rasely	D'Angelo	Engelman	Bodanya
E 8 May '37	Pelletier	Burke	Browning	Chamlee	Rasely	D'Angelo	Engelman	Bodanya

La Bohème (Puccini)

Date	Conductor	Mimi	Musetta	Rodolfo	Marcello	Schaunard	Colline	Benoit
> 1 Jan '32	Bellezza	Bori	Guilford	Gigli	De Luca	Frigerio	Pinza	Ananian
24 Dec '32	Bellezza	Müller	Morgana	Lauri-Volpi	Bonelli	Frigerio	Pinza	Ananian
23 Mar '35	Bellezza	Rethberg	Morgana	Jagel	De Luca	Picco	Pinza	Ananian
14 Mar '36	Papi	Moore	Gleason	Kullman	Morelli	Cehanovsky	Pinza	D'Angelo
15 Jan '38	Papi	Moore	Dickson	Landi	Tagliabue	Cehanovsky	Pinza	D'Angelo
10 Feb '40	Papi	Sayão	Dickey	Tokatyan	De Luca	Cehanovsky	Pinza	D'Angelo
12 Dec '42	Sodero	Moore	Greer	Jagel	Valentino	Engelman	Pinza	Baccaloni
4 Mar '44	Sodero	Sayão	Carroll	Martini	Brownlee	Cehanovsky	Lazzari	D'Angelo
29 Apr '44	Sodero	Albanese	Carroll	Kullman	Brownlee	Cehanovsky	Pinza	D'Angelo
3 Feb '45	Sodero	Sayão	Greer	Peerce	Valentino	Thompson	Moscona	Baccaloni
2 Mar '46	Sodero	Roman	Greer	Peerce	Brownlee	Kent	Vaghi	D'Angelo
31 Jan '48	Antonicelli	Sayão	Benzell	Tagliavini	Brownlee	Thompson	Moscona	Baccaloni
25 Dec '48	Antonicelli	Sayão	Benzell	Bjoerling	Valentino	Cehanovsky	Moscona	Baccaloni
25 Mar '50	Antonicelli	Albanese	Hunt	Tucker	Brownlee	Cehanovsky	Moscona	Pechner

Boris Godunov (Mussorgsky)

	Date	Conductor	Marina	Dimitri	Rangoni	Boris	Pimen	Varlaam	Schouisky
I	9 Dec '39	Panizza	Thorborg	Kullman	Warren	Pinza	Moscona	Cordon	De Paolis
I	13 Feb '43	Szell	Thorborg	Maison	Warren	*Kipnis	Moscona	Cordon	De Paolis
I	4 Dec '43	Szell	Thorborg	Tokatyan	Warren	Pinza	Moscona	Baccaloni	De Paolis
I	7 Dec '46	Cooper	Stevens	Tucker	Valentino	Pinza	Moscona	Baccaloni	De Paolis

*Kipnis sang in Russian

Carmen (Bizet)

	Date	Conductor	Carmen	Micaela	Frasquita	Mercedes	Don José	Escamillo	Zuniga
	1 Jan '36	Hasselmans	Ponselle	Fisher	Votipka	Olheim	Kullman	Pinza	D'Angelo
	28 Mar '36	Hasselmans	Ponselle	Fisher	Votipka	Olheim	Maison	Pinza	D'Angelo
	16 May '36	Papi	Castagna	Bodanya	Symons	Olheim	Tokatyan	Royer	Cordon
	9 Jan '37	Papi	Ponselle	Bodanya	Votipka	Olheim	Rayner	Huehn	D'Angelo
	17 Apr '37	Papi	Ponselle	Burke	Votipka	Olheim	Maison	Huehn	D'Angelo
	19 Mar '38	Papi	Castagna	Fisher	Votipka	Olheim	Maison	Brownlee	Cordon
>	21 Feb '41	Pelletier	Swarthout	Albanese	Votipka	Olheim	Jobin	Warren	D'Angelo
	15 Mar '41	Pelletier	Swarthout	Albanese	Votipka	Olheim	Kullman	Warren	D'Angelo
	24 Jan '42	Beecham	Djanel	Albanese	Votipka	Olheim	Kullman	Warren	Cordon
	27 Mar '43	Beecham	Djanel	Albanese	Votipka	Olheim	Jobin	Warren	Alvary
	22 Jan '44	Beecham	Djanel	Conner	Votipka	Browning	Jobin	Sved	Alvary
	6 May '44	Pelletier	Djanel	Albanese	Votipka	Browning	Jobin	Valentino	Alvary
	24 Mar '45	Pelletier	Djanel	Albanese	Votipka	Browning	Jobin	Valentino	D'Angelo
	22 Feb '47	Rudolf	Stevens	Conner	Votipka	Browning	Vinay	Merrill	Hargrave
	7 Feb '48	Pelletier	Stevens	Conner	Votipka	Browning	Vinay	Singher	Kinsman
	5 Mar '49	Pelletier	Stevens	Conner	Votipka	Lipton	Baum	Merrill	Alvary
	4 Feb '50	Perlea	Stevens	Conner	Votipka	Browning	Baum	Guarrera	Kinsman

Cavalleria Rusticana (Mascagni)

Date	Conductor	Santuzza	Lola	Lucia	Turiddu	Alfio
10 Apr '37	Papi	Rethberg	Petina	Kaskas	Rayner	Morelli
1 Feb '41	Calusio	Roman	Kaskas	Doe	Jagel	Warren
20 Mar '43	Sodero	Milanov	Kaskas	Olheim	Jagel	Valentino
25 Mar '44	Sodero	Flesch	Paulee	Votipka	Tokatyan	Valentino
28 Feb '48	Antonicelli	Resnik	Lipton	Turner	Berini	Brownlee

Les Contes d'Hoffmann (Offenbach)

Date	Conductor	Olympia	Giulietta	Antonia	Hoffmann	Coppelius, Miracle	Dappertutto	Servants
23 Jan '37	Abravanel	Bovy	Bovy	Bovy	Maison	Tibbett	Tibbett	Bada
26 Feb '44	Beecham	Munsel	Djanel	Novotna	Jobin	Pinza	Singher	De Paolis
12 Jan '46	Pelletier	Alarie	Thebom	Novotna	Jobin	Singher	Singher	Oliviero, De Paolis

Le Coq d'Or (*see* The Golden Cockerel)

The Daughter of the Regiment (*see* La Fille du Régiment)

Don Giovanni (Mozart)

Date	Conductor	Anna	Elvira	Zerlina	Ottavio	Giovanni	Leporello	Masetto	Commandant
17 Dec '32	Serafin	Ponselle	Müller	Fleischer	Schipa	Pinza	Pasero	Malatesta	Rothier
20 Jan '34	Serafin	Ponselle	Müller	Fleischer	Schipa	Pinza	Lazzari	D'Angelo	List
9 Feb '35	Panizza	Ponselle	Müller	Fleischer	Borgioli	Pinza	Lazzari	D'Angelo	List
1 Jan '38	Panizza	Giannini	Cigna	Farell	Crooks	Pinza	Lazzari	D'Angelo	List
14 Jan '39	Panizza	Rethberg	Jessner	Farell	Crooks	Brownlee	Lazzari	D'Angelo	Cordon
7 Mar '42	Walter	Bampton	Novotna	Sayão	Kullman	Pinza	Kipnis	Harrell	Cordon
3 Apr '43	Breisach	Milanov	Novotna	Sayão	Melton	Pinza	Baccaloni	Harrell	Cordon
9 Dec '44	Szell	Kirk	Steber	Sayão	Kullman	Pinza	Baccaloni	Harrell	Moscona
6 Dec '47	Rudolf	Resnik	Stoska	Conner	Kullman	Pinza	Baccaloni	Alvary	Hines

Don Pasquale (Donizetti)

Date	Conductor	Norina	Ernesto	Malatesta	Pasquale	Notary
23 Feb '35	Panizza	Bori	Schipa	De Luca	Pinza	Paltrinieri
21 Dec '40	Papi	Sayão	Martini	Valentino	Baccaloni	De Paolis
5 Jan '46	Busch	Sayão	Martini	Brownlee	Baccaloni	De Paolis

Elektra (R. Strauss)

Date	Conductor	Elektra	Chrysothemis	Klytemnestra	Aegisth	Orest	Overseer
12 Mar '32	Bodanzky	Kappel	Ljungberg	Branzell	Laubenthal	Schorr	Manski

The Elixir of Love (*see* L'Elisir d'Amore)

L'Elisir d'Amore (Donizetti)

Date	Conductor	Adina	Giannetta	Nemorino	Belcore	Dulcamara
3 Jan '42	Panizza	Sayão	Paulee	Landi	Valentino	Baccaloni
5 Feb '49	Antonicelli	Sayão	I. Manski	Tagliavini	Valentino	Tajo
24 Dec '49	Antonicelli	Sayão	Lenchner	Tagliavini	Valdengo	Baccaloni

The Emperor Jones (Gruenberg)

Date	Conductor	Native Woman	Jones	Smithers	Witch Doctor
7 Jan '33	Serafin	Besuner	Tibbett	Windheim	Winfield

Die Entführung aus dem Serail (*see* The Abduction from the Seraglio)

Falstaff (Verdi)

Date	Conductor	Alice	Nannetta	Meg Page	Quickly	Fenton	Falstaff	Ford
E 11 Mar '44	Beecham	Steber	Greer	Browning	Harshaw	Kullman	Warren	Brownlee
26 Feb '49	Reiner	Resnik	Albanese	Lipton	Elmo	Di Stefano	Warren	Valdengo

Faust (Gounod)

Date	Conductor	Marguerite	Siebel	Marthe	Faust	Valentin	Méphistophélès	Wagner
> 13 Feb '32	Hasselmans	Rethberg	Besuner	Wakefield	Thill	Basiola	Rothier	Ananian
17 Feb '34	Hasselmans	Norena	Swarthout	Wakefield	Martinelli	Tibbett	Pinza	Ananian
20 Mar '37	Pelletier	Jepson	Olheim	Bourskaya	Crooks	Bonelli	Pinza	Engelman
16 Mar '40	Pelletier	Jepson	Browning	Votipka	Crooks	Warren	Pinza	Engelman
6 Apr '40	Pelletier	Jepson	Olheim	Votipka	Crooks	Warren	Pinza	Engelman
14 Mar '42	Beecham	Albanese	Browning	Votipka	Kullman	Warren	Cordon	Engelman
30 Jan '43	Beecham	Albanese	Browning	Votipka	Jobin	Thomas	Pinza	Baker
15 Apr '44	Beecham	Albanese	Browning	Votipka	Jobin	Singher	Pinza	Baker
16 Dec '44	Pelletier	Albanese	Lipton	Votipka	Jobin	Singher	Pinza	Baker
4 Jan '47	Fourestier	Mazella	Stellman	Turner	Jobin	Singher	Pinza	Harbour
31 Dec '49	Pelletier	Kirsten	I. Manski	Turner	Di Stefano	Warren	Tajo	Thompson

Fidelio (Beethoven)

Date	Conductor	Leonore	Marzelline	Florestan	Jacquino	Pizarro	Rocco	Fernando
7 Mar '36	Bodanzky	Flagstad	Fleischer	Maison	Clemens	Hofmann	List	Huehn
31 Dec '38	Bodanzky	Flagstad	Farell	Maison	Laufkoetter	Schorr	List	Huehn
22 Feb '41	Walter	Flagstad	Farell	Maison	Laufkoetter	Huehn	Kipnis	Gabor
E 17 Mar '45	Walter	Resnik	Greer	Carron	Garris	Schon	Alvary	Janssen

La Fille du Régiment (Donizetti)

Date	Conductor	Marie	Marquise	Tonio	Sulpice	Hortensius	Duchess
28 Dec '40	Papi	Pons	Petina	Jobin	Baccaloni	D'Angelo	Savage

La Forza del Destino (Verdi)

Date	Conductor	Leonora	Preziosilla	Alvaro	Carlo	Guardiano	Melitone	Marqui
19 Jan '35	Bellezza	Rethberg	Swarthout	Martinelli	Borgioli	Pinza	Gandolfi	D'Angelo
23 Jan '43	Walter	Roman	Petina	Jagel	Tibbett	Pinza	Baccaloni	D'Angelo
27 Nov '43	Walter	Roman	Kaskas	Jagel	Tibbett	Pinza	Baccaloni	Lechner

Gianni Schicchi (Puccini)

Date	Conductor	Lauretta	Nella	Zita	Rinuccio	Schicchi	Simone	Spinelloccio
E 29 Feb '36	Papi	Burke	Symons	Bourskaya	Bentonelli	Huehn	Baromeo	Malatesta
12 Mar '49	Antonicelli	Albanese	Lenchner	Elmo	Di Stefano	Tajo	Lazzari	Luise

La Gioconda (Ponchielli)

Date	Conductor	Gioconda	Laura	Cieca	Enzo	Barnaba	Alvise
30 Dec '39	Panizza	Milanov	Castagna	Kaskas	Martinelli	Morelli	Moscona

The Golden Cockerel (Rimsky-Korsakov)

Date	Conductor	Queen	Amelfa	Cockerel	Astrologer	Guidon	Afron	Dodon	Polkan
E 10 Mar '45	Cooper	Munsel	Harshaw	Votipka	Marlowe	Manning	Thompson	Cordon	Gurney

Götterdämmerung (Wagner)

Date	Conductor	Brünhilde	Gutrune	Waltraute	Siegfried	Gunther	Alberich	Hagen
> 17 Mar '32	Bodanzky	Kappel	Manski	Doe	Melchior	Schützendorf	Gabor	Bohnen
> 31 Dec '32	Bodanzky	Ljungberg	Fleischer	Branzell	De Loor	Schorr	Schützendorf	Hofmann
> 17 Feb '33	Bodanzky	Leider	Manski	Olszewska	Melchior	Schorr	Schützendorf	Hofmann
11 Jan '36	Bodanzky	Lawrence	Manski	Meisle	Melchior	Schorr	Habich	Hofmann
12 May '39	Bodanzky	Flagstad	Manski	Thorborg	Melchior	Huehn	Gabor	List

Hänsel und Gretel (Humperdinck)

Date	Conductor	Hänsel	Gretel	Gertrud	Witch	Sandman	Dewfairy	Peter
25 Dec '31	Riedel	Fleischer	Mario	Wakefield	Manski	Flexer	Besuner	Schützendorf
26 Dec '32	Riedel	Fleischer	Mario	Wakefield	Manski	Bampton	Besuner	Schützendorf
25 Dec '33	Riedel	Fleischer	Mario	Wakefield	Manski	Flexer	Besuner	Schützendorf
25 Dec '34	Riedel	Fleischer	Mario	Wakefield	Manski	Flexer	Besuner	Schützendorf
24 Dec '36	Riedel	Jessner	Mario	Doe	Manski	Browning	Symons	Habich
10 Apr '37	Riedel	Jessner	Mario	Doe	Manski	Flexer	Andreva	Gabor
24 Dec '37	Riedel	Jessner	Mario	Doe	Manski	Browning	Symons	Gabor
26 Dec '38	Riedel	Jessner	Mario	Doe	Manski	Browning	Besuner	Gabor
E 11 Jan '47	Stiedry	Stevens	Conner	Turner	Votipka	Browning	Raymondi	Brownlee

Khovanchina (Mussorgsky)

Date	Conductor	Marfa	Susanna	Golitsin	Andrei	Shaklovity	Khovansky	Dossifé	Emma
E 25 Feb '50	Cooper	Stevens	Stoska	Kullman	Sullivan	Weede	Tibbett	Hines	Bollinger

Lakmé (Delibes)

Date	Conductor	Lakmé	Mallika	Ellen	Rose	Gerald	Frederic	Nilakantha	Hadji
> 27 Feb '32	Hasselmans	Pons	Swarthout	Ryan	Flexer	Jagel	De Luca	Rothier	Paltrinieri
> 24 Nov '32	Hasselmans	Pons	Swarthout	Doninelli	Falco	Martinelli	Cehanovsky	Rothier	Paltrinieri
6 Jan '40	Pelletier	Pons	Petina	Dickey	Browning	Tokatyan	Cehanovsky	Pinza	Massue
27 Dec '41	Pelletier	Pons	Petina	Dickey	Browning	Jobin	Cehanovsky	Pinza	Carter
9 Jan '43	Pelletier	Pons	Olheim	Greer	Browning	Gerard	Harrell	Cordon	Garris
23 Nov '46	Fourestier	Pons	Jordan	Farell	Stellman	Jobin	Singher	Vaghi	Carter

Lohengrin (Wagner)

	Date	Conductor	Elsa	Ortrud	Lohengrin	Telramund	Herald	King Henry
>	9 Jan '32	Bodanzky	Müller	Branzell	Lorenz	Schorr	Cehanovsky	Andresen
>	14 Jan '33	Bodanzky	Rethberg	Branzell	De Loor	Schorr	Cehanovsky	Hofmann
>	24 Mar '34	Bodanzky	Rethberg	Olszewska	Melchior	Schützendorf	Cehanovsky	Hofmann
	21 Dec '35	Bodanzky	Lehmann	Lawrence	Melchior	Schorr	Huehn	List
	27 Mar '37	Abravanel	Flagstad	Branzell	Maison	Huehn	Gabor	Hofmann
	19 Feb '38	Abravanel	Flagstad	Branzell	Melchior	Huehn	Cehanovsky	Hofmann
	27 Jan '40	Leinsdorf	Rethberg	Thorborg	Melchior	Huehn	Warren	List
	17 Jan '42	Leinsdorf	Varnay	Thorborg	Melchior	Janssen	Warren	Cordon
	2 Jan '43	Leinsdorf	Varnay	Thorborg	Melchior	Sved	Harrell	Cordon
	24 Feb '45	Leinsdorf	Varnay	Thorborg	Melchior	Sved	Harrell	Cordon
	26 Nov '45	Busch	Traubel	Thorborg	Ralf	Janssen	Thompson	Cordon
	22 Dec '45	Busch	Varnay	Thorborg	Melchior	Janssen	Thompson	Moscona
	25 Jan '47	Busch	Traubel	Harshaw	Melchior	Hawkins	Thompson	Ernster
	7 Jan '50	Stiedry	Traubel	Varnay	Melchior	Janssen	Guarrera	Ernster

Louise (Charpentier)

Date	Conductor	Louise	Mother	Camille	Julien	Father	Noctambulist, King of Fools
28 Jan '39	Panizza	Moore	Doe	Votipka	Maison	Pinza	De Paolis
20 Feb '43	Beecham	Moore	Doe	Votipka	Jobin	Pinza	De Paolis
10 Jan '48	Fourestier	Kirsten	Harshaw	Votipka	Jobin	Brownlee	Hayward, De Paolis

The Love of Three Kings (see L'Amore dei Tre Re)

Lucia di Lammermoor (Donizetti)

	Date	Conductor	Lucia	Alisa	Edgardo	Arturo	Ashton	Raimondo	Normanno
>	26 Nov '32	Bellezza	Pons	Egener	Schipa	Tedesco	De Luca	Rothier	Altglass
	3 Mar '34	Bellezza	Pons	Vettori	Martini	Tedesco	De Luca	Rothier	Bada
	29 Dec '34	Bellezza	Pons	Vettori	Martini	Tedesco	Bonelli	Lazzari	Paltrinieri
	27 Feb '37	Papi	Pons	Votipka	Jagel	Massue	Brownlee	Pinza	Bada
	12 Mar '38	Papi	Pons	Votipka	Jagel	Bada	Morelli	Pinza	Paltrinieri
	24 Dec '38	Papi	Pons	Votipka	Masini	Massue	Tagliabue	Pinza	Paltrinieri
	3 Feb '40	Papi	Pons	Votipka	Jagel	Massue	Bonelli	Lazzari	Oliviero
	28 Nov '42	St. Leger	Pons	Votipka	Peerce	Garris	Valentino	Moscona	Dudley
	8 Jan '44	Sodero	Pons	Votipka	Melton	De Paolis	Warren	Moscona	Dudley
	6 Jan '45	Sodero	Munsel	Votipka	Peerce	Manning	Warren	Moscona	Oliviero
	9 Mar '46	Cimara	Munsel	Votipka	Peerce	Hayward	Valentino	Moscona	Oliviero
	17 Jan '48	Cimara	Pons	Votipka	Tagliavini	Knight	Merrill	Moscona	Oliviero
*	1 Jan '49	Cimara	Pons	Votipka	Tagliavini	Knight	Valentino	Hines	Marlowe
	14 Jan '50	Cimara	Munsel	Votipka	Peerce	Hayward	Valentino	Hines	Chabay

*Broadcast on 2 Jan '49.

Madama Butterfly (Puccini)

Date	Conductor	Cio-Cio-San	Suzuki	Kate	Pinkerton	Sharpless	Goro	Bonze	Yamadori
25 Jan '41	Papi	Albanese	Browning	Stellman	Tokatyan	Brownlee	De Paolis	Gurney	Cehanovsky
19 Jan '46	Cimara	Albanese	Browning	Stellman	Melton	Brownlee	De Paolis	Hawkins	Cehanovsky
8 Feb '47	Sodero	Resnik	Browning	Stellman	Kullman	Brownlee	De Paolis	Hawkins	Cehanovsky
13 Dec '47	Antonicelli	Albanese	Altman	Jordan	Melton	Brownlee	De Paolis	Luise	Cehanovsky
18 Feb '50	Antonicelli	Albanese	Altman	Bollinger	Melton	Brownlee	De Paolis	Luise	Cehanovsky

The Magic Flute (Mozart)

Date	Conductor	Pamina	Queen	1st Lady	Papagena	Tamino	Papageno	Speaker	Sarastro
E 10 Jan '42	Walter	Novotna	Bok	Steber	Bodanya	Kullman	Brownlee	Schorr	Kipnis
E 26 Dec '42	Walter	Novotna	Antoine	Steber	Raymondi	Kullman	Brownlee	Cordon	Pinza
E 1 Apr '44	Walter	Conner	Bowman	Steber	Raymondi	Kullman	Brownlee	Moscona	Kipnis
E 1 Dec '45	Walter	Conner	Benzell	Resnik	Raymondi	Kullman	Thompson	Ezekiel	Pinza

Manon (Massenet)

Date	Conductor	Manon	Des Grieux	Lescaut	Count	Guillot	Brétigny
> 5 Mar '32	Hasselmans	Moore	Gigli	De Luca	Rothier	Bada	Cehanovsky
25 Feb '33	Hasselmans	Bori	Crooks	De Luca	Rothier	Bada	Cehanovsky
31 Mar '34	Hasselmans	Bori	Crooks	De Luca	Rothier	Bada	Cehanovsky
> 29 Mar '36	Hasselmans	Bori	Crooks	*	Rothier	*	*

*Act III, sc. 2 was the only broadcast portion of the Bori Farewell Gala.

Date	Conductor	Manon	Des Grieux	Lescaut	Count	Guillot	Brétigny
13 Feb '37	Abravanel	Sayão	Rayner	Bonelli	Baromeo	Bada	Cehanovsky
4 Dec '37	Abravanel	Sayão	Crooks	Brownlee	Rothier	Bada	Cehanovsky
25 Feb '39	Pelletier	Sayão	Kiepura	Brownlee	Rothier	De Paolis	Cehanovsky
13 Jan '40	Pelletier	Moore	Crooks	Brownlee	Moscona	De Paolis	Cehanovsky
16 Jan '43	Beecham	Sayão	Kullman	Brownlee	Moscona	De Paolis	Cehanovsky
20 Dec '47	Fourestier	Sayão	Kullman	Singher	Moscona	De Paolis	Cehanovsky

Manon Lescaut (Puccini)

Date	Conductor	Manon	Des Grieux	Lescaut	Geronte	Edmondo	Dancing Master	Innkeeper
10 Dec '49	Antonicelli	Kirsten	Bjoerling	Valdengo	Baccaloni	Hayward	De Paolis	Cehanovsky

The Man Without a Country (Damrosch)

Date	Conductor	Mary	Philip	Madrigal	A. Burr	Morgan	Reeve	Boatman	Admiral	Decatur
22 May '37	Pelletier	Traubel	Carron	Madeira	Royer	Gurney	Cehanovsky	D. Dickson	Rasely	D'Angelo

The Marriage of Figaro (see Le Nozze di Figaro)

The Masked Ball (see Un Ballo in Maschera)

Die Meistersinger von Nürnberg (Wagner)

Date	Conductor	Eva	Magdalene	Walther	David	Sachs	Kothner	Beckmesser	Pogner
22 Feb '36	Bodanzky	Rethberg	Branzell	Maison	Clemens	Schorr	Huehn	Habich	List
> 4 May '39	Bodanzky	Rethberg	Doe	Kullman	Laufkoetter	Schorr	Cehanovsky	Cehanovsky	List
2 Dec '39	Leinsdorf	Jessner	Branzell	Kullman	Laufkoetter	Schorr	Janssen	Olitzki	List
10 Feb '45	Szell	Steber	Thorborg	Kullman	Garris	Janssen	Harrell	Pechner	List
> 15 Dec '45	Szell	Steber	Thorborg	Kullman	Garris	Gynrod	Schon	Pechner	List
> 29 Nov '47	Martin	Stoska	Harshaw	Ralf	Garris	Janssen	Harrell	Pechner	Ernster

Merry Mount (Hanson)

Date	Conductor	Marigold	Plentiful	Desire	Gower	Bradford	Tewke	Morton	Tinker
10 Feb '34	Serafin	Ljungberg	Swarthout	Petina	Johnson	Tibbett	D'Angelo	Cehanovsky	Gabor

Mignon (Thomas)

Date	Conductor	Mignon	Philine	Frederic	Wilhelm	Laerte	Lothario	Jarno
30 Dec '33	Hasselmans	Bori	Pons	Swarthout	Schipa	Bada	Rothier	Ananian
4 Jan '36	Hasselmans	Bori	Antoine	Olheim	Crooks	Bada	Pinza	Wolfe
13 Mar '37	Pelletier	Swarthout	Antoine	Olheim	Hackett	Bada	Pinza	Cordon
15 May '37	Pelletier	Tourel	Antoine	Matyas	Tokatyan	Defrere	Rothier	Cordon
17 Dec '38	Pelletier	Stevens	Antoine	Olheim	Crooks	De Paolis	Pinza	Gurney
25 Dec '43	Beecham	Stevens	Munsel	Browning	Melton	De Paolis	Cordon	Gurney
27 Jan '45	Pelletier	Stevens	Benzell	Browning	Melton	Dame	Pinza	Gurney
4 Dec '48	Pelletier	Stevens	Cotlow	Madeira	Melton	Garris	Moscona	Hawkins

Norma (Bellini)

Date	Conductor	Norma	Adalgisa	Clotilde	Pollione	Flavio	Oroveso
> 26 Dec '31	Serafin	Ponselle	Swarthout	Egener	Lauri-Volpi	Bada	Pinza
20 Feb '37	Panizza	Cigna	Castagna	Votipka	Martinelli	Paltrinieri	Pinza
12 Feb '44	Sodero	Milanov	Castagna	Votipka	Jagel	De Paolis	Lazzari
30 Dec '44	Sodero	Milanov	Tourel	Votipka	Jagel	De Paolis	Cordon

Le Nozze di Figaro (Mozart)

Date	Conductor	Countess	Susanna	Cherubino	Marcellina	Almaviva	Figaro	Basilio	Bartolo
9 Mar '40	Panizza	Rethberg	Sayão	Novotna	Petina	Brownlee	Pinza	De Paolis	Lazzari
7 Dec '40	Panizza	Rethberg	Albanese	Novotna	Petina	Brownlee	Pinza	De Paolis	Baccaloni
20 Dec '41	Panizza	Rethberg	Sayão	Stevens	Petina	Brownlee	Pinza	De Paolis	Pechner
17 Apr '43	Breisach	Steber	Sayão	Novotna	Glaz	Brownlee	Pinza	De Paolis	Baccaloni
29 Jan '44	Walter	Steber	Sayão	Novotna	Petina	Brownlee	Pinza	De Paolis	Baccaloni
15 Mar '47	Busch	Steber	Schymberg	Novotna	Glaz	Brownlee	Pinza	De Paolis	Baccaloni
8 Jan '49	Busch	Steber	Sayão	Novotna	Turner	Brownlee	Tajo	De Paolis	Baccaloni
11 Feb '50	Reiner	Steber	Sayão	Novotna	Turner	Brownlee	Tajo	Klein	Baccaloni

Orfeo ed Euridice (Gluck)

Date	Conductor	Orfeo	Euridice	Amor	Spirit
26 Nov '38	Bodanzky	Thorborg	Jessner	Morel	Farell
20 Jan '40	Leinsdorf	Thorborg	Novotna	Farell	Dickey

Otello (Verdi)

Date	Conductor	Desdemona	Otello	Emilia	Cassio	Iago	Lodovico	Montano
12 Feb '38	Panizza	Rethberg	Martinelli	Votipka	Massue	Tibbett	Moscona	Cehanovsky
3 Dec '38	Panizza	Caniglia	Martinelli	Votipka	De Paolis	Tibbett	Moscona	Cehanovsky
24 Feb '40	Panizza	Rethberg	Martinelli	Votipka	De Paolis	Tibbett	Moscona	Cehanovsky
18 Jan '41	Panizza	Roman	Martinelli	Votipka	De Paolis	Tibbett	Moscona	Cehanovsky
23 Feb '46	Szell	Roman	Ralf	Lipton	De Paolis	Warren	Moscona	Schon
16 Nov '46	Busch	Roman	Ralf	Lipton	De Paolis	Warren	Moscona	Hargrave
29 Nov '48 *	Busch	Albanese	Vinay	Lipton	Garris	Warren	Moscona	Harvuot
18 Dec '48	Busch	Albanese	Vinay	Lipton	Garris	Warren	Moscona	Harvuot

*First telecast from the Met; no radio transmission.

Pagliacci (Leoncavallo)

Date	Conductor	Nedda	Canio	Beppe	Tonio	Silvio
10 Mar '34	Bellezza	Mario	Martinelli	Tedesco	Tibbett	Cehanovsky
29 Feb '36	Papi	Mario	Martinelli	Paltrinieri	Bonelli	Cehanovsky
26 Dec '38	Papi	Burke	Jagel	Paltrinieri	Tagliabue	Cehanovsky
1 Feb '41	Calusio	Greco	Martinelli	De Paolis	Tibbett	Valentino
20 Mar '43	Sodero	Farell	Martinelli	Dudley	Warren	Cassel
25 Mar '44	Sodero	Albanese	Jobin	Dudley	Warren	Valentino
28 Feb '48	Antonicelli	Quartararo	Vinay	Chabay	Warren	Thompson

Parsifal (Wagner)

Date	Conductor	Kundry	Parsifal	Amfortas	Klingsor	Gurnemanz	Titurel
> 25 Mar '32	Bodanzky	Kappel	Melchior	Whitehill	Schützendorf	Bohnen	Tappolet
> 9 Mar '33	Bodanzky	Leider	Melchior	Schorr	Schützendorf	Hofmann	Wolfe
15 Apr '38	*Bodanzky	Flagstad	Melchior	Schorr	Gabor	List	Cordon

*Leinsdorf conducted Act II.

Pelléas et Mélisande (Debussy)

Date	Conductor	Mélisande	Geneviève	Yniold	Pelléas	Golaud	Arkel	Physician
> 21 Jan '33	Hasselmans	Bori	Bourskaya	Sabanieeva	Johnson	Pinza	Rothier	Ananian
7 Apr '34	Hasselmans	Bori	Bourskaya	Dalossy	Johnson	Pinza	Rothier	D'Angelo
13 Jan '45	Cooper	Sayão	Harshaw	Raymondi	Singher	Tibbett	Kipnis	Alvary

Peter Grimes (Britten)

Date	Conductor	Ellen	Peter	Auntie	Mrs. Sedley	Balstrode	Boles	Swallow	Rev. Adams
13 Mar '48	Cooper	Stoska	Jagel	Turner	Lipton	Harrell	Hayward	Hines	Garris
12 Feb '49	Cooper	Stoska	Sullivan	Madeira	Lipton	Tibbett	Hayward	Hines	Garris

Peter Ibbetson (Taylor)

Date	Conductor	Mary	Mrs. Deane	Peter	Col. Ibbetson	Duquesnois
> 26 Mar '32	Serafin	Bori	Swarthout	Johnson	Tibbett	D'Angelo
17 Mar '34	Serafin	Bori	Swarthout	Johnson	Tibbett	Rothier

Prodaná Nevesta (*see* The Bartered Bride)

Das Rheingold (Wagner)

Date	Conductor	Freia	Fricka	Erda	Loge	Wotan	Alberich	Mime
>?: 26 Feb '32	Bodanzky	Ljungberg	Kappel	Schumann-Heink	Laubenthal	Bohnen	Schützendorf	Windheim
> 27 Jan '33	Bodanzky	Manski	Doe	Olszewska	Laubenthal	Schorr	Schützendorf	Windheim
3 Apr '37	Bodanzky	Manski	Branzell	Doe	Maison	Schorr	Habich	Laufkoetter

Rigoletto (Verdi)

Date	Conductor	Gilda	Maddalena	Duke	Rigoletto	Monterone	Sparafucile	Marullo
18 Feb '33	Bellezza	Pons	Swarthout	Lauri-Volpi	De Luca	Gandolfi	Pasero	Picco
28 Dec '35	Panizza	Pons	Olheim	Jagel	Tibbett	Gandolfi	Lazzari	Cehanovsky
5 Mar '38	Panizza	Sayão	Petina	Kiepura	Tagliabue	Cordon	Pinza	Cehanovsky
11 Mar '39	Papi	Pons	Olheim	Kiepura	Tibbett	Cordon	Lazzari	Cehanovsky
31 Jan '42	Panizza	Reggiani	Castagna	Landi	Weede	Hatfield	Moscona	Cehanovsky
18 Dec '43	Sodero	Pons	Kaskas	Kullman	Warren	Hawkins	Moscona	Cehanovsky
20 Jan '45	Sodero	Antoine	Kaskas	Kullman	Weede	Hargrave	Cordon	Cehanovsky
29 Dec '45	Sodero	Sayão	Lipton	Bjoerling	Warren	Hargrave	Cordon	Cehanovsky
1 Mar '47	Sodero	Schymberg	Lipton	Peerce	Warren	Hawkins	Vaghi	Cehanovsky
19 Mar '49	Cimara	Munsel	Lipton	Peerce	Warren	Schon	Ernster	Cehanovsky
4 Mar '50	Perlea	Munsel	Lipton	Peerce	Warren	Harvuot	Moscona	Cehanovsky

Roméo et Juliette (Gounod)

Date	Conductor	Juliette	Stephano	Gertrude	Roméo	Tybalt	Mercutio	Capulet	Laurence
> 9 Apr '32	Hasselmans	Moore	Swarthout	Wakefield	Gigli	Bada	De Luca	Whitehill	Rothier
26 Jan '35	Hasselmans	Norena	Swarthout	Wakefield	Hackett	Bada	De Luca	D'Angelo	Rothier
25 Dec '37	Abravanel	Sayão	Browning	Doe	Crooks	Bada	Brownlee	Cordon	Pinza
26 Jan '46	Cooper	Munsel	Greer	Kaskas	Jobin	Hayward	Singher	Valentino	Moscona
1 Feb '47	Cooper	Sayão	Benzell	Turner	Bjoerling	Hayward	Brownlee	Schon	Moscona

La Rondine (Puccini)

Date	Conductor	Magda	Lisette	Ruggero	Prunier	Rambaldo	Perichaud
21 Mar '36	Panizza	Bori	Fleischer	Martini	Windheim	D'Angelo	Cehanovsky

Der Rosenkavalier (R. Strauss)

Date	Conductor	Marschallin	Sophie	Octavian	Marianne	Singer	Faninal	Ochs	Valzacchi	Annina
5 Feb '38	Bodanzky	Lehmann	Fisher	Thorborg	Manski	Massue	Schorr	List	Bada	Doe
7 Jan '39	Bodanzky	Lehmann	Farell	Stevens	Manski	Massue	Schorr	List	Laufkoetter	Doe
19 Feb '44	Szell	Jessner	Conner	Novotna	Votipka	Baum	Olitzki	List	Garris	Glaz
16 Feb '46	Szell	Jessner	Conner	Novotna	Votipka	Hayward	Olitzki	List	De Paolis	Glaz
14 Dec '46	Busch	Jessner	Steber	Stevens	Votipka	Baum	Lechner	List	De Paolis	Glaz
14 Feb '48	Busch	Jessner	Steber	Novotna	Votipka	Baum	Lechner	List	De Paolis	Glaz
* 21 Nov '49	Reiner	Steber	Berger	Stevens	Votipka	Di Stefano	Thompson	List	Klein	Lipton

*Second telecast from the Met; no radio transmission.

Date	Conductor	Marschallin	Sophie	Octavian	Marianne	Singer	Faninal	Ochs	Valzacchi	Annina
3 Dec '49	Reiner	Steber	Berger	Stevens	Votipka	Di Stefano	Thompson	List	Klein	Lipton

Sadko (Rimsky-Korsakov)

Date	Conductor	Volkhova	Lubava	Sadko	Luka	Foma	Duda	Tsar	Guest
>F 12 Mar '32	Serafin	Fleischer	Bourskaya	Thill	Gandolfi	Altglass	D'Angelo	Ludikar	Anderson

Salome (R. Strauss)

Date	Conductor	Salome	Herodias	Page	Narraboth	Herod	Jokanaan	Nazarene	1st Jew
10 Mar '34	Bodanzky	Ljungberg	Manski	Doe	Clemens	Lorenz	Schorr	List	Windheim
12 Mar '49	Reiner	Welitsch	Thorborg	Glaz	Sullivan	Jagel	Janssen	Ernster	Chabay

Samson et Dalila (Saint-Saëns)

Date	Conductor	Dalila	Samson	Priest	Old Hebrew	Abimelech	Philistines		Messenger
26 Dec '36	Abravanel	Wettergren	Maison	Pinza	List	Gurney	Altglass,	Engelman	Bada
13 Dec '41	Pelletier	Stevens	Maison	Warren	Moscona	Cordon	Dudley,	Kent	Darcy
26 Nov '49	Cooper	Stevens	Vinay	Merrill	Ernster	Hawkins	Chabay,	Harvuot	Darcy

La Serva Padrona (Pergolesi)

Date	Conductor	Serpina	Vespone	Uberto
23 Feb '35	Bellezza	Fleischer	Bada	D'Angelo

Siegfried (Wagner)

Date	Conductor	Brünnhilde	Forest Bird	Erda	Siegfried	Mime	Wanderer	Alberich	Fafner
> 11 Mar '32	Bodanzky	Ljungberg	Fleischer	Schumann-Heink	Melchior	Clemens	Bohnen	Schützendorf	Tappolet
9 Feb '33	Bodanzky	Manski	Fleischer	Olszewska	Melchior	Windheim	Schorr	Schützendorf	Tappolet
30 Jan '37	Bodanzky	Flagstad	Andreva	Thorborg	Melchior	Laufkoetter	Schorr	Habich	List
10 Dec '38	Bodanzky	Flagstad	Bodanya	Kaskas	Hartmann	Witte	Schorr	Vogel	Cordon

Simon Boccanegra (Verdi)

Date	Conductor	Maria/Amelia	Gabriele	Simon	Paolo	Fiesco	Pietro	Maid
> 6 Feb '32	Serafin	Müller	Martinelli	Tibbett	Frigerio	Pinza	Ananian	Besuner
> 10 Dec '32	Serafin	Müller	Jagel	Tibbett	Frigerio	Pinza	Ananian	Besuner
16 Feb '35	Panizza	Rethberg	Martinelli	Tibbett	Gandolfi	Pinza	D'Angelo	Besuner
21 Jan '39	Panizza	Rethberg	Martinelli	Tibbett	Warren	Pinza	D'Angelo	Besuner
28 Jan '50	Stiedry	Varnay	Tucker	Warren	Valdengo	Székely	Alvary	Stellman

La Sonnambula (Bellini)

Date	Conductor	Amina	Lisa	Teresa	Elvino	Notary	Rodolfo	Alessio
11 Feb '33	Serafin	Pons	Doninelli	Bourskaya	Lauri-Volpi	Paltrinieri	Pinza	D'Angelo
2 Mar '35	Panizza	Pons	Besuner	Bourskaya	Tedesco	Paltrinieri	Lazzari	D'Angelo

Il Tabarro (Puccini)

Date	Conductor	Giorgetta	Frugola	Luigi	Tinca	Song Seller	Michele	Talpa
5 Jan '46	Sodero	Albanese	Harshaw	Jagel	De Paolis	Marlowe	Tibbett	Lazzari

The Tales of Hoffmann (see Les Contes d'Hoffmann)

Tannhäuser (Wagner)

Date	Conductor	Elisabeth	Venus	Tannhäuser	Wolfram	Landgrave	Biterolf	Shepherd
> 12 Feb '32	Bodanzky	Jeritza	Kappel	Melchior	Schorr	Bohnen	Gabor	Fleischer
> 16 Apr '32	Bodanzky	Rethberg	Manski	Melchior	Tibbett	Tappolet	Gabor	Doninelli
22 Feb '33	Bodanzky	Rethberg	Olszewska	Melchior	Schorr	Tappolet	Gabor	Doninelli
24 Feb '34	Bodanzky	Lehmann	Olszewska	Melchior	Schorr	Hofmann	Gabor	Fleischer
12 Jan '35	Bodanzky	Müller	Manski	Melchior	Bonelli	Hofmann	Gabor	Clark
18 Jan '36	Bodanzky	Flagstad	Halstead	Melchior	Tibbett	List	Gabor	Fleischer
25 Mar '39	Leinsdorf	Flagstad	Thorborg	Laholm	Janssen	List	Gabor	Farell
16 Dec '39	Leinsdorf	Flagstad	Pauly	Melchior	Janssen	List	Harrell	Stellman
4 Jan '41	Leinsdorf	Flagstad	Thorborg	Melchior	Janssen	List	Harrell	Stellman
14 Feb '42	Leinsdorf	Varnay	Thorborg	Melchior	Janssen	Kipnis	Kent	Stellman
19 Dec '42	Szell	Traubel	Thorborg	Melchior	Janssen	Kipnis	Hawkins	Stellman
5 Feb '44	Breisach	Varnay	Lawrence	Melchior	Huehn	Kipnis	Harrell	Stellman
6 Mar '48	Stiedry	Traubel	Varnay	Melchior	Janssen	Székely	Hawkins	Stellman

Tosca (Puccini)

Date	Conductor	Tosca	Cavaradossi	Scarpia	Spoletta	Angelotti	Sacristan	Sciarrone
7 Feb '42	Panizza	Moore	Jagel	Sved	De Paolis	Cehanovsky	Baccaloni	Engelman
8 Apr '44	Sodero	Moore	Kullman	Sved	De Paolis	Cehanovsky	Pechner	D'Angelo
9 Feb '46	Sodero	Moore	Peerce	Tibbett	De Paolis	Alvary	Baccaloni	Cehanovsky
15 Nov '47	Antonicelli	Dosia	Peerce	Valentino	De Paolis	Alvary	Luise	Cehanovsky
21 Jan '50	Antonicelli	Roman	Tagliavini	Sved	De Paolis	Alvary	Pechner	Harvuot

La Traviata (Verdi)

	Date	Conductor	Violetta	Flora	Alfredo	Gastone	Germont	Douphol	Dr. Grenvil
>	20 Feb '32	Serafin	Bori	Egener	Jagel	Bada	De Luca	Gandolfi	Ananian
	28 Jan '33	Serafin	Bori	Vettori	Tokatyan	Bada	Tibbett	Gandolfi	Wolfe
	5 Jan '35	Panizza	Ponselle	Vettori	Jagel	Bada	Tibbett	Gandolfi	Ananian
	6 Mar '37	Panizza	Sayão	Votipka	Kullman	Bada	Brownlee	Engelman	Cordon
	11 Dec '37	Panizza	Bovy	Votipka	Martini	Bada	Thomas	Engelman	Cordon
	23 Dec '39	Panizza	Jepson	Votipka	Crooks	De Paolis	Tibbett	Engelman	D'Angelo
	13 Apr '40	Panizza	Jepson	Votipka	Crooks	De Paolis	Brownlee	Engelman	Cordon
	29 Nov '41	Panizza	Novotna	Votipka	Peerce	De Paolis	Tibbett	Kent	D'Angelo
	5 Dec '42	Sodero	Albanese	Votipka	Kullman	De Paolis	Tibbett	Cehanovsky	Alvary
	24 Apr '43	Sodero	Sayão	Votipka	Kullman	De Paolis	Warren	Cehanovsky	Alvary
	1 Jan '44	Sodero	Albanese	Votipka	Peerce	Dudley	Tibbett	Cehanovsky	Alvary
	17 Feb '45	Sodero	Albanese	Votipka	Peerce	De Paolis	Tibbett	Cehanovsky	Alvary
	23 Mar '46	Sodero	Albanese	Votipka	Tucker	Manning	Warren	Cehanovsky	D'Angelo
	21 Dec '46	Sodero	Albanese	Votipka	Peerce	Chabay	Warren	Cehanovsky	Alvary
	22 Jan '49	Antonicelli	Steber	Votipka	Di Stefano	De Paolis	Merrill	Cehanovsky	Hawkins

Tristan und Isolde (Wagner)

	Date	Conductor	Isolde	Brangäne	Tristan	Sailor	Melot	Kurvenal	Marke
>	18 Feb '32	Bodanzky	Kappel	Doe	Melchior	Clemens	Gabor	Whitehill	Bohnen
>	3 Mar '33	Bodanzky	Leider	Olszewska	Melchior	Clemens	Gabor	Schorr	Hofmann
>	11 Mar '33	Bodanzky	Leider	Olszewska	Melchior	Clemens	Gabor	Schützendorf	Hofmann
	6 Jan '34	Bodanzky	Kappel	Doe	Melchior	Clemens	Gabor	Schorr	Hofmann
	9 Mar '35	Bodanzky	Flagstad	Branzell	Melchior	Clemens	Gabor	Schorr	Hofmann
	8 Feb '36	Bodanzky	Flagstad	Branzell	Melchior	Laufkoetter	Gabor	Huehn	Hofmann
	2 Jan '37	Bodanzky	Flagstad	Thorborg	Melchior	Laufkoetter	Gabor	Huehn	Hofmann
	29 Jan '38	Bodanzky	Flagstad	Wettergren	Melchior	Laufkoetter	Gabor	Huehn	List
	16 Apr '38	Bodanzky	Flagstad	Branzell	Melchior	Laufkoetter	Gabor	Huehn	List
	18 Feb '39	Bodanzky	Flagstad	Branzell	Melchior	Laufkoetter	Gabor	Janssen	List
	8 Apr '39	Bodanzky	Flagstad	Thorborg	Melchior	Witte	Gabor	Janssen	List
	23 Mar '40	Leinsdorf	Flagstad	Thorborg	Melchior	Marlowe	Cehanovsky	Huehn	List
	8 Feb '41	Leinsdorf	Flagstad	Thorborg	Melchior	Darcy	Darcy	Huehn	Kipnis
	6 Feb '43	Leinsdorf	Traubel	Thorborg	Melchior	Garris	Darcy	Huehn	Kipnis
	11 Dec '43	Beecham	Traubel	Thorborg	Melchior	Garris	Darcy	Janssen	Cordon
	23 Dec '44	Leinsdorf	Traubel	Thorborg	Melchior	Garris	Darcy	Janssen	Kipnis
	2 Feb '46	Busch	Traubel	Thorborg	Melchior	Garris	Darcy	Berglund	Kipnis
	30 Nov '46	Busch	Traubel	Harshaw	Svanholm	Garris	Darcy	Berglund	Ernster
	3 Jan '48	Busch	Traubel	Thebom	Melchior	Garris	Darcy	Berglund	Székely
	11 Dec '48	Busch	Traubel	Thebom	Melchior	Garris	Darcy	Janssen	Ernster
	17 Dec '49	Perlea	Traubel	Thebom	Melchior	Chabay	Darcy	Janssen	Székely

Il Trovatore (Verdi)

Date	Conductor	Leonora	Azucena	Inez	Manrico	Ruiz	Di Luna	Ferrando
> 16 Jan '32	Bellezza	Ponselle	Petrova	Egener	Lauri-Volpi	Paltrinieri	Danise	Pasero
15 Feb '36	Papi	Rethberg	Meisle	Votipka	Martinelli	Paltrinieri	Bonelli	Lazzari
> 29 May '37	Papi	Bampton	Castagna	Votipka	Carron	Oliviero	Morelli	Gurney
8 Jan '38	Papi	Milanov	Castagna	Votipka	Martinelli	Paltrinieri	Bonelli	Lazzari
4 Mar '39	Papi	Milanov	Castagna	Votipka	Martinelli	Paltrinieri	Bonelli	Lazzari
↙ 11 Jan '41	Calusio	Greco	Castagna	Stellman	Bjoerling	Oliviero	Valentino	Moscona
13 Mar '43	Sodero	Roman	Thorborg	Stellman	Carron	Oliviero	Valentino	Moscona
18 Mar '44	Sodero	Milanov	Harshaw	Stellman	Baum	Oliviero	Warren	Moscona
31 Mar '45	Sodero	Milanov	Castagna	Stellman	Baum	Oliviero	Warren	Moscona
15 Feb '47	Sodero	Milanov	Harshaw	Stellman	Baum	Oliviero	Warren	Vaghi
27 Dec '47	Cooper	Roman	Harshaw	I. Manski	Bjoerling	Oliviero	Warren	Vaghi

Die Verkaufte Braut (see The Bartered Bride)

Die Walküre (Wagner)

Date	Conductor	Sieglinde	Brünnhilde	Fricka	Siegmund	Wotan	Hunding
> 30 Jan '32	Bodanzky	Kappel	Ljungberg	Branzell	Melchior	Bohnen	Tappolet
> 3 Mar '32	Bodanzky	Ljungberg	Kappel	Claussen	Laubenthal	Schorr	Tappolet
> 2 Feb '33	Bodanzky	Stückgold	Leider	Olszewska	Melchior	Schorr	Tappolet
3 Feb '34	Bodanzky	Kappel	Leider	Branzell	Althouse	Hofmann	List
2 Feb '35	Bodanzky	Flagstad	Kappel	Olszewska	Althouse	Schorr	List
16 Jan '37	Bodanzky	Lehmann	Lawrence	Thorborg	Melchior	Schorr	List
18 Dec '37	Bodanzky	Flagstad	Lawrence	Thorborg	Melchior	Schorr	Hofmann
17 Feb '40	Leinsdorf	Lawrence	Flagstad	Branzell	Melchior	Huehn	List
30 Mar '40	Leinsdorf	Lehmann	Lawrence	Thorborg	Melchior	Schorr	List
6 Dec '41	Leinsdorf	Varnay	Traubel	Thorborg	Melchior	Schorr	Kipnis
27 Feb '43	Leinsdorf	Bampton	Traubel	Branzell	Melchior	Huehn	List
2 Dec '44	Szell	Bampton	Traubel	Thorborg	Melchior	Janssen	Kipnis
30 Mar '46	Breisach	Varnay	Traubel	Thorborg	Melchior	Berglund	List
8 Mar '47	Stiedry	Bampton	Varnay	Harshaw	Melchior	Janssen	Moscona
24 Jan '48	Stiedry	Bampton	Traubel	Thorborg	Melchior	Janssen	Székely
29 Jan '49	Stiedry	Bampton	Traubel	Thorborg	Lorenz	Berglund	Vichegonov
18 Mar '50	Stiedry	Bampton	Traubel	Thebom	Lorenz	Janssen	List

The Warrior (Rogers)

Date	Conductor	Delilah	Samson	Boy	Philistine Lords	Captains
11 Jan '47	Rudolf	Resnik	Harrell	Jordan	Marlowe, Knight	Garris, Hayward

Die Zauberflöte (see The Magic Flute)

Zolotoy Pyetushok (see The Golden Cockerel)

Maria Caniglia as Desdemona in *Otello*. Photography by Camuzzi.

Martial Singher as Dappertutto in *Les Contes d'Hoffmann*.

Metropolitan Opera
Historic Broadcast Recordings

The professionally mastered Historic Broadcast recordings are available from the Metropolitan Opera in return for a contribution to the Metropolitan Opera Fund. Inquiry may be made to:

Metropolitan Opera Association
Lincoln Center
New York, NY 10023

The Metropolitan Opera Historic Broadcast Centennial Collection 1935–59 features highlights from twenty-five seasons of broadcasts.

Carmen
17 April 1937

Carmen
Rosa Ponselle
Micaela
Hilda Burke
Frasquita
Thelma Votipka
Mercedes
Helen Olheim
Don José
René Maison
Escamillo
Julius Huehn
Dancaire
George Cehanovsky
Remendado
Giordano Paltrinieri
Zuniga
Louis d'Angelo
Morales
Wilfred Engelman
Conductor
Gennaro Papi

Der Rosenkavalier
7 January 1939

Marschallin
Lotte Lehmann
Octavian
Risë Stevens
Sophie
Marita Farell
Marianne
Dorothee Manski
Annina
Doris Doe
Orphans
Natalie Bodanya, Lucielle Browning, Anna Kaskas
Baron Ochs
Emanuel List
Faninal
Friedrich Schorr
Singer
Nicholas Massue
Valzacchi
Karl Laufkoetter
Commissioner
Norman Cordon
Majordomo, Innkeeper
Erich Witte

Notary
Arnold Gabor
Milliner
Pearl Besuner
Conductor
Artur Bodanzky

Simon Boccanegra
21 January 1939

Maria/Amelia
Elisabeth Rethberg
Maidservant
Pearl Besuner
Gabriele
Giovanni Martinelli
Simon Boccanegra
Lawrence Tibbett
Paolo
Leonard Warren
Fiesco
Ezio Pinza
Pietro
Louis d'Angelo
Captain
Giordano Paltrinieri
Conductor
Ettore Panizza

525

Otello
24 February 1940

Desdemona
Elisabeth Rethberg
Emilia
Thelma Votipka
Otello
Giovanni Martinelli
Iago
Lawrence Tibbett
Cassio
Alessio de Paolis
Lodovico
Nicola Moscona
Roderigo
Giordano Paltrinieri
Montano
George Cehanovsky
Herald
Wilfred Engelman
Conductor
Ettore Panizza

Le Nozze di Figaro
7 December 1940

Countess
Elisabeth Rethberg
Susanna
Licia Albanese
Cherubino
Jarmila Novotna
Marcellina
Irra Petina
Barbarina
Marita Farell
Count Almaviva
John Brownlee
Figaro
Ezio Pinza
Don Basilio
Alessio de Paolis
Dr. Bartolo
Salvatore Baccaloni
Don Curzio
George Rasely
Peasant girls
Helen Olheim, Pearl Besuner
Antonio
Louis d'Angelo
Conductor
Ettore Panizza

Un Ballo in Maschera
14 December 1940

Amelia
Zinka Milanov
Oscar
Stella Andreva
Ulrica
Bruna Castagna
Riccardo
Jussi Bjoerling

Renato
Alexander Sved
Silvano
Arthur Kent
Samuel
Norman Cordon
Tom
Nicola Moscona
Judge
John Carter
Servant
Lodovico Oliviero
Conductor
Ettore Panizza

Tannhäuser
4 January 1941

Elisabeth
Kirsten Flagstad
Venus
Kerstin Thorborg
Shepherd
Maxine Stellman
Tannhäuser
Lauritz Melchior
Wolfram
Herbert Janssen
Landgrave
Emanuel List
Walther
John Dudley
Biterolf
Mack Harrell
Heinrich
Emery Darcy
Reinmar
John Gurney
Conductor
Erich Leinsdorf

Tristan und Isolde
8 February 1941

Isolde
Kirsten Flagstad
Brangäne
Kerstin Thorborg
Tristan
Lauritz Melchior
Kurvenal
Julius Huehn
King Marke
Alexander Kipnis
Melot, Sailor's Voice
Emery Darcy
Shepherd
Karl Laufkoetter
Steersman
John Gurney
Conductor
Erich Leinsdorf

Fidelio
22 February 1941

Leonore
Kirsten Flagstad
Marzelline
Marita Farell
Florestan
René Maison
Don Pizarro
Julius Huehn
Don Fernando
Herbert Janssen
Jacquino
Karl Laufkoetter
Rocco
Alexander Kipnis
Prisoners
Emery Darcy, John Gurney
Conductor
Bruno Walter

Madama Butterfly
19 January 1946

Cio-Cio-San
Licia Albanese
Suzuki
Lucielle Browning
Kate Pinkerton
Maxine Stellman
Pinkerton
James Melton
Sharpless
John Brownlee
Goro
Alessio de Paolis
Yamadori
George Cehanovsky
Bonze
Osie Hawkins
Commissioner
John Baker
Conductor
Pietro Cimara

La Gioconda
16 March 1946

Gioconda
Zinka Milanov
Laura
Risë Stevens
Cieca
Margaret Harshaw
Enzo
Richard Tucker
Barnaba
Leonard Warren
Alvise
Giacomo Vaghi
Zuane
Osie Hawkins

Singers
Wellington Ezekiel, Richard Manning
Iseppo
Lodovico Oliviero
Monk
William Hargrave
Steersman
John Baker
Conductor
Emil Cooper

Roméo et Juliette
1 February 1947

Juliette
Bidú Sayão
Stephano
Mimi Benzell
Gertrude
Claramae Turner
Roméo
Jussi Bjoerling
Mercutio
John Brownlee
Tybalt
Thomas Hayward
Capulet
Kenneth Schon
Friar Laurence
Nicola Moscona
Duke of Verona
William Hargrave
Paris
George Cehanovsky
Benvolio
Anthony Marlowe
Gregorio
Philip Kinsman
Conductor
Emil Cooper

Salome
19 January 1952

Salome
Ljuba Welitch
Herodias
Elisabeth Hoengen
Page
Herta Glaz
Slave
Paula Lenchner
Herod
Set Svanholm
Narraboth
Brian Sullivan
Jokanaan
Hans Hotter
Nazarenes
Alois Pernerstorfer, Emery Darcy

Jews
Gabor Carelli, Thomas Hayward, Alessio de Paolis, Paul Franke, Gerhard Pechner
Soldiers
Norman Scott, Lubomir Vichegonov
Cappadocian
Osie Hawkins
Conductor
Fritz Reiner

Elektra
23 February 1952

Elektra
Astrid Varnay
Klytemnestra
Elisabeth Hoengen
Chrysothemis
Walburga Wegner
Confidant
Jean Madeira
Overseer
Thelma Votipka
Serving Women
Martha Lipton, Herta Glaz, Mildred Miller, Lucine Amara, Genevieve Warner
Trainbearer
Paula Lenchner
Aegisth
Set Svanholm
Orest
Paul Schoeffler
Old Servant
Lubomir Vichegonov
Young Servant
Paul Franke
Guardian of Orest
Alois Pernerstorfer
Conductor
Fritz Reiner

Andrea Chénier
4 December 1954

Maddalena
Zinka Milanov
Bersi
Rosalind Elias
Countess
Herta Glaz
Madelon
Sandra Warfield
Andrea Chénier
Mario del Monaco
Gérard
Leonard Warren
Mathieu
Salvatore Baccaloni
Fléville
George Cehanovsky

Abbé
Gabor Carelli
Spy
Alessio de Paolis
Fouquier
Norman Scott
Roucher
Frank Valentino
Dumas
Osie Hawkins
Schmidt
Lawrence Davidson
Majordomo
Louis Sgarro
Conductor
Fausto Cleva

Les Contes d'Hoffmann
3 December 1955

Olympia
Roberta Peters
Giulietta
Risë Stevens
Antonia
Lucine Amara
Nicklausse
Mildred Miller
Voice
Sandra Warfield
Hoffmann
Richard Tucker
Lindorf, Coppelius, Dappertutto, Miracle
Martial Singher
Spalanzani
Paul Franke
Andrès, Cochenille, Pitichinaccio, Frantz
Alessio de Paolis
Schlemil
Clifford Harvuot
Crespel
Norman Scott
Luther
George Cehanovsky
Nathanael
James McCracken
Hermann
Calvin Marsh
Conductor
Pierre Monteux

Tosca
7 January 1956

Tosca
Renata Tebaldi
Cavaradossi
Richard Tucker
Scarpia
Leonard Warren
Sacristan
Fernando Corena

[**Tosca,** continued]

Angelotti
   Clifford Harvuot
Spoletta
   Alessio de Paolis
Sciarrone
   George Cehanovsky
Jailer
   Calvin Marsh
Shepherd
   Peter Mark
Conductor
   Dimitri Mitropoulos

The first pirateer. Metropolitan Opera Librarian Lionel Mapleson recording excerpts from live performances at the Metropolitan Opera, 1901–1903.

Lawrence Tibbett as Brutus Jones in *The Emperor Jones*. Photography by Carlo Edwards.

Julius Huehn. Photography by Delar.

Select Bibliography

The primary source materials for this study have been the broadcasts themselves and material from the Metropolitan Opera Archives. Valuable information and a sense of period have been garnered from the pages of *Opera News* (volumes three through fifty-three), published by the Metropolitan Opera Guild, Inc. Several other magazines, *Opera, The Gramophone*, and *The Record Collector*, have provided similar materials. Mention also must be made of the memorable music critics of the New York newspapers early in the twentieth century whose writings have nourished and informed my thought for years: W. J. Henderson, Lawrence Gilman, Pitts Sanborn, Henry Krehbiel and Henry T. Finck. (Their prose may be sampled in Robert Tuggle's admirable recreation of *The Golden Age of Opera*.) Several contemporary critics, among them Conrad Osborne and Will Crutchfield, have given like enjoyment. While myriad autobiographies and biographies of singers have been read, few obtain the stature of Frances Alda's *Men, Women and Tenors* or Ira Glackens' biography of Lillian Nordica, *Yankee Diva*. Though too often hagiolatry obscures the subject, a few have been included in this selective bibliography.

Alda, Frances. 1937. *Men, Women and Tenors*. Boston: Houghton Mifflin Company.
Ardoin, John. 1977. *The Callas Legacy*. New York: Charles Scribner's Sons.
Beecham, Sir Thomas. 1943. *A Mingled Chime: An Autobiography*. New York: G. P. Putnam's Sons.
Belmont, Eleanor Robson. 1957. *The Fabric of Memory*. New York: Farrar, Straus and Cudahy.
Bing, Sir Rudolf. 1972. *5000 Nights at the Opera*. Garden City, NY: Doubleday & Company, Inc.
_____. 1981. *A Knight at the Opera*. New York: G. P. Putnam's Sons.
Caruso, Enrico, Jr., and Andrew Farkas. 1990. *Enrico Caruso: My Father and My Family*. Portland, OR: Amadeus Press.
Chapin, Schuyler. 1977. *Musical Chairs: A Life in the Arts*. New York: G. P. Putnam's Sons.
Christiansen, Rupert. 1984. *Prima Donna*. New York: Viking Penguin, Inc.
Davenport, Marcia. 1967. *Too Strong for Fantasy*. New York: Charles Scribner's Sons.
De Schauensee, Max. 1962. *The Collector's Verdi and Puccini*. Philadelphia: J. B. Lippincott Company.
Downes, Olin. 1957. *Olin Downes on Music*. New York: Simon and Schuster.

Eames, Emma. 1927. *Some Memories and Reflections*. New York: D. Appleton and Company.

Eaton, Quaintance. 1957. *Opera Caravan: Adventures of the Metropolitan on Tour 1883–1956*. New York: Farrar, Straus and Cudahy.

———. 1968. *The Miracle of the Met: An Informal History of the Metropolitan Opera 1883–1967*. New York: Meredith Press.

Erskine, John. 1950. *My Life in Music*. New York: William Morrow & Co.

Farkas, Andrew, ed. 1989. *Lawrence Tibbett: Singing Actor*. Portland, OR: Amadeus Press.

Farrar, Geraldine. 1938. *Such Sweet Compulsion*. New York: The Greystone Press.

Fitzgerald, Gerald, and Jean Seward Uppman, eds. 1989. *Annals of the Metropolitan Opera: The Complete Chronicle of Performances and Artists*. 2 vols. Boston: G. K. Hall & Co., and New York: The Metropolitan Opera Guild, Inc.

Flagstad, Kirsten, and Louis Biancolli. 1952. *The Flagstad Manuscript*. New York: G. P. Putnam's Sons.

Garden, Mary, and Louis Biancolli. 1951. *Mary Garden's Story*. New York: Simon and Schuster.

Goldovsky, Boris. 1984. *Good Afternoon, Ladies and Gentlemen!: Intermission Scripts from the Met*. Bloomington: Indiana University Press.

Eisler, Paul E. 1984. *The Metropolitan Opera: The First Twenty-Five Years 1883–1908*. Croton-on-Hudson, NY: North River Press, Inc.

Gatti-Casazza, Giulio. 1941. *Memories of Opera*. New York: Charles Scribner's Sons.

Hamilton, David, ed. 1987. *The Metropolitan Opera Encyclopedia: A Comprehensive Guide to the World of Opera*. New York: Simon and Schuster, and The Metropolitan Opera Guild, Inc.

Hines, Jerome. 1982. *Great Singers on Great Singing*. Garden City, NY: Doubleday & Company, Inc.

Jeritza, Maria. 1924. *Sunlight and Song: A Singer's Life*. Trans. Frederick H. Martens. New York: D. Appleton and Company.

Kolodin, Irving. 1936. *The Metropolitan Opera 1883–1935*. New York: Oxford University Press.

———. 1966. *The Metropolitan Opera 1883–1966: A Candid History*. New York: Alfred A. Knopf.

Lawrence, Marjorie. 1949. *Interrupted Melody*. New York: Appleton-Century-Crofts, Inc.

Lehmann, Lotte. 1938. *Midway in My Song*. New York: Bobbs-Merrill Company.

———. 1948. *My Many Lives*. New York: Boosey & Hawkes, Inc.

Leider, Frida. 1966. *Playing My Part*. Trans. Charles Osborne. New York: Meredith Press.

Leinsdorf, Erich. 1976. *Cadenza*. Boston: Houghton Mifflin Company.

Matz, Mary Jane. 1955. *Opera Stars in the Sun: Intimate Glimpses of Metropolitan Personalities*. New York: Farrar, Straus & Cudahy.

Mayer, Martin. 1983. *The Met: One Hundred Years of Grand Opera*. New York: Simon and Schuster, and the Metropolitan Opera Guild, Inc.

Mercer, Ruby. 1976. *The Tenor of His Time: Edward Johnson of the Met*. Toronto: Clarke, Irwin & Company, Ltd.

Merkling, Frank, John W. Freeman, and Gerald Fitzgerald. 1965. *The Golden Horseshoe: The Life and Times of the Metropolitan Opera House*. New York: The Viking Press.

Merrill, Robert, with Robert Saffron. 1976. *Between the Acts: An Irreverent Look at Opera and Other Madness*. New York: McGraw-Hill Company.

The Metropolitan Opera: The Radio and Television Legacy. Exhibition: 19 September–22 November 1986. New York: The Museum of Broadcasting.

Mili, Gjon and Mary Ellis Peltz. 1960. *The Magic of the Opera: A Picture Memoir of the Metropolitan*. New York: Frederick A. Praeger, Inc.

Moore, Grace. 1944. *You're Only Human Once*. Garden City and New York: Garden City Publishing Company.

Moran, William R., ed. 1990. *Herman Klein and The Gramophone.* Portland, OR: Amadeus Press.

Nash, Elizabeth. 1981. *Always First Class: The Career of Geraldine Farrar.* Washington, D.C.: University Press of America, Inc.

O'Connell, Charles. 1949. *The Other Side of the Record.* New York: Alfred A. Knopf.

Opera Cavalcade: The Story of the Metropolitan. 1938. New York: The Metropolitan Opera Guild, Inc.

Peltz, Mary Ellis. 1950. *Behind the Gold Curtain: The Story of the Metropolitan Opera: 1883 to 1950.* New York: Farrar Straus and Company.

Peltz, Mary Ellis, and Gerald Fitzgerald, eds. 1978. *Metropolitan Opera Annals: Third Supplement 1966–1976.* Clifton, NJ: James T. White & Company, and New York: The Metropolitan Opera Guild, Inc.

Pinza, Ezio, with Robert Magidoff. 1958. *Ezio Pinza: An Autobiography.* New York: Rinehart & Company, Inc.

Pleasants, Henry. 1966. *The Great Singers: From the Dawn of Opera to Our Own Time.* New York: Simon and Schuster.

Ponselle, Rosa, and James A. Drake. 1982. *Ponselle: A Singer's Life.* Garden City, NY: Doubleday & Company, Inc.

Porter, Andrew. 1978. *Music of Three Seasons: 1974–1977.* New York: Farrar Straus Giroux.

_____. 1981. *Music of Three More Seasons: 1977–1980.* New York: Alfred A. Knopf.

Prawy, Marcel. 1970. *The Vienna Opera.* New York: Frederick A. Praeger, Inc.

Rasponi, Lanfranco. 1982. *The Last Prima Donnas.* New York: Alfred A. Knopf.

Robinson, Francis. 1979. *Celebration: The Metropolitan Opera.* Garden City, NY: Doubleday & Company, Inc.

Rosenthal, Harold. 1958. *Two Centuries of Opera at Covent Garden.* London: Putnam.

Rubin, Stephen E. 1974. *The New Met in Profile.* New York: Macmillan Publishing Co., Inc.

Sachs, Harvey. 1978. *Toscanini.* Philadelphia and New York: J. B. Lippincott Company.

Scott, Michael. 1988. *The Great Caruso.* New York: Alfred A. Knopf.

_____. 1977. *The Record of Singing: To 1914.* New York: Charles Scribner's Sons.

_____. 1979. *The Record of Singing* [To 1925]. New York: Holmes & Meier Publishers, Inc.

Seltsam, William H., ed. 1947. *Metropolitan Opera Annals: A Chronicle of Artists and Performances.* New York: The H. W. Wilson Company, and The Metropolitan Opera Guild, Inc.

_____. 1957. *Metropolitan Opera Annals First Supplement: 1947–1957.* New York: The H. W. Wilson Company, and The Metropolitan Opera Guild, Inc.

_____. 1968. *Metropolitan Opera Annals Second Supplement: 1957–1966.* New York: The H. W. Wilson Company, and The Metropolitan Opera Guild, Inc.

Sheean, Vincent. 1956. *First and Last Love.* New York: Random House.

Smith, Patrick J. 1983. *A Year at the Met.* New York: Alfred A. Knopf.

Steane, J. B. 1974. *The Grand Tradition: Seventy Years of Singing on Record.* New York: Charles Scribner's Sons.

Stevens, Risë. 1959. *Subway to the Met: Risë Stevens' Story.* Garden City, NY: Doubleday & Company, Inc.

Thompson, Oscar. 1937. *The American Singer.* New York: The Dial Press.

Thomson, Virgil. 1947. *The Musical Scene.* New York: Alfred A. Knopf.

_____. 1967. *Music Reviewed: 1940–1954.* New York: Vintage Books.

Traubel, Helen, with Richard G. Hubler. 1959. *St. Louis Woman.* New York: Duell, Sloan and Pearce.

Tuggle, Robert. 1983. *The Golden Age of Opera: with the Photographs of Herman Mishkin.* New York: Holt, Rinehart and Winston.

Walter, Bruno. 1944. *Theme and Variations.* New York: Alfred A. Knopf.

Wayner, Robert J., ed. 1976. *What Did They Sing at the Met?* New York: Wayner Publications.

Nadine Conner as Zerlina in *Don Giovanni*. Photography by De Bellis.

Index

Years expressed in abbreviated form (e.g., '39) designate broadcast performances. References to illustrations appear in boldface type (e.g., **135**). Opera titles in subentries are shortened as follows:

Abduction (The Abduction from the Seraglio)
Amore (L'Amore dei Tre Re)
Ballo (Un Ballo in Maschera)
Barbiere (Il Barbiere di Siviglia)
Boccanegra (Simon Boccanegra)
Boris (Boris Godunov)
Butterfly (Madama Butterfly)
Cavalleria (Cavalleria Rusticana)
Elisir (L'Elisir d'Amore)
Figaro (Le Nozze di Figaro)
Fille (La Fille du Régiment)
Forza (La Forza del Destino)
Giovanni (Don Giovanni)
Grimes (Peter Grimes)

Hänsel (Hänsel und Gretel)
Hoffmann (Les Contes d'Hoffmann)
Ibbetson (Peter Ibbetson)
Lucia (Lucia di Lammermoor)
Meistersinger (Die Meistersinger
   von Nürnberg)
Orfeo (Orfeo ed Euridice)
Pasquale (Don Pasquale)
Pelléas (Pelléas et Mélisande)
Ring (Der Ring des Nibelungen)
Roméo (Roméo et Juliette)
Samson (Samson et Dalila)
Schicchi (Gianni Schicchi)
Tristan (Tristan und Isolde)

548 Index

Hitler, Adolf, 210
Hofmann, Ludwig, *bass,* 32, 145
    roles
        Bartered Bride (Kezal), '33, 31
        Götterdämmerung (Hagen), '36, 105, 106
        Lohengrin (King Henry), '34, 45; '37, 151
        Tannhäuser (Landgrave), '34, 44
        Tristan (Marke), '33, 32, 36; '34, 41; '35, 86; '37, 153, 154
        Walküre (Wotan), '34, 42, 43
Homer, Louise, *contralto,* 54, 74, 299, 460
Horowitz, Wanda Toscanini, 227
Horne, Marilyn, *mezzo soprano,* 22
Hoover, Herbert, 328
Huehn, Julius, *baritone,* 43, 262, 279, **530**
    compared with
        Schorr, 154
    debut
        Met (Herald), 1935, 151, 164
    roles
        Carmen (Escamillo), '37, 71
        Fidelio (Pizarro), '36, 103; '41, 260, 371
        Lohengrin (Telramund), '37, 151; '38, 151; '40, 161
        Meistersinger (Kothner), '36, 108
        Rheingold (Donner), '37, 146
        Tannhäuser (Wolfram), '44, 276–277
        Tristan (Kurvenal), '36, 103; '37, 153, 154; '38, 155; '41, 259; '43, 276
        Walküre (Wotan) Feb '40, 164–165; '43, 274
Humperdinck, Engelbert. *See Hänsel und Gretel*
Hunt, Lois, *soprano*
    roles
        Bohème (Musetta), '50, 484
Hurok, Sol, 292
Hutchins, Robert, 328

Idomeneo, 212, 321
Ilitsch, Daniza, *soprano*
    breaks down in *Aida* broadcast, 424
    career synopsis, 423
    compared with
        Milanov, Cerquetti, 424
    debut
        Met (Desdemona), 1947, 423
    roles, 423
        Ballo (Amelia), '47, 423–424
Intermezzo, 168
Intermissions, broadcast, 323–331. *See also*
    Abbott, Lawrence; Cross, Milton; Davenport, Marcia; Farrar, Geraldine; Goldovsky, Boris; Kennedy, John B.; "Opera News on, the Air"; "Opera Quiz"; "Singers' Roundtable"; Souvaine, Geraldine; Souvaine, Henry; Taylor, Deems
    and commercial sponsors, 323
    early practises during, 23, 323–327, 492
    and novel formats in 1940s, 327–328, 331
    procedures following Martinelli's collapse in *Aida,* 326
    and Rogers' *The Warrior,* 331

solicitation of funds during, 31–32, 219–220, 326–327
Iphigenia auf Tauris, 253
The Island God, 401

Jagel, Frederick, *tenor,* 75, 435
    debut
        Met (Radamès), 1927, 68, 243
    replaces Martinelli during *Aida* broadcast, 243, 326
    roles
        Africaine (Vasco), '34, 63
        Aida (Radames), '36, 110; '42, 243
        Bohème (Rodolfo), '35, 78; '42, 450
        Cavalleria (Turiddu), '41, 241; '43, 353
        Forza (Alvaro), '43, 342, 343, 345
        Gioconda (Enzo), '45, 356, 391
        Grimes (Peter), 1948, 403; '48, 404
        Lucia (Edgardo), **118;** '37, 117; '40, 200, 202
        Norma (Pollione), '44, 353, 354
        Rigoletto (Duke), '35, 111, 113
        Salome (Herod), '49, 446
        Tabarro (Luigi), '46, 379
        Tosca (Cavaradossi), '42, 247
        Traviata (Alfredo), '32, 24; '35, 68
✓ Janssen, Herbert, *baritone,* 277, 279, 410, 479, 488
    career synopsis, 155
    compared with
        Sved, 270
    debut
        Met (Wolfram), 1939, 155
    roles
        Fidelio (Fernando), '41, 260, 371
        Lohengrin (Telramund), '42, 268; '45, 377; '50, 482
        Meistersinger (Kothner), '39, 159
        Meistersinger (Sachs), **370;** '45, 368, 369
        Salome (Jokanaan), '49, 446
        Tannhäuser (Wolfram), '39, 159, 160; '40, xiii; '41, 258; '42, 272
        Tristan (Kurvenal), '39, 153, 155
    Steane on, 155
Jenkins, Florence Foster, *soprano,* 421
Jepson, Helen, *soprano,* 74, 326
    compared with
        Moore, 199
    in movies, 126
    roles
        Faust (Marguerite), **196;** '37, 136; '40, 197
        Pelléas (Mélisande), 199, 372
        Thaïs (Thaïs), 199
        Traviata (Violetta), 68; '39, 125–126; '40, 199
    student of Mario, 63
    throat ailment ends career, 199
✓ Jeritza, Maria, *soprano,* 26, 34, 262, 330
    returns in *Fledermaus,* 1951, 492
    roles, 13, 19, 246, 281
        Ägyptische Helena (Helena), **18**
        Tannhäuser (Elisabeth), 82; '32, 19, 25
✓ Jessner, Irene, *soprano*
    Johnson on, 157
    roles, 246
        Orfeo (Euridice), '38, 209